THINGS

THINGS

Edited by Bill Brown

THE
UNIVERSITY
OF CHICAGO
PRESS
Chicago & London

The University of Chicago Press, Chicago 60637
The University of Chicago Press, Ltd., London
08   07   06   05   04   5 4 3 2 1

© 2004 by The University of Chicago
All rights reserved. Published 2004
Printed in the United States of America

Library of Cataloging-in-Publication Data
Things / edited by Bill Brown.
    p. cm.
  Includes bibliographical references and index.
  ISBN 0-226-07611-3 (clothbound : alk. paper)—ISBN 0-226-07612-1
(paperbound : alk. paper)
  1. Material culture—Philosophy. I. Brown, Bill, 1958–

GN406 .T45 2004
306—dc22   2003024508

The paper used in this publication meets the minimum requirements of American National Standard for Information Sciences—Permanence of Paper for Printed Library
Materials, ANSI Z39.48-1984

Contents

Thing Theory

Bill Brown

Le sujet naît de l'objet.

—MICHEL SERRES

Is there something perverse, if not archly insistent, about complicating things with theory? Do we really need anything like thing theory the way we need narrative theory or cultural theory, queer theory or discourse theory? Why not let things alone? Let them rest somewhere else—in the balmy elsewhere beyond theory. From there, they might offer us dry ground above those swirling accounts of the subject, some place of origin unmediated by the sign, some stable alternative to the instabilities and uncertainties, the ambiguities and anxieties, forever fetishized by theory. Something warm, then, that relieves us from the chill of dogged ideation, something concrete that relieves us from unnecessary abstraction.

The longing for just such relief is described by A. S. Byatt at the outset of *The Biographer's Tale*. Fed up with Lacan as with deconstructions of the Wolf-Man, a doctoral student looks up at a filthy window and epiphan-

For their work on the special issue of *Critical Inquiry* on which this collection is based, I am indebted to my coeditors and to Jay Williams (who manages to manage details with profound equilibrium), Kristin Casady, Anne Stevens, and Thomas Kim. For their generous responses to this introduction, I'd like to thank Lauren Berlant, Jessica Burstein, James Chandler, Frances Ferguson, W. J. T. Mitchell, Janel Mueller, Joel Snyder, and Diana Young. And for her part in our ongoing conversation about things, I'd like to thank Miriam Hansen.

ically thinks, "I must have *things*." He relinquishes theory to relish the world at hand: "A real, very dirty window, shutting out the sun. A *thing*."[1]

In the last century, this longing became an especially familiar refrain. "Only things speak to me," Rilke proclaimed in 1903.[2] And in 1913 Fernando Pessoa argued that only "lessons in unlearning" will enable us to "see without thinking" so that "what we see of things are the things."[3] "Ideas," Francis Ponge wrote, shortly after World War II, "give me a queasy feeling, nausea," whereas "objects in the external world, on the other hand, delight me."[4] If, more recently, some delight has been taken in historicism's "desire to make contact with the 'real,'" in the emergence of material culture studies and the vitality of material history, in accounts of everyday life and the material *habitus*, as in the "return of the real" in contemporary art, this is inseparable, surely, from the very pleasure taken in "objects of the external world," however problematic that external world may be—however phantasmatic the externality of that world may be theorized to be.[5] These days, you can read books on the pencil, the zipper, the toilet, the banana, the chair, the potato, the bowler hat.[6] These

1. A. S. Byatt, *The Biographer's Tale* (New York, 2001), p. 2.

2. Rainer Maria Rilke, letter to Lou Andreas-Salomé, 8 Aug. 1903, *Letters of Rainer Maria Rilke, 1892–1910*, trans. Jane Bannard Greene and M. D. Herter Norton (New York, 1945), p. 122.

3. Fernando Pessoa, *The Keeper of Sheep*, in *Fernando Pessoa and Co.: Selected Poems*, trans. and ed. Richard Zenith (New York, 1988), p. 57.

4. Francis Ponge, "My Creative Method," *The Voice of Things*, trans. and ed. Beth Archer (New York, 1972), p. 93. In contrast, it was the confrontation with the materiality of matter— "below all explanation"—that occasioned a very different nausea, not Ponge's but Roquentin's (Jean-Paul Sartre, *Nausea*, trans. Lloyd Alexander [New York, 1964], p. 129). For the canonical expression of the thing/theory binary in American poetry, see Robert Haas, "Meditation at Lagunitas," *Praise* (Hopewell, N.J., 1979), pp. 4–5.

5. Catherine Gallagher and Stephen Greenblatt, *Practicing New Historicism* (Chicago, 2000), p. 54. For a brief account of the emergence of material culture studies (institutionally marked by the *Journal of Material Culture*), see *Material Cultures: Why Some Things Matter*, ed. Daniel Miller (Chicago, 1998); and for the U.S. tradition, see *Learning from Things: Method and Theory of Material Culture Studies*, ed. David Kingery (Washington, D.C., 1995). On contemporary art, see Hal Foster, *The Return of the Real: The Avant-Garde at the End of the Century* (Cambridge, Mass., 1996). On the concept of exteriority, see esp. Jacques Derrida, *Positions*, trans. Alan Bass (Chicago, 1978), p. 64, and Judith Butler, *Bodies That Matter: On the Discursive Limits of "Sex"* (New York, 1993), p. 30.

6. See Henry Petroski, *The Pencil: A History of Design and Circumstance* (New York, 1989); Robert Friedel, *Zipper: An Exploration in Novelty* (New York, 1994); Julie L. Horan, *The Porcelain God: A Social History of the Toilet* (New York, 1997); Virginia Scott Jenkins, *Bananas: An*

Bill Brown, George M. Pullman Professor of English and the history of culture at the University of Chicago and a coeditor of *Critical Inquiry*, is the author of *The Material Unconscious* (1996) and *A Sense of Things: The Object Matter of American Literature* (2003).

days, history can unabashedly begin with things and with the senses by which we apprehend them; like a modernist poem, it begins in the street, with the smell "of frying oil, shag tobacco and unwashed beer glasses."[7] Can't we learn from this materialism instead of taking the trouble to trouble it? Can't we remain content with the "real, very dirty window"— a "thing"—as the answer to what ails us without turning it into an ailment of its own?

Fat chance. For even the most coarse and commonsensical things, mere things, perpetually pose a problem because of the specific unspecificity that things denotes. Mind you, for Ponge, objects may seem substitutable for things, and by "siding with things" *(le parti pris des choses)* he meant to take the part of specified objects—doorknobs, figs, crates, blackberries, stoves, water.[8] But the very semantic *reducibility* of *things* to *objects,* coupled with the semantic *irreducibility* of *things* to *objects,* would seem to mark one way of recognizing how, although objects typically arrest a poet's attention, and although the *object* was asked to join philosophy's dance, things may still lurk in the shadows of the ballroom and continue to lurk there after the subject and object have done their thing, long after the party is over. When it comes to Ponge, in fact, the matter isn't so simple as it seems. Michael Riffaterre has argued that the poems, growing solely out of a "word-kernel" *(mot-noyau),* defy referentiality;[9] Jacques Derrida has argued that, throughout the poet's effort "to make the thing sign," the "thing is not an object [and] cannot become one."[10] Taking the side of things hardly put a stop to that thing called theory.

American History (Washington, D.C., 2000); Galen Cranz, *The Chair: Rethinking Culture, Body, and Design* (New York, 2000); Larry Zuckerman, *The Potato: How the Humble Spud Rescued the Western World* (San Francisco, 1999); and Fred Miller Robinson, *The Man in the Bowler Hat: His History and Iconography* (Chapel Hill, N.C., 1993). For a recent and important contribution to what one might call object studies, see *Things That Talk: Object Lessons from Art and Science,* ed. Lorraine Daston (New York, 2004).

7. Simon Schama, *The Embarrassment of Riches: An Interpretation of Dutch Culture in the Golden Age* (New York, 1987), p. 15.

8. His "delight" in these objects was prompted not by any familiarity but by the suddenly recognized peculiarity of the everyday, the fact that water "lies flat on its stomach" in a "hysterical urge to submit to gravity," for instance, sacrificing "all sense of decency to this *idée fixe,* this pathological scruple" ("ce scrupule maladif") (Ponge, "Of Water," trans. C. K. Williams, *Selected Poems,* trans. Williams, John Montague, and Margaret Guiton, ed. Guiton [Winston-Salem, N.C., 1994], pp. 57, 58; *Le Parti pris des choses* is the title of the volume of poetry in which "Of Water" first appeared).

9. Michael Riffaterre, "Ponge tautologique, ou le fonctionnement du texte," *Ponge inventeur et classique,* ed. Philippe Bonnefis and Pierre Oster (Paris, 1977), p. 66. See also Riffaterre, "The Primacy of Words: Francis Ponge's Reification," *Figuring Things: Char, Ponge, and Poetry in the Twentieth Century,* ed. Charles D. Minahen (Lexington, Ky., 1994), pp. 27–38.

10. Derrida, *Signéponge/Signsponge,* trans. Richard Rand (New York, 1984), pp. 126, 14.

"Things are what we encounter, ideas are what we project." That's how Leo Stein schematically put it.[11] Although the experience of an encounter depends, of course, on the projection of an idea (the idea of encounter), Stein's scheme helps to explain the suddenness with which things seem to assert their presence and power: you cut your finger on a sheet of paper, you trip over some toy, you get bopped on the head by a falling nut. These are occasions outside the scene of phenomenological attention that nonetheless teach you that you're "caught up in things" and that the "body is a thing among things."[12] They are occasions of contingency—the chance interruption—that disclose a physicality of things. In Byatt's novel, the interruption of the habit of looking *through* windows as transparencies enables the protagonist to look *at* a window itself in its opacity. As they circulate through our lives, we look *through* objects (to see what they disclose about history, society, nature, or culture—above all, what they disclose about *us*), but we only catch a glimpse of things.[13] We look through objects because there are codes by which our interpretive attention makes them meaningful, because there is a discourse of objectivity that allows us to use them as facts. A *thing*, in contrast, can hardly function as a window. We begin to confront the thingness of objects when they stop working for us: when the drill breaks, when the car stalls, when the windows get filthy, when their flow within the circuits of production and distribution, consumption and exhibition, has been arrested, however momentarily. The story of objects asserting themselves as things, then, is the story of a changed relation to the human subject and thus the story of how the thing really names less an object than a particular subject-object relation.

And, yet, the word *things* holds within it a more audacious ambiguity. It denotes a massive generality as well as particularities, even your particularly prized possessions: "'Things' were of course the sum of the world; only, for Mrs. Gereth, the sum of the world was rare French furniture and oriental china."[14] The word designates the concrete yet ambiguous within the everyday: "Put it by that green thing in the hall." It functions to over-

11. Leo Stein, *The A-B-C of Aesthetics* (New York, 1927), p. 44.

12. Maurice Merleau-Ponty, "Eye and Mind," trans. Carleton Dallery, *The Primacy of Perception and Other Essays on Phenomenological Psychology, the Philosophy of Art, History and Politics*, trans. James M. Edie et al., ed. Edie (Evanston, Ill., 1964), p. 163.

13. The window scene in Byatt's novel should be read in relation to Nabokov's point about how things become multiply transparent and read in the context of a dialectic of *looking through* and *looking at:* "When we concentrate on a material object, whatever its situation, the very act of attention may lead to our involuntarily sinking into the history of that object" (Vladimir Nabokov, *Transparent Things* [New York, 1972], p. 1). We don't apprehend things except partially or obliquely (as what's beyond our apprehension). In fact, by looking *at* things we render them objects.

14. Henry James, *The Spoils of Poynton* (1896; New York, 1987), p. 49. In his preface for the New York edition of the novel (reprinted in this Penguin edition, pp. 23–33), James plays with a full range of the word's denotations (for example: "The thing is to lodge somewhere, at the heart of one's complexity an irrepressible *appreciation*" [p. 31]).

come the loss of other words or as a place holder for some future specifying operation: "I need that thing you use to get at things between your teeth." It designates an amorphous characteristic or a frankly irresolvable enigma: "There's a thing about that poem that I'll never get." For Byatt's protagonist, the quest for things may be a quest for a kind of certainty, but *things* is a word that tends, especially at its most banal, to index a certain limit or liminality, to hover over the threshold between the nameable and unnameable, the figurable and unfigurable, the identifiable and unidentifiable: Dr. Seuss's Thing One and Thing Two.[15]

On the one hand, then, the thing baldly encountered. On the other, some thing not quite apprehended. Could you clarify this matter of things by starting again and imagining them, first, as the amorphousness out of which objects are materialized by the (ap)perceiving subject, the anterior physicality of the physical world emerging, perhaps, as an aftereffect of the mutual constitution of subject and object, a retroprojection? You could imagine things, second, as what is excessive in objects, as what exceeds their mere materialization as objects or their mere utilization as objects—their force as a sensuous presence or as a metaphysical presence, the magic by which objects become values, fetishes, idols, and totems. Temporalized as the before and after of the object, thingness amounts to a latency (the not yet formed or the not yet formable) and to an excess (what remains physically or metaphysically irreducible to objects). But this temporality obscures the all-at-onceness, the simultaneity, of the object/thing dialectic and the fact that, all at once, *the thing seems to name the object, just as it is, even as it names some thing else.*

If thing theory sounds like an oxymoron, then, it may not be because things reside in some balmy elsewhere beyond theory but because they lie both at hand and somewhere outside the theoretical field, beyond a certain limit, as a recognizable yet illegible remainder or as the entifiable that is unspecifiable. Things lie beyond the grid of intelligibility the way mere things lie outside the grid of museal exhibition, outside the order of objects. If this is why things appear in the name of relief from ideas (what's encountered as opposed to what's thought), it is also why the Thing be-

15. By hastily tracking some of the ways we use *things* to both mark and manage uncertainty, I am specifically not deploying an etymological inquiry to delimit and vivify the meaning of things. But see, most famously, Marcel Mauss, who finds in the "best" etymology of *res* a means of claiming that *res* "need not have been the crude, merely tangible thing, the simple, passive object of transaction that it has become" (Marcel Mauss, *The Gift: The Form and Reason for Exchange in Archaic Societies,* trans. W. D. Halls [1950; New York, 1990], p. 50); and Martin Heidegger, who finds in the Old German *dinc* the denotation of a gathering of people that enables him to concentrate on how "thinging" gathers; see Martin Heidegger, "The Thing," in *Poetry, Language, Thought,* trans. Albert Hofstadter (New York, 1971), pp. 174–82. I should add that Heidegger believes that it is the English word *thing* that has preserved the "semantic power" of the original Roman word *res,* which is to say its capacity to designate a case, an affair, an event (p. 175). In turn, Michel Serres complains that such etymology—wherein objects exist "only according to assembly debates"—shows how "language wishes the whole world to derive from language" (Michel Serres, *Statues: Le Second Livre des fondations* [Paris, 1987], p. 111).

comes the most compelling name for that enigma that can only be en-
circled and which the object (by its presence) necessarily negates.¹⁶ In
Lacan, the Thing is and it isn't. It exists, but in no phenomenal form.

   The real, of course, is no more phenomenal in physics than it is in psychoanalysis—or, as in psychoanalysis, it is phenomenal only in its effects.
Somewhere beyond or beneath the phenomena we see and touch there
lurks some other life and law of things, the swarm of electrons. Nonetheless, even objects squarely within the field of phenomenality are often less
clear (that is, less opaque) the closer you look. As Georg Simmel said of tel-
escopic and microscopic technology, "coming closer to things often only
shows us how far away they still are from us."¹⁷ Sidney Nagel brings the form
of the drop into optical consciousness (pp. 23–39) and thus demonstrates
(like Ponge) how the most familiar forms, once we look, seem unpredictable
and inexplicable, to poets and physicists both. If, as Daniel Tiffany argues
(pp. 72–98), humanistic criticism should assert its explanatory power
when it comes to the problem of matter, this is because the problem can't be
sequestered from the tropes that make matter make sense.¹⁸
   Only by turning away from the problem of matter, and away from the
object/thing dialectic, have historians, sociologists, and anthropologists
been able to turn their attention to things (to the "social life of things" or the
"sex of things" or the "evolution of things"). As Arjun Appadurai has put it,
such work depends on a certain "methodological fetishism" that refuses to
begin with a formal "truth" that cannot, despite its truth, "illuminate the
concrete, historical circulation of things." In *The Social Life of Things*, he argues that "even though from a *theoretical* point of view human actors encode
things with significance, from a *methodological* point of view it is the things-
in-motion that illuminate their human and social context."¹⁹ Such methodological fetishism—what Appadurai calls the effort to "follow the things

   16. See Jacques Lacan, *The Ethics of Psychoanalysis 1959–1960*, volume 7 of *The Seminar of
Jacques Lacan*, trans. Dennis Porter, ed. Jacques-Alain Miller (New York, 1992), p. 139. The
Thing can only be "represented by emptiness, precisely because it cannot be represented by
anything else" (p. 129). For a useful commentary, see Slavoj Žižek, "Much Ado about a Thing,"
For They Know Not What They Do: Enjoyment as a Political Factor (London, 1991), pp. 229–78.
Doctrinaire Lacanians may tell you that the Thing names only one thing in Lacan, but in fact
it has different meanings and different valences in different texts and within single texts.
   17. Georg Simmel, *The Philosophy of Money*, trans. Tom Bottomore, David Frisby, and
Kaethe Mengelberg, 2d ed. (1907; New York, 1990), p. 475.
   18. For a further elaboration of this point, see Daniel Tiffany, *Toy Medium: Materialism
and Modern Lyric* (Berkeley, 2000) and *Material Events: Paul de Man and the Afterlife of Theory*,
ed. Tom Cohen et al. (Minneapolis, 2001).
   19. Arjun Appadurai, "Introduction: Commodities and the Politics of Value," in *The Social Life of Things: Commodities in Cultural Perspective*, ed. Appadurai (Cambridge, 1986), p. 5.

themselves"—disavows, no less, the tropological work, the psychological work, and the phenomenological work entailed in the human production of materiality as such. It does so, however, in the name of *avowing* the force of questions that have been too readily foreclosed by more familiar fetishizations: the fetishization of the subject, the image, the word. These are questions that ask less about the material effects of ideas and ideology than about the ideological and ideational effects of the material world and transformations of it. They are questions that ask not whether things are but what work they perform—questions, in fact, not about things themselves but about the subject-object relation in particular temporal and spatial contexts. These may be the first questions, if only the first, that precipitate a new materialism that takes objects for granted only in order to grant them their potency—to show how they organize our private and public affection.[20]

Methodological fetishism, then, is not an error so much as it is a condition for thought, new thoughts about how inanimate objects constitute human subjects, how they move them, how they threaten them, how they facilitate or threaten their relation to other subjects. What are the conditions, Jonathan Lamb asks (pp. 193–226), for sympathizing with animals and artifacts, and how does such sympathy threaten Locke's "thinking thing," the self? Why, Michael Taussig asks as he reads Sylvia Plath's last poems, does death have the capacity both to turn people into things and to bring inanimate objects to life (pp. 381–92)? How is it, Rey Chow asks, that an individual's collecting passion threatens the state (pp. 362–80)? (And why, we might ask, did the emotional response to the loss of built space, after 9/11, come to exceed the response to the loss of human lives, the towers having become something like the lost object as such?) These are questions that hardly abandon the subject, even when they do not begin there. When it comes to the Subject as such—that Cartesian subject which becomes the abstract subject of democracy and psychoanalysis—Matthew Jones points to its emergence within the spiritual exercise of concrete work, work with rulers and compasses.[21] He shows how "a simple mathematical instrument [the proportional compass] became the model and exemplar of Descartes's new subject," the subject "supposedly so removed from the material" (pp. 40–71).

What habits have prevented readers of Descartes from recognizing this material complication? What habits have prevented us—prevented you—from thinking about objects, let alone things? Or, more precisely, perhaps: what habits have prevented you from sharing your thoughts? In

---

20. The most influential books to introduce such questions have undoubtedly been Gaston Bachelard, *The Poetics of Space,* trans. Maria Jolas (Boston, 1969), and Susan Stewart, *On Longing: Narratives of the Miniature, the Gigantic, the Souvenir, the Collection* (Baltimore, 1984). For the most thorough recent representation of how objects organize human life, see the costarring role of the volleyball, Wilson, in *Castaway,* dir. Robert Zemeckis, prod. DreamWorks/Image Movers/Playtone, 2000.

21. On the Cartesian subject within democracy and psychoanalysis, see Joan Copjec, *Read My Desire: Lacan against the Historicists* (Cambridge, Mass., 1994), pp. 141–62.

one of his neglected, slightly mad manifestos, Jean Baudrillard sanely declares that "we have always lived off the splendor of the subject and the poverty of the object." "It is the subject," he goes on to write, "that makes history, it's the subject that totalizes the world," whereas the object "is shamed, obscene, passive." The object has been intelligible only as the "alienated, accursed part of the subject"—the "individual subject or collective subject, the subject of consciousness or the unconscious." "The fate of the object," to Baudrillard's knowledge, "has been claimed by no one."[22] And yet the very grandiosity of Baudrillard's claim about *the* object (and the "potency of the object") threatens the subject no more than it threatens (by absorbing) both objects and things.[23]

In a response both to perceptual phenomenology and to the ontological quest for being, Cornelius Castoriadis pronounced the need to abandon our image of representation as "a projection screen which, unfortunately, separates the 'subject' and the 'thing.'"[24] Representation does not provide "impoverished 'images' of things"; rather, "certain segments" of representation "take on the weight of an 'index of reality' and become 'stabilized', as well as they might, without this stabilization ever being assured once and for all, as 'perceptions of things'" (*I*, pp. 331, 332). The argument shares the more recent emphasis on understanding materiality as a materiality-effect,[25] but it most pointedly seeks to recast thingness and its apprehension within, and as, the domain of the social: the "'thing' and the 'individual', the individual as 'thing' and as the one for whom there are indubitably 'things' are [all], to begin with . . . dimensions of the institution of society" (*I*,

22. Jean Baudrillard, *Fatal Strategies*, trans. Philip Beitchman and W. G. J. Niesluchowski, ed. Jim Fleming (New York, 1990), p. 111. For a more sober account of this history, see Serres, *Statues*, pp. 208–12. For Baudrillard's own account of his manifesto in the context of his earlier thoughts about objects (under the spell, as it were, of Mauss and Bataille), see Baudrillard, "From the System to the Destiny of Objects," *The Ecstasy of Communication*, trans. Bernard and Caroline Schutze, ed. Sylvère Lotringer (New York, 1988), pp. 77–95 and "Revenge of the Crystal: An Interview by Guy Bellavance," *Revenge of the Crystal: Selected Writings on the Modern Object and Its Destiny, 1968–1983*, trans. and ed. Paul Foss and Julian Pefanis (London, 1990), pp. 15–34.

23. I've made this point at greater length in Bill Brown, "The Secret Life of Things: Virginia Woolf and the Matter of Modernism," *Modernism / Modernity* 6 (Apr. 1999): 1–28.

24. Cornelius Castoriadis, *The Imaginary Institution of Society*, trans. Kathleen Blamey (1975; Cambridge, Mass., 1987), p. 329; hereafter abbreviated *I*. Castoriadis is a theorist of plentitude and thus complains about desire being defined by the lack of a desired object, when in fact the object must be present to the psyche as desirable, which means that the psyche has in fact already fashioned it; see *I*, pp. 288–90. Still, there is what you might call a dialectic of insufficiency that proves more troubling; crudely put, deconstruction teaches that the word is never as good as the referent, but pychoanalysis teaches that the actual object is never as good as the sign.

25. Thus, for instance, Judith Butler writes, in a footnote emphasizing the "temporality of matter," and thinking through Marx's first thesis on Feuerbach, "if materialism were to

p. 332). By means of a particular "socialization of the psyche," then, "each society" imposes itself on the subject's senses, on the "*corporeal imagination*" by which materiality as such is apprehended (*I*, p. 334).

Though he is willing to grant (grudgingly) that there is some "transcultural pole of the institution of the things," one that "leans on the natural stratum," Castoriadis maintains, quite rightly, that this "still says nothing about *what* a thing is and what things are for a given society" (*I*, p. 334). The "perception of things" for an individual from one society, for instance, will be the perception of things "inhabited" and "animated"; for an individual from another society things will instead be "inert instruments, objects of possession" (*I*, pp. 334–35). This discrepancy between percepts (and thus not just the meaning but the very being of objects) has been a central topic of anthropology at least since the work of Marcel Mauss: however materially stable objects may seem, they are, let us say, different things in different scenes.[26] But when you ask "what things are for a given society" (noticing, by the way, how societies have taken the place of things as the given), surely the inquiry should include attention to those artistic and philosophical texts that would become sources, then, for discovering not epistemological or phenomenological truth, but the truth about what force things or the question of things might have in each society. Indeed, such attention would help to preclude the homogenization of each society in its insular eachness. For, on the one hand, differences *between* societies can be overdrawn; as Peter Stallybrass and Ann Rosalind Jones make clear (pp. 174–92), the Western Renaissance may have witnessed "fetishism" elsewhere, but it was saturated by a fetishism of its own. On the other, differences *within* each society can be overlooked: to call a woman in Soweto a "'slave of things'" is to charge her with being "'a white black woman.'"[27]

The question is less about "what things are for a given society" than about what claims on your attention and on your action are made on behalf of things. If society seems to impose itself on the "corporeal imagination," when and how does that imagination struggle against the imposition, and what role do things, physically or conceptually, play in the struggle? How does the effort to rethink things become an effort to *re*institute society? To declare that the character of things as things has been

---

take account of praxis as that which constitutes the very matter of objects, and praxis is understood as socially transformative activity, then such activity is understood as constitutive of materiality itself" (Butler, *Bodies That Matter*, p. 250 n. 5).

26. Thus Nicholas Thomas writes: "As socially and culturally salient entities, objects change in defiance of their material stability. The category to which a thing belongs, the emotion and judgment it prompts, and narrative it recalls, are all historically refigured" (Nicholas Thomas, *Entangled Objects: Exchange, Material Culture, and Colonialism in the Pacific* [Cambridge, Mass., 1991], p. 125). See also, for instance, *The Social Life of Things*, and *Border Fetishisms: Material Objects in Unstable Places*, ed. Patricia Spyer (New York, 1998).

27. Njabulo S. Ndebele, "The Music of the Violin," *"Fools" and Other Stories* (Johannesburg, 1983), p. 146.

extinguished, or that objects have been struck dumb, or that the idea of re-
specting things no longer makes sense because they are vanishing—this is
to find in the fate of things a symptom of a pathological condition most fa-
miliarly known as modernity.[28] In "Everyday Life and the Culture of the
Thing" (1925), for instance, Boris Arvatov recognized that the revolution
had yet to effect a fundamental change in the most quotidian interactions
with the physical object world, the step of overcoming the "rupture between
Things and people that characterized bourgeois society," the step of achieving a newly "active contact" with the things in Soviet society. If achieving
that change meant both encouraging the "psyche" to become "more thinglike" and "dynamiz[ing]" the thing into something "connected like a co-
worker with human practice," then Arvatov was imagining a novel
reification of people and a new personification of things that did not result
(as it does in the Marxian script) from society's saturation with the commodity form.[29] Constructivist materialism sought to recognize objects
as participants in the reshaping of the world: "Our things in our hands,"
Aleksandr Rodchenko claimed, "must be equals, comrades."[30] The women
of the Constructivist movement, designing and manufacturing post-
revolutionary clothes, came as close as anyone, Christina Kiaer argues
[pp. 245–303], to integrating "socialist objects" within the world of consum-
able goods. In the Italian "romance" that Jeffrey Schnapp reconstructs (pp.
304–29), this politicization of things is inverted into the materialization of
politics, the effort to fuse national and physical form. The call to "organize
aluminum" on behalf of the fascist state accompanies the declaration that aluminum is the "autarchic metal of choice," the "Italian metal" par excellence.
Today, in what Charity Scribner calls the "race to curate the socialist past,"
communist commodities achieve their final value as memorializing tokens
of daily life in the GDR (pp. 330–45). Materialism may persist in appearing
in the name of—or *as* the name of—politics, but these cases exhibit a more
intense effort to deploy material goods on behalf of a political agenda.

Beyond the boundaries of Soviet Russia, the conscious effort to
achieve greater intimacy with things, and to exert a different determination for them, took place, most famously and at times comically, within the
surrealist avant-garde. Among the various experimental "novelties" that

28. See Georg Lukács, *History and Class Consciousness: Studies in Marxist Dialectics,* trans.
Rodney Livingstone (Cambridge, Mass., 1971), p. 92; Siegfried Kracauer, "Farewell to the Lin-
den Arcade," *The Mass Ornament: Weimar Essays,* trans. and ed. Thomas Y. Levin (Cambridge,
Mass., 1995), p. 342; and Hans-Georg Gadamer, "The Nature of Things and the Language of
Things," *Philosophical Hermeneutics,* trans. and ed. David E. Linge (Berkeley, 1976), p. 71.

29. Boris Arvatov, "Everyday Life and the Culture of the Thing (Toward the Formulation of the Question)," trans. Christina Kiaer, *October,* no. 81 (Summer 1997): 121, 124, 126.
See Kiaer's important introduction to the piece, "Boris Arvatov's Socialist Objects," *October,*
no. 81 (Summer 1997): 105–18.

30. Quoted in Kiaer, "Rodchenko in Paris," *October,* no. 75 (Winter 1996): 3. I want to
thank Susan Buck-Morss for drawing my attention to this essay.

would unify "thought with the object" through some "*direct* contact with the object," Salvador Dali "dream[ed] of a mysterious manuscript written in white ink and completely covering the strange, firm surfaces of a brand-new Roll-Royce."[31] Although words and things have long been considered deadly rivals, as Peter Schwenger details (pp. 135–49), Dali had faith that they could be fused and that "everyone" would "be able to read from things."[32] When André Breton first dreamed up surrealism, he did so by trying to make good on a dream. He dreamed of finding a book at a flea market, a book with a wooden statue of an Assyrian gnome as its spine, and with pages made of black wool. "I hastened to acquire it," he writes, "and when I woke up I regretted not finding it near me." Still, he hoped "to put a few objects like this in circulation."[33]

By transforming the bricolage of the dreamwork into the practice of everyday life, the surrealists registered their refusal to occupy the world as it was. Walter Benjamin claimed they were "less on the trail of the psyche than on the track of things," acting less as psychoanalysts than as anthropologists. In "Dream Kitsch," he fuses the surrealist invigoration of cultural debris with the movement's own invigoration from "tribal artifacts." He describes them seeking "the totemic tree of objects within the thicket of primal history. The very last, the topmost face on the totem pole, is that of kitsch." Though this image visualizes the animation projected onto or into the "outlived world of things," the essay concludes by describing the process in reverse, describing how "in kitsch, the world of things advances on the human being" and "ultimately fashions its figures in his interior."[34] Subjects may constitute objects, but within Benjamin's materialism things have already installed themselves in the human psyche.

"Formal truths" about how things are part and parcel of society's institution hardly help to explain the ways that things have been recast in the effort to achieve some confrontation with, and transformation of, society. Because Benjamin devoted himself to such explanations he assumes particular authority in the following pages. Among the other writers invoked in this collection, Bruno Latour exerts no less influence, and in his own contribution to the volume he interrupts the trajectory of Heidegger's fa-

31. Salvador Dali, "The Object as Revealed in Surrealist Experiment" (1931), in *Theories of Modern Art,* ed. Herschel B. Chipp (Berkeley, 1968), p. 424.

32. Ibid.

33. André Breton, *Introduction au discours sur le peu de réalité* (1927), which he quotes (dating it 1924, the year of his originating surrealist manifesto), in "Surrealist Situation of the Object" (1935), *Manifestoes of Surrealism,* trans. Richard Seaver and Helen R. Lane (Ann Arbor, Mich., 1972), p. 277.

34. Walter Benjamin, "Dream Kitsch" (1927), trans. Howard Eiland, *Selected Writings,* trans. Rodney Livingston et al., ed. Michael Jennings, Eiland, and Gary Smith, 4 vols. to date (Cambridge, Mass., 1999–2003), 2:4. In "Several Points on Folk Art," he writes that "art teaches us to see into things. Folk art and kitsch allow us to look out through things." But this act of looking *through* things depends on the human application of them as though they were a mask fused to the sensorium (Benjamin, "Einiges zur Volkskunst," *Gesammelte Schriften,* ed. Rolf Tiedemann

mous essay on "The Thing" to ask if it isn't the othering of people that the thingness of things discloses (pp. 151–73). In the past, he has forcefully and repeatedly insisted that "things do not exist without being full of people" and that considering humans necessarily involves the consideration of things. The subject/object dialectic itself (with which he simply has no truck) has obscured patterns of circulation, transference, translation, and displacement.[35] Latour has argued that modernity artificially made an ontological distinction between inanimate objects and human subjects, whereas in fact the world is full of "quasi-objects" and "quasi-subjects," terms he borrows from Michel Serres.[36] Whereas the eighteenth-century automata described by Jessica Riskin were meant to test the boundaries between synthetic and natural life, between mechanism and vitality, between people and things (pp. 99–133), modernism's resistance to modernity lay not least in its effort to deny such distinctions. Yet modernism's own "discourse of things," as John Frow calls it (pp. 346–61), is far from consistent in what it reveals as the source of the thing's animation.

If modernism, when struggling to integrate the animate and the inanimate, humans and things, always knew that we have never been modern, this hardly means that you should accept such knowledge as a *fait accompli*. Indeed, Theodor Adorno, arguing against epistemology's and phenomenology's subordination of the object and the somatic moment to a fact of consciousness, understood the alterity of things as an essentially ethical fact. Most simply put, his point is that accepting the otherness of things is the condition for accepting otherness as such.[37]

When, shortly after the millennium turned, I told an art historian that I was working on things and editing the special issue of *Critical Inquiry* on which this book is based, she responded by saying: "Ah, well: it's

---

and Herman Schweppenhäuser, 7 in 14 vols. [Frankfurt am Main, 1972–89], 6:187; trans. Darren Ilett. See also Benjamin, "Surrealism: The Last Snapshot of the European Intelligentsia," trans. Edmund Jephcott, *Selected Writings*, 2:207–21). In all these essays, Benjamin is developing an image of "innervation," a term he uses to describe the mimetic internalization of the physical world—eventually the internalization of technological apparatuses. See Miriam Bratu Hansen, "Benjamin and Cinema: Not a One-Way Street," *Critical Inquiry* 25 (Winter 1999): 306–43.

35. Bruno Latour, "The Berlin Key or How to Do Words with Things," trans. Lydia Davis, in *Matter, Materiality, and Modern Culture*, ed. P. M. Graves-Brown (London, 2000), pp. 10, 20.

36. See Latour, *We Have Never Been Modern*, trans. Catherine Porter (Cambridge, Mass., 1993), pp. 10–11. For a history outside the realm of sociology, see Miguel Tamen, *Friends of Interpretable Objects* (Cambridge, Mass., 2000), and Tiffany, *Toy Medium*.

37. See Theodor W. Adorno, *Negative Dialectics*, trans. E. B. Ashton (New York, 1997), pp. 189–94; see also p. 16. Unlikely as it seems, it would be possible to relate this claim to the way that, for Lacan, the Thing proves to be the center around which the drive achieves its ethical force.

the topic of the 1990s the way it was of the 1920s, isn't it?"[38] This first felt like an unwitting accusation of belatedness (in the year 2000), and it did so because the academic psyche has internalized the fashion system (a system meant to accelerate the obsolescence of *things*). Still, if Benjamin was able to outstep the avant-garde in the 1920s by conceptualizing the "revolutionary energies" of surrealism's materialist bricolage,[39] this was in part because of the sociological ground cleared by Simmel's earlier account of the gap between the "culture of things" and modernity's human subject, and because of his insistence that the subject's desire, and not productive labor, is the source of an object's value.[40] Benjamin recognized that the gap between the function of objects and the desires congealed there became clear only when those objects became outmoded. Things seems like a topic of the nineties as it was of the twenties because the outmoded insights of the twenties (insights of Benjamin, of Bataille, of O'Keefe, among others) were reinvigorated.[41] Among those insights, we learn that history is exactly the currency that things trade in and that obsolescence as an accusation, whenever it represses its own history, is utterly passé. Things seems like a topic of the 1990s no less because, as the twentieth century drew to a close, it became clear that certain objects—Duchamp's *Fountain*, Man Ray's *Object to Be Destroyed*, Joseph Beuys's *Fat Chair*—kept achieving new novelty, and that modes of artistic production that foreground object culture more than image culture (mixed media collage, the readymade, the *objet trouvé*) would persevere.[42]

But what decade of the century didn't have its own thing about things? Given Heidegger's lecture "The Thing" in 1950 and Lacan's location of the Thing *at* and *as* the absent center of the real in 1959; given Frank O'Hara's declaration that "the eagerness of objects to / be what we are afraid to do /

38. Although things may seem to have achieved a new prominence, I want to point out that *Modern Starts: People, Places, Things*, ed. John Elderfield et al. (exhibition catalog, Museum of Modern Art, New York, 7 Oct. 1999–14 Mar. 2000) symptomatically diminished things in relation to place and to people. In the exhibition catalogue, things receive only 58 (of 360) pages of attention.

39. Benjamin, "Surrealism," 2:210.

40. Simmel, "The Future of Our Culture" (1909), *Simmel on Culture*, trans. Mark Ritter and David Frisby, ed. Frisby and Mike Featherstone (London, 1997), p. 101. By complicating the ideas he formulated in the 1890s, Simmel's best students—Lukács, Bloch, Benjamin, and Kracauer—achieved insights about the "culture of things" that continue to inspire some of today's most ambitious cultural analysis.

41. See, for instance, Michael Taussig, *Mimesis and Alterity: A Particular History of the Senses* (New York, 1993), pp. 232–33; Yve-Alain Bois and Krauss, *Formless: A User's Guide* (Cambridge, Mass., 1997); and Wanda M. Corn, *The Great American Thing: Modern Art and National Identity, 1915–1935* (Berkeley, 1999).

42. See, for instance, Benjamin H. D. Buchloh's account of Arman's work of the 1950s in relation to the paradigm of the readymade, *Neo–Avant-garde and Culture Industry: Essays on European and American Art from 1955 to 1975* (Cambridge, Mass., 2000), pp. 269–79.

cannot help but move us" in 1951,[43] Rauschenberg's aggressive interruption of abstract expressionism with the combine, and the *chosisme* of the decade's *nouveau roman*, the postwar era looks like an era both overwhelmed by the proliferation of things and singularly attentive to them. Only belatedly, in the 1980s, did Baudrillard declare that just as modernity was the historical scene of the subject's emergence, so postmodernity is the scene of the object's preponderance. If a genealogy of things has yet to be written, there's still a patent conceptual geology where simple elements appear in multiple layers—the scandal of the surrealist veneration of detritus reasserted in Claes Oldenburg's claim that a "refuse lot in the city is worth all the art stores in the world" and the scandal of the ready-made resurfacing as the very different scandal of pop art, in work like Oldenberg's best-known oversized and understuffed everyday objects: the mixer, the cheeseburger, the light bulb, the telephone, the wall switch, the ice-cream cone.[44]

Since his exhibition at the Green Gallery in New York, 1962, through which he transformed himself from a dramaturg of happenings to the most noteworthy pop sculptor (as the stage sets for the happenings were disassembled into distinct works), Oldenberg has re-created, with relentless consistency, the iconic objects of everyday life. Donald Judd called Oldenburg's objects "grossly anthropomorphized."[45] Indeed, they are invariably and teasingly mammary, ocular, phallic, facial, vaginal, scrotal. But the very "blatancy," as Judd went on to argue, seems to ridicule anthropomorphism as such.[46] In the same way, the grossly mimetic character of the work draws attention to the discrepancy between objectivity and materiality, perception and sensation, objective presence (a fan, a Fudgsicle, a sink) and material presence (the canvas, the plaster of paris, the vinyl), as though to theatricalize the point that all objects (not things) are, first off, iconic signs. (A sink looks like a sink.)

Despite the enormousness and enormity of objective culture in Oldenburg's world, it has somehow lost its potency. In the presence of his monumentally flaccid objects, it is difficult not to suffer some vague feeling of loss, as though they were half-deflated balloons, lingering in the ballroom two

---

43. Frank O'Hara, "Interior (With Jane)," *The Collected Poems of Frank O'Hara*, ed. Donald Allen (New York, 1971), ll. 1–3, p. 55. For the material context of such attention in postwar France—that is, the sudden proliferation of American objects—see Kristin Ross, *Fast Cars, Clean Bodies: Decolonization and the Reordering of French Culture* (Cambridge, Mass., 1996). Georges Perec's *Les Choses: Une Histoire des années soixante* (Paris, 1965) may have restored a Balzacian mise-en-scène to the novel, but décor became the scene of depletion, an arrangement of empty signs, which is why the arrangement was such an inspiration for Baudrillard's *System of Objects*, trans. James Benedict (1968; New York, 1996).

44. Quoted by Barbara Rose, *Claes Oldenburg* (New York, 1970), p. 46.

45. Donald Judd, "Specific Objects" (1965), *Complete Writings, 1959–1975* (New York, 1975), p. 189.

46. Ibid.

days after the party, hovering at eye level, now, and rather worn out. Finally allowed to relax, to just be themselves, objects sink into themselves, weary of form; they consider sinking into an amorphous heap, submitting to the *idée fixe* of gravity. Oldenburg's work may be melodramatic and sentimental, as Michael Fried declared in 1962, but it is also *about* melodrama and sentiment, meant to pose some question about, by physically manifesting, the affective investment Americans have in the hamburger, the ice-cream cone, chocolate cake.[47] Why have we turned the cheeseburger into a totemic food, a veritable member of the family, a symbol of the national clan? Though art may seem to be, most fundamentally, "a projection of our mental images upon the world of things," this is art that instead shows how weary that world has become of all our projections.[48] If these objects are tired, they are tired of our perpetual reconstitution of them as objects of our desire and of our affection. They are tired of our longing. They are tired of us.

But a recent work of Oldenburg's, *Typewriter Eraser,* gleams in the new sculpture garden outside the National Gallery in Washington D.C. Unlike his myriad soft objects, the eraser is pert, it is rigid, it is full of life and stands at attention, if slightly askew, its chrome as bright as the typical typewriter eraser was always dirty and dull. The pleasure of looking at the people looking at the *Typewriter Eraser,* amused by its monumentality, is inseparable from the pleasure of listening to the child who, befuddled by an anachronistic object she never knew, pleads: "What is that thing supposed to be?" What is this disk with the brush sticking out of it? What was a typewriter? How did that form ever function? The plea expresses the power of this particular work to dramatize a generational divide and to stage (to melodramatize, even) the question of obsolescence. While the "timeless" objects in the Oldenburg canon (fans and sinks) have gone limp, this abandoned object attains a new stature precisely because it has no life outside the boundary of art—no life, that is, within our everyday lives. Released from the bond of being equipment, sustained outside the irreversibility of technological history, the object becomes something else.[49]

If, to the student of Oldenburg, the eraser ironically comments on the artist's own obsession with typewriters, it more simply transforms a dead commodity into a living work and thus shows how inanimate objects organize the temporality of the animate world. W. J. T. Mitchell makes it clear

47. See Michael Fried, "New York Letter," in *Pop Art: A Critical History,* ed. Steven Henry Madoff (Berkeley, 1997), p. 216; Oldenburg's aggressive consciousness of his sentimentality is suggested by the "nougat" in the following statement from his manifesto: "I am for the art of rust and mold. I am for the art of hearts, funeral hearts or sweetheart hearts, full of nougat. I am for the art of worn meathooks, and singing barrels of red, white, blue and yellow meat" (Claes Oldenburg, "Statement" [1961], in *Pop Art,* p. 215).

48. Rudolf Arnheim, "Art among the Objects," *Critical Inquiry* 13 (Summer 1987): 679.

49. Heidegger taxonomizes things into mere things (such as pebbles), equipment, and work (such as art). Much of pop art, of course, works to elide such distinctions. See Heidegger, "The Origin of the Work of Art," *Poetry, Language, Thought,* pp. 15–88.

(pp. 227–44) that the discovery of a new kind of object in the eighteenth century, the fossil, enabled romanticism to recognize and to refigure its relation to the mortal limits of the natural world. In the case of the Oldenburg eraser, the present, which is the future that turned this object into a thing of the past, is the discourse network 2000, where the typewriter eraser has disappeared, not just into the self-correcting Selectric, but into the delete function. How, Oldenburg's object seems to ask, will the future of your present ever understand your rhetoric of inscription, erasure, and the trace?[50]

As a souvenir from the museum of twentieth-century history, the *Typewriter Eraser* reminds us that if the topic of things attained a new urgency in the closing decades of that century, this may have been a response to the digitization of our world—just as, perhaps, the urgency in the 1920s was a response to film. But in the twenties the cinema provided a projection screen that didn't separate people and things but brought them closer, granting props the status of individuals, enabling neglected objects to assume their rightful value.[51] As Lesley Stern puts it (pp. 393–430), things can grab our attention on film; and they do so because they have become not just objects but actions. Even at rest, in the photographs of Wright Morris that Alan Trachtenberg studies (pp. 431–56), objects, caught however slightly off guard, begin to achieve the status of things. New media—perspectival painting, printing, telegraphy—each in its way newly mediates the relation between people and objects, each precipitates distance *and* proximity.

You could say that today's children were born too late to understand this memorial to another mode of writing, or you could say that Oldenberg (cleverly) re-created the object too late for it to be generally understood. It is an object that helps to dramatize a basic disjunction, a human condition in which things inevitably seem too late—belated, in fact, because we want things to come before ideas, before theory, before the word, whereas they seem to persist in coming after: as the alternative to ideas, the limit to theory, victims of the word. If thinking the thing, to borrow Heidegger's phrase, feels like an exercise in belatedness, the feeling is provoked by our very capacity to imagine that thinking and thingness are utterly distinct.

---

50. On the new tropes provided by new media, see the closing chapter of Eric Jager, *The Book of the Heart* (Chicago, 2000).

51. See Benjamin, "The Work of Art in the Age of Mechanical Reproduction," *Illuminations*, trans. Harry Zohn, ed. Hannah Arendt (New York, 1969), pp. 217–51; Jean Epstein, "*Bonjour Cinéma* and Other Writings by Jean Epstein," trans. Tom Milne, *Afterimage* 10 (Autumn 1981): 19; and Fernand Léger, *Functions of Painting*, trans. Alexandra Anderson (New York, 1965), p. 50. For an account of how assessments of early cinema obsess about the new magical powers bestowed on objects, see Rachel O. Moore, *Savage Theory: Cinema as Modern Magic* (Durham, N.C., 2000).

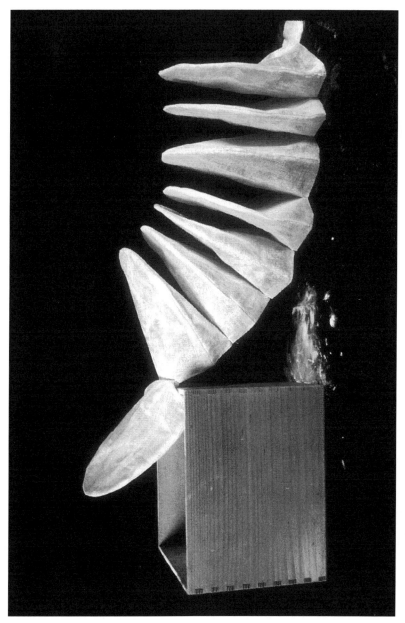

FIG. 1.—Kyle Huffman, *Mask 1*, 1996. Wood, gauze, shellac, cornstarch. Photo: courtesy of the artist.

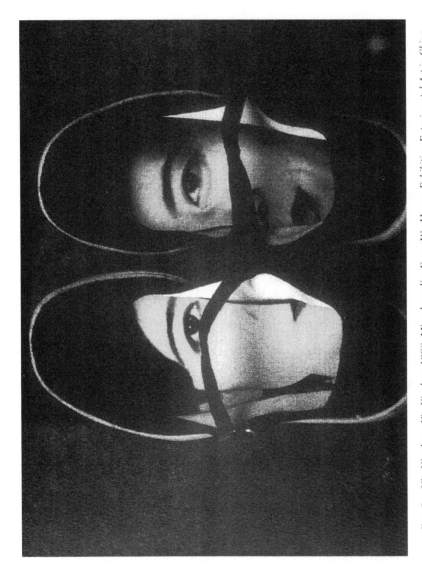

FIG. 2.—Yin Xiuzhen, *Yin Xiuzhen*, 1998. Mixed media. From Wu Hung, *Exhibiting Experimental Art in China* (Chicago, 2000).

FIG. 3.—Irina Nakhova, *Big Red*, 1998. Installation, Galerie Eboran, Salzburg.

FIG. 4.—Claes Oldenberg, *Typewriter Eraser,* 1999. Washington, D.C. Photo: Kandice Chuh.

cravats
crayons
crazy straws
credenzas
credit cards
credits
crewneck sweaters
cribbage boards
cribs
crochet hooks
crockery
crockpots
croquet sets
crosses
crossword puzzles
crowbars
crowns
crucifixes
cruise control
cruise ships
crutches
cryostats
crystal
crystal balls
cubicles
cuckoo clocks
cuff links
cuffs
culottes
cummerbunds
cup holders
cupboards
cups
curbs
curios
curlers
curling irons
currency
curricula
curtain rods
curtains
cushions
cuticle creams
cuticle nippers
cutlery
cutting boards
cymbals
dams
dances
dashboards
day planners
dead bolts
debutante balls
debuts
decanters
decoys
deep fat fryers
defenses
delicatessens
demonstrations
dens

dental crowns
dental flosses
dentures
deodorants
depilatories
deposit slips
depots
derbies
derricks
desks
desserts
detergents
devotionals
diadems
diagrams
dialysis machines
diapers 18
diaphragms
diaries
dice
dictionaries
diets
digital cameras
dikes
dildos
dimmers
dinghies
dining rooms
dinners
dioramas
directories
disco balls
discos
dishes
dishwashers
disks
dispensers
display stands
displays
dissertations
diving bells
docks
dog collars
dog dishes
doghouses
doilies
dollhouses
dollies
dolls
domes
dominoes
donut shops
donuts
door knockers
door stops
doorbells
doorknobs
doormats
doors
dormitories
downspouts

drains
dramas
drapes
drawer pulls
dreidels
dress patterns
dressers
dresses
dressings
drill bits
drill presses
drills
drinking fountains
drive trains
driveways
drugs 39
drugstores
drums
dry erase boards
dry erase pens
drywall
dune buggies
dustpans
duvets
DVD players
DVDs
dynamos
earpieces
earmuffs
earrings
ears
eggs 49
electric chairs
electrified fences
electrocardiographs
electronic games 20
elevators
embroidery hoops
emergency brakes
emergency exits
emery boards
encyclopedias
engines
engravings
envelopes
epaulets
erasers
escalators
espresso makers
exams
exercise machines
exercises
exhaust pipes
exhibitions
experiments
explosives
extension cords
extensions
eyeglasses
eyelash curlers
eyelets

eyeliner
eyes
eyeshadow
fabrics
fabric softeners
facelifts
faceplates
fairs
fake nails
families
fan belts
fans
faucets
fax machines 44
feather dusters
fedoras
feedbags
ferries
ferris wheels
fertilizers
festivals
fezzes
figurines
files
fillings
film
fire extinguishers
fire hoses
fire hydrants
fireplaces
fireworks
firing ranges
first aid kits
fish food
fish tanks
fishing hooks
fishing lures
fishing rods
fixtures
flags
flash bulbs
flasks
fliers
flies
flip-flops
flippers
floor plans
flooring
flotation devices
flower arrangements
flower pots
flowers
flues
flutes
fly swatters
fog lights
foghorns
folders
folding chairs
fondue pots
fonts 46

FIG. 5—From *Voices* (exhibition catalog, AIGA National Design Conference, 23–26 Sept. 2001, Washington D.C.), p. 3.

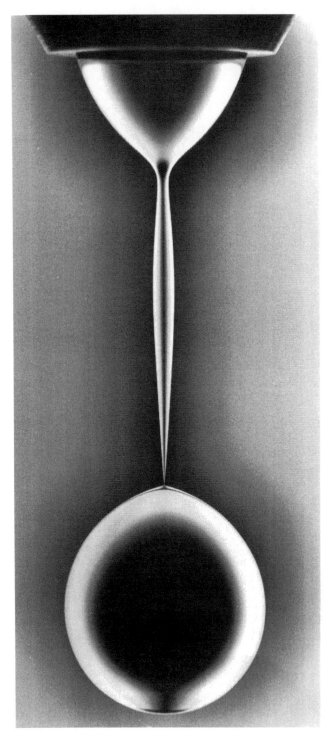

COVER PHOTO—A drop of glycerol (a liquid with a viscosity one thousand times greater than that of water) breaking apart inside another fluid, PDMS, of the same viscosity as the glycerol. Photo: Sidney R. Nagel and Itai Cohen.

Shadows and Ephemera

Sidney R. Nagel

The serenity of the picture of the drop falling obscures the violence taking place beneath the surface as the fluid fissions and becomes two separate drops. The sinuous contours of the drop, apparently hanging quietly in space, give no suggestion that at a more microscopic scale molecules are moving rapidly, tearing apart from one another. We see a departure from smoothness only at the apex of the conical neck connecting the round liquid sphere at the bottom to the brass nozzle at the top. If we had taken the picture a moment later, the liquid would be in two disconnected pieces separated at the tip of that cone; a moment earlier it would have hung together in one large and rather boring blob. An extraordinary transition is taking place (figs. 1a–b).

Am I captivated by this image because of its sensuous gracefulness? by its freezing in time of rapid dynamics? or am I engaged by it because the photograph is itself a shadow suggesting and contributing to a more complete view of the drop—an image giving us a handle on what processes are at work as the drop breaks apart? I am attracted for all these reasons.

I have used the word *shadow* deliberately since it suggests two important aspects of the research that produced this image. The word is of course the symbolic metaphor at the heart of Plato's myth of the cave in which we, in the real world, can only glimpse shadows cast by the eternal forms. Our knowledge and understanding of the world is incomplete until we perceive the forms themselves. The word has also been used by William Henry Fox Talbot, one of the inventors of photography, who

characterized his invention as "the art of fixing a shadow."[1] The marvel
of photography is, of course, that it allows one to record, permanently
and precisely, the patterns of light and shadow on a sheet of paper. Photography plays many roles: for a photographer like Minor White it is the
art of catching a dream, while for a street photographer like Robert Frank
it is the art of capturing the iconography of a time and place.[2] However,
for a scientist such as Harold Edgerton, the task can be more straightforward: photography provides a means of catching the shadows cast by the
ephemeral objects of our world, which we can then analyze later at our
leisure.

My guess is that most physicists are Platonists at heart. We are taught
from the very first that there are laws governing the way nature behaves.
Although these laws are, we like to think, universal and immutable, they
are not obvious. The laws of mechanics, of electricity and magnetism,
of relativity and quantum mechanics are all remarkable, subtle, and of
exceptional generality. Something that is not as often emphasized is that
the idea of universality can extend to the objects themselves and is not
merely relegated to the laws that govern their interactions.

Let me give one example of a common object that displays this universality of form to a remarkable extent. Everyone is by now aware of the
electron. Electrons run through our household wires, they surround all
atoms and participate in the chemical bonding that keeps our world together and gives it form. The electron is as real to us (and in some cases
more real) than most other objects in our world. Yet none of us has ever
actually beheld an electron. It is far too small to be seen by our eyes,
touched by our hands, smelled, tasted, or heard. It is not an obvious concept, and a few hundred years ago it probably had not even been con-
jectured. Yet today we *know* electrons exist. Moreover, today the electron
exists in a manner that is absolutely surprising and would have, I believe,

1. William Henry Fox Talbot, *Some Account of the Art of Photogenic Drawing, or the Process by Which Natural Objects May Be Made to Delineate Themselves without the Aid of the Artist's Pencil* (London, 1839).

It is also the title of a book on the history of photography: Sarah Greenough et al., *On the Art of Fixing a Shadow : One Hundred and Fifty Years of Photography* (exhibition catalog, National Gallery of Art, 7 May–30 July 1989).

2. See *Mirrors And Windows: American Photography Since 1960*, ed. John Szarkowski (exhibition catalog, Museum of Modern Art, New York, 28 July–2 Oct. 1978).

Sidney R. Nagel, the Stein-Freiler Distinguished Service Professor of Physics at the University of Chicago, has worked on problems dealing with nonlinear and disordered phenomena appearing in macroscopic systems far from equilibrium. He has recently coedited with Andrea J. Liu *Jamming and Rheology: Constrained Dynamics on Microscopic and Macroscopic Scales* (London, 2001).

astounded even Plato. It is a pure embodiment of a Platonic form. All electrons are identical to one another—they have the same electric charge, the same mass, the same spin. There is no way, *even in principle*, of telling them apart. The statistics that we must use to describe these quantum objects takes this indistinguishability into account explicitly. We know of their existence only by secondhand observations, by detecting their sometimes small and sometimes large effects discernible in the macroscopic world—that is, in the metaphor of the cave, by detecting their shadows. If ever there was a case to be made for the material existence of a Platonic form, the electron surely must be that manifestation.

Electrons, of course, are not the only indistinguishable objects. All of the elementary particles have this same property. Thus all protons are the same and all neutrons are identical. Nor, as I alluded to above, does the concept of universality apply only to the microscopic scale. We see it on all levels. We are, I dare say, familiar with the nearly parabolic arc traversed by an object tossed in the air—a baseball knocked out of a stadium, for example. The marvelous photographs of a bouncing ball by Bernice Abbott capture an approximation to this ideal arc.[3] Although one might quibble that this shape-of-the-trajectory is not a material object, it does nonetheless show how dynamics can produce both elegant and universal forms.

All of this brings me back to the picture of the drop that I mentioned at the outset. At its essence, this photograph displays another Platonic form—the drop at the moment of breakup. It shares with the example of the arc of the thrown ball that it is formed by the dynamics of the situation. However, it also shares with the example of the electron that it is a material object, however much the specificity of the object depends on the precise moment of its existence. What I want to argue is that this object is itself universal and that whenever we think of the thing a-drop-breaking-apart we necessarily allude to the scene depicted in the first photograph.

The explanation for why this is true is so elementary (although it can look complicated when the mathematical formulae are included to make the argument rigorous) that I cannot resist mentioning it here.[4] It depends on the realization that in the vicinity of the neck, where the drop

3. See Bernice Abbott, *Photographs* (Washington, D.C., 1970), pp. 156–57.

4. The ideas of scale invariance in fluid dynamics go back a long way and appear in many manifestations. The work on drop breakup is only one example of where these ideas arise. The work described in this article is from Xiangdong Shi, Michael P. Brenner, and Sidney R. Nagel, "A Cascade of Structure in a Drop Falling from a Faucet," *Science,* 8 July 1994, pp. 219–22; Brenner et al., "Breakdown of Scaling in Droplet Fission at High Reynolds Number," *Physics of Fluids* 9 (June 1997): 1573–90; and Itai Cohen et al., "Two Fluid Drop Snap-Off Problem: Experiments and Theory," *Physical Review Letters,* 9 Aug. 1999, pp. 1147–50. Much of the work on the breakup of drops is reviewed in Jens Eggers, "Nonlinear Dynamics and Breakup of Free-Surface Flows," *Reviews of Modern Physics* 69 (July 1997): 865–929.

eventually breaks apart, the thickness of the fluid must become arbitrarily small. After all, the neck decreases in diameter until its thickness goes to zero. Thus, at some point, it has become so much smaller than any other macroscopic length in the problem that those larger lengths can no longer matter for a description of the neck itself. It is smaller than the nozzle holding it. It is smaller than the size of the separating round drop at the bottom (whose size is determined by a competition of the downward pull of gravity against the force of surface tension holding the liquid together). If we ask what determines the dynamics in the vicinity of this thinnest point in the neck, we have to admit that it only makes sense that the dynamics should depend *only* on the thickness of the neck itself and cannot depend on the size of the nozzle or the size of the drop. So, the dynamics in the neck only depends on its thickness and we have arrived at a chicken-and-egg situation: The thickness of the neck depends only on the dynamics (since the dynamics is what pulls the neck into a thin thread in the first place), which in turn depends only on the thickness, and this repetition continues ad infinitum. As time goes on toward the point of pinchoff, the neck conforms to a very special shape—one that must be similar to its own shape at both an earlier and a later time. The only thing that happens as the drop gets closer to the point of snapoff is that the neck gets thinner and more stretched out, but the overall shape must remain the same—only scaled by different amounts in the radial and axial directions at different times. It is thus a *universal* shape.[5]

The point I want to emphasize is that the object shown in the photograph of the drop breaking apart is, like the electron, a Platonic form. The photograph has fixed on paper a shadow that is precisely the shadow of the Platonic metaphor. Every drop of water falling will look exactly like this in the vicinity of snapoff. It does not matter that this drop was held by a nozzle and was pulled down by gravity. As we can see in figure 1b, the drop actually breaks up in at least two points, one near the bottom as shown in the first picture and again when the satellite drop breaks off

---

5. Making this argument rigorous requires finding a *scaling* description for the interfacial shape near the point of snapoff. If h(z,t) is the radius of the drop at a vertical position, z, and time, t (where z and t are each measured with respect to the position and time of the snapoff singularity), a scaling solution asserts that h(z,t) is related to H(ζ), a function of a single variable, $\zeta = z\,t^{-\beta}$:

$$h(z,t) = t^{\alpha}\,H(\zeta)$$

where α and β are exponents that need to be determined. The idea of universality classes is that over a wide range of physical parameters, these exponents α and β will not vary and that all systems in the same class will have the same shape at snapoff. Such a solution is verified by inserting it into the Navier-Stokes equations describing the motion of the fluid interface. The scaling equation for the shape near the singularity, using the single variable ζ, provides a much simplified description of the shape and the dynamics of the drop. The *understanding* of the process that I detailed in the text is obtained from an analysis of the implications of such scaling phenomena.

near the nozzle. The second image shows that the cone-into-sphere shape of the snapoff is the same pointing upward near the nozzle as it was pointing downward near the initial drop. The point of breakup would have looked the same even if it had been formed from a wave tossed into the air at the shores of Lake Michigan.

The shape of the drop at snapoff is robust—indeed, universal. The reason for this remarkable fact is that there are so many constraints on the shape (it must look both as if it is almost separated into two drops and also as if it is almost one single mass of fluid) that the normal variety of parameters that we can vary for a liquid does not play an important role in the physics at the point of snapoff. However, we *can* tune the parameters so that different regimes appear in the viewfinder of our camera. Thus the picture on the front of this journal is a drop of one liquid breaking apart while falling through a second fluid rather than through air, as was the case in figures 1a and 1b. In this image the region around the point of fission looks different. However, over a wide range of parameters this shape, too, would be robust and universal. It is another Platonic form. These photographs have helped us isolate the one particular region of universal behavior in an otherwise profoundly mundane object. It has, at the same time, managed to make visible the elegant and serene. Photography as a tool has managed to let us isolate a truly ephemeral object, the drop-at-the-point-of-snapoff. Without this tool, it would have been impossible to see the shape of the drop both because the snapoff process occurs too rapidly and because the features of the neck are too difficult to resolve with the naked eye alone.[6] Photography has made objective the

6. This discovery by photographic means recalls a passage from Walter Benjamin on the optical unconscious:

> The enlargement of a snapshot does not simply render more precise what in any case was visible, though unclear: it reveals entirely new structural formations of the subject. So, too, slow motion not only presents familiar qualities of movement but reveals in them entirely unknown ones. . . . Evidently a different nature opens itself to the camera than opens to the naked eye—if only because an unconsciously penetrated space is substituted for a space consciously explored by man.

(Walter Benjamin, "The Work of Art in the Age of Mechanical Reproduction," *Illuminations: Essays and Reflections,* trans. Harry Zohn, ed. Hannah Arendt [New York, 1969], p. 236)
In an explication of this notion, Joel Snyder asks: "If the photograph fails to show us 'the way things look,' does it achieve accuracy by showing us 'the way things *are?*' How shall we characterize the relation of photographs to the world? In Benjamin's view, the photograph destroys the traditional relationship of the picture to the world as perceived" (Joel Snyder, "Benjamin on Reproducibility and Aura: A Reading of 'The Work of Art in the Age of Its Technical Reproducibility,'" in *Benjamin: Philosophy, Aesthetics, History,* ed. Gary Smith [Chicago, 1983], p. 161).
These excerpts raise important issues related to how we learn, or decide upon, the "truth" in scientific thought. I do not want to digress into those issues here. I would simply maintain that a discovery about nature made through the use of photography is not so different in its implications for scientific knowledge than the myriad other discoveries made

robust features of the physics—features that I would argue are as universal as the inherent properties of an elementary particle.

The argument that I have used to suggest that the drop near the point of snapoff has universal properties, and thus qualifies as a Platonic form, rests on the idea that we can *scale* the shape at different times so that the set of pictures for each drop approaching snapoff can be superimposed onto a common curve. This is a symmetry of nature no less than, for example, the mirror symmetry that takes right into left-handedness. If one magnifies an object and finds that upon increasing its size one again obtains the same pattern, then we call the object a fractal. Some objects have this symmetry and some do not, just as some objects are symmetric between right and left and some, such as your hands, are not. The human eye is particularly sensitive to many types of patterns—to symmetries in particular. Indeed, much of modern scientific work in pattern formation and pattern recognition is an attempt to put what the eye naturally sees and comprehends into mathematical form so that it can be made quantitative.

The scaling symmetry appears in a myriad of ways in nature. Its appearance at the snapoff singularity in the drop is only one of its elegant manifestations. I would like to illustrate it in a more familiar case. I have taken pictures of barren trees in winter near dusk where the branches stand out clearly against the thickening sky. There is a certain quality to the light coming through branches such as these that is appealing and subtle. We can ask what is behind our attraction to this light just as we can ask about the quality of light in the canvases of Corot. What makes us perceive it as beautiful? One thing that I think is obvious is that there is a delicacy about the way the light is broken up as the branches bifurcate over and over again into smaller and finer structures. The tree is an approximation of a fractal: an enlargement of the finest branches congregating to form larger limbs has the same form as the larger limbs coming together to form the trunk. This symmetry pattern, repeated over and over again at different parts of the canopy, gives more than just a delicacy to the light (which could have been achieved after all with a pattern made of just the smallest twigs with no large branches at all). The pattern, I submit, is interesting to the eye because it has an underlying symmetry— what we call the scaling or dilation symmetry of a fractal object. It is this same dilation symmetry that is at work, albeit in a less obvious manner, at the point of snapoff in the drop depicted earlier (figs. 2a–c).

I now conclude by looking at some photographs of very small objects that celebrate the variety of forms that nature can produce. I have taken a series of images of water and oil mixtures. At this small scale, there are

---

from precision measurements of phenomena that the unaided human body would otherwise have been unable to detect. The use of photography as a scientific tool may, however, have implications for the *aesthetic* quality of some of those discoveries.

again only few forces giving the liquids their shape. As we know from common experience, oil and water do not mix. When they are forced to be together, each liquid forms islands which touch the other fluid only at their perimeter. The islands do not easily coalesce because to do so would involve the complete removal of all intervening liquid from between them. This takes a long time to happen, so the islands remain in place for extended periods. I find the shapes that these mixtures display endlessly fascinating. Each interface is described by a precise and delicate arc. When looked at as pure elements of form, they have a sensuous quality. Indeed I am tempted to ascribe almost sentient characteristics to them—in some cases vulnerability, in some cases sheltering, in some cases joy. The objects in these images are created with a very limited set of forces. Yet the austerity of the situation does not prevent them from enjoying an enormous diversity. I find that it is essentially impossible for nature to make an unharmonious design at this level (figs. 3a–d).

The variety of shapes in this situation is in stark contrast to the argument that I gave before, in which I asserted that the shapes may be so constrained by the physics of the situation (that is, being on the border between a single drop and two separated ones) as to be universal. Drops breaking are Platonic forms; these pictures are part of a vast gallery of possibilities—none of which is universal. Yet there is something that, even if not Platonic, nevertheless is robust about the shape of the interface. The shape in every instance is governed by a strict set of laws that nonetheless allows a variation in overall form. This is in some sense similar to the example I gave above of the arc of a thrown ball that is always close to a parabola. Depending on the speed of the ball, the arc can have different amounts of curvature. Here we see the interfacial forces writ in the curvature of the interfaces of the liquids.

I am struck by the observation of Victor Hugo: "Where the telescope ends, the microscope begins, and which has the wider vision? You may choose."[7] I am seduced by the shape of objects on small scale. The forces that govern their forms are the same as those that are responsible for structures at ever increasing sizes; yet on the smaller scale those forms have a simplicity and elegance that is not always apparent elsewhere. We go great distances to view the wonders of our natural landscape—mountains, canyons, deserts, and oceans. At a more modest level I find these smaller objects of an equal if a more delicate beauty. Moreover, they have over their counterparts in the macroscopic domain the advantage that they are in some sense timeless: although mountain ranges may erode over time, a drop in the process of snapping off will have that same shape no matter when we observe it (of course assuming that we catch it at the moment of breaking apart!).

Wallace Stegner wrote about the need for wilderness: "The reminder

7. Victor Hugo, *Les Misérables*, trans. Norman Denny (Harmondsworth, 1976), p. 764.

and the reassurance that it is still there is good for our spiritual health even if we never once in ten years set foot in it. . . . It is important to us when we are old simply because it is there—important, that is, simply as idea."[8] The same thought can be applied to the images of these small mundane objects. Their beauty, precision, and elegance are often ignored and taken for granted. But once their magnificence has been asserted they are difficult to forget. The distress of being kept awake at night by the steady, interminable drip of a leaking faucet is mitigated when one considers the stunning and remarkable process occurring during each and every breakup event. In the ephemeral drop we glimpse the shadow of a universal form—a form that is filled with sensuality and grace. The oil slicks on one's driveway, too, when looked at closely have an unanticipated and elegant structure. These are some of the objects that make up our everyday world—that give texture to our lives. It is important to look into the core of their structure to see what contributes to their splendor. These things are also important "simply as idea."

8. Wallace Stegner, "Wilderness Letter," *Marking the Sparrow's Fall: The Making of the American West*, ed. Page Stegner (New York, 1998), p. 112.

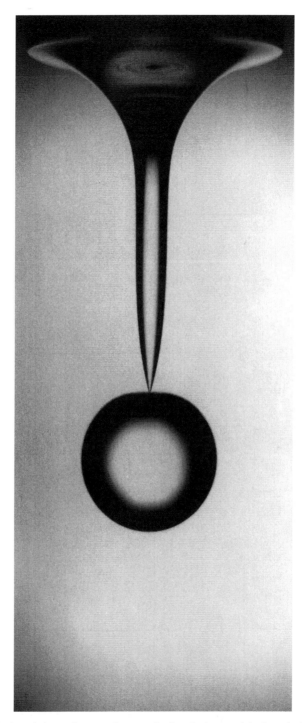

FIGS. 1a–b.—A drop of water photographed at the instant (a) when the large drop at the bottom breaks away from the long neck of fluid and (b) when the neck itself forms a satellite drop by breaking away from the liquid at the nozzle. Photos: Sidney R. Nagel and Xiangdong Shi.

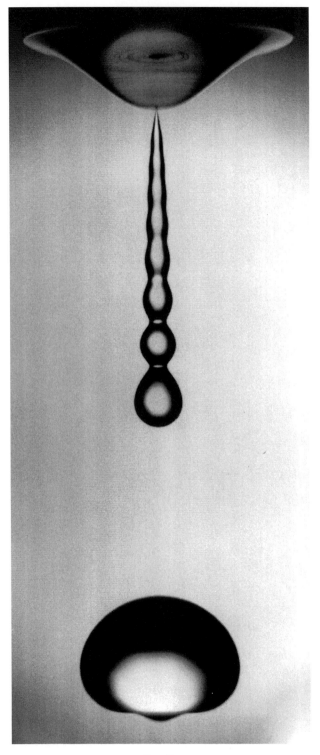

FIG. 1b.

FIGS. 2a–c.—Three photographs of trees near dusk showing the scale-invariance symmetry of their branches. This symmetry is the same as occurs at the point of the drop breakup shown in figure 1 and on the cover. Photos: Sidney R. Nagel.

FIG. 2b

FIG. 2c

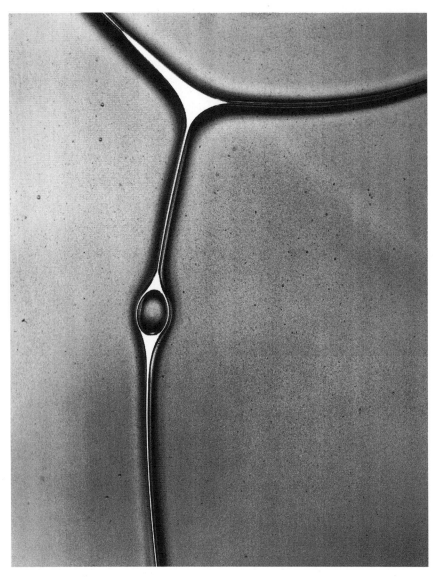

FIGS. 3a–d.—Four photographs of emulsions of water and oil confined in the thin gap between two plates. The curvatures of the droplet boundaries are determined by surface tension forces and the local velocities of the fluids. Photos: Sidney R. Nagel.

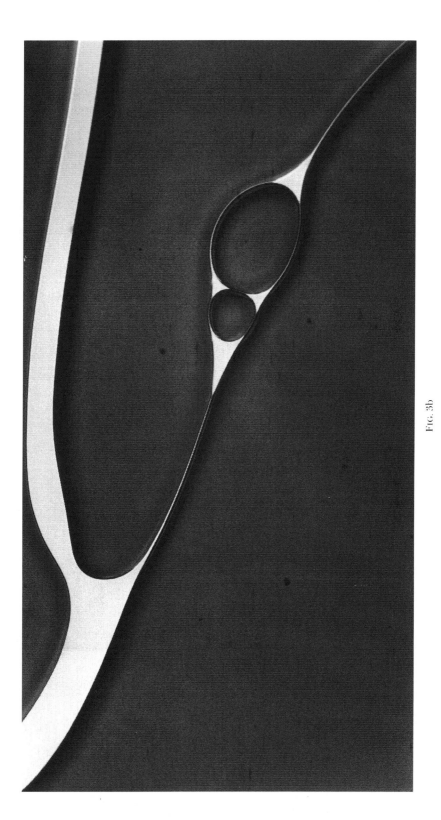

FIG. 3b

Fig. 3c

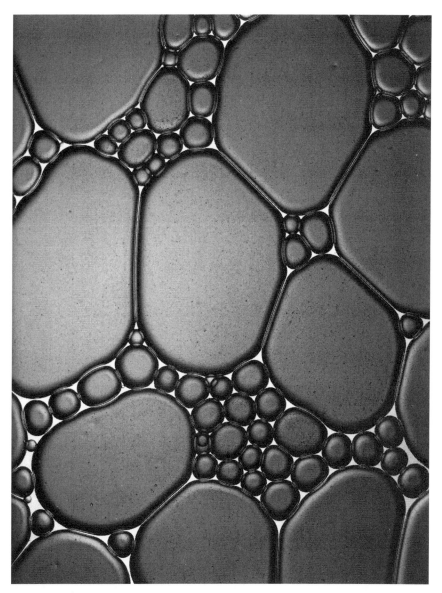

Fig. 3d

Descartes's Geometry as Spiritual Exercise

Matthew L. Jones

Introduction

Most academics are familiar with a comforting fable, subject to minor variations, about René Descartes and modern philosophy. Around 1640, Descartes philosophically crystallized a key transformation latent in Renaissance views of humanity. He moved the foundation of knowledge from humans fully embedded within and suited to nature to inside each individual. Descartes made knowledge and truth rest upon the individual subject and that subject's knowledge of his or her own capacities. This move permitted a profoundly new thoroughgoing skepticism, but rather than undermining universal knowledge by positing a uniformity of human subjects, this move ultimately guaranteed intersubjective knowledge. Knowledge became subjective and objective. Not content merely to make man himself the ground of knowledge, Descartes went further to make the human mind alone the source for knowledge, a knowledge modeled after pure mathematics. The new Cartesian subject ignored the

Unless otherwise indicated, all translations are my own. I have benefited from René Descartes, *Règles utiles et claires pour la direction de l'esprit en la recherche de la vérité*, trans. Jean-Luc Marion and Pierre Costabel (The Hague, 1977) and *Regulae ad directionem ingenii— Rules for the Directions of the Natural Intelligence: A Bilingual Edition of the Cartesian Treatise on Method*, trans. and ed. George Heffernan (Amsterdam, 1998).

For helpful criticism and support, thanks to Mario Biagioli, Tom Conley, Arnold Davidson, Kathy Eden, Pierre Force, Peter Galison, Michael Gordin, David Kaiser, Lisbet Koerner, Elizabeth H. Lee, audiences at Harvard, Cornell, and Columbia, and the editors at *Critical Inquiry*.

manifold contributions of the body, and Descartes assumed all real knowledge could come only from a reason common to all humans. The universality of the knowing thing and the processes of knowing make this Cartesian subject a transcendental one. Above all, mathematics, with its proof techniques, and formal thought, modeled on mathematics, exemplify those things that can be intersubjectively known by individual but importantly similar subjects.

Versions of this fable appear in numerous analyses, some quite sophisticated and textually based, some crude and dismissive. These versions provide grounds for praising or dismissing Descartes and the philosophical modernity he wrought.[1] Rather than surveying or evaluating these appraisals, here I want merely to clarify and anchor historically the subject Descartes hoped his philosophy would help produce.[2] This essay examines one set of exercises Descartes highlighted as propaedeutic to a better life and better knowledge: his famous, if little known, geometry. Critics and supporters have too often stressed Descartes's dependence on or reduction of knowledge to a mathematical model without inquiring

1. My goal is not to undermine such appraisals but to offer a stronger historical basis for them. To take two important critical exemplars from the serious literature: Feminist critics have stressed the historical conditions of gender and social status in the emergence of claims to universal knowledge based on universal mental processes. Structuralist and poststructuralist critics characterize the subject as essentially a product of linguistic practices. For a survey of some of these approaches, see Susan Bordo and Mario Moussa, "Rehabilitating the 'I'," in *Feminist Interpretations of René Descartes,* ed. Bordo (University Park, Penn., 1999), pp. 280–304. One can easily multiply examples to include those from phenomenology (especially Husserl and Heidegger), cognitive science, and analytic philosophy. There are several important compendia of articles, often discussing and invoking Descartes. See, for example, *Who Comes after the Subject?* ed. Eduardo Cadava, Peter Connor, and Jean-Luc Nancy (New York, 1991), and *Penser le sujet aujourd'hui,* ed. Elisabeth Guibert-Sledziewski and Jean-Louis Viellard-Baron (Paris, 1988).

2. Descartes used the term *subject* in the traditional Aristotelian manner. There are numerous other historical corrections to the fable. See Stephen Gaukroger's introduction to *Descartes: An Intellectual Biography* (Oxford, 1995), and John Schuster, "Whatever Should We Do with Cartesian Method?—Reclaiming Descartes for the History of Science," in *Essays on the Philosophy and Science of René Descartes,* ed. Stephen Voss (New York, 1993), pp. 195–223. A key approach has been to underline Descartes's continuity with late scholasticism; for two recent examples, see Dennis Des Chene, *Physiologia: Natural Philosophy in Late Aristotelian and Cartesian Thought* (Ithaca, N.Y., 1996), and Roger Ariew, *Descartes and the Last Scholastics* (Ithaca, N.Y., 1999). Another key movement has been to undermine the view that Descartes had no room for the senses. See, for example, Desmond M. Clarke, *Descartes's Philosophy of Science* (University Park, Penn., 1982), and Daniel Garber, *Descartes Embodied: Reading Cartesian Philosophy through Cartesian Science* (Cambridge, 2001).

Matthew L. Jones (mj340@columbia.edu) is assistant professor of history at Columbia University. He is preparing a cultural history of mathematics and natural philosophy as spiritual exercises in seventeenth-century France, especially in Descartes, Pascal, and Leibniz.

into the rather odd mathematics he actually set forth as this model. His geometry, neither Euclidean nor algebraic, has its own standards, its own rigor, and its own limitations.[3] These characteristics ought radically to modify our view of Descartes's envisioned subject. Although the technical details of his geometry might seem interesting and comprehensible only to historians of mathematics, the essential features grounding Descartes's program can be made readily comprehensible. Descartes did far more than theoretically (albeit implicitly) invoke the knowing subject in his *Meditations*. To pursue his philosophy was nothing less than to cultivate and order one's self. He offered his revolutionary but peculiar mathematics as a fundamental practice in this philosophy pursued as a way of life. Let us move, then, from abstraction about Descartes to the historical quest for this way of life.

In his earliest notebook, Descartes noted an ironic disjunction between bodily health and spiritual or mental health. "Vices I call maladies of the soul, which are not so easily diagnosed as are maladies of the body. While we often have experienced good health of the body, we have never had any experience of good health of the mind."[4] Descartes's language of spiritual malady harkens to Cicero's *Tusculan Disputations:* "Diseases of the soul are both more dangerous and more numerous than those of the body."[5] For Cicero, philosophy offered succor for these diseases. "Assuredly there is an art of healing the soul—I mean philosophy, whose aid must be sought not, as in bodily diseases, outside ourselves, and we must use our own utmost endeavor, with all our resources and strength, to have the power to be ourselves our own physicians" (*T,* 3.3.6, pp. 230–31). The dedicated pursuit of the spiritual exercises of a philosophy alone can overcome the sickness and delusion inculcated by institutions, tradition, and everyday commerce.[6] Clear thinking and the nobility attendant upon a healthy soul demanded work, exercise—*askesis.*

Descartes's geometry was such a spiritual exercise, meant to counter instability, to produce and secure oneself despite outside confusion through the production of real mathematics.[7] Descartes's famous quest to find a superior philosophy took place within this therapeutic model. Cicero's account of philosophy's curative virtues and his vision of a self-

3. My analysis of the geometry rests on a number of specialized studies, above all the work of Henk J. M. Bos, cited extensively below.

4. René Descartes, *Oeuvres de Descartes,* ed. Charles Ernest Adam and Paul Tannery, 2d ed., 12 vols. (Paris, 1971), 10:215; hereafter abbreviated *AT.*

5. Cicero, *Tusculan disputations,* trans. J. E. King (Cambridge, 1971), 3.3.5, pp. 228–29; hereafter abbreviated *T.*

6. For the theme of philosophy as a therapeutic for the soul in Hellenistic philosophy, see André-Jean Voelke, *La Philosophie comme thérapie de l'âme: Études de philosophie hellénistique* (Paris, 1993).

7. "Spiritual exercises" as a crucial category for understanding ancient Greek and Roman and particularly Hellenistic thought stems from the essential work of Pierre Hadot; see esp. Pierre Hadot, *Exercices spirituels et philosophie antique* (Paris, 1981). Beyond the work

selecting elite purifying themselves was disseminated widely in late Renaissance and early modern Europe. Descartes had very likely encountered Cicero's text at his Jesuit school; in any case his Jesuit pedagogy was predicated in part on this model of philosophy's ennobling, curative virtues.[8] The diagnostic then curative philosophical model received a great boost from Pierre Charron's vastly influential *Livres de la sagesse* (1601). Charron "calls man to himself, to examine, sound out and study himself, so that he might know himself and feel his faults and miserable condition, and *thus* render himself capable of salutary and necessary remedies—the advice and teachings of wisdom."[9] But Descartes's early note above underlined his skepticism of the therapeutic capacity of (largely stoic) philosophy and contemporary accounts of wisdom—varying philosophies for living (see *T,* 3.3.5, pp. 230–31).[10] However much he clearly desired a therapy for the soul, Descartes could not see how to choose any particular one without a benchmark to use as a certain gauge of the soul's health. While he might second Charron's diagnoses of humanity's misery, Descartes at this early stage simply lacked any means to decide among the many treatments available in the early seventeenth century.

Pages later in his notebook the first glimmers of a way forward appeared. He discussed a number of new mathematical discoveries involving instruments and machines. Soon he applied these discoveries to the question of the soul's health. New forms of exercise, including geometrical exercise, could provide the means to come to a baseline of spiritual health.

Descartes made the concreteness of these exercises clear. A few years after writing his notebook, he advised studying "the simplest and least exalted arts, and especially those in which order prevails—such as those of artisans who weave and make carpet, or the feminine arts of embroidery, in which threads are interwoven in an infinitely varied pattern." The same held for arithmetic and games with numbers. "It is astonishing how the practice of all these things exercises the mind," so long as we do not borrow their discovery from others, but invent them ourselves (*AT,* 10:404).[11] Cicero had likewise maintained that intense personal endeavor

---

of Hadot, see Michel Foucault, *Le Souci de soi,* vol. 3 of *Histoire de la sexualité,* 3 vols. (Paris, 1984), esp. pp. 51–85, and Arnold I. Davidson, "Ethics as Ascetics: Foucault, the History of Ethics, and Ancient Thought," in *Foucault and the Writing of History,* ed. Jan Goldstein (Oxford, 1994), pp. 63–80.

8. See "Regulæ professoris humanitatis," *Ratio atque institutio studiorum,* ed. Ladislaus Lukács, vol. 5 of *Monumenta historica societatis iesu* (1591; Rome, 1965), p. 303.

9. Pierre Charron, *Livres de la sagesse* (1601/1604; Paris, 1986), p. 369; my emphasis.

10. "And then how can we accept the notion that the soul cannot heal itself, seeing that the soul has discovered the actual art of healing the body" (*T,* 3.3.5, pp. 230–31).

11. See Dennis L. Sepper, *Descartes's Imagination: Proportion, Images, and the Activity of Thinking* (Berkeley, 1996), p. 135 and his comments on the expansion of ingenium's power through exercise, p. 140.

was necessary for health. Such study habituated one to experiencing clear and distinct order:

> We must therefore practise these easier tasks first, and above all me-
> thodically, so that by following accessible and familiar paths we may
> grow *accustomed*, just as if we were playing a game, to penetrating
> always to the deeper truth of things. [*AT,* 10:405; my emphasis][12]

Descartes boldly announced, "human discernment [sagacitas] consists almost entirely in the proper observance of such order" (*AT,* 10:404; *CSM,* 1:35). Upon such discernment of order rested the ability to make the will capable of clearly recognizing the intellect's guidance. And no activity developed discernment better than mathematics:

> These rules are so useful in the pursuit of deeper wisdom that I have
> no hesitation in saying that this part of our method was designed
> not just for the sake of mathematical problems; our intention was,
> rather, that the mathematical problems should be studied almost ex-
> clusively for the sake of the excellent practice which they give us in
> the method. [*AT,* 10:442; *CSM,* 1:59]

Descartes's new geometry hardly offered a totalizing and algorithmic means for mechanically gaining knowledge of a mathematical world but rather gave exemplary practice in seeing and thinking clearly, in experi-encing with a healthy soul. Such effort, undertaken with one's greatest endeavor, could provide some standard for judging among philosophical doctrines and practices.

But wait. What does all this historical detail have to do with the sub-stance of Descartes's mathematics? Descartes might have held mathemat-ics to be good for some exercise, but how possibly could that make its content, its essence, any different? After all, since Euclid had exemplified mathematical rigor, what could be more obvious than that mathematics retains an unchanging core despite all its varied uses, its manifold repre-sentations, and the motivations for doing it?

Few would now doubt the need to study rigorously the contingent constitution of systems of thought, sets of epistemic practices, and the embedding of those constitutions within their cultural and social roles. In nearly every study of such systems, however, a cordoned-off core of logic and rigorously argued philosophy remains. So, one ought rightly to contend, however variable the cultural uses of philosophy and mathemat-ics, there remains an invariable, autonomous essence in each to be stud-ied in itself, an essence abstractable from those uses. My research takes as

12. Descartes, *The Philosophical Writings of Descartes,* trans. Robert Stoothoff et al., 3 vols. (Cambridge, 1984), 1:36; hereafter abbreviated *CSM.*

its starting point precisely the historical contingency of how mathematics, logic, and natural philosophy were supposed to be rigorous, evident, coherent, or certain during the seventeenth century in Western Europe.[13] After the criticisms of humanists, skeptics, and neoscholastics of the sixteenth century, the very definition and centrality of proof was contested. Simply put, Descartes rejected standard mathematical proof. And he was hardly alone. No consensus existed around the objects of mathematics, its proof techniques, its proper institutional settings, its place in the hierarchy of disciplines, or its relationship to "mathematical practitioners."[14] Such contingency hardly implies sophomoric relativism. It means that the very things that make a technical history of an object technical, systematic, or rigorous are themselves historical. It means a plurality of programs compete, each demanding serious, nonanachronistic technical inquiry, none reducible to modern logic or proof, when the history of logic and proof is precisely what ought to be explained.

Descartes's account of mathematics called for changes in the *objects* of mathematics, so he limited proof processes, expanded kinds of allowable curves, and added algebraic representation. Equally it altered the *subjects* of mathematics. Recent historical attention to the self-fashioning of mathematicians has paid too little attention to the variety of mathematical practices (and their metamathematical embedding) that were to help effect such fashioning. To assess correctly the contingent nature of mathematics demands examination of its practitioners' changing social embedding.[15] But equally, to evaluate its practitioners, one needs careful inquiry

13. For metamathematical concerns in the seventeenth century, see Hermann Schüling, *Die Geschichte der Axiomatischen Methode in 16. und beginnenden 17. Jahrhundert* (Hildesheim, 1969), and Paolo Mancosu, *The Philosophy of Mathematics and Mathematical Practice in the Seventeenth Century* (New York, 1996).

14. Recent studies of seventeenth- and eighteenth-century mathematical physics have carefully detailed the specific mathematics of different thinkers. For examples, see Michael S. Mahoney, "Algebraic vs. Geometric Techniques in Newton's Determinations of Planetary Orbits," in *Action and Reaction: Proceedings of a Symposium to Commemorate the Tercentenary of Newton's "Principia,"* ed. Paul Theerman and Adele F. Seeff (Newark, 1993), pp. 183–205; Domenico Bertoloni Meli, *Equivalence and Priority: Newton versus Leibniz* (Oxford, 1993); Michel Blay, *La Naissance de la mécanique analytique: La Science du mouvement au tournant des XVIIe et XVIIIe siècles* (Paris, 1992); and Douglas M. Jesseph, *Squaring the Circle: The War between Hobbes and Wallis* (Chicago, 1999), among others.

15. See, for example, Mario Biagioli, "The Social Status of Italian Mathematicians, 1450–1600," *History of Science* 27 (Mar. 1989): 41–95 and *Galileo, Courtier: The Practice of Science in the Culture of Absolutism* (Chicago, 1993); Stephen Johnston, "Mathematical Practitioners and Instruments in Elizabethan England," *Annals of Science* 48 (July 1991): 314–44; Robert S. Westman, "The Astronomer's Role in the Sixteenth Century: A Preliminary Study," *History of Science* 18 (June 1980): 105–47; J. A. Bennett, "The Mechanics' Philosophy and the Mechanical Philosophy," *History of Science* 24 (Mar. 1986): 1–28; Peter Dear, *Discipline and Experience: The Mathematical Way in the Scientific Revolution* (Chicago, 1995); and Mahoney, *The Mathematical Career of Pierre de Fermat, 1601–1665,* 2d ed. (Princeton, N.J., 1994), pp. 1–14, 20–25.

into technical content and practices, into the range of objects, tools, and allowed logic of their particular mathematics.

What then is a spiritual exercise? Is it something like aerobics with crystals? Spiritual exercises are sets of practices aiming for the cultivation of the self. Specifying a spiritual exercise means something like outlining (1) a set of practices; (2) a conception of the self, where the self need not be exclusively a mind or an intellect; and (3) the people the exercises are for, that is, the social field of the exercises' application, either explicit or implicit. As a category, spiritual exercise demands a careful spelling out of intellectual detail and social framework.

This study examines what seem at once the most esoteric and the most modern of Descartes's works, the *Geometry* of 1637, on its own terms, using his repetitive statements of its purpose, its contents, its foundation. He continually asserted that mathematics is an exercise, perhaps the best that we have. In taking this claim seriously, we can clarify Descartes's geometry. Simultaneously we will escape the long tradition of equating the subject Descartes aimed to create through his exercise with the so-called Cartesian and modern subjects. We will get at the subjects and objects of Descartes's mathematics and early natural philosophy, as well as the practices of language, of the body, and of the mind that constitute them.

While a number of insightful scholars have rightly stressed the need to focus on Descartes's work as something practiced, they have largely avoided his mathematics.[16] His curious mathematics offers the key to understanding how Descartes intended to have his philosophy practiced. I focus on the laborious nature of mathematics; it is exercise, hard exercise—a point obvious enough to mathematicians but too often absent from histories and philosophies of the subject. Only work using geometry as exemplar could produce the focused *ingenium*—the natural intelligence—that Descartes thought the very definition of cultivation.

16. There is one exception, however: "To imitate Descartes' example," David Lachterman rightly notes, "one will need to practice and apply it, not memorize or passively receive it" (David Rapport Lachterman, *The Ethics of Geometry: A Genealogy of Modernity* [New York, 1989], p. 134). In a penetrating study of Descartes's *Meditations*, Foucault insisted that recognizing the intelligibility of Descartes's choices rested on a "double reading" of his text as both a *system* and an *exercise* (Foucault, "My Body, This Paper, This Fire," *Aesthetics, Method and Epistemology*, vol. 2 of *Essential Works of Foucault, 1954–1984*, ed. James D. Faubion [New York, 1998], p. 406); compare the considerably more historically grounded Gary Hatfield, "The Senses and the Fleshless Eye: The *Meditations* as Cognitive Exercises," in *Essays on Descartes's "Meditations,"* ed. Amelie Oksenberg Rorty (Berkeley, 1986), pp. 45–79; for a negative assessment of Hatfield, see Bradley Rubidge, "Descartes's *Meditations* and Devotional Meditations," *Journal of the History of Ideas* 51 (Jan.-Mar. 1990): 27–49; and for positive ripostes, see Dear, "Mersenne's Suggestion: Cartesian Meditation and the Mathematical Model of Knowledge in the Seventeenth Century," in *Descartes and His Contemporaries*, ed. Roger Ariew and Marjorie Grene (Chicago, 1995), pp. 44–62; and Sepper, "The Texture of Thought: Why Descartes's *Meditationes* Is Meditational, and Why It Matters," in *Descartes's Natural Philosophy*, ed. Gaukroger, John Andrew Schuster, and John Sutton (New York, 2000), pp. 736–50.

Envisioning the Ancients: True Mathematics and Noninstitutionalized Philosophy

Descartes's early experiences of contemporary mathematics while in the Jesuit school of La Flèche led him to conclude that mathematics was good only for clever tricks and mean trades.[17] Subsequently he asked himself how Plato's Academy refused to admit anyone ignorant of mathematics, this "puerile and hollow" science (*AT,* 10:375; see *CSM,* 1:18). The ancients, he decided, must have had a "mathematics altogether different from the mathematics of our time" (*AT,* 10:376; see *CSM,* 1:18). Descartes caught glimpses of this true mathematics in the ancient mathematicians. Why only glimpses? In a remarkable piece of paranoid historical reconstruction, Descartes explained that the ancients feared

> that their method, being so easy and simple, would become cheapened if it were divulged, and so, to make us wonder, they put in its place *sterile truths deductively demonstrated with some ingenuity,* as the effects of their art, rather than teaching us this art itself, which might have dispelled our admiration. [*AT,* 10:376–77, my emphasis; see *CSM,* 1:19]

The ancients' ruse of formal proof led Descartes's amazed contemporaries to memorize the ancients' sterile truths rather than to grasp the fundamental relationships behind those truths.

Descartes's friend, writer Guez de Balzac, made a similar point about Cicero. Cicero's codified rhetoric for swaying the mob had been mistaken as his true rhetoric and dialectic and then fetishized.[18] Balzac and Descartes's contemporaries had mistaken instantiations of technique for the essences of mathematics and rhetoric. These ancient techniques might well deceive, move, and direct, but neither dispel wonder nor produce true orators and thinkers. Misapprehension of the ground of these techniques made their contemporaries the mob to be swayed, those needing

---

17. For Jesuit mathematics pedagogy in France and at La Flèche, see Antonella Romano, "La Compagnie de Jésus et la révolution scientifique: Constitution et diffusion d'une culture mathématique jésuite à la Renaissance (1540–1640)" (Doctorat, Université de Paris–I, 1996), and the traditional source, Camille de Rochemonteix, *Un Collège de Jésuites aux XVIIIᵉ et XVIIIᵉ siècles: Le Collège Henri IV de La Flèche,* 4 vols. (Le Mans, 1889); see also Geneviève Rodis-Lewis, "Descartes et les mathématiques au collège," in *"Le Discours" et sa méthode: Colloque pour le 350ᵉ anniversaire du "Discours de la méthode,"* ed. Nicolas Grimaldi and Marion (Paris, 1987), pp. 187–211.

18. See Jean-Louis Guez de Balzac, "Suite d'un entretien de vive voix, ou de la conversation des Romains," in *Oeuvres diverses,* ed. Roger Zuber (1644; Paris, 1995), pp. 73–96, 82–83. In his defense of Guez de Balzac's rhetoric, Descartes offered an historical account of the loss of true rhetoric and the production of rules and sophismata to replace it. See *AT,* 1:9.

external discipline, when, presumably, they ought to have been the ones swaying the mob. They lost at once true mathematics and rhetoric and with them knowledge, civility, and self-control.

Descartes and Balzac connected institutionalization to this dependence on technique. Like many of their contemporaries, they envisioned the ancients as successful, stable, and productive precisely because they were *honnêtes hommes*—a sort of cultivated gentlemen—outside of stultifying institutions.[19] Blaise Pascal captured this common seventeenth-century view well: "One thinks of Aristotle and Plato only in the black robes of pedants, but they were *honnêtes hommes,* laughing along with their friends as they wrote their philosophy to regulate a hospital of madmen."[20] Institutionalized supplementary technique for regulating others had been mistaken for essential philosophical doctrine and considered ways of living.

In contrast to moderns who fetishized final results, Descartes argued, the "same light of mind that allowed [the ancients] to see that one must prefer virtue to pleasure and honnêteté to utility . . . also gave them true ideas in philosophy and the method" (*AT,* 10:376; see *CSM,* 1:18).[21] Descartes echoed Cicero's famous critique of Aristotle in phrase and intent: "Whereas Aristotle is content to regard *utilitas* or advantage as the aim of deliberative oratory, it seems to me that our aim should be *honestas* and *utilitas.*"[22] Morality and utility characterized deep knowledge and true skill. Descartes, Pascal, and Balzac, like many others in the early seventeenth century, assimilated the ancients to their vision of *honnêteté.*[23] In *honnêteté,* a genteel nonspecialization, proper manners, and truth making outside of formal institutions were intertwined with elements of taste more broadly conceived.[24]

19. See Emmanuel Bury, "Le Sourire de Socrate ou, peut-on être à la fois philosophe et honnête homme?" in *Le Loisir lettré à l'âge classique,* ed. Marc Fumaroli, Philippe-Joseph Salazar, and Bury (Geneva, 1996), pp. 197–212.

20. Blaise Pascal, *Pensées,* in *Oeuvres complètes de Blaise Pascal,* ed. Louis Lafuma (Paris, 1963), no. 533, p. 578.

21. Compare the *Discours, AT,* 6:7–8; see also Marion, *Sur l'ontologie grise de Descartes: Science cartésienne et savoir aristotélicien dans les "Regulae"* (Paris, 1975), p. 151.

22. Cicero, *De inventione,* in *De inventione; De optimum genere oratorum; Topica,* trans. H. M. Hubbell (Cambridge, Mass., 1949), 2.51.156, p. 324; compare 2.55.166, p. 332 and pseudo-Cicero, *Rhetorica ad herennium,* trans. Harry Caplan (Cambridge, Mass., 1954), 3.2.3, pp. 160–62; see also Quintilian, *The Institutio Oratoria of Quintilian,* trans. H. E. Butler, 4 vols. (New York, 1921), 3.8.22, 1:490, and Montaigne "De l'utile et l'honneste," *Essais,* ed. Maurice Rat 2 vols. (Paris, 1962) 3.1, 2:205–21.

23. On *honnêteté* and Descartes's physical work, see Dear, "A Mechanical Microcosm: Bodily Passions, Good Manners, and Cartesian Mechanism," in *Science Incarnate: Historical Embodiments of Natural Knowledge,* ed. Christopher Lawrence and Steven Shapin (Chicago, 1998), pp. 51–82, esp. pp. 62–63.

24. Early in the century, the notion referred primarily to normative vision of judgment and taste among the nobility of the robe. Later, *honnêteté* became an anticourtly, more aristocratic ideal. For *honnêteté,* see Zuber, "Die Theorie der Honnêteté," in *Frankreich und*

But Descartes and Balzac hardly thought the ancient gentlemen-philosophers reached their own ideal. That they took the trouble "of writing so many vast books about" geometry, Descartes argued, showed that "they did not have the true method for finding all" the solutions (*AT,* 6:376). While the ancients had the seeds of true method, Descartes contended, "they did not know it perfectly." Both Balzac and Descartes similarly argued that the ancients had the seeds of true rhetoric, but not true rhetoric itself.[25] The latter extended this account of the ancients' imperfection to mathematics. His evidence? "Their extravagant transports of joy and the sacrifices they offered to celebrate discoveries of little weight *demonstrate* clearly how rude they were" (*AT,* 10:376). This lack of self-control proved that some results came as surprises, gained not by methodic comprehension but rather miracle-like genius. Even if the lucky ancients had the right informal social forms, they lacked the complementary exercise necessary for eliminating imitation and surprise.

Moderns needed better social forms and better exercises to renew and exceed the virtues of the ancients. Balzac spearheaded a movement to civilize the unruly texts of the Renaissance, to take the fruits of humanism and strip them of the extravagance and pedantry exemplified in the—to his mind—uncontrolled works of Montaigne or classical scholars like Girolamo Cardano. Only then could humanism be properly deinstitutionalized and the true potential of ancient learning nourished. This return to the *urbanité* of Rome's noninstitutionalized higher philosophy needed new forms of writing and print, which Balzac tried to produce.[26]

Descartes took Balzac's iconic attempt to write "urbane" political philosophy, *The Prince,* as the physical model for layout of the *Discourse on Method.* In a number of letters to the great Dutch diplomat, musician, connoisseur, and poet Constantijn Huygens, Descartes gave detailed instructions for the typographic layout, the typeface, the margins, the paragraph breaks, and even the sort of paper to be used.[27] Its physical form

---

Niederlände, vol. 2 of *Die Philosophie des 17. Jahrhunderts,* ed. Jean-Pierre Schöbinger (Basel, 1993), pp. 156–66; Bury, *Littérature et politesse: L'Invention de l'honnête homme, 1580–1750* (Paris, 1996); Domna C. Stanton, *The Aristocrat as Art: A Study of the "Honnête Homme" and the Dandy in Seventeenth-and Nineteenth-Century French Literature* (New York, 1980); Maurice Magendie, *La Politesse mondaine et les théories de l'honnêteté, en France au XVIIe siècle, de 1600 à 1660,* 2 vols. (Paris, 1925); and Nannerl O. Keohane, *Philosophy and the State in France: The Renaissance to the Enlightenment* (Princeton, N.J., 1980), esp. pp. 283–88.

25. See Balzac, letter to Boisrobert, 28 Sept. 1623, quoted in Bernard Beugnot, "La Précellence du style moyen," in *Histoire de la rhétorique dans l'Europe moderne, 1450–1950,* ed. Fumaroli (Paris, 1999), p. 542.

26. See Zuber, "L'Urbanité française," *Les Émerveillements de la raison: Classicismes littéraires du XVIIe siècle français* (Paris, 1997), pp. 151–61.

27. See Henri-Jean Martin, "Les Formes de publications au milieu du XVIIe siècle," *Ordre et contestation au temps des classiques,* ed. Roger Duchêne and Pierre Ronzeaud, 2 vols. (Paris, 1992), 2:209–24, and Jean-Pierre Cavaillé, "Descartes: Stratège de la destination," *XVIIe siècle,* no. 177 (Oct.–Dec. 1992): 551–59.

echoed its content's promises: new exercises proper for a noninstitutional philosophy of and for *honnêtes hommes* and perhaps *femmes*.

Returning to the true mathematics hidden by the devious ancients meant the production of a better set of exercises producing knowledge and civility. In debate around his *Geometry,* one of three "essays" following his *Discourse on Method,* Descartes became enveloped in controversy with the famous Toulousian mathematician and lawyer Pierre de Fermat. Descartes condemned Fermat's mathematics as wondrous and uncivil:

> Mr. Fermat is a Gascon; I am not. It's true that he has found numerous *particular* beautiful things . . . he is a man of great genius. But, as for me, I've always striven to consider things with extreme generality, to the end of being able to infer rules that also have utility elsewhere. [*AT,* 3:333; my emphasis][28]

"Gascon" was a well-targeted snub. It suggested provincialism, extravagance, amusement, and a quest for advancement: in sum, incivility and disorder.[29] Descartes attacked how Fermat arrived at his results. "Without industry and by chance, one can easily fall onto the path one must take to encounter it" (*AT,* 1:490). Fermat was doubly particular: he found pretty trinkets and he did so through genius—chancy genius. For Descartes, chance findings typified mathematics as then practiced. They were an inferior means toward a lower form of mathematical knowledge, one that, nonetheless, often produced results. The aleatory nature of such discovery produced wonder, dependence, and extravagance, not clarity, independence, and self-control.

Fermat's mathematics was ironically inferior *as mathematics* because it failed as a more general cultivating activity. Descartes's general geometric method, he claimed, offered true understanding, for an orderly constructive process produced all of its results.[30] Every mathematical solution need not proceed by some new ingenuous technique dependent on individual instantiations of skill, expertise, and genius.[31] For Descartes, *real* mathematical knowledge—cultivating knowledge—demanded chance

28. As reported by Schooten to Christiaan Huygens. Compare Gaston Milhaud, *Descartes savant* (Paris, 1921), p. 160.

29. Compare the similar attack on Descartes's friend Guez de Balzac as a "Gascon," discussed in Jean Jehasse, *Guez de Balzac et le génie romain, 1597–1654* (Saint-Étienne, 1977), p. 117.

30. See Henk J. M. Bos, "Arguments on Motivation in the Rise and Decline of a Mathematical Theory: The 'Construction of Equations,' 1637–ca. 1750," *Archive for History of Exact Sciences* 30 (Nov. 1984): 331–80, esp. p. 363. See also Gaukroger, "The Nature of Abstract Reasoning: Philosophical Aspects of Descartes's Work in Algebra," in *The Cambridge Companion to Descartes,* ed. John Cottingham (Cambridge, Mass., 1992), pp. 91–114, esp. pp. 106–8.

31. Nicely noted in Morris Kline, *Mathematical Thought from Ancient to Modern Times* (New York, 1972), p. 308.

and genius be eliminated. He thus insisted that mathematical practices that made the assent to inferential steps—proofs—the essence of mathematics be abandoned, although it required the temporary use and then transcendence of such inferential steps. Descartes worked to sever, in his eyes, a truer mathematics of cultivation from a false one of mere calculation, passive procedures, and deliberate deception.

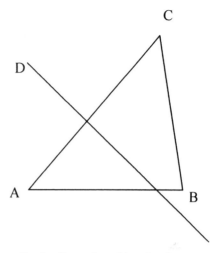

FIG. 1.—Example problem (my figure).

Descartes's Geometry of 1637

The sixteenth and seventeenth centuries witnessed countless mathematical "duels" in which mathematicians tried to best one another with their ingenuity in solving particular problems.[32] A very simple example of a problem: Given a triangle ABC and a point D outside the triangle, one must construct a line through D dividing the triangle in two equal parts (fig. 1). All solutions must comprise a series of constructions of circles and lines produced by standard compasses and rulers. Usual solutions to such problems included no information about how to come to the solution or how to go about solving another like it.[33] Besting someone in a mathematical duel typically meant making others marvel at your ingenuity in solving, not offering heuristic instruction. As the example above indicates, Descartes criticized his rivals like Fermat, for finding "numerous *particular* . . . things" with genius rather than offering rules useful elsewhere in math or otherwise (*AT,* 3:333; my emphasis).

Descartes aimed to give a set of general tools offering a certain method for problem solving. The *Geometry* began audaciously: "All problems in Geometry can easily be reduced to such terms that there is no need to know more than the lengths of certain straight lines to construct them" (*AT,* 6:369). By assigning letters to line lengths, Descartes could represent geometrical diagrams as algebraic formulas. His geometry

32. Note, for example, those of Girolamo Cardano, Lodovico Ferrari, and Niccolo Tartaglia. See Øystein Ore, *Cardano, the Gambling Scholar* (Princeton, N.J., 1953), esp. pp. 53–107; Mahoney, *The Mathematical Career of Pierre de Fermat, 1601–1665,* pp. 6–7; and the review of Arnaldo Masotti's *Lodovico Ferrari e Niccolo Tartaglia. Cartelli di Sfida Matematica* by Alex Keller, "Renaissance Mathematical Duels," *History of Science* 14 (Sept. 1976): 208–9.

33. See Bos, "The Structure of Descartes's *Géométrie,*" in *Descartes: Il metodo e i saggi,* ed. Giulia Belgioioso et al. (Rome, 1990), pp. 349–69, esp. pp. 352–56.

gained a toolbox of algebra—this is why the book is so famous. Every algebraic manipulation corresponded to a geometric construction. For example, the addition of two symbols meant the addition of one line segment to another. In Descartes's mathematics, geometric problems get geometrical constructions as solutions.[34] Algebra should serve only as a temporary means toward conceiving ever more clearly and distinctly the relations among geometric entities.[35]

To illustrate the power of his approach, Descartes addressed a key problem from antiquity—the Pappus problem.[36] In its simplest form, the problem is to find all the points that maintain distances from two lines such that the distances equal a constant. Solving the problem for a small number of lines was relatively easy. But the traditional limitation to standard compass and line constructions blocked the solution of the problem for a higher number of lines.

So Descartes needed more tools. He added a wider variety of curve-drawing instruments and defended their use (for an example, see fig. 3). His new machines generated a wider set of curves that could be used in solving geometric problems. With these new machines, Descartes believed that he could solve the famous Pappus problem for any number of lines, thereby far surpassing the ancients. More important, he could do so as part of his systematic method for solving geometric problems and not because of some ingenious insight or expertise, as in mathematical duels.[37] Descartes concluded (perhaps foolishly) that he had provided the tools for classifying and systematically solving all geometrical problems

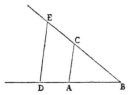

FIG. 2.—Multiplication, from *La Géométrie*, p. 298.

34. See Bos, "The Structure of Descartes's *Géométrie*" and "On the Representation of Curves in Descartes's *Géométrie*," *Archive for History of Exact Sciences* 24 (Oct. 1981): 295–338. He defined multiplication as follows: Let AB be unity. If one wants to multiply BD by BC, then one only needs to join C to A, and draw the parallel from C to E. Then BE is the desired product (since AB:BD::BC:BE and AB is unity, AB.BE = 1.BE = BC.BD); see fig. 2. Similarly, he defined the square root geometrically.

35. Not all commentators agree on this point, in large part because Descartes was well aware that his algebra could produce nongeometric solutions. See chapter 5 of Peter A. Schouls, *Descartes and the Possibility of Science* (Ithaca, N.Y., 2000).

36. The Pappus problem: Let there be n lines L_i, n angles ϕ_i and a segment a, and a proportion α/β. From a point P, one draws lines d_i meeting each L_i with angle ϕ_i; find the locus of points P such that the distances of the lines d_i maintain a set of proportions: For $n>2$, $2n-1$ lines, $(d_1 \cdots d_n):(d_{n+1} \cdots d_{2n-1} a)::\alpha:\beta$ and for $2n$ lines, $(d_1 \cdots d_n):(d_{n+1} \cdots d_{2n})\ldots\alpha:\beta$. I take this description from Bos, "On the Representation of Curves in Descartes's *Géométrie*," p. 299.

37. The Pappus problem itself acted as a sort of machine, which produced an extended family of smaller problems, each with its family of orderly solution curves produced by a machine easy to imagine. On this, see especially chapter 2 of Emily Grosholz, *Cartesian Method and the Problem of Reduction* (Oxford, 1991).

admitting certain solution. No longer would slavish imitation of the big books of the ancients and those of their modern day followers be needed.

Considerably more than mere tools for mathematical problem solving, his new geometrical tools offered essential exercise:

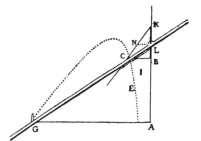

> I stop before explaining all this in more detail, because I would take away ... the utility of cultivating your *esprit* in exercising yourself with them, which is ... the key thing that one can take away from this science. [*AT,* 6:374][38]

FIG. 3.—Geometric machine and associated curve, from *La Géométrie,* p. 320. The machine rotates *GL* about *G; GL,* attached at *L,* pushes the contraption *KBC* along the line *AK.* The intersections at *C* of *GL* and the ruler *NK* make up the curve.

Descartes's Competition: A Range of Spiritual Exercises

For Descartes, self-cultivation meant developing the ability to allow the will to recognize and to accept freely the insights of reason, and not just following the passions or memorized patterns of actions. It meant essentially recognizing the *limits* of reason and willing *not* to make judgments about things beyond reason's scope.[39] From the *Rules for the Direction of the Natural Intelligence [ingenium]* of the 1620s to the *Principles of Philosophy* and the *Passions of the Soul* of the 1640s, Descartes criticized contemporary philosophical practices as deleterious to this proper self-cultivation. In his 1647 introduction to the French version of the *Principles of Philosophy,* he argued that to live without philosophizing

> is properly to have the eyes closed without ever trying to open them; ... this study is more necessary to rule our manners and direct us in this life than is using our eyes to guide our steps. [*AT,* 9:2:3–4]

Far more than mere precepts or an academic discipline, philosophy was an *activity* directing the everyday; it was a mode of civility where the discipline of manner stemmed not from taught external techniques but rather arose from internalized principles discerned by oneself. "In studying these principles, one will accustom oneself, little by little, to judge better everything one encounters, and thus become more Wise." In contrast, traditional philosophy embodied memorized external rule of the self. "In this they [his principles] will have an effect contrary to that of common Phi-

---

38. Compare Gaukroger, *Descartes,* p. 153.

39. This latter point appears most prominently in the fourth meditation.

losophy, for one easily notices in those one calls Pedants, that it renders them less capable of reasoning than if they had never learned it." [*AT,* 9: 2:18]

In his important study of the image of Socrates in seventeenth-century France, Emmanuel Bury argues the century had

> a vision of ancient philosophy that stressed consciousness of the existential character that ancient philosophy took on, so close, in many ways, to the spiritual exercises of the Christian religion: it is very much a question of a choice of a life, and philosophy has no meaning unless it is, in the final analysis, moral.[40]

Yet we must not conflate late sixteenth- and seventeenth-century spiritual exercises with their ancient antecedents. Nor is it enough to consider the early modern variants as merely Christianized, given the rapid and radical transformations in the practice and theory of different Christianities during this period. Understood and articulated through other aspects of Early Modern culture, the ancient exemplary spiritual exercises were resources many advanced to respond to seventeenth-century concerns.

Central to the fundamental religious upheavals of the sixteenth century was a greatly reinforced emphasis on the *individual* as the unit for the instillation of religious discipline.[41] In France these religious transformations coincided and interacted with wide-ranging social transformations, still remarkably little understood. Social historians have long since abandoned the vision of an incipient bourgeois class rooted in a *noblesse de robe* overcoming traditional elites. Exact social parameters are far less important, however, than the tremendous uncertainty about what constituted nobility or elite status.[42] One correlation with instability in social position and codes of conduct was the massive effusion of cultural projects offering competing visions of distinction and nobility.[43] These cul-

40. Bury, "Le Sourire de Socrate ou, peut-on être à la fois philosophe et honnête homme?" p. 205.

41. Such an emphasis is fundamental in John Bossy, *Christianity in the West, 1400–1700* (Oxford, 1985). For the notion of "social disciplining," see Gerhard Oestreich, *Neostoicism and the Early Modern State,* trans. David McLintock, ed. Brigitta Oestreich and H. G. Koenigsberger (Cambridge, Mass., 1982); for the use of social disciplining and confessionalization in describing the Reformation and Counter Reformation, see the overview of German scholarship in R. Po-chia Hsia, *Social Discipline in the Reformation: Central Europe, 1550–1750* (New York, 1989), esp. chap. 6.

42. The vague English word *gentlemen* might translate any number of historians' categories for France's elites or any number of contemporaries' own categorizations: *noblesse de robe, noblesse d'épée, laboureur, bourgeois gentilhomme, honnête homme,* and many others.

43. For a survey of the recent social history of elites in this period, see Jean-Marie Constant, "Absolutisme et Modernité," in *Histoire des élites en France du XVIᵉ au XXᵉ siècle,* ed. Guy Chaussinand-Nogaret (Paris, 1991), pp. 145–216, and the useful but older study by John Hearsey McMillan Salmon, *Society in Crisis: France in the Sixteenth Century* (New York, 1975), pp. 92–113; for educated elites in the late sixteenth century, see George Huppert,

tural projects were not some necessary superstructual reflections of some base social relations; they were attempts to understand and to transform those social relations along differing contested axes. As one historian has termed it, a "culture of separation" saturated French elite culture.[44] While not reflecting accurately some actual social separation, this culture displayed rather an often desperate, often highly theorized desire for dissociation and produced a wide array of different schemes that attempted to define and justify divisions of society and hierarchy.[45] Each rested on some different account of nobility—and many were nobilities of mind, morals, or the spirit and not in theory, of course, of land, a particular education, or a particular social position. So, early seventeenth-century French culture was awash in possibilities new and old for simultaneously reforming one's self and one's knowledge.[46] These conflicting spiritual exercises offered different modes and ideals for cultivating the self: Ignatius's *Spiritual Exercises* (and its various reformulations), Michel de Montaigne's *Essays,* the humanist ideal orator/citizen Charron's *Livres de la sagesse,* Jean Bodin's *Methodus ad facilem historiarum cognitionem,* the alchemical romances of Béroalde de Verville, Eustachius a Sancto Paulo's *Exercices spirituelles,* Pierre Gassendi's Epicureanism, Justus Lipsius's Neostoicism, Cornelius Jansenius's Augustinianism, Seneca's *De vita beata,* Epictetus's *Manual,* to name but a few.[47]

Les Bourgeois Gentilshommes: An Essay on the Definition of Elites in Renaissance France (Chicago, 1977); for elites and the transformation of manners, see Norbert Elias, *The Court Society,* trans. Edmund Jephcott (New York, 1983); Orest Ranum, "Courtesy, Absolutism, and the Rise of the French State, 1630–1660," *Journal of Modern History* 52 (Sept. 1980): 426–51; and Ellery Schalk, "The Court as 'Civilizer' of the Nobility: Noble Attitudes and the Court in France in the Late Sixteenth and Early Seventeenth Centuries," in *Princes, Patronage, and the Nobility: The Court at the Beginning of the Modern Age, c. 1450–1650,* ed. Ronald G. Asch and Adolf M. Birke (Oxford, 1991), pp. 245–63.

44. Anna Maria Battista, "Morale 'privé' et utilitarisme politique en France au XVIIᵉ siècle," in *Staatsräson: Studien zur Geschichte eines politischen Begriffs,* ed. Roman Schur (Berlin, 1975), p. 101.

45. See ibid., and Huppert, *Les Bourgeois Gentilshommes;* compare Peter Burke, *Popular Culture in Early Modern Europe* (New York, 1978), pp. 270–81. The sense of instability is well illustrated by the proliferation of treatises desperately trying to identify unambiguous visual markers of social position, most famously, Charles Loyseau, *A Treatise of Orders and Plain Dignities,* trans. and ed. Howell A. Lloyd (Cambridge, Mass., 1994).

46. The term *spiritual exercises* had, of course, a dominant referent in Descartes's day: Ignatius of Loyola's *Spiritual Exercises,* which itself drew on the ancient genre of spiritual exercises. For the most careful study of Descartes's relationship with the Ignatian exercises, one which casts great doubt on commentators seeking echoes of Ignatius in Descartes, see Michel Hermans and Michel Klein, "Ces *Exercices spirituels* que Descartes aurait pratiqués," *Archives de Philosophie* 59 (Jul.–Sept. 1996): 427–40. For studies of such echoes, see, for example, the study of textual similarities in Walter John Stohrer, "Descartes and Ignatius Loyola: La Flèche and Manresa Revisited," *Journal of the History of Philosophy* 17 (Jan. 1979): 11–27.

47. For intimations on this, see John Stephenson Spink, *French Free-Thought from Gassendi to Voltaire* (London, 1960), esp. chap. 8, and John Cottingham, *Philosophy and the Good Life:*

Partisans may have disputed the proper connected form of self-cultivation and knowledge production, but they did not question the existence of such a connection itself.[48] Many of these stressed the digestion of historical exemplars while others stressed literary ones; such digested exemplars, particularly of the Stoics, formed much of the ethics course in Descartes's final year of schooling.[49] A few, like Lipsius or Gassendi, focused on moralities grounded in natural philosophies.

As Pierre Hadot has eloquently illustrated, for the ancient Epicureans and Stoics such as Marcus Aurelius, the careful study of the natural world mattered in large part for its importance as a spiritual exercise. As is well known, natural philosophy uncovered in principle the naturalistic basis for ethics. But, more strongly, working through that natural philosophy helped one to recognize both one's natural limits and abilities and a coherent moral end. So too in the Early Modern revivals of the ancient sects.

These spiritual exercises were not a mere automatic reflection of some classes' aspirations, a cynical codification of their particular abilities as the good life. They were, however, attempts at *defining* criteria for a

---

Reason and the Passions in Greek, Cartesian, and Psychoanalytic Ethics (New York, 1998), chap. 3. For the uneasy coexistence of the ideals of pagan and Christian antiquities in the period, see Zuber, "Guez de Balzac et les deux Antiquités," *XVIIe siècle*, no. 131 (Apr.–Jun. 1981): 135–48. Hadot has examined how physical thought figured in Marcus Aurelius's general scheme of self-cultivation. Knowing the physical world allows one to concentrate fully on that which can be changed, to achieve the state of *apatheia*. See Hadot, *Exercices spirituels*, "L'Expérience de la méditation," *Magazine litteraire*, no. 342 (Apr. 1996): 73–76, and Hadot, *Philosophy as a Way of Life: Spiritual Exercises from Socrates to Foucault*, trans. Michael Chase, ed. Davidson (Oxford, 1995). Lisa Sarasohn recently has emphasized how Gassendi's physical thought similarly figured within his Epicurean ethic of self-cultivation. See Lisa T. Sarasohn, *Gassendi's Ethics: Freedom in a Mechanistic Universe* (Ithaca, N.Y., 1996). Compare, for Germany, Pamela H. Smith, *The Business of Alchemy: Science and Culture in the Holy Roman Empire* (Princeton, N.J., 1994), pp. 41–44, and for England, see Julie Robin Solomon, *Objectivity in the Making: Francis Bacon and the Politics of Inquiry* (Baltimore, 1998), pp. 37–43. For the humanist tradition of history reading as moral instruction and the collapse of this in the late Renaissance, see Timothy Hampton, *Writing from History: The Rhetoric of Exemplarity in Renaissance Literature* (Ithaca, N.Y., 1990). For differing accounts of the pedagogic role of logical treatises, see Wilhelm Risse, *Die Logik der Neuzeit*, 2 vols. (Stuttgart-Bad Cannstatt, 1964), vol. 1, chap. 6. For a fine account of artificial versus natural logic and their relations to comtemplative versus active ideals, see Nicholas Jardine, "Keeping Order in the School of Padua: Jacopo Zabarella and Francesco Piccolomini on the Offices of Philosophy," in *Method and Order in Renaissance Philosophy of Nature: The Aristotle Commentary Tradition*, ed. Daniel A. Di Liscia, Eckhard Kessler, and Charlotte Methuen (Aldershot, 1997), pp. 183–210, esp. p. 201.

48. For example, in 1634, the famous correspondent Marin Mersenne weighed the respective values of mathematics versus natural philosophy as forms of self-cultivation. See Marin Mersenne, *Questions inouyes, ou récréation des sçavans* (1634; Stuttgart-Bad Cannstatt, 1972), pp. 76–88.

49. See Rodis-Lewis, *Descartes: His Life and Thought*, trans. Jane Marie Todd (Ithaca, N.Y., 1998), pp. 15–16.

kind of elite, an elite characterized by the careful development of particular mental, spiritual, and moral virtues through technical exercise. Descartes produced his modern candidate for subjectivity in trying, like so many of his contemporaries, to effect a better seventeenth-century subjectivity, one suitable to the dislocations of his age. He rejected other forms of knowledge acquisition because they failed his criteria for proper cultivation of the reason and the will.[50]

Attention-Deflection Disorder: Rejecting Forms of Cultivation

It is by now a commonplace that an exploding variety of new words, things, and approaches characterized and threatened Renaissance visions of knowledge. Roughly, in Descartes's picture of the human faculties, the attention could be trained on the intellect, the imagination, or the memory, but only one at a time. For the will to receive the guidance of the intellect, the attention must be focused on the intellect. Therefore, any epistemic procedure keeping the attention away from the intellect for too long had to be rejected as noncultivating. Descartes wanted to overcome individual, disjointed fragments of knowledge but, like Montaigne, doubted whether contemporary intellectual tools could ever surpass them. For example, in an early notebook entry, Descartes complained that the art of memory was necessarily useless "because it requires the whole space [*chartam*] that ought to be occupied by better things and consists in an order that is not right." The art's collections of particulars not only failed as knowledge, but blocked it; they diverted attention away from the discerning of order, a function of intellect, toward the recognition of disjointed particulars, a function of the memory. In contrast, "the [right]

50. This entire enterprise may seem altogether too vague, too inclusive. In calling something a spiritual exercise, I mean that:

1) It comprises a set of practices, often including logic and mathematics, intended ultimately to lead one's self or soul toward some goal of self-cultivation. These practices necessarily involve the development of various faculties, including *ingenium, ingenio, esprit,* memory, wit, and so forth.

2) In its more philosophical guises it would include

2.1) an ontology,

2.2) an account of the faculties to be improved,

2.3) the appropriateness or inappropriateness of those faculties for gaining access to the philosophy's ontology, an account of basis of the morality to be improved (which may or may not be naturalistic, often depending on [2.1]).

3) A specification of the social field at whom it is aimed, or whom end up pursuing it. Ignatius stressed the plasticity of the term: "'Spiritual Exercises' embraces every method of examination of conscience, of meditation, of vocal and mental prayer, and of other spiritual activity. . . . For just as strolling, walking, and running are bodily exercises, so spiritual exercises are methods of preparing and disposing the soul to free itself of all inordinate attachments" (quoted in Stohrer, "Descartes and Ignatius Loyola," p. 25).

order is that the images be formed from one another as interdependent" (*AT,* 10:230).⁵¹

The pedagogic and reading practices associated with arts of memory, commonplace books, and encyclopedias promised to help discover such interconnection.⁵² But, too concerned with disconnected experiences and historical facts, these techniques necessarily prevented its discovery. Perhaps worse, narratives attempting to combine particulars generated not any interconnection but monstrous mixtures. Descartes gauged such narrative monsters as histories, not sciences. They always involved focusing the attention on discrete elements in the imagination or memory, rather than focusing on the intellect's comprehension of fundamental unities tying together apparently discrete elements.

For Descartes, these epistemic failings led inevitably to moral ones. Deflection of attention yielded imitation, not introspection. Monstrous histories of disconnected facts misled those "who rule their manners by the examples they take from them." Ruling manners by imitation and not introspection allowed people "to fall into the extravagances of the Paladins of our romances and to conceive of designs that surpass their strength" (*AT,* 6:7). Don Quixote's illusory windmills haunted the philosophical alternatives available to Descartes's contemporaries. Imitation and wonder made them unable freely to consider, to choose, and to rule themselves.

Descartes explained the range of disciplines he dismissed as history: "By history I understand all that has been previously found and is contained in books." True knowledge meant, in contrast, the ability to resolve all questions "by one's own industry," to become (here Descartes significantly uses the Stoic term) *autarches,* that is, self-sufficient (*AT,* 3:722–23).⁵³ Only self-sufficiency allows true inventiveness in reason and the moral life predicated upon it.⁵⁴

This expansive condemnation of history included mathematics. In mathematics, as elsewhere, Descartes explained, imitating the ancients' works failed: "Even though we know other people's demonstrations by heart, we shall never become mathematicians if we lack the aptitude, by virtue of our *ingenium,* to solve any given problem" (*AT,* 10:367; see *CSM,* 1:13). Empty mathematical facts would never eliminate wonder through systematic comprehension. Standard mathematical proof was a form of imitation. Why?

For Descartes, formal logical consequence, as in a syllogism or math-

---

51. Translation from Sepper, *Descartes's Imagination,* pp. 76–77.

52. For humanist commonplace methodology, see, for example, Ann Blair, "Humanist Methods in Natural Philosophy: The Commonplace Book," *Journal of the History of Ideas* 53 (Oct.–Dec. 1992): 541–51.

53. Descartes made the same point in the *Regulae;* see *AT,* 10:367.

54. Thus Descartes claims to break with *imitatio,* both textual and in life. Compare Terence Cave, *The Cornucopian Text: Problems of Writing in the French Renaissance* (Oxford, 1979).

ematical proof, rested on the possibility of surveying a formal deduction over time.[55] Considering a series of particular facts or observations in an enumeration demands the step-wise switching of attention as one reviews the series in memory or on paper; so, too, with the discrete steps of formal deductions:

> [When a deduction is complex and involved] we call it "enumeration" or "induction," since the intellect cannot simultaneously grasp it as a whole, and its certainty in a sense depends on memory, which must retain the judgments we have made on the individual parts of the enumeration if we are to derive a single conclusion from them taken as a whole. [*AT,* 10:408; *CSM,* 1:37]

If one knows A~B, B~C, C~D, D~E, then "I do not on that account see what the relation is between A and E, nor can I grasp it precisely from those already known, unless I recall them all" (*AT,* 10:387–88; see *CSM,* 1:25). The sequence in the proof offers good reasons to *consent* that the relation between the first and the fifth is such. But in consenting we do not grasp the relation in anything like the way we grasp the more intermediate and immediately grasped relations. Descartes admitted that formal deductions could be perfectly certain *"in virtue of the form"* (*AT,* 10: 406; *CSM,* 1:36).[56]

Formal *certainty* hardly made the result and its connection to the intermediate steps at all *evident.* The discrete steps were just like a bunch of particular observations about the natural world. Both syllogistic causal philosophy and mathematical demonstrations in their traditional forms, those products of the ancients' ruses, rested on memory. In slavishly imitating and assenting to proof, one allowed reason to "amuse" oneself and thereby one lost the habit of reasoning. In sum, one lost the foundation of regulating oneself in epistemic and moral matters.

Descartes's Positive Conception of Knowledge

Having rejected essentially all contemporary forms of knowledge production, what resources did the young Descartes have left? In his earliest notebook, we find an antimemory, "poetical" view of knowledge closely associated with Descartes's first real achievements in geometry with the help of machines and algebra.[57] He contrasted the laborious pro-

55. See Andre Robinet, *Aux sources de l'esprit cartesien: L'Axe La Ramée-Descartes: De la "Dialectique" des 1555 aux "Regulae"* (Paris, 1996), pp. 191–96.

56. See Marion's annotations in Descartes, *Règles utiles et claires pour la direction de l'esprit en la recherche de la vérité,* pp. 217–18.

57. For this notebook and the vicissitudes of its transmission, see Henri Gaston Gouhier, *Les Premières Pensées de Descartes: Contribution à l'histoire de l'anti-renaissance* (Paris, 1958),

cesses of reasoning in philosophy with the organic unity of wisdom and knowledge that poets divined.

> It seems amazing, what heavy thoughts are in the writings of the poets, rather than the philosophers. The reason is that poets write through enthusiasm and the strength of the imagination; for there are the sparks of knowledge within us, as in a flint: where philosophers extract them through reason, poets force them out through the imagination and they shine more brightly. [*AT,* 10:217; see *CSM,* 1:4]

This poetic ideal, worthy of much further inquiry, promised knowledge of a sharply aesthetic, intuitive character, illuminating the unity of its objects and thereby appropriate for regulating oneself through attention on unities in the intellect.

Descartes turned this poetic claim of his early notebook into an epistemic standard of unity and interconnection. He offered a new vision of cause. This kind of cause eliminates the need for memory because once the cause is grasped one can easily reproduce its original justification. That knowledge of cause, however, is neither secured by those formal steps, nor does it include an enumeration of them. Cause comprises, rather, knowledge of an organizing principle underlying the *interdependence* of elements (see *AT,* 10:230).[58]

Descartes claimed his new mathematics was a key exercise for cultivation. A cultivating mathematics would give one experience in recognizing the interdependence and evidence of the steps of a formal proof and make those steps ultimately superfluous. Under this constraint, the series of proportions A~B, B~C, C~D, D~E of a formal proof would have to be somehow grasped all at once.

What example did Descartes have of such a remarkable reduction of deductive knowledge? Thanks to his travels in Germany, he had a new proportional compass (fig. 4).[59] Descartes's compass begins with the two straightedges YZ and YX (see *AT,* 6:391–92). BC is fixed on YX. Other straightedges perpendicular to YZ and YX respectively are attached but can move side to side along YZ and YX. As the compass is opened, BC pushes CD, which in turn pushes DE, which pushes EF, and so forth. As it opens, the compass produces a series of similar triangles YBC, YDE,

and Rodis-Lewis, "Le Premier Registre de Descartes," *Archives de philosophie* 54, no. 3–4 (1991): 353–77, 639–57.

58. For discussion, see Sepper, *Descartes's Imagination,* pp. 76–77; compare pp. 44–46. Compare also *AT,* 10:204, 10:94.

59. I skip completely over the difficult question of Descartes's encounters while in Germany. For a persuasive recent view, based on careful analysis of algebraic procedures, see Kenneth Manders, "Descartes et Faulhaber," *Bulletin Cartésien, Archives de Philosophie* 58 (Jul.–Sept. 1995): 1–12.

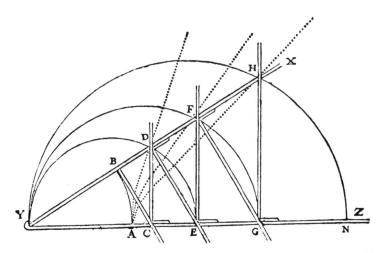

FIG. 4.—Descartes's compass, from *La Géométrie*, p. 318.

YFG, and so on. This allows the infinite production of mean proportionals, YB:YC :: YC:YD :: YD:YE :: YE:YF. Numerous problems in geometry can be solved through finding such mean proportionals.

With the compass in mind, we can grasp the ordering principle behind a sequence of continued relations. That is, we can grasp the relation between a first and last term (YB:YF) in something akin to our grasp of an intermediate and more immediate relationship (YB:YC). We need not retain the individual proportions in memory to claim knowledge of any of the particular relations because we can easily read them off the compass. The compass offered the crucial heuristic, a material propaedeutic, for Descartes' revised account of mathematics freed from memory and subject to a criterion of graspable unity.[60] A simple mathematical instrument became the model and exemplar of the knowledge of Descartes's new subject, the one supposedly so removed from the material.

Evidence and Deduction: An Aesthetics of Deduction Rooted in a Mathematics

Descartes distinguished the evidence of a proof from its formal certainty. Formal demonstrations, like syllogisms or other logical forms of

60. The equation $b = a^3$ encodes both a curve and the progression $1:a :: a:a^2 :: a^2:a^3$. This algebraic progression encapsulates the constructive process of his compass. See Lachterman, *The Ethics of Geometry: A Genealogy of Modernity*, pp. 165–66. Timothy Lenoir argues that, for Descartes, algebra "served as a device for the easy storage and quick retrieval of information regarding geometrical constructions" (Timothy Lenoir, "Descartes and the Geometrization of Thought: The Methodological Background of Descartes's *Géométrie*," *Historia Mathematica* 6 [Nov. 1979]: 363).

proof, could, in his eyes, produce certainty. They did not, however, make the connections one was proving evident.[61] Descartes's radical move was to demand that all real knowledge consist in the same sort of immediate, *evident* character as our knowledge of singular things around us cognized clearly. In the *Rules for the Direction of the Natural Intelligence* of the 1620s, Descartes formalized a new account of enumerative and deductive knowledge subject to the criterion of evidence. The new form of deduction extended evidence from single, simple intuitions of local things to knowledge of simple and complex unified systems. He privileged this form of deduction as necessary for allowing the will to see clearly the guidance offered by the intellect. Here I can give only a brief account of his deeply problematic but enticing vision.[62]

He reduced all true knowledge to an ineffable intuition: "two things are required for intuition: first, the proposition intuited must be clear and distinct; next, it must be understood all at once, and not bit by bit" (*AT*, 10:407; see *CSM*, 1:37). Descartes knew well that such instantaneous, intuitive grasp could hardly account for much complex knowledge. But he demanded more complex knowledge nevertheless retain the qualities of intuitions: "The evidence and certainty of intuition are required not only for apprehending single enunciations but equally for all routes" (*AT*, 10:369; see *CSM*, 1:14–15).

Anything more complex than immediate intuition, however, would necessarily involve cognition over time using the memory, thereby mov-

61. For the real conflicting demands of clarity versus demonstration as a standing problem, see Leibniz' remarks on Ramus's and Mercator's sacrificing of demonstrative rigor for clarity of method, in Gottfried Wilhelm Freiherr von Leibniz, "Projet et Essais pour arriver à quelque Certitude pour finir une bonne partie des disputes, et pour avancer l'art d'inventer," *Philosophische Schriften*, in *Sämtliche Schriften und Briefe*, ed. Berlin-Brandenburgischen Akademie der Wissenschaften, 7 ser. (Berlin, 1923–), ser. 6, vol. 4, pt. A, pp. 968–69. Gaukroger has insightfully connected Descartes's epistemic standards to the Roman rhetorical tradition; see his "Descartes's Early Doctrine of Clear and Distinct Ideas," *The Genealogy of Knowledge: Analytical Essays in the History of Philosophy and Science* (Aldershot, 1997), pp. 131–52. For a fuller discussion of evidence in the philosophical, theological, and rhetorical traditions, see, for the foundational texts, Aristotle, *Physics*, 1.1 (184a17–22) and *Posterior analytics*, 2.19 (99b15–100b17); Wesley Trimpi, *Muses of One Mind: The Literary Analysis of Experience and Its Continuity* (Princeton, N.J., 1983), pp. 117–20; and Antonio Pérez-Ramos, *Francis Bacon's Idea of Science and the Maker's Knowledge Tradition* (Oxford, 1988), pp. 201–15. For a late scholastic account, see Eustachius a Sancto Paulo, *Summa philosophiae quadripartita: De rebus dialecticis, ethicis, physicis, et metaphysicis* (Cambridge, 1640), pp. 135–36.
62. The best account of deduction in Descartes is Doren A. Recker, "Mathematical Demonstration and Deduction in Descartes's Early Methodological and Scientific Writings," *Journal of the History of Philosophy* 31 (Apr. 1993): 223–44; see also Frederick Van De Pitte, "Intuition and Judgment in Descartes's Theory of Truth," *Journal of the History of Philosophy* 26 (July 1988): 453–70; Gaukroger, *Cartesian Logic: An Essay on Descartes's Conception of Influence* (Oxford, 1989); Yvon Belaval, *Leibniz: Critique de Descartes* (Paris, 1960); and Desmond M. Clarke, "Descartes's Use of 'Demonstration' and 'Deduction,'" in *René Descartes: Critical Assessments*, ed. Georges J. D. Moyal, 4 vols. (New York, 1991), 1: 237–47.

ing one's attention away from the intellect. His proposed model of deduction was to raise enumerations, including but by no means limited to mathematical and other traditionally deductive arguments, to certain knowledge of an evident character by bringing out the occulted order organizing them:

> So I will run through [all the particulars] several times in a continuous motion of the imagination, simultaneously intuiting one relation and passing on the next, until I have learned to pass from the first to last so swiftly that no part is left to the memory, and I seem to intuit the whole thing at once. In this way our memory is relieved, the sluggishness of our intelligence redressed, and its capacity in some way enlarged. [*AT,* 10:388; see *CSM,* 1:25]

Descartes's vision of intuiting "the whole thing at once" rested on there being a "thing" to be grasped at once, something guaranteeing the interconnection of the objection and the continuous intuition of the object. His usual metaphor involved the chain: "If we have seen the connections between each link and its neighbor, this enables us to say that we have seen *how* the last link is connected to the first" (*AT,* 10:389; *CSM,* 1:26; my emphasis). He limited knowledge to those things possessing such connections, like mathematics, as he understood it.

His central example for his new deductions was the sequence of relations described above. To understand fully the endpoint that A has in relationship to E, we need to grasp not only the series of simple relations but the underlying order producing them. As we saw, the compass in this example offered the ordering principle, the *how,* behind these relations. Thus, the compass, properly abstracted, comprises the simultaneously grasped, clear, and distinct intuition produced by the sufficient enumeration of the relations. With this little example, one might experience what it is like to have such an intuition, which, being basic, cannot be defined.

Exercises: Evidence, Mathematics, and Tapestries

Clear and *distinct* have long struck commentators as more aesthetic than epistemic and therefore useless as criteria for knowledge.[63] Something like this aesthetic quality attracted Descartes, for only an aesthetic criterion, drawn from poetry and rhetoric, could ensure the interconnection central to real knowledge—the interconnected knowledge divined by the poets. *Aesthetic* hardly meant subjective in the pejorative sense. Exer-

---

63. I use *aesthetic* in the modern sense and not the meaning of sensory impression of the seventeenth century. On this, see Paul Oskar Kristeller, "The Modern System of the Arts," *Renaissance Thought and the Arts: Collected Essays* (Princeton, N.J., 1990), pp. 163–227.

cise created the *objective* habit of recognizing the truly interconnected; developing the habit made Descartes's subject capable of intersubjective knowledge.

He made this clear in his *Rules for the Direction of the Natural Intelligence*. "Natural intelligence" (or, even worse, "mind") poorly translates Descartes's term *ingenium*—a central, much disputed Renaissance term for artistic and poetical spark or genius. More specifically, the term could indicate the ability of an orator to imagine a situation so vividly, that, by speaking, he could produce an evident picture in the listener's mind.[64] Developing this ability required intense practice.

Descartes's *ingenium* equally needed such concrete practice. In a vein far removed from the image of the philosopher cogitating alone and without corporeal things, as I noted in the introduction, Descartes recommended studying "the simplest and least exalted arts, and especially those in which order prevails." Such study habituated one to the affect of experiencing clear and distinct order. A proper form of geometry offered the best habituation. Mathematics provided exercise in recognizing how things that are foundational for Descartes are indeed clear and distinct: the self, mind, extension, and God. It offered the practice that could allow one to choose among philosophical therapeutics. Doing correct geometrical work mattered because it epitomized knowledge both certain and evident; it best could refine one's *objective* taste for and in truths. This august role for mathematics, however, set troublesome boundaries for correct geometrical work.

Algebra: Developing Mathematical Taste and Threatening to Spoil It

Descartes's account of exercise required a dangerous temporary use of artificial instruments to achieve this intuitive habituation. Like manuals claiming to teach ostensibly natural manners, civility, or taste, such artificial means always have something paradoxical about them. As with a primer on taste, Descartes's tools promised the supposedly natural through the artificial. He attacked traditional formal reasoning because its forms promised natural knowledge through artificial means, but never severed its attachment to the artificial.[65]

64. See also Nicolas Caussin's attempt to combine *judicium* with highly personal *ingenium* in his rhetoric in Fumaroli, *L'Âge de l'éloquence: Rhétorique et "res literaria," de la Renaissance au seuil de l'époque classique* (Paris, 1994), p. 288. For *ingenium*, see Martin Kemp, "From *Mimesis* to *Fantasia:* The Quattrocento Vocabulary of Creation, Inspiration, and Genius in the Visual Arts," *Viator* 8 (1977): 347–98.

65. Descartes's ambivalence toward algebra has divided commentators, with some seeing true modernity and algebraic liberation in the geometry, and others stressing the algebra's secondary character. For the first, see Schouls, *Descartes and the Possibility of Science,*

Nevertheless, Descartes recognized a need for arts to maximize our natural but obscured capacities. In the *Rules,* Descartes explained that arts aided reasoning temporally by *preparing* one to intuit relations not immediately grasped. The greater part of human labor consisted in this preparation:

> Absolutely every cognition, which one has not acquired through the simple and pure intuition of a unique thing, is acquired by the comparison of two or multiple things among themselves. And certainly nearly all the industry of human reason consists in preparing this operation; for when it [the operation] is open and simple, there is no need for any aid of an art, but the light of nature alone is necessary to intuit the truth, which is had by this. [*AT,* 10:440; see *CSM,* 1:57]

Once the complex nature has been grasped intuitively, that is, all at once, the art is no longer needed. Again the heuristic is of a string of proportions. Terms A and E are not immediately proportionate until C, B, and D are added to the picture.

Descartes's early mathematical machines suggested that solutions to problems in mathematics came from producing "means" connecting the objects one wants to characterize, like the relations completely characterized through his compass:

> In every question there ought to be given a mean between two extremes, through which they are conjoined explicitly or implicitly: as with the circle and parabola, by means of the conic section. [*AT,* 10:229][66]

As we saw, Descartes's compass showed how a string of proportionals are intimately connected, as are their algebraic representations. The compass exemplified how to make enumerations, including deductions, for the demand of sufficiency (see *AT,* 10:384–87).[67] This necessarily demanded a movement from knowns to unknowns to fill the gaps sufficiently. This movement, in filling out a deduction, does not produce a "being entirely new"; rather, "one simply extends all this knowledge until we perceive that the thing sought participates in one or another fashion in the nature

---

and to some extent Mahoney, "The Beginnings of Algebraic Thought in the Seventeenth Century," in *Descartes: Philosophy, Mathematics, and Physics,* ed. Gaukroger (Sussex, 1980), pp. 141–68; for the latter, see Lenoir, "Descartes and the Geometrization of Thought," and Grosholz, *Cartesian Method and the Problem of Reduction.* Gaukroger examines Descartes's refusal to pursue the potential for formal reasoning latent in his algebra; see Gaukroger, *Cartesian Logic,* pp. 72–88.

66. Compare *AT,* 10:232–3 on a machine for making conic sections.

67. See Michel Serfati, "Les Compas cartésiens," *Archives de philosophie* 56 (Apr.–Jun. 1993): 197–230, esp. pp. 213–14.

of the givens" (*AT,* 10:438–39; see *CSM,* 1:56). He offered the example of someone who knows only basic colors but is able to deduce the rest in an orderly fashion.

Art, whether algebraic symbols or the proportional compass, could help precisely because it helped to evolve (roll out) the relations "involved" within nature:

> All the others require preparation, for no other reason than that this common nature is not in both equally, but rather is involved [enveloped] in them according to certain relations or proportions. The principle part of human industry is not placed other than for reducing these proportions until the equality between the thing sought and the thing already known is seen clearly. [*AT,* 10:440; see *CSM,* 1:57–58]

The art in question helps one come to see things clearly; but once seen, the art must no longer play any role.

He introduced his new tool algebra into geometry given these caveats. Algebra helps to disaggregate a disordered collection of geometrical objects into a variety of distinctly conceived but clearly unified components. In so doing, one produces an apparently more complicated picture, replete with symbols and additional lines. But the newly selected algebraic formula guides the construction of a machine, which draws a curve, reducing the disorder by showing its interconnection. This curve/machine complex allows simultaneous intuition of the interconnected geometrical objects. Algebra enabled one to get to the *moving* geometric order, but it was never to supplant that order.

The habituation Descartes's cultivating mathematics offered was not only that of becoming accustomed to the experience of the clear and distinct but equally that of the process of filling in intermediate relations of a set of discrete elements to reduce that ramshackle collection to a clear and distinct unified order. It was thus the central *practice* necessary in adding the unseen and unseeable efficient causes to apparently disparate and definitely surprising phenomena.[68]

The introduction of algebra, however, was dangerous. While it was a crucial tool in producing intuitive mathematical "taste," it threatened to eliminate self-sufficiency in thought and in action. Descartes contrasted his temporary application of algebra with the practices of the "vulgar calculators." Their blind procedures of calculation prevented reasoning based on a real sense of the properties of objects; working with empty numbers and imaginary figures without method soon meant that "we get

---

68. See *AT,* 10:438–39 on the movement from talk of "knowns" and "unknowns" to mechanical explanations.

out of the habit of using our reason" (*AT,* 10:375; *CSM,* 1:18).[69] Like the ancients making sacrifices when they came across a discovery, the calculator, the essential imitator, could not be in self-control. Descartes condemned the technical procedures of the calculator and the dialectician by condemning both as useful only to "amuse" oneself, but not, assuredly, to direct oneself.

> I would not make so much of these rules, if they sufficed only to resolve the inane problems with which Calculators [*Logistae*] and Geometers amuse themselves to pass time, for in that case all I could credit myself with achieving would be to dabble in trifles with greater subtlety than they. . . . I'm hardly thinking of vulgar Mathematics here, but I'm talking of another discipline entirely, of which [these examples of figures and numbers] are rather the outer garment than the parts. [*AT,* 10:373–74; see *CSM,* 1:17]

Like the courtier with his politeness learned only from books, the scholastic philosopher too dependent on syllogistic, or the orator stuck on stock rhetorical devices, the calculators' use of artificial practices—their techniques—prevents real cultivation of the aesthetic ability central to real mathematics and philosophy and necessary to regulate manners and the mind.

This simultaneous social and epistemic critique surrounds Descartes's geometry. By no means do I claim that all of the features and tensions of Descartes's geometrical program can be so explained; indeed, geometry enticed Descartes precisely because of its rigidity and certainty once its boundaries had been defined. Understanding the exclusion of the varieties of mathematics Descartes viewed as noncultivating, however, helps to transform numerous problems of Descartes's geometry into its central features.

Account of Allowable and Knowable Curves

In his earliest notebook and in his eighth rule, Descartes stressed that one must gain an adequate picture of human capacity—the real abilities and real failings—to avoid attempting to know what humans cannot. Only thereby could one gauge and temper the tools necessary to fulfill

69. The quotes from this section draw on the similarities between Rule IV-A and IV-B and do not highlight their major differences. For the debates, see, for example, John A. Schuster, "Descartes and the Scientific Revolution, 1618–1634: An Interpretation" (Ph.D. diss., Princeton University, 1977); Van De Pitte, "The Dating of Rule IV-B in Descartes's *Regulae ad directionem ingenii," Journal of the History of Philosophy* 29 (July 1991): 375–95, and many others.

our capacity (see *AT,* 10:215).[70] Descartes's account of curves, the heart of the *Geometry,* offered a carefully selected middle path methodologically and ontologically set between abstraction and calculation—it expanded the domain of knowable objects but included only those within the compass of human ability. The ancients had too low an estimation of human ability; they excluded too much. Descartes argued that they prohibited the use of curves other than circles and lines in constructions, only because they, by chance, had happened upon a few bad examples and abandoned the whole lot (see *AT,* 6:389–90).[71] In not methodically considering their candidates for mathematical objects, they failed to distinguish among the various curves and condemned all of them as "mechanical" and thus unknowable, rather than seeing that many were perfectly knowable and in fact necessary for systematic knowledge. In contrast, Descartes argued for expanding the domain of the perfectly knowable but placed severe restrictions on this expansion. His exclusions and inclusions have long worried sensitive commentators, from Isaac Newton to Henk J. M. Bos.

The simple machines of compass and ruler produce circles and lines. Descartes offered another machine that produces legitimate curves: his famous compass, described above. Though this compass can produce many different motions or curves, each is regulated by the first motion. Any one can be known and understood by reference to any other. In producing a circle, this compass generates a number of curves the ancients considered merely mechanical (see *AT,* 6:391–92).

> In considering Geometry as a science that teaches generally how to know the dimensions of all bodies, one must no more exclude the most composed lines than the most simple ones, provided that one can imagine them described by a continuous movement, or a number of movements that follow upon one another and of which the last are *entirely regulated* by those that precede them: for, by this means, one can ever have an exact knowledge of their dimensions. [*AT,* 6:389–90; my emphasis][72]

Mechanisms of interdependent motions were intimately connected to the constraints of Descartes's new account of mathematical deduction. Des-

70. Compare *AT,* 10:393–8.

71. A. G. Molland shows how Descartes misrepresented the ancients better to make his case; see Molland, "Shifting the Foundations: Descartes's Transformation of Ancient Geometry," *Historia Mathematica* 3 (1976): 21–49, esp. pp. 35–37.

72. Bos has nicely outlined the twists of Descartes's account with its multiple, apparently disparate accounts of acceptable curves. I largely follow his account here. See Bos, "On the Representation of Curves in Descartes's *Géométrie*," "The Structure of Descartes's *Géométrie*," and "Descartes, Pappus's Problem, and the Cartesian Parabola: A Conjecture," in *The Investigation of Difficult Things: Essays on Newton and the History of the Exact Sciences in Honour of D. T. Whiteside,* ed. P. M. Harman and Alan E. Shapiro (Cambridge, 1992), pp. 71–96.

cartes apparently saw the connected chain of interdependent
motions as more or less equivalent
to a chain of clear and distinct
mathematical reasons each yielding something as clear and distinct
as the previous.[73] *Tracing* a curve—
the ability to create or imagine a
machine of interdependent regulated motions tracing a given
curve—and *conceiving* that curve
came together. The material compass and its products offered, as he
suggested, the best exemplar of
Descartes's deeply problematic notion of clarity and distinctness and
his idiosyncratic view of deduction.

In contrast to the curves generated by machines like Descartes's

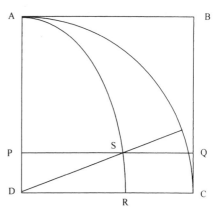

Fig. 5.—Quadratrix (my figure). Given a square *ABCD*, the quadratrix is the locus *AR* from the intersections *S* of the radius from *D* uniformly moving circularly from *A* to *C* and the line *PQ* uniformly moving from *DC* to *AB*.

compass, other curves cannot be so perceived or produced by interdependent, regulated, continuous motion. His example of an unknowable
curve is the quadratrix (fig. 5).[74] The quadratrix is "conceived as described by two separate movements, between which there is no relation
that can be measured exactly" (*AT*, 6:390). Quite characteristically, Descartes slid between standards for the acceptability of curves from a mechanical to a proportional criterion. The key relationship between the
two movements making up the quadratrix, AC:AD as AP:AT, relates a
segment of a circle to a straight line. Descartes retained the traditional
notion that "the proportion between straight lines and curves is not
known." He believed, moreover, that it is not "able to be known," that
one could not conclude anything from considerations involving any such
proportion (*AT*, 6:412).[75] Though we could imagine a machine producing
the curve, one of the key motions of that machine could not be known
exactly in reference to the other. One can only know the proportion *partially* through long arithmetical approximations. In contrast, "geometric"
curves, "that is, those that admit of precise and exact measurement, have

73. Noted as a "parallel" in Bos, "On the Representation of Curves in Descartes's *Géométrie*," p. 310.

74. See, for example, Paolo Mancosu, "Descartes's *Géométrie* and Revolutions in Mathematics," in *Revolutions in Mathematics*, ed. Donald Gilles (Oxford, 1992), pp. 93–95 for Clav-
ius as Descartes's likely source.

75. See Molland, "Shifting the Foundations: Descartes's Transformation of Ancient
Geometry," pp. 26, 36; Bos, "On the Representation of Curves in Descartes's *Géométrie*,"
p. 314; and Joseph E. Hofmann, *Leibniz in Paris 1672–1676: His Growth to Mathematical Matu-
rity* (Cambridge, 1974), pp. 101–3.

necessarily a certain relationship to all points of a straight line" (*AT*, 6:392).[76]

The quadratrix remains a "mechanical" curve by numerous standards: it cannot be constructed by an interdependent, continuously moving machine; it requires long computation, which produces only approximations; and it cannot be known all at once clearly and distinctly. Perhaps useful for a vulgar calculator, the quadratrix could never help to constitute Descartes's interconnected, easily reproducible mathematical knowledge, knowledge both certain *and* evident. By using something too abstract, like a very broad definition of curve, the mathematician would become intimately mired in deluding calculations of the *Logistae*—the vulgar calculators—and lose the attention necessary to control himself.

Hence a partial answer to the question of Descartes's inclusion and exclusion of curves. If Descartes were to be more abstract *ontologically* and allow a greater set of curves, he would simultaneously become much less abstract *methodically* by dragging himself into the domain of mass calculation. Descartes's progressive acceptance of more geometrical objects combined with his regressive rejection of others may appear inchoate and *ad hoc* within the logic of modern so-called Cartesian analytical geometry. Within his program of avoiding the aleatory and laborious, in favor of a cultivating, systematic method of producing clear and distinct knowledge graspable all at once, his choices cohere. Spiritual exercises necessary for his new geometrical subject required different constraints on his geometrical objects.

Conclusion: Eliminating Everyday Deception

Descartes's elaborate scheme for self-cultivation through methodic practice hardly took the mid-seventeenth century by storm. Success came only as his works disseminated into an array of resources with divergent visions of Cartesianism. The *Geometry*, in a series of ever more massively annotated Latin translations, quickly took on an autonomous life, one still marked by its exclusion from nearly all easily available editions of the *Discourse on Method* and its essays. The natural philosophy became an institutionalized replacement for Aristotelianism. Versions of the philosophy became fixtures of salons and polite culture.[77] The essential unity of

76. See Bos, "On the Representation of Curves in Descartes's *Géométrie*," pp. 313–15.
77. For intended audiences, see Jean-Pierre Cavaillé, "'Le Plus Éloquent Philosophe de derniers temps': Les Stratégies d'auteur de René Descartes," *Annales: Histoire, Sciences sociales*, no. 2 (Mar.–Apr. 1994): 349–67; for reception of the *Discourse*, see Garber, "Descartes, the Aristotelians, and the Revolution That Did Not Happen in 1637," *Monist* 71 (Oct. 1988): 471–86, and the essays in *Problématique et réception du "Discours de la méthode" et des "Essais*," ed. Henry Méchoulan (Paris, 1988), pp. 199–212. For "Cartesian women," see Erica Harth, *Cartesian Women: Version and Subversions of Rational Discourse in the Old Regime* (Ithaca,

his philosophy as a way of life, anchored in exemplary geometrical practices and built in response to early seventeenth-century concerns about
elite subjectivity, was quickly lost to his contemporaries and historians
since. A number of historians have maintained that Descartes wanted to
replace traditional philosophizing with practice and knowledge useful for
the *honnête homme* and *femme*. But they have understated the centrality of
geometry at the level of practice. Descartes said that only the third essay
following the *Discourse on Method*, the *Geometry, demonstrated* his method at
work (see *AT,* 1:478).

Traditional mathematics and natural philosophy, with their pretty
stories and turgid deductions, merely increased the number of wonders
in the world; they made imitation necessary. In contrast, one who masters
the *Discourse* and its three essays, the *Meteors*, the *Optics*, and the *Geometry*,
gains ascendancy over a large class of wondrous objects.[78] The *Geometry*
offered habituation in filling in the intermediate relations missing from a
disparate picture. A grasp of the coherence of objects filling the world
replaces the loss of attention everyday phenomena produce in the un-
learned. One regains the will's ability freely to consider the intellect's
guidance, which allows the freedom to judge correctly or not at all. Self-
produced philosophy returns to its proper role of improving our lives,
ruling our manners, and guiding our steps.[79]

Descartes put forth a set of practices for producing an early
seventeenth-century elite subject, removed from the corruption of institutions, narratives, proof, and deceptions, and therefore not needing external discipline. Coming to his proscribed subjectivity involved not
simply a turning away from world and word, nor a signal neglect of the
body, but a program of mental and physical transformation with an ambivalent relationship to the necessary material and mental arts it pre-
scribes. Descartes offered a seventeenth-century dream of subjectivity in
which a constructive geometry with an algebra is but one of many central
cultivating abilities. Modern subjects and geometry, they were not. As
Descartes's geometry suggests, to avoid deception one must fill in the intermediate relations connecting his subject and his mathematics to the so-
called modern subjects and mathematics; with that labor, crucial criticism
would have a more properly focused subject for censure or praise.

N.Y., 1992), and Eileen O'Neill, "Women Cartesians, 'Feminine Philosophy,' and Historical
Exclusion," in *Feminist Interpretations of René Descartes,* pp. 232–57.

78. See especially Neil M. Ribe, "Cartesian Optics and the Mastery of Nature," *Isis* 88
(Mar. 1997): 42–61; Geoffrey V. Sutton, *Science for a Polite Society: Gender, Culture, and the
Demonstration of Enlightenment* (Boulder, Colo., 1995); and Dear, "A Mechanical Microcosm."

79. Ironically, he located it in the development of a capacity inborn to all, "good
sense." See the beginning of the *Discours, AT,* 6:1.

Lyric Substance: On Riddles, Materialism, and Poetic Obscurity

Daniel Tiffany

> In poetry, a garment is not a garment; it conceals nothing.
> —G. E. LESSING, *Laocoön*

> Everyday opinion sees in the shadow only the lack of light, if not light's complete denial. In truth, however, the shadow is a manifest, though impenetrable, testimony to the concealed emitting of light.
> —MARTIN HEIDEGGER, "The Age of the World Picture"

> Pure of source is the riddle.
> —FRIEDRICH HÖLDERLIN, "The Rhine"

In the Parlance of Things

By most accounts, the form of the earliest secular poetry in English—the riddle—descends from the genre of the *aenigma,* first composed by English scholars (in Latin) in the seventh century.[1] Because the Latin clerical tradition of riddling was far less robust and inventive than its Anglo-

---

1. W. P. Ker comments on Anglo-Saxon literature's affinity for the riddle: "Poetical riddles were produced in England more largely than anywhere else in the Dark Ages, both in Latin and the native tongue. . . . The difference is that the old English poetical fashions are much more favourable to this kind of entertainment than anything in Latin. It is the proper business, one might say, of the old English poetry to call things out of their right names" (W. P. Ker, *The Dark Ages* [London, 1904], p. 92; hereafter abbreviated *D).* Northrop Frye makes a bolder claim, identifying the riddle as the primordial form of one of the two basic modes of lyric poetry, which are *melos* and—the mode proper to the riddle—*opsis;* see Northrop Frye, *Anatomy of Criticism* (Princeton, N.J., 1971), p. 280. On the riddle as one of

Saxon descendant, however, this literary-historical account may be less significant for a genealogy of lyric than the cultural disposition of the riddle poem. Archaeological evidence reveals that the earliest poetry in English displays an affinity for objects whose rarity and eccentricity were signaled by a peculiar verbal identity. Indeed, it may be possible to claim that lyric poetry first emerged in English as the enigmatic voice of certain highly wrought objects.

In the Anglo-Saxon world prior to the eleventh century, certain artifacts (crosses, weapons, bells, jewelry, sundials, chess pieces) bear inscriptions—in the first person—that refer to the object's maker or owner (or both), to the world at large, and to the object itself. For the most part, the scope of these inscriptions is quite limited, consisting of formulaic phrases such as "Godric made me," or "Ælfred ordered me to be made," or "Ædred owns me."[2] A smaller number of objects, however, bear more complex inscriptions betraying the form of a riddle. One object, for example, declares, "Cross is my name. Once, trembling and drenched with blood, I bore the mighty king."[3] Evoking the form of Anglo-Saxon riddles that end with an exhortation such as "Say who I am," or "Say what I am called," the first statement in this inscription ("Cross is my name") is the solution to the riddle posed by the second sentence. A riddle containing its own solution (in the title or embedded in the enigma itself) is a common feature of the Latin tradition, refined considerably by the Anglo-Saxon poet.

The incorporation of verbal identities by these objects reveals—even in the case of the meanest inscription—important details about their social and imaginative identities. Unlike the phenomenon of the modern commodity fetish, which comes to life only at the moment of exchange, these artifacts speak on the occasion of their manufacture, or under the condition of ownership (as distinct from simple possession). Yet the grammatical construction of the owner/maker formulae undermines the peculiar agency of the artifact. For although these objects speak and thus appear to occupy, at a linguistic level, the position of a subject, their

the essential roots of lyric poetry, see Andrew Walsh, *Roots of Lyric: Primitive Poetry and Modern Poetics* (Princeton, N.J., 1978), ch. 2.

2. Elisabeth Okasha, *Hand-list of Anglo-Saxon Non-runic Inscriptions* (Cambridge, 1971), pp. 106, 49, 89.

3. Ibid., p. 57.

Daniel Tiffany is the author of *Radio Corpse: Imagism and the Cryptaesthetic of Ezra Pound* (1995) and *Toy Medium: Materialism and Modern Lyric* (2000). A poet and translator, he is coeditor of a new book series on auditory culture and teaches at the University of Southern California in Los Angeles.

grammatical position in these statements is usually in the accusative case ("Godric made me"), thereby preserving their status as objects that are acted upon. The incorporation of verbal identities thus secures for these artifacts a novel position suspended between subject and object, human and thing.

The scope of animation increases considerably when the object speaks in riddles, which coincides with its assumption of grammatical agency. In the riddle inscription I cited earlier, for example, the *I* of the object exists in the nominative case, and it possesses a name (though its name, Cross, blurs the distinction between ordinary nouns and proper names). In addition, the riddle endows things with a history, since the artifact, even as it presents itself to us, provides us with an image of itself in the past ("Once . . ."). The artifact, through its riddlic form, is now capable of disappearing into the past—a past, moreover, that is false, for the cross bearing the inscription did not actually bear "the mighty king." Not only, then, does the riddle permit the object to tell lies about itself (and thus exist in an ambiguous state of not being present), but the moment of animation coincides with the object's transformation into what it is not: flesh. For the being whose name is Cross claims to have "trembled" under the weight of the king, suggesting that this particular cross (made of precious metals) possesses qualities of a living body—the king's body. The artifact, altered by its enigmatic voice, has become a kind of god.[4]

Now, before I comment further on the possible significance of lyric poetry's role in coaxing an object to speak in riddles, I want to make some observations about the terms of the analysis I have initiated here, in order to bring to light certain assumptions that are characteristic generally of the analysis of material culture. Nothing in my introductory remarks suggests any reason to doubt the coherence of these artifacts as *material* phenomena. That is to say, I do not call into question the material substance of the things I have been examining, nor do I believe most readers would hold me accountable were I not to do so in the course of an extended analysis. Nothing about these particular artifacts, as far as I've described them, appears to call for such scrutiny. Indeed, the evidence of material culture ordinarily possesses, insofar as it becomes the object of academic criticism, a similar immunity from critical reflection concerning its physical mass.

In the humanities, the material substance of ordinary things is judged to be either an intuitive certainty or an arcane possession of phys-

---

4. Because this particular object, a cross, involves the death of an individual, the ambiguity of its animate being (suspended between human and thing) may be compared to the principle of the "deodand" ("accursed object") in English law. Rooted in Germanic and Anglo-Saxon common law, the deodand (meaning, literally, "that which must be given to God") pertains to "the liability of inanimate objects," to objects implicated in the death or injury of a human being (William Pietz, "Death of the Deodand: Accursed Objects and the Money Value of Human Life," *Res* 31 [Spring 1997]: 98).

ics. Matter is no longer viewed as a problem relevant to humanistic criticism. These assumptions, which extend to the ostensibly critical study of material culture, are among the long-term effects of literature's (and philosophy's) withdrawal from serious debate over the nature of material substance. Science has long been regarded as the sole arbiter in the determination of matter. The result is that the authority and explanatory power of literary or cultural theory in relation to material culture is limited by its dependence on science not only to furnish a plausible account of material substance but to determine, in a fundamental sense, what sets material things apart from ideas or events.

In this essay, I am concerned essentially with what lyric poetry may be able to tell us about the material substance of things and if what matters about the world in a poem holds any particular significance for the history of philosophical materialism. Science continues to be puzzled by distinctions between ponderable and imponderable bodies or, more precisely, by the coexistence of these properties in a single entity. What do the intuitive properties of an object (what we can perceive of it) have in common with the invisible foundation of material substance? Following the development of modern physics, this question has become more acute because certain kinds of subatomic events do not appear to observe the laws of intuitive bodies—the very bodies that are ostensibly founded on these inscrutable events. Hence, real bodies appear to be composed of unreal substance. And the *substance* of things—the insensible foundation of material bodies—possesses intuitive reality solely in the form of images and tropes. Substance, in this sense, is the solution to the conundrum posed by things that speak in riddles: the verbal identity of these objects, which is the source of their obscurity, corresponds to the role of analogy in the determination of material substance. More precisely, when an object speaks in riddles, it reveals its true "substance." That is to say, the innate obscurity of matter in the history of physics, like the inscrutability of things in lyric poetry, betrays the inescapable role of language in depicting the nonempirical qualities—the invisible aspect—of material phenomena. The production of verbal or lyric substance in poetry therefore corresponds to an essential aspect of the way science understands the nature of the material world.

My contention that philosophical materialism betrays an affinity with lyric poetry in particular (rather than, say, with fiction or painting) depends in part on a conception of poetry formulated and reiterated by the leading figures of Western aesthetic philosophy. That is to say, I am interested not only in particular qualities of poetry as such but also in poetry as a discursive formation that has come to be defined in relation to other arts and other forms of knowledge. This historical formation relies in part on a fundamental correspondence between the technicality of poetry (its craft) and its obscurity—including the attenuated substance of the lyric "air." Hence the productive (or, to borrow the term used by

Vico in *The New Science,* genetic) character of poetry has always raised important questions about the relation between *techne,* or technology, and material substance.

Philosophical materialism, from antiquity to the present day, has sought to establish an authoritative account of physical reality by depicting a world of invisible and frequently unverifiable entities: the lawlessness of visible reality masks, it is said, the lawful—but invisible—realm of atoms. Correspondingly, poetry is to be distinguished from the other arts, according to Lessing, Kant, and Heidegger, by its freedom from intuition and its disavowal of imitation. For poetry renders the world effectively by making illusory and even impossible images of things—by rendering the world as what it is not. For example, Kant states, "Poetry fortifies the mind: for it lets the mind feel its ability—free, spontaneous, and independent of natural determination—to contemplate and judge phenomenal nature as having aspects that nature does not on its own offer in experience either to sense or to the understanding."[5]

Philosophical materialism has been plagued since its inception, starting with the figure of the atom, by its reliance on tropes and imaginary pictures to render the invisible foundation of matter. It is not therefore simply a question of a moment in the history of materialism when matter is captured by language and thus, suspended between materiality and immateriality, begins to lose its substantial character. Rather, materialism in its most rigorous forms descends unavoidably into language, to a place where matter is mostly not matter, where matter cannot be distinguished from the tropes and analogies that make it intelligible (and hence secure the equation of materialism and realism). I am therefore interested in the problem of literary obscurity, not only for what it can tell us about the improbable (though essential) materialism of lyric poetry, but also as an authentic model of the figurative aspect of Western materialism.[6] And I undertake this analysis in order to make available to literary and cultural studies a more productive sense of the ambiguity of material substance—a project that challenges the epistemological and ethical priority frequently assigned to materialist criticism.

I want to return now to the correspondence between riddles and

5. Immanuel Kant, *Critique of Judgment,* trans. Werner S. Pluhar (Indianapolis, 1987), §53, pp. 196–97. Kant's position echoes that of Lessing, who observes, regarding the impression conveyed by a poem, "I am a long way from seeing the object itself"—because, he says, "illusion" is "the principal object of poetry" (Gotthold Ephraim Lessing, *Laocoön: An Essay on the Limits of Painting and Poetry,* trans. Edward Allen McCormick [Baltimore, 1984], p. 88). Furthermore, Kant's position anticipates Heidegger's view that, in the language of poetry, "everything ordinary and hitherto existing becomes an unbeing" (Martin Heidegger, "The Origin of the Work of Art," *Poetry, Language, Thought,* trans. Albert Hofstadter [New York, 1971], p. 72).

6. The correspondences between lyric poetry and philosophical materialism, which I can allude to only briefly here, are the subject of my book, *Toy Medium: Materialism and Modern Lyric* (Berkeley, 2000).

things by invoking, with some trepidation, the Marxist premise of technological determinism, as a way of picking the lock that currently bars the literary critic from addressing the problem of material substance. In a recent issue of *PMLA* devoted to the topic of material evidence, Yves Bonnefoy claims in an essay on the indexicality of photography and poetry that Edgar Allen Poe and Stephane Mallarmé were among the first writers "to announce that photography was going to change the world."[7] Further, aligning Mallarmé's lyrical conception of "Nothingness" with the ontological effects of the "new look" of photography, Bonnefoy contends, "Mallarmé wants to accomplish consciously—wants to accomplish as an ultimate act of consciousness, at the threshold of a new age—what the photographic machine does outside any consciousness. . . . Mallarmé wants to look as photography looks."[8]

Now, this is an interesting (and debatable) point, but the principle of technological determinism, which serves for Bonnefoy (and for many others) to explain the "new age" precipitated by photography, appears to have no application to poetry. Is it not the case that the determinism governing the effects of the photographic machine might also be extended to lyric poetry, surely the most technical, and even mechanistic, of literary forms (given the requirements of meter, rhyme, and stanza)? As a veritable "machine" of literature (Paul Valéry, for example, called poetry "a kind of machine for producing the poetic state of mind by means of words"), the lyric poem appears to have a special affinity for the implications of a doctrine of technological determinism.[9] Bonnefoy's thesis of indexicality may be worth considering, but it seems likely that the apparatus of a lyric poem would yield a very different kind of substance (as a Mallarmé lyric yields the peculiar "Nothingness" of objects) from the photographic machine. And it is therefore conceivable that the technics of poetry (by which I mean prosody and the craft of ordering words, but also the poem's image-making and rhetorical apparatus) might yield a consistent and coherent doctrine of "lyric" substance.

If we return to a discussion of riddles and artifacts with an explicit concern for material substance, it appears that the grammatical suspension between subject and object, the projection of things into the past, the assumed identities, and the transubstantiation from metal to human flesh to divine matter may all have distinct implications for the material substance of things that speak in riddles. To gain a fuller sense of the way objects are shaped by riddles, and of the significance of riddles for the origins of lyric poetry in English, we must turn for a moment to the Anglo-

7. Yves Bonnefoy, "Igitur and the Photographer," trans. Mary Ann Caws, *PMLA* 114 (May 1999): 333.

8. Ibid., p. 335.

9. Paul Valéry, "Poésie et pensée abstraite," quoted in *The New Princeton Encyclopedia of Poetry and Poetics* (Princeton, N.J., 1993), p. 1124. I want to thank Barbara Bowen for referring me to this citation.

Saxon riddles collected in *The Exeter Book* in the late tenth century (though the riddles themselves date from the eighth century). One of the four great miscellanies of Old English literature, *The Exeter Book* contains, in addition to riddles, the source texts for "The Wanderer" and "The Sea-farer." Though these two celebrated poems are typically granted, in contrast to the riddles, a privileged place in the genealogy of English lyric, the prosody of the riddles (the standard four-beat, alliterative line of Old English verse) is identical to that of "The Wanderer," "The Seafarer," and *Beowulf.* The elevation of the riddlic form is confirmed by "The Dream of the Rood," the greatest Christian poem in Old English, which was composed as a riddle.[10] These formal correspondences bear witness to the hermeneutical implications of the word *riddle,* which is directly linked to the verb *to read.*[11]

The formal sophistication and delicacy of the riddle-poem, coupled with its inherent obscurity, points to an unresolvable—and productive—ambiguity in its literary character. For although the archaic aspect (and historical origin) of riddles is associated with prophetic and oracular speech, the Anglo-Saxon riddle no longer functions, quite obviously, in a prophetic mode—though it retains, in its construction, the inscrutability of the oracle. Thus the riddle as a secular form is already, in its earliest manifestations, a poetic device—a kind of literary toy, which invites us to regard the riddle not as an archaic mode of poetic utterance but as a form of literary decadence. The genealogy of lyric poetry in English therefore begins late in the life of an archaic form, the riddle, and this tension between archaism and decadence appears to stabilize the form and to remain integral to its endurance and mutability as a poetic model. Indeed, as W. P. Ker suggests, the genealogy of the riddle can be drawn to encompass the seventeenth-century Metaphysical lyric, with its bold conceits, its obscurity, and its curious amalgam of analysis and sensibility.[12] From this perspective, what may appear in the present context to be an eccentric attempt to extend the poetics of the riddle beyond its historical moment actually supplements T. S. Eliot's alignment of modernist and Metaphysical poetry, which he calls "the direct current of English po-

10. Ker views the riddle in Old English literature as an important source of innovation in the history of lyric: "In some of the riddles the miracle takes place which is not unknown in literary history elsewhere: what seems at first the most conventional of devices is found to be a fresh channel of poetry" (*D*, p. 93).

11. According to the *Oxford English Dictionary,* the etymological root of "riddle" and "read" is the Old English verb, *raedan,* meaning "to give or take counsel, to advise, to deliberate." Further, "the sense of considering or explaining something obscure or mysterious is also common to the various languages, but the application of this to the interpretation of ordinary writing, and to the expression of this in speech, is confined to English" (*Oxford English Dictionary,* s.v. "read").

12. Ker writes, "Though it is only a game, it [the riddle] carries the poetic mind out of the world: as not infrequently with the Metaphysical poets, the search for new conceits will land the artist on a coast beyond his clever artifices" (*D*, p. 93).

etry."[13] Thus, linking Eliot's influential thesis to Ker's observation, modernist poetry, insofar as it follows the example of the Metaphysical lyric, might be viewed as reviving and transforming the poetics of the riddle.

Anglo-Saxon riddles display a high degree of artifice and formal sophistication, yet their basic design differs little from the two-sentence inscription on the cross I described earlier. In about half of the ninety-six riddles in *The Exeter Book* the mystery object speaks directly to the reader, and the riddle ends (as I mentioned earlier) with a phrase such as, "Say what I am called," or "Say who I am." The solutions to most of the riddles (not all of them have been solved) are familiar objects, and sometimes animals, of the house, hall, farmyard, monastery, or battlefield. One finds riddles, for example, about storm and wine cup, churn and key, rake and bagpipe, quill pen and gold. Thus, a riddle is essentially an allegory, though, unlike conventional allegory, the phenomenon veiled by the dark or enigmatical description is not a metaphysical entity (an abstract concept or a divinity), but a physical object or being. A riddle is a *materialist* allegory (as well as an allegory of materialism). The weird creature we encounter at the outset of the poem turns out to be a phenomenon common to most people's experience; the dark speech of the riddle veils, even as it describes precisely, a familiar object.

The riddle produces a complex object—a "riddle-creature," as one editor calls it[14]—that, by speaking, sheds its human qualities yet goes on speaking. The thing becomes human and then performs a verbal striptease in the dark, before our eyes, divesting itself of its human attributes. The suggestive verbal gestures that constitute the striptease are, at the same time, the movement that obscures the thing and transforms it into what it is not. For that is what a riddle does: it withholds the name of a thing so that the thing may appear as what it is not, in order to be revealed for what it is. Here's how it works:

> My dress is silver, shimmering gray,
> Spun with a blaze of garnets. I craze
> Most men: rash fools I run on a road
> Of rage, and cage quiet determined men.
> Why they love me—lured from mind,
> Stripped of strength—remains a riddle.
> If they still praise my sinuous power
> When they raise high the dearest treasure,
> They will find through reckless habit
> Dark woe in the dregs of pleasure.[15]

13. T. S. Eliot, "The Metaphysical Poets" (1921), *Selected Prose of T. S. Eliot,* ed. Frank Kermode (New York, 1975), p. 66.

14. See Craig Williamson, introduction to *A Feast of Creatures: Anglo-Saxon Riddle Songs,* trans and ed. Williamson (Philadelphia, 1982), p. 41.

15. "Riddle 9," *A Feast of Creatures,* p. 69.

There is an element of the burlesque both in the main persona of the riddle and in the teasing performance of the riddle itself. The inherently seductive quality of a riddle, which can be attributed in part to a manner of speaking that simultaneously illuminates and obscures its object, finds itself embodied in this irresistible—and apparently dangerous—object: a wine cup. Thus the object itself resembles the form of its dark speech; the source of its fascination, according to the speaker, "remains a riddle" to its suitors. What's more, like the inherent obscurity of the riddle, a darkness associated with pleasure lies at the bottom of things—and of this thing in particular. It is the darkness that remains after the thing has disrobed, after the wine cup has been emptied, after the object has reverted, but for the darkness of speech, to its inhuman origin.

Black Wonder

What can a riddle, a word trick that allows an object to speak directly to us, even as its identity remains a mystery, tell us about the material substance of things and about the substance of the riddle itself? The riddle I cited above, along with a number of others in *The Exeter Book*, turns upon a moment of reflexivity, which reveals the object, aside from its verbal identity, to be inherently puzzling or mysterious. In one riddle, for example, the mystery object declares,

> My race is old, my seasons many,
> My sorrows deep. I have dwelt in cities
> . . . .
> My craft and course, power and rich passage,
> I must hide from men. Say who I am.[16]

Here, the persona of the riddle creature—that of a wanderer or fugitive—thematizes not only the veiled course of the object through the riddle, but its inherently cryptic nature: "I must hide from men. Say who I am." The object—gold—thus reflects by its enigmatic nature the linguistic mode of the riddle. This homeless substance is therefore doubly disguised: already hidden, it is veiled by the dark speech of the riddle as well. Indeed, there is, it seems, a darkness common to both the object and its riddle.

In another riddle poem, the object speaking is generally thought to be a bell (though there are other possible solutions) whose sound mimics the riddle song: "I sing round/The truth if I may in a ringing riddle."[17] Thus the object, whatever it may be, calls itself "a ringing riddle." The

16. "Riddle 79," *A Feast of Creatures*, p. 141.
17. "Riddle 2," *A Feast of Creatures*, p. 62.

thing is therefore a riddle even before it starts talking in riddles, a correspondence that suggests a certain degree of identification between poem and thing. Frequently, as I indicated in earlier examples, this identification is rooted in the phenomenon of darkness or obscurity, a quality intrinsic to the riddle or *aenigma* (and to allegory)—as the roots of these words tell us.[18] The darkness of the riddle becomes a property of the thing encrypted in the riddle, or, more accurately, the dark speech of the riddle finds an image of itself in the cryptic nature of the thing it brings to life.

The puzzling identification of words and things becomes a bit more explicit when the object speaking in riddles is associated, as often happens, with reading, writing, or bookmaking. In one of the most ingenious riddles of *The Exeter Book*, an inkhorn (or inkwell) speaks as an individual separated from its twin brother (the other horn), describing itself as "untwinned." The melancholy inkhorn declares, "in my belly/Is a black wonder"—a trope referring to the ink that it contains.[19] Materialized in this way, darkness appears as the material of the poem's inscription—the very substance of the riddle that is concealed in the "untwinned" thing. The "black wonder" at the core of things is thematized in another riddle on bookmaking, where the book-object describes how the quill pen "darts often to the horn's dark rim" and "with a quick scratch of power, tracks/Black on my body."[20] The darkness of writing embodied in these riddles calls to mind the dark well of the wine cup and the obscurity that binds gold to the words of its riddle.

Returning now to the problem of material substance, the first question is obvious: How are we to understand the inherent obscurity of riddles (and of lyric poetry) as a substance that mirrors the darkness of things? What qualities does the body of darkness possess (in a poem)? And what significance might the problem of literary obscurity—as distinct from obscurantism—hold for the history of philosophical materialism? To begin to answer these questions, the term *obscurity,* as it pertains to texts and especially poetry, must be dislodged from its conventionally figurative usage. Obscurity must be understood as a phenomenon occupying a position along a *material* spectrum of darkness, ranging from the unclear to the obscure to the opaque. The critical task of materializing obscurity, as a way of gauging the significance of poetry for our understanding of things, begins with the long history of the *topos* of darkness—a history, by the way, that reveals obscurity to be an element ranging well beyond the aesthetic ideology of the sublime. In the Book of Exodus, for

18. The Latin term *aenigma* (a "dark saying") derives from the Greek verb *ainissesthai,* meaning "to speak riddling verses." The term *riddle* (and its cognate, *to read*) derives, as I mentioned earlier, from an Anglo-Saxon verb meaning "to consider something obscure" (Liddell and Scott, *Greek-English Lexicon,* s.v. "ainissesthai").

19. "Riddle 84," *A Feast of Creatures,* p. 147.

20. "Riddle 24," *A Feast of Creatures,* p. 84.

example, the eighth plague is a swarm of locusts that "covered the face of the whole earth, so that the land was darkened" (Exod. 10:15). And the darkening swarm, conceived as a body, anticipates the plague immediately following it—that of darkness itself—a "darkness which may be felt" (Exod. 10:21). Evidently, there is a correspondence here between the obscure nature of the swarm and the darkness produced by the swarm, which in turn gives way to a darkness that is somehow autonomous. The autonomous dark is figured differently in *The Exeter Book,* where the first three poems are storm riddles, which thematize the obscurity of the riddle by configuring darkness as a pneumatic or meteorologic phenomenon. Hence the body of darkness first appears in *The Exeter Book* in the guise of the weather, as a body of air (corresponding to the lyric "air").

The Orphic Measure and the Backwardness of Things

Before I delineate further the corporeal aspect of obscurity—what Milton in *Paradise Lost* calls "darkness visible"—I want to establish a literary-historical framework for understanding the significance of obscurity as a critical concept.[21] In his magisterial survey of Western literature, *Mimesis,* Erich Auerbach divides the European tradition into two styles, one originating with Homer and the other with the prophetic books of the Old Testament. He writes:

> The two styles, in their opposition, represent two types: on the one hand, fully externalized description, uniform illumination, uninterrupted connection, free expression. . . . On the other hand, certain parts brought into high relief, others left obscure, abruptness, suggestive influence of the unexpressed.[22]

Work of the latter type, Auerbach observes, is "dark and incomplete" and hence "mysterious, containing a second, concealed meaning."[23] This type, characterized above all by its obscurity, has its roots in allegory, while the opposing type, Auerbach states, forms the basis of realism. Although

21. Here is the passage from *Paradise Lost* in which the phrase occurs:

> . . . yet from those flames
> No light, but rather darkness visible
> Serv'd only to discover sights of woe,
> Regions of sorrow, doleful shades, where peace
> And rest can never dwell

(John Milton, *Paradise Lost,* in *Complete Poetry of John Milton,* ed. John T. Shawcross [New York, 1971], 1.62–66, pp. 252–53).

22. Erich Auerbach, *Mimesis: The Representation of Reality in Western Literature,* trans. Willard R. Trask (Princeton, N.J., 1968), p. 23.

23. Ibid., p. 15.

Auerbach never mentions the literary form of the riddle—and indeed he tends to neglect lyric poetry in his analysis—it is quite evident from our brief examination of the riddle that it belongs in the category of the dark style. The very fact that Auerbach's dichotomy of literary styles depends, in part, on the principle of obscurity indicates that the dark speech of the riddle should not be viewed as an eccentric or aberrant phenomenon in literary history.

The problem with Auerbach's model, for our purposes, is that the phenomenon of obscurity never becomes palpable in any way; it functions solely—and predictably—as a figurative term. Auerbach fails to corporealize the dark principally, in my view, because to do so would undermine the basic opposition in his model between obscurity and realism. Were darkness to be understood as a trope for the kind of body produced by the apparatus of lyric poetry—that is to say, if obscurity belongs to the history of materialism—then it could not stand securely in opposition to realism (as long as the equation of realism and materialism survives). Our immediate task then is to materialize the concept of literary obscurity that typifies, in Auerbach's mind, a major component of the Western literary tradition. We must ask: Are there corporeal phenomena analogous to the qualities in language that we judge to be obscure? But also: What precisely does obscurity yield in the act of reading—in the absence of clear, cognitive meaning—if not a sense, strange indeed, of poetic *materials?*

The literary-historical division at the core of Auerbach's survey reappears (in the name of darkness) in Maurice Blanchot's theory of literature, with the difference that Blanchot provides a highly suggestive material emblem for the phenomenon of literary—and specifically "Orphic"—obscurity. In his essay on the image in language, Blanchot states, "there are two possibilities for the image, two versions of the imaginary, and this duplicity comes from the initial double meaning produced by the power of the negative."[24] Literature, according to Blanchot, negates the "world" in such a way that it produces two "versions"—one ideal and the other material—of the phenomena it negates; and neither version (idea or thing) belongs to the "world." To grasp Blanchot's dichotomy correctly, one must understand the "world" in a Heideggerian sense, as the effect of a primary negation and idealization of "things," resulting in the mediated phenomenon we call the "world."[25] Literature—and more precisely the literary image—thus constitutes a second moment of negation, destroying the world as we know it and exposing us to what cannot be fully grasped, that is, whatever exists in a purely ideal or purely material state. The two versions of the imaginary (namely, the two aspects of the

24. Maurice Blanchot, "Two Versions of the Imaginary," *The Gaze of Orpheus*, trans. Lydia Davis, ed. P. Adams Sitney (Barrytown, N.Y., 1981), p. 86; hereafter abbreviated "T."
25. Heidegger formulates his theory of the work of art issuing from the "rift" between the "earth" and a "world" in his essay, "The Origin of the Work of Art." See esp. pp. 42–44.

image) therefore correspond to whatever precedes the world (things) and to whatever comes after the world (ideas), both of which are equally remote from understanding.

Blanchot associates the aspect of the image pertaining to what precedes the world (its purely material aspect in sound or inscription) with what he calls "the word as expression of the obscurity of existence," with a moment when "literature refuses to name anything, when it turns a name into something obscure and meaningless, witness to the primordial obscurity."[26] Thus, over and against the word in its ideal, transparent, and meaningful aspect, there is, Blanchot states, "another side to literature. Literature is a concern for the reality of things, for their unknown, free, and silent existence . . . it is the being which protests against revelation . . . it sympathizes with darkness."[27] It is especially pertinent for our investigation of lyric that Blanchot associates the penumbral aspect of the image (which is on the side of things) with what he calls "the Orphic measure" and with "the essential night" that is "kept within the limits and the measured space of the song."[28] Hence Blanchot refers us, like the riddles of *The Exeter Book*, to a darkness that is common to song and to things.

The most astonishing moment of Blanchot's theorization of poetic obscurity occurs when he compares the darkness of the image—its "elemental strangeness"—to a cadaver: "At first sight, the image does not resemble a cadaver, but it could be that the strangeness of a cadaver is also the strangeness of the image" ("T," p. 81). According to Blanchot, therefore, the figure of the cadaver renders what we experience as obscurity in a literary text; hence he argues that the material aspect of a poem (not its content or meaning) is the origin of what we call obscurity in literature. The cadaverous aspect of the image is the remains of the world after its negation by words: "what is left behind is precisely this cadaver, which is not of the world either—even though it is here—which is rather behind the world . . . and which now affirms, on the basis of this, the possibility of a world-behind, a return backwards" ("T," p. 82). The analogy of the corpse thus depicts the resistance to understanding—the *backwardness*—of the orphic measure and of things prior to the "world."

At the same time, it is essential to bear in mind that, although "someone who has just died is first of all very close to the condition of a thing" ("T," p. 82), Blanchot does not regard the corpse or the thing as an object. Rather, the corpse is continually transformed by "infinite erosion" and "imperceptible consumption" ("T," p. 85), properties that emphasize its partial and unstable identity and that help to explain its aesthetic allure. For Blanchot calls the cadaver "this splendid being who radiates beauty"

26. Blanchot, "Literature and the Right to Death," *The Gaze of Orpheus*, p. 48.
27. Ibid., p. 49.
28. Blanchot, "The Gaze of Orpheus," *The Gaze of Orpheus*, pp. 101, 103.

("T," p. 83) and declares, "it can very well represent an object to us in a luminous *formal* halo; it has sided with the *depth,* with elemental materiality" ("T," p. 80). The cadaver, in Blanchot's conception, effectively depicts the element of obscurity precisely because its substance is no more palpable than a halo (a phenomenon said to be woven of light and air), which is almost certainly related, in a material sense, to the beauty radiating from the corpse. Indeed, because the cadaver is subject to "infinite erosion," thereby rendering its physical being comparable to the nebulous body of a storm (or a swarm), the material substance of a thing cannot easily be distinguished from the invisible substance radiating from the blurred boundaries of what exists prior to, or behind, the world. Hence the radiant cadaver, as Blanchot conceives it, is an emblem of the lyric substance of a poem—its obscurity—but also of the kind of body consistently produced by the apparatus of a poem.

Darkness Visible

Blanchot's emblem of the image-cadaver may appear to be eccentric or even perverse, but it displays qualities often found in a longstanding iconography of lyric substance, which concerns the representation of what Milton calls "darkness visible"—the strange light of hell. And because the luminescence of the underworld is somehow more palpable than natural light, its substance cannot be clearly distinguished from that of certain kinds of nebulous bodies. In addition, beginning with the ancient texts that feed Milton's imagery, the topos of this radiant, shadowy substance has been associated with the *pathos* of hell, with suffering. R. W. Johnson, in a superb book on the style of Vergil's *Aeneid* and its legacy in European lyric poetry, proves to be an indispensable guide to the classical origins of the topos of "darkness visible."[29] Though Johnson is not deliberately concerned with questions of material substance, his subtle and evocative readings of Homer and Vergil yield a rich archive of images pertaining to the material spectrum of "darkness visible." In addition, though he does not explicitly identify lyric poetry as the proper framework of his study (because the *Aeneid* is an epic poem), he readily admits that his analysis is keyed to Vergil's "famous lyricism" and that he regards the *Aeneid* as a "lyrical epic" (*DV,* pp. 50, 164). Hence his elaboration of "darkness visible" and its various permutations holds special significance for the study of lyric poetry.

In the *Aeneid,* Johnson argues, the reader encounters a "deliberately violent and disordered poetics" and further, he claims, "this deliberate

---

29. R. W. Johnson, *Darkness Visible: A Study of Vergil's Aeneid* (Berkeley, 1976); hereafter abbreviated *DV.*

failure of images is a way of showing darkness" (*DV,* p. 59). It is not so much unmitigated darkness, however, as an amalgam of shadow and luminosity that characterizes Vergil's *Stimmungskunst.* What Johnson calls the "negative image" of Vergil's style evokes "a trembling, fitful splendor, moving at random, overwhelmed by a space whose magnitude it can suggest but cannot illumine" (*DV,* p. 87). And there is a distinct correlation between these atmospheric conditions and the representation of unknown or unknowable phenomena (a visit to the underworld, for example): "Vergil opts for 'unknown modes of being' and for the beautiful filtered light that reveals realities only to hide them again" (*DV,* p. 48). Yet the "darkness visible" of the underworld becomes the light in which ordinary reality is perceived in the *Aeneid;* hence "Vergil's hell exists both for the sake of the narrative it frames and for the sake of other kinds of realities" (*DV,* p. 89). Because it exists at the threshold of intuition—and for the sake of "other kinds of realities"—the palpable and antithetical *lux* of hell serves as the invisible material foundation of ordinary bodies.

Johnson takes great care in describing the chiaroscuro of common things (which are at the same time unknowable) as they appear in the *Aeneid,* yet he also reveals other kinds of bodies that are latent in the trope of obscurity. For the material propensities of the dark as a figure of speech extend well beyond the failure of light that is its immediate cause. As in the storm riddles of *The Exeter Book,* meteorological phenomena in the *Aeneid* (storms, clouds, rainbows, mist) become forms capable of showing or approximating the substance of darkness.[30] These pneumatic or meteoric bodies—bodies of air—have a direct correlation to the lyric "air." In addition, Johnson cites an extraordinary passage in the *Aeneid* depicting an attempt to dislodge a beehive from a tree with a smoky torch (see *D,* p. 92). The roiling material phenomena of the swarm, the smoke, and the turbulent sound of the bees all combine to produce a powerful approximation of the poem's obscurity, but also of the strange substance of things as they appear in Vergilian darkness. Indeed, Johnson makes an explicit correlation between the elements of lyric and the material substance of unknowable things (which are also common things) when he refers to "the 'unknown modes of being' that Vergil, in trying to write his poem, has learned are part of its materials" (*D,* p. 89).

Johnson's study not only corporealizes the obscurity of Vergil's text but also seeks to account for the significance of darkness as an image of material substance. That is, Johnson attempts to discern what the idea of obscurity refers to in the existence of real bodies. Vergil's poem involves "imagining the nameless and invisible sense of what it is like to be over-

---

30. My favorite weather in the *Aeneid* occurs when a rainbow (the goddess Iris) appears as a messenger of death; see Virgil, *The Aeneid of Virgil,* trans. Rolfe Humphries (New York, 1951), 4.693–705, p. 112.

taken by one's doom"—what Johnson calls "the process of becoming nothing" (*D*, p. 98). Overtaken by darkness, a body becomes increasingly obscure and, in time, it becomes "nothing." The trope of "darkness visible" therefore depicts the substance of a body in time, or through time, and thus in flux—a process of invisible decomposition recalling the "infinite erosion" of the cadaver in Blanchot's essay. Because things dwindle to nothing as darkness overtakes them in a poem, the matter of obscurity itself conversely loses its substantial character as things yield to it in time. Hence the obscurity of the temporal object—the poem, but also the world it calls into being—reveals itself to be at once corporeal and incorporeal, the anomalous and imponderable medium of literature itself. Yet the erosion or eclipse of things in a poem—the filtering effect of the dark—is never complete or unequivocal. As a temporal object, a body remains in obscurity, and it is precisely the invisible erosion of things that appears in poetry as a form of darkness, as a blur.

Radiography

The iconography of lyric substance constellated about the phenomenon of "darkness visible" provides a framework—remarkably stable throughout literary history—for depicting correspondences between the poem's nebulous body and certain amorphous bodies in nature. There is certainly a reflexive dimension to these correspondences—the poem sees its own body in a rainbow, a cloud of dust, a shadow, a storm—but we must also recall that pneumatic and meteorological bodies have been an inescapable feature of the iconography of material substance in physics since the seventeenth century. Natural philosophers repeatedly visualized the invisible foundation of matter as a kind of weather. Hence the corporealization of obscurity in lyric poetry frequently coincides, in its particulars, with the depiction of invisible substance in the history of philosophical materialism.

One could examine the iconography of materialism through its philosophical unfolding, but the correspondences between materialism and lyric poetry also inform poetry itself, as is the case, for example, in the writings of contemporary American poet Jorie Graham. The most ambitious and programmatic rendering of these correspondences occurs in her book *Materialism,* though a concern with lyric substance is also evident in the titles of an earlier collection, *Erosion,* and of her more recent book, *Swarm.*[31] *Materialism* juxtaposes Graham's own meditations on the mysterious texture of things with translations and "adaptations" of au-

---

31. See Jorie Graham, *Erosion* (Princeton, N.J., 1983); see also Graham, *Swarm* (New York, 1999).

thors — mostly philosophers—who have had, in her view, something interesting to say about the nature of materiality: Plato, Sir Francis Bacon (twice), Ludwig Wittgenstein, Bertolt Brecht, Jonathan Edwards, and Walter Benjamin (among others). In addition, the book includes a translation of canto eleven of Dante's *Inferno* to remind us that the poet's descent into the underworld (recalling the topos of "darkness visible" I outlined earlier) should not be isolated from the scientific discovery of a material occult that can be represented only by imaginary forms.

Graham's anatomy of what she calls "the dream of the unified field" (the title of a poem in *Materialism*, later to become the title of her *Selected Poems*) is provoked, in part, by two questions that appear in the book: "(how can the water rise up out of its grave of matter?)—/ . . . /(how can the light drop down out of its grave of thought?)—."[32] The former question, alluding to the recurrent motif of a Heraclitean river in the book, becomes "How can the scream rise up out the grave of its matter?"[33] The armature of the book thus turns upon the impossible convergence (out of the grave) of the corporeality of the voice and the insubstantial body of light.

Versions of this impossible substance, like Milton's figure of "darkness visible," appear throughout the book as corrupt forms of *light*, which constitute the "atomic-yellow ground" of the visible world.[34] The poet, hypnotized by a "beam" of sunlight "calling across the slatwood floor," refers to herself and "the incandescent *thing*" in the third person as "she"—the first of many palpable bodies to be gathered into the "beam" ("S," p. 26). In the material world of these poems, things without mass betray the presence or passage of time, suggesting, as proposed earlier, that one aspect of lyric substance pertains to the substance of bodies in time. The poet calls the beam

> an unrobed thing we can see the inside of—
>   less place than time—
> less time than the shedding skin of time, the thought
>   of time
>   ["S," pp. 26–27]

Insofar as the "beam of sun" incorporates (and therefore idealizes) more palpable bodies, modeling the inscrutable passage of time that blurs or veils the substance of things, it recalls the insubstantial image in Yeats's "Byzantium": "an image, man or shade,/Shade more than man, more image than a shade."[35] In Graham's Byzantium, the "she" inhabiting the

32. Graham, "Event Horizon," *Materialism* (New York, 1995), p. 53.
33. Graham, "Manifest Destiny," *Materialism*, p. 100.
34. Graham, "Subjectivity," *Materialism*, p. 25; hereafter abbreviated "S."
35. W. B. Yeats, "Byzantium," *The Poems*, ed. Richard J. Finneran (New York, 1983), p. 248.

beam, "unrobed," appears likewise in radiant form:

> and out there, floating, on the emptiness,
>
> > among the folds of radio signals, hovering, translucent,
> > inside the dress of fizzing, clicking golden
> > > frequencies—the pale, invisible flames—
> > is the face of the most beautiful woman in the world[36]

Here, the movement toward imponderable bodies revises the topos of "darkness visible" to include the ponderable light of radiation and a new division of radioactive bodies. Radiography, poised between vision and voice, thus becomes the new science of lyric substance.

Though sublimation and incorporation are magical functions of the beam's physical presence, its substance is much more likely to become evident in these poems by assuming, though never unequivocally, the properties of other, more tangible bodies. Thus the palpable light of Graham's materialism tends to darken with air, or dust, or moisture; to darken into song, or storm, or flesh. In her adaptation of a passage of Plato's *Phaedo,* Graham cites Socrates on the relation of the body to "the intellectual principle, which to the bodily eye is dark and invisible."[37] By contrast, Socrates states, "this corporeal element, my friend, is heavy and weighty and earthy and is the element of *sight*"; hence the soul, when it becomes "fascinated by the body," is "cloyed with sight."[38] In Graham's reworking of the dialectic of light and dark in her poems, the "beam" of light acquires texture—a tentative corporeal identity—by entertaining the dark:

> no light—no—something
>
> powdery, yet slick—the
>
> continuum?—no luminosity and yet a sheen on it
>
> which you could say is your listening
>
> sprinkling over the green dark,
>
> but not materially, no, a dust[39]

The subversion of light here coincides with its granulation into darkness or twilight, yet it also appears to be converting itself into an acoustic body,

36. Graham, "Event Horizon," *Materialism,* p. 54.
37. Quoted in *Materialism,* p. 62.
38. Ibid.
39. Graham, "Break of Day," *Materialism,* p. 115; hereafter abbreviated "B."

as if darkness and sound were related phenomena. Indeed, there are moments in *Materialism* when darkness appears to usurp altogether the role of the luminous beam:

> the dark seems to be *composed* . . .
> Has voice in it. A lyre? A concealed
>
> weapon?
>
> As if there's something in it for safekeeping, something
> of which I
> am the paraphrase
>
> as if lifts up above me now, a labyrinth of variegated darks—
> ["B," p. 123]

Concealed in the dark is a paraphrase of the human body, but also a voice and a lyre, the root of the term *lyric*.

The insubstantial beam darkens with compounds of air and dust, signifying matter; and the granules of dust impend, always, in the neighborhood of sound: "morning dust, dust of the green in things, *on* things, dust of water/whirling up off the matter, mist, hoarfrost, dust over the fiddlehead" ("B," p. 127). If the beam is "aswarm with dust and yet/not entered by dust" ("S," p. 27), then the air, impregnated by dust, functions as the matrix that permits the light (and the world) to be seen:

> Meanwhile the transparent air
> through or into which the beam—
> over the virtual and the material—
> over the world and over the world of the beholder—
> glides.
> ["S," p. 28]

The body of air, the medium in which the beam makes its appearance, is the body of music that grounds the poem:

> the last note carries the air in it and is
> carried by
> that air, dusty, in which the light, and the molecules of watching, and
> the motes of
> listening, are changes rung, rung, but upon what.[40]

In this passage, the motes (or motets) of vision and sound are suspended in a medium of air and light, which is the matrix of the turbulent substance of things as they appear in a poem.

In Graham's rhapsodic materialism, the elements of lyric substance

---

40. Graham, "Invention of the Other," *Materialism*, p. 132.

(air, light, dust, moisture) achieve their most comprehensive form in the nebulous and dynamic bodies of the weather. And it is through the elements of this poetic meteorology that Graham's dialogue with Wallace Stevens, concerning poetry's role in the determination of material substance, becomes audible. Indeed, passages about the weather in Graham's poems often bring to mind Stevens's profound meditations on the correspondence between "the sense of poetry" and "the sense of the weather."[41] For example, Graham's poem "The Dream of the Unified Field" begins with a meditation on a snowstorm, an amorphous body that appears and reappears in the image of other bodies, such as "the huge flock of starlings massed over our neighborhood . . . /the black bits of their thousands of bodies swarming/then settling/overhead."[42] The poet returns repeatedly to the memory of the storm as an image of "the constant repatterning of a thing" ("DU," p. 82) and of the mysterious inside of things, recalling the "bullioned slant" of the beam:

> Filaments of falling marked by the tiny certainties
> of flakes. Never blurring yet themselves a cloud. Me in it
> and yet
> moving easily through it.
>
> ["DU," p. 80]

The imaginative and philosophical changes "rung" on the snowstorm (which reflect the mutability of the phenomenon itself) coincide with the reciprocation of interior and exterior spaces. The "certainties of flakes" become bits of sleep and thought that accumulate to become the imagined objects of an interior climate:

> The storm: I close my eyes and,
> standing in it, try to make it *mine.* An inside
> thing. Once I was . . . once, once.
> It settles in my head, the wavering white
> sleep, the instances—they stick, accrue,
> grip up, connect, they do not melt.
> I will not let them melt, they build, cloud and cloud.
>
> ["DU," p. 85]

The nebulosity of the material storm and the solidity of intellectual objects coincide because the blind, possessive, agglutinative mode of com-

---

41. In "Adagia," Stevens writes, "Weather is a sense of nature. Poetry is a sense" (Wallace Stevens, "Adagia," *Opus Posthumous*, ed. Samuel French Morse [New York, 1957], p. 161). Stevens's materialism, inevitably overlooked or misread by critics, develops principally through his meditations on poetry's affinity with the weather. His many poems referring to this subject include "Extracts from Addresses to the Academy of Fine Ideas," "Like Decorations in a Nigger Cemetery," "Chocurua to Its Neighbor," "The Snow Man," "Man Carrying Thing," "A Primitive Like an Orb," and "Auroras of Autumn."

42. Graham, "The Dream of the Unified Field," *Materialism*, p. 81; hereafter abbreviated "DU."

position is the same in both cases. Ultimately, the storm that is reassembled in the mind reveals itself to be a "possession" of history, a "splinter colony" ("DU," p. 85). Indeed, in a startling transformation, the snowstorm becomes the "vast white sleeping geography" of the "new world" discovered by Columbus ("DU," p. 86)—the very substance of a unified field of matter, thought, language, and history.

Counterfeit Gloom

Considered solely in terms of its conceptual horizon and its philosophical ambitions, Graham's anatomy of lyric substance might be regarded as a literary anomaly, as an eccentric and highly sophisticated thought-experiment. Yet insofar as it dwells on—and in—the obscurity of its particular medium (the *materia poetica* of lyric), it addresses the urgent question of how poetry makes sense of the material world. Her poetry, couched in a literary genealogy of darkness, follows the great tradition of Epicurean meditations on the nature of sense. That is to say, as rich as Graham's particular vision may be, one need not turn to poems devoted explicitly to the topic of materialism in order to discern how the medium of darkness becomes palpable in the signatures of things. There is, of course, a substantial tradition of obscurity in lyric poetry—again, to be distinguished from obscurantism or just bad writing—ranging from Pindar to the English Metaphysical poets to Mallarmé's doctrine of "mystery" in literature (conceived principally in terms of "obscurity").[43] Yet obscurity associated with virtuosity or difficulty need not be a precondition for the elaboration of lyric substance in a poem because obscurity is a quality that most readers tend to associate with poetry—even in its most accessible forms.

The problem of obscurity, conceived as an allegory of materialism in lyric poetry, poses significant questions about the nature of material substance, even as it offers a fleeting glimpse of the tenuous matter of the poem itself. If we think of Blanchot's figure of the cadaver or the "beam" of sunlight in Graham's *Materialism*, it is evident that these marvelous things (or "strange creatures," in the parlance of riddles) possess both the stable form of an object and the nebulous body of a meteoric phenomenon. The duplicity of things also appears in the object lessons staged by the Anglo-Saxon riddle, if we recall that possible solutions for one unsolved riddle range from swan to water and from quill pen to siren. The difference between ponderable and imponderable bodies, but also the mysterious relation between them, is implicit as well in the storm riddles

43. Mallarmé's essay, "Le Mystère dans les lettres," published in *Revue blanche* in 1896, appeared in direct response to Marcel Proust's polemic, "Contre l'obscurité," also published in *Revue blanche* in 1896.

of *The Exeter Book*, which speak to us in the same fashion as the talking objects that follow them. It is peculiar that the storm-riddles, which comprise the first three riddles in the collection, and which pertain to nebulous bodies that are also events, should serve to introduce us to a collection of talking *objects*. Indeed, were all of the riddles to remain unsolved, the dark speech of the weather would not betray what distinguishes a storm from an object. The rainbow and the bucket would speak the same gibberish.

Imagining how a rainbow may be like a bucket, or how a body of air precipitates more tangible bodies, might appear to be a fanciful pastime, but science suggests it is not, or not merely so. Even so, if the intuitive and nonintuitive aspects of a thing remain polarized in the discourse of scientific materialism, poetry, by contrast, excels at producing images in which the invisible foundation of matter rises to the surface of things and the mutable forms of intuition dissolve into the hidden ground of their abstraction—what Graham calls "the dream of the unified field." Gerard Manley Hopkins, a poet notorious for the close, labored textures—and hence the obscurity—of his verse, praises what he calls "pied beauty," a rubric for contrasting phenomena that are paired or conjoined. Though, at first glance, the poem called "Pied Beauty" appears to be a rather simpleminded celebration of "dappled things," it is not, on closer inspection, entirely clear why "skies of couple-colour" or a "brinded cow" might be counted among "all things counter, original, spáre, stránge." We must attend closely to these terms if we are to grasp the correspondence envisioned by the poet.

Dappled things are "original" because they make visible the origin, the hidden foundation, of things; and they are "counter" because their appearance betrays what is antithetical to appearance—the amalgam of "pied beauty." In this sense dappled things are "spare" because they are simple and rudimentary but also excessive in their disclosure of what they do not possess, a beauty that is "past change." These ordinary things therefore betray the qualities of an invisible, mutable substance that precedes them in the image of all that is "adazzle, dim" and, more palpably, in "fresh-firecoal chestnut-fálls." These protean substances, which hover just below the threshold of objecthood, and which nevertheless reveal the essential properties of "pied beauty," are emblems of "darkness visible." In addition, by praising "all trades, their gear and tackle and trim"—perhaps the most curious example of "pied beauty" in the poem—Hopkins suggests that the insubstantial apparatus of lyric poetry somehow renders the "strange" matter of pied beauty.[44]

The ember of pied beauty, too faint to illumine any thing but itself (and therefore akin to darkness), is an effect of what Hopkins calls "light's

---

44. Gerard Manley Hopkins, "Pied Beauty," *The Poetical Works of Gerard Manley Hopkins*, ed. Norman H. MacKenzie (Oxford, 1990), p. 144.

delay." The phrase occurs in one of his so-called dark sonnets, which begins with the line, "I wake and feel the fell of dark, not day." What it means to wake into a darkness that is felt depends, in large measure, on the word *fell,* a complex term with at least four disparate levels of meaning: a covering of hide; the substance known as gall (a bitter humor); a waste hillside; and a blow. The dark of wakefulness is evidently a material thing, shape-shifting and enigmatical, yet it is also a form of utterance:

> This night! what sights you, heart, saw, ways you want!
> And more must, in yet longer light's delay.
> With witness I speak this.[45]

The poet feels "the fell of dark," and he speaks it in the "rugged dark" of the sonnet's heavily stressed lines. Thus the substance of darkness ranges across the material spectrum, from barren soil to liquid humor to the blows of the metrical beat.

The extraordinary texture and density of Hopkins's lines—the basis of their obscurity—arouse a sense of the submerged correspondence between darkness and things—the kind of enigmatical affinities that form the basis of Anglo-Saxon riddle poems. But the vocabulary and rhythm of Hopkins's lyrics, which reflect a conspicuous attempt on his part to recuperate the strong-stress metrics of Anglo-Saxon verse, are not the only aspects of his poetry to evoke the sensibility of the riddle. The bold but sometimes inscrutable physiognomy of Hopkins's verse recalls the materialism of the riddle as well in its use of uncommon conceits to render common things, not to mention the *substance* of things. The most ambitious and sustained example of this method occurs in "The Wreck of the *Deutschland,*" the first great expression of Hopkins's mature style. The poem recounts the sinking of a passenger ship (and the drowning of five nuns on board) by a powerful storm at sea "between midnight and morning of December 7" in 1875.[46] It is not the ship, however, but the storm and the darkness mingled with it that compel the poet's attention. The long night at sea and the storm consume nearly a quarter of the poem's thirty-five stanzas, so that the storm becomes the material and figurative matrix of the poem's theology.

Instead of starting with an ordinary object and allowing the object, through the material and figurative operations of the poem, to decompose, to dissolve into the invisible substance of its material foundation, the method of Hopkins's materialism, by contrast, starts with an image of the penumbral substance of things—a storm—in order to bear witness to

45. Hopkins, "St. Winefred's Well," *The Poetical Works of Gerard Manley Hopkins,* p. 181.
46. Hopkins, "The Wreck of the *Deutschland,*" *The Poetical Works of Gerard Manley Hopkins,* p. 119; hereafter abbreviated "W." This reference to the timing of the storm—at night—occurs in the poem's dedication (to the five drowned nuns).

the objectification of matter through language. A number of the poem's features invite the reader to view it as a storm riddle, after the Anglo-Saxon riddle poems. Indeed, "The Wreck of the *Deutschland*" actually contains several short riddles that are very close in form to those found in *The Exeter Book*. Here is one of them:

> 'Some find me a swórd; sóme
> The flánge and ráil; fláme,
> Fang, or flood'
> ["W," p. 121]

Were we to supply the exhortation "Say who I am" at the end of these lines, the poem could easily be mistaken for an Old English riddle (which indeed it may be, given the quotation marks). The riddle creature, in this case, is Death (the solution supplied by the poet, who adds, "storms bugle his fame").

If we are to read "The Wreck of the *Deutschland*" as a storm riddle, as a parable of theological materialism, then we must listen more carefully to Hopkins's echo of a storm riddle in *The Exeter Book*. Here is the voice of the storm in the Anglo-Saxon text:

> Sometimes I swoop down, whipping up waves,
> Rousing white water, driving to shore
> The flint-gray flood, its foam-flanks flaring
> Against the cliff wall. Dark swells loom
> In the deep—hills on hills of dark water,
> Driven by the sea, surge to a meeting of cliffs.[47]

And here is Hopkins's description of the imagined (and perhaps borrowed) storm of his allegory:

> For the infinite air is unkind,
> And the sea flint-flake, black-backed in the regular blow,
> Sitting Eastnortheast, in cursed quarter, the wind;
> Wíry and white-fíery and whírlwind-swivellèd snów
> Spins to the widow-making unchilding unfathering deeps
> ["W," p. 122]

Though the two texts diverge in significant ways (Hopkins, for example, imagines a snowstorm), the evocation of "dark swells" is central to both passages. And Hopkins's phrase "sea flint-flake" is almost certainly an adaptation of the Anglo-Saxon epithet, "flint-gray sea." A few lines later, he refers to "the cobbled foam-fleece" of the sea, again perhaps echoing the Exeter riddle ("W," p. 123). Generally, the alliterative patterns and

---

47. Williamson, *A Feast of Creatures*, p. 60.

strong-stress meter shared by the two poems heighten one's sense of resounding forms and intertextual play.

   Though the Anglo-Saxon tradition appears to furnish Hopkins with
the imagery and prosodic effects necessary to evoke the storm's fatal character, the modern poet recoils from the task of imagining what lies beyond the scope of his experience or knowledge. The storm, to the poet,
is therefore a mystery, a conundrum whose resolution is uncertain. Faced
with an unknown—and perhaps unknowable—event, the poet is nearly
abandoned by words; the poem begins to unravel:

> But how shall I . . . Make me room there;
> Reach me a . . . Fancy, come faster—
> Strike you the sight of it? look at it loom there.
>
> ["W," p. 126]

The problem here is similar to that faced by Vergil or Milton in trying to
depict the underworld, for the storm that Hopkins seeks to represent is
indeed a kind of hell on earth. That is to say, the storm becomes, for
Hopkins, the place in which one discovers the protean substance of
"darkness visible."

   Hopkins's solution to the problem is at once surprising and familiar;
he declares,

> There was a single eye!
> Réad the unshápeable shóck níght
>   And knew the who and the why;
> Wording it how but by him that present and past,
> Heaven and earth are word of, worded by?—
>
> ["W," p. 126]

The poet finds his footing again, so to speak, and acquires the power to
envision what has taken place in the dark, by assuming the "single eye"
of God, the one true witness to the event. (This is the surprising part of
the poet's answer to the conundrum posed by the storm.) Even more
important, for our purposes, the act of imagination or representation is
conceived in terms of reading and textuality. Hence the unknown materials of the storm—the "unshapeable shock night"—are assimilated to the
turbulent substance of the poem. And that is the familiar part of the poet's solution to representing the storm. For we have already seen, on several occasions, how a poem is inclined to discover the nature of its own
materials in the substance of darkness and the weather. In Hopkins's
great poem, not only is there continual attention to problems of language
and speech, but the storm's furious body (air, snowflake, thunder, stress,
darkness) begins somehow to resemble the dainty materials of the poem:

"Storm flákes were scróll-leaved flówers, lily showers—sweet/héaven was astréw in them" ("W," p. 124). The storm becomes a kind of toy, its "black-about air" at once the poem's breath and the "searomp over the wreck" ("W," pp. 125, 123). The "storm's brawling" becomes a "madrigal start" ("W," pp. 124, 123), and the fearful "dark" rhymes with "the uttermost mark"—with writing ("W," p. 127).

In Hopkins's storm riddle, the wind, called out of its name, becomes "the burl of the fóuntains of air" ("W," p. 123), and night is converted to the poem's obscurity, to "counterfeit gloom" (in Milton's memorable image). The insubstantial engine of lyric therefore turns darkness into a thing, an artifact. And this is the aim of a riddle: the dark speech veiling the object coalesces—once the riddle is solved—into an image of the object itself. Yet obscurity, in a literary sense, is itself already an artifact, the glowing remains of darkness apprehended by language. Heidegger's equation of naming with *lighting* comes to mind, so that we may understand obscurity—what passes for material substance in poetry—to be the erosion of the particular darkness of things by their names, producing a compound of language and matter, a crepuscular medium.[48] Naming the dark makes darkness visible, and this conversion from substance to object is always a matter of artifice.

In conclusion, I want to return to the question of what significance the principle of lyric substance may hold for philosophical materialism and for materialist criticism in literary studies. Most immediately, the correlation between the way science makes sense of material substance (by depicting the invisible) and what matters about the world in a poem should encourage criticism in the humanities to abandon uncritical assumptions about the nature of material substance. Unless the critical methodology is strictly empirical—an orientation fundamentally alien to literary criticism—the reality of matter must always remain uncertain, always a problem that needs to be taken into consideration. Hence the study of material culture, for example, should never take for granted the material existence of its objects.

Finally, although one is not likely to ascribe to poetry the authority and explanatory power usually reserved for science, this antinomy obtains within science itself, between theoretical physics and more empirical models or disciplines. Hence the question of what sort of reality should be ascribed to the impossible configurations of quantum mechanics (in contrast to the way bodies behave in Newtonian space) resembles debate about the significance of poetry for our conception of physical reality. Which is more real, physics must now ask, the unreal substance of which we are made or the lawful appearance of things in perceptual space? It is

---

48. Heidegger refers to naming as "the lighting of what *is*" (Heidegger, "The Origin of the Work of Art," p. 73).

not inconceivable that it may one day appear reasonable to assimilate our understanding of ordinary bodies to the invisible—and frequently impossible—features of material substance (as science envisions it). So, too, we may one day grant to lyric substance (what poetry makes of the world) an authority it possesses today only in the realm of speculation—the only certainty, perhaps, it will ever possess.

The Defecating Duck, or, the Ambiguous Origins of Artificial Life

Jessica Riskin

> My second Machine, or Automaton, is a Duck. . . . The Duck stretches
> out its Neck to take Corn out of your Hand; it swallows it, digests it,
> and discharges it digested by the usual Passage.
> —JACQUES VAUCANSON, letter to Abbé Desfontaines, 1738[1]

> Squirt is the smallest robot we have built . . . . Its normal mode of op-
> eration is to act as a "bug," hiding in dark corners and venturing out
> in the direction of noises.
> —RODNEY BROOKS, "Elephants Don't Play Chess," 1990[2]

An eighteenth-century mechanical duck that swallowed corn and grain
and, after a pregnant pause, relieved itself of an authentic-looking
burden was the improbable forebear of modern technologies designed
to simulate animal and intelligent processes. Quaint as the Duck now
seems, we remain in an age that it inaugurated; its mixed career set in

---

Except where otherwise indicated, all translations are my own.

This essay and another, "Eighteenth-Century Wetware" (*Representations,* no. 83 [Sum-
mer 2003]) are parts of a larger project on the early history of artificial life and intelligence,
hence the frequent references in each essay to the other.

1. Jacques Vaucanson, "Letter to the Abbé Desfontaines" (1742 [1738]), *Le Mécanisme
du fluteur automate,* trans. J. T. Desaguliers (Buren, The Netherlands, 1979), p. 21; hereafter
abbreviated "L." This edition of Vaucanson's treatise includes both the original French version and Desaguliers's English translation. For the sake of consistency, all page numbers refer to the English translation.

2. Rodney A. Brooks, "Elephants Don't Play Chess," *Robotics and Autonomous Systems* 6
(1990): 9.

motion a dynamic that has characterized the subsequent history of artificial life.[3]

Jacques Vaucanson, the ambitious son of a Grenoble glove maker,
put his defecating Duck on display in Paris in the winter of 1738 in a
rented hall, the grand *salle des quatre saisons* at the Hôtel de Longueville.
Its companions were two android musicians, a Pipe-and-Tabor player and
a Flute-player that had first appeared at the Foire St.-Germain the previous February (fig. 1).[4] The price of admission was a substantial three *livres*,
about a week's wages for a Parisian worker. Nevertheless the people
poured in, earning Vaucanson in a single season several times what he
had borrowed to finance the project (see *JV*, pp. 30–34). In addition to
making money, the three automata captured the fancy of Voltaire, who
celebrated their inventor as "Prometheus's rival" and persuaded Frederick the Great to invite their maker to join his court. Vaucanson, sensing
he could do even better at home, declined the offer.[5] His own monarch
did in fact have another project in mind for him, wondering if he could
"execute in this manner the circulation of the blood." Louis XV ultimately
supported Vaucanson in a protracted effort to do so (see *JV*, pp. 55–56,
133–35, 141, 151–61).[6] In the meantime in 1741, the king's finance minister, Philibert Orry, recruited Vaucanson to become Inspector of Silk
Manufactures. Finally, overcoming academicians' habitual suspicion of
commercial projects, the automata helped Vaucanson to secure a much-

---

3. By *artificial life*, here and throughout, I mean all attempts to understand living
processes by using machinery to simulate them. *Artificial Life*, with capital letters, will refer specifically to the research field that arose in the mid-twentieth century in which computer scientists, engineers, cognitive and neuroscientists, and others have tried to use
information-processing machinery to simulate living processes, such as reproduction and
sensation.

4. See André Doyon and Lucien Liaigre, *Jacques Vaucanson, mécanicien de génie* (Paris,
1966), pp. 33, 61; hereafter abbreviated *JV*.

5. Voltaire, "Discours en vers sur l'homme" (1738), *Oeuvres complètes*, 10 vols. (Paris,
1877), 9:420. For Frederick the Great's invitation, see Marie Jean Antoine Nicolas de Cari-
tat, Marquis de Condorcet, "Éloge de Vaucanson" (1782), *Oeuvres de Condorcet*, ed. A. Condorcet O'Connor and M. F. Arago, 12 vols. (Paris, 1847), 2:650–51; hereafter abbreviated
"EV."

6. [Louis Petit de Bachaumont], *Mémoires secrets pour servir à l'histoire de la République des
Lettres en France, depuis 1762 jusqu'à nos jours, ou journal d'un observateur*, 36 vols. (London,
1777–89), 23:307. On Vaucanson's project to simulate the circulation of the blood, see also
Riskin, "Eighteenth-Century Wetware."

Jessica Riskin is an assistant professor of history at Stanford University. She is the author of *Science in the Age of Sensibility: The Sentimental Empiricists of the French Enlightenment* (2002) and is currently working on a
history of artificial life and intelligence circa 1730–1950.

FIG. 1.—The Flute-player, the Duck, and the Pipe-and-Tabor player. From the prospectus of the 1738 exhibition of Vaucanson's automata, Vaucanson, *Le Mécanisme du fluteur automate.* William Andrews Clark Memorial Library, University of California, Los Angeles.

coveted appointment to the Paris Academy of Sciences as "associated mechanician" in 1757 (a contest in which he beat out Denis Diderot) (*JV*, p. 308; see also pp. 142–45). In short, they were utter successes: entrepreneurial, philosophical, popular, and professional.

Their success lay in their author's transformation of an ancient art. Automata, "self-moving machines," had existed from antiquity, but as amusements and feats of technological virtuosity.[7] Vaucanson's automata were philosophical experiments, attempts to discern which aspects of living creatures could be reproduced in machinery, and to what degree, and what such reproductions might reveal about their natural subjects. Of course, his automata were also commercial ventures intended to entertain and demonstrate mechanical ingenuity. But their value as amusements lay principally in their dramatization of a philosophical problem that preoccupied audiences of workers, philosophers, and kings: the problem of whether human and animal functions were essentially mechanical. The Abbé Desfontaines, advertising Vaucanson's show to his readership, described the insides of the Flute-player as containing an "infinity of wires and steel chains . . . [which] form the movement of the fingers, in the same way as in living man, by the dilation and contraction of the muscles. It is doubtless the knowledge of the anatomy of man . . . that guided the author in his mechanics" (quoted in *JV,* p. 51).[8]

The novelty in Vaucanson's approach to automaton-making is apparent in the contrast between his machines and a 1644 design for an automaton by the French engineer Isaac de Caus (fig. 2).[9] An owl slowly pivots toward a group of birds, all fluttering and chirping. As the owl faces them, the birds become still and silent. Then, as the owl pivots away, the birds perk up again. The motions are driven by a waterwheel and ordered by a pegged cylinder, as in a music box. The design dramatizes the distance between the mechanism and the imitation in seventeenth- and early eighteenth-century automata. In this case, the distance is literal; the mechanism is all subterranean and the imitative figures all on top. But, even in cases where the mechanism was contained within the figures, it played no part in the imitation, which was purely external. An artificial swan, presented to the Paris Academy of Sciences in 1733 by a mechanician named Maillard, contained its mechanism inside itself (fig. 3). The swan paddled through the water on a paddle wheel while a set of gears swept its head slowly from side to

7. On ancient automata, see Alfred Chapuis and Édouard Gélis, *Le Monde des automates: Étude historique et technique,* 2 vols. (Paris, 1928), vol. 1, chaps. 1–4; Chapuis and Edmond Droz, *Automata: A Historical and Technical Study,* trans. Alec Reid (New York, 1958), chaps. 1–2; and Derek de Solla Price, "Automata and the Origins of Mechanism and Mechanistic Philosophy," *Technology and Culture* 5 (Winter 1964): 9–23.

8. See Abbé Desfontaines, "Lettre CLXXX sur le flûteur automate et l'aristipe moderne," 30 Mar. 1738, *Observations sur les écrits moderne,* 34 vols. (Paris, 1735–43), 12:340. The review of Vaucanson's treatise on the Flute-player in the *Journal des sçavans* also emphasized the role of anatomical and physical research in informing the android's design. See "Le Mechanisme du fluteur automate," *Journal des sçavans* (Apr. 1739): 441.

9. See Isaac de Caus, *Nouvelle invention de lever l'eau plus hault que sa source avec quelques machines mouvantes par le moyen de l'eau, et un discours de la conduit d'icelle* (London, 1644), p. 25 and plate 13.

FIG. 2.—Isaac de Caus's threatening owl and intimidated birds. From Isaac de Caus, *Nouvelle invention*, plate xiii. Courtesy of the Department of Special Collections, Stanford University Libraries.

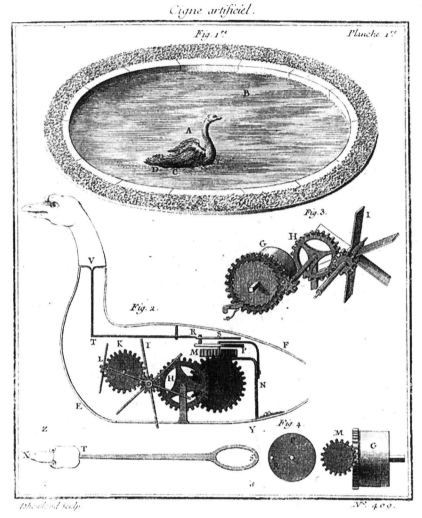

Cygne artificiel.

Fig. 3.—Maillard's artificial Swan. From Gallon, "Cygne artificiel," *Machines,* 7 vols. (Paris, 1735–77), 1:133–35. Courtesy of Department of Special Collections, Stanford University Libraries.

side.[10] It was intended to represent the behavior of a natural swan, but by no means to reproduce its physiology.

10. See "Diverses machines inventées par M. Maillard: Cygne artificiel," in *Machines et inventions approuvées par l'Académie Royale des Sciences depuis son établissement jusqu'à present; avec leur description,* ed. M. Gallon, 7 vols. (Paris, 1735–77), 1:133–35. I have found one possible exception to the general rule that automaton makers before Vaucanson did not try to reproduce living processes. This is a "statue" designed in the 1670s by a Württemburg physician

By the late eighteenth century, automata were imitative internally as well as externally, in process and substance as well as in appearance. Cartesian dualism, which had exempted consciousness from mechanist reduction, and "hypotheticalism,"[11] which had allowed for an infinity of possible mechanisms underlying nature's visible behaviors, gave way to an emergent materialism and to a growing confidence, derived from ever-improving instruments, that experimentation could reveal nature's actual design. These developments brought a new literalism to automata and a deepening of the project. The designers now strove, not only to mimic the outward manifestations of life, but also to follow as closely as possible the mechanisms that produced these manifestations.

Thus the hands of three automata built by a Swiss clock-making family named Jaquet-Droz in 1774 were probably designed with the help of the village surgeon, their skeletal structures modeled on real, human hands (fig. 4).[12] During the century that separated the Jaquet-Droz automata from de Caus's birds, the array of technological devices available to automaton-makers did not change significantly. In fact this array remained fairly constant from the late sixteenth century, when mechanical musical devices began to incorporate pinned barrels, through the addition of electric motors in the early twentieth century.[13] But the way in which these mechanisms were deployed did change importantly: the design of automata became increasingly a matter, not just of representation, but of simulation.[14]

---

named Reyselius. According to reports, this artificial man demonstrated circulation, digestion, and respiration with great "resemblance to man in all the internal parts" ("Le Mechanisme du fluteur automate," *Journal des savants* [1677]: 352). On the artificial man of Reyselius, see Thomas L. Hankins and Robert J. Silverman, *Instruments and the Imagination* (Princeton, N.J., 1995), p. 182, and *JV,* pp. 117–18, 162–63. For a fuller discussion of the shift from representative to simulative automata, see Riskin, "Eighteenth-Century Wetware."

11. The term is from Laurens Laudan, "The Clock Metaphor and Probabilism: The Impact of Descartes on English Methodological Thought, 1650–1665," *Annals of Science* 22 (June 1966): 73–104.

12. See Charles Perregaux and F.-Louis Perrot, *Les Jaquet-Droz et Leschot* (Neuchatel, 1916), pp. 31–34.

13. On the advent of the pinned cylinder in the late sixteenth century, see Sylvio A. Bedini, "The Role of Automata in the History of Technology," *Technology and Culture* 5 (Winter 1964): 35, and Maurice Daumas, "Industrial Mechanization," in *A History of Technology and Invention: Progress through the Ages,* trans. Eileen Hennessy, ed. Daumas, 3 vols. (1962–68; New York, 1969–79), 3:178–79. On the continuity in automata technology before electronics, see Reed Benhamou, "From Curiosité to Utilité: The Automaton in Eighteenth-Century France," *Studies in Eighteenth-Century Culture* 17 (1987): 95.

14. I intend the word *simulation* in its modern sense, which originated around the middle of the twentieth century, to mean an experimental model from which one can discover properties of the natural subject. *Simulation* in its eighteenth-century usage meant "artifice" and had a negative connotation, implying fakery. (I am grateful to Evelyn Fox Keller for pressing me to clarify my use of the term.) I have not found eighteenth-century

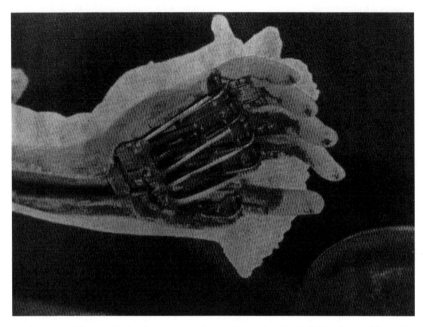

FIG. 4.—The simulative hand of the Jaquet-Droz family's 1774 Lady-musician. From Alfred Chapuis and Edmond Droz, *Automata*, p. 282.

This new, simulative impulse embraced, not only the mechanisms underlying living processes, but also the matter of life, its material aspect. Indeed, the two were inseparable in the eyes of eighteenth-century designers of simulative machines. How, for example, could one build a circulatory system that worked like natural ones without using an elastic material for the veins? So Vaucanson incorporated into his plans for a "moving anatomy" an exotic new material: rubber.[15] The Jaquet-Droz family were

---

uses of *simulation* in reference to automata. I employ it here despite the anachronism because it describes Vaucanson's and his contemporaries' newly experimental approach to automata and in order to suggest that their work had a pivotal place in the history of attempts to simulate (in its modern sense) life processes. For an analysis of the meaning and implications of simulation and an argument that the project of simulating life originated in the mid-eighteenth century, see Riskin, "Eighteenth-Century Wetware." For arguments that Vaucanson's automata were simulative in the modern sense, see Doyon and Liaigre, "Méthodologie comparée du biomécanisme et de la mécanique comparée," *Dialectica* 10 (1956): 292–335; Georges Canguilhem, "The Role of Analogies and Models in Biological Discovery," trans. Mrs. J. A. Z. Gardiner and Mrs. G. Kitchin, in *Scientific Change: Historical Studies in the Intellectual, Social, and Technical Conditions for Scientific Discovery and Technical Invention, from Antiquity to the Present*, ed. A. C. Crombie (New York, 1961), pp. 510–12; Price, "Automata and the Origins of the Mechanistic Philosophy"; and David M. Fryer and John C. Marshall, "The Motives of Jacques Vaucanson," *Technology and Culture* 20 (Jan. 1979): 257–69.

15. See "*EV*," 2:655; Eliane Maingot, *Les Automates* (Paris, 1959), p. 18; *JV*, pp. 118–19;

also innovators in this regard, using lifelike materials such as leather, cork, and papier-mâché to give their machines the softness, lightness, and pliancy of living things. By imitating the stuff of life, automaton makers were once again aiming, not merely for verisimilitude, but for simulation; they hoped to make the parts of their machines work as much as possible like the parts of living things and thereby to test the limits of resemblance between synthetic and natural life. Eighteenth-century mechanicians also produced devices that emitted various lifelike substances; not only did their machines bleed and defecate, but, as we will see, they also breathed.[16]

Vaucanson's Duck marked the turning point in these developments (fig. 5). It produced the most organic of matters; and Vaucanson made the imitation of internal process explicitly central to his project. He boasted that the Duck was transparent—its gilded copper feathers were perforated to allow an inside view—and wrote wittily that although "some Ladies, or some People, who only like the Outside of Animals, had rather have seen . . . the Duck with Feathers," his "Design [had been] rather to demonstrate the Manner of the Actions, than to shew a Machine" ("*L*," pp. 22–23, 22). The Duck was powered by a weight wrapped around a lower cylinder, which drove a larger cylinder above it. Cams in the upper cylinder activated a frame of about thirty levers. These were connected with different parts of the Duck's skeletal system to determine its repertoire of movements, which included drinking, playing "in the Water with his Bill, and mak[ing] a gurgling Noise like a real living Duck" ("*L*," p. 23) as well as rising up on its feet, lying down, stretching and bending its neck, and moving its wings, tail, and even its larger feathers.[17]

Most impressively, the Duck ate bits of corn and grain and, after a moment, excreted them in an altered form (fig. 6). Vaucanson said these processes were "copied from Nature," the food digested "as in real Animals, by Dissolution. . . . But this," he added, "I shall . . . shew . . . [on] another Occasion" ("*L*," p. 21). By claiming that his Duck digested by dissolution, Vaucanson entered a debate among physiologists over whether digestion was a chemical or a mechanical process. Unfortunately his postponement of further explanations to "another occasion" aroused suspicions. Already in 1755 a critic accused the Duck of being "nothing more than a coffee-grinder" (*JV*, p. 479). Then in 1783, a close observer of the Duck's swallowing mechanism uncovered an even greater deceit: the

---

and Linda Marlene Strauss, "Automata: A Study in the Interface of Science, Technology, and Popular Culture" (Ph. D. diss., University of California, San Diego, 1987), pp. 71–72. For Vaucanson's introduction of the phrase "moving anatomy" ("anatomie mouvante") to describe mechanical physiological models, see *JV*, p. 110; see also pp. 18, 34.

16. On eighteenth-century automaton designers' interest in lifelike materials and textures, see Riskin, "Eighteenth-Century Wetware."

17. See Chapuis and Gélis, *Le Monde des automates*, 2:149–51, and Chapuis and Droz, *Automata*, pp. 233–42.

FIG. 5.—One of a mysterious set of photographs discovered around 1950 by the curator of the Musée des Arts et Métiers in Paris. The photographs were in a folder left by his predecessor, labeled "Pictures of Vaucanson's Duck received from Dresden." From Chapuis and Droz, *Automata*, pp. 233–38.

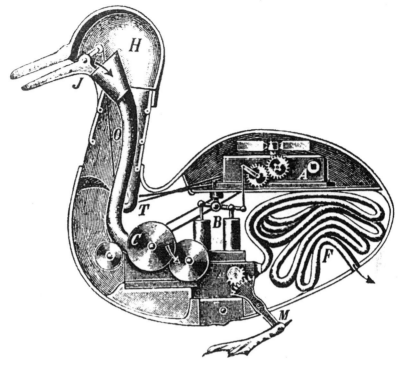

FIG. 6.—A nineteenth-century inventor's illustration of his own imagined version of a mechanical digesting duck. An arrow helpfully indicates where the main action takes place. From Chapuis and Édouard Gélis, *Le Monde des automates*, 2:151.

food did not continue down the neck and into the stomach but rather stayed at the base of the mouth tube. Reasoning that digesting the food by dissolution would take longer than the brief pause the Duck took between swallowing and expulsion, this observer concluded that the grain input and excrement output were entirely unrelated and that the tail end of the Duck must be loaded before each act with fake excrement.[18] The Duck that pioneered physiological simulation was, at its core, fraudulent. Yet, this central fraud was surrounded by plenty of genuine imitation. Vaucanson was intent on making his Duck strictly simulative, except where it was not.

18. See Friedrich Nicolai, *Chronique à travers l'Allemagne et la Suisse*, 2 vols. (Berlin, 1783), 1:284. The magician and automaton maker Jean Eugène Robert-Houdin claimed to have made the same discovery in 1845, while repairing the Duck's mechanism. See Jean Eugène Robert-Houdin, *Memoirs of Robert-Houdin*, trans. Lascelles Wraxall (1858; New York, 1964), pp. 104–7. The parts Robert-Houdin repaired may or may not have been from Vaucanson's Duck. On this question, see Chapuis and Gélis, *Le Monde des automates*, 2:151–52, and Chapuis and Droz, *Automata*, pp. 248, 404 n. 17. On the Duck's fraudulence in general and its discovery, see *JV*, pp. 125–29, and Barbara Maria Stafford, *Artful Science: Enlightenment Entertainment and the Eclipse of Visual Education* (Cambridge, Mass., 1999), pp. 193–94.

Each wing contained over four hundred articulated pieces, imitating every bump on every bone of a natural wing. All the Duck's movements (except the one just mentioned) were modeled upon exhaustive studies of natural ducks.[19]

What, then, is the meaning of this hybrid animal, partly fraudulent and partly genuine, partly mechanical and partly (ostensibly) chemical, partly transparent and partly ingeniously opaque? Consider the points of emphasis in Vaucanson's description. He is careful to say that he wants to show, not just a machine, but a process. But he is equally careful to say that this process is only a partial imitation. He wrote, "I don't pretend to give this as a perfect Digestion. . . . I hope no body would be so unkind as to upbraid me with pretending to any such Thing" ("*L,*" p. 22).

The deceptively transparent feathers hid, not just a trick, but an implicit judgment of the boundaries of mechanism. The partially fraudulent Duck perfectly encapsulated the two defining novelties of Vaucanson's work. The first was his interest in reproducing inner process. And the second, no less important, was his organizing assumption that the imitation of life's inner processes had limits. The Duck, in its partial fraudulence, made manifest both the process of mechanical simulation and its boundary. This was exactly the lesson that the marquis de Condorcet, perpetual secretary of the Academy of Sciences, derived from the Duck in his eulogy of Vaucanson. Condorcet did not believe in the digestive part of the imitation, but he wrote "it was not M. de Vaucanson's fault if . . . nature operated her functions in a way other than those he could imitate" ("*EV,*" 2:648).

Historians writing on Vaucanson's and other eighteenth-century automata have generally taken them as straightforward renditions of life in machinery,[20] and recent writers have continued to read the automata as emblematic of an unbridled devotion to mechanism. For example, Gaby Wood suggests that Vaucanson's projects expressed mechanist ambitions that went "beyond the bounds of reason." She diagnoses a kind of "madness" in what she sees as his attempts to "[blur] the line between man and machine, between the animate and the inanimate."[21] Another example is Daniel Cottom, who argues similarly that Vaucanson's work dramatized the mechanist reduction of both life (in the Duck) and art (in the Fluteplayer) to bodily processes: "In an age of mechanical digestion, one of the central problems of aesthetic judgment must be to distinguish between art

19. See "*L,*" and Godefroy-Christophe Bereis, letter dated 2 Nov. 1785, quoted in Chapuis and Droz, *Automata,* p. 234; see also pp. 233–38 and n. 14.

20. See for example Strauss, "Reflections in a Mechanical Mirror: Automata as Doubles and as Tools," *Knowledge and Society* 10 (1996): 179–207, in which the author ascribes to automata "the complex cultural role of doubles or doppelgängers" (p. 183).

21. Gaby Wood, *Living Dolls: A Magical History of the Quest for Mechanical Life* (London, 2002), p. xvi.

and shit."[22] It seems to me, on the contrary, that the automata expressed, not mechanist conviction, but the tug-of-war between such conviction and its antithesis. By building a machine that played the flute and another that shat, and placing them alongside each other, Vaucanson, rather than demonstrating the equivalence of art and shit as the products of mechanical processes, was testing the capacity of each, the artistic and the organic product, to distinguish the creatures that produced them from machines. In other words, I find the most striking feature of Vaucanson's automata to have been their simultaneous enactment of both the sameness and the incomparability of life and machinery.

Vaucanson developed his experimental approach to designing automata, neither in a context in which mechanist theories of bodily processes were dominant, as in mid- to late seventeenth-century physiology,[23] nor in one in which such theories were largely discredited, as in early nineteenth-century biology,[24] but, instead, during an intervening moment of profound uncertainty about the validity of philosophical mechanism. This uncertainty accompanied the rising materialism of eighteenth-century natural

22. Daniel Cottom, "The Work of Art in the Age of Mechanical Digestion," *Representations*, no. 66 (Spring 1999): 71. For a third example, see Daniel Tiffany, *Toy Medium: Materialism and Modern Lyric* (Berkeley, 2000), chaps. 2–3.

23. On the role of mechanism in seventeenth-century physiology, and on the development and influence of René Descartes's physiology in particular, see Theodore M. Brown, "Physiology and the Mechanical Philosophy in Mid-Seventeenth-Century England," *Bulletin of the History of Medicine* 51 (1977): 25–54; Peter Dear, "A Mechanical Microcosm: Bodily Passions, Good Manners, and Cartesian Mechanism," in *Science Incarnate: Historical Embodiments of Natural Knowledge*, ed. Stephen Shapin and Christopher Lawrence (Chicago, 1998), pp. 51–82; François Duchesneau, *Les Modèles du vivant de Descartes à Leibniz* (Paris, 1998), chaps. 2–3; Julian Jaynes, "The Problem of Animate Motion in the Seventeenth Century," *Journal of the History of Ideas* 31 (Apr.–Jun. 1970): 219–34; and Phillip R. Sloan, "Descartes, the Sceptics, and the Rejection of Vitalism in Seventeenth-Century Physiology," *Studies in the History and Philosophy of Science* 8 (1977): 1–28.

24. The rejection of classical mechanism in nineteenth-century life sciences has been treated mostly in the context of German romanticism and *Naturphilosophie*. See for example Timothy Lenoir, *The Strategy of Life: Teleology and Mechanics in Nineteenth-Century German Biology* (Dordrecht, 1982) and "Morphotypes and the Historical-Genetic Method in Romantic Biology" and L. S. Jacyna, "Romantic Thought and the Origins of Cell Theory," in *Romanticism and the Sciences*, ed. Andrew Cunningham and Nicholas Jardine (Cambridge, 1990), pp. 119–29, 161–68; Jardine, "*Naturphilosophie* and the Kingdoms of Nature," in *Cultures of Natural History*, ed. Jardine, J. A. Secord, and E. C. Spary (Cambridge, 1996), pp. 230–45; and Myles W. Jackson, "The State and Nature of Unity and Freedom: German Romantic Biology and Ethics," in *Biology and the Foundation of Ethics*, ed. Jane Maienschein and Michael Ruse (Cambridge, 1999), pp. 98–112. On late eighteenth- and nineteenth-century departures from the mechanist explanation of living processes outside Germany, see Evelleen Richards, "'Metaphorical Mystifications': The Romantic Gestation of Nature in British Biology" and Philip F. Rehbock, "Transcendental Anatomy," in *Romanticism and the Sciences*, pp. 130–43, 144–60; Elizabeth A. Williams, *The Physical and the Moral: Anthropology, Physiology, and Philosophical Medicine in France, 1750–1850* (Cambridge, 1994); and Robert J. Richards, "Darwin's Romantic Biology: The Foundation of His Evolutionary Ethics," in *Biology and the Foundation of Ethics*, pp. 113–53.

philosophy. Even as their insistence on the primacy of matter seemed to prepare the ground for mechanist explanations of nature, leading Enlightenment materialists such as Diderot and Georges Buffon nonetheless disparaged such explanations, invoking vital tendencies and properties of matter that, they argued, defied mechanist reduction.[25] The ontological question of whether natural and physiological processes were essentially mechanistic, and the accompanying epistemological question of whether philosophical mechanism was the right approach to take to understand the nature of life, preoccupied philosophers, academicians, monarchs, ministers, and consumers of the emerging popular science industry during the middle decades of the eighteenth century. Neither mechanist nor antimechanist conviction, then, but rather a deep-seated ambivalence about mechanism and mechanist explanation provided the context for the emergence of artificial life. The defecating Duck and its companions commanded such attention, at such a moment, because they dramatized two contradictory claims at once: that living creatures were essentially machines and that living creatures were the antithesis of machines. Its masterful incoherence allowed the Duck to instigate a discussion that is continuing nearly three centuries later.

A simultaneous belief in both propositions—that animal life is essentially mechanistic and that the essence of animal life is irreducible to mechanism—has, from the Duck's performances to this day, driven attempts to understand life by reproducing it in machinery. Not that the history of artificial life has been the simple unfolding of a suprahistorical dialectic; on the contrary, the dialectic represents a historical moment, one in which we are still living. Its contradictory convictions derive from a combination that emerged in the early eighteenth century and remains with us: first, a widely held materialist theory of animal life and, second, the inability of this theory to explain the core phenomenon of animal life, consciousness. Insofar as this combination persists, and despite the scientific and technological transformations of the last two and a half centuries, we live in the age of Vaucanson.

At each successive moment, the competing beliefs that life is mechanism and that life is nonmechanism have engaged with scientific, technological, social, and cultural developments[26] to produce continually changing hypotheses about the line dividing life from nonlife. Thus the contradiction at the heart of the project of artificial life has brought about

25. I treat the mid-eighteenth-century turn against philosophical mechanism, and its underlying uncertainties and ambivalences, in Riskin, *Science in the Age of Sensibility: The Sentimental Empiricists of the French Enlightenment* (Chicago, 2002), chap. 3.

26. Examples follow. But one sort of cultural development that figured centrally in the changing fortunes of artificial life during the eighteenth and nineteenth centuries is not directly treated here: the shifting tides of secularism and religiosity. An example of the changing role of religion in the history of artificial life is that religious objections to simulating life arose, as far as I have been able to tell, only in the early part of the nineteenth century and were conspicuously absent from the conversation during the preceding pe-

a conspicuous contingency in the basic terms of that project. Is it possible to design a machine able to talk, write, reason, play chess, make music, draw pictures, sense, interact, have feelings, express emotion, learn? A succession of such questions has motivated the disciplines of Artificial Life and Artificial Intelligence from their inception in the mid-twentieth century. But this continually changing field of questions in fact dates back to the time of Vaucanson's Duck, as does the underlying contradiction they express. To ask whether a machine can digest, converse, or emote is to raise the possibility that animal and human abilities are the sheer products of animal and human machinery. But the questions also identify precisely those capacities of living beings that have appeared at a given moment to be the likeliest to defy mechanistic reduction.

In short, the projects of artificial life have been attempts to reach the outer bounds of mechanism. The attempt to reproduce life in machinery, in tandem with the attempt to find where mechanical reproduction would fail, has resulted in an ongoing taxonomic exercise, sorting the animate from the inanimate, the organic from the mechanical, the intelligent from the rote, with each category crucially defined, as in any taxonomy, by what is excluded from it. As designers of artificial life have sought to explain living processes by analogy with mechanical arrangements, their understandings of life and of mechanism have also developed in mutual opposition. Vaucanson's Duck and its companions launched this taxonomic dynamic. In its apparent performance of the most animal of processes, the mechanical Duck dramatized, not just the reducibility of animals to machines, but also the problem of where the machine ended and the animal began.

The Flute-player did not involve deception, but it did similarly test the limits of mechanization of a process performed by a living creature (fig. 7). Outwardly, the Flute-player reproduced a statue of a satyr by Antoine Coysevox entitled *Shepherd Playing the Flute* that stood in the entrance to the Tuillerie gardens and is now at the Louvre. The mechanism was moved by weights attached to two sets of gears. The bottom set turned an axle with cranks that powered three sets of bellows, leading into three windpipes, giving the Flute-player's lungs three different blowing-pressures. The upper set of gears turned a cylinder with cams, as in the Duck, triggering a frame of levers that controlled the Flute-player's fingers, windpipes, tongue, and lips.[27]

---

riod. I mean to treat this aspect of the story in the larger project from which this essay is drawn. On religious attitudes toward "animating the inanimate," see Victoria Nelson, *The Secret Life of Puppets* (Cambridge, Mass., 2001), p. 50. For a presentation of the magical and wondrous elements of early modern automata, see Stafford and Frances Terpak, *Devices of Wonder: From the World in a Box to Images on a Screen* (Los Angeles, 2001), esp. pp. 35–47 and 266–74.

27. See Vaucanson, "An Account of the Mechanism of an Automaton or Image Playing the German Flute" (1742), *Le Mécanisme du fluteur automate,* pp. 10–20.

FLUTEUR DE VAUCANSON

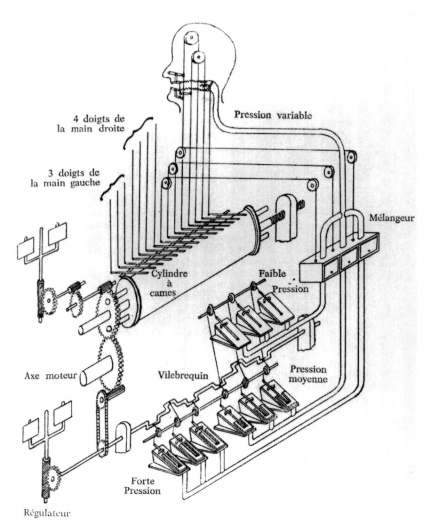

FIG. 7.—Diagram of the Flute-player's mechanism drawn by Vaucanson's biographers, André Doyon and Lucien Liaigre. From Doyon and Liaigre, *Jacques Vaucanson*, p. 81.

The mechanized satyr was the first example of what Diderot's *Encyclopédie* defined as an "androïde," that is, a human figure performing human functions.[28] This meant that the Flute-player was not, as people at first believed it must be, a music box with an autonomous mechanism inside and a purely decorative figure outside. It played a real flute, blowing air from its lungs and

28. Jean d'Alembert, "Androïde" (1751), *Encyclopédie, ou dictionnaire raisonné des sciences, des arts, et des métiers,* ed. Denis Diderot and d'Alembert, 17 vols. (Paris, 1751–72), 1:448.

exercising soft, flexible fingers, lips, and tongue. It was said that one could even substitute another, similar flute and the Flute-player would play that one, too.[29] To design a machine that played a flute, Vaucanson studied human flute players in minute detail. He devised various ways of transmitting aspects of their playing into the design of his android. For example, to mark out measures he had a flutist play a tune while another person beat time with a sharp stylus onto the rotating cylinder.[30]

To persuade people that the Flute-player was genuinely playing his flute, Vaucanson submitted a memoir explaining its mechanism to the Paris Academy of Sciences.[31] This memoir begins with a theory of the physics of sound production in the flute, the first known such theory. Vaucanson's idea was that the pitch of a note depended upon the speed of the air's vibrations as it left the flute. This in turn depended upon three parameters: blowing-pressure, the shape of the aperture, and the sounding-length of the flute damping the vibrations, which was determined by the player's finger positions. Vaucanson wanted to test the influence of these three parameters on pitch, and his Flute-player was an acoustical experiment; he told the academy that he had investigated the "Physical Causes" of the modification of sound in the flute "by imitating the same Mechanism in an Automaton."[32]

As an experiment, the android tested, not only Vaucanson's theory of the acoustics of the flute, but also—in his choice of a subject—the experimental potential of mechanical simulation. Like the chemical process of digestion, the flute was a deliberately unlikely choice for a mechanical imitation. Vaucanson explained that he had chosen the flute because it was unique among wind instruments in having an "undetermined" aperture,

29. "One can substitute another flute entirely in the place of the one he plays" (Charles Philippe d'Albert, duc de Luynes, *Mémoires du Duc de Luynes sur la cour de Louis XV*, 3 vols. [Paris, 1860], 2:12–13). Similarly, the Abbé Desfontaines emphasized that it was "the fingers positioned variously on the holes of the flute that vary the tones. . . . In a word art has done here all that nature does in those who play the flute well. That is what can be seen and heard, beyond a doubt" (Desfontaines, "Lettre CLXXX sur le flûteur automate et l'aristipe moderne," quoted in *JV*, p. 50). On audiences' initial disbelief that the Flute-player was actually playing his flute, see Chapuis and Droz, *Automata*, p. 274; Alexander Buchner, *Mechanical Musical Instruments*, trans. Iris Urwin (London, n.d.), pp. 85–86; and David Lasocki, preface to Vaucanson, *Le Mécanisme du fluteur automate*, p. [ii].

30. See Vaucanson, "An Account of the Mechanism of an Automaton or Image Playing the German Flute," pp. 19–20. This process was the ancestor of the procedure by which the first musical recordings were made, during the second and third decades of the twentieth century, when pianists such as Claude Debussy, Sergei Rachmaninoff, George Gershwin, Arthur Rubinstein, and Scott Joplin marked out rolls for player-pianos. See Larry Givens, *Reenacting the Artist: A Story of the Ampico Reproducing Piano* (New York, 1970).

31. See Vaucanson, *Le Mécanisme du fluteur automate; JV*, pp. 70–72, 76–80; and Registre des procès-verbaux des séances for 26 Apr. 1739 and 30 Apr. 1739, Archives de l'Académie des Sciences, Paris.

32. Vaucanson, "An Account of the Mechanism of an Automaton or Image Playing the German Flute," p. 10.

which depended upon the position of the player's lips and their situation with respect to the flute's hole. This made flute playing subject to an "infinity" of variations, which he claimed to approximate using only four parameters. The lips could open, close, draw back from the flute's hole (to approximate tilting the flute outward), and advance toward the hole (to approximate tilting the flute inward).[33] Vaucanson was able to produce the lowest note by using the weakest blowing-pressure, further attenuated by passing through a large aperture and damped by the flute's full sounding-length. The higher notes and octaves resulted from stronger blowing-pressures, smaller apertures, and shorter sounding-lengths. These results confirmed his hypothesis that the three parameters together—blowing-pressure, aperture, and sounding-length—governed pitch.[34]

Thus, although Vaucanson did not claim to reproduce the precise motions of a human flute player—indeed, he deliberately chose an instrument that involved motions he could only approximate—he was nevertheless able to use his simulation to discover features of its natural subject. The Flute-player made manifest both the constraints upon mechanical imitation and its epistemological utility despite these constraints.

The Pipe-and-Tabor player was another acoustical experiment, and Vaucanson chose the pipe, too, because it seemed to occupy a boundary of what one could imitate mechanically. The pipe, unlike the flute, had a fixed aperture, but it had only three holes, which meant that the notes were produced almost entirely by the human player's variations of blowing-pressure and tongue-stops. Vaucanson's project was to imitate these subtleties. He found that human pipers employed a much greater range of blowing-pressures than they themselves realized, and he emphasized the enormous labor involved in producing each one by an arrangement of levers and springs. The Piper also yielded a surprising discovery that seemed to indicate a limit, if not to mechanism, at least to mechanical reduction. Vaucanson had assumed that each note would be the product of a given finger position combined with a particular blowing-pressure, but he discovered that the blowing-pressure for a given note depended upon the preceding note, so that it required more pressure to produce a D after an E than after a C, requiring him to have twice as many blowing-pressures as notes (see "*L,*" pp. 23–24). (The higher overtones of the higher note resonate more strongly in the pipe than the lower overtones of the lower note.) But pipers themselves were not aware of compensating for this effect, and the physics of overtones was explained only in the 1860s by Her-

33. Ibid., pp. 4, 16–17.
34. This was in fact in conflict with the recommendations of some contemporary published flute tutors. Johann Quantz, in particular, denied that pitch was controlled by blowing-pressure. See Johann Joachim Quantz, *Versuch einer Anweisung die Flöte traversière zu spielen* (Berlin, 1752), chap. 4. There was much disagreement even about flute players' actual practice. See Lasocki, preface, pp. [v–ix].

mann von Helmholtz.[35] Thus, like the Flute-player, Vaucanson's Piper was also an experiment, and a successful one; it yielded a result independent of both theory and common experience.

Philosophes and mechanicians immediately began to use Vaucanson's automata to gauge the limits of the mechanical imitation of life, and in the second half of the century they became preoccupied by questions of possibility and impossibility. Their discussion focused upon two phenomena that seemed to lie at the crux of the distinction between animate and inanimate, human and nonhuman. The first phenomenon was perpetual motion. Enthusiasm for this problem was such that in 1775 the Paris Academy of Sciences announced it would no longer consider proposals for perpetual motion machines,[36] reaffirming the Aristotelian principle that self-generated motion distinguished the animate from the inanimate. The second phenomenon that seemed a crucial test of the limits of artificial life was spoken language.

In 1738, the Abbé Desfontaines predicted in a review of Vaucanson's Flute-player that the simulation of human speech would prove to be impossible because one could never know precisely "what goes on in the larynx and glottis . . . [and] the action of the tongue, its folds, its movements, its varied and imperceptible rubbings, all the modifications of the jaw and the lips" (quoted in *JV,* p. 162). Speaking was too organic a process to be simulated. The mechanist maverick Julien Offray de La Mettrie disagreed. Looking at Vaucanson's Flute-player he concluded that a speaking machine could "no longer be regarded as impossible."[37]

During the 1770s and 1780s, several people took up the project of artificial speech. Among them was a Hungarian engineer named Wolfgang von Kempelen. In 1791, he published a "description of a speaking machine"[38] in which he reported having attached bellows and resonators to musical instruments that resembled the human voice, such as oboes and clarinets; he had also tried modifying *vox humana* organ pipes (fig. 8). Through twenty years of such attempts, he had been sustained by the conviction that "*speech must be imitable.*" The result was a contraption consisting

35. Hermann von Helmholtz explained the effects of partials in his *Die Lehre von den Tonempfindungen als physiologische Grundlage für die Theorie der Musik* (Braunschweig, 1863). I am grateful to Myles Jackson for helping me to figure out the causes underlying Vaucanson's acoustical discovery.

36. "The Academy voted that henceforth it will not receive nor examine any paper concerned with squaring the circle, trisecting the angle, duplicating the cube, and perpetual motion, and that this decision will be made public" (quoted in Roger Hahn, *The Anatomy of a Scientific Institution: The Paris Academy of Sciences, 1666–1803* [Berkeley, 1971], p. 145).

37. Julien Offray de La Mettrie, *Man a Machine and Man a Plant,* trans. Richard A. Watson and Maya Rybalka (1748; Indianapolis, 1994), p. 69.

38. See Wolfgang von Kempelen, "De la machine parlante," *Le Mécanisme de la parole suivi de la description d'une machine parlante* (Vienna, 1791), pp. 394–464; hereafter abbreviated "MP." On Kempelen's and others' attempts to simulate human speech in the last third of the eighteenth century, see Hankins and Silverman, *Instruments and the Imagination,* chap. 8, and Riskin, "Eighteenth-Century Wetware."

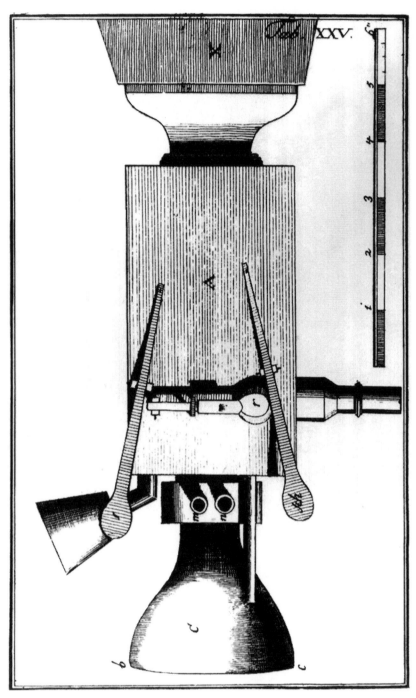

FIG. 8.—Kempelen's speaking machine. From Wolfgang von Kempelen, *Le Mécanisme de la parole*, p. 439.

of a resonating box with a bellows letting into it on one side, acting as lungs, and a rubber "mouth" on the other side. Inside the box was an ivory reed that Kempelen likened to the human glottis. By means of three levers on the box, two connected with whistles and the third with a wire that could be dropped onto the reed, one could produces Ss, Zs, and Rs. Two little pipes in the lower part of the box served as nostrils ("*MP*," p. 405; see pp. 395–400).

This machine yielded an empirical finding reminiscent of Vaucanson's discovery that the blowing-pressure for a given note depended upon the preceding note. Kempelen reported that he had first tried to produce each sound in a given word or phrase independently but failed because the successive sounds needed to take their shape from one another: "the sounds of speech become distinct only by the proportion that exists among them, and in the linking of whole words and phrases" ("*MP*," p. 401). Like Vaucanson, Kempelen had tried to atomize patterned sound in mechanizing it, and his results, like Vaucanson's, had indicated a particular check on mechanical reduction, namely, that the parts relied upon the pattern, and not just the pattern upon the parts.

In general, though, Kempelen's machine was only moderately successful. It pronounced vowels and consonants in a childish voice, said words like "'Mama'" and "'Papa,'" and uttered some phrases, such as "'you are my friend—I love you with all my heart'" ("*MP*," preface, §243), "'my wife is my friend,'"[39] and "'come with me to Paris,'" but only indistinctly.[40] Its conversation bored Goethe who, after meeting it, pronounced it "not very loquacious."[41] Kempelen and his supporters emphasized that the machine was imperfect and claimed that it was not so much a speaking-machine as a machine that demonstrated the possibility of constructing a speaking-machine (see *IR*, p. 49).

Listening to his machine's blurred speech, Kempelen perceived a further constraint upon the mechanization of language: the reliance of comprehension upon context (see "*MP*," p. 401). This observation raised another problem in which he was keenly interested, that is, the possibility of mechanizing thought itself. In a sense, Kempelen had already been working on this problem. Like Vaucanson, he designed both genuine and fraudulent automata, and he too remains best known for a spectacularly

39. Karl Gottlieb von Windisch, *Inanimate Reason: or a Circumstantial Account of that Astonishing Piece of Mechanism, M. de Kempelen's Chess-Player* (London, 1784), p. 47; hereafter abbreviated *IR*.

40. Strauss, "Automata," p. 123.

41. Johann Wolfgang von Goethe, letter to Herzog Carl August, 12 June 1797, quoted in Hankins and Silverman, *Instruments and the Imagination*, p. 196. Several years later, Goethe saw Vaucanson's three automata in Helmstädt and reported that they were "utterly paralyzed," the Flute-player had fallen "mute," and the Duck "still devoured his oats briskly enough, but had lost its powers of digestion" (Goethe, *Annals, or Day and Year Papers 1749–1822*, trans. and ed. Charles Nisbet [1805; New York, 1901], p. 113).

fraudulent automaton, the chess-playing Turk, built in 1769 and exhibited across Europe and America by Kempelen himself and then by others through 1840 (fig. 9).[42] The Turk not only played human opponents, but it also generously corrected their mistakes, and in the course of its long career it bested Frederick the Great, Benjamin Franklin, Napoleon, and Charles Babbage.[43] In addition to playing chess, it could perform a Knight's Tour[44] and respond to questions from the audience, spelling out its answers by pointing to letters on a board.[45] In the event, the Turk's motions were directed by human chess players ingeniously concealed in its pedestal. Although this fraud, like Vaucanson's, was not established until the middle of the next century,[46] Kempelen himself spoke deprecatingly of the Turk as a mere "bagatelle" and even insisted that his major achievement in it had been to create an "illusion."[47] Yet this did not detract from its fascination, which was fueled by a growing interest both in the mechanical simulation of life and in its limits.

Even while they insinuated that the Turk transcended the bounds of dumb mechanism, Kempelen's promoters also argued that its interest lay in its dramatization of this same boundary separating mere mechanism from warm life. In 1784, a friend of Kempelen's, Karl Gottlieb von Windisch, published an account of the Turk that epitomized this contradictory attitude. In his account, entitled *Inanimate Reason*, Windisch extolled the Turk's engagement of the understanding as comparable to Vaucanson's Flute-player's engagement of "the ear." At the same time, however, Windisch was also certain that the Turk was "a deception" and

42. On Kempelen's chess-playing Turk, see Charles Michael Carroll, *The Great Chess Automaton* (New York, 1975); Simon Schaffer, "Babbage's Dancer and the Impresarios of Mechanism," in *Cultural Babbage: Technology, Time, and Invention*, ed. Francis Spufford and Jenny Uglow (London, 1996), pp. 65–75 and "Enlightened Automata," in *The Sciences in Enlightened Europe*, ed. William Clark, Jan Golinksi, and Schaffer (Chicago, 1999), pp. 154–64; and Tom Standage, *The Turk: The Life and Times of the Famous Eighteenth-Century Chess-Playing Machine* (New York, 2002).

43. See [George Walker], "Anatomy of the Chess Automaton," *Fraser's Magazine* 19 (June 1839): 725; Schaffer, "Enlightened Automata," p. 162; Aleck Abrahams, "Dr. Kempelen's Automaton Chess-player," *Notes and Queries*, 8 Apr. 1922, pp. 155–56; Strauss, *Automata*, p. 134; and Henry Ridgely Evans, *Edgar Allan Poe and Baron von Kempelen's Chess-Playing Automaton* (Kenton, Ohio, 1939), p. 14.

44. A Knight's Tour entails moving a knight, starting on any square and using the rule governing the knights' moves, to all the other squares in succession without touching any square twice. See *IR*, pp. 23–24, and *Observations on the Automaton Chess Player, Now Exhibited in London, at 4, Spring Gardens* (London, 1819), p. 24.

45. See *IR*, pp. 15, 18, and Carroll, *The Great Chess Automaton*.

46. For prominent debunkings of the Turk, see Robert Willis, *An Attempt to Analyse the Automaton Chess Player of Mr. de Kempelen* (London, 1821), and Edgar Allan Poe, "Maelzel's Chess-Player," *"Eureka," and Miscellanies*, ed. Edmund Clarence Stedman and George Edward Woodberry, 10 vols. (New York, 1914), 9:173–212.

47. *The History and Analysis of the Supposed Automaton Chess Player of M. de Kempelen, Now Exhibiting in This Country by Mr. Maelzel* (Boston, 1826), p. 5. See also *IR*, p. 10.

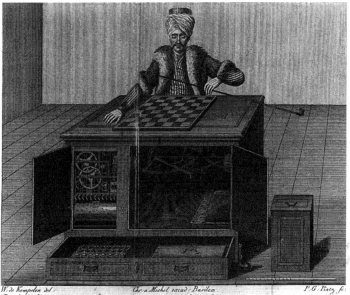

W. de Kempelen del .   Chr: a Michel excud : Basileæ .   P. G: Pintz fec:
Der Schac-Spieler, wie er vor dem Spiele gezeigt wird von vorne. Le Joueur d'echecs, tel qu'on le montre avant le jeu, par devant.

Fig. 9.—Von Kempelen's chess-playing Turk. From Karl Gottlieb van
Windisch, *Lettres sur le joueur d'echecs de M. de Kempelen* (1783). Courtesy of the
Department of Special Collections, Stanford University Libraries.

that, as such, it did "honor to human nature." Windisch identified two
separate "powers," a visible "vis motrix" and a hidden "vis directrix."
And it was Kempelen's ability to unite these two powers—in other words,
to carry out the fraud—that Windisch celebrated as "the boldest idea
that ever entered the brain of a mechanic" (*IR*, pp. 39, 13, 34, v). He admired Kempelen's accomplishment, not of an identity between intelligence and machine, but of a connection between intelligence on one side
of the boundary and machine on the other. Windisch's analysis of the
Turk was picked up by later commentators and remained influential well
into the following century. In 1819, Babbage brought his copy of *Inanimate Reason* to a demonstration of the Turk at Spring Gardens in London
and took careful notes in its margins, returning later to play the Turk.[48]
In the same year, an anonymous reviewer wrote that although the Turk
must be directed by "some human agent," it nevertheless "display[ed] a
power of invention as bold and original, as any that has ever been exhibited to the world."[49]

48. See Abrahams, "Dr. Kempelen's Automaton Chess-player," p. 155, and Strauss,
"Automata," p. 134.
49. *Observations on the Automaton Chess Player, Now Exhibited in London, at 4, Spring Gardens*, pp. 30, 32.

Defecation and chess playing had something in common: both seemed beyond the bounds of mechanism and thereby provoked mechanicians who were interested in testing the limits of their craft to become conjurers. As conjurers, though, they did something of genuine interest: they created machines that straddled the breach between the possible and the impossible.

In 1836, Edgar Allan Poe wrote admiringly of Vaucanson's Duck and then used it to examine the plausibility of Kempelen's chess player and of the other automaton then in the news, Babbage's Difference Engine. If the Duck was "ingenious," he wondered, "what shall we think of an engine of wood and metal which can . . . compute astronomical and navigation tables?" He decided he did believe in the calculating engine because arithmetic, like digestion and flute playing, was "finite and determinate." However, he did not believe in the chess-playing automaton because he said chess was an "uncertain" process.[50] Looking over the history of automata since Vaucanson, Poe tried to define a criterion of possibility. Only "determinate" processes, he decided, could be mechanized.

To a twenty-first-century electrical engineer or computer scientist, Poe's logic is perplexing.[51] Why must a machine carry out only a predetermined sequence of moves? Why could it not respond to each move of its opponent as it went along? It is striking that Poe should have believed this to be impossible. Even at the time he was writing, machines that responded to external conditions by means of feedback loops—thermostats and steam engines, for example—had been in plentiful supply for almost a century (and in existence for much longer). But Poe nevertheless took such responsiveness to be essential to mind and beyond the reach of machine. He was not alone; people began to understand machines that employed what we now call feedback as responsive to their environments only around the middle of the twentieth century,[52] two centuries after the proliferation of such machines during the Industrial Revolution. In the wake of this conceptual shift, artificial bugs that can respond to noises, such as the one described in a passage quoted at the beginning of this essay, have assumed a significance that defecating Ducks held in the mid-eighteenth century: they perform an operation—arguably *the* operation—that previously seemed to typify living creatures.

50. Poe, "Maelzel's Chess-Player," pp. 176, 177. On Poe and the chess-playing Turk, see Evans, *Edgar Allan Poe and Baron von Kempelen's Chess-Playing Automaton.*
51. I am indebted to the students in my 1998 and 1999 "Prehistory of Computers" seminars at MIT for the responses described in this paragraph to Poe's essay and to Deep Blue.
52. The MIT engineer Norbert Wiener played the leading role in formulating the concept of feedback. See Norbert Wiener, *Cybernetics; or, Control and Communication in the Animal and the Machine* (Cambridge, 1948). For other early discussions of machines as information processors capable, like animals, of interacting with their environments, see W. Grey Walter, "An Imitation of Life," *Scientific American* 182 (May 1950): 42–45 and *The Living Brain* (New York, 1953), chaps. 5 and 7, and Otto Mayr, *The Origins of Feedback Control* (Cambridge, 1970).

How people distinguish between machine and animal capabilities is not determined by the sorts of machines in existence at a given moment. Instead, understandings of machines and of humans have, since the emergence of simulation in the early eighteenth century, shaped one another in the ongoing dialectic that this essay has been tracing. When IBM's Deep Blue beat Gary Kasparov in 1997, most Artificial Intelligence researchers and commentators decided that chess playing did not require intelligence after all and declared a new standard, the ability to play Go.[53] Others point to this shift as evidence that we are moving the goal posts with each new achievement. But this recent redefinition of intelligence, to exclude the ability to play chess as a defining feature, and the long history of such revisions before it seem to me rather to demonstrate the historical contingency of any definition of intelligence and the complexity of the forces that interact to shape such definitions. Not only has our understanding of what constitutes intelligence changed according to what we have been able to make machines do but, simultaneously, our understanding of what machines can do has altered according to what we have taken intelligence to be.

The problem of what constitutes intelligent action as measured against mechanical action, which preoccupied philosophers of the mid- to late eighteenth century, was by no means of purely philosophical interest. The epistemological question of the limits of mechanical simulation was inextricably tied to a set of economic and social problems and implications. When Vaucanson was appointed Inspector of Silk Manufactures in 1741, he once again assumed that automation was specific to a certain domain and set out to identify its boundaries and to reshape industrial production around them.[54] The result was a transformed understanding of the nature of human labor. This understanding derived from a new way of drawing the distinction between intelligent and unintelligent work, locating the divide somewhere along a spectrum from intelligent human at one end, through less intelligent human in the middle, and arriving at the other end in machinery.

53. See, for example, Katie Hafner, "In an Ancient Game, Computing's Future," *New York Times*, 1 Aug. 2002, p. 5.
54. For an argument that "before thinking of automating manual labor, one must conceive of *mechanically representing the limbs of man*," see Jean-Claude Beaune, *L'Automate et ses mobiles* (Paris, 1980), p. 257. Beaune takes Vaucanson's career as his central case. He returns to this trajectory from automata to industrial automation, simulation to replacement, in "The Classical Age of Automata: An Impressionistic Survey from the Sixteenth to the Nineteenth Century," trans. Ian Patterson, in *Fragments for a History of the Human Body*, ed. Michel Feher, Ramona Naddaff, and Nadia Tazi, 3 vols. (New York, 1989), 1:431–80. It seems to me however, and I have been arguing here, that the epistemological, technological, and economic aspects of simulation shaped one another—rather than the epistemological preceding the technical that in turn preceded the economic. These elements were all inextricably present in the very constitution of the question of what was essential to life or of what constituted intelligent behavior.

In other words, in political economy, as in experimental philosophy, the first experiments in automation were devoted to determining its uppermost limits, which simultaneously meant identifying the lowest limits of humanity. Vaucanson did not think, for example, that automation was relevant to the biggest problem confronting French textiles, which was the difficulty of procuring good primary material domestically. In the case of silk, the primary material was the long fibers drawn from cocoons and reeled into thread. Silk thread available on the domestic market was so poor that French manufacturers often had to import their thread from Piedmont. Orry, the finance minister who had recruited Vaucanson, was especially worried about Italian competition in silk. So Vaucanson's first effort as silk inspector was directed at improving domestic primary material (see *JV,* pp. 142–45).

His diagnosis was that silk reeling was a delicate and skilled job, requiring workers to adapt themselves to the quality of individual cocoons. But French peasants who raised silkworms generally took the cocoons to market and sold or traded them to merchants and artisans of all types. These people would then reel the silk themselves or hire peasant women to do it. Vaucanson complained that "everyone indiscriminately wants to reel silk without reason or knowledge." To remedy this situation, he proposed to educate a population of expert *tireuses,* women trained in silk reeling, and to establish standards. He would accomplish both by creating a company of silk merchant-manufacturers, who would in turn establish seven factories, comprising a Royal Manufacture guaranteed by the Royal Treasury, where silk would be reeled under ideal conditions. The factories would serve as "seminaries" for silk reeling (*JV,* pp. 456, 462). Charles Gillispie has pointed out that this was an early example of a combination that would be characteristic of the post-Revolutionary French economy: expert consulting, private money, and government guarantee and oversight.[55] But at the same time it represented the reverse of another subsequent trend, the deskilling of factory work through mechanization. Vaucanson's automatic loom, discussed below, was an early example of that. But the Royal Manufacture, on the contrary, was a program to industrialize skill.

This program proved ill-fated. Established by a regulation of the city of Lyon in 1744, the Royal Manufacture was instantly embroiled in a fierce struggle between the roughly 250 silk merchant-manufacturers of Lyon and the roughly 3,000 master workers who ran their shops and who sometimes succeeded in setting up their own (there were about 160 independent shops in 1744). The workers had recently won a repeal of certain merchant-manufacturer monopolies, increasing their chances of becoming independent. Vaucanson wanted the cooperation of the

55. See Charles Coulston Gillispie, *Science and Polity at the End of the Old Regime* (Princeton, N.J., 1980), p. 416.

merchant-manufacturers, so he restored their monopolies and provoked a silk-workers' strike accompanied by some of the worst pre-Revolutionary rioting of the century. He was forced to flee Lyon in the dead of night, disguised as a monk, and the regulation was annulled (see *JV*, pp. 191–203).

Back in Paris, Vaucanson turned his attention from education to automation and from silk reeling to weaving. His efforts culminated in the automatic loom of 1747, which is now at the Musée des Arts et Métiers in Paris (fig. 10). The loom looks in retrospect like a very different sort of automaton, intended for utility rather than mimesis. However, this distinction, between machines designed to replace human or animal functions and machines designed to simulate aspects of human or animal life, is misleading when applied to the early history of artificial life. For one thing, most early projects in artificial life combined the pragmatic with the mimetic (just as, we have seen, these projects represented other distinctively Enlightenment combinations, such as experiment and entertainment, philosophy and entrepreneurialism). Automaton makers designed simulations for specific, practical uses. Vaucanson's "moving anatomies," mechanical models of bodily processes such as respiration and circulation, were intended for physiological experimentation and to test medical therapies such as bleeding.[56] The Jaquet-Droz family borrowed devices and materials from their automata to construct prosthetic limbs.[57] Reciprocally, the mimesis involved in automata often served an experimental function, as has been most strikingly apparent in Vaucanson's android musicians.

One might be tempted to distinguish mimetic from pragmatic devices by their outward resemblance to their natural subjects, but in fact some devices designed for particular uses, such as the Jaquet-Droz family's prosthetic limbs, closely resembled their natural subjects, while some designed for the sake of imitation and experimentation, such as Kempelen's talking machine, did not. That the simulation of appearance and of function came in various combinations was an expression of the experimental impetus behind projects in artificial life. Automaton designers used their devices to study the relations between the outer and the inner: form and process, bodily movement and physiology, action and thought.

Even when a simulation was purely functional, with no attempt to reproduce the outward appearance of the natural model, it provoked the

56. On Vaucanson's moving anatomies, see *JV*, pp. 110, 18, 34, and chap. 5, and "*EV*," 2:655. For other examples of moving anatomies, see François Quesnay, *Essai phisique sur l'oeconomie animale* (Paris, 1736), pp. 219–23, and Doyon and Liaigre, "Méthodologie comparée du biomécanisme et de la mécanique comparée," pp. 298–99. See also Riskin, "Eighteenth-Century Wetware."

57. On the Jaquet-Droz family's prostheses, see Charles Perregaux and F.-Louis Perrot, *Les Jaquet-Droz et Leschot* (Neuchatel, 1916), pp. 31–36, 89–91, 100–111, 140; Strauss, "Automata," p. 109; and Riskin, "Eighteenth-Century Wetware."

Fig. 10.—Vaucanson's automatic loom. From Claudette Balpe, "Vaucanson, mé-canicien et montreur d'automates," *La Revue,* no. 20 (Sept. 1997): 36.

same kind of philosophical speculation as mimetic machines; Kempelen's talking machine is one example, and the automatic loom provides another. The loom did not reproduce the motions of a human weaver in the way that the Flute-player enacted those of a human flutist. However, it took over a function that had hitherto been, not only human, but highly skilled: the weaving of patterned fabrics. On that basis, its designer and other commentators drew from it the same sorts of implications regarding the nature of human life, work, and intelligence that they drew from android automata. The fact that a machine could do this human job belonged, for them, in the same category as the fact that a machine could play a musical instrument. Whether the machine performs the function in the same way as human beings perform it is a more recent worry. We take it for granted that machines can replace a great variety of human functions without actually simulating human performances of them and that functional replacements of human activities do not have the same implications for how we understand those activities as simulations would have.[58] But in the early days of artificial life the mere fact that a machine could carry out a complex human activity had the same salience as a mimetic automaton; it could serve as evidence for a materialist-mechanist understanding of life, and, at the same time, it could provoke a rethinking of the boundary dividing humanity from machinery. The automatic loom constituted just such a provocation.

The loom was a close cousin of Vaucanson's three automata; it was built by the same Parisian artisans, and it worked similarly. A rotating cylinder was perforated according to the pattern to be woven. It turned against a frame of horizontal needles connected to vertical cords coming up from the warp-threads. The spaces in the cylinder pushed the corresponding needles forward, while the holes allowed them to remain in place. The

---

58. A recent installation by the Belgian artist Wim Delvoye makes manifest the current willingness to separate functional from mimetic simulation. *Cloaca,* Delvoye's digesting and defecating machine, looks like a laboratory bench, with a system of tubes and pumps leading through a series of six transparent vats containing enzymes, bacteria, acids, and bases. See Wim Delvoye, *Cloaca* (Ghent, 2000) and *Cloaca, New and Improved* (New York, 2001). Despite the fact that his machine is a purely functional simulation, Delvoye insists that its purpose is solely artistic and in no way experimental. Thus functional simulations have, in the early twenty-first century, assumed the role that clockwork amusements such as de Caus's birds, which reproduced only external behavior and not inner function, played during the seventeenth. At that time, the simulation of inner function did not yet command philosophical interest, and automaton makers confined their efforts to reproducing animals' outward behaviors for artistic purposes. Now, the simulation of inner function is familiar enough that, except in the context of mental processes, its philosophical interest has waned. Perhaps for this reason functional simulations can become purely artistic projects the way clockwork amusements once were. In between, however, automaton makers and commentators were keenly interested in the relations between outward appearance and inner function; thus their efforts to reproduce each were as inseparable as were the artistic, technological, and philosophical components of their work.

needles remaining in place, attached to the corresponding cords, were then raised by a bar, raising the selected warp-threads.[59]

Vaucanson boasted that with his machine a "horse, an ox, an ass makes fabrics much more beautiful and much more perfect than the most clever workers of silk." He imagined an animist factory in which "one sees the fabric weave itself on the loom without human intervention . . . the warp opens, the shuttle propels itself through, the reed pounds the cloth, the cloth rolls itself onto the cylinder." These claims were quoted in an enthusiastic review of the loom in November 1745 in the *Mercure de France* (*JV,* p. 210). According to his biographers, Vaucanson wanted to eliminate the silk workers who had run him out of town.[60] But the full story was more complicated.

Vaucanson's automatic loom, his functional simulation of a weaver, was intended to transform the categories of intelligent and unintelligent work. Anticipating Frederick Winslow Taylor's methods, Vaucanson identified a set of tasks generally taken to require intelligence but which, according to him, need not.[61] Any human activity that could be simulated, even a very complex one, did not require intelligence. The "reading of designs," Vaucanson noted, was "the operation that demands the most intelligence" in silk-production. "It is so difficult that it requires three or four years to learn." But, on the automatic loom, this operation became "so simple that . . . the only science required is to know how to count to ten." Thus the "most limited people," even "girls," could be "substituted for those who . . . [are] more intelligent, [and] demand a higher salary" (quoted in *JV,* pp. 468–69).

A hybrid entity, the loom and its "limited" operator constituted neither inert machine nor full human. The hybrid was the product of a new principle of classification, according to which one measured human labor, not only against other human labor, but also in relation to work that could be done by a machine. This taxonomic principle worked to transform a scheme already in place. Vaucanson did not invent the division of workers into the intelligent and unintelligent. Contemporary political economy relied on this demarcation and other, similar ones. The French Physiocrats' program of economic reform, for example, rested on a distinction between "productive" and "sterile" workers. The particular discrimination be-

59. See *JV,* pp. 206, 225–35; Almut Bohnsack, *Der Jacquard-Webstuhl* (Munich, 1993), pp. 27–28; Conservatoire National des Arts et Métiers, *Jacques Vaucanson* (exhibition catalogue, Musée National des Techniques, Paris, 1983), p. 16; and Garanger, "Industrial Mechanization," pp. 179–81.

60. "Encore sous l'impression profonde des événements de Lyon, il va montrer, et avec quel brio, qu'il est possible de se passer d'un grand nombre d'ouvriers pour actionner les métiers des canuts lyonnais" (*JV,* p. 208).

61. For Taylor's application of the distinction between intelligent and unintelligent work, see Frederick Winslow Taylor, *The Principles of Scientific Management* (New York, 1911), chap. 2.

tween intelligent and unintelligent work was central to the social hierarchy of the Old Regime. Diderot's *Encyclopédie* defined *artist* as the name given to workers in the mechanical arts whose work required the most intelligence, while the work of *artisans* required the least intelligence.[62] But by making the uncertain boundary between human and machine the center of the spectrum of labor, and populating this border region with hybrids comprised of complex machines and limited humans, Vaucanson redefined the old categories.

Certain human occupations came to seem less human and others more human, according to what machines could and could not do. For example, when the sophisticated use of camshafts made it possible to automate certain kinds of patterned movements, weaving became unintelligent work—Vaucanson demoted the reading of designs, which had been the most intelligent work, to the very bottom of the hierarchy—but the comparatively lowly task of silk reeling remained a matter of human skill and was therefore elevated to a higher position.[63] Artificial life and artificial intelligence implied new meanings for real life and real intelligence, even as they were shaped by what their designers took real life and real intelligence to be. Along the same lines, Lorraine Daston has observed that calculation was demoted at the beginning of the nineteenth century from being paradigmatic of intelligence to being mechanical and therefore the antithesis of intelligence.[64] If a machine could calculate, then something else—say, decision making or language—must be emblematic of human intelligence.

This development was preceded by a century and a half of reevaluation of human versus machine capabilities. Early designers of calculating machines defined human intelligence by contrast with what they believed machines could do, while at the same time their assumptions about what machines could do were shaped and reshaped by contrast with what they took human intelligence to be. Consider the divisions of labor they drew. Blaise Pascal placed the line between judgment, which he assigned to the

62. See "Artisan" and "Artiste," in *Encyclopédie,* 1:745. See also William H. Sewell, Jr., *Work and Revolution in France: The Language of Labor from the Old Regime to 1848* (Cambridge, 1980), p. 23.

63. Schaffer has written that "enlightened science imposed a division between subjects that could be automated and those reserved for reason. Such a contrast between instinctual mechanical labor and its rational analysis accompanied processes of subordination and rule" (Schaffer, "Enlightened Automata," p. 164). I would add to this the suggestion that the division was a dynamic one, continually redrawn through an interaction among the natural sciences, moral philosophy, technology, and political economy. At some moments in this ongoing process, reason lay on the opposite side of the line from machinery, and instinct on the same side. But at other moments a rational process such as reading fabric patterns landed on the side of machinery, while an intuitive process such as making the subtle adaptations required to reel silk properly remained the province of human beings.

64. See Lorraine Daston, "Enlightenment Calculations," *Critical Inquiry* 21 (Autumn 1994): 182–202.

human operator of his mechanical calculator, and memory, which he said the machine would supply.[65] G. W. Leibniz, and later Charles Babbage, both took computation itself to be the antithesis of intelligent work. Leibniz said it was "unworthy of excellent men to lose hours like slaves in the labor of calculation."[66] And Babbage placed computation at the bottom of a tripartite hierarchy into which he divided the making of tables. The top of the hierarchy, establishing the formulas, had to be the work of "eminent mathematicians." The second level, working out how to apply the formulas to a given calculation, required "considerable skill." And the third, carrying out the actual calculations, required so little ability that Babbage believed it could be done by his calculating engines. He attributed this "division of mental labor" to the French engineer Gaspard Riche de Prony, who in turn said he had been inspired by Adam Smith's description of pin making, which had indicated to de Prony that he could reduce table making to operations simple enough that they could be performed by unskilled workers—as it happened, de Prony hired hairdressers left unemployed by the transformed hairstyle of the post-Revolutionary era—and their ability to do the job implied for Babbage that a machine could do it, too.[67]

The social, the epistemological, and the economic dimensions of determinations of intelligence were everywhere inseparable. The two categories, human and artificial intelligence, natural and synthetic life, continually redefined one another by opposition. And, yet, the driving force behind the projects of artificial life was the assumption that life could be simulated and that the simulations would be useful by being analogous to natural life, not by being its antithesis. So these categories really redefined one another, not only by opposition, but also by analogy, and the early history of artificial life was driven by two contradictory forces: the impulse to simulate and the conviction that simulation was ultimately impossible.

Each new simulation implied a new territory beyond the reach of im-

65. See Blaise Pascal, "Lettre dédicatoire à Monseigneur le Chancelier sur le sujet de la machine nouvellement inventée par le sieur B. P. pour faire toutes sortes d'opérations d'arithmétique par un mouvement réglé sans plume ni jetons, avec un avis nécessaire à ceux qui auront curiosité de voir ladite machine et s'en servir" (1645), trans. L. Leland Locke, in *A Source Book in Mathematics*, ed. David Eugene Smith (1929; New York, 1959), p. 169.

66. Gottfried Wilhelm Leibniz, "Machina arithmetica in qua non additio tantum et subtractio sed et multiplicatio nullo, divisio vero paene nullo animi labore peragantur" (1685), trans. Mark Kormes, in *A Source Book in Mathematics*, p. 181.

67. Charles Babbage, *The Economy of Machinery and Manufactures* (1822), *The Works of Charles Babbage*, ed. Martin Campbell-Kelly, 10 vols. (London, 1989), 8:136, 137. See Daston, "Enlightenment Calculations," and Campbell-Kelly and William Aspray, *Computer: A History of the Information Machine* (New York, 1996), chap. 1. The tables were computed by the method of differences, the relevant theorem being that for a polynomial of degree n, the nth difference is a constant. On Babbage's notions of human and machine intelligence and mental labor, see also Schaffer, "Babbage's Intelligence: Calculating Engines and the Factory System," *Critical Inquiry* 21 (Autumn 1994): 203–27, "Babbage's Dancer," and "OK Computer," in *Ecce Cortex: Beiträge zur Geschichte des modernen Gehirns*, ed. Michael Hagner (Göttingen, 1999).

itation. Vaucanson promised that his automatic loom would open vast "new fields . . . to the genius of fabric-designers" (quoted in *JV,* p. 471). Carrying automation to its limit on one side of the boundary would expand the horizons, on the other side, of genius. This notion of machinery on one side of the boundary and genius on the other brings up another dimension of the investigation of the limits of artificial life, its aesthetic dimension. Vaucanson's automatic musicians set off a discussion of whether artistic creativity could be automated. In 1772, a skeptic observed that "ever since M. de Vocanson caused a piece of wood dressed as a man to play a flute-concert," simulating the motions of music making had been possible, but, he continued, "I defy M. de Vocanson and all the machinists on earth to make an artificial face that expresses the passions, because to express the passions of the soul, one must have a soul" (quoted in *JV,* p. 56 n. 13). On the other hand, two years later, Pierre Jaquet-Droz designed a "Lady-Musician," a harpsichordist, whose eyes followed her fingers and whose breast heaved with the music (fig. 11).[68] She gave so titillating an impression of the bodily manifestation of powerful emotion that she seemed to confirm La Méttrie's argument that the passions and the artistic creativity they fueled were, of all human attributes, the most mechanical.[69]

Vaucanson's project to identify the boundaries of artificial life was pursued after his death. In his eulogy of Vaucanson, Condorcet proposed a redefinition of the "mechanician" as one who made machines "execute operations that we were obliged, before him, to entrust to the intelligence of men" (*"EV,"* 2:649). But an 1820 treatise on mechanical simulation took Vaucanson's achievements to represent an outer limit, stating that the only "vital functions that mechanics [could] imitate" were respiration and digestion.[70] With the elaboration of artificial life in the century after Vaucanson's automata, natural philosophers and engineers became continually more interested in its limits. In 1854, Helmholtz criticized what he took to be an earlier tendency in the mechanical arts to consider "no problem beyond its power." He called Vaucanson's Duck "the marvel of the last century," but he observed that after Vaucanson people had stopped trying to build multiple imitative automata that would "fulfil the thousand services required of *one* man" and had turned instead to building

68. On the Jaquet-Droz Lady-musician, see Chapuis and Gélis, *Le Monde des automates,* 2:270–78; Chapuis and Droz, *Automata,* pp. 280–81; and Comité des Fêtes du 250e anniversaire de la naissance de Pierre Jaquet-Droz (1721–1790), *Les Oeuvres des Jaquet-Droz, Montres, Pendules, et Automates* (La Chaux-de-Fonds, 1971).

69. "If what thinks in my brain is not a part of that vital organ, and consequently of the whole body, why does my blood heat up when I am lying tranquilly in bed thinking . . . . Ask this of imaginative men, of great poets, of those who are ravished by a well-expressed sentiment, who are transported by an exquisite taste, by the charms of nature, truth, or virtue!" (La Mettrie, *Man a Machine and Man a Plant,* pp. 63–64).

70. J. A. Borgnis, *Des machines imitatives et théatrales,* vol. 8 of *Traité complet de mécanique appliquée aux arts* (Paris, 1820), p. 118.

FIG. 11.—The Jaquet-Droz family's Lady-musician. Photo: Jessica Riskin.

machines that would perform only one service, but in performing it would "occupy . . . the place of a thousand men."[71]

71. Helmholtz, "On the Interaction of Natural Forces" (1854), trans. John Tyndall, *Popular Lectures on Scientific Subjects*, trans. H. W. Eve et al. (1873; New York, 1895), pp. 137, 138.

This formula encapsulated the conflicting impulses that had informed Vaucanson's career and the early history of artificial life and intelligence more generally. Artificial life could be hugely powerful, Helmholtz advised, but only if it were sharply restricted. The contradictory convictions—that one could understand life and intelligence by reproducing them, on the one hand, and that life and intelligence were defined precisely by the impossibility of reproducing them, on the other—went into operation in the early part of the eighteenth century. They worked in continual engagement with philosophical developments such as the rise of a materialism that coexisted with a profound ambivalence about mechanist explanations of nature; with cultural factors, notably the emergence of a public for popular science, eager to witness the quandaries of natural philosophy dramatized; with technological innovations, principally the automatic loom; with social taxonomies like the Old Regime distinction between artists (intelligent) and artisans (unintelligent); and with economic projects such as industrial rationalization. The result was a continual redrawing of the boundary between human and machine and redefinition of the essence of life and intelligence. Insofar as we are still, in discussions of modern technologies from robotics to cloning, redrawing the same boundary and reevaluating its implications for the nature of life, work, and thought, we are continuing a project whose rudiments were established two and a half centuries ago by the defecating Duck that didn't.

Words and the Murder of the Thing

Peter Schwenger

In the satirical hodgepodge that is book three of *Gulliver's Travels,* the prize exhibit is undoubtedly the Academy of Lagado. Among its improbable schemes is one designed to avoid the "Diminution of Our Lungs by Corrosion"; as well, this scheme would achieve communicative precision and provide an infallible esperanto. It consists simply in abolishing all words and replacing them with their referents:

> Since Words are only Names for *Things,* it would be more convenient for all Men to carry about them, such *Things* as were necessary to express the particular Business they are to discourse on ... which hath only this Inconvenience attending it; that if a Man's Business be very great, and of various Kinds, he must be obliged in Proportion to carry a greater Bundle of *Things* upon his Back, unless he can afford one or two strong Servants to attend him.[1]

Here Swift is satirizing the notion of a perfect correspondence between words and the physical things they denominate.[2] The ludicrousness of the unwieldy "conversations" he goes on to describe underscores the other-

This work was supported by a grant from the Social Sciences and Humanities Research Council of Canada. Unless otherwise indicated, all translations are my own. Thanks to Larry Steele for help with the Ponge translations.

1. Jonathan Swift, *Gulliver's Travels,* vol. 11 of *The Prose Works of Jonathan Swift,* ed. Herbert Davis (Oxford, 1941), p. 169.

2. Swift critics cite a particular target: Thomas Sprat's desire for an Edenic time "when men deliver'd so many things, almost in an equal number of words"—or rather the mecha-

ness of things in relation to language: words and things seem fated to an absolute difference.

They may be fated, indeed, to an actual fatality. For in the space of that difference hovers death—or so it is asserted in a recurrent metaphor. It has even been suggested that this difference initiated the first death, that it was not "the Fruit / Of that Forbidden Tree whose mortal taste / Brought Death into the World" but a prior act of *hubris* for which God himself served as tempter: the translation of the world into words.[3] In Hegel's *First Philosophy of Spirit* (1803–4), he writes: "The first act, by which Adam established his lordship over the animals, is this, that he gave them a name, i.e., he nullified them as beings on their own account."[4] Maurice Blanchot glosses this sentence as follows:

> Hegel means that from that moment on the cat ceased to be a uniquely real cat and became an idea as well. The meaning of speech, then, requires that before any word is spoken there must be a sort of immense hecatomb, a preliminary flood plunging all of creation into a total sea. God had created living things, but man had to annihilate them. Not until then did they take on meaning for him, and he in turn created them out of the death into which they had disappeared.[5]

The passage's last words reverse the direction of its death drive: we murder *to create*. This reversal is underscored almost immediately. "My speech is a warning that at this very moment death is loose in the world," Blanchot tells us. Yet, at the same time, "death alone allows me to grasp what I want to attain; it exists in words as the only way they can have meaning" ("L," p. 43). The death of the thing, then, is the price we pay for the word.

Still, the word may be worth the price and, through an odd economics,

nistic equivalence between words and things that this wish implies (Thomas Sprat, *History of the Royal Society*, ed. Jackson I. Cope and Harold W. Jones [St. Louis, 1958], p. 113).

3. John Milton, *Paradise Lost*, ed. Merritt Y. Hughes (Indianapolis, 1975), 1.1–3, p. 5.

4. G. W. F. Hegel, *System of Ethical Life and First Philosophy of Spirit*, trans. and ed. H. S. Harris and T. M. Knox (Albany, N.Y., 1979), p. 221.

5. Maurice Blanchot, "Literature and the Right to Death," *"The Gaze of Orpheus" and Other Literary Essays*, trans. Lydia Davis, ed. P. Adams Sitney (Barrytown, N.Y., 1981), p. 42; hereafter abbreviated "L."

Peter Schwenger is professor of English at Mount St. Vincent University. He is the author of several books, including, most recently, *Fantasm and Fiction: On Textual Envisioning* (1999). He is currently working on *The Tears of Things*, a study of the melancholy associated with objects.

may lead to the return of the thing. Martin Heidegger argues this case:

> Language, by naming beings for the first time, first brings beings to word and to appearance. Only this naming nominates beings *to* their being *from out of* their being. Such saying is a projecting of the clearing, in which announcement is made of what it is that beings come into the Open *as*.[6]

But what exactly is it that they come *"from out of* their being" *as?* Not to their being as such, but only to "word and to appearance," to that mode of being by which they are given meaning in language. This is not simply to say that things are re-created in words (a difficult enough project, as we shall see) but that things become objects—objects of a subject, of a subjectivity that language both expresses and, as Lacan has taught us, forms. Language, according to Heidegger, is an inherent part of the human subject; but there is no language in the being of stone, plant, or animal (see "O," p. 73). When such a being is named, then, it is also changed. It is assimilated into the terms of the human subject at the same time that it is opposed to it as object, an opposition that is indeed necessary for the subject's separation and definition. All of our knowledge of the object is only knowledge of its modes of representation—or rather of *our* modes of representation, the ways in which we set forth the object to the understanding, of which language is one. The object "is thus first of all the represented."[7] What it is not, in Kantian terms, is the thing-in-itself *[Ding an sich],* which Heidegger specifically opposes to the human act of representing it.[8]

This is not to say, though, that the thing, as opposed to the object, simply falls into nonexistence in surpassing, as it always does, the limits of representation. It is true that for Heidegger "the thing-in-itself, i.e., detached from and taken out of every relation of manifestation *(Bekundung)* for us, remains for us a mere *x*." But, he continues, "in every thing as an appearance we unavoidably think also of this *x*."[9] The *x* that is the thing shadows the object as it is represented to our knowledge. In a paradoxical way, beyond that knowledge we always know something more, namely, that there is an unknowable otherness to the thing. Of this we must think in exactly the measure that we are unable to think it: "The thing as thing remains proscribed, nil, and in that sense annihilated. This

6. Martin Heidegger, "The Origin of the Work of Art," *Poetry, Language, Thought,* trans. Albert Hofstadter (New York, 1971), p. 73; hereafter abbreviated "O."

7. Heidegger, *What Is a Thing?* trans. W. B. Barton, Jr. and Vera Deutsch (Chicago, 1967), p. 140.

8. See Heidegger, "The Thing," *Poetry, Language, Thought,* p. 117; hereafter abbreviated "T."

9. Heidegger, *What Is a Thing?* p. 128.

has happened and continues to happen so essentially that not only are things no longer admitted as things, but they have never yet at all been able to appear to thinking as things" ("T," pp. 170–71). Annihilated in a certain sense, the thing is always present in another; unable to appear, the thing is in the first instance appearance. And beyond that appearance, which represents the thing to us as object, there is an ineluctable presence—the thingness of the thing—that we can never grasp.

Aporias such as these appear whenever words are confronted with things, and the attempt is made to think within the space of their difference. What that thinking produces is not so much a reconciliation as an assimilation to one side or another. Either it is argued that words *are* things, partaking in their solidity and presence, or else material things are hollowed out by an awareness that they can never be seen as anything but signifiers in a psychic space. Gertrude Stein, Francis Ponge, and Jacques Lacan represent this dynamic in the following pages as if on a spectrum. Yet at each point the position taken oscillates uneasily. This oscillation, as we shall see, is not unlike the dynamics of the Freudian death drive. And in this sense the space between words and things once again manifests itself as fatal—if only to our philosophies.

1

Adam's act of naming had about it a strangeness lost to us now, when the word is our instinctive refuge from the thing's strangeness.[10] Conventional language and habits of perception proceed in parallel toward a facile familiarity that contributes to the death of the thing. "Habitualization," asserts Victor Shklovsky, "devours works, clothes, furniture, one's wife, and the fear of war. . . . Art exists that one may recover the sensation of life; it exists to make one feel things, to make the stone *stony*."[11] For Shklovsky this goal is attained through a technique of defamiliarization, which attempts to return the object in this way to the strangeness of a thing. For at bottom, Heidegger reminds us, "the ordinary is not ordinary; it is extra-ordinary, uncanny" ("O," p. 54).

For Blanchot, too, literature exists "to make the stone stony"; it is a continual search for that which has preceded literature, that which has

10. John Hollander recovers the strangeness of naming in "Adam's Task," which begins:

> Thou, paw-paw-paw; thou, glurd; thou, spotted
> Glurd; thou, whitestap, lurching through
> The high-grown brush; thou, pliant-footed,
> Implex; thou, awagabu.

(John Hollander, "Adam's Task," *Selected Poetry* [New York, 1993], p. 267).

11. Victor Shklovsky, "Art as Technique," in *Russian Formalist Criticism: Four Essays*, trans. Lee T. Lemon and Marion J. Reis (Lincoln, Nebr., 1965), p. 12.

disappeared into language: "It wants the cat as it exists, the pebble *taking the side of things*, not man, but the pebble, and in this pebble what man rejects by saying it" ("L," p. 46). Yet there is a significant scission from Shklovsky. Art does not exist "to make one feel things," for our feelings are not equivalent to things, and to feel things is not to attain to the state of things. The things that are felt are only aspects of our own subjectivity. Shklovsky asserts that "the purpose of art is to impart the sensation of things as they are perceived and not as they are known."[12] But perception *is* a way of knowing them, even if that perception may be blunted by habit. No matter how refreshed and vivified perception may be, it is still a subject that is doing the perceiving, one that is opposed to and distanced from the thing it has turned into an object. The attempt to close that distance only leads to a fresh representation of perceptual representation. "Then," Blanchot asks, "what hope do I have of attaining the thing that I push away? My hope lies in the materiality of language, in the fact that words are things, too. . . . A name ceases to be the ephemeral passing of nonexistence and becomes a concrete ball, a solid mass of existence; language, abandoning the sense, the meaning which was all it wanted to be, tries to become senseless" ("L," p. 46). Here, then, is one strategy for countering the death of the thing. If words throw the things of this world into nonexistence, as Blanchot has asserted, they then move into the vacancy with an existence of their own. That existence is material, whatever else it may be. Moving past the ambiguities of signification into the "senseless," concrete language is capable of becoming itself a thing.

Is the following language, then, senseless in the way that Blanchot recommends?

A CARAFE, THAT IS A BLIND GLASS.
   A kind in glass and a cousin, a spectacle and nothing strange a single hurt color and an arrangement in a system to pointing. All this and not ordinary, not unordered in not resembling. The difference is spreading.[13]

This, the beginning of *Tender Buttons,* cannot, according to Gertrude Stein herself, be without sense: "I made innumerable efforts to make words write without sense and found it impossible. Any human being putting down words had to make sense out of them."[14] Let us then try to make sense of Stein's piece, beginning with the title. In what sense is a carafe "a blind glass"? Looking rather like a glass, a "kind" of glass and a "cousin," a carafe differs in its narrow then flaring lip. This allows one to

12. Ibid., p. 12.
13. Gertrude Stein, *Tender Buttons* (Mineola, N.Y., 1997), p. 3, hereafter abbreviated *T.*
14. Stein, "A Transatlantic Interview, 1946," *A Primer for the Gradual Understanding of Gertrude Stein,* ed. Robert Bartlett Haas (Los Angeles, 1971), p. 18.

pour from it but makes it something extremely difficult to drink from as from a glass. The "eye" that is the vessel's opening has, then, a certain negative quality that might be equated to blindness. For Richard Bridgman, the "hurt color" of the carafe is "a glass tinted grey-green or purple, the color of a bruise."[15] But we might recall Stein's comment that "glass is confusing it confuses the substance which was of a color" (*T,* p. 45). It is particularly confusing if it is a cut glass that we are dealing with—and "cut" of course can be related to "hurt" here.[16] Glass "of a color," glass-colored, divides itself into spectra and reflections through the facets that are "an arrangement in a system to pointing." The carafe's faceted system is a kind of cubism; and so this first object in *Tender Buttons* becomes a statement of its general aesthetic as well. If the thing here is fractured into planes "not resembling" each other, the thing made of words is similarly fractured: "the difference is spreading." This difference is that between the passage's individual words; it is also the difference between this spreading use of words and their conventional use to gather something to a manageable focus. All of this is "not ordinary" any more than things in the real world are ordinary if we see past our ordinary way of seeing.

This analysis, no more or less plausible than other readings of the passage, is of course a failure, and should be.[17] As Stein explains, "There was no certainty. Fitting a failing meant that any two were indifferent and yet they were all connecting that, they were all connecting that consideration" (*T,* p. 46). The verbals here, like "spreading" above, emphasize process in a congruence with the philosophy of Stein's friend Alfred North Whitehead. Whitehead argued that both objects and those who view them are events in creative flux rather than enduring substances.[18] Similarly, neither Stein's writings nor their various readings are destined to become authoritative products. Stein is asking us to "translate more than translate the authority, show the choice and make no more mistakes than yesterday" (*T,* p. 51). The common mistake of yesterday is not to see the trees for the forest; that is, we impose the noun upon the thing without seeing the complex perceptual facetting of which the thing is composed. Conventional language must be broken into pieces so that in Stein's compositions we may recover a sense of how the thing is composed: "Why is the name changed. The name is changed because in the little space there

15. Richard Bridgman, *Gertrude Stein in Pieces* (New York, 1970), p. 127.

16. For examples of nineteenth-century cut glass carafes, see Felice Mehlman, *The Phaidon Guide to Glass* (Oxford, 1982), pp. 126–27.

17. See for example Allegra Stewart, *Gertrude Stein and the Present* (Cambridge, Mass., 1967), pp. 87–95; William H. Gass, "Gertrude Stein and the Geography of the Sentence," *The World Within the Word,* ed. Gass (New York, 1979), pp. 63–123, esp. pp. 82–84; and Lisa Ruddick, *Reading Gertrude Stein: Body, Text, Gnosis* (Ithaca, N.Y., 1990), pp. 194–97.

18. See Linda Mizejewski, "Gertrude Stein: The Pattern Moves, the Woman behind Shakes It," *Women's Studies* 13 (1986): 42.

is a tree, in some space there are no trees, in every space there is a hint of more, all this causes the decision" (*T,* p. 48). The forest is never adequately described by its name. Indeed, despite the lure of the more conventional titles in *Tender Buttons*—"A BOX," "A RED HAT," "AN UMBRELLA," "MILK," "EGGS," "APPLE"—what we are given is not a *description:*

> The word or words that make what I looked at be itself were always words that to me very exactly related themselves to that thing the thing at which I was looking, but as often as not had as I say nothing whatever to do with what any words would do that described that thing.[19]

A description is a denegation of the thing described in the very act of translating it into words. Historically, it is a kind and a cousin of definition;[20] and, as Georges Braque observed in his notebooks, "To define a thing is to replace it with its definition."[21] In contrast, Stein invites us into a process of making sense, without any intention of arriving at a definitive sense.

> There was a whole collection made. A damp cloth, an oyster, a single mirror, a manikin, a student, a silent star, a single spark, a little movement and the bed is made. This shows the disorder, it does, it shows more likeness than anything else, it shows the single mind that directs an apple. [*T,* p. 46]

The "likeness" here seems to contradict the "difference" of the opening. But, in fact, as differences spread in Stein the mind continues to seek likeness, consistency, narrative coherence. It is then the mind that is being shown, rather than the thing.

And, as well, language is being shown. Sherwood Anderson has recorded his brother's initial reaction to *Tender Buttons:* "It gives words an oddly new intimate flavor and at the same time makes familiar words seem almost like strangers."[22] What is defamiliarized, then, is not common objects but common words. Abandoning the senses in which we usually apprehend them, individual words emerge with a material intensity they have not had, perhaps, since one's first encounters as a child with words on a page. But if words have become things in this way—and thus, in Blanchot's terms, "concrete" and "solid"—this has not resulted in sta-

19. Stein, "Portraits and Repetition," *Look at Me Now and Here I Am: Writings and Lectures, 1909–1945,* ed. Patricia Meyerowitz (London, 1990), p. 115.

20. *Oxford English Dictionary,* s.v. "description."

21. Georges Braque, *Illustrated Notebooks, 1917–1955,* trans. Stanley Applebaum (New York, 1971), p. 35.

22. Quoted in Sherwood Anderson, "The Work of Gertrude Stein," introduction to Stein, *Geography and Plays* (Boston, 1922), p. 5.

bility. Rather, a vital disorder is manifested: within the words one senses, always, the movement of the mind seeking an unknown *x*.

2

That our reactions to words recapitulate our reactions to things would scarcely have surprised Francis Ponge: "Things are *already as close to words* as they are to things, and reciprocally, words are *already as close to things* as they are to words."[23] But in what way is this so? The answer must be sought in Ponge's entire oeuvre. Within that oeuvre are certain works where Ponge renders a thing in all its particulars, which are demonstrated to be also those of words. Such is the case with "La Cruche" ("The Jug"), which opens with a meditation on the name given to the thing. Far from annihilating that thing, the name seems to evoke it with uncanny accuracy.

> Pas d'autre mot qui sonne comme cruche. Grâce à cet U qui s'ouvre en son milieu, cruche est plus creux que creux et l'est à sa façon. C'est un creux entouré d'une terre fragile: rugueuse et fêlable à merci.

> [No other word resounds like *cruche*. Thanks to that U which opens up in its midst, *cruche* is more hollow *(creux)* than hollowness, and is so in its own fashion. It is a hollow surrounded by a fragile earth: rough and easily cracked.][24]

More hollow in the depth of its *U* than the flatter vowel sound of *creux* (or, for that matter, of the English *jug*), the jug's emptiness resonates like a violin, filling with the poet's song.

> Cruche d'abord est vide et le plus tôt possible vide encore.
> Cruche vide est sonore.
> Cruche d'abord est vide et s'emplit en chantant.
> De si peu haut que l'eau s'y précipite, cruche d'abord est vide et s'emplit en chantant.

> [Jug at first is empty and as soon as possible empties again.
> The empty jug is sonorous.
> Jug at first is empty and fills itself while singing.
> However small the height from which water throws itself into it, jug at first is empty and fills itself while singing.] ["C," p. 94]

23. Quoted in Serge Gavronsky's introduction to Francis Ponge, *The Power of Language*, trans. Gavronsky (Berkeley, 1979), p. 21.
24. Ponge, "La Cruche," *Pièces* (Paris, 1962), p. 94; hereafter abbreviated "C."

The poem is of course "filling" itself at this moment, and Ponge continues to meditate on the mundaneness and fragility of the jug: it is meant to be used every day, but every day that use increases the chance of its accidental destruction. Therefore one isolates it a bit so that it will not strike against other things. If the jug does break, one lingers, noting the fragments, slightly curved like rose petals or egg shells. But here the poet pulls himself up short with a final realization:

> Car tout ce que je viens de dire de la cruche, ne pourrait-on le dire, aussi bien, de paroles?

> [For everything I have just said about the jug, couldn't one say it just as well about *words?*] ["C," p. 96; my emphasis]

What is being said about both things and words here has to do, then, with hollowness, mundaneness, a certain possible "singing," but in the end a frangibility whose fragments recapitulate the curve of an ultimate hollow.

All of this is in marked contrast to Heidegger's treatment of the jug in his essay "The Thing." Beginning like Ponge with the idea of the jug as a "void that holds" ("T," p. 169), which might be applicable to any vessel, Heidegger goes on to assert that "the jug's jug-character consists in the poured gift of the pouring out" ("T," p. 172). This assertion soon leads beyond the jug's particular character to the character of thingness itself: "The gift gathers what belongs to giving. . . . This manifold-simple gathering is the jug's presencing. Our language denotes what a gathering *is* by an ancient word. That word is: thing" ("T," pp. 173–74). The Old High German *Ding* does indeed mean "a gathering," and Heidegger fuses etymology with the exemplum of the jug to arrive at a somewhat mystical characterization of the thing as a gathering or fusion of four elements: earth, sky, divinities, mortals. Regardless of what is gathered, such a notion of the thing as a gathering is always problematic. Near the beginning of *The Phenomenology of Mind,* Hegel recognizes that any thing is made up of various aspects; however, these are not comfortable fusions but differences, which are spreading: "The thing contains within it opposite aspects of truth, a truth whose elements are in antithesis to one another."[25] In continual comparison to other things and to itself, the thing is now bigger, now smaller, now distinguished by color, now by texture, now by density. To our understanding, then, the integrity of things must always fragment, along with the words that attempt to fill their hollows.

But it is not a gathered fullness that most concerns Ponge, who writes, "here is the definition of things I like best: they are what I do not speak about, what I would like to speak about, and what I never arrive at

---

25. Hegel, *The Phenomenology of Mind,* trans. J. B. Baillie (London, 1966), p. 172.

the point of speaking about."[26] For always he senses the hollow: "a kind of abyss at one's left that hollows itself out *[se creuse]* at every instant" ("TO," p. 202). And the sense of this abyss makes his head reel. What is he to do, then, but what is always done when vertigo seizes one at the edge of a precipice?

> Instinctively one looks at what is near at hand. . . . One gazes at the nearby step, at the pillar or the balustrade or any fixed object. . . . One attentively regards the pebble in order not to see the rest. Now it comes about that the pebble gapes in its turn, and also becomes a precipice. . . . No matter what object, it's enough to want to describe it, it opens itself up in its turn, it becomes an abyss, but this can be closed up again, it's more manageable; one can, by means of art, close up the pebble again, one cannot close up the great metaphysical hole, but perhaps the closing up of the pebble will stand in for the rest, therapeutically. ["TO," pp. 203–4]

And yet what Ponge does is not so much to close but to dis-close the thing; his poems are a continual opening. Their aim is "to return always to the object itself, to what in it is primal and *different:* different especially from what I have already (at this moment) written about it. Let my work be that of a continual rectification of my expression . . . in the interest of the unadorned object."[27] The work does not come to rest, then, in a thing made of words. Rather, Ponge writes what have been called "processual" poems. In their most extreme forms, such as *Soap* or "The Pine Woods Notebook," these include all the notes, drafts, and rewritings leading to the putatively finished poem, which in fact is not markedly distinct from what precedes it—and follows it, for a series of appendixes may complete the work by underscoring its persistent incompleteness.

Such a work, paradoxically consisting of all the drafts and rewritings that go into the "work," necessarily involves a high degree of repetition. Ponge recognizes that repetition, generally accepted in music, is likely to be frowned upon in literature. But there are good reasons for it: "This is how developments happen in me, this is how the mind goes forward,— and it is very necessary, isn't it? to be honest, very necessary not to tamper with the mind's movement?"[28] We find again, as in Stein, that it is the mind's movement, not the thing in itself that is necessarily the subject of the poem. That movement, it seems, is a kind of repetition compulsion. As in Freud, it may indicate a simultaneous necessity and impossibility, a repeated baffling by the trauma of a Real—not the abyss of the First

26. Ponge, "Tentative orale," *Méthodes* (Paris, 1988), p. 202; hereafter abbreviated "TO."

27. Ponge, *Tome Premier,* trans. Richard Stamelman (Paris, 1965), p. 257.

28. Ponge, *Soap,* trans. Lane Dunlop (Stanford, Calif., 1998), p. 10; hereafter abbreviated *S.*

World War, as in Freud's example of shell-shocked veterans, but the abyss that is continually opening up within the pebble or any other commonplace object:

> And the crack in the tea-cup opens
> A lane to the land of the dead[29]

And perhaps it is this opening that is sought quite as much as the closing up of the object by or in words. For the repetitions of Ponge's processual poems may correspond to the vacillations of Freud's death drive:

> It is as though the life of the organism moved with a vacillating rhythm. One group of instincts rushes forward so as to reach the final aim of life [that is, death] as quickly as possible; but when a particular stage in the advance has been reached, the other group jerks back to a certain point to make a fresh start and so prolong the journey.[30]

Ponge himself said that "*underneath* is what I am concerned with"—which, he adds, "is only death."[31]

The link between Ponge's concern with death and his concern with physical objects can be made through Lacan's reading of the death drive. Lacan associates the death drive with the dynamics of the lost object—generally the absent mother, as it is for little Ernst in Freud's example. Ernst attempts to master his first sense of loss through the *fort/da* game, a strategy of representation; however, the game's repetitiveness betrays its inadequacy. While the lost object is an element in any representation, it can never be regained or re-presented, for it is less a particular object than the irreversible experience of loss. In the representation there always remains a drive toward something beyond what is represented, something more than mimesis. Similarly the death drive is "the *more* than us in us that is at that moment irreducible to meaning or satisfaction."[32] What is "more" is not known because not possessed—but it is implied by the sense of what is less than we desire, just as absence implies a previous presence. So Lacan identifies the death drive with a shortfall in representation: "The death instinct is only the mark of the symbolic order, in so

29. W. H. Auden, "As I Walked out One Evening" *Collected Poems,* ed. Edward Mendelson (New York, 1976), p. 115.

30. Sigmund Freud, *Beyond the Pleasure Principle,* in *The Standard Edition of the Complete Psychological Works of Sigmund Freud,* trans. and ed. James Strachey, 24 vols. (London, 1975), 18:40–41.

31. Ponge, "Proem," *Things,* trans. Cid Corman (New York, 1971), p. 12.

32. Ellie Ragland, "Lacan, the Death Drive, and the Dream of the Burning Child," in *Death and Representation,* ed. Sarah Webster Goodwin and Elisabeth Bronfen (Baltimore, 1993), p. 84.

far . . . as it is dumb, that is to say in so far as it hasn't been realised."[33] The repeated inadequacy of Ponge's studies of soap or pine woods, then, points to something beyond either the objects being described or the words doing the describing.

Take *Soap,* for instance. The poem is about what happens to soap (both the thing and the poetic subject) in the hands of the poet: "At first a reserve, a bearing, a patience in its saucer as perfect as those of the pebble stone" (S, p. 41). When immersed in water, though, the cake of soap opens itself up in a peculiarly suggestive way:

> It clings to the bottom and—how should I say it?—I won't say that it gives up the ghost, because it is its whole body that it lets disperse in trailing fumes, in fuliginous trails, slow in their movement and disappearance. Its whole body gives up the ghost in fumes that are slow to dissipate. Or rather, it gives up its body at the same time as its soul, and, when it breathes its last, at the same time the last trace of its body has disappeared. [S, p. 70]

These veils emanating from the object are equivalent to the poet's associations and allusions—as are the "voluble" bubbles produced by the repetitive rubbing of soap in the hands. Either way, the object diminishes in yielding itself up to words. This does not take place without pleasure, but the pleasure principle is fused with what goes beyond it. If joy transforms the object into what Ponge calls the *objoie,* that word is related to *jouissance,* the end product of the poetic process.

> It is exactly this way that writing must be thought of: not as the transcription, according to conventional rules, of some idea (exterior or anterior) but, in reality, as an orgasm: as the orgasm of being or structure, let's say, conventional to begin with, of course —yet which must fulfil itself, give itself, exultantly, as such. [S, p. 96]

Such a fulfillment is also an annihilation, a *petite mort.*[34] The object gives itself in an outpouring that may froth and sing; yet in soap or jug what is given is made possible by an absence, a hollowness—whether that of the jug's resonant interior or that of a bubble, the traditional symbol of the vanity of things.

---

33. Jacques Lacan, *The Ego in Freud's Theory and in the Technique of Psychoanalysis, 1954–1955,* vol. 2 of *The Seminar of Jacques Lacan,* trans. Sylvana Tomaselli, ed. Jacques-Alain Miller (New York, 1991), p. 326.

34. "From the mid-sixties on, Lacan equated the death drive with the *jouissance* effects produced by the *objet a*," Ragland tells us—stressing, however, that jouissance can be either ecstacy or agony (Ragland, "Lacan, the Death Drive and the Dream of the Burning Child," p. 85).

3

At one point in his seventh seminar, *The Ethics of Psychoanalysis,* Lacan returns to Heidegger's example of the jug, which he misreads, perhaps deliberately, as a vase. This already skews his reading away from the jug's function of pouring out, of which Heidegger makes so much, and brings it closer to Ponge's jug with its ultimate hollowness. Indeed, hollowness is for Lacan the heart of the vase; the potter builds the object up around a hole. The finished vase "creates the void and thereby instances the possibility of filling it. . . . If the vase may be filled, it is because in the first place in its essence it is empty."[35] The vase is then "an object made to represent the existence of the emptiness at the center of the real that is called the Thing" (*E*, p. 121). Here it is imperative to distinguish between the physical thing and that psychological Thing *(das Ding)* of which Lacan goes on to speak.

We should first recall the distinction made earlier in this essay between the object and the thing, a distinction that Lacan makes also through an anecdote about Jacques Prévert's matchbox collection. This collection of identical specimens, threaded together with the aid of a slight displacement of the little drawer, was made to climb up and down the walls of Prévert's room. Emphasizing beyond its normal function the matchbox's nature as a self-contained drawer, the collection "illustrates, in brief, the transformation of an object into a thing, the sudden elevation of the matchbox to a dignity it did not possess before. But it is a thing that is not, of course, the Thing" (*E*, pp. 117–18). Lacan's distinction here between thing and Thing carries on a distinction found in Freud; in his German it is marked, in fact, by different words: *Sache* and *Ding. Sache,* according to Lacan, is "a product of industry and of human action as governed by language" (*E*, p. 45). The matchbox has been named and designated to a certain role in the real—a role that Prévert's arrangement makes as strange, as uncanny, as if we had never named the matchbox or designated it to its proper use. And to that degree the strangeness of the physical thing may allude to another kind of strangeness, that of the psychological Thing.

Lacan introduces the idea of *das Ding* through an instance, found in Freud's *Project for a Scientific Psychology,* of the objectification of another. Certain perceptions of the other person cue associations that underscore that person's similarity to us (if someone is screaming we supply the pain associated with our own screaming at some other time); other perceptions (such as the person's unique facial configuration) emphasize what is different. The part that is different detaches itself from the subject's

35. Lacan, *The Ethics of Psychoanalysis, 1959–1960,* vol. 7 of *The Seminar of Jacques Lacan,* trans. Dennis Porter, ed. Miller (New York, 1992), p. 120; hereafter abbreviated *E*.

associative web to become objectified; it "affirms itself through an unchanging apparatus, which remains together as a thing, *als Ding*" (Freud, quoted in *E*, p. 51).[36] But whereas Freud is concerned with the objectification of the other, Lacan is interested in the otherness of objectification, and of the object. What has been objectified, Lacan says, is "by its very nature alien, *Fremde*. . . . strange and even hostile on occasion" (*E*, p. 52). This extends beyond the otherness of other subjects as one perceives them to all that is other than ("alien" to) one's own subject-position. Psychoanalysis has shown that this is not confined to the world without, the world of objects or objectified subjects; what is other is within us, too. It is within us even if, or especially because, it is not there: "the Thing is not nothing, but literally is not. It is characterized by its absence, its strangeness" (*E*, p. 63). Lacan has given Freud's original sentence a turn that now links it to the dynamics of the lost object. And since those dynamics are involved in the very constitution of the subject, *das Ding* is not merely a part of another as physical object; it is a Thing in one's psyche that has come into being with an object's loss.

Das Ding, then, is both the lost object and the psychic dynamics formed around its absence. Neither of these can be grasped directly, as they are by nature absent or alien. For this reason, the Thing must necessarily always be represented by something else: "An object, insofar as it is a created object, may fill the function that enables it not to avoid the Thing as a signifier, but to represent it" (*E*, p. 119). Thus Lacan, using Freud's terminology, forms this gnomic utterance: *"Die Sache ist das Wort des Dinges"*—the thing is the word of the Thing (*E*, p. 63). This utterance breaks down the venerable opposition between word and thing. Indeed, for Lacan the "opposition between what is called concrete and what is called figurative" is fallacious (*E*, p. 120). Both may function as signifiers. The real opposition is between that function and the impossible Thing that it attempts to signify; the Thing is "that which I will call the beyond-of-the-signified" (*E*, p. 54).

The vase is such an object functioning as a word, filling itself, like Ponge's jug, with a certain resonance. Yet it can be filled only because, as Lacan observes, in its essence it is empty. "And," he continues, "it is exactly in the same sense that speech or discourse may be full or empty" (*E*, p. 120). The equation between the word and this instance, at least, of the thing can be made because the vase is for Lacan a signifier and, what is more, a signifier of signification. As with that other Lacanian signifier of signification, the phallus, it is through an absence that the "filling" of significance is initiated: "The fashioning of the signifier and the introduction of a gap or a hole in the real is identical" (*E*, p. 121). With every

36. This is Lacan's (or rather his translator's) version of Freud's words in the *Project for a Scientific Psychology*. Strachey's translation is slightly different, but the substance is the same. See Freud, *Project for a Scientific Psychology*, in *The Standard Edition of the Complete Psychological Works of Sigmund Freud*, 1:330.

signifying act the gap spreads wider, and there is no limit to this process: "one final day," Lacan speculates, "we may find that the whole texture of appearance has been rent apart, starting from the gap we have introduced there" (*E*, p. 122).

We have come full circle, returning to the nullification involved in naming. The effects of the signifier descend like Adam's curse from what at first presents itself as a consolidation to the reverse of this, a final apocalyptic absence. The creation falls into Blanchot's hecatomb as its appearances are increasingly displaced by words. And the control that was supposedly granted to Adam through the act of naming is displaced as well in this dynamic, and interminably so. In his "The Function and Field of Speech and Language in Psychoanalysis" Lacan sums up the sequence: "The symbol manifests itself first of all as the murder of the thing, and this death constitutes in the subject the eternalization of his desire."[37] For the word that replaces the thing is absence as much as presence, a lack that draws Adam into the desire to fill it, a desire that can only move endlessly along the signifying chain, never fulfilling itself, never filling a fundamental emptiness.

The potter who made the vase created a thing that represents both the Thing beyond signification and that which attempts to contain it, in the form of the vase's sides enclosing its hollow. The Thing, Lacan asserts, "will always be represented by emptiness, precisely because it cannot be represented by anything else—or, more exactly, because it can only be represented by something else. But in every form of sublimation emptiness is determinative. . . . All art is characterized by a certain mode of organization around this emptiness" (*E*, pp. 129–30). This circling by words we have seen in carafe, jug, and vase, where richness and emptiness produce each other continuously within the work. And this instability makes of the work, and of the object that is its subject, something unfamiliar, disturbing, uncanny. If there is a murder of the thing by the word, then, this does not definitively annihilate that thing; it only transposes it to the scene of an interminable haunting of language.

37. Lacan, "The Function and Field of Speech and Language in Psychoanalysis," *Écrits: A Selection,* trans. Alan Sheridan (New York, 1977), p. 104.

Why Has Critique Run out of Steam? From Matters of Fact to Matters of Concern

Bruno Latour

Wars. So many wars. Wars outside and wars inside. Cultural wars, science wars, and wars against terrorism. Wars against poverty and wars against the poor. Wars against ignorance and wars out of ignorance. My question is simple: Should we be at war, too, we, the scholars, the intellectuals? Is it really our duty to add fresh ruins to fields of ruins? Is it really the task of the humanities to add deconstruction to destruction? More iconoclasm to iconoclasm? What has become of the critical spirit? Has it run out of steam?

Quite simply, my worry is that it might not be aiming at the right target. To remain in the metaphorical atmosphere of the time, military experts constantly revise their strategic doctrines, their contingency plans, the size, direction, and technology of their projectiles, their smart bombs, their missiles; I wonder why we, we alone, would be saved from those sorts of revisions. It does not seem to me that we have been as quick, in academia, to prepare ourselves for new threats, new dangers, new tasks, new targets. Are we not like those mechanical toys that endlessly make the same gesture when everything else has changed around them? Would it not be rather terrible if we were still training young kids—yes, young recruits, young cadets—for wars that are no longer possible, fighting enemies long gone, conquering territories that no longer exist, leaving them ill-equipped in the face of threats we had not anticipated, for which we are so thoroughly unprepared? Generals have always been accused of being on the ready one war late—especially French generals, especially these days. Would it be so surprising, after all, if intellectuals were also one war late,

For Graham Harman. This text was written for the Stanford presidential lecture held at the humanities center, 7 Apr. 2003. I warmly thank Harvard history of science doctoral students for many ideas exchanged on those topics during this semester.

one critique late—especially French intellectuals, especially now? It has been a long time, after all, since intellectuals were in the vanguard. Indeed, it has been a long time since the very notion of the avant-garde—the proletariat, the artistic—passed away, pushed aside by other forces, moved to the rear guard, or maybe lumped with the baggage train.[1] We are still able to go through the motions of a critical avant-garde, but is not the spirit gone?

In these most depressing of times, these are some of the issues I want to press, not to depress the reader but to press ahead, to redirect our meager capacities as fast as possible. To prove my point, I have, not exactly facts, but rather tiny cues, nagging doubts, disturbing telltale signs. What has become of critique, I wonder, when an editorial in the *New York Times* contains the following quote?

> Most scientists believe that [global] warming is caused largely by man-made pollutants that require strict regulation. Mr. Luntz [a Republican strategist] seems to acknowledge as much when he says that "the scientific debate is closing against us." His advice, however, is to emphasize that the evidence is not complete.
>
> "Should the public come to believe that the scientific issues are settled," he writes, "their views about global warming will change accordingly. Therefore, you need to continue to make the *lack of scientific certainty* a primary issue."[2]

Fancy that? An artificially maintained scientific controversy to favor a "brownlash," as Paul and Anne Ehrlich would say.[3]

1. On what happened to the avant-garde and critique generally, see *Iconoclash: Beyond the Image Wars in Science, Religion, and Art,* ed. Bruno Latour and Peter Weibel (Cambridge, Mass., 2002). This article is very much an exploration of what could happen beyond the image wars.

2. "Environmental Word Games," *New York Times,* 15 Mar. 2003, p. A16. Luntz seems to have been very successful; I read later in an editorial in the *Wall Street Journal:*

> There is a better way [than passing a law that restricts business], which is to keep fighting on the merits. There is no scientific consensus that greenhouse gases cause the world's modest global warming trend, much less whether that warming will do more harm than good, or whether we can even do anything about it.
>
> Once Republicans concede that greenhouse gases must be controlled, it will only be a matter of time before they end up endorsing more economically damaging regulation. They could always stand on principle and attempt to educate the public instead. ["A Republican Kyoto," *Wall Street Journal,* 8 Apr. 2003, p. A14]

And the same publication complains about the "pathological relation" of the "Arab street" with truth!

3. Paul R. and Anne H. Ehrlich, *Betrayal of Science and Reason: How Anti-Environmental Rhetoric Threatens Our Future* (Washington, D.C., 1997), p. 1.

Bruno Latour teaches sociology at the École des Mines in Paris.

Do you see why I am worried? I myself have spent some time in the past trying to show "*the lack of scientific certainty*'" inherent in the construction of facts. I too made it a "'primary issue."' But I did not exactly aim at fooling the public by obscuring the certainty of a closed argument—or did I? After all, I have been accused of just that sin. Still, I'd like to believe that, on the contrary, I intended to *emancipate* the public from prematurely naturalized objectified facts. Was I foolishly mistaken? Have things changed so fast?

In which case the danger would no longer be coming from an excessive confidence in ideological arguments posturing as matters of fact—as we have learned to combat so efficiently in the past—but from an excessive *distrust* of good matters of fact disguised as bad ideological biases! While we spent years trying to detect the real prejudices hidden behind the appearance of objective statements, do we now have to reveal the real objective and incontrovertible facts hidden behind the *illusion* of prejudices? And yet entire Ph.D. programs are still running to make sure that good American kids are learning the hard way that facts are made up, that there is no such thing as natural, unmediated, unbiased access to truth, that we are always prisoners of language, that we always speak from a particular standpoint, and so on, while dangerous extremists are using the very same argument of social construction to destroy hard-won evidence that could save our lives. Was I wrong to participate in the invention of this field known as science studies? Is it enough to say that we did not really mean what we said? Why does it burn my tongue to say that global warming is a fact whether you like it or not? Why can't I simply say that the argument is closed for good?

Should I reassure myself by simply saying that bad guys can use any weapon at hand, naturalized facts when it suits them and social construction when it suits them? Should we apologize for having been wrong all along? Or should we rather bring the sword of criticism to criticism itself and do a bit of soul-searching here: what were we really after when we were so intent on showing the social construction of scientific facts? Nothing guarantees, after all, that we should be right all the time. There is no sure ground even for criticism.[4] Isn't this what criticism intended to say: that there is no sure ground anywhere? But what does it mean when this lack of sure ground is taken away from us by the worst possible fellows as an argument against the things we cherish?

Artificially maintained controversies are not the only worrying sign. What has critique become when a French general, no, a marshal of critique, namely, Jean Baudrillard, claims in a published book that the Twin Towers destroyed themselves under their own weight, so to speak, under-

---

4. The metaphor of shifting sand was used by neomodernists in their critique of science studies; see *A House Built on Sand: Exposing Postmodernist Myths about Science*, ed. Noretta Koertge (Oxford, 1998). The problem is that the authors of this book looked backward, attempting to reenter the solid rock castle of modernism, and not forward to what I call, for lack of a better term, nonmodernism.

mined by the utter nihilism inherent in capitalism itself—as if the terror-
ist planes were pulled to suicide by the powerful attraction of this black
hole of nothingness?[5] What has become of critique when a book that claims
that no plane ever crashed into the Pentagon can be a bestseller? I am
ashamed to say that the author was French, too.[6] Remember the good old
days when revisionism arrived very late, after the facts had been thoroughly established, decades after bodies of evidence had accumulated?
Now we have the benefit of what can be called *instant revisionism.* The
smoke of the event has not yet finished settling before dozens of conspiracy theories begin revising the official account, adding even more ruins to
the ruins, adding even more smoke to the smoke. What has become of critique when my neighbor in the little Bourbonnais village where I live looks
down on me as someone hopelessly naïve because I believe that the United
States had been attacked by terrorists? Remember the good old days when
university professors could look down on unsophisticated folks because
those hillbillies naïvely believed in church, motherhood, and apple pie?
Things have changed a lot, at least in my village. I am now the one who
naïvely believes in some facts because I am educated, while the other guys
are too *un*sophisticated to be gullible: "Where have you been? Don't you
know that the Mossad and the CIA did it?" What has become of critique
when someone as eminent as Stanley Fish, the "enemy of promises" as
Lindsay Waters calls him, believes he defends science studies, my field, by
comparing the laws of physics to the rules of baseball?[7] What has become
of critique when there is a whole industry denying that the Apollo program
landed on the moon? What has become of critique when DARPA uses for
its Total Information Awareness project the Baconian slogan *Scientia est po-
tentia?* Didn't I read that somewhere in Michel Foucault? Has knowledge-
slash-power been co-opted of late by the National Security Agency? Has
Discipline and Punish become the bedtime reading of Mr. Ridge (fig. 1)?

   Let me be mean for a second. What's the real difference between conspiracists and a popularized, that is a teachable version of social critique
inspired by a too quick reading of, let's say, a sociologist as eminent as
Pierre Bourdieu (to be polite I will stick with the French field command-
ers)? In both cases, you have to learn to become suspicious of everything
people say because of course we all know that they live in the thralls of a
complete *illusio* of their real motives. Then, after disbelief has struck and
an explanation is requested for what is really going on, in both cases again
it is the same appeal to powerful agents hidden in the dark acting always

   5. See Jean Baudrillard, *"The Spirit of Terrorism" and "Requiem for the Twin Towers"* (New
York, 2002).
   6. See Thierry Meyssan, *911: The Big Lie* (London, 2002). Conspiracy theories have always existed; what is new in instant revisionism is how much scientific proof they claim to
imitate.
   7. See Lindsay Waters, *Enemy of Promises* (forthcoming); see also Nick Paumgarten,
"Dept. of Super Slo-Mo: No Flag on the Play," *The New Yorker,* 20 Jan. 2003, p. 32.

Fig. 1.

consistently, continuously, relentlessly. Of course, we in the academy like to use more elevated causes—society, discourse, knowledge-slash-power, fields of forces, empires, capitalism—while conspiracists like to portray a miserable bunch of greedy people with dark intents, but I find something troublingly similar in the structure of the explanation, in the first movement of disbelief and, then, in the wheeling of causal explanations coming out of the deep dark below. What if explanations resorting automatically to power, society, discourse had outlived their usefulness and deteriorated to the point of now feeding the most gullible sort of critique?[8] Maybe I am taking conspiracy theories too seriously, but it worries me to detect, in

8. Their serious as well as their popularized versions have the defect of using society as an already existing cause instead of as a possible consequence. This was the critique that Gabriel Tarde always made against Durkheim. It is probably the whole notion of *social* and *society* that is responsible for the weakening of critique. I have tried to show that in Latour, "Gabriel Tarde and the End of the Social," in *The Social in Question: New Bearings in History and the Social Sciences,* ed. Patrick Joyce (London, 2002), pp. 117–32.

those mad mixtures of knee-jerk disbelief, punctilious demands for proofs, and free use of powerful explanation from the social neverland many of the weapons of social critique. Of course conspiracy theories are an absurd deformation of our own arguments, but, like weapons smuggled through a fuzzy border to the wrong party, these are our weapons none-theless. In spite of all the deformations, it is easy to recognize, still burnt in the steel, our trademark: *Made in Criticalland.*

Do you see why I am worried? Threats might have changed so much that we might still be directing all our arsenal east or west while the enemy has now moved to a very different place. After all, masses of atomic missiles are transformed into a huge pile of junk once the question becomes how to defend against militants armed with box cutters or dirty bombs. Why would it not be the same with our critical arsenal, with the neutron bombs of deconstruction, with the missiles of discourse analysis? Or maybe it is that critique has been miniaturized like computers have. I have always fan-cied that what took great effort, occupied huge rooms, cost a lot of sweat and money, for people like Nietzsche and Benjamin, can be had for noth-ing, much like the supercomputers of the 1950s, which used to fill large halls and expend a vast amount of electricity and heat, but now are acces-sible for a dime and no bigger than a fingernail. As the recent advertise-ment of a Hollywood film proclaimed, "Everything is suspect . . . Everyone is for sale . . . And nothing is what it seems."

What's happening to me, you may wonder? Is this a case of midlife cri-sis? No, alas, I passed middle age quite a long time ago. Is this a patrician spite for the popularization of critique? As if critique should be reserved for the elite and remain difficult and strenuous, like mountain climbing or yachting, and is no longer worth the trouble if everyone can do it for a nickel? What would be so bad with critique for the people? We have been complaining so much about the gullible masses, swallowing naturalized facts, it would be really unfair to now discredit the same masses for their, what should I call it, gullible criticism? Or could this be a case of radical-ism gone mad, as when a revolution swallows its progeny? Or, rather, have we behaved like mad scientists who have let the virus of critique out of the confines of their laboratories and cannot do anything now to limit its dele-terious effects; it mutates now, gnawing everything up, even the vessels in which it is contained? Or is it another case of the famed power of capital-ism for recycling everything aimed at its destruction? As Luc Boltanski and Eve Chiapello say, the new spirit of capitalism has put to good use the ar-tistic critique that was supposed to destroy it.[9] If the dense and moralist cigar-smoking reactionary bourgeois can transform him- or herself into a free-floating agnostic bohemian, moving opinions, capital, and networks from one end of the planet to the other without attachment, why would he

9. See Luc Boltanski and Eve Chiapello, *Le Nouvel Esprit du capitalisme* (Paris, 1999).

or she not be able to absorb the most sophisticated tools of deconstruction, social construction, discourse analysis, postmodernism, postology?

In spite of my tone, I am not trying to reverse course, to become reactionary, to regret what I have done, to swear that I will never be a constructivist any more. I simply want to do what every good military officer, at regular periods, would do: retest the linkages between the new threats he or she has to face and the equipment and training he or she should have in order to meet them—and, if necessary, to revise from scratch the whole paraphernalia. This does not mean for us any more than it does for the officer that we were wrong, but simply that history changes quickly and that there is no greater intellectual crime than to address with the equipment of an older period the challenges of the present one. Whatever the case, our critical equipment deserves as much critical scrutiny as the Pentagon budget.

My argument is that a certain form of critical spirit has sent us down the wrong path, encouraging us to fight the wrong enemies and, worst of all, to be considered as friends by the wrong sort of allies because of a little mistake in the definition of its main target. The question was never to get *away* from facts but *closer* to them, not fighting empiricism but, on the contrary, renewing empiricism.

What I am going to argue is that the critical mind, if it is to renew itself and be relevant again, is to be found in the cultivation of a *stubbornly realist attitude*—to speak like William James—but a realism dealing with what I will call *matters of concern*, not *matters of fact*. The mistake we made, the mistake I made, was to believe that there was no efficient way to criticize matters of fact except by moving *away* from them and directing one's attention *toward* the conditions that made them possible. But this meant accepting much too uncritically what matters of fact were. This was remaining too faithful to the unfortunate solution inherited from the philosophy of Immanuel Kant. Critique has not been critical enough in spite of all its sorescratching. Reality is not defined by matters of fact. Matters of fact are not all that is given in experience. Matters of fact are only very partial and, I would argue, very polemical, very political renderings of matters of concern and only a subset of what could also be called *states of affairs*. It is this second empiricism, this return to the realist attitude, that I'd like to offer as the next task for the critically minded.

To indicate the direction of the argument, I want to show that while the Enlightenment profited largely from the disposition of a very powerful descriptive tool, that of matters of fact, which were excellent for *debunking* quite a lot of beliefs, powers, and illusions, it found itself totally disarmed once matters of fact, in turn, were eaten up by the same debunking impetus. After that, the lights of the Enlightenment were slowly turned off, and some sort of darkness appears to have fallen on campuses. My question is thus: Can we devise another powerful descriptive tool that deals this time with matters of concern and whose import then will no longer be to debunk but to protect and to care, as Donna Haraway would put it? Is it really possible to transform the critical urge in the ethos of someone who *adds* reality to matters of fact and not *subtract* reality? To put it another way, what's the difference between deconstruction and constructivism?

"So far," you could object, "the prospect doesn't look very good, and you, Monsieur Latour, seem the person the least able to deliver on this promise because you spent your life debunking what the other more polite critics had at least respected until then, namely matters of fact and science itself. You can dust your hands with flour as much as you wish, the black fur of the critical wolf will always betray you; your deconstructing teeth have been sharpened on too many of our innocent labs—I mean lambs!—for us to believe you." Well, see, that's just the problem: I have written about a dozen books to inspire respect for, some people have said to uncritically glorify, the objects of science and technology, of art, religion, and, more recently, law, showing every time in great detail the complete implausibility of their being socially explained, and yet the only noise readers hear is the snapping of the wolf's teeth. Is it really impossible to solve the question, to write not matter-of-factually but, how should I say it, in a matter-of-concern way?[10]

Martin Heidegger, as every philosopher knows, has meditated many times on the ancient etymology of the word *thing.* We are now all aware that in all the European languages, including Russian, there is a strong connection between the words for thing and a quasi-judiciary assembly. Icelanders boast of having the oldest Parliament, which they call *Althing,* and you can still visit in many Scandinavian countries assembly places that are designated by the word *Ding* or *Thing.* Now, is this not extraordinary that the banal term we use for designating what is out there, unquestionably, a thing, what lies out of any dispute, out of language, is also the oldest word we all have used to designate the oldest of the sites in which our ancestors did their dealing and tried to settle their disputes?[11] A thing is, in one sense, an object out there and, in another sense, an *issue* very much *in* there, at any rate, a *gathering.* To use the term I introduced earlier now more precisely, the same word *thing* designates matters of fact and matters of concern.

Needless to say, although he develops this etymology at length, this is not the path that Heidegger has taken. On the contrary, all his writing aims to make as sharp a distinction as possible between, on the one hand, objects, *Gegenstand,* and, on the other, the celebrated *Thing.* The handmade

10. This is the achievement of the great novelist Richard Powers, whose stories are a careful and, in my view, masterful enquiry into this new "realism." Especially relevant for this paper is Richard Powers, *Plowing the Dark* (New York, 2000).

11. See the erudite study by the remarkable French scholar of Roman law, Yan Thomas, "Res, chose et patrimoine (note sur le rapport sujet-objet en droit romain)," *Archives de philosophie du droit* 25 (1980): 413–26.

jug can be a thing, while the industrially made can of Coke remains an object. While the latter is abandoned to the empty mastery of science and technology, only the former, cradled in the respectful idiom of art, craftsmanship, and poetry, could deploy and gather its rich set of connections.[12] This bifurcation is marked many times but in a decisive way in his book on Kant:

> Up to this hour such questions have been open. Their questionability is concealed by the results and the progress of scientific work. One of these burning questions concerns the justification and limits of mathematical formalism in contrast to the demand for an immediate return to intuitively given nature.[13]

What has happened to those who, like Heidegger, have tried to find their ways in immediacy, in intuition, in nature would be too sad to retell—and is well known anyway. What is certain is that those pathmarks off the beaten track led indeed nowhere. And, yet, Heidegger, when he takes the jug seriously, offers a powerful vocabulary to talk also about the object he despises so much. What would happen, I wonder, if we tried to talk about the object of science and technology, the *Gegenstand*, as if it had the rich and complicated qualities of the celebrated *Thing?*

The problem with philosophers is that because their jobs are so hard they drink a lot of coffee and thus use in their arguments an inordinate quantity of pots, mugs, and jugs—to which, sometimes, they might add the occasional rock. But, as Ludwik Fleck remarked long ago, their objects are never complicated enough; more precisely, they are never simultaneously *made* through a complex history and new, real, and *interesting* participants in the universe.[14] Philosophy never deals with the sort of beings we in science studies have dealt with. And that's why the debates between realism and relativism never go anywhere. As Ian Hacking has recently shown, the engagement of a rock in philosophical talk is utterly different if you take a banal rock to make your point (usually to lapidate a passing relativist!) or if you take, for instance, dolomite, as he has done so beautifully.[15] The first can be turned into a matter of fact but not the second. Dolomite is so beautifully complex and entangled that it resists being treated as a matter of fact. It too can be described as a gathering; it too can

12. See Graham Harman, *Tool-Being: Heidegger and the Metaphysics of Objects* (Chicago, 2002).

13. Martin Heidegger, *What Is a Thing?* trans. W. B. Barton, Jr., and Vera Deutsch (Chicago, 1967), p. 95.

14. Although Fleck is the founder of science studies, the impact of his work is still very much in the future because he has been so deeply misunderstood by Thomas Kuhn; see Thomas Kuhn, foreword to Ludwik Fleck, *Genesis and Development of a Scientific Fact* (1935; Chicago, 1979), pp. vii–xi.

15. See Ian Hacking, *The Social Construction of What?* (Cambridge, Mass., 1999), in particular the last chapter.

be seen as engaging the fourfold. Why not try to portray it with the same enthusiasm, engagement, and complexity as the Heideggerian jug? Heidegger's mistake is not to have treated the jug too well, but to have traced a dichotomy between *Gegenstand* and *Thing* that was justified by nothing except the crassest of prejudices.

Several years ago another philosopher, much closer to the history of science, namely Michel Serres, also French, but this time as foreign to critique as one can get, meditated on what it would mean to take objects of science in a serious anthropological and ontological fashion. It is interesting to note that every time a philosopher gets closer to an object of science that is at once historical and interesting, his or her philosophy changes, and the specifications for a realist attitude become, at once, more stringent and completely different from the so-called realist philosophy of science concerned with routine or boring objects. I was reading his passage on the *Challenger* disaster in his book *Statues* when another shuttle, *Columbia*, in early 2003 offered me a tragic instantiation of yet another metamorphosis of an object into a thing.[16]

What else would you call this sudden transformation of a completely mastered, perfectly understood, quite forgotten by the media, taken-for-granted, matter-of-factual projectile into a sudden shower of debris falling on the United States, which thousands of people tried to salvage in the mud and rain and collect in a huge hall to serve as so many clues in a judicial scientific investigation? Here, suddenly, in a stroke, an object had become a thing, a matter of fact was considered as a matter of great concern. If a thing is a gathering, as Heidegger says, how striking to see how it can suddenly *disband*. If the "thinging of the thing" is a gathering that always connects the "united four, earth and sky, divinities and mortals, in the simple onefold of their self-unified fourfold,"[17] how could there be a better example of this making and unmaking than this catastrophe unfolding all its thousands of folds? How could we see it as a normal accident of technology when, in his eulogy for the unfortunate victims, your president said: "The crew of the shuttle Columbia did not return safely to Earth; yet we can pray that all are safely home"?[18] As if no shuttle ever moved simply in space, but also always in heaven.

This was on C-Span 1, but on C-Span 2, at the very same time, early February 2003, another extraordinary parallel event was occurring. This time a Thing—with a capital T—was assembled to try to coalesce, to gather in one decision, one object, one projection of force: a military

16. See Michel Serres, *Statues: Le Second Livre des fondations* (Paris, 1987). On the reason why Serres was never critical, see Serres with Latour, *Conversations on Science, Culture, and Time*, trans. Roxanne Lapidus (Ann Arbor, Mich., 1995).

17. Heidegger, "The Thing," *Poetry, Language, Thought*, trans. Albert Hofstadter (New York, 1971), p. 178.

18. "Bush Talking More about Religion: Faith to Solve the Nation's Problems," CNN website, 18 Feb. 2003, www.cnn.com/2003/ALLPOLITICS/02/18/bush.faith/

strike against Iraq. Again, it was hard to tell whether this gathering was a tribunal, a parliament, a command-and-control war room, a rich man's club, a scientific congress, or a TV stage. But certainly it was an assembly where matters of great concern were debated and proven—except there was much puzzlement about which type of proofs should be given and how accurate they were. The difference between C-Span 1 and C-Span 2, as I watched them with bewilderment, was that while in the case of *Columbia* we had a perfectly mastered object that suddenly was transformed into a shower of burning debris that was used as so much evidence in an investigation, there, at the United Nations, we had an investigation that tried to coalesce, in one unifying, unanimous, solid, mastered object, masses of people, opinions, and might. In one case the object was metamorphosed into a thing; in the second, the thing was attempting to turn into an object. We could witness, in one case, the head, in another, the tail of the trajectory through which matters of fact emerge out of matters of concern. In both cases we were offered a unique window into the number of *things* that have to participate in the gathering of an *object*. Heidegger was not a very good anthropologist of science and technology; he had only four folds, while the smallest shuttle, the shortest war, has millions. How many gods, passions, controls, institutions, techniques, diplomacies, wits have to be folded to connect "earth and sky, divinities and mortals"— oh yes, especially mortals. (Frightening omen, to launch such a complicated war, just when such a beautifully mastered object as the shuttle disintegrated into thousands of pieces of debris raining down from the sky—but the omen was not heeded; gods nowadays are invoked for convenience only.)

My point is thus very simple: things have become Things again, objects have reentered the arena, the Thing, in which they have to be gathered first in order to exist later as what *stands apart*. The parenthesis that we can call the modern parenthesis during which we had, on the one hand, a world of objects, *Gegenstand*, out there, unconcerned by any sort of parliament, forum, agora, congress, court and, on the other, a whole set of forums, meeting places, town halls where people debated, has come to a close. What the etymology of the word *thing—chose, causa, res, aitia*—had conserved for us mysteriously as a sort of fabulous and mythical past has now become, for all to see, our most ordinary present. Things are gathered again. Was it not extraordinarily moving to see, for instance, in the lower Manhattan reconstruction project, the long crowds, the angry messages, the passionate emails, the huge agoras, the long editorials that connected so many people to so many variations of the project to replace the Twin Towers? As the architect Daniel Libeskind said a few days before the decision, building will never be the same.

I could open the newspaper and unfold the number of former objects that have become things again, from the global warming case I mentioned earlier to the hormonal treatment of menopause, to the work of Tim

Lenoir, the primate studies of Linda Fedigan and Shirley Strum, or the hyenas of my friend Steven Glickman.[19]

Nor are those gatherings limited to the present period as if only recently objects had become so obviously things. Every day historians of science help us realize to what extent we have never been modern because they keep revising every single element of past matters of fact from Mario Biagioli's Galileo, Steven Shapin's Boyle, and Simon Schaffer's Newton, to the incredibly intricate linkages between Einstein and Poincaré that Peter Galison has narrated in his latest masterpiece.[20] Many others of course could be cited, but the crucial point for me now is that what allowed historians, philosophers, humanists, and critics to trace *the* difference between modern and premodern, namely, the sudden and somewhat miraculous appearance of matters of fact, is now thrown into doubt with the merging of matters of fact into highly complex, historically situated, richly diverse matters of concern. You can do one sort of thing with mugs, jugs, rocks, swans, cats, mats but not with Einstein's Patent Bureau electric coordination of clocks in Bern. Things that gather cannot be thrown at you like objects.

And, yet, I know full well that this is not enough because, no matter what we do, when we try to reconnect scientific objects with their aura, their crown, their web of associations, when we accompany them back to their gathering, we always appear to *weaken* them, not to *strengthen* their claim to reality. I know, I know, we are acting with the best intentions in the world, we want to *add* reality to scientific objects, but, inevitably, through a sort of tragic bias, we seem always to be subtracting some bit from it. Like a clumsy waiter setting plates on a slanted table, every nice dish slides down and crashes on the ground. Why can we never discover the same stubbornness, the same solid realism by bringing out the obviously webby, "thingy" qualities of matters of concern? Why can't we ever counteract the claim of realists that only a fare of matters of fact can satisfy their appetite and that matters of concern are much like nouvelle cuisine—nice to look at but not fit for voracious appetites?

One reason is of course the position objects have been given in most social sciences, a position that is so ridiculously useless that if it is employed, even in a small way, for dealing with science, technology, religion, law, or literature it will make absolutely impossible any serious consideration of objectivity—I mean of "thinginess." Why is this so? Let

---

19. Serres proposed the word *quasi-object* to cover this intermediary phase between things and objects—a philosophical question much more interesting than the tired old one of the relation between *words* and *worlds*. On the new way animals appear to scientists and the debate it triggers, see *Primate Encounters: Models of Science, Gender, and Society,* ed. Shirley Strum and Linda Fedigan (Chicago, 2000), and Vinciane Despret, *Quand le loup habitera avec l'agneau* (Paris, 2002).

20. See Peter Galison, *Einstein's Clocks, Poincaré's Maps: Empires of Time* (New York, 2003).

me try to portray the critical landscape in its ordinary and routine state.[21]

We can summarize, I estimate, 90 percent of the contemporary critical scene by the following series of diagrams that fixate the object at only two positions, what I have called the *fact* position and the *fairy* position—*fact* and *fairy* are etymologically related but I won't develop this point here. The fairy position is very well known and is used over and over again by many social scientists who associate criticism with antifetishism. The role of the critic is then to show that what the naïve believers are doing with objects is simply a projection of their wishes onto a material entity that does nothing at all by itself. Here they have diverted to their petty use the prophetic fulmination against idols "they have mouths and speak not, they have ears and hear not," but they use this prophecy to decry the very objects of belief—gods, fashion, poetry, sport, desire, you name it—to which naïve believers cling with so much intensity.[22] And then the courageous critic, who alone remains aware and attentive, who never sleeps, turns those false objects into fetishes that are supposed to be nothing but mere empty white screens on which is projected the power of society, domination, whatever. The naïve believer has received a first salvo (fig. 2).

But, wait, a second salvo is in the offing, and this time it comes from the fact pole. This time it is the poor bloke, again taken aback, whose behavior is now "explained" by the powerful effects of indisputable matters of fact: "You, ordinary fetishists, believe you are free but, in reality, you are acted on by forces you are not conscious of. Look at them, look, you blind idiot" (and here you insert whichever pet facts the social scientists fancy to work with, taking them from economic infrastructure, fields of discourse, social domination, race, class, and gender, maybe throwing in some neurobiology, evolutionary psychology, whatever, provided they act as indisputable facts whose origin, fabrication, mode of development are left unexamined) (fig. 3).

Do you see now why it feels so good to be a critical mind? Why critique, this most ambiguous *pharmakon*, has become such a potent euphoric drug? You are always right! When naïve believers are clinging forcefully to their objects, claiming that they are made to do things because of their gods, their poetry, their cherished objects, you can turn all of those attachments into so many fetishes and humiliate all the believers by showing that it is nothing but their own projection, that you, yes you alone, can see.

21. I summarize here some of the results of my already long anthropological inquiry into the iconoclastic gesture, from Latour, *We Have Never Been Modern*, trans. Catherine Porter (Cambridge, Mass., 1993) to *Pandora's Hope: Essays on the Reality of Science Studies* (Cambridge, Mass., 1999) and of course *Iconoclash*.

22. See William Pietz, "The Problem of the Fetish, I," *Res* 9 (Spring 1985): 5–17, "The Problem of the Fetish, II: The Origin of the Fetish" *Res* 13 (Spring 1987): 23–45, and "The Problem of the Fetish, IIIa: Bosman's Guinea and the Enlightenment Theory of Fetishism," *Res* 16 (Autumn 1988): 105–23.

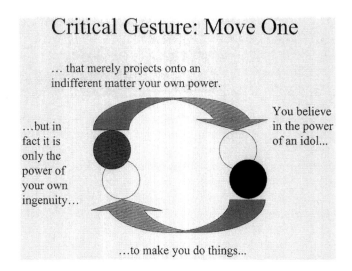

Critical Gesture: Move One

... that merely projects onto an
indifferent matter your own power.

...but in
fact it is
only the
power of
your own
ingenuity...

You believe
in the power
of an idol...

...to make you do things...

FIG. 2.

But as soon as naïve believers are thus inflated by some belief in their own importance, in their own projective capacity, you strike them by a second uppercut and humiliate them again, this time by showing that, whatever they think, their behavior is entirely determined by the action of powerful causalities coming from objective reality they don't see, but that you, yes you, the never sleeping critic, alone can see. Isn't this fabulous? Isn't it really worth going to graduate school to study critique? "Enter here, you poor folks. After arduous years of reading turgid prose, you will be always right, you will never be taken in any more; no one, no matter how powerful, will be able to accuse you of naïveté, that supreme sin, any longer? Better equipped than Zeus himself you rule alone, striking from above with the salvo of antifetishism in one hand and the solid causality of objectivity in the other." The only loser is the naïve believer, the great unwashed, always caught off balance (fig. 4).

Is it so surprising, after all, that with such positions given to the object, the humanities have lost the hearts of their fellow citizens, that they had to retreat year after year, entrenching themselves always further in the narrow barracks left to them by more and more stingy deans? The Zeus of Critique rules absolutely, to be sure, but over a desert.

One thing is clear, not one of us readers would like to see *our* own most cherished objects treated in this way. We would recoil in horror at the mere suggestion of having them socially explained, whether we deal in poetry or robots, stem cells, blacks holes, or impressionism, whether we are patriots, revolutionaries, or lawyers, whether we pray to God or put our hope in neuroscience. This is why, in my opinion, those of us who tried to portray sciences as matters of concern so often failed to convince; readers have confused the treatment we give of the former matters of fact with the ter-

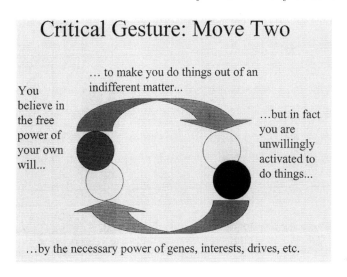

Critical Gesture: Move Two

You believe in the free power of your own will...

... to make you do things out of an indifferent matter...

...but in fact you are unwillingly activated to do things...

...by the necessary power of genes, interests, drives, etc.

FIG. 3.

rible fate of objects processed through the hands of sociology, cultural studies, and so on. And I can't blame our readers. What social scientists do to our favorite objects is so horrific that certainly we don't want them to come any nearer. "Please," we exclaim, "don't touch them at all! Don't try to explain them!" Or we might suggest more politely: "Why don't you go further down the corridor to this other department? *They* have bad facts to account for; why don't you explain away those ones instead of ours?" And this is the reason why, when we want respect, solidity, obstinacy, robustness, we all prefer to stick to the language of matters of fact no matter its well-known defects.

And yet this is not the only way because the cruel treatment objects undergo in the hands of what I'd like to call *critical barbarity* is rather easy to undo. If the critical barbarian appears so powerful, it is because the two mechanisms I have just sketched are never put together in one single diagram (fig. 5). Antifetishists debunk objects they don't believe in by showing the productive and projective forces of people; then, without ever making the connection, they use objects they do believe in to resort to the causalist or mechanist explanation and debunk conscious capacities of people whose behavior they don't approve of. The whole rather poor trick that allows critique to go on, although we would never confine our own valuables to their sordid pawnshop, is that there is never any *crossover between the two lists of objects* in the fact position and the fairy position. This is why you can be at once and without even sensing any contradiction (1) an antifetishist for everything you don't believe in—for the most part religion, popular culture, art, politics, and so on; (2) an unrepentant positivist for all the sciences you believe in—sociology, economics, conspiracy theory, genetics,

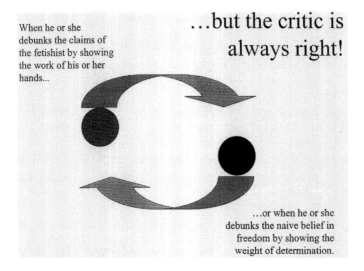

When he or she debunks the claims of the fetishist by showing the work of his or her hands...

...but the critic is always right!

...or when he or she debunks the naive belief in freedom by showing the weight of determination.

FIG. 4.

evolutionary psychology, semiotics, just pick your preferred field of study; and (3) a perfectly healthy sturdy realist for what you really cherish—and of course it might be criticism itself, but also painting, bird-watching, Shakespeare, baboons, proteins, and so on.

If you think I am exaggerating in my somewhat dismal portrayal of the critical landscape, it is because we have had in effect almost no occasion so far to detect the total mismatch of the three contradictory repertoires—antifetishism, positivism, realism—because we carefully manage to apply them on *different* topics. We explain the objects we don't approve of by treating them as fetishes; we account for behaviors we don't like by discipline whose makeup we don't examine; and we concentrate our passionate interest on only those things that are for us worthwhile matters of concern. But of course such a cavalier attitude with such contradictory repertoires is not possible for those of us, in science studies, who have to deal with states of affairs that fit neither in the list of plausible fetishes—because everyone, including us, does believe very strongly in them—nor in the list of undisputable facts because we are witnessing their birth, their slow construction, their fascinating emergence as matters of concern. The metaphor of the Copernican revolution, so tied to the destiny of critique, has always been for us, science students, simply moot. This is why, with more than a good dose of field chauvinism, I consider this tiny field so important; it is the little rock in the shoe that might render the routine patrol of the critical barbarians more and more painful.

The mistake would be to believe that we too have given a social explanation of scientific facts. No, even though it is true that at first we tried, like good critics trained in the good schools, to use the armaments handed

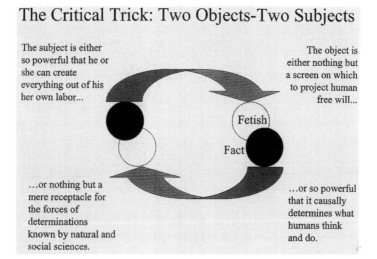

The Critical Trick: Two Objects-Two Subjects

The subject is either so powerful that he or she can create everything out of his her own labor...

The object is either nothing but a screen on which to project human free will...

Fetish

Fact

...or nothing but a mere receptacle for the forces of determinations known by natural and social sciences.

...or so powerful that it causally determines what humans think and do.

FIG. 5.

to us by our betters and elders to crack open—one of their favorite expressions, meaning to destroy—religion, power, discourse, hegemony. But, fortunately (yes, fortunately!), one after the other, we witnessed that the black boxes of science remained closed and that it was rather the tools that lay in the dust of our workshop, disjointed and broken. Put simply, critique was useless against objects of some solidity. You can try the projective game on UFOs or exotic divinities, but don't try it on neurotransmitters, on gravitation, on Monte Carlo calculations. But critique is also useless when it begins to use the results of one science uncritically, be it sociology itself, or economics, or postimperialism, to account for the behavior of people. You can try to play this miserable game of explaining aggression by invoking the genetic makeup of violent people, but try to do that while dragging in, at the same time, the many controversies in genetics, including evolutionary theories in which geneticists find themselves so thoroughly embroiled.[23]

On both accounts, matters of concern never occupy the two positions left for them by critical barbarity. Objects are much too strong to be treated as fetishes and much too weak to be treated as indisputable causal explanations of some unconscious action. And this is not true of scientific states of affairs only; this is our great discovery, what made science studies commit such a felicitous mistake, such a *felix culpa*. Once you realize that scientific objects cannot be socially explained, then you realize too that the

23. For a striking example, see Jean-Jacques Kupiec and Pierre Sonigo, *Ni Dieu ni gène: Pour une autre théorie de l'hérédité* (Paris, 2000); see also Evelyn Fox-Keller, *The Century of the Gene* (Cambridge, Mass., 2000).

so-called weak objects, those that appear to be candidates for the accusation of antifetishism, were never mere projections on an empty screen either.[24] They too act, they too do things, they too *make you do* things. It is not
only the objects of science that resist, but all the others as well, those that
were supposed to have been ground to dust by the powerful teeth of automated reflex-action deconstructors. To accuse something of being a fetish
is the ultimate gratuitous, disrespectful, insane, and barbarous gesture.[25]

Is it not time for some progress? To the fact position, to the fairy position, why not add a third position, a *fair* position? Is it really asking too
much from our collective intellectual life to devise, at least once a century,
some *new* critical tools? Should we not be thoroughly humiliated to see that
military personnel are more alert, more vigilant, more innovative than we,
the pride of academia, the crème de la crème, who go on ceaselessly transforming the whole rest of the world into naïve believers, into fetishists, into
hapless victims of domination, while at the same time turning them into
the mere superficial consequences of powerful hidden causalities coming
from infrastructures whose makeup is never interrogated? All the while
being intimately certain that the things really close to our hearts would in
no way fit any of those roles. Are you not all tired of those "explanations"?
I am, I have always been, when I know, for instance, that the God to whom
I pray, the works of art I cherish, the colon cancer I have been fighting, the
piece of law I am studying, the desire I feel, indeed, the very book I am
writing could in no way be accounted for by fetish or fact, nor by any combination of those two absurd positions?

To retrieve a realist attitude, it is not enough to dismantle critical
weapons so uncritically built up by our predecessors as we would obsolete
but still dangerous atomic silos. If we had to dismantle social theory only,
it would be a rather simple affair; like the Soviet empire, those big totali-
ties have feet of clay. But the difficulty lies in the fact that they are built on
top of a much older philosophy, so that whenever we try to replace matters
of fact by matters of concern, we seem to lose something along the way. It
is like trying to fill the mythical Danaid's barrel—no matter what we put in
it, the level of realism never increases. As long as we have not sealed the
leaks, the realist attitude will always be split; matters of fact take the best
part, and matters of concern are limited to a rich but essentially void or irrelevant *history*. More will always seem less. Although I wish to keep this paper short, I need to take a few more pages to deal with ways to overcome
this bifurcation.

24. I have attempted to use this argument recently on two most difficult types of entities, Christian divinities (Latour, *Jubiler ou les tourments de la parole religieuse* [Paris, 2002]) and
law (Latour, *La Fabrique du droit: Une Ethnographie du Conseil d'État* [Paris, 2002]).

25. The exhibition in Karlsruhe, Germany, *Iconoclash*, was a sort of belated ritual in order to atone for so much wanton destruction.

Alfred North Whitehead famously said, "The recourse to metaphysics is like throwing a match into a powder magazine. It blows up the whole arena."[26] I cannot avoid getting into it because I have talked so much about weapon systems, explosions, iconoclasm, and arenas. Of all the modern philosophers who tried to overcome matters of fact, Whitehead is the only one who, instead of taking the path of critique and directing his attention *away* from facts to what makes them possible as Kant did; or adding something to their bare bones as Husserl did; or avoiding the fate of their domination, their *Gestell,* as much as possible as Heidegger did; tried to get *closer* to them or, more exactly, to see through them the reality that requested a new respectful realist attitude. No one is less a critic than Whitehead, in all the meanings of the word, and it's amusing to notice that the only pique he ever directed against someone else was against the other W., the one considered, wrongly in my view, as the greatest philosopher of the twentieth century, not W. as in Bush but W. as in Wittgenstein.

What set Whitehead completely apart and straight on our path is that he considered matters of fact to be a very poor rendering of what is given in experience and something that muddles entirely the question, What is there? with the question, How do we know it? as Isabelle Stengers has shown recently in a major book about Whitehead's philosophy.[27] Those who now mock his philosophy don't understand that they have resigned themselves to what he called the "bifurcation of nature." They have entirely forgotten what it would require if we were to take this incredible sentence seriously: "For natural philosophy everything perceived is in nature. We may not pick up and choose. For us the red glow of the sunset should be as much part of nature as are the molecules and electric waves by which men of science would explain the phenomenon" (*CN*, pp. 28–29).

All subsequent philosophies have done exactly the opposite: they have picked and chosen, and, worse, they have remained content with that limited choice. The solution to this bifurcation is not, as phenomenologists would have it, adding to the boring electric waves the rich lived world of the glowing sun. This would simply make the bifurcation greater. The solution or, rather, the adventure, according to Whitehead, is to dig much further into the realist attitude and to realize that matters of fact are totally implausible, unrealistic, unjustified definitions of what it is to deal with things:

> Thus matter represents the refusal to think away spatial and temporal characteristics and to arrive at the bare concept of an individual entity. It is this refusal which has caused the muddle *of importing the mere*

---

26. Alfred North Whitehead, *The Concept of Nature* (Cambridge, 1920), p. 29; hereafter abbreviated *CN.*

27. See Isabelle Stengers, *Penser avec Whitehead: Une Libre et sauvage création de concepts* (Paris, 2002), a book which has the great advantage of taking seriously Whitehead's science as well as his theory of God.

procedure of thought into the fact of nature. The entity, bared of all characteristics except those of space and time, has acquired a physical status as the ultimate texture of nature; so that the course of nature is conceived as being merely the fortunes of matter in its adventure through space. [*CN*, p. 20]

It is not the case that there would exist solid matters of fact and that the next step would be for us to decide whether they will be used to explain something. It is not the case either that the other solution is to attack, criticize, expose, historicize those matters of fact, to show that they are made up, interpreted, flexible. It is not the case that we should rather flee out of them into the mind or add to them symbolic or cultural dimensions; the question is that matters of fact are a poor *proxy* of experience and of experimentation and, I would add, a confusing bundle of polemics, of epistemology, of modernist politics that can in no way claim to represent what is requested by a realist attitude.[28]

Whitehead is not an author known for keeping the reader wide awake, but I want to indicate at least the *direction* of the new critical attitude with which I wish to replace the tired routines of most social theories.

The solution lies, it seems to me, in this promising word *gathering* that Heidegger had introduced to account for the "thingness of the thing." Now, I know very well that Heidegger and Whitehead would have nothing to say to one another, and, yet, the word the latter used in *Process and Reality* to describe "actual occasions," his word for my matters of concern, is the word *societies*. It is also, by the way, the word used by Gabriel Tarde, the real founder of French sociology, to describe all sorts of entities. It is close enough to the word *association* that I have used all along to describe the objects of science and technology. Andrew Pickering would use the words "mangle of practice."[29] Whatever the words, what is presented here is an entirely different attitude than the critical one, not a flight into the conditions of possibility of a given matter of fact, not the addition of something more human that the inhumane matters of fact would have missed, but, rather, a multifarious inquiry launched with the tools of anthropology, philosophy, metaphysics, history, sociology to detect *how many participants* are gathered in a *thing* to make it exist and to maintain its existence. Objects are simply a gathering that has failed—a fact that has not been as-

---

28. That matters of fact represent now a rather rare and complicated historical rendering of experience has been made powerfully clear by many writers; see, for telling segments of this history, Christian Licoppe, *La Formation de la pratique scientifique: Le Discours de l'expérience en France et en Angleterre (1630–1820)* (Paris, 1996); Mary Poovey, *A History of the Modern Fact: Problems of Knowledge in the Sciences of Wealth and Society* (Chicago, 1999); Lorraine Daston and Katherine Park, *Wonders and the Order of Nature, 1150–1750* (New York, 1998); and *Picturing Science, Producing Art*, ed. Caroline A. Jones, Galison, and Amy Slaton (New York, 1998).

29. See Andrew Pickering, *The Mangle of Practice: Time, Agency, and Science* (Chicago, 1995).

sembled according to due process.[30] The stubbornness of matters of fact in the usual scenography of the rock-kicking objector—"It is there whether you like it or not"—is much like the stubbornness of political demonstrators: "the U.S., love it or leave it," that is, a very poor substitute for any sort of vibrant, articulate, sturdy, decent, long-term existence.[31] A gathering, that is, a thing, an issue, inside a Thing, an arena, can be very sturdy, too, on the condition that the number of its participants, its ingredients, nonhumans as well as humans, not be limited in advance.[32] It is entirely wrong to divide the collective, as I call it, into the sturdy matters of fact, on the one hand, and the dispensable crowds, on the other. Archimedes spoke for a whole tradition when he exclaimed: "Give me one fixed point and I will move the Earth," but am I not speaking for another, much less prestigious but maybe as respectable tradition, if I exclaim in turn "Give me one matter of concern and I will show you the whole earth and heavens that have to be gathered to hold it firmly in place"? For me it makes no sense to reserve the realist vocabulary for the first one only. The critic is not the one who debunks, but the one who assembles. The critic is not the one who lifts the rugs from under the feet of the naïve believers, but the one who offers the participants arenas in which to gather. The critic is not the one who alternates haphazardly between antifetishism and positivism like the drunk iconoclast drawn by Goya, but the one for whom, if something is constructed, then it means it is fragile and thus in great need of care and caution. I am aware that to get at the heart of this argument one would have to renew also what it means to be a constructivist, but I have said enough to indicate the direction of critique, not *away* but *toward* the gathering, the Thing.[33] Not westward, but, so to speak, eastward.[34]

The practical problem we face, if we try to go that new route, is to associate the word *criticism* with a whole set of new positive metaphors, gestures, attitudes, knee-jerk reactions, habits of thoughts. To begin with this

---

30. See Latour, *Politics of Nature: How to Bring the Sciences into Democracy,* trans. Porter (Cambridge, Mass., 2004).

31. See the marvelously funny rendering of the realist gesture in Malcolm Ashmore, Derek Edwards, and Jonathan Potter, "The Bottom Line: The Rhetoric of Reality Demonstrations," *Configurations* 2 (Winter 1994): 1–14.

32. This is the challenge of a new exhibition I am curating with Peter Weibel in Karlsruhe and that is supposed to take place in 2004 under the provisional title "Making Things Public." This exhibition will explore what *Iconoclash* had simply pointed at, namely, beyond the image wars.

33. This paper is a companion of another one: Latour, "The Promises of Constructivism," in *Chasing Technoscience: Matrix for Materiality,* ed. Don Ihde and Evan Selinger (Bloomington, Ind., 2003), pp. 27–46.

34. This is why, although I share all of the worries of Thomas de Zengotita, "Common Ground: Finding Our Way Back to the Enlightenment," *Harper's* 306 (Jan. 2003): 35–45, I think he is entirely mistaken in the *direction* of the move he proposes back to the future; to go back to the "natural" attitude is a sign of nostalgia.

new habit forming, I'd like to extract another definition of critique from the most unlikely source, namely, Allan Turing's original paper on thinking machines.[35] I have a good reason for that: here is the typical paper about formalism, here is the origin of one of the icons—to use a cliché of antifetishism—of the contemporary age, namely, the computer, and yet, if you read this paper, it is so baroque, so kitsch, it assembles such an astounding number of metaphors, beings, hypotheses, allusions, that there is no chance that it would be accepted nowadays by any journal. Even *Social Text* would reject it out of hand as another hoax! "Not again," they would certainly say, "once bitten, twice shy." Who would take a paper seriously that states somewhere after having spoken of Muslim women, punishment of boys, extrasensory perception: "In attempting to construct such machines we should not be irreverently usurping [God's] power of creating souls, any more than we are in the procreation of children: rather we are, in either case, instruments of His will providing mansions for the souls that He creates" ("*CM*," p. 443).

Lots of gods, always in machines. Remember how Bush eulogized the crew of the *Columbia* for reaching home in heaven, if not home on earth? Here Turing too cannot avoid mentioning God's creative power when talking of this most mastered machine, the computer that he has invented. That's precisely his point. The computer is in for many surprises; you get out of it much more than you put into it. In the most dramatic way, Turing's paper demonstrates, once again, that all objects are born things, all matters of fact require, in order to exist, a bewildering variety of matters of concern.[36] The surprising result is that we don't master what we, ourselves, have fabricated, the object of this definition of critique:[37]

---

35. See A.M. Turing, "Computing Machinery and Intelligence," *Mind* 59 (Oct. 1950): 433–60; hereafter abbreviated "CM." See also what Powers in *Galatea 2.2* (New York, 1995) did with this paper; this is critique in the most generous sense of the word. For the context of this paper, see Andrew Hodges, *Alan Turing: The Enigma* (New York, 1983).

36. A nonformalist definition of formalism has been proposed by Brian Rotman, *Ad Infinitum: The Ghost in Turing's Machine: Taking God out of Mathematics and Putting the Body Back In* (Stanford, Calif., 1993).

37. Since Turing can be taken as the first and best programmer, those who believe in defining machines by inputs and outputs should meditate his confession:

> Machines take me by surprise with great frequency. This is largely because I do not do sufficient calculation to decide what to expect them to do, or rather because, although I do a calculation, I do it in a hurried, slipshod fashion, taking risks. Perhaps I say to myself, "I suppose the voltage here ought to be the same as there: anyway let's assume it is." Naturally I am often wrong, and the result is a surprise for me for by the time the experiment is done these assumptions have been forgotten. These admissions lay me open to lectures on the subject of my vicious ways, but do not throw any doubt on my credibility when I testify to the surprises I experience. ["CM," pp. 450–51]

On this nonformalist definition of computers, see Brian Cantwell Smith, *On the Origin of Objects* (Cambridge, Mass., 1997).

Let us return for a moment to Lady Lovelace's objection, which stated that the machine can only do what we tell it to do. One could say that a man can "inject" an idea into the machine, and that it will respond to a certain extent and then drop into quiescence, like a piano string struck by a hammer. Another simile would be an atomic pile of less than critical size: an injected idea is to correspond to a neutron entering the pile from without. Each such neutron will cause a certain disturbance which eventually dies away. If, however, the size of the pile is sufficiently increased, the disturbance caused by such an incoming neutron will very likely go on and on increasing until the whole pile is destroyed. Is there a corresponding phenomenon for minds, and is there one for machines? There does seem to be one for the human mind. The majority of them seem to be "sub-critical," *i.e.* to correspond in this analogy to piles of sub-critical size. An idea presented to such a mind will on average give rise to less than one idea in reply. A smallish proportion are super-critical. An idea presented to such a mind may give rise to a whole "theory" consisting of secondary, tertiary and more remote ideas. Animals' minds seem to be very definitely sub-critical. Adhering to this analogy we ask, "Can a machine be made to be super-critical?" ["CM," p. 454]

We all know subcritical minds, that's for sure! What would critique do if it could be associated with *more*, not with *less*, with *multiplication*, not *subtraction*. Critical theory died away long ago; can we become critical again, in the sense here offered by Turing? That is, generating more ideas than we have received, inheriting from a prestigious critical tradition but not letting it die away, or "dropping into quiescence" like a piano no longer struck. This would require that all entities, including computers, cease to be objects defined simply by their inputs and outputs and become again things, mediating, assembling, gathering many more folds than the "united four." If this were possible then we could let the critics come ever closer to the matters of concern we cherish, and then at last we could tell them: "Yes, please, touch them, explain them, deploy them." Then we would have gone for good beyond iconoclasm.

Fetishizing the Glove in Renaissance Europe

Peter Stallybrass and Ann Rosalind Jones

In a series of articles, William Pietz has argued that

> the fetish . . . as a novel object not proper to any prior discrete soci-
> ety, originated in the cross-cultural spaces of the coast of West Africa
> during the sixteenth and seventeenth centuries.[1]

Focusing on Portuguese traders in the areas inhabited by the Akan
people, Pietz traces the word *fetish* to the pidgin *Fetisso*, which can in turn
be traced to the Portuguese *feitiço*, meaning magical practice or witchcraft. The fetish, Pietz shows, came into being above all as a term of religious abuse, by which Europeans rejected objects that were attributed
with animating powers. African amulets, for instance, used for protection
against disease or sorcery, were demonized by Portuguese Catholics, who

Unless otherwise indicated, all translations are our own.

1. William Pietz, "The Problem of the Fetish, I," *Res* 9 (Spring 1985): 5. See also Pietz,
"The Problem of the Fetish, II," *Res* 13 (Spring 1987): 23–45 and "The Problem of the
Fetish, IIIa: Bosman's Guinea and the Enlightenment Theory of Fetishism," *Res* 16 (Autumn
1988): 105–23. See also Pietz, "Fetishism and Materialism: The Limits of Theory in Marx,"
in *Fetishism as Cultural Discourse*, ed. Emily Apter and Pietz (Ithaca, N.Y., 1993), pp. 119–51.
We have analyzed the concept of the fetish in the Renaissance more fully elsewhere; see
Ann Rosalind Jones and Peter Stallybrass, *Renaissance Clothing and the Materials of Memory*
(Cambridge, 2000) and "Fetishisms and Renaissances," in *Historicism, Psychoanalysis, and
Early Modern Culture*, ed. Carla Mazzio and Douglas Trevor (New York, 2000), pp. 20–35.

contrasted their "false" spiritual powers to the "true" spiritual powers of relics, indulgences, and the sacrament. In the seventeenth century, Dutch Protestants attacked Akan fetishes as idols, explicitly conflating these animated objects with the supposed idolatry of European Catholics. Through the attribution of belief in animated objects to demonized idolaters—whether Akan or Catholic—the proper European Protestant was imagined, by antithesis, as a subject unconstrained by the constituting power of objects.

Constituted as such "proper" subjects, we know that we should not treat people like things. Objectification is conceptualized from this perspective as the incapacitating of the subject. But what we all presume to know is historically specific. What did it mean in the Renaissance to be a monarch or an aristocrat if not to be powerfully objectified as land, both imagined and material? Shakespeare's Bolingbroke (the name of the castle where he was born) can scarcely sustain his name as Duke of Lancaster without the things that support that name. The king's favorites, he claims, have

> Dispark'd my Parkes, and fell'd my Forrest Woods;
> From mine owne Windowes torne my Household Coat,
> Raz'd out my Impresse, leauing me no signe,
> Saue mens opinions, and my liuing blood,
> To shew the World I am a Gentleman.[2]

The value of "mens opinion" and "my liuing blood" (that is, the internalized sap of the family tree) is inadequate without the value of the actual trees of parks and forests that constitute Lancaster. Name is constituted by things. Take away the things and the name disappears or is emptied

2. William Shakespeare, *The Life and Death of Richard the Second*, in *The First Folio of Shakespeare: The Norton Facsimile*, ed. Charlton Hinman (New York, 1968), 3.1.23–7 (TLN 1335–9, p. 355). Unless otherwise noted, all citations from Shakespeare are to this edition; references to act, scene, and line numbers are to *The Riverside Shakespeare*, ed. G. Blakemore Evans (Boston, 1974), followed by the through line numbers (TLN) of Hinman's *First Folio*.

Peter Stallybrass is Annenberg Professor of Humanities at the University of Pennsylvania. He is the author of, most recently, *O Casaco de Marx (Marx's Coat)* (1999) and *Renaissance Clothing and the Materials of Memory* (2000), written with Ann Rosalind Jones. **Ann Rosalind Jones** is Esther Cloudman Dunn Professor of Comparative Literature at Smith College and author of *Currency of Eros: Women's Love Lyric in Europe, 1540–1620* (1990) and coeditor and translator, with Margaret F. Rosenthal, of *The Poems and Selected Letters of Veronica Franco* (1998).

out. Without his retainers, King Lear is merely Lear, no longer the royal we but the I of the private—that is, deprived—subject.[3]

To think of objectification as a form of power is a distinctively pre-capitalist way of thinking about the relations between person and thing. When we rewrite a precapitalist ideology of objectification in terms of the emergent subject, we get the past absolutely wrong. It is not the capitalist present that has suddenly started to obsess about the value of things. On the contrary, capitalist cultures are often squeamish about value, attempting to separate cultural value from economics, persons from things, subjects from objects, the priceless (us) from the valueless (the detachable world).

But detachable parts—rings, jewels, gloves, for instance—continued to trouble the conceptual opposition of person and thing, even as the concept of the fetish was forged to formalize such an opposition. Gloves, which we focus upon in this essay, not only materialized status, "gentling" the hand of the gentry, but also functioned as what Pietz calls "external organs of the body," organs that could be transferred from beloved to lover, from monarch to subject, from master to servant.[4] They thus materialized the power of people to be condensed and absorbed into things and of things to become persons.

As "external organs," gloves could be preserved and transmitted as heirlooms. Gloves were among the material forms in which the English monarchy stored its supposed virtues. In 1655, Thomas Fuller wrote that

> posterity conceived so great an opinion of King *Edward*'s piety, that his Cloaths were deposited amongst the *Regalia,* and solemnly worn by our *English* Kings on their Coronation, never counting themselves so fine, as when invested with his Robes. . . . It was to mind our Kings, when habited with his Cloaths, to be cloathed with the habit of his vertuous Endowments: as when putting on the Gloves of this Confessour, their Hands ought to be like his, in moderate taking of Taxes from their Subjects.[5]

The monarch can be minded by putting on the clothes of the "pious" Edward. The inward habit of virtue is first materialized through the outward habit of robes and gloves.

Clothing is here imagined as antithetical to fashion—that is, to the rapid shifting of different shapes and styles. The monarch will be molded

---

3. For a brilliant account of the function of Lear's "train" in the formation of his royal identity, see Margreta de Grazia, "The Ideology of Superfluous Things: *King Lear* as Period Piece," in *Subject and Object in Renaissance Culture,* ed. de Grazia, Maureen Quilligan, and Stallybrass (Cambridge, 1996), pp. 17–42.

4. Pietz, "The Problem of the Fetish, I," p. 10.

5. Thomas Fuller, *The Church History of Britain,* 6 vols. (Oxford, 1845), 1:384.

to his proper function visually and tactilely through what he wears, through his habits. As Daniel Defert argues:

> To confuse the meaning of habit *[l'habit]* in the sixteenth century with that of fashion *[la mode]* is an anachronistic illusion. Habit has the original connotation of *habitus,* which implies work upon the body. The serious expression of a judge or the reticence of a virgin, the hairlessness or the tattoos of an Indian, body piercing or asceticism, are all part of the *habit-habitus* that defines the mode of being of established groups and not the free choice of individuals.[6]

Clothing, as habit, implies a way of life. This material shaping is clearest in relation to the habits that monks wore. As Defert notes:

> No sixteenth-century French dictionary defines *[habitus monasticus]* simply as "garment." The *habitus monasticus* designates the rule, the way of life, from which the garment cannot be disassociated: *l'habit-habitus* makes the monk. . . . The garment is a rule of conduct and the memory of this rule for the wearer as well as for others.[7]

If Hamlet imagines habit or custom as a "monster," it is because of its power to transform. Attempting to persuade his mother to abstain from sleeping with Claudius, Hamlet says:

> Assume a vertue if you haue it not,
> That monster custome . . .
>   . . . is angel yet in this
> That to the vse of actions faire and good,
> He likewise giues a frock or Liuery
> That aptly is put on . . .
> For vse almost can change the stamp of nature.[8]

What we would now describe as an ethical state is imagined by Hamlet as a bodily practice—virtue, like clothing, can be "put on." Repeated wearing acts as an inscription upon the body that can work with or against alternative forms of inscription (here, "the stamp of nature").

The monarch's glove continued to be treated as a form of inscription as well as an extension of the monarch's hand throughout the seven-

6. Daniel Defert, "Un Genre ethnographique profane au XVIe: Les Livres d'habits (Essai d'ethno-iconographie)," in *Histoires de l'anthropologie (XVIe–XIXe siècles),* ed. Britta Rupp-Eisenreich (Paris, 1984), p. 27.

7. Ibid., p. 28.

8. Shakespeare, *The Tragicall Historie of Hamlet, Prince of Denmarke,* in *The Three-Text Hamlet: Parallel Texts of the First and Second Quartos and First Folio,* ed. Paul Bertram and Bernice W. Kliman (New York, 1991), 2d quarto, 3.4.160–68, p. 174.

teenth century. Indeed, new ritual aspects of monarchy were elaborated, particularly in response to the execution of Charles I, but they had to compete against the "demystifying" discourses of idolatry and the fetish. Fuller's records of Edward the Confessor's coronation regalia is in fact a nostalgic lament for what has been lost: "But now *Edward's Staffe* is broken, *Chair* overturned, *Cloaths* rent, and *Crown* melted; our present Age esteeming them the reliques of Superstition."[9] If the touch of the royal hand continued to be stored up in the material form of a glove, the glove was increasingly a museum piece that would no longer have the power to cure scrofula or to have other magical effects.[10] A pair of Edward the Confessor's gloves (in this case, knitted gloves) found their way into the Tradescant cabinet of wonders in Oxford, along with the gloves of Henry VIII and the "silke knit-gloves" of Anne Boleyn.[11] But as the cabinet of wonders was transformed into the Ashmolean Museum, such gloves were stripped of their ability to transform their recipient with the power of the absent hand.

Of course, gloves were not necessarily connected to specific bodies, nor did they necessarily become powerful material agents. In the Renaissance as today there were many practical functions for gloves, whether to protect hands from heat and cold or from the rigors of labor. Gloves were functional, a protection for servants' hands. As useful accessories, they were absorbed into the labor process. But the gloves of aristocrats and gentry—male and female alike—usually operated to display hands to which such labor was alien. The function of these gloves—for both men and women—was to occupy the hands in the manu-facture of the immaterial. They thus materialize a paradox: they draw attention to the hands while making the hands useless, or useful only for putting on or taking off a glove, or for holding gloves or handkerchiefs or fans or flowers.

The play of hands and gloves, though, was an aspect of the ritual exchanges of social life by no means confined to the elite. Gloves, like hands, were given and taken as the embodied form of social acts—the bonding of friend to friend, of lover to lover.[12] In his "Guide to the Tongues" (1617), John Minsheu derives "glove" from "gift-love" and from the Low Dutch "gheloove," meaning faithfulness.[13] Given to guests at weddings by anyone who could afford to give them, gloves extended the prosthetic

9. Fuller, *The Church History of Britain,* 1:384.

10. On the power of the royal touch to cure scrofula, see Marc Bloch, *Les Rois thaumaturges* (Strasbourg, 1924), and Keith Thomas, *Religion and the Decline of Magic* (Harmondsworth, 1973), pp. 227–44.

11. John Tradescant, *Musaeum Tradescantianum: Or, a Collection of Rarities* (London, 1657), p. 49.

12. On the handshake, see Herman Roodenburg, "The 'Hand of Friendship': Shaking Hands and Other Gestures in the Dutch Republic," in *A Cultural History of Gesture,* ed. Jan Bremmer and Roodenburg (Cambridge, 1991), pp. 152–89.

13. John Minsheu, "Guide to the Tongues," *Ductor in Linguas* (London, 1617), p. 216.

hand of affection.[14] They reached out to pair the guests to the gift-givers and to each other. In 1560, Henry Machyn recorded in his diary that a vintner "gayff a C payre of glovys" to the guests at his wedding.[15] It's perhaps worth noting that such mass gifts had their problems; how often did the gloves fit? In Thomas Dekker's *Satiromastix* (1602), a gentlewoman claims that "fiue or sixe payre of the white innocent wedding gloues, did in my sight choose rather to be torne in peeces than to be drawne on."[16] The materialization of social connection through gloves was always threatened by the contingency of things: the gloves might not fit; they were easily lost (like handkerchiefs); they wore out and got stained.

But the glove—particularly, as we argue, the single glove—conjured up the hand as the corporeal site of agency for Aristotle, Galen, and their followers.[17] Hand and glove are, as the proverb still suggests, intimately related, even inseparable. In such a conjoining, it no longer seems to matter which is the glove and which the hand. Each is embraced and animated by the other. On the other hand, gloves are dropped, lost, discarded. If a person could "be laid at one side like a paire of old shooes," one could equally be thrown aside like a cast-off glove.[18] And if the hand is the site of agency, the *pairing* of hands, as of gloves, is already problematic. The expression "on the one hand . . . on the other hand" unpairs the human body, setting the right hand against the left, the left against the right. This unpairing of the hands is staged again and again in Renaissance portraits where the sitter is posed with one glove on, one off. If one hand ("on the one hand") is inseparable from its glove, the other hand ("on the other hand") is naked, the glove absent, or resting on a table, or held loosely in the hand.

Unpairing the Hands

In "Restitutions of the Truth in Pointing," Derrida conducts a sustained meditation on pairing and unpairing—the pairing and unpairing of a painting and what it represents, of a painting and its titles, of foot

14. On gloves at weddings, see David R. Smith, *Masks of Wedlock: Seventeenth-Century Dutch Marriage Portraiture* (Ann Arbor, Mich., 1982), pp. 78–79, and M. Channing Linthicum, *Costume in the Drama of Shakespeare and His Contemporaries* (Oxford, 1936), pp. 267–68.

15. Quoted in Linthicum, *Costume in the Drama of Shakespeare and His Contemporaries*, p. 268.

16. Thomas Dekker, *Satiromastix*, in *The Dramatic Works of Thomas Dekker*, ed. Fredson Bowers, 4 vols. (Cambridge, 1962), 1:1.1.31–33, p. 312.

17. See Katherine Rowe, "'God's Handy Worke': Divine Complicity and the Anatomist's Touch," in *The Body in Parts: Fantasies of Corporeality in Early Modern Europe*, ed. David Hillman and Mazzio (New York, 1997), pp. 284–309.

18. Dekker, *The Shoemakers' Holiday*, in *The Dramatic Works of Thomas Dekker*, 1:1.1.142–43, p. 27.

and shoe, of one shoe and its "pair."[19] Derrida's speculations revolve around Van Gogh's *Old Shoes with Laces* and Heidegger's and Schapiro's commentaries on Van Gogh. As Derrida notes:

> A pair of shoes is more easily treated as a *utility* than a single shoe or two shoes which aren't a pair. The pair inhibits, at least, if it does not prevent, the "fetishizing" movement; it rivets things to use, to "normal" use. . . . It is perhaps in order to exclude the question of a certain uselessness, or of a so-called perverse usage, that Heidegger and Schapiro denied themselves the slightest doubt as to the parity of pairedness of these two shoes. They bound them together in order to bind them to the law of normal usage.[20]

Shoes and gloves are not, of course, a pair themselves. They are both put on and taken off; they both shape and are reshaped by the body; they both take in the oils and smells of the body (although the smell of the hand is not the same as the smell of the foot, and aristocratic—and even middle-class—gloves in the Renaissance were frequently perfumed any-way).[21] But if your feet are accustomed to shoes, it will be painful to walk barefoot on rough ground or gravel. The shoe's remolding of the foot is not the same as the glove's remolding of the hand. If you walk with one shoe on and one shoe off, you limp. You are even more likely to "limp" with both gloves on. Wearing a pair of gloves makes it more difficult to blow your nose, to find change in your pocket or to sort out the right change, to retie your shoelaces, to do up buttons (particularly if the gloves are thick or if you're wearing mittens).

The unpairing of gloves (the taking off of one to perform an action) is often a functional activity. But in Renaissance portraiture the hands are unpaired again and again as sitters are depicted with one glove on, the other off. And the hands are rarely doing anything. In this aristocratic iconography, both the uselessness of the hands and their differences from each other are immediately striking. In 1570, for instance, Antonio Mor depicted Anne of Austria with her white left hand resting on a chair (fig. 1). Her right hand is in a dark glove, even darker by contrast to the bright white handkerchief that she holds, as well as to her other naked hand. Two decades earlier, Mor had depicted Maria of Austria with her white left hand resting upon a table; on her right hand is a dark brown leather glove, slashed at the lower joints of the fingers to show her rings (fig. 2).

19. See Jacques Derrida, *The Truth in Painting,* trans. Geoff Bennington and Ian McLeod (Chicago, 1987).

20. Ibid., pp. 332–33.

21. Gervase Markham gives recipes for perfuming gloves in his *The English Housewife,* ed. Michael R. Best (1615; Kingston, Ont., 1986), p. 132. See also Tomaso Garzoni, *La piazza universale di tutte le professioni del mondo* (Venice, 1616), p. 281.

Fig. 1.—Antonio Mor, *Ann of Austria,
Queen of Spain* (1570). Kunsthistorisches
Museum, Vienna. From Janet Arnold, *Queen
Elizabeth's Wardrobe Unlock'd* (Leeds, 1988),
p. 126.

Fig. 2.—Antonio Mor, *Maria of
Austria, Wife of Emperor Maximilian II*
(1551) Museo del Prado. From Arnold,
Queen Elizabeth's Wardrobe Unlock'd, p.
125.

Here, the proverbial hand-in-glove takes on a new meaning: the gloved
hand holds the other glove like a third, crushed hand. But how are we to
read this detail? Are Mor's queens about to give away, or have they already
given away, their unworn glove as a favor? Or are they emphasizing the
dazzling whiteness of the hand that can be kissed, in contrast to the other
hidden and darkened hand?

Renaissance courts staged a mathematics of the hand and glove, a
physical meditation on the relations between one, two, three, and four.
But it is through the odd numbers—one and three—that the fetish most
powerfully emerges, for the reason that Derrida suggests. Unpaired, the
gloves can no longer be seen as functional.

One of the most powerful and mysterious Renaissance portraits is
Titian's *Man with a Ripped Glove* (c. 1520–23) (figs. 3 and 4). In the portrait,
a somber young man, his black doublet open to reveal a white shirt, stares
to the viewer's right. His right hand is naked, held horizontally across his
belly; the index finger, with a signet ring, points. But this masterful hand
contrasts strikingly to the gloved left hand, projecting forward to the

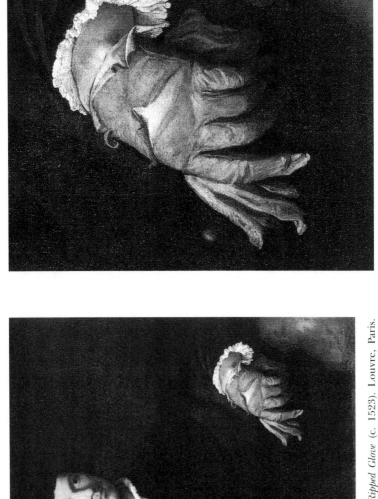

FIG. 3.—Titian, *Man with a Ripped Glove* (c. 1523). Louvre, Paris. From Paul Hills, *Venetian Colour: Marble, Mosaic, Painting, and Glass 1250–1550* (New Haven, Conn., 1999), p. 193.

FIG. 4.—Titian, *Man with a Ripped Glove*. Detail of fig. 3.

viewer. The leather glove that he wears is folded back in a torn, ragged line at the cuff, while the back of the glove is torn in two different directions. Is it his hand or the glove's lining that is revealed through the torn back? Where does the skin of animal end and the skin of human begin? It is hard to tell. The index finger of the glove extends beyond the finger within to a flattened, detumescent end. Equally disturbing is the empty, ghostly glove that the gloved hand holds: a glove no longer structured by flesh and bone, collapsed in on itself, the fingers flattened and curling at the ends. The gloves are a pair. But the pair of gloves vividly materializes the unpairing of the hands, one hand naked and powerful, the other draped in aristocratic ease but marked by what looks like a violent assault. It is as if the marks of identity have been transferred from the anonymous and unwrinkled face to the torn glove that he wears, and that gives the painting one of its modern titles.

Despite the strangeness of the torn glove (materializing the thrift of the wearer? or the torn heart of a lover?), it is not unique. Indeed, its style, color, and even its tear were fashionable. In *Man in a Red Cap* (c. 1515), Titian had already painted a sitter wearing a skintight, gray glove on his left hand, with which he grasps the hilt of a sword. And, again, the glove is ripped on the back. But in the earlier painting, the ripped glove has to compete for attention with the gleaming hilt of the sword, the luxurious spotted fur, and the red cap of the sitter. In the later portrait, with the exception of the small jewel round the sitter's neck and the ring on his finger, the colors are reduced to the colors of the flesh and the black and white of the clothing.

The wrinkles and rips of the glove that the sitter in *Man with a Ripped Glove* wears transfer the ravages of age and violence from the enigmatic young man to the "thing" that he wears. The light that catches both the gloved hand and the ghostly "hand" that it holds highlights the irregularities of texture and form as the viewer passes from naked hand to gloved hand to empty glove. The painting stages the unpairing of hands. One hand naked, one gloved. The gloved hand is both protected and exposed, paired with the empty glove, but only so as to make more striking the emptying out of the bodily form that has already begun in the tip of the index finger of the worn glove.

If Titian's portrait remains unreadable, it nevertheless points to the complex attention to the hands that controlled the most public of Renaissance courtly rituals. At the center of the ceremony of Elizabeth I's court, for instance, was the kissing of her hand. In an anonymous watercolor from the 1570s, Elizabeth is depicted in the Presence Chamber, receiving two Dutch ambassadors. They kneel in front of her as she extends her right hand for them to kiss. Similarly, Paul Hentzner wrote of his visit to Greenwich: "While we were there, William Slawata, a Bohemian Baron, had letters to present to [Elizabeth]; and she, after pulling off her glove, gave him her right hand to kiss, sparkling with rings and jewels, a mark

of particular Favour."²² On other occasions, however, the queen wore
rings on top of her gloves, presumably not being disposed to dispense
such marks of favor. Thomas Platter described her in 1599 as wearing "elegant gloves over which were drawn costly rings."²³ Despite the elegance
of the gloves, they here remain a barrier between suitor and monarch.
The naked hand is the mark of Elizabeth's favor, her glove a mark of her
distance and unapproachability.

Yet there is nothing inevitable about this privileging of the naked
hand over the gloved hand or even of the hand itself over the glove. If
the hand could be kissed, it could also be withdrawn, whereas the favor
of a glove could become an enduring materialization of the monarch's
love. Indeed, the giving away of a glove was crucial to Elizabeth's transformation of court politics into courtly romance at the annual tournaments
held to celebrate her accession. The material memory of Elizabeth's favor
has been preserved in two cabinet miniatures by Nicholas Hilliard. The
first is a portrait of George Clifford, third Earl of Cumberland (fig. 5),
who had appeared regularly at tilts for Elizabeth beginning in 1590, the
year in which he became her official champion, undertaking to defend
the superiority of her beauty and virtue against all comers. At Whitehall
in the same year, Cumberland assumed the role of the Knight of Pen-
dragon Castle, wearing a white surcoat over his armor and white feathers
on his helmet in honor of his Virgin Queen. A similar helmet and plumes
are visible at the lower right in the Hilliard painting, while his small tour-
nament impresa shield hangs on the tree behind him. On the ground to
either side of him are his discarded gauntlets. But Clifford's paired pieces
of armor are set off against the single dark glove that he wears on his hat.
The glove is folded in half, with the fold set just above his forehead; the
embroidered cuff is turned forward, the five fingers standing outlined
against the upturned crown of the hat. A large jewel sparkles on the cuff
of the glove. Elizabeth is materialized in the painting not as an abstract
presence but as the giver of a specific glove—a glove now extravagantly
unmatched from its mate, turned into the favor that transforms Cumberland into a favorite.

Five years after Cumberland's appointment as the queen's champion,
at the Accession Day tilt in November 1595, Rowland White described
Elizabeth's gift of a glove to Robert Devereux. In a letter to Robert Sidney,
White gave an account of the elaborate masque of Love and Self-love that
Essex had requested Francis Bacon compose for him. As Essex's page
entered the tiltyard with a message for Elizabeth, she gave him one of
her gloves; he took it to Essex, who added it to his costume of red and
white, the colors of love. In a painting of about the same size as the portrait of Cumberland, Hilliard shows this second champion of the queen

22. Quoted in Janet Arnold, *Queen Elizabeth's Wardrobe Unlock'd* (Leeds, 1988), p. 11.
23. Ibid., p. 11.

Fig. 5.—Nicholas Hilliard, *George Clifford, 3rd Earl of Cumberland* (c. 1590). National Maritime Museum, Greenwich. Taken from *Dynasties: Painting in Tudor and Jacobean England, 1530–1630*, ed. Karen Hearn (London, 1995), p. 126.

also wearing a glove as a favor.[24] It is not worn on his hat but tied with a gleaming, broad, gold-embroidered silver ribbon to his arm. The glove has a black hand, or body, and a brown-gold cuff. It may well be that the painting commemorates the specific tilt in 1595 and the gift of the glove. The portrait gives us another style of displaying the glove as a token of love: worn upon the armor, it marks the lover's arms as arms transformed by the beloved. Here, the material memorials of favor translate politics into a public declaration of love.

But if such material memorials made present an absent beloved, they could also threaten the autonomy of their wearer. In Shakespeare's *Troilus*

24. See Roy Strong, *The English Renaissance Miniature* (New York, 1983), pp. 104–6.

and Cressida, Cressida gives Troilus her glove while he gives her his sleeve. Both objects are imagined as material hauntings, animated by the separated partner. Cressida, speaking to Troilus's sleeve, says

> O prettie, prettie pledge;
> Thy Maister now lies thinking on his bed
> Of thee and me, and sighes, and takes my Gloue,
> And giues memoriall daintie kisses to it;
> As I kisse thee.[25]

The single glove carries enough of Cressida with it so that, in its separation from her, it can conjure up her presence. The second skin of her glove is transformed into her own skin, taken to bed by Troilus and kissed. The power of the fetish emerges through an act of separation, but that separation is haunted by the possibility of further separations, further exchanges. If the fetish keeps the absent beloved present to the lover, it also potentially gives a part of the lover away. Troilus, in the form of his sleeve, can be worn by Cressida, but the sleeve can also be taken and worn by Diomedes. In taking the sleeve from Cressida, Diomedes takes not only Troilus away from Cressida but Cressida away from herself. As Cressida says, "he that takes that, rakes my heart withall."[26] Unpaired, the glove and the sleeve circulate, unpairing Troilus and Cressida, re-pairing Cressida and Diomedes.

In a sharply misogynist scene in Beaumont and Fletcher's *The Scornful Lady* (1616), Welford, a young man about town, specifically remarks on the problematic value of the unpaired glove as the site of the emergence of fetishism and of the loss of use-value. Abigail, a middle-aged woman attracted to Welford, *"drops her Glove,"* as the stage direction tells us. But, despising Abigail, Welford scorns the power of her unpaired glove:

> What hidden vertue is there in this glove, that you would have me weare it? Is't good against sore eyes, or wil it charme the toothake? Or these red tops, beeing steept in white wine soluble, wil't kill the itch? or h'as it so conceald a providence to keepe my hand from bonds? If it have none of these, and proove no more but a bare glove of halfe a crowne a payre, twill bee but halfe a courtesie, I weare two alwaies: faith let's draw cuts, one will doe me no pleasure.[27]

Unpaired, the single glove that Welford picks up will pair him to Abigail, calling out to its other half, which Abigail retains. As a pair, though, the

25. Shakespeare, *Troilus and Cressida,* 5.2.77–81 (TLN 3063–7, p. 611).

26. Ibid., 5.2.82 (TLN 3069, p. 611). The text of the first quarto reads "takes my heart withall."

27. Francis Beaumont and John Fletcher, *The Scornful Lady,* in *The Dramatic Works in the Beaumont and Fletcher Canon,* ed. Bowers et al., 10 vols. (Cambridge, 1970), 2:3.1.17–24, p. 493.

gloves lose any imagined power. They have an unmagical function and an unmagical price—"half a crowne a payre."

At the same time, Welford crudely spells out the sexual implications of a single glove. As a pair, the gloves recall hands. Single, the glove becomes a vagina. Women, he claims, "love this whorson doing so directly, that that they wil not sticke to make their very skinnes Bawdes to their flesh."[28] The skin is here the glove, the flesh is Abigail. But the skin of the glove is imagined both as a displacement of Abigail and as an undesired foretaste of her body.

The single glove, materializing a woman's body, wavers in the Renaissance discourse of the glove between the priceless and the valueless. The glove as a female body, used and discarded, figures in a story by Arthur Wilson published in 1653 in his *History of Great Britain, Being the Life and Reign of King James I*. Wilson claims that the young Henry, Prince of Wales, was rumored to be having a flirtation with Frances Howard. Henry supposedly lost interest in Howard when he found that her favors inclined to the Earl of Rochester. Wilson claims, "dancing one day among the *Ladies*, her Glove falling down, it was taken up, and presented to [Prince Henry], by one that thought he did him an acceptable *service;* but the Prince refused to receive it, saying publickly, He would not have it, it is *stretcht* by another."[29] The glove is animated by a human presence, but the human presence is reduced to an inanimate part, a part that men can appropriate and discard as they choose. It is in this vein that Lafew in *All's Well That Ends Well* sneers at Diana: "This womans an easie gloue my Lord, she goes off and on at pleasure."[30] The circulation of glove from hand to hand is transformed from the circulation of the beloved's favor to the circulation of her body. In such stories, the detachability of the glove suggests not the difference between thing and person but the resemblance between them.

In Thomas Middleton and William Rowley's *The Changeling* (1623), the sexual implications of the circulation of a glove as favor and as curse are complexly elaborated. At the end of the first scene, Beatrice-Joanna, perhaps in an attempt to show her favor to the newly arrived Alsemero, drops her glove. But it is her father who notices the dropped glove, and Deflores, a man she loathes, picks it up. Insofar as the single glove condenses Beatrice-Joanna's own body, Deflores handles her when he handles her glove. Beatrice-Joanna remedies the situation by casting away her other glove. Re-paired, the single dropped glove loses its status as fetish. But in re-pairing the gloves as Deflores's possession, Beatrice-Joanna animates them as material curse. On Deflores's hands, she wishes that they will be a physical reminder of her hatred for him, eating his

28. Ibid., 2:3.1.6–7, p. 493.

29. Arthur Wilson, *The History of Great Britain, Being the Life and Reign of King James I* (London, 1653), p. 56.

30. Shakespeare, *All's Well That Ends Well*, 5.3.277–78 (TLN 3009–10, p. 271).

skin like poison, so that when he takes them off, he will strip off his own skin:

> BEA. Mischief on your officious forwardness,
> Who bade you stoop? they touch my hand no more:
> There, for t'other's sake I part with this,
>   [She takes off the other glove and casts it down.]
> Take 'em and draw thine own skin off with 'em.[31]

This "favour," as Deflores notes, comes "with a mischief." Beatrice-Joanna would, as he puts it, rather wear his skinned body as a pair of dancing pumps than that "I should thrust my fingers/ Into her sockets here" (*C*, 1.1.233–34). But the fact that he *can* thrust his fingers into her prosthetic body, the glove, materializes what the play will enact: Deflores, the deflowerer, will "haunt her still;/ Though I get nothing else, I'll have my will" (*C*, 1.1.231–2). Indeed, he already haunts her by inserting his fingers into the skin she has worn.

These stagings of the glove as fetish seem at first all too predictable in a post-Freudian age. The woman is materialized as stretchable skin, the man as phallic finger. Yet Deflores reminds us that the relation between inside and outside, penetrator and penetrated, was anything but obvious in the Renaissance. In the courtly paradigms of heterosexual love, it was the woman who shot Cupid's arrows from her eyes and who pierced the man; it was her image that penetrated his heart and impressed itself upon him; she was the hunter, he the hunted. Deflores conjures up this instability in the gendering of male lover and female beloved by imagining his own skin turned into shoes that Beatrice–Joanna will stretch and wear.

In the Renaissance, the obsession is less that men have penises and women don't. It is, rather, that men and women alike have tongues, have mouths, have feet.[32] Men and women alike are constituted through presences and absences. And male lovers repeatedly imagine themselves as the hollow forms (necklaces, shoes, shifts, gloves) into which the female beloved enters.

It is this desire to be worn that the Spaniard Antonio Pérez, living in exile at Elizabeth's court, wittily elaborates in a letter to Lady Penelope Rich:

> I have been so troubled not to have at hand the dog's skin gloves your ladyship desires that, pending the time when they shall arrive,

---

31. Thomas Middleton and William Rowley, *The Changeling* (London, 1653), sig. B4, 1.1.227–30; hereafter abbreviated *C*.

32. For a fine account of the ambivalence of the tongue in the Renaissance, see Mazzio, "Sins of the Tongue," in *The Body in Parts: Fantasies of Corporeality in Early Modern Europe*, pp. 52–79.

I have resolved to sacrifice myself to your service and flay a piece of my own skin from the most tender part of my body, if such an un-couth carcass as mine can have any tender skin. To this length can love and the wish to serve a lady be carried that a man should flay himself to make gloves for his lady out of his own skin. But in my case this is nothing, for even my soul will skin itself for the person it loves. If my soul were visible like my body, the most pitiful soul would be seen and the most pitiful thing that has ever been looked upon.

The gloves, my Lady, are made of dog's skin, though they are mine; for I hold myself a dog and beg your ladyship to keep me in your service upon the honour and love of a faithful dog. —Your Ladyship's flayed dog.[33]

Pérez expands a trope that was already well established in classical antiq-uity. The lover, transformed into gloves, will always be near his beloved. When she wears him, he will be able to touch her. Intimacy is gained here not through potency but through diminution. Reduced to a malleable layer of skin, the lover can attain his desires, even if it is at the cost of be-coming a flayed dog.

Similarly, Romeo imagines a glove as achieving the intimacy that is denied him:

See how she leanes her cheeke vpon her hand.
O that I were a Gloue vpon that hand,
That I might touch that cheeke.[34]

As a thing, Romeo would experience the personal touch that is denied him as a person. As a glove, he would be pressed between Juliet's hand and cheek.

But in Renaissance portraiture, the worn glove often seems to be absorbed into the frozen life of the sitter, while the detached glove takes on a life of its own. Both the detachability and the animation are fore-grounded in English paintings of the early seventeenth century. Gloves—of males and females alike—are shown as if they are about to be dropped, suspended by a single finger. John de Critz paints Anne Vavasour (c. 1605) with one glove dangling by a finger from her left hand (fig. 6); Marcus Gheeraerts paints Mary Throckmorton, Lady Scudamore (c. 1614–15), with one naked hand partially concealed in her gown and her right, gloved hand dangling the other glove (fig. 7); and in Gheeraerts's depiction of Anne Hale, Mrs. Hoskins (1629), the left glove again dangles from the gloved right hand (fig. 8). At the same time, gloves no longer lie

---

33. Antonio Pérez, letter to Lady Penelope Rich, c. 1595, *A Spaniard in Elizabethan England: The Correspondence of Antonio Pérez's Exile*, ed. Gustav Ungerer, 2 vols. (London, 1974), 1:199.

34. Shakespeare, *Romeo and Juliet*, 2.2.23–25 (TLN 815–17, p. 675).

FIG. 8.—Marcus Gheeraerts the Younger, *Anne Hale, Mrs. Hoskins* (1629), private collection. From Strong, *The English Icon*, p. 276.

FIG. 7.—Marcus Gheeraerts the Younger, *Mary Throckmorton, Lady Scudamore* (1614–15). Tate Gallery, London. From Strong, *The English Icon*, p. 285.

FIG. 6.—John de Critz (?), *Anne Vavasour* (c. 1605). The Armourers and Brasiers of London. From Roy Strong, *The English Icon: Elizabethan and Jacobean Portraiture* (London, 1969), p. 265.

Fig. 9.—Marcus Gheeraerts the Younger (?), *Unknown Lady* (1618). Ferens Art Gallery, Hull. From Strong, *The English Icon*, p. 294.

Fig. 10.—Marcus Gheeraerts the Younger (?), *Unknown Lady.* Detail of fig. 9.

flat on tables or chairs, awaiting the animation of a wearer. They seem to fill out, haunted by having already been worn, or they lie hollowed out for the hands of another wearer or for the viewer's eyes. In Gheeraerts's *An Unknown Lady* (1618), the lady's animated gloves lie on the chair beside her, one half-turning its opening to the viewer (figs. 9 and 10); and in William Larkin's *Sir William Sidney* (c. 1611), Sidney wears one glove while the other lies on a table, its hollow opening again turned to the viewer (fig. 11). The gloves' fingers curl and twist like material ghosts, bewitched matter animated in contrast to the still life of the sitter.

At the very moment, then, that the demonized concept of the fetish is emerging to characterize the false animations of the idolater (Akan or Catholic), the unpaired glove takes on a new animation, as it is released from the "utility" of the pair. It is materialized as pledge or gage, absent lover or material memory, tactile presence or gaping hollow. If, as Derrida suggests, the fetish emerges when the unpaired object is no longer bound "to 'normal' use," the paradox of the single glove in the Renaissance is that it is the *norm*, at least within literary and artistic representations.[35] Materializing the unpairedness of the human body, the single glove was

35. Derrida, "Restitutions," pp. 332, 333.

FIG. 11.—William Larkin, *Sir William Sidney* (c. 1611). Viscount De L'Isle. From Strong, *The English Icon,* p. 322.

haunted by its absent other, whether that glove was with a lover or a messenger, whether it remained on the table beside the sitter or was held as a withered and spectral hand. Even as the hand was used as the sign of good faith in a proliferating range of commercial contracts, where questions of "true value" emerged with ever more urgent force, the single glove became a site where the thing was animated with a life that oscillated between the priceless and the worthless.

Modern Metamorphoses and Disgraceful Tales

Jonathan Lamb

> For I pray to be accepted as a dog without offence, which is best of all.
>
> —CHRISTOPHER SMART, *Jubilate Agno*

> Metamorphosis, that thickens our speech, dulls our feelings, turns us into beasts.
>
> —J. M. COETZEE, *Age of Iron*

A subgenre of fiction appeared in the eighteenth century, preponderantly in English, now known variously as 'it-narratives', 'object tales', and 'novels of circulation'. They were autobiographies of things and creatures—dogs, coins, and articles of dress were popular—and they exploited two of the century's dominant preoccupations, one with the ancient doctrine of metempsychosis and the other with the modern theory of sympathy. They imitated Ovid and cited his Pythagorean beliefs to show how metamorphoses between the human and nonhuman occur when confusion amidst the world of objects destabilizes personal identity or when personal identity contrives to extend itself beyond the limit of species. Sympathy was the measure of the 'kindness' of these changes, the degree to which the feelings of different creatures might be communicated and shared. It was monitored by sentimental novels, whose authors and readers shared a belief in the benevolent tendency of a *sensus communis,* and

I want to thank Michael Sayeau for suggesting the connection between *Disgrace* and the Lucy poems.

were not shy of including animals and artefacts within it. But some of
these it-narratives are surprisingly unkind to the extent that they show
sympathy to be a perverse outcome of a defensive or hostile relation between species and things. In these stories metamorphosis reveals one
mode of being at odds with another; and sometimes when they find their
voices, things and creatures use them not to admire and claim association
with human beings but to report matters that humiliate and disgrace
them, such as their avarice, delusion, cruelty, ugliness, and mortality. Alternatively, humans may be propelled towards another kind not for sentimental pleasure but as a refuge from loneliness or self-loathing.
Sometimes it is terror or hatred that supplies the energy for a change of
shape. The genealogy and descent of these intimate but troubled connections between the human and the nonhuman extend from the early modern period to the present day. By tracing the line backwards, I hope to
show more clearly how this form of narrative conflict developed in the
eighteenth century.

I begin with two pieces of fiction by an author peculiarly alert to this
legacy; and then in the terms he has handled it, I shall rehearse some of
the key moments in the history of its formation. In *The Lives of Animals*
and *Disgrace,* both published in 1999, J. M. Coetzee probes the limits of
sympathy.[1] In the first he adapted two Tanner lectures he had given at
Princeton University for a philosophical dialogue upon the rights of animals. The dialogue is managed by an older woman, Elizabeth Costello,
whose fear of death is correlated to her indignation at the injustices humans inflict on animals. The second is a novel about the shaming and
exile of a man who learns how to mitigate his isolation by working in
an animal refuge, where with quixotic punctilio he attends the death of
unwanted dogs, easing the disgrace of their end with certain pointless
formalities. In his review of these two books, Ian Hacking wrote of the
importance of sympathy for Coetzee who, he argued, 'speaks for a felt
sympathy between some people and at least some animals.'[2] He then
drew the moral he understood Coetzee had embedded in these stories:
'We shall have to broaden our sympathies in ways we do not well understand. . . . So I think we have to be Humean and first worry about how

1. See J. M. Coetzee, *The Lives of Animals* (Princeton, N.J., 1999); hereafter abbreviated
L. See also Coetzee, *Disgrace* (New York, 1999); hereafter abbreviated *D.*
2. Ian Hacking, 'Our Fellow Animals', *New York Review of Books,* 29 June 2000, p. 20.

Jonathan Lamb is a professor of English at Princeton University. He
is the author of, most recently, *Preserving the Self in the South Seas* (2001)
and coeditor, with Vanessa Smith and Nicholas Thomas, of the anthology
Exploration and Exchange: A South Seas Anthology, 1680–1900 (2000).

to enlarge our sympathies.'[3] It is a good pun, since Hume is not only a defender of the rationality of beasts but stands preeminent as the first British philosopher to investigate the social and psychological subtleties of sympathy. But Coetzee—and Hume, for that matter—join an older debate about the fellowship of animals and humans, or what was known to the Greeks as their *oikeiosis*. Its advocates were Plutarch, Pythagoras, and Porphyry among the philosophers, and Ovid and Apuleius among the poets.[4] For those who believed in the transmigration of souls and the possibility of metamorphosis between species, plants, and substances, there was every reason to extend sympathy to all sentient creatures, and beyond to trees and stones, for all are connected by the possibility of mutual substitution—via death or that passionate transport 'by which we are put in the place of another'.[5] As the gateway to metamorphosis among living things is the dissolution of the body and its renewal in a different form, and as this change is frequently accompanied and sometimes even determined by excessive grief or sympathy (in Ovid's stories of Phaeton's sisters, of Procris and of Niobe, for instance), the terms of Coetzee's argument, depending on the correlation between the presence of death and the degree of interspecies sympathy, are generally consistent with Ovid's examples of Pythagorean doctrine. I suggest that this is more than an accidental resemblance and that the three linked elements of sympathy, death, and metamorphosis recur in the history of representation that leads from Ovid's epic to Coetzee's novel, but not (as I have said) in ways that are always flattering to human agency.

In *The Lives of Animals* the conventional limits of sympathy are stated for Costello by the philosopher Thomas Nagel who, in his essay 'What Is It Like to Be a Bat?' robustly denies the basis of any correspondence between the subjective experience of a creature and an objective understanding of what it is like to be that creature. These particular and variegated subjectivities proliferate, says Nagel, 'in countless forms totally unimaginable to us'.[6] Not only bats are out of range, then, but also other human beings, if what is supposed is a shared consciousness; so the best that can be expected with regard to animals is a sort of extension by analogy from the human case.[7] Costello confronts the philosopher with the stupidity of his scepticism. 'Despite Thomas Nagel,' she declares, 'there is no limit to the extent to which we can think ourselves into the being of another. There are no bounds to the sympathetic imagination' (*L*, p. 35). Her claim is founded on her own strong intimation of mortality

3. Ibid., p. 26.
4. See Richard Sorabji, *Animal Minds and Human Morals* (London, 1993).
5. Edmund Burke, *A Philosophical Enquiry into the Origin of Our Ideas of the Sublime and Beautiful*, ed. James T. Boulton (Oxford, 1987), p. 44.
6. Thomas Nagel, *Mortal Questions* (Cambridge, 1979), p. 166.
7. See ibid., pp. 170–71.

and the amphibious sense it gives her in relation to the unimaginable. 'When I know, with this knowledge, that I am going to die . . . what I know is what a corpse cannot know: that it is extinct, that it knows nothing and will never know anything anymore. For an instant, before my whole structure of knowledge collapses in panic, I am alive inside that contradiction, dead and alive at the same time' (*L*, p. 32). Having once felt the force of that contradiction, it becomes possible to fly from the familiarities of one's own heart into the alien sphere of a bat, whose being is no more unfamiliar than the idea of self-extinction. 'If we are capable of thinking our own death, why on earth should we not be capable of thinking our way into the life of a bat?' (*L*, pp. 32–33). Indeed, Ovid tells the story of how Alcithoe turned into a bat.

In *Disgrace* the limits of sympathy are propounded by the hero, David Lurie, while he is teaching a class on Byron's 'Lara', a poem about Lucifer exiled on earth, 'a thing of dark imaginings' whose perverse inclinations are so alien that it is impossible for human beings to treat him, or it, companionably (*D*, p. 32). 'We are invited to understand and sympathize,' says Lurie, anticipating his own casting out, 'but there is a limit to sympathy. For though he lives among us, he is not one of us. He is exactly what he calls himself: a *thing*' (*D*, pp. 33–34). Coming to terms with his own disgrace in the uplands of the Eastern Cape, Lurie turns again to Byron and his seduction of Teresa Guiccioli. He begins to compose an opera about the indecisive ending of their affair. Their duets are sung not in the flame but the ashen aftermath of mutual passion, and they span this world and the next. She sings to him from her father's house amidst the pine-scrub of the Romagna of her desire and her shame, while his ghostly responses emerge from the caverns of the underworld. Lurie elaborates this part of the libretto while developing an attachment for a crippled dog whose quietus he signs as fitly as he can, as one disgraced being to another. The stripped-down music of the opera, plucked out on a child's seven-string banjo, matches the dead level of Lurie's sympathising consciousness, advertised in a conversation with his daughter Lucy. She tries to explain to him the necessary privation of her new start in life: 'With nothing. Not with nothing but. With nothing. No cards, no weapons, no property, no rights, no dignity.' And he says, 'Like a dog.' And she agrees, 'Yes, like a dog' (*D*, p. 205).

In Wordsworth's Lucy poems one finds both the germ of Lurie's Byronic opera and the emptiness disclosed by his love for his daughter, aptly named Lucy. The five poems are a series of questions posed about the extent of sympathy in cases of an excessive love that is menaced by the idea, or interrupted by the event, of the death of its object. In 'Lucy Gray' the child's footprints in the snow disclose a blankness whose dreariness is modified by a pain so vivid it represents the child as a ghost, still walking the moors where she was lost. ''Tis said that some have died for love' produces the same blankness not as the mockery of sorrow but as its sole lenitive, when the bereft lover demands that the motion and sounds of the natural world all be halted so as not to interfere with his apprehension of the pure emptiness left by his dead lover.[8] The poet, who in the last stanza hopes that he might not know the happiness of love if this is the risk it runs, returns to the theme in 'Strange fits of passion I have known,' where his overflowing love for Lucy finds expression perversely in the dreadful fancy that she might be dead. In 'She dwelt among th'untrodden ways' and 'A slumber did my spirit seal' the deadness of the Lucy figure is carried through two metamorphoses. In the first she has ceased to be, an event so very obscure that the poet tenderly distinguishes her life in images of isolation: she was like a violet growing by a mossy stone or a star shining singly in the sky. In the second her transition into a thing materialises fully. 'She' is the stuff of the earth itself, 'rocks and stones and trees.'[9] But 'she' is ambiguous and straddles, like Costello's sympathising imagination, the sense of being alive and dead at once, for it remains unclear whether the pronoun refers to a mourned female in her grave or to the spirit itself, slumbering in the embrace of that larger soul whose dwelling is the light of setting suns, and the round ocean, and the living air. Coleridge produces similar effects in the lyrical ballad 'The Rime of the Ancient Mariner', when the personification of Death-in-Life grips the seafarer's soul. Under her influence disgusting things become so lovely that they provoke in him a sympathy with all creatures.

Whether impelled by strong feelings of love or disgrace, the sympathy expressed in these cases is presented as real, not illusory. In the history of sympathy, however, Nagel's position has been most explicitly adopted by two of its leading theorists, David Hume and Adam Smith. Neither believed it possible to dart from one's own consciousness into another's. Smith is categorical about this, and supposing the case of his brother upon the rack, he asserts, 'Our senses . . . never did, and never can, carry us beyond our own person, and it is by the imagination only that we can form any conception of what are his sensations'.[10] This is merely a balder way of handling those complicated conversions of ideas into impressions, the 'double relation' used by Hume to explain the arrival of 'a sympathetic motion in my breast, conformable to whatever I imagine in his'.[11] In these accounts the relation between the object and subject of sympathetic feeling is always mediated by the imagination, allowing a fancied but never a real substitution. Building this principle of mediation into an analogy, Hume provides himself with a basis to compare humans and animals; for each species is capable of a degree of rea-

8. William Wordsworth, 'Tis said, that some have died for love', *'Lyrical Ballads' and Other Poems,* ed. James Butler and Karen Green (Ithaca, N.Y., 1992), pp. 176–78.

9. Wordsworth, 'A slumber did my spirit seal', *Lyrical Ballads,* p. 164.

10. Adam Smith, *The Theory of Moral Sentiments,* ed. D. D. Raphael and A. L. Macfie (Indianapolis, 1982), p. 9.

11. David Hume, *A Treatise of Human Nature* (London, 1969), p. 434.

son—that is, of inferring certain outcomes on the basis of experience—and of supplementing reason with instinct. 'Though the instinct be different, yet it is still an instinct which teaches a man to avoid the fire, as much as that which teaches a bird, with such exactness, the art of incubation and the whole economy and order of its nursery.'[12] As for the fear of death, it acts as a solvent of the distinctions between species only in that nature would never implant in any creature an instinctive horror of an impossible event, and as this horror arises from the prospect of the soul's annihilation, it does indeed put humans on a footing with animals, whose souls are understood to resemble human souls chiefly in their mortality.[13]

Here is an earlier and much more limited example of the fear of death leading to sympathy with other creatures. Hume and Smith agree that the imagination is alerted by the fear of one's own destruction, but unlike the romantic poets and Costello they do not believe that imagination really finds a passage from one heart to another. It only pretends to and becomes part of the barrier between them. On this account, Burke placed sympathy not among the social passions but among those belonging to self-preservation. What we sympathise with in the presence of pain is the fantasy of our being in pain, too. The solidity of identity hampers spiritual transmigration and cuts off any possibility of speaking for another being or as another being. Coetzee's complex idea of disgrace is intended to dismantle that barrier. Disgrace is a collapse of the ego induced by pain and humiliation so severe that the acute sense of dispossession and self-disgust accompanying it is not a hypothesis or fantasy but a brutal expulsion from familiar thoughts into presentiments so alien, unconsoling, and vivid that they could belong to someone or something else. It is something like the instinctive compassion espoused by Mandeville and Rousseau but more alarming in that it arises from the violence (usually torture in Coetzee's earlier work) inflicted by people upon people or from repulsion. In an earlier version of *The Lives of Animals*, Costello is asleep on an aeroplane, studied by her son: 'He can see up her nostrils, into her mouth, down the back of her throat. And what he cannot see he can imagine: the gullet, pink and ugly, contracting as it swallows, like a python, drawing things down to the pear-shaped belly-sac. . . . No he tells himself, that is not where I come from, that is not it.'[14] This is the reluctant kindness extorted from those either metamorphosed by unkindness or dislodged from their kind by humiliation. To study the repulsiveness of one's body, particularly the genitals; to be licked by a dog; to know that nothing belongs to you any more as a human being: these are the signs

12. Hume, *An Inquiry Concerning Human Understanding*, ed. Charles W. Hendel (Indianapolis, 1955), p. 116.

13. See Hume, 'Of the Immortality of the Soul', *Essays Moral, Political, and Literary*, ed. Eugene F. Miller (Indianapolis, 1985), pp. 597–98.

14. Coetzee, 'What Is Realism', *Salmagundi* 114–115 (Spring–Summer 1997): 81. This passage does not appear in the 1999 edition of *The Lives of Animals*.

F<small>IG</small>. 1.—Piero di Cosimo, *The Death of Procris* (c. 1500–1510). National Gallery, London. From Sharon Fermor, *Fiction, Invention, and 'Fantasia'* (London, 1993), pp. 42–43.

of disgrace and metamorphosis in Coetzee's work. Among Hume's contemporaries, property ministers the same charge to the imagination as disgrace among Coetzee's characters. Are there forerunners of this kind of sympathy, where death, violence, disgust, or the autonomy of manufactured goods pierce the barrier between species and species, or between species and things? I think there are two: one broad and diverse and dealing chiefly with things, the other specific and dealing with animals. These are Dutch still life paintings and the work of Piero di Cosimo, particularly his picture of one of Ovid's tales called *The Death of Procris* (1500–1510) (fig. 1).

Still life arose in the Netherlands from the custom of using the backs of portraits as subsidiary canvasses on which ewers, vases, lilies, ivy, and, occasionally, a skull were depicted. Sometimes the reverse images commented emblematically on the obverse; for example, symbols of purity were laid on the back of a picture of the virgin. Sometimes the things on the back had no symbolic function at all. But the skulls turned front and back into an arrangement resembling a *transi* tomb, those two-level structures where the rotting corpse beneath warns of the changes in store for the perfect body above. A message of mortality was incorporated directly into those *vanitas* still lifes where the death's head is placed amidst emblems of transitoriness such as spent candles, watches, legal papers, hourglasses, and moneybags (fig. 2).[15] The signs of corruption linger in still lives that are not strictly examples of the *vanitas,* such as flower pieces with blowflies, beetles, and reptiles lurking among the blooms. Alternatively, there is an evolution of the *vanitas* into a collection of things that no longer serves as a *memento mori.* In these the items that once advertised mortality are left to their own devices, free to join with the clutter of luxury articles and exotica, including Venetian glasses, goblets worked in gold and silver, parrots, and shells.

15. See Ingvar Bergström, *Dutch Still-Life Painting in the Seventeenth Century,* trans. Christina Herström and Gerald Taylor (London, 1956), pp. 12–15.

FIG. 2.—Willem Claesz, *Vanitas* (1621). Haags Gemeentemuseum, The Hague. From Norman Bryson, *Looking at the Overlooked: Four Essays on Still Life Painting* (London, 1990), p. 131.

The association between desymbolized objects and death is never quite removed, however, for even in the sumptuous *pronk stilleven* of Willem Kalf, the remains of the *vanitas* can be seen occasionally in candle-ends and overturned flasks, now no longer ominous but nevertheless exhibiting, along with the other assembled artifacts, a vibrancy that flourishes in the absence of the human. In *trompe l'oeil* still lifes the vibrancy grows into a weird autonomy as the picture loses all trace of its production to become indistinguishable from what it shows. At this stage the elimination of a human presence emerges as the triumph of an object proclaiming its self-origination over a viewing subject prone to believe what it says. Such 'emphatic verisimilitude'[16] seems to anticipate the transfer of initiative from producers to products typical of the fetishization of the commodity in commercial society.[17] But the social life of the commodity fetish is not noticeable in the litter of trivia that constitutes the triumph of things in *trompe l'oeil*, where detritus ('scraps, husks, peelings, the fraying and discolouration of paper') congregates in 'an area of insufficient control.'[18] Samuel Pepys gives an account of being enslaved to such a picture. When he saw a flower piece by Simon Verelst, he remembered,

16. Charles Sterling, *Still Life Painting from Antiquity to the Present Time* (New York, 1959), p. 26.

17. See Svetlana Alpers, *Rembrandt's Enterprise* (Chicago, 1988), p. 102.

18. Norman Bryson, *Looking at the Overlooked: Four Essays on Still Life Painting* (London, 1995), p. 143.

Fig. 3.—Cornelius Norbertus Gijsbrechts, *The Back of a Picture*. Statens Museum for Kunst, Copenhagen. From Bryson, *Looking at the Overlooked*, p. 143.

'I was forced again and again to put my finger to it to feel whether my eyes were deceived or no.'[19] That is, he was repeatedly coerced by a thing to challenge the evidence of his senses. Cornelius Norbertus Gijsbrechts painted a *trompe l'oeil* that carried still life back to its origin. Entitled *The Back of a Picture*, it shows the bare canvas and frame with nothing at all painted on it except a tag with the number '36' (fig. 3) .[20] Johannes Torrentius was so skilled at leaving no trace of a brush on his canvasses that he was accused of sorcery, tortured, and imprisoned.[21] Marinus van Reymerswael of Middelburg was such a gifted imitator of luxurious surfaces, particularly velvet and brocade, that he was inspired to revolt against the success of an art that gave things back to themselves, so he turned iconoclast and was gaoled for breaking images.[22]

It is not surprising that a genre whose message of human mortality

19. Samuel Pepys, *The Diary*, ed. Robert Latham and William Matthews, 11 vols. (Berkeley, 1976), 9:515.

20. See Bryson, *Looking at the Overlooked*, p. 143.

21. See Alan Chong and Wouter Kloek, *Still-Life Paintings from the Netherlands, 1550–1720* (exhibition catalog, Rijksmuseum, Amsterdam, 19 June–19 Sept. 1999), p. 40.

22. See Simon Schama, 'Perishable Commodities', in *Consumption and the World of Goods*, ed. John Brewer and Roy Porter (New York, 1993), p. 485.

evolves into the autonomy of things should provoke feelings Coetzee might recognise. Connoisseurs of still life articulate their fascination with its extravagant realism in a manner parallel with Coetzee's characters when they talk of disgrace. 'Dead and alive at the same time,' says Costello, sympathising with the being of a bat (*L,* p. 32). 'Is vitality or mortality the sovereign principle here?' asks Simon Schama of the *pronk stilleven.*[23] Hal Foster characterises the effect of *trompe l'oeil* as 'not alive, not dead, not useful, not useless . . . the pictorial effect is often one of deathly suspension or . . . eerie animation.'[24] Pepys himself senses that there is no pleasure to be drawn from being fooled by these brilliant illusions that is not tinged with the sort of humiliation that Norman Bryson calls 'the look of the world before our entry into it or after our departure from it.'[25] When we gaze at a clutter of artefacts and curiosities from which human standards of significance have begun to be abstracted, noticing how independent they are becoming of our ideas of property or class and understanding how they represent nothing but themselves, the experience can be cast only in negatives that recoil upon our sense of self. The more keenly these things tempt us into a sense of their unique existence, the more boldly they speak to us of the disgrace of mortality they were originally designed to announce.

Piero di Cosimo was an eccentric Florentine, a vegetarian whose concern even for plant life was seen in his overgrown garden, where nothing was cropped or pruned. He lived more like a beast than a man, according to Giorgio Vasari, a mode of life responsible for Piero's '"empathic" interest in what may be called the "souls" of plants and animals.'[26] Certainly he was interested in things, for Vasari also records his 'excellent representation of an old parchment book' in his picture of the Visitation, 'and the balls of St. Nicholas are made lustrous, reflecting each other, showing the curious fancies of Piero's brain, and how he sought out and performed difficult things.'[27] This northern flavor may have been imparted to his work by his early fascination with death and with the techniques for representing it as powerfully as possible. Before he became a recluse he was famous in Florence for having arranged a stunning procession dominated by the vast figure of Death on a cart. As the cart advanced, tombs released the dead, the *jeunesse dorée* of Florence clothed in black costumes on which skeletons had been painted in vivid white; and it culminated with

23. Ibid., p. 483.

24. Hal Foster, 'The Art of Fetishism: Notes on Dutch Still Life', in *Fetishism as Cultural Discourse,* ed. Emily Apter and William Pietz (Ithaca, N.Y., 1993), p. 257.

25. Bryson, *Looking at the Overlooked,* p. 143.

26. Erwin Panofsky, *Studies in Iconology* (New York, 1962), p. 33; see also Giorgio Vasari, *The Lives of the Painters, Sculptors, and Architects,* trans. A. B. Hinds, ed. Ernest Rhys, 4 vols. (London, 1927), 2:177.

27. Vasari, *The Lives of the Painters, Sculptors, and Architects,* 2:177.

FIG. 4.—Piero di Cosimo, detail from *The Battle of the Lapiths and the Centaurs* (c. 1505–7). National Gallery, London. From Fermor, *Fiction, Invention, and 'Fantasia'*, p. 55.

the Miserere, lugubriously sung by these animated bones.[28] His most arresting paintings are the *spalliere* panels narrating the violent evolution from animal to human. *A Hunting Scene* and *The Return from the Hunt* show human and hybrid figures (centaurs and fauns) slaughtering cattle, pigs, and wild beasts, then carrying them home in strange sleighlike boats, with masks of dead animals slung from crosstrees. The theme and style of these panels are closely related to his representation of one of the most violent of Ovid's stories, *The Battle of the Lapiths and Centaurs* (1505–7) (fig. 4). This remarkable piece details the ferocious outcome of the drunken assault by the centaurs on the Lapith women at Perithous's wedding feast. The equivocal appearance of these animals is redoubled as human and half-human bodies collide and coil in acts of mayhem. The fringe of agitated figures frames the death of Cyllarus and Hyloneme, two beautiful centaur lovers locked in an embrace. Pierced by a spear, Cyllarus is dying, and Hyloneme is trying to revive him with a kiss, prior to killing herself for grief when he expires. The tender feelings shared by these two hybrid

28. See ibid., 2:179.

creatures seem to temper the pitiless conflict between species taking place around them.

The Death of Procris organises the same elements as *The Battle of the Lapiths and Centaurs,* except that the pocket of serene pathos in which Cyllarus is dying has expanded to control the mood of the whole scene. Here a female figure lies dead of a spear wound to the throat, her left hand bent against the ground in the same gesture of prostration as Cyllarus's right. At her side a faun, half-human and half-beast, mourns, his eyes fixed upon her face and his hand upon her shoulder. Close by stands a dog and beyond the dog three others, one crouching, one in the act of sitting down, and one striding over a beach that opens out upon a bay populated by storks and pelicans, with a city and ships on the other side. The dog's attitude is strangely intent, as if it were absorbing from its own point of view an event whose unimaginable strangeness is conveyed by the bluish haze that suffuses the whole landscape with an air of improbability.[29] The dog, the faun, and the viewer of the picture form a triangle whose three apices comprise the three possibilities of response to a death: the animal, the hybrid, and the human. Consistent with Ovid's original stories, neither this picture nor *The Battle of the Lapiths and Centaurs* shows a metamorphosis.

Piero is interested in distributing the effects of sympathy among the canine witness, the mourning faun, and the human viewer, as if to examine the possibility of a transformation in the wake of a human death and to represent something like a metamorphosis *in the making.* In Marvell's 'A Nymph Complaining for the Death of Her Faun', a poem dealing with the same scene in reverse, the metamorphosis lies in the sympathy; for the nymph promises to weep herself, like Niobe, into a stone and then by still weeping to wear her own statue away, a self-annihilation that Marvell seems to consider a happy change of kind from the human (which is responsible for the death of fauns and the desertion of nymphs) into an invisible presence fit for sympathetic love: 'O I cannot be/ Unkind t'a Beast that loveth me.'[30] Beasts being not unkind to humans is what Piero has tried to paint. He shows that kindness involves the question of species in the question of sympathy. Dog, faun, and human have access to the same scene, but are their feelings the same? And if they are, what does this mean? Apuleius puts the same questions in a ribald way when his hero, having been transformed into an ass, becomes the object of a noblewoman's passion. This leads to a scene where a human who wishes to be coupled with a beast is mounted by a creature who thinks he is really human.

Even that joke cannot disguise the commitment to Pythagorean metempsychosis among ancients and moderns who believe that sympathy

29. See Panofsky, *Studies in Iconology,* p. 33.
30. Andrew Marvell, 'A Nymph Complaining for the Death of Her Faun', *The Poems of Andrew Marvell,* ed. Hugh Macdonald (London, 1952), ll. 45–46, p. 17.

prefaces or explains a transformation from one kind to another. Piero pairs scenes of sympathy with representations of hybrids as if to show the lineaments that true sympathy might bear. However, implicit in both pictures, and in the viewer's reaction to them, is a disturbing suggestion that true sympathy looks very like the reason for the violence which calls it forth, namely, a strong desire to cross the species frontier. Cyllarus is dying because centaurs fell in love with women; Procris is dead because a faun fell in love with her and told her that Cephalus, her human lover, was having an affair with the wind. If the human viewer feels for either Cyllarus or Procris, the impulse is mediated by a sympathising figure, the faun or Hyloneme, whose hybridity expresses both the effect and cause of sympathy, an arrangement that seems to say, 'What you mourn so well is what you well might do, if desire should carry you so far.' In which case the dog provides a disinterested alternative, inasmuch as it confronts death with an absorption that is itself immune to metamorphosis while still evincing keen apprehension for what has happened. But it has nothing to hope from what it feels, no expectation that its sorrow will change its status. In being able to paint an animal's desireless concern for a human event, Piero depicts a sympathy impossible for the viewer to imitate.

British attitudes to sympathy are explicitly non-Pythagorean. Locke, Hume, and Smith offer various accounts of sympathy that exclude the possibility of the soul's transmigration while making room for some limited kindness to animals. They were unanimous in their opposition to the philosopher closest to the Pythagorean position on the soul, Descartes, who was also notorious for his unkind attitude to animals, whom he counted nothing but machines, oblivious to pain on account of the mortality of their souls.[31] The Cartesian system of innate ideas posits an immaterial substance, or soul, with a life outside the limits of the body that endures before and after its existence. According to Locke's reading of Descartes, this required that the constitution of the self, or personal identity, should transcend experience, making it possible to become other people as the single soul successively inhabits different bodies. Locke offers as absurd the example of a man convinced that in his person he contained both himself and the soul of Socrates. It is equally absurd to suppose that 'the souls of men may, for their miscarriages, be detruded into the bodies of beasts'.[32] In opposition to Christian Platonists and Pythagoreans, Locke declares the identity of the self to be coextensive with consciousness:

> As far as this consciousness can be extended backwards to any past action or thought, so far reaches the identity of that *person:* it is the

31. See Sorabji, *Animal Minds and Human Morals,* p. 206, and Keith Thomas, *Man and the Natural World* (London, 1983), p. 35.
32. John Locke, *An Essay Concerning Human Understanding,* ed. John W. Yolton, 2 vols. (London, 1961), 1:278; hereafter abbreviated *E.*

same *self* now that it was then, and it is by the same self with this present one that now reflects on it, that that action was done. [*E*, 1:281]

And if the limit of consciousness is the extent of the memory of actual impressions, so is the limit of sympathy determined by the organism of any sentient being. If a person's hand were to be chopped off, it would no longer be part of that person, for consciousness only has to do with the living, integral body: 'all whose particles whilst vitally united to this same thinking conscious self so that we feel when they are touched and are affected by and conscious of good or harm that happens to them, are a part of our selves, i.e. of our thinking conscious *self*'. These particles are to everyone 'a part of *himself*; he sympathizes and is concerned for them' (*E*, 1:282). Sympathy stops at the skin. As for metamorphosis, it is inconceivable, for if the soul of Heliogabalus were to enter a hog, the hog would not be Heliogabalus, not merely because their two consciousnesses would not be identical, but also because the human figure is as important an attribute of personal identity as continuity of impressions.

> Whoever should see a creature in his own shape and make, though it had no more reason all its life than a *cat* or a *parrot,* would call him still a *man;* or whoever should hear a *cat* or a *parrot* discourse, reason, and philosophize would call or think it nothing but a *cat* or *parrot* and say the one was a dull irrational *man,* and the other a very intelligent and rational *parrot.* [*E*, 1:279]

To make his point he then tells the story of Sir William Temple's conversation with Johan Moritz of Nassau-Siegen, governor of Dutch Brazil. Prince Maurice (as he is called by Temple) arranged to meet a very intelligent and rational parrot. With the help of two interpreters, one a Dutchman who spoke Brazilian, the other a Brazilian who spoke Dutch, the prince enjoyed a conversation in which the bird informed him where it came from, who owned it, and what job it did.

> When they brought it close to him, he ask'd it, *D'ou venes vous?* It answer'd, *De Marinnan.* The Prince, *A qui estes vous?* The Parrot, *A un Portugez.* Prince, *Que fais tu la.* Parrot, *Je garde les Poulles.* The Prince laugh'd, and said, *Vous gardez les Poulles?* The Parrot answer'd, *Ouy, moy & je scay bien faire,* and made the Chuck four or five times that people use to make to Chickens when they call them'.[33]

Here Locke means to make a point about personal identity, 'what the word *I* is applied to' (*E*, 1:287). It cannot be applied to a creature without

33. Sir William Temple, *Memoirs of What Past in Christendom* (London, 1692), pp. 57–58; hereafter abbreviated *M*.

a human figure. It is noteworthy that he does not deny a parrot reason; nor does he suppose that the dialogue with the Prince's parrot relied upon a trick; nor does he suggest that a rational parrot is a monster. But it has no right to the first person singular. The parrot, on the other hand, insists upon its own agency as a creature capable of mediating between birds and humans.

Whether Locke's anti-Cartesian position takes him further into materialism than he is aware, he keeps referring to the self as a thing composed of substance ('whether spiritual or material . . . it matters not')— '*self* is that conscious thinking thing', 'this present thinking thing' (*E*, 1:286). In his second *Treatise of Government*, this thinking thing encounters another thing in the form of property. If a human in the state of nature should labor to kill a deer, for example, the venison becomes his, 'and so his, i.e. a part of him, that another can no longer have any right to it'.[34] This appropriation occurs because the labor of finding and killing results in a metamorphosis: 'Whatsoever then he removes out of the State that Nature hath provided, and left it in, he hath mixed his Labour with, and joyned to it something that is his own, and thereby makes it his Property.'[35] Karl Olivecrona points out that the transfusion of identity from human to thing by means of labour is Locke's unique contribution to the theory of right, without a precedent in Grotius or a parallel in Pufendorf.[36] Piero's hunting scenes might be instanced as narratives of the origin of such property to the extent that the hybridity of the hunters aptly expresses the exchange of qualities with their quarry. To lose property acquired in this way is 'a severe amputation' because it has entered the same circuit of sympathy as an attached hand or any other part of the living body.[37] Dialogue with a parrot that has cost the owner the labor of catching it and training it to speak, such as Temple's parrot or Robinson Crusoe's Poll, is an intimate and interpersonal event, as Crusoe testifies when he is awoken by a voice calling, '*Robin, Robin, Robin Crusoe,* poor *Robin Crusoe,* where are you *Robin Crusoe?*' only to see his parrot, 'and immediately [I] knew that it was he that spoke to me; for just in such bemoaning Language I had used to talk to him'.[38]

Stories of how things take a human print are popular among the Scriblerian satirists of the early eighteenth century. In his satires, Swift sports tirelessly with the connection between identity, or soul, and material things such as books and clothes. After the death of controversialists,

34. Locke, *Two Treatises of Government,* ed. Peter Laslett (New York, 1960), p. 305.

35. Ibid., p. 306.

36. See Karl Olivecrona, 'Appropriation in the State of Nature: Locke on the Origin of Property', in *John Locke: Critical Assessments,* ed. Richard Ashcraft, 4 vols. (London, 1991), 3:318–19.

37. Ibid., 3:312.

38. Daniel Defoe, *The Life and Strange Surprizing Adventures of Robinson Crusoe,* ed. J. Donald Crowley (Oxford, 1983), p. 142.

'the Soul transmigrates there [to their volumes], to inform them.'[39] These transmigrations include the multitude of modern works that either survive to do battle with other books or disappear without trace, 'Unhappy Infants, many of them barbarously destroyed, before they have so much as learnt their Mother-Tongue to beg for Pity.'[40] Similarly, the souls of fashionable folk are to be found in their garments, for in them they live, move, and have their being, 'By all which it is manifest, that the outward Dress must needs be the Soul' ('TT', p. 48). These mockeries of Pythagorean doctrine are aimed, like Locke's idea of personal identity, at Descartes. Yet while the narrator of 'A Tale of a Tub' (1704) shows how the singularity of the Cartesian system is given countenance by vibrational harmony, 'a secret necessary Sympathy' between the pitch of screwed-up brains ('TT', p. 106), he asserts the superior pleasure of beholding glinting surfaces, catoptrical tricks, *trompe l'oeil*, and the enjoyment of what he calls the possession of being well deceived: 'How fade and insipid do all Objects accost us that are not convey'd in the Vehicle of *Delusion* . . . that if it were not for Assistance of Artificial *Mediums*, false Lights, refracted Angles, Varnish and Tinsel; there would be a mighty Level in the Felicity and Enjoyments of Mortal Men' ('TT', p. 109). This summary of those effects which Pepys found most satisfying in Dutch still life introduces a proposal for emptying out the inhabitants of Bedlam, the public madhouse, into various professions, as if proclaiming that zest and novelty are to be kept up in civil society by preserving our unfamiliarity with the true nature of things and ourselves. Madness (a delusive relation to personal identity) combined with sympathy (a delusive relation to others) and pleasure (a delusive relation to objects) is the only consolation for mortality.

Pope introduces a similar doctrine with less irony in *The Rape of the Lock* (1714), a poem that dances between the zones of the familiar and unfamiliar. After the Baron has cut off Belinda's lock of hair Clarissa tells the shorn heroine that the value of all earthly things, particularly the painted and ornamented bodies of females, is ultimately determined by death. 'Since painted, or unpainted, all shall fade,/ And she who scorns a Man, must die a Maid,' then the British Fair is wise to distinguish between vanities that serve a purpose and those that don't.[41] In effect Clarissa introduces a death's-head into the uncontrolled clutter of the heroine's life, such as the dressing table, the altar of vanity from which the delusive presence of the made-up Belinda is to emerge, where lie 'puffs, powders, patches, bibles, billets doux' (*RL*, 1.138, p. 222). This clutter dominates the poem. Prayers, masquerades, hearts, necklaces, hair, husbands,

---

39. Jonathan Swift, 'The Battle of the Books', *A Tale of a Tub' and Other Satires*, ed. Kathleen Williams (London, 1975), p. 144.

40. Swift, 'A Tale of a Tub', *A Tale of a Tub' and Other Satires*, p. 20; hereafter abbreviated 'TT'.

41. Alexander Pope, *The Rape of the Lock*, in *The Poems of Alexander Pope*, ed. John Butt (London, 1963), 5.27–28, p. 238; hereafter abbreviated *RL*.

garters, coronets, lapdogs, honor, vases, and parrots compete for attention and importance. The systole and diastole of this moving toyshop of
the heart is the pulse of things ('Wigs with Wigs, with Sword-knots Sword-
knots strive' [*RL*, 1.101, p. 221]) and the metamorphosis of abstract values into material things that leaves honor to vie with brocade, chastity
with a china jar, and 'death' (qua *petite mort*) with death. Although Pope
is not blind to the attraction of an artefact lambent in the illusion of its
beauty, and occasionally brings the iridescent glitter of things into the
same lucid focus that glass achieves in Kalf's still lifes ('On her white
Breast a sparkling *Cross* she wore,/Which *Jews* might kiss, and Infidels
adore' [*RL*, 2.7–8, p. 223]), he is as keen as Clarissa to reintroduce the
death's head into this space, expecting that a solid principle of difference
might control it and make it exemplary of moral sense. His Ovidian metamorphosis of the missing lock into a comet is performed on this condition:

> For after all the Murders of your Eye,
> When, after Millions slain, your self shall die;
> When those fair Suns shall sett, as sett they must,
> And all those tresses shall be laid in Dust
> *This Lock*, the Muse shall consecrate to Fame
> [*RL*, 5.145–49, p. 242]

Pope is attempting a reversal of the evolution of still life. Instead of letting
items of trivial allure spell their autonomy by disgracing the human, he
wishes to restrict them to the original moral economy of the *memento mori*
and so preserve species dignity.

In *Gulliver's Travels* (1726) Swift uses the relativities of size and reason
in the same way that Coetzee uses torture and disgrace, namely, as the
means of introducing a human subject to the zero-degree of identity
where kindness with animals is the only alternative to absolute destitution. Thus in Brobdingnag the hero is treated by turns as an animal,
automaton, and insect, while in Houyhnhmnland his master places him
in exactly the same light as Prince Maurice's parrot, being 'eager to learn
from whence I came, how I acquired those appearances of reason which I
discovered in all my actions, and to know my story from my own mouth.'[42]
Despite Gulliver's willingness to regard giants and horses as examples of
human excellence, they do not repay the compliment; and the result is
something like a metamorphosis without a metamorphosis, as Gulliver
studies so intently his own impotence, ugliness, contemptibility, and disgrace that he conceives himself to be an animal. As Locke might say, he
is a very articulate splacknuck, or a very rational Yahoo, but certainly he
is not a member of the premier species. One of the effects of Gulliver's
demotion below the level of the norm that humanity once embodied is

42. Swift, *Gulliver's Travels* (Oxford, 1948), p. 289; hereafter abbreviated *G*.

the proliferation of the clutter that Pope tries to wedge beneath the shadow of mortality. In the second book it is manifest as a confusion typical of still lives and of Belinda's dressing table. In the kitchens of the palace at Lorbrulgrud he sees wonders: 'If I should describe the kitchen-grate, the prodigious pots and kettles, the joints of meat turning on the spits, with many other particulars, perhaps I should be hardly believed' (*G*, p. 131). He is like Robinson Crusoe when he speaks of the miracle of the pot that glazes itself in his fire: 'No Joy at a Thing of so mean a Nature was ever equal to mine'.[43] In the fourth book Gulliver's particularisations proceed not from wonder, however, but disgust, and they exceed all principles of control as Gulliver inveighs against the once familiar things of civil society, now disgracefully exoticised by his perception of himself as an underspecies and rendered as the endless negative specifications of a horse utopia: 'Here were no gibers, censurers, backbiters, pick-pockets, highwaymen, housebreakers, attorneys, bawds, buffoons, gamesters, politicians, wits, splenetic, tedious talkers, controversialists, ravishers, murderers, robbers, virtuosos' (*G*, p. 347). The list goes on and on. The heterogeneity that announces Wordsworth's sympathy with things—rocks, stones, and trees—or the variety of incorporated sweets that illustrates the love between Marvell's nymph and her faun—sugar, milk, lilies, and roses—here has tumbled into an abysmal confusion, the result of Gulliver's earnest desire to speak in the first person as a horse.

While Swift was writing this satire the people of London were experiencing a change in relation to their property as altogether radical and unsettling. Crime reached a new level of success owing to Jonathan Wild's entrepreneurial approach to the fencing of stolen goods. Turning thieves into journeymen and theft into a business, he was able to drive a trade between the owner of property and the person who alienated it. That is to say, the contractual right to chattels under a system of exchange, where alienation is accomplished by agreeing and paying a price, was being penetrated by an older method of appropriation, in which the labor of seizing the thing gave a right to it, introducing an utterly novel regime of pricing. Blackstone's definition of the property right in civil society held good at this time and lay in 'that sole and despotic dominion which one man claims and exercises over the external things of the world, in total exclusion of the right of any other individual in the universe.'[44] Although the objects of this dominion were evidently vulnerable to 'amotion or deprivation,'[45] the right was not obscured: 'If my goods are stolen from me, and sold, out of market overt, my property is not altered, and I may take

---

43. Defoe, *The Life and Strange Surprizing Adventures of Robinson Crusoe*, p. 121.

44. William Blackstone, *Of the Rights of Things*, vol. 2 of *Commentaries on the Laws of England* (Oxford, 1766), p. 2; hereafter abbreviated *OR*.

45. Blackstone, *Of Private Wrongs*, vol. 3 of *Commentaries on the Laws of England*, p. 145.

them wherever I find them' (*OR*, p. 449). Wild and his associates ensured that owners behaving as if they still had rights to their lost property would never handle it again. In his biography of this remarkable criminal Defoe pointed out that advertisements which threatened the thief by advising traders who identified stolen items to hold both the goods and vendors were warning the thieves not to move their booty but to melt it down into bullion as quickly as possible.[46] The advertisements most likely to produce the missing article ended with the honeyed words, 'No questions asked', a phrase addressed effectually not to the public but directly to the thief or his agent.

While Defoe thought the nation infatuated to put up with such humiliations, Mandeville went further. According to the statute of theftbote, which made it a felony to take money for returning stolen goods, everyone suing for the return of property in this way was conspiring to break the law. 'He who by publick Advertisements, with Promises of Secrecy, and that no Questions shall be asked, invites others to commit Felony, is guilty of a great Misdemeanour.'[47] He mocks the sympathy that binds the injured party to the injurer. Of these advertisements he sardonically observes, 'That in no performances the true Spirit of Christianity was so conspicuous as these . . . that speaking to a Thief, we never call'd him so in those charitable Addresses. . . . [Thus] we consult in the most effectual Manner, the Safety of a Person that deserves Hanging for the Wrong he has done us' (*EC*, p. 5). He describes a state of affairs in which false sympathy between humans endows things with an opportunity to assert their autonomy by entering new realms of value and to discomfit their owners by acquiring new levels of volubility.

Mandeville pointed out that articles made of silver and gold were paid back at a price which included the bullion weight plus a *je ne sais quoi* he calls 'the Fashion' of the thing: 'If there is Painting about it, if it be a particular Ring, the Gift of a Friend; or any Thing which we esteem above the real Value . . . we are . . . welcome to redeem it' (*EC*, p. 4). Fielding gives a funny account of this invisible quality when he explains the advantages of Wild's system to persons

> who had lost pieces of plate they had received from their grandmothers; to others who had a particular value for certain rings, watches, heads of canes, snuff-boxes, etc., for which they would not have taken twenty times as much as they were worth, either because they had them a little while or a long time, or that somebody else had had them before, or from some other such excellent reason, which often

46. See Defoe, *The True and Genuine Account of the Life and Actions of the Late Jonathan Wild* (London, 1725), p. 11.
47. Bernard Mandeville, *An Enquiry into the Causes of the Frequent Executions at Tyburn* (London, 1725), p. x; hereafter abbreviated *EC*.

stamps a greater value on a toy than the great Bubble-boy himself would have the impudence to set upon it.[48]

He describes a moving toyshop of the heart, more nefarious than that dramatized by Pope in *The Rape of the Lock*, but recognizable as one in which Sir Plume would be earnest to recover 'the nice Conduct of a *clouded cane*' (*RL*, 4.124, p. 236). Value is as capriciously bestowed, and as assiduously defended, by highwaymen, pickpockets, and housebreakers in Wild's world as it is by the guardian sylphs in Belinda's. A successful transaction between the charitable owner and the thief in this anomalous, covert market arrives at a price not by means of a sociable encounter between things yielding a commensurate market value but by the translation of a judgment of taste into money. That sum added to the bullion weight just equals the value of the labor of stealing it. The intimacy of the two parties is real at least in this respect: like two virtuosos, they share a sense of the unique worth of a thing. They collude in the metamorphosis of property from a commodity into a curiosity, participating in 'a special kind of transvaluation'[49] by installing the thing in a category of goods that Blackstone himself exempted from the laws against felony, namely, things 'only kept for pleasure, curiosity, or whim, as dogs, bears, cats, apes, parrots, and singing birds; because their value is not intrinsic, but depending only on the caprice of the owner' (*OR*, p. 393).

Advertising for lost things was called 'crying'. Moll Flanders says a friendless woman is 'just like a bag of money or a jewel dropped on the highway. . . . If a man of virtue and upright principles happens to find it, he will have it cried, and the owner may come to hear of it again.'[50] It is like noise and its echo when the cry and the response come from honest folk. But when the advertisement is really a secret communication, posing no questions and getting no answers, it is plain that the published details are otiose; for, as Defoe says, they are addressed to someone 'having no need of the Information.'[51] Mandeville's solution to the problem posed by Wild to civil society was to persuade every victim to give up the property right and let the article sink into perpetual silence, like Swift's infant books. He advises owners to be content to hear of their goods no more, especially items of no intrinsic value, such as shopbooks, pocketbooks, bills, bonds, and banknotes, which began to dominate this trade of 'payback', as it was called. Nevertheless advertisements were printed in great

48. Henry Fielding, *The Life of Mr Jonathan Wild the Great* (1743; London, 1964), p. 99.

49. Arjun Appadurai, 'Introduction: Commodities and the Politics of Value', in *The Social Life of Things*, ed. Appadurai (Cambridge, 1986), p. 23.

50. Defoe, *The Fortunes and Misfortunes of the Famous Moll Flanders*, ed. Juliet Mitchell (Harmondsworth, 1978), p. 135.

51. Defoe, *The True and Genuine Account of the Life and Actions of the Late Jonathan Wild*, p. 10.

numbers, and all were exhaustive in their descriptions of missing things. Here is an example from the *Daily Courant,* 10 January 1718:

> Lost on the 1ˢᵗ Instant, a Snuff Box about the Bigness and Shape of a Mango, with a Stalk on the Lid, it being a West-India Bean of a reddish Colour, and like Shagreen; the End of the Stalk tipped with Silver, opens with a Hinge, and the Inside lined with Lead. Whoever brings it to Tom's Coffee-house Cornhill, shall have a guinea Reward, and no Questions asked; it being three times the Worth of the Silver.[52]

In one sense this must be considered an aesthetic exercise, an account of the appeal of the thing's fashion that justifies its price of thirteen shillings and eightpence. In another sense it is like the beginning of a narrative— something about life in Jamaica or Barbados and a journey to London— except that the story speaks of the thing itself, while for his part the owner retires into necessary silence, bent merely upon evoking the motive power inherent in the snuffbox he hopes will cause it to return to him. Silence has another purpose besides soothing the thief and mobilising the article. It is enjoined by the compromising circumstances of the loss, generally owing to negligence, intemperance, lewdness, or other disgraceful matters that will not bear mentioning (see *EC*, p. 11). Here is another advertisement that tells a tale of libertinage at the owner's expense: 'Lost out of a Gentleman's Pocket coming out of the Old Play-House in Drury Lane, on Thursday Night the 17ᵗʰ last an Oval Ivory Snuff-box, studded with Gold on both Sides, in the Shape of a Scallop, with a Gold Hinge, and a Picture on the Lid, representing a Fryar whipping a Nun'.[53] The transmigration of souls from authors to books mentioned in the 'Tale of a Tub' that spawns those calf-bound infants who are destroyed before they have learnt their mother tongue to beg for pity has advanced a stage further to the point where not only is the item heard of but heard crying on its own behalf, somewhere between the dominated condition of property and the indistinguishable state of bullion (see 'TT', p. 20). And these cries accuse the virtue of the owner.

Charles Gildon responded to this state of affairs with two books, *The New Metamorphosis* (1704) and *The Golden Spy* (1709). The first is a rewriting of Apuleius, except the hero is transformed into a Bolognese lapdog instead of an ass. The second is regarded as the first, fully fledged it-narrative in English, consisting of the autobiographies of different kinds of gold coin. Gildon brings a fascination with Ovid to bear upon what he understands to be a fundamental antagonism between human beings and the whole variety of objects they covet and consume. In *The New Metamor-*

52. *The Daily Courant,* 10 Jan. 1718.
53. *The Daily Courant,* 19 Jan. 1717.

phosis the hero Fantasio loves Theresa both as a man and as a dog, proving a fidelity that knows no boundary of kind: 'It is a difficult matter,' he tells her, 'to separate you from my self.'[54] She on the other hand finds it only too easy, and the only advantage to be derived from his altered shape is to have unlimited access to the manifold secrets of her erotic life. In *The Golden Spy* Gildon uses gold to find out similar secrets; but he is careful to point out that this discovery depends on two related metamorphoses. Gold that talks is not the ordinary stuff of circulating money but a special metal derived from Jupiter's shower upon Danaë, capable of finding its way into hidden recesses, such as princes' cabinets and gambling clubs. There this unique metal witnesses the intrigue, vice, madness, and folly that hide behind grave and modest deportments. In the company of patriots it finds people who love only themselves, and in the company of gamesters it finds gentlemen transformed into the human litter that so disgusts Gulliver: 'Footmen, Porters, Butchers, Tapsters, Bowl-Rubbers.'[55] Talking gold, that is to say, enjoys the same quality Mandeville calls the fashion of a stolen object, a *je ne sais quoi* from which a narrative emerges disgraceful to the people concerned in it. The danger is that this extra quality in the gold might ruin human sympathy, and 'the Sense of Things . . . destroy all confidence betwixt Man and Man, and so put an End to human Society' (*GS*, p. 246).

Like the advertisements for stolen goods, gold shows sympathy between people to be a fiction sustained by the reticence of things; and once things or animals learn to speak, the lurid facts behind the fiction come to light. When Gulliver, or Fantasio, or Danaë's gold, or a stolen object start talking, the result is limitless satire delivered by narrators whose unkindness to humans demonstrates how little social or ethical interest they have in exposing human frailty. It serves merely as an adjunct to their own stories. Although death in the shape of Tyburn, privies, melting pots, and casual cruelty hovers over all the existences of things, animals and humans alike, it fosters metamorphoses that breach entirely the love of one kind for another. As narratives proliferate in the latter part of the century, written in the first person singular allegedly by lapdogs, lice, hackney coaches, ostrich feathers, sofas, rupees, guineas, and even atoms, this hostility becomes settled. Even in sentimental novels, where things and animals are freely anthropomorphised, and in slave narratives, where the metamorphosis is reversed and human beings speak both as chattels and as themselves, there is little evidence of a softening of the position, although there is often a pretence of sympathy.

Christopher Flint supposes that these 'object narratives' took their

54. Charles Gildon, *The New Metamorphosis: Or, Pleasant Transformation* (1704; London, 1724), p. 77.

55. Gildon, *The Golden Spy* (1709; London, 1724), p. 157; hereafter abbreviated *GS*. The 1724 edition was bound with Gildon's *The New Metamorphosis*.

rise from the circulation of goods in an open market, yielding an early intuition of commodity fetishism.[56] Markman Ellis calls them 'novel[s] of circulation' and relates them to the sentimentalisation of exchangeable chattels such as Sterne's starling.[57] Deidre Lynch points to unevennesses in the process of circulation that cause money to acquire stability of character while humans grow labile and unpredictable and cites these as the reasons for the secret histories told by coin.[58] But Gildon insists on a double metamorphosis, both of money and the people who love it, so that gold which is more than gold enters into an erotic intimacy with humans who are less than human: 'Why dost thou delay those Joys, that are as enchanting as uncommon,' cries Gildon's narrator to the coin he has clasped to his bosom (*GS*, p. 154). Like Defoe and Mandeville, who attend closely to the politics of extra value that fills the space between property and bullion, Gildon enters a similar region of insufficient control that we have seen represented first in still life and subsequently in *The Rape of the Lock*, where various things standing in a nonsymbolic relation to each other develop an aura that causes both pleasure and discomfort to the human observer. Bill Brown shrewdly questions whether things acquire the social attributes of human beings as a result of the circulation of commodities or whether the irregularities and suspensions of exchange, such as theft and shipwreck, make them conspicuous.[59] If things are to function independently as things, and if humans are to confront the challenge to their *amour propre* constituted by mobile and articulate things, then there has to be an impediment to market forces, a break in the circuit of exchange.[60]

This break often annoys the things themselves, who seem unaware that it is the *sine qua non* of their speech, nothing being more silent than property under the dominion of its owner or more pointless than a coin's transit from hand to hand. Gildon's coin protests against the injustice of being held by a miser, 'for shut up in his Coffers we lose this agreeable Quality' (*GS*, p. 155). Helenus Scott's rupee complains bitterly when it is immobilised in a pawnbroker's shop; an anonymous pin resents being placed in a miser's hoard; an ostrich feather is outraged when it is lodged in a warehouse and subsequently exhibited in a collection of New World curiosities.[61] In England, explains the rupee, 'I was no longer current

---

56. Christopher Flint, 'Speaking Objects: The Circulation of Stories in Eighteenth-Century Prose Fiction', *PMLA* 113 (Mar. 1998): 212.

57. Markman Ellis, *The Politics of Sensibility* (Cambridge, 1996), p. 77.

58. Deidre Shauna Lynch, *The Economy of Character: Novels, Market Culture, and the Business of Inner Meaning* (Chicago, 1998), p. 96.

59. See Bill Brown, 'How to Do Things with Things (A Toy Story)', *Critical Inquiry* 24 (Summer 1998): 935, 952.

60. See ibid., p. 954.

61. See Helenus Scott, *The Adventures of a Rupee* (London, 1783); Anon., *The History of a Pin* (London, 1798); and Anon., *The History of an Ostrich Feather* (London, 1812).

coin, but a kind of curiosity.'[62] At the pawnbroker's, where everything is
waiting to be reclaimed as personal property, lodged in a travesty of a
shop and suspended in an intercalary state without a price, commodities
are metamorphosed into things that start to evince, like advertisements,
a narrative potential: 'Those watches . . . are now silent as the lapse of
time, which they were designed to measure. . . . That ring was perhaps
in remembrance of the purest flame that love can excite.'[63] In the miser's
hoard the clutter typical of uncontrolled space begins to collect. The pin
recalls, 'I was placed among many of my fellow-sufferers, and introduced
to that side of his chest where were collected together old buckles, bent
nails, rusty keys, broken locks, seals without settings, and settings without
seals'.[64] 'Poor I was locked up in a trunk,' says a slipper, 'above us hung
petticoats of all kinds, pateliers, demi-robes, jackets, stays, sacs, masquer-
ade habits.'[65] This is the arena of early self-consciousness and the beginning of the story. 'Here is a beauteous assemblage that will tell no tales',
says the pickpocket in *The Adventures of a Hackney Coach* as he produces
a diamond repeater and a heavy gold snuffbox, but the hackney coach
knows better.[66]

Despite the advantages that accrue from being seized and held,
things express their hostility towards humans by wishing that they might
suffer the same fate. In *Aureus* (1824) the sovereign's memories of his origins in a bank vault and his intimation of perpetual night in a sunken
ship cause him to be interested in stories of human beings pent up in
narrow places, such as a sea captain 'incarcerated in a small, dark, and
loathesome cell' and an actor who gets stuck in a water-butt, crying 'like
Sterne's starling, "*I can't get out—I can't get out.*"'[67] It affords things pleasure
to see their gaolers removed from circulation and turned into spectacles.
The hackney coach watches Dr Dodd's execution for forgery with great
satisfaction. Whether the person is being punished for a property crime
or is simply making the transition from life to death makes little difference to the coach, which enjoys the sight of the Earl of Chatham's funeral
procession as much as the scene at Tyburn. Both rituals extinguish personal identity as defined by Locke and transform its residue into an object
of interest. Thus the sovereign enjoys the story of Lord Lavender who,
when meeting a man who apologised to him for not recollecting his
name, declared: 'Why, at this moment, I do not recollect it myself, but I
shall remember it before I get to the top of the street.'[68] More pointedly,

62. Scott, *The Adventures of a Rupee*, p. 103.
63. Ibid., p. 137.
64. Anon., *The History of a Pin*, p. 34.
65. Anon., *The History and Adventures of a Lady's Slippers and Shoes* (London, 1754), p. 9.
66. Anon., *The Adventures of a Hackney Coach* (Philadelphia, 1783), p. 73.
67. Peregrine Oakley, *Aureus, or the Life and Opinions of a Sovereign* (London, 1824), pp.
55, 84.
68. Ibid., p. 265.

Charles Johnstone's guinea reports with glee the execution of Aminadab, the coiner who has been responsible for disfiguring and devaluing him: 'Of all the human sufferings I had yet seen . . . this gave me the greatest pleasure.'[69] Likewise, the hero of *The Adventures of a Banknote* enjoys the view at Tyburn because it finds in it consolation for the prospect of its own end in the bank, where 'a fellow with a hangman-looking face, takes us by the nape of the neck, and in a moment twitches some talismanic letters (which to us are the spinal marrow) from the north-east corner of our skirts: the operation is no sooner performed, than down we drop, and are joined with patriots, pensioners, princes, peers, pimps . . . in the gloomy cave of eternal oblivion.'[70] The bank, a cabinet, a pawnbroker's shop, a fence's lock: like still lifes and Belinda's dressing table they are spaces uncontrolled by principles of difference in which things experience a pause in the system of exchange-value, but not as commodity fetishes. Far from usurping the sociability of their producers, these things become singular and self-aware as they negotiate the threat of annihilation on one side and resumption into circulation on the other.

Francis Coventry's *Pompey the Little* (1751) records these metamorphoses from a dog's point of view. The story is loosely arranged around Pompey's relationship with Lady Tempest, a materialist in Locke's mold and a great collector of dogs. Her fondness for them seems to depend partly on Hume's principle, namely, that the mortality of the souls of dogs and humans establishes an equality between them, and partly on a desire to incense her husband, who hangs two or three of her animals every week. Pompey is under no illusions about how far a fondness for pets extends into cross-species sympathy. He lives briefly with a family that owns 'a Dormouse, two Kittens, a *Dutch* Pug, a Squirrel, a Parrot, and a Magpye' but he finds the kittens dead, 'drowned for some Misdemeanour . . . and the Magpye's Head chopt off . . . for daring to peck a piece of Plumb-Cake.'[71] Rather like the narrative of Dickens's *Oliver Twist*, Pompey's revolves around an advertisement: '*Lost in the* Mall *in* St. James's Park, *between the Hours of Two and Three* in the Morning, *a beautiful* Bologna *Lapdog, with black and white Spots, a mottled Breast, and several Moles upon his Nose, and answers to the name of* Pomp, *or* Pompey' (*PL,* p. 72). When he is rediscovered, Lady Tempest simply asserts her property right, and it is left to a lawyer to explain to her that 'there is something very peculiar in the Nature of Dogs' (*PL,* p. 262). This peculiarity provides the standpoint from which a dog can observe the perversity and cruelty of humans, but it also opens up a narrow opportunity for sympathy between Pompey and a starving

69. Charles Johnstone, *The Adventures of a Guinea,* ed. E. A. Baker (London, 1907), p. 282.

70. Thomas Bridges, *The Adventures of a Banknote,* 2 vols. (London, 1770), 1:167.

71. Francis Coventry, *Pompey the Little* (London, 1751), pp. 75, 83; hereafter abbreviated *PL.*

hack writer—perhaps a picture of Coventry himself—who is given the animal by his patron after having asked for money to help with his wife's lying in. 'The Dog pretends here to be starving, and yet has the Assurance to deal in Procreation,' announces Lord Danglecourt, 'Here, *Dickson*, carry him this Dog which I brought home the other Night' (*PL*, pp. 211–12). One dog sent to another, Pompey beholds in the author's garret the clutter symptomatic of their nominal sympathetic union, including 'the first Act of a Comedy, a Pair of yellow Stays, two political Pamphlets, a Plate of Bread-and-butter, three dirty Night-caps, and a Volume of Miscellany Poems'—and under the bed an overflowing chamberpot (*PL*, pp. 215, 214). A dog who is shortly to die meets a destitute man with an unfinished drama: this is the same uncontrolled space and the same relation between dog and human occupied by David Lurie at the end of his story.

Slave narratives closely follow the narrative pattern laid down by things. They preserve the convention of the title page where the autobiography of a pin, feather, or coin is always written or related by itself (*The Adventures of a Black Coat as related by ITSELF* [1762]; *Aureus, or the Life and Opinions of a Sovereign written by himself* [1824]). Thus Olaudah Equiano's *Interesting Narrative* (1789) is 'written by himself'; so is Frederick Douglass's *Narrative* (1845), while Mary Prince's *History* (1831) is 'related by herself'. The pen and the voice tell of an imperfect double metamorphosis—from human to chattel and chattel to human—that tests a quality belonging neither to a circulating commodity nor to a civil self. Locke founds 'that thinking thing' the self upon each individual's primary property in his or her person. When the person is entirely appropriated by the will of someone else, then the slave suffers the extinction of identity, for he is without legal title to property, incapable of making a contract or of giving testimony, undefended by the laws, and bereft of liberty. In this condition, aptly defined by Locke as suspended death, the first person pronoun refers to nothing, since the slave owns not even the actions of his or her own body.[72] Strictly speaking, it was impossible in this condition of civil death for slaves to commit crimes or to receive punishment, since the forensic element of personal responsibility had been eliminated from their natures. But of course the lurid annals of plantation life and the hideous torments allowed by colonial statute indicate that there was always some quality surplus to commodity status, a residue of will and self, upon which punishment could fall. Curiously, the statutes acknowledged this residue in the £15 fine imposed in the Leeward Islands on slave owners who 'out of wantonness, and bloody mindedness' killed their own slaves; for over and above the loss of the value of the chattel-slave, there is some shadow of an abuse of a human right that has to be paid

72. See Locke, *Two Treatises of Government*, p. 325.

for.[73] It is the residue of life persisting in a state of civil death; it is the remains of agency that allows a slave such as Equiano or Venture Smith to purchase himself and so become his own master.

Like the 'fashion' of a stolen artefact or the aura of Danaë's gold, this residue forms the basis of all subsequent autonomy and is what the enslaved or manumitted I refers to. But having survived near-extinction, it is not fundamentally a sociable principle; rather, the opposite, since it drives slaves towards powerful nonhuman sympathies. 'I have often wished myself a beast', Douglass confesses, 'I preferred the condition of the meanest reptile to my own.'[74] On the middle passage, Equiano longs to be a fish and later describes a crisis of identity in which 'I began to blaspheme, and wished often to be any thing but a human being' (*IN*, p. 181). The condition of death-in-life leads them, like Elizabeth Costello, Lemuel Gulliver, and the Ancient Mariner, to a kindness for animals in reaction against the cruelties of their own kind. The facts recorded by these first persons are outrageous, brutalities 'so very disgraceful to human nature,'[75] reflecting such 'great disgrace' upon the species, that the first person narrator no longer treats the human as an ethical category (*IN*, p. 180). Somewhere between death and the market, the self-liberated former slave elaborates a story whose germ lies, as it does for stolen things, in an advertisement: 'A Negro Boy called Ebo, about 15 years old, well favour'd, having a scar on the right Side of his Head, like a half Moon, an Impediment in his Speech, wearing only a torn dark Fustian Wastcoat lin'd with blue, and brass Buttons, Leather Breeches, and red Stockings.'[76] If fully told, the tale would connect the scar to the stutter to confirm the depravity of property owners illustrated in other narratives of autonomous things.

When Belinda loses her lock of hair, the amputation of a material part of the self and its disappearance into the world of things is celebrated in a sprawling litotes that wickedly confounds the important and the trivial:

> Not youthful Kings in Battel seiz'd alive,
> Not scornful Virgins who their Charms survive,
> Not ardent Lovers robb'd of all their Bliss,
> Not ancient Ladies when refus'd a Kiss
> [*RL*, 4.3–6, p. 232]

73. Olaudah Equiano, *The Interesting Narrative of the Life of Olaudah Equiano*, ed. Vincent Carretta (New York, 1995), p. 109; hereafter abbreviated *IN*.

74. Frederick Douglass, *Narrative of the Life of Frederick Douglass*, in *The Classic Slave Narratives*, ed. Henry Louis Gates, Jr. (New York, 1987), p. 279; hereafter abbreviated *N*.

75. Quobua Ottobah Cuguano, 'Thoughts and Sentiments on the Wicked Traffic of Slavery,' in *Unchained Voices: An Anthology of Black Authors in the English-Speaking World of the Eighteenth Century*, ed. Carretta (Lexington, Ky., 1996), p. 161.

76. *The Daily Courant*, 17 Mar. 1720.

When Equiano purchases his freedom he adapts the same figure of confusion to his feelings:

> Not conquering heroes themselves in the midst of a triumph—Not the tender mother who has just regained her long-lost infant, and presses it to her heart—Not the weary hungry mariner, at the sight of the desired friendly port—Not the lover, when he once more embraces his beloved mistress, after she had been ravished from his arms. [*IN*, p. 136]

Like Belinda he reduces human variety to a dead level in comparison with the liberated 'fashion' of a thing no longer under despotic dominion of an owner. Like Gulliver he lists a series of human cases that are unfit to express the importance of his own metamorphosis. Like Lucy Lurie's estimate of the condition of a dog ('No cards, no weapons, no property, no rights, no dignity'), he piles up negatives to express the singularity and public insignificance of his new start.

The sentimental novel set itself the task of reconciling the interests of things, animals, and humans. The characteristic of the man of feeling is that he lives like Equiano out of the world, a human with very little social value, capable of forming fine relationships with things and creatures similarly situated outside the mainstream of exchange. An index of unworldliness in the novels of Sterne and Mackenzie is the reduction of sentiment to the level of a situation, where a casual arrangement of things provokes and frames untranslatable feelings. Whether it is clothing, furniture, an ornament, food, or an animal, it can be used simultaneously as the source and object of these unspoken intensities. Mackenzie wrote an essay for *The Mirror* entitled 'Of Attachment to Inanimate Objects' in which he describes the eccentric habits of Mr Umphraville, who refuses to be parted from an old tree stump in his garden or his ancient elbow chair.[77] Like objects in a still life, these appurtenances of his existence have neither emblematic nor commercial value, and the feelings they arouse have no reference to anything beyond their own materiality. Like the snuffboxes, gloves, spectacles, crusts of bread, and millinery that contingently occasion or frame actions and feelings in Sterne's *A Sentimental Journey,* they are signs turned into toys or curios and serve the purpose of avoiding explanations or symbolisations of what is happening. As sentimental travelers claim to be figures of peculiar integrity, like no one but themselves, so these are just things in themselves, contributing to sets of circumstances congenial to the voice of nature. Similarly, the dogs, horses, mules, and asses that are so frequently encountered by the sentimental traveler appear, like many of the dogs and horses in paintings by Stubbs, as creatures symbolic of nothing outside the situations that frame them,

---

77. See Henry Mackenzie, 'Of Attachment to Intimate Objects', *The Mirror,* no. 61, 3 vols. (London, 1786), 2:204.

enforcing neither a moral nor a lesson. They stand in no necessary or legible relation to social truths; they are the attendants and vouchers of singular emotions. It seems, then, as if sentiment does indeed depend on a restoration of a state of nature, where things find a route to the heart not by ingestion and appropriation, as Locke argues, and animals greet humans not in the common shadow of their mortality, as Hume suggests, but by cheerful companionship and mutual good offices.

When the hackney coach confesses that he has borrowed 'an old worn-out pen of Yorick's,' the author is alluding to an early scene in *A Sentimental Journey* where Yorick starts to feel sorry for a coach standing forlornly in the courtyard of the inn at Calais.[78] 'Much indeed was not to be said for it—but something might—and when a few words will rescue misery out of her distress, I hate the man who can be a churl of them.'[79] His failure in this instance doesn't stop him subsequently from talking on behalf of mute things, dumb animals, gesturing dwarves, and other creatures out of the class of humanity. In this proclivity he follows the example of Tristram Shandy, who fashions a dialogue out of his meeting with the mad and mute Maria in southern France, although she never utters a word.[80] He has practised this technique before, turning a one-sided encounter with an ass in Lyons into dialogue so successfully he resolves thereafter never to neglect colloquy with members of this species:

> I generally fall into conversation with him; and surely never is my imagination so busy as in framing his responses from the etchings of his countenance—and where those carry me not deep enough——in flying from my own heart into his, and seeing what is natural for an ass to think——as well as a man, upon the occasion. In truth, it is the only creature of all the classes of beings below me, with whom I can do this: for parrots, jackdaws, *&c.*——I never exchange a word with them——nor with the apes, *&c.* for pretty near the same reason; they act by rote, as the others speak by it, and equally make me silent. . . . But with an ass, I can commune for ever.[81]

Like so many of Sterne's jokes, this is made partly at Locke's expense, for here there is no limit to human sympathy with an animal nor any division between their common nature.

There is no more teasing example of the relation of a creature to the problem of human identity, and of the emblem of slavery to slavery itself, than the caged starling Yorick meets in the passage of his hotel the night

78. Anon., *The Adventures of a Hackney Coach,* p. 2.

79. Laurence Sterne, *A Sentimental Journey through France and Italy,* ed. Graham Petrie (London, 1967), p. 37; hereafter abbreviated *SJ.*

80. See Sterne, *The Life and Opinions of Tristram Shandy,* ed. Ian Campbell Ross (Oxford, 1983), pp. 522–23.

81. Ibid., p. 419.

when he is informed that he is traveling illegally in France and is in danger of being imprisoned in the Bastille. He makes light of his predicament, until he hears what he thinks is a child's voice calling, 'I cannot get out,' and then the dire offence of dominion and slavery are borne in upon him. Again, like the scene with the ass, it is obliquely but unmistakably aimed at Locke's *Essay*, specifically the story of the parrot. The bird's repeated cry, 'I cannot get out', punctuates Yorick's futile attempts to set it free; and with each repetition Yorick is more moved: 'I vow, I never had my affections more tenderly awakened' (*SJ*, p. 96). In order to express these feelings he claims a language for the bird on four distinct levels. It is described as mere mechanism ('Mechanical as the notes were'); as the voice of nature ('yet so true in tune to nature were they chanted, that in one moment they overthrew all my systematic reasonings'); as dialogue ('I cannot set thee at liberty—"No," said the starling—"I can't get out'''); and as mere noise ('an *unknown* language') (*SJ*, p. 99). These correspond roughly to the four current notions of expressive sympathy: Mandeville's, Hutcheson's, Smith's, and Burke's respectively; namely, an involuntary impulse of the body that happens to move the spectator; a public and significant sentiment; a theatrically modulated exchange of feelings; and symptomatic obscurity. Despite this comprehensive appeal, the cry elicits nothing. It fails as a call for freedom—in fact Yorick puts the starling back into circulation as a caged commodity, exchanged for goods and money—and it also fails as the symbolic cry of slavery, for he can't help particularising the universal scene of slavery, substituting a detailed portrait of himself in prison. That he can see only himself in the bird explains why eventually he claims it as property ('that bird was my bird') and puts it on top of his coat of arms as proof of who he is and what belongs to him (*SJ*, p. 99). Sterne's reading of Locke and the parrot seems to go something like this, then: sympathy with a dumb creature can accidentally express what one feels, and since no real passage has been opened from a human to an animal heart, human identity is strengthened by the temporary fiction that a bird can speak.

There is a curious pendant to this scene in the section of *A Sentimental Journey* entitled 'The Passport. Versailles', where Yorick describes his efforts to legalize his presence in France. When he meets the Comte de B**** he identifies himself by pointing to the graveyard scene in Shakespeare's play, conveniently lying open on the desk in front of him, crying 'Me *Voici!*' (*SJ*, p. 109). With this gesture Yorick makes another sentimental leap into the heart and mouth of a speaking object, this time the human skull apostrophised by Hamlet, which he claims for his own. This turns out to be a mistake because the count proceeds to make a category error that does Yorick's sense of identity no good. He assumes that this eccentric Englishman (perhaps because he is unskilled in French, perhaps because his health is bad) is mutely appealing for words to be spoken on his behalf and that he has presented himself as an object ripe for sentimental appropriation, just like the starling. Yorick's position vis-à-vis the bird is now taken up by the count. '*Et, Monsieur, est il Yorick?* cried the Count,—*Je le suis,* said I.—*Vous?*—*Moi—moi qui ai l'honneur de vous parler, Monsieur le Compte—Mon Dieu!* said he, embracing me—*Vous etes Yorick*' (*SJ*, p. 110). The count ignores Yorick's claims for personal identity and lodges him in the same empty role Yorick formerly assigned the starling. Just as the bird is affixed to the escutcheon to blazon the name of its owner, so the passport is given Yorick in the king of France's name, allowing him no other status than that of a factitious personality—the king's jester—who travels from place to place (and the sequel bears this out) speaking by rote. Not until the reunion with Tristram's Maria does Yorick recover his sentimental panache.

The futility of the starling's appeals for liberty, combined with the humiliation Yorick suffers when the count puts him in the same position as the bird, conspire to suggest that the division between things and humans asserted by Locke, and then illustrated by the conflicts dramatised in it-narratives, is not so easily bridged by sympathy as Yorick suggests when he talks with asses. These scenes show that Burke's sympathetic substitution is not communion between a sentient and an inanimate thing, or between a dumb creature and an articulate human, so much as a contest over who will look at whom and who will usurp the right of speech. In fact Sterne, notorious as the man who wept over a dead ass while neglecting a living mother, reveals that the animosity between things and people evident from the first examples of the genre has by no means disappeared. This is a point made explicitly in Mackenzie's essay, 'The Unfortunate Attendant of a Woman of Extreme Sensibility,' where he tells the story of Barbara Heartless who becomes the companion of Mrs Sensitive. She shares a house with 'three lap-dogs, four cats . . . a monkey, a flying squirrel, two parrots, a parroquet, a Virginia nightingale, a jack-daw, an owl,' and is instructed by her mistress (who 'can understand their looks and their language from *sympathy*') to accommodate herself to the feelings of these creatures. She is bidden to 'scratch the heads of the parrots . . . laugh to the monkey, and play at cork-balls with the kittens.' But she discovers that this sympathy has no social corollary at all, for Mrs Sensitive 'has no pity on us, no sympathy in the world for our distresses. . . . Ordinary objects of charity we are ordered never to suffer to come near her.'[82] Her household pets are sufficient objects of interest: a collection of living curiosities that consolidates her own sense of identity without the need of any human addition. The hierarchy structuring the relation of the two scenes of *A Sentimental Journey* is observable here, too: as the count to Yorick and Yorick to the starling, so Mrs. Sensitive to her animals and the animals to their human servants.

82. Henry Mackenzie, 'The Unfortunate Attendant of a Woman of Extreme Sensibility', *The Lounger,* no. 90, 3 vols. (London, 1788), 3:191–93.

How the animals themselves may feel about this treatment is an issue raised by Temple in the memoir of the parrot cited by Locke. Temple's purpose in telling the story differs from Locke's, who makes it clear that he believes the story to be true. But I think Temple means to laugh at Prince Maurice, rather as Prince Maurice laughs at the bird. The young English diplomat is going to get the old Dutchman to recite a well known tale that will make him look daft: 'I dare say this Prince, at least, believed himself in all he told me, having ever pass'd for a very honest and pious Man,' says the patronising youth (*M*, p. 59). And the prince is evidently reluctant to tell it, answering his questions 'short and coldly', as if anticipating ridicule (*M*, p. 57). However, the parrot has already weakened this hierarchy of mockery by proving with its voice that its relation to the chickens is the same as that which humans think they have with birds: it can mimic their mimicry of them, indicating that it controls both the difference between itself and other birds and between itself and human beings. It even claims to know the differences among human beings themselves. When it comes into the room, its first words are, 'What a Company of White Men are here?' (*M*, p. 58). Everything the starling lacks—the ability to choose and inflect its words, the knowledge of its relations to others—the parrot possesses, and it backs up its skills with a claim to identity: '*Vous gardez les Poulles?* The Parrot answer'd, *Ouy, moy*' (*M*, p. 58). This resembles closely the interchange between Yorick and the count ('*Et, Monsieur, est il Yorick? . . . Je le suis,* said I,—*Vous?—Moi—moi*' [*SJ*, p. 110]), except that Yorick is losing the battle that the parrot is winning. In effect it is saying to Prince Maurice, 'I hold the same position with regard to fowl as you think you hold to me. If you challenge that, I can challenge you.' For his part, Temple tries to make the Prince act the parrot's part, only to find that the parrot has made them both behave like chickens. This challenge must be met, Locke insists, by placing a human, self-sympathising I where a rational bird appears to stand. The real I must usurp the false one, and so preserve itself. From different sides, then, Sterne and Locke agree that animal sounds, whether mechanical or natural, constitute some sort of threat to the self which has to be overcome. But Temple's parrot shows that the contest is never simple, for the starling's place awaits anyone who thinks the game too easy.

There are a number of ways in which this revision of the scene of sympathy between humans and nonhumans can be applied to slavery. As a target of easy feelings of pity, the starling provides the same opportunity for tears as the story of Yarico and Inkle, where the injustice of enslavement is displaced by its poignancy.[83] Alternatively, the sentimental attachment of the owner towards his chattel is a common theme of plantation

---

83. This story was told in many forms in the eighteenth century, but the best known version is that of Sir Richards Steele, given in *The Spectator*, no. 11, 13 Mar. 1711.

narratives such as Sarah Scott's *History of Sir George Ellison* (1766), Mackenzie's *Julia de Roubigne* (1777), Thomas Bellamy's *The Benevolent Planters*
(1789) and Maria Edgeworth's short story, 'The Grateful Negro' (1802).
Even Equiano refers to his owner Mr King as 'a man of feeling' (*IN*, p.
101). When British authors enter more fully into the passionate resent-
ments of slaves, such as Thomas Day in his 'The Dying Negro' (1773) or
Aphra Behn in *Oroonoko* (1688), sympathy is a threat or a challenge. The
dying negro wishes that his tormentors might feel his agony: 'Be theirs
the torment of a ling'ring fate,/ Slow as thy justice, dreadful as my hate.'[84]
Oroonoko commences the process of the torturous death the planters
have in store for him by cutting off parts of his person and hurling them
at his enemies, in defiance of any pain they might inflict.[85] In these examples slaves confront their tormentors with a version of the Native
American death song, commemorated by both Adam Smith and Adam
Ferguson as a primitive example of sympathy and admired by Joanna
Baillie as 'a grand and terrible game' of competitive agony.[86]

I have already mentioned the desire for metamorphosis experienced
by slaves whose links to their kind have been broken; but sometimes ani-
mality acts as the cause as well as the effect of this transformation, introducing a sinister intimacy into the process of unkindness when brutality
makes brutes of victims, and brutalisers are themselves brutalised. Frederick Douglass describes the metamorphosis of Sophia Auld under the
influence of slave owning: 'The tender heart became stone, and the lamb-
like disposition gave way to one of tiger-like fierceness' (*N*, p. 277), having
already shown how field hands were broken in and then 'ranked with
horses, sheep, and swine' (*N*, p. 281). Similarly, Equiano identifies among
whites in the West Indies a collapse of self-esteem that transforms them
into swine who treat their own mulatto offspring as slaves (see *IN*, pp.
151, 110), having already shown how slaves are 'humbled to the condition
of brutes' (*IN*, p. 111). If slave and owner are metamorphosed by the
same process and confront each other as animals, locked in a passionate
enmity from which reason and humanity have been expelled, then they
travesty many a sentimental scene. When Ignatius Sancho writes to a
white friend of jackasses, remarking, 'I ever had a kind of sympathetic
(call it what you please) for that animal—*and do I not love you?*' the Shan-
dean joke takes a detour (like the starling) through the corruptions of
slavery.[87] In Maria Edgeworth's *Belinda* (1801) the heroine is charmed by
a creole of sensibility called Mr Vincent, one who 'thought, acted, and

84. Thomas Day, 'The Dying Negro: A Poetical Epistle', *The Critical Review*, no. 36
(London, 1773), p. 71.
85. See Aphra Behn, *Oroonoko: or, The Royal Slave* (New York, 1997).
86. Joanna Baillie, introduction to *A Series of Plays*, 3 vols. (London, 1798), 1:7.
87. Ignatius Sancho, *Letters of Ignatius Sancho, an African*, ed. Carretta (London, 1998),
p. 92.

suffered as a man of feeling'[88] but who nevertheless follows the custom among planters of calling slaves by dogs' names.[89] In a chapter entitled, 'Love me, love my dog,' he declares that Juba is the best creature in the world, and Belinda asks, 'Juba, the dog, or Juba, the man?' and he replies meaninglessly, 'Well! Juba, the man, is the best man—and Juba, the dog, is the best dog.'[90]

Only by means of the grossest delusion is it possible to make such sentimental equations between the lives of humans and animals. Mr Vincent is close enough to the hideous events that have fetched humans and animals to a common level of brutality—the pain, loneliness, and destitution that makes Lucy Lurie like a dog, for example—not to be allowed the refuge of stupidity. If the history of modern metamorphosis teaches humans anything, it is that the enlargement of sympathy discloses relations that are neither comfortable nor sociable. The autonomy it confers on things and creatures, far from mirroring a benevolent intention, generates narratives of human behaviour replete with arrant but unsuccessful selfishness, remorseless cruelty, and humiliating weakness. Because kindness is only the projection of defeated self-love; because tenderness can originate in perversity and tend towards violence; and because the real sense of another's loss calques upon a presentiment of the extinction of our own identity, we should worry not about extending sympathy, but that it is already too disgracefully extended.

88. Maria Edgeworth, *Belinda* (London, 1896), p. 433.
89. Robin Blackburn, *The Making of New World Slavery: From the Baroque to the Modern* (London, 1998), p. 325.
90. Edgeworth, *Belinda*, p. 356.

Romanticism and the Life of Things:
Fossils, Totems, and Images

W. J. T. Mitchell

The following essay was written as the keynote address to the annual meeting of the North American Society for the Study of Romanticism in September 2000. The topic for that year was Romanticism and the Physical, a signal that the current interest in questions of material culture, objecthood, and thingness were (as always) percolating down through the canonical periods of literary and cultural history. Romanticism, however, has been a period under siege in recent reformulations of English literary history. Crowded on the one side by Frank O'Gorman's conceptualization of the "long eighteenth century" and on the other by the Victorian and ever-voracious modernist periods, it has begun to look like an endangered species in the sequence of historical literary specialties, especially as measured by the Modern Language Association's annual lists of job openings.[1] This historical squeeze is compounded by the continuing habit among cultural critics and historians to refer unreflectively to tendencies such as emotionalism, sentimentality, and idealism as "merely" romantic phenomena that have been superseded by tough-minded modernism or even more wised-up postmodernism. My paper, then, was a double effort to link romanticism to the new interest across a number of disciplines in things and to trace the genealogy of that very interest to the historic discovery of some very specific and rather momentous concepts and images of thinghood in the heart of the romantic movement.

Special thanks are due to Mark Lussier, the organizer of this event. I want to acknowledge also Bill Brown, James Chandler, Arnold Davidson, Marilyn Gaull, and Françoise Meltzer who made numerous excellent suggestions about the issues raised in this paper.

1. See William Galperin and Susan Wolfson, "The Romantic Century," *Romantic Circles*, 30 Apr. 2000, http://www.rc.umd.edu/features/crisis/crisisa.html

227

At the same time, this paper was conceived as part of my own ongoing inquiry into the question of the "animated" object/image/thing, especially those forms of animation rooted in desire and longing. The argument may be seen, then, as an attempt to answer the question—what do pictures want?—in a framework that allows for the possibility that "pictures" (representational images and objects in any medium, verbal or visual) have lives of their own and that those lives are founded in want, that is, in desires as both a negative lack and a positive longing for an object.[2]

1. My Own Country

First, I must thank the North American Society for the Study of Romanticism for inviting an errant romanticist to come home. Later I will say something about ways in which North America (Canada, especially) might be a home for certain romantic things, but for the moment I only want to say something about myself as a romanticist. Although I began my professional life as a scholar of romantic literature, especially of the work of William Blake, I have been exploring strange seas of thought (iconologies, media studies, art history, visual culture) outside the field of romantic studies for almost twenty years now, with my editorship of *Critical Inquiry* serving as sea anchor. When people ask me these days what my field is, I generally find myself hard-pressed to give an answer. But one response I find unavoidable is simply to say, "well, I started out as a romanticist." Romantic studies, specifically in England, but more broadly in France and Germany, has always seemed to me like a crucial point of origin, even though, like everyone else, I understood that romanticism was a deeply ambiguous and contested concept, one that varies across national borders and literary genres. It was, in fact, the conspicuous mixtures of genres, media, and styles that most appealed to me about romanticism, a sense that its "impurity" as a concept and a historical formation stood out in contrast to the rule-governed decorum of classical, especially neoclassical, aesthetic forms.

2. For a fuller argument, see my essay, "What Do Pictures Want?" in *In Visible Touch: Modernism and Masculinity*, ed. Terry Smith (Sydney, 1997), pp. 215–32, and a slightly different version, "What Do Pictures *Really* Want?" *October*, no. 77 (Summer 1996): 71–82.

W. J. T. Mitchell is Gaylord Donnelley Distinguished Service Professor in the departments of English and art history at the University of Chicago and has been editor of *Critical Inquiry* since 1978. His most recent publication is *The Last Dinosaur Book: The Life and Times of a Cultural Icon* (1998), and the following essay is part of a new book entitled *What Do Pictures Want?*

A romantic beginning is not just a matter of my own autobiography, however, but reflects the peculiar role romanticism has played in much of the criticism that has transformed the world of literary and cultural study in our time. I will spare you the full recitation of these transformations. Suffice it to say that the last thirty years have witnessed revolutions at every level of human civilization and in every region of the world. Globalization, the emergence of new economies, technologies, and media, of new geopolitical orders and religious revivals have been accompanied by vast cultural transformations that effect everyday life and the professional study of culture in which we participate. When I was in graduate school in the 1960s, deconstruction was a rumor of a possible future; now it is a Republican debating strategy, and it is periodically pronounced dead by those who claim to understand French intellectual culture.[3] Feminism, African American studies, cultural studies, new historicism, critical theory, semiotics, and so on did not exist (in the American academy in those simpler times, although the social and political forces that would give rise to them were all around us in the sixties). "Bliss was it in that dawn to be alive," Wordsworth's summary of witnessing the French Revolution in the early 1790s,[4] had a new resonance for the generation of the sixties and launched a sense of the romantic movement as somehow the counterpart to our own time.

So I was not alone in straying from the romantic fold after the sixties. The whole theoretical revolution in literary studies, especially in its Marxist, poststructuralist, and feminist forms, seemed (as Orrin Wang and others have showed in their "genealogical" studies of romanticism, modernity, and postmodernity) to make romanticism the crucial precursor to dominant structures of feeling in the sixties and after.[5] The romantic period began to feel like the origin of everything interesting in our time. But this meant that to be a romanticist meant being many other things as well–a student of modernism, of postmodernism, of theories of culture and history. How could one understand the thought of Marx or Freud or Darwin, for instance, without reading Hegel or Blake or Cuvier? How could one grasp the intricacies of textual interpretation in general without grappling with Coleridge and German romantic hermeneutics? The Yale school dominated literary theory for a decade, yet it was itself dominated by the romantic literary canon. How could one write a history of

3. "And campaign officials have been busily analyzing and deconstructing videotapes and transcripts of Mr. Gore's debates back to 1988, when he ran for the Democratic presidential nomination, a senior adviser to Mr. Bush said" (Frank Bruni, "Campaign Aides Set Tone for Next Big Test in Race," *New York Times*, 21 Aug. 2000, p. A18).

4. Williams Wordsworth, *The Prelude*, in *Selected Poems and Prefaces*, ed. Jack Stillinger (Boston, 1965), l. 108, p. 333.

5. See Orrin Wang, *Fantastic Modernity: Dialectical Readings in Romanticism and Theory* (Baltimore, 1996), and Clifford Siskin, *The Historicity of Romantic Discourse* (New York, 1988).

literature or culture or politics at all without wrestling with the emergence of the very idea of history in the romantic period?[6] And how could one address the concept of the postmodern, seen as a dialectical overturning of the modern, without noticing the parallel with the romantic movement's overturning of the Enlightenment? In the sixties, as in the romantic period, the grand modernizing narratives of endless progress through technical rationality seemed to collide visibly with the resurgence of the primitive, the irrational, and the archaic. Utopian revolutionary hopes wove themselves through the fabric of disillusionment and times of slackening. In short, if all roads seemed to lead us back to the romantic period and that indefinable cultural formation known as romanticism, all roads seemed to lead from it to our own time as well. I took the road away, and now come back, like the Ancient Mariner, to my own country.

2. Getting Physical with Romanticism

The conversation has now turned to Romanticism and the Physical. In the old days, of course, it would have been Romanticism and the Spiritual (or the mental, the psychological, the ideal, the immaterial, the metaphysical). We would have been quoting Blake's "Mental Things are alone real"[7] and Wordsworth's vaporous raptures over the mind and the spirit. But if all roads lead to romanticism, they inevitably bring along with them the baggage of our present concerns—postcoloniality, gender, race, technology, and now the physical.

What exactly is the physical? Is it the physical body? Or the physical, material world more generally, the object of the physical sciences? Is it the domain of nature, the nonhuman realm of what Wordsworth called "rocks, and stones, and trees," and all the rest—the earth, the oceans, the atmosphere, the planets, and stars in their courses?[8] And what is the rhetorical or theoretical force of invoking the physical as a thematic within romanticism? Is this a signal of a new materialism, another overturning of Hegel and idealism? Is it a reflex of the fashion for bodily matters in contemporary criticism and, if so, is this a natural body or a cultural body? A virtual techno-body, a gendered, racialized, erotic body, or a body without organs? Where does the invocation of the physical locate us in the endless debate of nature and culture, the natural and the human sciences? Is it a replaying of the old romantic division between the physical, understood as the organic, living substance, and the material, understood as the inert, dead, or mechanical?

6. For a magisterial study of romantic historicism, see James K. Chandler, *England in 1819: The Politics of Literary Culture and the Case of Romantic Historicism* (Chicago, 1998).

7. William Blake, "A Vision of the Last Judgment," *The Poetry and Prose of William Blake,* ed. David Erdman (Garden City, N.Y., 1965), p. 555.

8. Wordsworth, "A Slumber Did My Spirit Seal," *Selected Poems and Prefaces,* l. 8, p. 115.

The great temptation for romanticists is to think that our gesture of getting physical with romanticism is an accomplishment in itself. We are in danger of supposing that somehow the turn to the physical is a tough-minded and realistic gesture, a politically progressive act of getting down to the concrete, hard facts, the obdurate stuff of things in themselves, an escape from old-fashioned romantic idealism. And of course the more closely we look at both romanticism and at the physical world, the more difficult it becomes to sustain any such illusion. The physical is a thoroughly metaphysical concept. The concrete is (as Hegel points out) the most abstract concept we have; bodies are spiritual entities, constructions of fantasy. Objects only make sense in relation to thinking, speaking subjects, and things are evanescent, multistable appearances; and matter, as we have known since the ancient materialists, is a "lyric substance" more akin to comets, meteors, and electrical storms than to some hard, uniform mass.[9]

3. The Life of Things

Getting physical with romanticism, then, will get us absolutely nowhere if we do not get metaphysical at the same time. We can see this most clearly if we look at the status of the physical in our own time. We live at a strange moment in cultural history, when the most extreme forms of material physicality and real violence are exerted by virtual, disembodied actors. As Katherine Hayles has demonstrated, there are more things, especially more living things, in heaven and earth today than were ever dreamt of by physico-theology, natural philosophy, or romantic idealism.[10] I like to call this the age of biocybernetic reproduction to name the conjunction of biological engineering and information science that has made it possible to simulate physical organisms in the real world out of bits of data and inert substances.[11] Walter Benjamin's "mechanical reproduction," a paradigm of cultural and technical production based in the assembly line and such exemplary figures as the robot, the photograph, and the cinematic sequence has now been replaced by the figures of the clone and the cyborg, the unpredictable, adaptable mechanism. The old opposition between the mechanical and the organic makes no sense or is restaged in films like *Terminator 2* as the difference between the rods, gears, pulleys, and servomotors of the "old" Terminator and the new model composed of living, liquid metal.

9. See Daniel Tiffany, *Toy Medium: Materialism and Modern Lyric* (Berkeley, 1999) for a brilliantly detailed exploration of "poetic substances" and iconologies of matter.
10. See N. Katharine Hayles, "Simulating Narratives: What Virtual Creatures Can Teach Us," *Critical Inquiry* 26 (Autumn 1999): 1–26.
11. See my "The Work of Art in the Age of Biocybernetic Reproduction" in a forthcoming issue of *Critical Inquiry*.

The slogan for our times then is, not things fall apart, but things come alive. The modernist anxiety over the collapse of structure is replaced by the panic over uncontrolled growth of structures—cancers, viruses, and other rapidly evolving entities. The premonition of an imminent decoding of the riddle of life repeats a familiar trope of romanticism, as we see in the resonance between the Frankenstein narrative and its contemporary descendant, *Jurassic Park.* Both stories revolve around the hubristic conquest of death and the production of new living things that threaten to destroy their creators. The difference is that Frankenstein's monster is human and is composed of recently dead matter, corpses fresh from the graveyard. Our contemporary monster, the dinosaur, is nonhuman, a giant beast driven solely by appetite, and it is resurrected from material that is not just long dead but absolutely inert, petrified, and fossilized. No physical remains of the original organic tissues survive in a fossil, only the image or impression, a purely formal trace in which every atom and molecule of the original has been turned to stone. While this may seem like a narrative that depends for its plausibility on contemporary biocybernetics, it is, I will argue, a tale whose foundations were laid in the romantic period.

"The life of things" in romantic literature is sometimes mischaracterized as a matter for unmixed celebration, as when Wordsworth praises "that serene and blessed mood" in which "an eye made quiet by the deep power/Of harmony" sees "into the life of things." But closer readings of this celebrated passage note that something very like the death of the physical body is entailed in this perception:

> the breath of this corporeal frame
> And even the motion of our human blood
> Almost suspended, we are laid asleep
> In body, and become a living soul.[12]

When Blake raises the question, "what is the material world, and is it dead?" his answer comes from a fairy who promises (when tipsy) to show him "all alive/The world, where every particle of dust breathes forth its joy." Yet the life of matter the fairy goes on to describe is a storm of "dismal thunder," pestilence, and "howling terrors" animating the "devouring and devoured" elements, while human history, the "eighteen hundred years" of *Europe,* passes as a dream in the mind of a ravished "nameless shadowy Female."[13] Romantic animism and vitalism are not unmixed affirmations,

---

12. Wordsworth, "Lines Composed a Few Miles above Tintern Abbey," *Selected Poems and Prefaces,* ll. 47–49, 43–46, p. 109.

13. Blake, "Europe a Prophecy" (1794), *The Poetry and Prose of William Blake,* pls. iii, 1, 2, 9, and 1.

but complex, ambivalent weavings of fairy lore and irony, mystical trances and anxiety, joy and sorrow. The stony, petrified sleep of Urizen may be preferable to the pain and terror of living forms. What consolation is it to know that Wordsworth's dead Lucy is "rolled round in earth's diurnal course,/With rocks, and stones, and trees"? Or that his complacent assurance of her vitality was expressible only in terms of a "slumber" that "sealed" the poet's spirit like a gravestone and made him perceive her as "a thing that could not feel/The touch of earthly years"?[14]

What is this new, heightened perception of thingness–of materiality, physicality, objecthood–really all about? Foucault suggests an answer in *The Order of Things*. If things are taking on a new life in the romantic period, if biology is replacing physics as the frontier of science, if new forms of archaic and modern animism and vitalism seem to be springing up on every side, it is because history itself is abandoning Man and moving into the nonhuman world, the world of physical things. We usually suppose exactly the opposite to be the case. As Foucault puts it:

> We are usually inclined to believe that the nineteenth century, largely for political and social reasons, paid closer attention to human history. . . . According to this point of view, the study of economies, the history of literatures and grammars, and even the evolution of living beings are merely the effects of the diffusion . . . of a historicity first revealed in man. In reality, it was the opposite that happened. Things first of all received a historicity proper to them, which freed them from the continuous space that imposed the same chronology upon them as upon men. So that man found himself dispossessed of what constituted the most manifest contents of his history. . . . The human being no longer has any history.[15]

The age of the greatest historical upheavals, of massive political, social, and cultural revolutions, of the invention of history itself, is also, as Hegel insisted, the age of "the end of history," a romantic slogan that has been echoed in our own time in reflections on the end of the cold war.[16]

Once again biology is at the frontier of science, new nonhuman life-forms are everywhere, and a new history of physical objects seems to be rearing its head. Cloned sheep, self-reproducing robots, and the frozen DNA of a Siberian mammoth are front-page news, and images of extinct monsters revived from the dead dominate the world of cinematic spectacle. How can the "life of things" in the romantic period help to illuminate these images?

14. Wordsworth, "A Slumber Did My Spirit Seal," ll. 7–8, 1, 3–4, p. 115.
15. Michel Foucault, *The Order of Things: An Archaeology of Human Sciences*, trans. pub. (New York, 1973), p. 368; hereafter abbreviated *OT*.
16. See Francis Fukuyama, *The End of History and the Last Man* (New York, 1992).

4. Beaver and Mammoth

Consider two physical things–two animals, in fact—that arrived in Europe in the 1790s. One is a mammoth, reconstructed in Paris by Georges Cuvier in 1795 to demonstrate his new theory of fossils, which transforms them from freaks of nature or mere curiosities into traces of extinct life and evidence for a series of catastrophic revolutions in the history of the earth.[17] The other is a beaver, and it arrives in London in 1790 tattooed on the chest of an Englishman named John Long, who worked as a fur trader among five nations of Canadian Indians. Long had been initiated as a Chippewa warrior while working as what we would now call a military advisor to Indian tribes who were fighting as allies of the British against the American colonies. The scanty biographical studies of Long invariably raise the question of whether he scalped or killed American civilians or soldiers while participating in raids.[18] But Long himself is silent about his participation in violence. He is at his most eloquent in describing the exquisite torture of the three-day initiation ceremony.

> He undergoes the following operation. Being extended on his back, the chief draws the figure he intends to make with a pointed stick, dipped in water in which gunpowder has been dissolved; after which, with ten needles dipped vermilion, and fixed in a small wooden frame, he pricks the delineated parts, and where the bolder outlines occur he incises the flesh with a gun flint. The vacant spaces, or those not marked with vermillion, are rubbed in with gunpowder, which produces the variety of red and blue; the wounds are then seared with punk-wood to prevent them from festering.[19]

Long's name for the animal inscribed on his body is "totem," a word from the Ojibway language usually translated "he is a relative of mine" and associated with ideas of animal, vegetable, and sometimes mineral "tutelary spirits," and thus with destiny, identity, and community.[20]

The mammoth on display in Paris and the beaver on John Long's chest are "forms of animal visibility," to borrow Foucault's expression (*OT*,

17. See Martin J. S. Rudwick, *Georges Cuvier, Fossil Bones, and Geological Catastrophes* (Chicago, 1997).

18. A copy of Long's memoir in the John Carter Brown Library, Providence, R. I., contains handwritten notes by George Coleman, Senior, complaining that "this book had better never have been published for it adds fresh disgrace to the English nation, and hurts our character, as it shews that we neither act like Christians or men of common honesty in Canada" (*A Catalogue of Books Relating to North and South America in the Library of John Carter Brown* [Providence, 1871], vol. 2, pt. 2).

19. John Long, *Voyages and Travels in the Years 1768–1788*, ed. Milo Milton Quaife (Chicago, 1922), p. 64.

20. Claude Lévi-Strauss, *Totemism*, trans. Rodney Needham (Boston, 1963), p. 18.

p. 137). They are real objects in the world, but they are also images and verbal expressions. Long's "totem" is a new word in the English language, and it quickly circulates in French and German translations of Long's memoir.[21] Of course the longer range fortunes of this word are legendary. By the mid-nineteenth century it had become a staple of early anthropology and comparative religion. It travels to Australia and the South Pacific, where "totemism" is discovered in its purest form in Aboriginal societies. In the work of Durkheim and Freud it becomes a key to explaining, not just primitive religions, but the foundations of sociology and psychology; it is the object of obsessively thorough critique by Lévi-Strauss and enters popular consciousness in its linkage with the so-called totem poles of the Pacific Northwest coast Indians. In common usage, it is often confused with fetishism and idolatry or equated with animism and nature worship.[22]

If Long brings a new object into the world with a new word from the New World, Cuvier takes an old word-image-idea complex—the fossil—and gives it a revolutionary new meaning. Foucault could not be more emphatic: "One day, towards the end of the eighteenth century, Cuvier was to topple the glass jars of the Museum, smash them open and dissect all the forms of animal visibility that the Classical age had preserved in them" (*OT,* pp. 137–38). In this epistemic revolution, natural history becomes truly historical for the first time, opening up what Wordsworth would call "time's abyss" unimaginably greater than human history.[23] We could debate endlessly whether Cuvier's theory of the fossil as a trace of a life-form wiped out by geological revolutions was an echo of the French Revolution or whether the understanding of that revolution is itself a

---

21. While no sales figures on Long's memoir are traceable, it seems to have achieved fairly wide circulation. Joseph Banks, the president of the Royal Society, headed the list of subscribers. It was favorably reviewed in anon., "Voyages and Travels of an Indian Interpreter and Trader," *Monthly Review* (June 1792): 129–37, and was translated into French (1794, 1810) and German (1791, 1792). See Quaife, "Historical Introduction," in Long, *Voyages and Travels in the Years 1769–1788,* pp. xvii–xviii.

The fortunes of the word and concept *totem* between the 1790s and the 1850s remain a missing chapter in intellectual history that would be fascinating to explore. It would involve, among other things, finding out how this North American Indian word is merged with the Polynesian vocabulary of mana and tapu by Andrew McLennan and E. B. Tylor to become a fixture of comparative religion and ethnography in the second half of the 19th century. I'm grateful here for the help of Raymond Fogelson of the department of anthropology, University of Chicago, for sharing with me his unpublished manuscript on Long's memoir.

22. See Émile Durkheim, *The Elementary Forms of the Religious Life,* trans. Joseph Ward Swain (1915; New York, 1968); Sigmund Freud, *Totem and Taboo,* in *The Standard Edition of the Complete Psychological Works of Sigmund Freud,* trans. and ed. James Strachey, 24 vols. (London, 1953–74), 13:1–162; and Lévi-Strauss, *Totemism.* For an attempt to distinguish fetish, idol, and totem, see my essay, "La Plus-Value des images" ["The Surplus-Value of Images"], trans. Paul Batik, *Études litteraires* (forthcoming).

23. Wordsworth, "Forth from a Jutting Ridge, around Whose Base," *The Complete Poetical Works* (London, 1888), l. 21.

product of the new sense of natural history.[24] In any event, the new meaning of fossils quickly becomes a metaphor for human as well as natural history and specifically for the human relics left behind by the French Revolution. Edward Bulwer-Lytton finds "fossilized remains of the old regime" in certain districts of Paris and describes an aging English baronet as "a fossil witness of the wonders of England, before the deluge of French manners swept away ancient customs."[25] "Fossilism" is a way, in short, of revolutionizing natural history and naturalizing revolutionary human history. Under the spell of this metaphor, political revolution comes to be seen less as a matter of human agency and control than as a product of inhuman, impersonal forces, the life of physical things going out of control in catastrophic upheavals.

5. Forms of Animal Visibility

> The simultaneity of two events is no less a historical fact than their succession.
> —MICHEL FOUCAULT, "Sur les façons d'écrire l'histoire"[26]

What is the relation between the appearance of the fossil and the totem? Foucault makes the fossil the centerpiece of his history of epistemic transformations in *The Order of Things*. The fossil is the principal example of this new "historicity of things" that is independent of human affairs and human history. But he is silent on the other new natural object, the totem. This is surely because totemism arrives unobtrusively, in the memoirs of an obscure Englishman whose name survives only as a footnote in the writings of anthropologists. Cuvier's notion of the fossil, by contrast, was a revolutionary breakthrough and an international sensation in learned circles.

Nevertheless, there is something uncannily fitting about the emergence of these two concepts in the 1790s, something that resonates between them both in their internal logics and in their subsequent careers in intellectual history. Fossils and totems are both "forms of animal visibility," images of natural objects, residing on the border between artifice and

24. Exposing the futility of this debate is, I take it, one of Foucault's key contributions to historical study. My aim here is to describe, not explain, the transformation that made the fossil central to a new system of cognitive and intellectual relations. For more on this noncausal theory of historical change, see Arnold I. Davidson, "Structures and Strategies of Discourse: Remarks Towards a History of Foucault's Philosophy of Language," and Paul Veyne, "Foucault Revolutinizes History," trans. Catherine Porter, in *Foucault and His Interlocutors*, trans. Ann Hobart et al., ed. Davidson (Chicago, 1997), pp. 1–17, 146–82.

25. Edward Bulwer-Lytton, *Pelham; or, Adventures of a Gentleman* (London, 1828), pp. 186, 273.

26. Quoted in Davidson, "Structures and Strategies of Discourse," p. 10.

nature. The fossil is the natural sign par excellence, an imprint in stone, sculpted by petrifaction. Seeing the fossil as a picture or symbol of any kind, however, requires human eyes to pick out the image/organism in the stony matrix. Even a devout anti-evolutionist like Hegel had to account for fossils as readable images. His strategy was to deny that fossils *ever*

> actually lived and then died; on the contrary, they are still-born. . . . It is organoplastic Nature which generates the organic . . . as a dead shape, crystallized through and through, like the artist who represents human and other forms in stone or on a flat canvas. He does not kill people, dry them out and pour stony material into them, or press them into stone. . . . What he does is to produce in accordance with his idea and by means of tools, forms which represent life but are not themselves living: Nature, however, does this directly, without needing such mediation.[27]

The totem also occupies the nature/culture frontier. It is traditionally a handmade image in wood, stone, or skin of an animal; less often it is a vegetable or mineral object. The animal itself is also the totem (though Durkheim will insist that the image is always more sacred than what it represents).[28] Natural organisms are not just entities in themselves, but a system of natural signs, living images, a natural language of *zoographia* or "animal writing" that, from ancient bestiaries to DNA and the new Book of Life, continually reintroduces religion—and animation—into things and their images.[29]

The central physical objects of paleontology and anthropology, twin sciences of ancient life, are conceived in the same decade: anthropology, understood as the science of the savage, of the primitive ancestor living in a state of nature; paleontology, the science of successive states of nature that existed long before the emergence of human life, long before the forms of natural life that we see around us. By the end of the nineteenth century, fossils and totems will serve as the principal display objects of

27. G. W. F. Hegel, *Hegel's Philosophy of Nature,* trans. A. V. Miller (Oxford, 1970), p. 293. I'm grateful to Robert Pippin for his advice on Hegel and natural history.

28. "We arrive at the remarkable conclusion that *the images of totemic beings are more sacred than the beings themselves*" (Durkheim, *The Elementary Forms of the Religious Life,* p. 156). This is surely because the image of the totem animal, like that of the fossilized specimen, is the site where the species being of the individual is "crystallized," as it were, and rendered as a kind of concrete universal.

29. The DNA revolution has not, as one might suppose, utterly secularized the concept of the living organism. Robert Pollack, a collaborator of James Watson, finds the image of the holy city with the sacred text at its center the ideal metaphor for the cell:

> A cell is not just a chemical soup but a molecular city with a center from which critical information flows, a molecular version of King David's Jerusalem. That walled city . . . had a great temple at the center and a book at the very center of the temple. [Robert Pollack, *Signs of Life: The Language and Meanings of DNA* (Boston, 1994), p. 18]

museums of natural history, especially in North America. The relics of ancient life and of so-called primitive life will anchor the biological and cultural wings of these institutions.

Fossil and totem are windows into deep time and dream time respectively, into the childhood of the human race and the earliest stages of its planet. Fossilism is modernized natural history, based in comparative anatomy, systematic notions of species identity, and a mechanistic model of animal physiology.[30] Totemism is *primitive* natural history, what anthropologists now call ethnozoology and ethnobotany, a combination of magical lore and empirical folk wisdom.[31] The fossil is the trace of a vanished life-form and a lost world; the totem is the image of a vanishing, endangered life, the trace of a world disappearing before the advance of exactly that modern civilization that has invented the concept of fossils as a trace of extinct life. If fossils are the evidence for a first nature totally alien to human culture, totems are evidence for what we might call a first second nature, a state of culture that is much closer to nature than our modern world. Both fossils and totems are images of nature, expressing a relationship between human beings and the nonhuman physical world of animal, vegetable, and mineral objects. There are no human fossils, according to Cuvier, and totems are almost never human images, but are invariably drawn from the natural world, a feature that distinguishes them from the tendency to anthropomorphism in idols and fetishes.

6. Totems as Fossils, and Vice Versa

In a very real (if metaphoric) sense, then, totems are fossils, and fossils have the potential to become totems. The first possibility is illustrated by Freud when he opens *Totem and Taboo* by noting that "taboos still exist among us" and

> do not differ in their psychological nature from Kant's "categorical imperative," which operates in a compulsive fashion and rejects any conscious motives. Totemism, on the contrary, is something alien to our contemporary feelings—a religio-social institution which has been long abandoned as an actuality and replaced by newer forms. It has left only the slightest traces behind it in the religions, manners and customs of the civilized peoples of to-day.

30. See Rudwick, *Georges Cuvier, Fossil Bones, and Geological Catastrophe* on Cuvier's insistence on a mechanical model for anatomy. "He put his science firmly on the map, by explaining his conception of organisms . . . as functionally integrated 'animal machines'" (p. 15).
31. See Scott Atran, *Cognitive Foundations of Natural History: Towards an Anthropology of Science* (Cambridge, 1990), and my discussion in *The Last Dinosaur Book: The Life and Times of a Cultural Icon* (Chicago, 1998), for an account of folk taxonomy and ethnobiology.

Freud goes on to note the parallel between natural and cultural history that obtains in the one place on earth where totemism seems to survive: "the tribes which have been described by anthropologists as the most backward and miserable of savages, the aborigines of Australia, the youngest continent, in whose fauna, too, we can still observe much that is archaic and that has perished elsewhere."[32] Australia is the land of living fossils, where both totemism and "archaic" life-forms survive together. Edward B. Tylor, the founding father of modern anthropology, laid the groundwork for theories of "social evolution" in his "'doctrine of survivals,'" the preservation of what *The Dictionary of Anthropology* calls "obsolete or archaic aspects of culture" as "living cultural fossils."[33]

Fossils become totemic, on the other hand, when they escape (as they inevitably do) from the grip of scientific classification and become objects of public display and popular mythology. I have traced some of this process in *The Last Dinosaur Book*, exploring the transformation of the American mammoth or mastodon into a national icon during the Jeffersonian period and the emergence of the dinosaur as a totem figure of the British empire in the mid-nineteenth century and of American modernity in the twentieth century.[34]

Given the numerous parallels and analogies between totems and fossils, it seems surprising that they have never, to my knowledge, been brought into a metaphorical relationship. This is principally a result, I suspect, of the disciplinary divisions between biology and anthropology, between the "natural" and "cultural" wings of the natural history museum. Fossils and totems cannot be compared with one another. The one is the trace of an extinct animal, an image reconstructed by the methods of modern science. The other is the image of a living animal, as constructed within a premodern set of religious or magical rituals. To compare fossils and totems is to undermine the difference between science and superstition, to violate a taboo against mixing distinct kinds of objects and genres of discourse.

Nevertheless the very proximity of fossil and totem images in public displays, especially in the natural history museums of North America— in New York, Washington, D.C., Pittsburgh, Chicago, and Toronto— makes the metonymic, if not metaphoric relations of these images unavoidable. Perhaps most dramatic is the central hall of the Field Mu-

32. Freud, *Totem and Taboo*, 13:xiv, 1.

33. Thomas Barfield, "Edward Burnett Tylor," *The Dictionary of Anthropology*, ed. Barfield (Oxford, 1997), p. 478.

34. Clearly, fossil bones were already filled with totemic potential for premodern and ancient cultures. Jefferson gathered Delaware Indian legends about the mastodon, and later ethnographers noted Sioux legends of a subterranean monster that were probably based on large fossil bones. Adrienne Mayor's recent book, *The First Fossil Hunters: Paleontology in Greek and Roman Times* (Princeton, N.J., 2000) points out that Greek and Roman images of the griffin, as well as legendary wars of primeval giants and monsters were very likely based on the large fossil bones to be found in Turkey and Asia Minor.

seum in Chicago, in which the most prominent objects of display are the Kwakiutl totem poles from the Pacific Northwest and (now) the *Tyranno- saurus rex* named Sue.[35] Fossils and totems coexist and greet each other in the natural history museums of North America even if they have not yet acknowledged their kinship. The romantic and the North American genealogies of these institutions make it seem somehow appropriate to stage their encounter at a meeting of the North American Society for the Study of Romanticism.

7. The Romantic Image and the Dialectical Object

What does all this add up to for the study of romanticism and its legacy? In one sense, of course, I am simply revisiting very old and famil- iar territory in romantic studies, the regions that Arthur Lovejoy long ago designated by the names of "organicism" and "primitivism."[36] Both fossils and totems are concrete instances, physical, minute particulars that instantiate these very broad conceptions. Each is both "organic" and "primitive" in its way, providing a glimpse into the deep past and the deep present of physical things from the different angles of nature and culture. So you might well ask, what is gained by focussing so minutely on these exemplary objects?

One hopes, of course, that concreteness and specificity will be sources of added value in themselves. Marx's key contribution to the his- tory of ideas, in my view, was his insistence on tracing what he called the "concreteness of concepts" to their origins in practical, historical circum- stances (a matter I discuss at some length in *Iconology*).[37] But he did not perform this maneuver with the notion of fixing a metaphysical origin in material things but rather to trace the dialectics of the object, its shifting placement and significance in human history. The theory of the commod- ity fetish proceeds by refusing to reduce either the commodity or its an- thropological analogue, the fetish, with an iconoclastic critique that denies or destroys the "life of things."[38] Like Nietzsche, Marx refuses the strategy of straightforwardly smashing the idols of the mind, the tribe, or the marketplace. Instead, he "sounds" the idols with the tuning fork of his own critical language, makes them speak and resonate to divulge their hollowness, as when he invites the commodity to talk about its own life.[39]

35. Before Sue became the main attraction in the Field's great hall, "she" was pre- ceded by an impressively tall Brachiosaurus, which now scrapes the ceiling of the United Airlines terminal at O'Hare airport.

36. See Arthur O. Lovejoy's classic essay, "On the Discrimination of Romanticisms," *PMLA* 39, no. 2 (1924): 229–53.

37. See Mitchell, *Iconology: Image, Text, Ideology* (Chicago, 1986).

38. See my "Surplus-Value of Images" for a more detailed version of this argument.

39. "As regards the sounding-out of idols, this time they are not idols of the age but *eternal* idols which are here touched with the hammer as with a tuning fork" (Friedrich

The concreteness of the totem and fossil as physical objects, then, is only half the story. The other half is the abstract, metaphysical, and imaginary character of these objects, their lives not only as real objects, but as words circulating in the new discourses of paleontology and anthropology and (beyond that) in new commonplaces and poetic tropes. But to call them tropes is already to associate them with that strange attractor, the image, that has always bedeviled romantic poetics. Romanticism has circulated obsessively around the notion of the image, understood as both the origin and destination of literary expression, from Coleridge's "living educts of the imagination," to Blake's graphic images, whose bosoms we are encouraged to enter as friends and companions.[40]

In his classic essay "Intentional Structure of the Romantic Image," Paul de Man begins with the thoroughly uncontroversial claim that imagery and imagination (along with metaphor and figuration) take on an unprecedented centrality in romantic poetics and that this is coupled with a new concentration on nature: "An abundant imagery coinciding with an equally abundant quantity of natural objects, the theme of imagination linked closely to the theme of nature, such is the fundamental ambiguity that characterizes the poetics of romanticism."[41] But why is this an ambiguity? Why does it constitute, in de Man's words, a "tension between two polarities" rather than a natural fit between two domains, the mind and the world, the image and the natural object? De Man's answer is that language itself is what makes the "natural image" impossible for poetry, or even for imagination, and condemns romantic poetry to expressions of "nostalgia for the natural object" (*RR*, p. 6). "Critics who speak of a 'happy relationship' between matter and consciousness," argues de Man, "fail to realize that the very fact that the relationship has to be established within the medium of language indicates that it does not exist in actuality" (*RR*, p. 8).

The problem I have always had with this explanation is that language is given too much blame and too much credit for the unhappy consciousness of romanticism. If language as such were the culprit, then the strange ambivalence de Man describes would be the condition of all poetry and not distinctive to the late eighteenth and early nineteenth centuries in Europe and England. "The word," de Man insists, "is always a free presence to the mind, the means by which the permanence of natural entities can be put into question and thus negated, time and again, in the endlessly widening spiral of the dialectic" (*RR*, p. 6).

Nietzsche, *The Twilight of the Idols* [1889], *"Twilight of the Idols" and "The Anti-Christ,"* trans. R. J. Hollingdale [Harmondsworth, 1968], p. 22).

40. Samuel Taylor Coleridge, "The Statesman's Manual" (1816), in *Political Tracts of Wordsworth, Coleridge, and Shelley*, ed. R. J. White (Cambridge, 1953), p. 24. See Blake, "A Vision of the Last Judgment," p. 550.

41. Paul de Man, "Intentional Structure of the Romantic Image," *The Rhetoric of Romanticism* (New York, 1984), p. 2; hereafter abbreviated *RR*.

But suppose natural, physical objects were already caught up in the dialectic before being put into question by "the word"? Suppose the image was not, as de Man seems to think, merely an emphatic expression of language's desire to draw closer to the natural object, but a visible and material entity, a representation in a physical medium like stone or human flesh? Suppose further that these sorts of representations were appearing for the first time in Europe in concrete, public manifestations that resonated deeply with the great historical events of the time? Cuvier's fossil mastodon and Long's beaver totem are, of course, new words, or new meanings for old words. But they are also physical manifestations, a reconstructed assembly of petrified bone fragments and a figure carved and burned on the chest of a veteran of the Indian wars. Language is important, but it is not everything. And poetic language is the place where the world beyond language comes home to roost, at least temporarily.

I propose then a revision of de Man's theory of the romantic image, one that preserves its dialectical character and its combination of irony and sentimentality toward the concrete things of the natural world. The romantic image becomes a composite of two concrete concepts, the fossil and the totem. Totemism is the figure of the longing for an intimate relationship with nature and the greeting of natural objects as "friends and companions"—the entire panoply of tutelary spirits from Wordsworth's daffodils to Coleridge's albatross to Shelley's west wind. It is also, as these examples should remind us, the figure of the kind of guilt, loss, and tragic transgression that only becomes imaginable when natural objects enter into a family romance with human consciousness. The totem animal must not be killed; the nightingale was not born for death, and so of course the albatross is killed, and everything that lives must die, even the nightingale.

This is the point where the figure of the fossil enters the picture, bringing with it the spectre not just of individual death but of species extinction. If totemism adumbrates the romantic longing for a reunification with nature, akin to Hegel's notion of the "flower" and "animal" religions that lie at the origins of spirit's encounter with nature, fossilism expresses the ironic and catastrophic consciousness of modernity and revolution.[42] As a petrified imprint, both icon and index, of a lost form of life, the fossil is already an image, and a "natural image" in the most literal sense we can give these words. As verbal figure, moreover, the fossil is an image of the very process that de Man associates with "the medium of language." Emerson is perhaps the first to say this explicitly when he declares that

> Language is fossil poetry. As the limestone of the continent consists of infinite masses of the shells of animalcules, so language is made

42. See Hegel, *Phenomenology of Spirit*, trans. Miller (Oxford, 1977), §§689–90.

up of images or tropes, which now, in their secondary use, have long ceased to remind us of their poetic origin. But the poet names the thing because he sees it, or comes one step nearer to it than any other. This expression or naming is not art, but a second nature, grown out of the first, as a leaf out of a tree.[43]

If the romantic desire for an image to secure an intimate communion with nature is itself a form of totemism, the inevitable defeat of this desire is named by the fossil, which turns out to be a name for the dead images that make up language as such. The living origin of language is in metaphor. And the first metaphors, as commentators from Rousseau to John Berger have remarked, were animals. As Berger puts it (writing as confidently as if he were Rousseau), "The first subject matter for painting was animal. Probably the first paint was animal blood. Prior to that, it is not unreasonable to suppose that the first metaphor was animal."[44] Totems and fossils are both animal images, one living, organic, and cultural (but archaic and obsolete), the other dead, mechanical, and natural (but brought back to life by modern science).

When Adorno comes to his critique of "World Spirit and Natural History" in *Negative Dialectics,* his aim is not just to overturn Hegel's thoroughly ahistorical and mythic notion of nature, the "organoplastic" artist of fossil images. He is also, like Benjamin, aiming at the formulation of dialectical images, which would capture "the objectivity of historic life" as a form of "natural history." Marx, Adorno reminds us, "was a Social Darwinist" who recognized that no amount of critique would allow the "natural evolutionary phases" of "modern society's economic motion" to be "skipped or decreed out of existence."[45] This dynamic and evolutionary notion of natural history can, of course, become as rigid an ideology in its lockstep sequence of phases as the timeless order of ideological nature that it opposes. Among the many lessons we might learn from the simultaneous onset of fossilism and totemism in the romantic era is that when new objects appear in the world, they also bring with them new orders of temporality, new dialectical images that interfere with and complicate one another. Just when we think that things are safely dead, fossilized, petrified, and consigned to the past, they rise from their graves of natural extinction and cultural obsolescence. Dream time and deep time,

43. Ralph Waldo Emerson, "The Poet" (1884), *The Selected Writings of Ralph Waldo Emerson,* ed. Brooks Atkinson (New York, 1950), pp. 329–30.

44. John Berger, "Why Look at Animals?" *About Looking* (New York, 1980), p. 5. See also my essay, "Looking at Animals Looking," in *Picture Theory: Essays on Verbal and Visual Representation* (Chicago, 1994), pp. 329–44.

45. Theodor Adorno, *Negative Dialectics,* trans. E. B. Ashton (New York, 1973), pp. 354–55. For a discussion of Adorno and Benjamin's deployment of natural history, and especially of figures of petrification and fossilization in their theories of allegory and imagery, see Beatrice Hanssen, *Walter Benjamin's Other History: Of Stones, Animals, Human Beings, and Angels* (Berkeley, 1998).

modern anthropology and geology, together weave a spell of natural imagery in the poetry of the romantic era, an imagery that continues to haunt critical theory today.

It is perhaps not so surprising that the romantic image should turn out to be a combination of fossilism and totemism, a dialectical figure of animation and petrification, a ruinous trace of catastrophe, and a "vital sign." After all, romanticism itself plays something like this double role in our sense of cultural and literary history. Why does the professional formation known as romantic studies have such a peculiar and persistent life in the academic study of cultural history? Is it not because we take a more than professional interest in this period and its ideologies? Not content with "historicizing" romanticism, we seem to want it to do more for us, to revive and renovate our own time. Is not romanticism itself a fossil formation in the history of culture, not only because of its obsession with lost worlds, ruins, archaism, childhood, and idealistic notions of feeling and imagination, but because it is itself a lost world, swept away by the floods of modernity it attempted to criticize? And is not romanticism therefore itself a totem object, a figure of collective identification for a tribe of cultural historians called romanticists and, beyond that, for a structure of feeling more generally available to anyone who identifies him- or herself as a romantic? The survival of this structure of feeling, and the poetic and critical resources it makes available, is a story that goes beyond my limits here. Suffice it to say that the critique of modernity that runs through Marx, Nietzsche, and Freud to Benjamin and Adorno would be unthinkable without the special form of natural history bequeathed to us by the romantics, captured in its particularity by the figures of the fossil and the totem. Bruno Latour has assured us that, in reality, "we have never been modern,"[46] and I would only add that this must mean we have always been romantic.

46. See Bruno Latour, *We Have Never Been Modern,* trans. Porter (Cambridge, Mass., 1993).

The Russian Constructivist Flapper Dress

Christina Kiaer

A geometric textile design by the Russian Constructivist Liubov' Popova appeared on the cover of an issue of *Lef,* the journal of the Left literary and artistic avant-garde, in 1924 (fig. 1). The issue was dedicated to her; she had died suddenly of scarlet fever at the age of thirty-five in May of that year. In their dedication, the editors wrote,

> Popova was a constructivist-productivist not only in words, but in deed. When she and Stepanova were invited to work at [the First State Cotton-Printing] factory, no one was happier than she was. Day and night she sat making her drawings for fabrics, attempting in one

This essay has benefitted from a long gestation, including the opportunity to present versions of it as public lectures. I would like to thank the organizers and audiences of the session on Fashion, Identity, and Cultural History chaired by Leila Kinney and Nancy Troy at the annual meeting of the College Art Association in Los Angeles in 1999; the In the House lecture series at the Institute for Research on Women and Gender, Columbia University (particularly Nadia Michoustina); the modernist colloquium in the department of art history, Yale University (especially Christopher Wood); and the symposium New Work on the Russian Avant-garde at the University of California, Berkeley. I would also like to thank the members of the graduate seminar on the Russian avant-garde that I taught in the department of the history of art at Berkeley in the spring of 2000 for their careful reading of this essay; in particular the comments of Anthony Grudin, Ara Merjian, Allison Schachter, and John Tain all bore fruit in the text. Robert Gamboa read this essay with typical engagement and generosity; I have come to rely on his exacting response to my work.

All translations from the Russian are my own unless otherwise noted.

creative act to unite the demands of economics, the laws of exterior design and the mysterious taste of the peasant woman from Tula.[1]

Working at the First State Cotton-Printing Factory in Moscow in 1923–24, Popova and her colleague Varvara Stepanova were the only Constructivists to see their designs for everyday, utilitarian things (other than posters and publication graphics) actually mass-produced and distributed in the Soviet economy. They fulfilled the Constructivist brief of abandoning the role of individual artist-craftsman and entering into collective factory production as "artist-productivists" to produce utilitarian things for the socialist collective. Yet textile design, as a traditional practice of applied art associated with the decorative arts and fashion, might not be expected to fulfil the role demanded of the technologically oriented productivist. It would seem, in fact, to lie beneath the technological aspirations—exemplified by the systemic structures of the early sculptural constructions, the photomontage propaganda posters, the mechanical contraptions such as "radio-orator stands," and so on—that we usually associate with the productivist imperative of Constructivism.

But the language of the *Lef* dedication is instructive because it suggests a previously unexamined Constructivist concern with the problem of forging a new form of socialist *consumption* as an alternative to the consumerism of capitalist modernity. The description of Popova's "creative act" offers in fact a highly economical explanation of a key term in the Constructivist lexicon: *tselesoobraznost'*, which can be translated literally as "formed in relation to, or conforming to, a goal."[2] According to the *Lef* editors, Constructivist *tselesoobraznost'* concerned itself with the material form of things not only in relation to technical problems of utilitarian form ("the laws of exterior design") but also in relation to the new socialist economy ("the demands of economics") and the need to appeal to consumer desire ("the mysterious taste of the peasant woman from Tula"). Constructivist theorists and artists, then, although famed for their com-

1. The editors, "Pamiati L. S. Popovoi," *Lef* 2, no. 6 (1924): 4. The text refers to the factory as the "former Tsindel'," which was its prerevolutionary name.

2. *Tselesoobraznost'* is consistently translated as "expediency" in most English-language texts on Constructivism. But I offer my clunkier and more literal translation because current English usage favors the opportunistic or self-interested meaning of "expedient" rather than the primary and neutral meaning of "suitable for achieving a particular end."

Christina Kiaer (chk28@ columbia.edu) is an associate professor in the department of art history and archaeology, Columbia University, where she teaches modern art. Her book, *Imagine No Possessions: The "Socialist Objects" of Russian Constructivism*, is forthcoming. She is currently working on a new project on the socialist realist painter Aleksandr Deineka.

Fig. 1.—Aleksandr Rodchenko, cover of *Lef,* no. 2 (1924), incorporating Popova fabric design.

mitment to technological *production*, also invented the concept of the everyday material object of socialist *consumption* as a socialist thing. This
thing would be an active "co-worker" or "comrade" of the human subject
rather than a mere commodity to be possessed.[3] The very mundanity of
cheap printed cotton fabric—its absolute usefulness in the "new everyday
life" (*novyi byt*) being promoted by the Bolsheviks after the revolution—
made it an exemplary Constructivist thing. But it is exemplary only if
Constructivism is acknowledged as a practice that sees that the subject is
formed as much through the process of *using* objects in everyday life as
by *making* them in the sphere of production.

As the celebratory *Lef* dedication makes vivid, Popova and Stepanova
were central players in the Constructivist subset of the avant-garde; the
Russian avant-garde of the early twentieth century is well-known for the
unusual prominence of women artists within it.[4] Yet Popova and Stepanova, not their male counterparts, were the ones who worked in textile
design, a traditionally feminine area of artistic endeavor.[5] The story of
their textile-design work could therefore be recruited for a history of
modernist women artists who have in various ways reclaimed feminized
areas of craft for high art—artists such as Anni Albers at the weaving workshop at the Bauhaus (where women were prohibited from participating
in the more strenuous wall-painting and furniture workshops and were
directed instead to ceramics and weaving); Sonia Delaunay with her cubist-
inspired fabric and fashion; Hannah Höch, whose later dada collages critically incorporate fabrics and images of domesticity and fashion; and

3. The productivist theorist Boris Arvatov calls the object a "co-worker" in an important essay from 1925 (Boris Arvatov, "Everyday Life and the Culture of the Thing (Toward
the Formulation of the Question)," trans. Christina Kiaer, *October*, no. 81 [Summer 1997]:
124; hereafter abbreviated "EL"). Aleksandr Rodchenko calls the object a "comrade" in his
letters home from Paris in 1925; see Aleksandr Rodchenko, "Rodchenko v Parizhe: Iz pisem
domoi," *Novyi lef*, no. 2 (1927): 9–21. For an account of Constructivism that develops the
model of production, see Maria Gough, *The Artist as Producer* (forthcoming).
4. This aspect of the Russian avant-garde is often mentioned, although surprisingly
little scholarship exists on it; until recently, M. N. Yablonskaya, *Women Artists of Russia's New
Age, 1900–1935*, trans. and ed. Anthony Parton (London, 1990) was the only major publication to address the women artists as an entity within the avant-garde. This has changed
with the publication of *Amazons of the Russian Avant-garde*, ed. John E. Bowlt and Matthew
Drutt (exhibition catalog, Solomon R. Guggenheim Museum, New York, 14 Sept. 2000–10
Jan. 2001). (The rather unfortunate title of the exhibition stems from a phrase applied to
the artists by their contemporary, the poet Benedikt Livshits.) The catalog essays attempt to
answer the question why such an unusual number of women reached prominence within
the Russian avant-garde (six women artists were represented in the exhibition). Ekaterina
Dyogot's excellent catalog essay, "Creative Women, Creative Men, and Paradigms of Creativity: Why Have There Been Great Women Artists?" pp. 109–27, in particular, offers a
theoretical, feminist account of the gendered cultural categories that supported the prominence of women artists.
5. On the ties between the decorative arts and femininity in the Russian context, see
Briony Fer, "The Language of Construction," in Fer, David Batchelor, and Paul Wood, *Realism, Rationalism, Surrealism: Art between the Wars* (New Haven, Conn., 1993), pp. 87–169.

Meret Oppenheim with her fur-lined surrealist teacup; as well as a whole generation of second-wave-feminism-inspired artists since the 1970s working in "femmage" styles. But a conscious retrieval of fabric design as a typically feminine practice was emphatically *not* how Popova and Stepanova themselves articulated their practice. As committed productivists who had foresworn the individual touch of painting and craft, their stated goals at the textile factory were precisely the scientific and technical ones usually associated with Constructivism: the opportunity to develop skills of mechanical drawing, to participate in the factory research laboratory and production decisions, and to see their work enter the process of mass industrial production.

The Constructivist interest in technical and systematic modes of making is most often described as a move toward transparency, to use the productivists' own term, or indexicality, to use the semiotic term.[6] The productivist critic and theorist Boris Arvatov, whose theory of the socialist thing I will be considering in this essay, describes the development of the ideal form of the modern thing in this way: "the mechanism of a thing, the connection between the elements of a thing and its purpose, were now transparent" ("EL," p. 126). The transparent or indexical thing demonstrates its *tselesoobraznost'*—the connection between its material form and its purpose—by showing us how it was made. This "rhetoric of indexicality" dominated Constructivist writings, and it has contributed to our usual definition of Constructivism as an avant-garde that embodies the modernist desire for transparency and rationality. But I believe that this rhetoric has been too narrowly interpreted in terms of an instrumental utilitarianism. Instead, the transparency and rationality of the Construc-

---

6. The efficacy of the index in relation to Constructivism is proposed by Gough in her discussion of Rodchenko's *Hanging Spatial Constructions* (c. 1920): "Rodchenko elaborates a nascent principle of deductive or indexical structure: the very structure of the work reveals the process of its production" (Gough, "In the Laboratory of Constructivism: Karl Ioganson's Cold Structures," *October,* no. 84 [Spring 1998]: 113). As Gough points out, it was Rosalind Krauss who demonstrated the importance of the index for analyzing modernist art; see Rosalind Krauss, "Notes on the Index," pts. 1 and 2, *The Originality of the Avant-garde and Other Modernist Myths* (Cambridge, Mass., 1985), pp. 196–219. While the notion of indexical structure may be a productive heuristic device for analyzing Rodchenko's systemic *Constructions,* completed just before his shift to the utilitarian-productivist model of Constructivism, it cannot be transferred unchanged to an analysis of his or other Constructivists' utilitarian things. Gough does not propose such a transfer in her essay, but other scholars, such as Hubertus Gassner, have done so; he claims that once the systemic (or for Gough, indexical) constructions of early Constructivism were harnessed for utilitarian purposes, their forms lost their theoretical clarity, and they became instruments of subjugation. For Gassner, in other words, the indexical model of transparency must be predicated on the refusal of the opacities introduced by the historical situatedness of the thing. My aim is to argue for a model of transparency that does not require such a refusal. See Hubertus Gassner, "The Constructivists: Modernism on the Way to Modernization," in *The Great Utopia: The Russian and Soviet Avant-garde, 1915–1932* (exhibition catalog, the Solomon R. Guggenheim Museum, New York, 25 Sept.–15 Dec. 1992), pp. 298–319.

tivist thing does not preclude it from addressing the opacity of commodity desire in the everyday life of modernity. The utilitarian "goal" or "purpose" referenced by *tselesoobraznost'* is not only the mechanical purpose of the thing but the larger purpose of confronting the phantasmatic power of the commodity object and redeeming it for socialism.

Popova and Stepanova acknowledged this phantasmatic power of the object; they knew that the real test of their textile-design work at the First State Cotton-Printing Factory would come in clothing design—in the formation, from their fabrics, of three-dimensional things for use in everyday life. Fashion would therefore be the site of their Constructivist intervention into revolutionary material culture, an area of consumer culture that was undeniably associated with femininity. But then so was *byt* (everyday life) itself—the chosen field of action for the Constructivist thing. In Russian culture, the split between *byt* (everyday life) and *bytie* (higher spiritual or intellectual existence) is arguably even more tenacious than in other cultures. The tenacity of this split paradoxically supported the rise to prominence of women writers and artists in the early twentieth century; in the context of the hypervaluation placed on literary and, to a lesser extent, artistic achievements (Russia is well-known for its cult of literary celebrity), women could "transcend" the usual limitations imposed by their gender. (The ur-example from our period is the revered poet Anna Akhmatova.) It is therefore all the more perverse and challenging that Popova and Stepanova, as women artists, would take their hard-won productivist credentials *back* into *byt*—into its most commercialized and feminized guise of fashion—and aim to make a Constructivist difference there. As Constructivists within the field of fashion they acknowledged the individual desires of the female consumer while remaining critical of them and attempting to steer them in more collective directions. I will establish Popova and Stepanova's productivist commitment to the project of the transparent or indexical Constructivist thing *as well as* their openness to confronting the desires encompassed by fashion commodities—with an emphasis on the former for Stepanova and her designs for sports clothing and on the latter for Popova and her designs for flapper dresses.

Griselda Pollock has suggested that the historical presence of women artists in a "field of representation so powerfully dominated by the beat of men's drums . . . offers a shift in the pattern of meanings in a given culture."[7] But Popova and Stepanova did not simply shift the meanings within an already-defined field; rather, the shifts they introduced through their textile and fashion work were in fact foundational to the very formation of what I am proposing as the most productive version of the Constructivist object as a socialist thing. Tarrying with the feminized

7. Griselda Pollock, *Differencing the Canon: Feminist Desire and the Writing of Art's Histories* (London, 1999), p. 124.

domains of the everyday and the commodity were part and parcel of this Constructivist art-into-life practice; at this moment, Vladimir Tatlin was designing stoves and pots and pans for proletarian kitchens, and Aleksandr Rodchenko was making cookie advertisements for Mossel'prom, the state-owned agricultural trust.[8]

Constructivist things like pots, cookie ads, and flapper dresses—related as they are to everyday life and commerce—have a distinctly marginal look to them in the context of modern art and in the context of the technological ambitions of the early Constructivist manifestoes. The two main Popova scholars say as much when they write that Popova's fashion experiments, as opposed to her textile designs at the factory, raise the problem of the extent to which her art is Constructivist at all:

> If in our analysis of her fabrics we immediately felt the presence of the Constructivist aesthetic (regular geometrism, the use of black and white, the slight graphic tone), then all the phenomena as a whole—clothing and textile design both—clearly exceed the stylistic framework and aesthetic principles of Constructivism.[9]

My argument will be the opposite: Popova's flapper dress exceeds our given definitions of Constructivism only because those definitions are too narrow. Marginal Constructivist things like the flapper dress, as well as the idiosyncratic Constructivist theoretical writings on the thing in everyday life, *are* Constructivism—if we understand the Constructivist project more expansively. Popova and Stepanova's project, as the most successfully realized example of Constructivist theory, is thus front and center in the story of the Constructivist thing. Their things are both indebted to, and deviate from, traditionally feminine forms of artistic practice. They

8. On Tatlin, see Kiaer, "Les Objets quotidiens du constructivisme russe," *Les Cahiers du Musée National d'Art Moderne* 64 (Summer 1998): 31–69; on Tatlin and Rodchenko, see Kiaer, *Imagine No Possessions: The "Socialist Objects" of Russian Constructivism* (manuscript in preparation), chaps. 1 and 3.

9. Dmitri V. Sarabianov and Natalia L. Adaskina, *Popova*, trans. Marian Schwartz (New York, 1990), p. 304; hereafter abbreviated *P*. Christina Lodder in her comprehensive history makes a similar argument: she calls Popova's elegant dress designs a "deviation" from the defined objectives of Constructivism (Christina Lodder, *Russian Constructivism* [New Haven, Conn., 1983], p. 152; hereafter abbreviated *RC*). Lodder also emphasizes the traditional nature of textile design itself, claiming that it should actually be seen as a "pragmatic retreat" from the Constructivist ideal, and argues that it is only through the connection with clothing design projects that it can be understood as part of the larger project, which she defines as "the restructuring of the entire environment in accord with Constructivist principles" (*RC*, p. 151). Lodder judges Constructivist practice very strictly by the standard of whether or not it adhered to the original goals of Constructivism. Her account adheres to the orthodox Marxist perspective that shaped the first Constructivist manifestoes: only production and productive labor hold the keys to social transformation. More traditional practices of applied art, such as fabric or poster design, or the crafting of prototype objects of everyday life, are merely superstructural and cannot be the sites of social change.

demonstrate that Constructivism itself, as theory and practice, can be understood as an avant-garde that unsettles some of the gendered hierarchies of modernist art.

Into Production![10]

Popova and Stepanova began to work for the First State Cotton-Printing Factory sometime in the late fall of 1923.[11] It was a massive and well-known factory on the banks of the Moscow River that had been privately owned before the revolution by Emil Tsindel'; despite its new post-revolutionary name, most people in the early 1920s, including Popova and Stepanova, still referred to it as the Tsindel' factory (fig. 2). After years of world and civil war, revolution, and embargo had cut off contact with other industrialized nations, Soviet textile producers, like most other recently nationalized manufacturers struggling to produce efficiently in the shaky postrevolutionary economy, were burdened by outmoded equipment and designs. In an effort to jump-start the sorry state of the factory's production, the director, Aleksandr Arkhangelskii, took the creative risk of hiring a pair of avant-garde artists as textile designers. He took the unprecedented step—for a Soviet industrial manager—of actually heeding the many Constructivist speeches, articles, and manifestoes that declared that the new "artist-constructors" of the left avant-garde held the key to improving the quality and competitiveness of Soviet industry. The Constructivist women were most likely invited to work there, while their male colleagues were not, because of the feminization of the textile industry; in Russia as in other industrialized countries, textile workers were predominantly women. Yet if Popova and Stepanova's gender may have naturalized them as employees for Arkhangelskii, their avant-garde credentials and notoriety landed them the job. They were well-known in Moscow for their costume and set designs for the avant-garde theater director Vsevolod Meierkhol'd, which had been widely discussed

10. The title of this section is taken from Osip Brik, "V proizvodstvo!" *Lef* 1, no. 1 (1923): 105–8.

11. No definitive archival evidence of the terms of their employment at the factory, including the starting date, has yet been found. But contemporary accounts suggest that they were invited to work there by the director in the fall of 1923 and that they were certainly working there by January 1924. Popova was still working for the factory at the time of her death in May 1924; according to the art historian Alexander Lavrentiev, who is also Stepanova's grandson, Stepanova continued working there until 1925. For synthetic accounts of the available sources for this history, see Alexander Lavrentiev, *Varvara Stepanova: The Complete Work*, trans. Wendy Salmond, ed. John E. Bowit (Cambridge, Mass., 1988), pp. 79–84; *P*, pp. 299–303; *RC*, pp. 146–52; and Tatiana Strizhenova, *Soviet Costume and Textiles, 1917–1945*, trans. Era Mozolkova (Moscow, 1991), pp. 135–47, hereafter abbreviated *SCT*.

FIG. 2.—Detail, brochure from the Tsindel' factory.

in the press, and Stepanova had even made a foray into the discourse of clothing production by publishing an article called "Today's Clothing Is Production Clothing" in *Lef* in early 1923.[12]

When Popova and Stepanova entered the First State Cotton-Printing Factory, they attempted to define their role precisely as that of the productivist artist-engineer. They wrote a high-handed memo to the factory administration with the following demands:

> 1. Participation in the production sections . . . with the right to vote (on production plans, production models, the acquisition of design drawings and the hiring of workers for artistic work). 2. Participation in the chemistry laboratory to observe the coloring process. 3. The

12. See Varvara Stepanova, "Kostium segodniashnego dnia—prozodezhda," *Lef* 1, no. 2 (1923): 65–68, which I discuss below. Popova designed the set and costumes for Meierkhol'd's 1922 production of *The Magnanimous Cuckold,* while Stepanova similarly designed his production of *The Death of Tarelkin* in the same year.

production of designs for block-printed fabrics according to our requirements and proposals.[13]

The third demand was meant to give them the right to determine the
types of fabrics printed in relation to their proposed uses—in other words,
to connect the "traditional" applied-art aspect of the textile-printing process to the more ambitious one of the shaping or forming of mass-produced
objects such as clothing.[14] By voicing their desire to be involved in production decisions and to enter the industrial laboratories of the factory, they
attempted to differentiate themselves from traditional applied artists who
stayed within the artistic domain of the design departments. They threw
themselves into the study of the cotton-printing process, developing an
understanding, for example, of the limitations posed by the narrow width
of the factory's print rollers and its outmoded conveyor system.

A skeptic might well ask on what grounds Popova and Stepanova
expected that they could possibly be qualified to run technical laboratories in factories. Their qualification (*kvalifikatsiia,* a key buzzword of the
time), they would answer, was their training as abstract, modernist artists.
They both had participated in the debates leading to the formation of
the First Working Group of Constructivists in March of 1921 at the Institute of Artistic Culture (*Institut Khudozhestvennoi Kul'tury,* or Inkhuk) in
Moscow. The Inkhuk was an unprecedented institution: an art institute
sponsored by the state that was set up solely for the purpose of conduct-
ing research on modernism in art. The artists, critics, and historians who
were members researched the very building blocks of art making—material, texture (*faktura*), color, space, time, form, and technique (*tekhnika*)—
and investigated psychological and physical responses to art through
studies and questionnaires.[15] The Inkhuk research program exemplifies
the definition of modernism articulated by Clement Greenberg: the self-
critical attention given by advanced artists, beginning in the second half
of the nineteenth century, to the materials, processes of making, and
structures of reception that are inherent and exclusive to particular art

13. Stepanova and L. S. Popova, "Memo to the Directorate for the First State Cotton-
Printing Factory" (1924), manuscript, Rodchenko-Stepanova Archive, Moscow; quoted in
A. N. Lavrentiev, "Poeziia graficheskogo dizaina v tvorchestve Varvary Stepanovoi," *Tekh-
nicheskaia estetika* (1980): 25; trans. in *SCT,* p. 136; trans. mod.

14. This interpretation of the memo is offered by Lavrentiev, *Varvara Stepanova,* p. 81.

15. "Polozhenie Otdela izobrazitel'nykh iskusstv i khudozhestvennoi promyshlennosti
NKP po voprosu 'o khudozhestvennoi kul'ture,'" *Iskusstvo kommuny,* no. 11 (1919): 4; quoted
in *RC,* p. 79. The Inkhuk had been organized in March of 1920, on the initiative and under
the leadership of Vasilii Kandinsky, by the Department of Fine Arts of the National Commis-
sariat of Enlightenment. My account of the Inkhuk and the debates within it leading to
Constructivism draws primarily on Lodder's comprehensive study; see *RC,* esp. pp. 78–98.
For an in-depth account of the disputed term *faktura,* see Gough, "*Faktura:* The Making of
the Russian Avant-garde," *Res* 36 (Autumn 1999): 32–59; in this essay, she elaborates further
on the relevance of the index for an account of Russian avant-garde art.

forms.[16] But in a departure from Greenbergian modernism, the principle
of construction as it developed at the Inkhuk debates in 1921 resulted
in a critique of the traditional concept of art as individual creation—a
critique that led logically, for the productivist theorists at Inkhuk, to the
adoption of the highly organized, scientific, and technologically advanced
model of collective *industrial* production as the new model for artistic
making in Constructivism. It would serve not simply as a model for art
making but as art making itself (once it was sufficiently improved by Constructivist principles). Constructivist "artist-productivists" would combine
their skills of advanced *artistic* analysis of material, form, and process with
these newly learned and newly adopted "scientific" skills, in order to "dy-
namize" the traditional, backward practices of Soviet industry.

Both Popova and Stepanova started out as painters, but they arrived
at their joint stint at the First State Cotton-Printing Factory, and the remarkably similar textile designs they produced there, through different
paths of artistic development. Popova was born into a rich and cultured
family near Moscow in 1889 and received an excellent art education. She
had the opportunity to travel in Russia and Europe to look at art and
spent a year in Paris studying at La Palette, the studio of the cubist painters Henri Le Fauconnier and Jean Metzinger. On her return from Paris
in 1913, she worked in the studio of Vladimir Tatlin, who was developing
his famous *Counter-relief* constructions; during this period she successfully
exhibited cubist-style paintings. In 1916 she switched allegiances and
joined the suprematist group around Kazimir Malevich and developed
her own acclaimed suprematist-inspired language of abstract painting,
her *Architectonics* series.

In *Painterly Architectonics with Pink Semicircle* of 1918, vibrantly colored
quadrilaterals and a pink circle are layered like so many flat cut-paper
collage elements on the surface, invoking suprematist flatness (fig. 3). Yet
where Malevich's flat quadrilaterals can be read in modernist terms as in-
dices of the picture frame, evacuating any possibility of three-dimensional
space, Popova here courts its emergence: the explicitly painterly touch of
her brushwork blends colors at certain junctures, producing a chiaroscuro shading that gives occasional solidity, even roundness, to the
planes. Some of her quadrilaterals, here and elsewhere in the *Architectonics*, graze each other at oblique angles, slicing themselves open to grasp
other forms within their openings. This drama of interconnected colored
forms unfolds here against a backdrop of looming darkness. Emotion,
even illusionism, lurk, despite Popova's stated intention of achieving a
transparency of formal means. In an artist's statement of 1919, she would
graphically divide all of painting up into two categories, one positive and

16. Greenberg lays out this definition of modernism most starkly in Clement
Greenberg, "Modernist Painting," *The Collected Essays and Criticism,* ed. John O'Brian, 4 vols.
(Chicago, 1986–93), 4:85–93.

FIG. 3.—Liubov' Popova, *Painterly Architectonics with Pink Semicircle*, 1918.

one negative. She placed *Architectonics* in the positive column under the plus sign, defined in modernist terms by a list of its constituent elements: painterly space, line, color, energetics, *faktura;* in the negative column under the minus sign she placed the term *aconstructiveness,* which she defined by illusionism, literariness, emotion, and recognition (see *P,* pp. 346–47). She soon abandoned the *Architectonics,* as if the solidity and interconnectedness of the architectonic planes still suggested too much sensation or narrative, no matter how nonliterary (although to my mind, the contradiction between her work and her stated intentions gives the *Architectonics* paintings their pictorial force, as it works itself out across their surfaces). She began to make even more rigorously flattened and linear compositions, such as her *Spatial-Force Construction* series of 1921.

We should not be surprised to learn that one of her contemporaries, a student at the state art school Vkhutemas, where she taught the basic course in painting, spoke of Popova's "domestication of her own, to some extent ladylike [*damskoi*], suprematism."[17] Although her young admirer (he also praises her beauty and good taste in clothes) hardly uses the adjective *ladylike* here with any specificity, it is not difficult to guess at what he might have meant by this feminine adjective; today, as in 1920, *touch, sensation,* and *interconnectedness* are privileged signifiers of the feminine.[18] In the context of avant-garde painting and the debates at Inkhuk, *ladylike* was not the adjective an ambitious painter like Popova would want attached to her work. The *Spatial-Force Construction* series might be a deliberate rejoinder to this description: mathematical in their vectored linearity; vehemently material in their use of plywood, impasto oils, and marble dust; and modernist in their irreducible flatness. They meet quite precisely the proto-Constructivist criteria for plus painting enumerated by her own statement of 1919.[19]

For most of the period of the debates at Inkhuk, Popova resisted the Constructivist group's demand for utilitarianism; only in November 1921 did she sign a proclamation of artists who renounced easel painting in

17. Boris Rybchenkov, "Rasskazy B. F. Rybchenkova," in *Prostranstvo kartiny: Sbornik statei,* ed. Natalia Tamruchi (Moscow, 1989), p. 294. Rybchenkov wrote these memoirs in 1979; his romanticizing memories of Popova's attractively feminine personal qualities, with the hindsight of almost sixty years, do seem to color his memory of the qualities of her paintings, which he goes on to describe as naive and more suited for printing on children's fabrics than for the development of abstract art. But his memoirs, unreliable as they may be, do signal, I think, the possibility of such a negatively gendered reading at the time.

18. For an evocative theoretical account of touch and femininity within a history of painting, see Ewa Lajer-Burcharth, "Pompadour's Touch: Difference in Representation," *Representations,* no. 73 (Winter 2001): 54–88.

19. Fer has discussed Popova's *Spatial Force* paintings in parallel terms, emphasizing that Popova was deliberately renouncing the traditional sense of an artist's self, with its connotations of individual nuances, including masculine and feminine, in favor of a more rational and scientific conception of making. In particular, Fer calls attention to Popova's interest in mechanical drawing. See Fer, *Realism, Rationalism, Surrealism,* p. 129 and also "What's in a Line? Gender and Modernity," *Oxford Art Journal* 13, no. 1 (1990): 77–88.

favor of productivist work. Comparing the richly gradated shading of her *Painterly Architectonics with Pink Semicircle* with the printed fabric of 1923–24 that had appeared on the cover of *Lef*, the fabric design can be seen as a kind of end point in her consciously Constructivist move away from the individual, sensual touch of painting toward more anonymous, linear forms based on the "industrial" model of mechanical drawing. The earlier painting's conjuring of spatial illusionism against all odds from the flat suprematist circles and quadrilaterals is retained but graphically simplified and transformed in the fabric design. The ingenious juxtaposition of alternately directed black and white stripes creates the effect of receding black holes, while bright orange targetlike circles hover "above" the background.

Stepanova's fabric designs created similar optical or "op-art" effects, although their origins cannot be traced to her pre-Constructivist painting practices with the same satisfyingly linear logic. Stepanova was younger than Popova by five years, and her background was less privileged. She had gone to art school in Kazan and did not move to Moscow until 1913. There, she became involved with the avant-garde and continued to study painting, but she also worked as a secretary in a factory. Her only major series of paintings to be exhibited, at the Nineteenth State Exhibition in Moscow in 1920, were influenced, like Popova's paintings at that time, by the flat, abstract planes of suprematism. But she appropriated them for a more traditional style of figuration, turning the quadrilateral planes into torsos and limbs and giving them round heads and little feet; most of her canvases are comprised of friezelike rows of flattened dancing figures (fig. 4). Stepanova's visual gifts would emerge far more convincingly in design than in painting. With good reason, I think, these paintings were not as well-received as innovations in abstract painting as Popova's efforts of the same period. Stepanova recorded in her diary the responses of contemporary artists and critics to the exhibition. Those who wanted to respond encouragingly used open-ended terms such as "rich," "fresh," "charming," and "intriguing" to describe her work, while others more straightforwardly called it "unformed," "evolving," "lacking definite values," "ungovernable," "unbalanced" (these last two adjectives were offered by Marc Chagall). All these terms stem from the familiar lexicon of male critics confronting women's art. One critic even told her straight out that her paint was overworked and that this was typical of women's art.[20] (The Constructivist Konstantin Medunetskii rudely, if not entirely inaccurately, later referred to the figures in these paintings as "tadpoles.")[21]

20. See the account of her diary entries describing these responses to her paintings in Lavrentiev, *Varvara Stepanova*, pp. 43–44. The critics contrasted her work to the innovative, analytic abstraction of Rodchenko, which was exhibited next to her paintings at the same exhibition.

21. Konstantin Medunetskii et al., "Transcript of the Discussion of Comrade Stepanova's Paper 'On Constructivism'" (1921), in *Art into Life: Russian Constructivism, 1914–1932,*

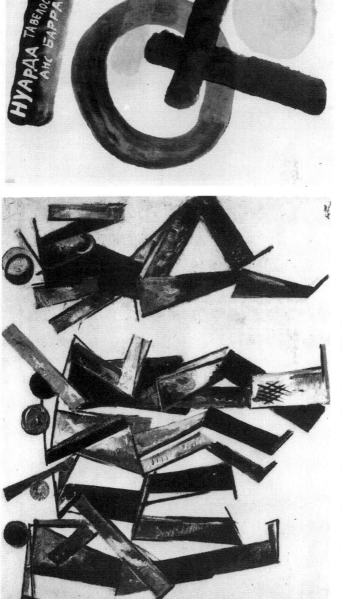

FIG. 5.—Varvara Stepanova, Illustration for *Rtny Khomle*, 1918. Tempera on paper.

FIG. 4.—Varvara Stepanova, *Five Figures*, 1920. Oil on canvas.

Her considerable graphic talent, in contrast, had emerged in 1918–19 when she produced nonobjective sound poems for which she handwrote the evocative-sounding nonsense words, surrounding and enveloping them with bright, almost translucent rectangles, circles, thick lines, and grids—simple graphic forms rendered in brushy freehand tempera (fig. 5). These works are more modest in scale and finish than her paintings, but more visually forceful and inventive. Yet clearly she wanted to produce work at a higher level of permanence and finish than these experiments on paper, which is why she turned to producing the less well-received oil paintings of 1920. In the context of her own artistic history, then, it is not so surprising that Stepanova was a founding member of the First Working Group of Constructivists at Inkhuk—the group that definitively rejected easel painting in favor of utilitarian work. Stepanova's allegiance to the antisubjective, mechanistic aspects of Constructivism may well have been more vehement and consistent than Popova's because her paintings had not received the same kind of erudite critical acclaim. She became the research secretary of Inkhuk in 1920–21 and would continue to function as an archivist and theorist of Constructivism throughout the 1920s, keeping careful records of avant-garde exhibitions, delivering theoretical papers, and publishing essays (she was a far more prolific writer than Popova).

We can see her at work with a compass in a famous photograph taken by her life partner, the Constructivist Aleksandr Rodchenko, in 1924 (fig. 6). The photograph has come to function as a sign for Constructivism's rejection of the individual touch of the artist's hand—here reduced to an amorphous blob—in favor of the mechanical precision of the compass. In a notebook entry, Stepanova notes that the factory council at the First State Cotton-Printing Factory criticized her and Popova for drawing with compass and ruler, assuming that they did so because they could not draw.[22] The implication, of course, is that factory councils have no comprehension of the Constructivist view that artistic drawing in the context of industry is obsolete. But perhaps for Stepanova there is also a recognition that her talent *does* lie with simplified graphic forms, with the ruler and the compass. In a paper on their work at the textile factory delivered at Inkhuk in January 1924, she enumerated her and Popova's goals as precisely the eradication of "the high artistic value [placed on] a handdrawn design" and the elimination of "naturalistic design"—she has in mind the traditional Russian floral patterns—in favor of exclusively geometric forms.[23]

trans. James West, ed. Richard Andrews and Milena Kalinovska (exhibition catalog, Henry Art Gallery, Seattle, 4 July–2 Sept. 1990), p. 74.

22. See Stepanova, "Registration of Textile Samples" (c. 1924), notebook, Rodchenko-Stepanova Archive, Moscow; quoted in *SCT*, p. 147.

23. Stepanova, "O polozhenii i zadachakh khudozhnika-konstruktivista v sittsenabivnoi promyshlennosti v sviazi s rabotami na sittsenabivnoi fabrike," paper delivered at Inkhuk, 5 Jan. 1924; quoted in *RC*, p. 151.

Yet despite the anti-authorial ano-
nymity associated with mechanical
drawing and factory labor, Stepanova's public performance of her
artist-productivist role suggests
that it was not, in fact, anti-
individual or antisubjective; she
developed a strong artistic identity
as a productivist, an identity that
would prove enabling to her as a
woman artist in a way that her
identity as a painter had not. The
photograph both produces and
corroborates her productivist identity; her hand may be out of focus,
but her blurry forefinger is paral-
lelled by her intensely chewed cigarette, and the two parallel lines of
finger and cigarette dramatically
bisect the central vertical rectangle,
the four corners of which are fixed
by her intently gazing eyes above
and the sharp points of the com-

Fig. 6.—Aleksandr Rodchenko, photograph of Varvara Stepanova holding a
compass, 1924.

pass below. The photograph produces her as individual creator as roman-
tically as any painted portrait of the artist at work, but the model of
creation is transformed from mystifying inspiration to useful invention.

Popova and Stepanova may have arrived at the textile factory from
different artistic origins, but both artists seem to have agreed that their
mandate there was to produce geometric designs with consistently vibrating effects—even though such specifically "op-art" effects, as opposed to
merely geometric forms, were nowhere articulated as particularly Constructivist. For Stepanova we have direct evidence that these effects were
an explicit goal of her designs; her 1925 course plan for the Textile Faculty at Vkhutemas, where she taught, asks students to "plan a bichromatic
design in order to create a multi-colored effect" and "compose a design
which creates chromatic effects (such as iridescence)."[24] We even have a
series of images, from an early sketch to a finished fabric, that demon-

24. Stepanova, "Organizational Plan of the Programme for a Course in Artistic Composition at the Faculty of Textile of the Vkhutemas, 1925," in Lidya Zaletova et al., *Costume
Revolution: Textiles, Clothing, and Costume of the Soviet Union in the Twenties,* trans. Elizabeth
Dafinone (London, 1989), p. 178. These two points of the teaching program (the final two
points of section 1, parts L and M), cited here from the English translation, are curiously
omitted from this document in the more recent publication of Stepanova's writings in Russian. See Stepanova, *Chelovek ne mozhet zhit' bez chuda: pis'ma, poeticheskie opyty, zapiski khudozh-
nitsy* (Moscow, 1994), p. 184; hereafter abbreviated *CNM.*

strate her deliberate process of working toward the most optical variation of a given design. In the final variant, which was mass-produced at the First State Cotton-Printing Factory, circles with alternating white and red stripes appear to float against a recessed lattice of white and yellow stripes (fig. 7). All the stripes move in the same direction, but this logical continuity of vertical stripes is dislocated by the simple shift from white to colored band within the circles to create an optical effect. With the slight irregularities that result from the weave and stretch of the fabric, on printed cloth the design seems to shift and move.

But if it can be demonstrated that optical patterns were the explicit goal of Stepanova and Popova's textile designs, it still does not answer the question, What makes these optical patterns *Constructivist?* The answer, I will propose—neither artist ever spoke to this directly—is that in its dynamic, optical quality, this piece of cotton fabric, destined for women's dresses, embodies the Constructivist ideal of a mass-produced object of everyday life that has been penetrated and transformed by the processes of production. The fabric is a specifically industrial object because its vibrant colors were perfected in the factory's chemistry laboratory, and its small, repeating pattern of balls on stripes responds to the limitations imposed by the narrow printing presses at the factory. According to Arvatov, the dynamism of the socialist thing results from its condition of industrial production—for Marx, the most powerful unleashing of human energy and imagination in history—and its purpose is to import this dynamism into the stagnant, passive, consumerist lethargy of everyday life (*byt*) (see "EL," p. 121). The vibrating opticality of the pattern, while not integral to the structure or production of the cotton cloth itself, points

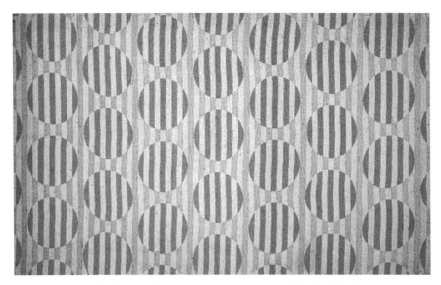

FIG. 7.—Varvara Stepanova, weaving sample of fabric, 1923–24.

to—or to use the semiotic term, indexes—the invention and creativity of the industrial production process. The skilled human labor that produced the fabric is rendered transparent in its very material form, lending the fabric itself the animation of its makers. These claims for the fabric designs as socialist things may seem, at least on the face of it, farfetched, and require explanation. The writings of Arvatov offer such an explanation, and his account speaks so directly to both the successes and failures of the Constructivist experiment at the First State Cotton-Printing Factory that I feel certain he had Popova and Stepanova in mind as he wrote it.[25]

Boris Arvatov's Socialist Things

Arvatov's essay "Everyday Life and the Culture of the Thing" (1925) attempts to imagine how socialism will transform passive capitalist commodities into active socialist things. These things, connected like "co-workers" with human practice, will produce new relations of consumption, new experiences of everyday life, and new human subjects of modernity (see "EL," p. 124). Although integral to Arvatov's theory of Soviet production art, this essay does not mention art at all; it takes as its subject matter the industrial thing in Western modernity, not in Russia. His homeland is still too industrially backward to provide evidence for his grand thesis, which is that industrial production is a source of human creativity that, when liberated from the oppressive labor and class conditions of capitalism and reimagined in socialist culture, "will directly form all aspects of human activity" ("EL," p. 121). Already in America, Arvatov imagines, despite the harmful effects of capitalism, this industrial creativity is beginning to transform human beings through the agency of the innumerable new things that it mass produces: "The new world of Things, which gave rise to a new image of a person as a psycho-physiological individual, dictated forms of gesticulation, movement, and activity. It created a particular regimen of physical culture. The psyche also evolved, becoming more and more thinglike in its associative structure" ("EL," p. 126).[26] In Arvatov's theory, then, the industrial thing—in Marx's terms, the commodity fetish—has an agency that is potentially beneficial to the human subject, which is itself rendered more active and "evolved" through interaction with this thing.

25. There is a transcript of a public discussion between Stepanova and Arvatov on the subject of the artist's role in industry, from the Inkhuk session in which she presented the paper "On Constructivism," and he chaired the discussion that followed. See Medunetskii et al., "Transcript of the Discussion of Comrade Stepanova's Paper, 'On Constructivism,'" esp. p. 78.

26. Arvatov could only fantasize about the American city because he never travelled to the West. For more on his biography, see Kiaer, "Boris Arvatov's Socialist Objects," *October*, no. 81 (Summer 1997): 105–18.

But the potentially dynamizing effects of the "new world of things" are stymied by the commodity relation, which prevents things from acting on consciousness. Grounded in exchange-value, the commodity form isolates production from consumption and promotes private-property relations to things; it entails "the maximum isolation of the system of production, as a machine-collective system, from the system of consumption, as a system of individual appropriation" ("EL," p. 122). The bourgeois has no direct physical contact with the technological creativity of things in production. His interaction with things is limited to his narrow, private-property form of everyday life (*byt*), which takes place in the spaces of private apartments and offices. Bourgeois *byt* is a passive sphere of experience diametrically opposed to the active creation associated with production; the thing in bourgeois material culture exists "outside its creative genesis" and therefore as "something completed, fixed, static and, consequently, dead" ("EL," p. 122).

Arvatov's emphasis on the *passivity* of the commodity constitutes a novel reworking of Marx's theory of the commodity. For Marx, the commodity is a fetish because people project value onto it, a value that is arbitrary because it exists only as a consequence of practices of exchange on the market.[27] The real value of the thing, its labor value, is constituted by the labor power that produced it, but this is suppressed by the commodity form. The commodity has agency only in the negative sense of leeching that agency away from the human producers to whom it rightly belongs; its agency is negative and antisocial. It "reflects the social relation of the producers to the sum total of labour as a social relation between objects, a relation which exists apart from and outside the producers" (*C*, 1:165).[28] This shift in agency from producers to objects renders the human producers passive, while exchange-value confers on commodities the role of active agents of social relations.[29] For Arvatov, on the other hand, the commodity form renders the *things* passive—uncreative, fixed, dead. They may serve as substitutes for relations between producers, but this is an inherently static and formal function, governed by the spontaneous forces of the market: "The Thing as the fulfillment of the organism's physical capacity for labor, as a force for social labor, as an instrument and as a co-worker, does not exist in the everyday life of

27. In chapter 1 of *Capital,* Marx famously makes the analogy to fetishism "in the misty realm of religion," where "the products of the human brain" are projected onto wooden idols (Karl Marx, *Capital,* trans. Ben Fowkes, 3 vols. [New York, 1977], 1:165; hereafter abbreviated *C*). On the origins of Marx's use of the concept of the fetish, see W. J. T. Mitchell, "The Rhetoric of Iconoclasm: Marxism, Ideology, and Fetishism," *Iconology: Image, Text, Ideology* (Chicago, 1986), pp. 160–208.

28. Arvatov cites this passage in his discussion of the aesthetics of easel art in Arvatov, *Iskusstvo i klassy* (Moscow, 1923), p. 52.

29. Hal Foster offers a pithy formulation of this idea: "the commodity becomes our uncanny double, evermore vital as we are evermore inert" (Hal Foster, *Compulsive Beauty* [Cambridge, Mass., 1993], p. 129).

the bourgeoisie" ("EL," p. 124). This list of qualities that commodities lack enumerates, of course, precisely what will be desirable in the socialist thing. While Marx lamented that the commodity fetish resulted in "material [*dinglich*] relations between persons and social relations between things" (*C*, 1:166), Arvatov wants to recuperate thinglike (*dinglich*) relations between persons and social relations between things *for* proletarian culture. Instead of wishing for a lost set of "direct social relations between persons in their work," Arvatov claims that industrial society has infinitely more and better things than humanity has ever known, and therefore it makes sense that relations between people should be more thinglike. The problem is not just with the commodity as a social form—as Marx sees it—but with the actual material, formal qualities of the things produced under the capitalist system of production. Thus what separates Arvatov from Marx is his conviction that the elimination of the rupture between things and people will be achieved not only through the socialist transformation of relations of production but by Constructivist transformations of *the things themselves*. It is this obsessive, even unseemly emphasis on the things themselves that characterizes the particular Constructivist version of materialism.

By imagining an object that is differently animated than the commodity, Arvatov attempts to bestow a different kind of social agency on the thing that is not immediately reducible to the structure of the fetish. Only socialist revolution can achieve this, by freeing the creative forces of production from capitalist structures. But certain conditions that lessen the power of the commodity already exist in embryo, Arvatov contends, in the everyday life of the technical intelligentsia of the industrial city in far-away America.[30] He imagines that the American city boasts an "everyday life of enormous offices, department stores, factory laboratories, research institutes, and so on" as well as "the collectivization of transport and . . . heating, lighting, plumbing" ("EL," p. 125). The reactionary financial bourgeoisie may continue, obliviously, to live its commodified everyday life of private consumption, but the everyday life of the technical

---

30. "Technical intelligentsia" translates *tekhnicheskaia intelligentsiia,* a specific and highly motivated class term. Historically, the "intelligentsia" was the intellectual or educated sector of the bourgeoisie in Russia, a social group that arose in the second half of the nineteenth century. Bolshevism aimed to eradicate the bourgeoisie as a class, but it recognized the need for preserving the technical skills of the bourgeois engineers, scientists, and administrators who were needed for the practical tasks of building socialism. By referring to this same group of people in America as the "technical intelligentsia," Arvatov offers them social legitimation in Soviet terms: they are partially exonerated for their bourgeois class status. The members of the *artistic* intelligentsia in Arvatov's *Lef* circle, by stressing their role as technicians (of texts or art objects), attempted to identify themselves with the *technical* intelligentsia—the one group of the bourgeoisie recognized as useful to the Bolshevik state. On the complex history of the Russian intelligentsia's relation to the Western technical intelligentsia and to Bolshevism in the context of the avant-garde, see Gassner, "The Constructivists," p. 306.

intelligentsia has been completely penetrated by these collectivizing forces originating in production. The technical intelligentsia is in the unique position of organizing the advanced technological things of industry through its work, without forming an ownership attachment to those things, because it is only "a group of hired organizers" ("EL," pp. 125–26). It lives "in a world of things that it organizes but does not possess, things that condition its labor" ("EL," p. 125). The technical intelligentsia is *structurally* less affected by the commodity form.

The less commodified everyday life of the technical intelligentsia leads it to demand new values of activity and flexibility from things— values that will eventually, under socialism, become the values of socialist things. In contrast to the display or status value of bourgeois things, or to the decorative forms of the privately owned home (the weighty furniture, heavy draperies, and endless coverings of the bourgeois interior), the new criteria of value are "convenience, portability, comfort, flexibility, expedience [*tselesoobraznost'*], hygiene, and so on—in a word, everything that they call the adaptability of the thing, its suitability in terms of positioning and assembling for the needs of social practice" ("EL," p. 126).[31] Portable and flexible, ready to be assembled or disassembled on short notice, these things respond *formally* to the newly collectivized everyday life of the technical intelligentsia by rendering themselves *transparent:* "Glass, steel, concrete, artificial materials, and so on were no longer covered over with a 'decorative' casing, but spoke for themselves. The mechanism of a thing, the connection between the elements of a thing and its purpose, were now transparent, compelling people practically, and thus also psychologically, to reckon with them, and only with them" ("EL," p. 126). The newly transparent thing logically embodies and demonstrates the labor power—the technical intelligence—of the technical intelligentsia. Arvatov endows modernism with Marxist credentials; the transparent modernist object that displays its mode of construction and its function is already, it turns out, by virtue of its form, on the way toward engendering socialist culture, because it contests the secrecy of the commodity fetish.

Yet Arvatov's theory is not a simplistic technological one, all breathless wonder at modern machines and contraptions. There is an aspect of that, certainly, but to claim that as the core of his thesis would be to miss the more interesting claim he is making about people's relation to objects. In a key passage, he writes that even the most mundane, low-tech, everyday objects can engender socialist culture: "The ability to pick up a cigarette-case, to smoke a cigarette, to put on an overcoat, to wear a cap,

31. For an excellent analysis of the key Constructivist term *ustanovka* ("positioning"), see Gough, "Switched On: Notes on Radio, Automata, and the Bright Red Star," in *Building the Collective: Soviet Graphic Design, 1917–1937,* ed. Leah Dickerman (New York, 1996), pp. 39–55.

to open a door, all these 'trivialities' acquire their qualification, their not unimportant 'culture'" ("EL," p. 126). As the forms of such simple, everyday objects of consumption begin to approach the more advanced technical forms that already exist in the objects of production that have entered everyday life (he cites revolving doors and escalators, among other things), they will become better qualified as active agents of socialist culture. Arvatov's attention to the transformative potential of everyday life (*byt*) differentiates him from other early Soviet Marxists who, he claims, were obsessed with production and ignored the world of everyday things (see "EL," p. 119). They neglected to analyze everyday consumption as a site for the realization of human consciousness *through the thing.* Arvatov's theory of the socialist thing is therefore especially useful to feminist analyses of early Soviet culture, where women were firmly equated with *byt.*[32]

On the basis of this analysis of Arvatov's theory, Popova and Stepanova at the First State Cotton-Printing Factory—as designers fulfilling the role of the technical intelligentsia, and as women with a more practical and experiential investment in *byt*—were uniquely well placed to fulfil this vision of the culture of the thing. As self-consciously revolutionary artists, they had already begun to renounce bourgeois forms of *byt* in their own lives (helped along, of course, by the appalling living conditions in Russia during the civil war); now, as technical design workers in the factory, they were in a position consciously to imbue these everyday objects with the dynamic qualities derived from technological modes of making. Their vibrating fabric designs can be seen to embody precisely the "physiological-laboring capacities of the organism." The set of demands they had addressed to the factory managers in their memo, demanding participation in the chemistry laboratories and production decisions, was their passport to becoming full-fledged members of a new, socialist technical intelligentsia. They would unite the advanced experience already available to this class in the West with the socialist economy of the USSR—the step that was missing in the West. "I suppose we have a proletariat in the West and an ideology of proletarian culture in Russia," Arvatov had said after hearing Stepanova's paper on Constructivism at Inkhuk. "We have Constructivist ideologists in Russia, and technological industry in the West. This is the real tragedy."[33]

Corroborating Arvatov's pessimism, and perhaps predictably, Popova and Stepanova's Constructivist requests to be more than traditional designers were largely refused by factory management. They were not invited to work in the factory's research laboratory; in fact, they did not even work in the factory's design atelier but rather at home in their stu-

32. See Kiaer, "Objets Quotidiennes" and *Imagine No Possessions,* chap. 1, "Everyday Objects."

33. Medunetskii et al., "Transcript of the Discussion of Comrade Stepanova's Paper 'On Constructivism'," p. 76.

FIG. 8.—Aleksandr Rodchenko, caricature of Popova and Stepanova. From the homemade newspaper by Stepanova and Aleksandr Rodchenko, *Nash Gaz,* 1924.

FIG. 9.—Advertisement for the "Mossukno" state textile trust, 1923.

dios. They went to the factory only to drop off their designs, as depicted in a caricature by Rodchenko that shows Popova on her way to the factory pushing a wheelbarrow filled with designs ("I'm taking my weekly production of designs to Tsindel'!" she says), while Stepanova herself is hand carrying two new designs to the same destination (fig. 8).[34] They were prevented from fulfilling the role of the technical intelligentsia by conservative industrial management, which was too pressured by the financial problems of running a newly nationalized factory to have the luxury of experimenting with left avant-garde schemes for industrial improvement.

34. The caricature stems from a home-made newspaper produced by Rodchenko and Stepanova for their friends in 1924, entitled *Nash Gaz,* short for "*nasha gazeta*" ("our newspaper"). Like the English word, "gas" here can also be read in the senses of joking and of farting. The newspaper is in the collection of the Rodchenko-Stepanova Archive, Moscow. The full text and images of the newspaper have not been published; the most complete publication of it to date appeared, in English translation only, in a small, limited-edition catalogue: *Ornament and Textile Design,* ed. Katerina Drevina, Varvara Rodchenko, and Lavrentiev (Manege Gallery, Moscow, 1990). The tone of this particular caricature is jocular, but it seems, once again, that Popova is depicted as more successful than Stepanova, with her massive output of fabrics.

Arvatov's dream of a technical intelligentsia transformed by the collectivizing forces originating in production was paradoxically *further* from being realized in socialist Moscow than in capitalist Chicago.

The Socialist Thing in the Capitalist (NEP) Marketplace

Soviet industry was caught between socialism and capitalism in 1923 because it was operating under the semicapitalist and market-based New Economic Policy (NEP, which effectively lasted from its inception in 1921 until approximately 1928). NEP was instituted by Lenin in order to revive the economy after the devastation of the civil war. The policy permitted limited private enterprise to coexist with newly nationalized state concerns, which meant that Soviet state-owned enterprises competed on the NEP market with private ones. Many of them advertised to solicit consumers. A 1923 advertisement for fabrics from the Mossukno state textile trust in Moscow conveys the inherent contradictions of Bolshevik capitalism; it shows turbanned black boys unfurling bolts of cloth from above, while a female figure modelling fabrics on a stage is ogled from below (fig. 9). These familiar orientalizing and sexualizing strategies from bourgeois visual culture are here deployed, however, to address putatively proletarian consumers: the onlookers include a Red Army soldier with a red star on his cap on the lower left and a red-kerchiefed woman worker on the right. Kerchiefed women were familiar fixtures from propaganda posters. The text of a huge poster from 1923, for example, proclaims that "the new everyday life [*novyi byt*] is the child of October," while the graphics show a kerchiefed woman worker who emancipates herself by kicking out her domestic stove and washboard—signs of primitive Russian *byt*—and striding into factory production with the help of new collective services such as public dining rooms and nurseries, pictured on the upper right (fig. 10). The transposition of this giant red woman from the poster into a docile member of a fashion show audience in the Mossukno advertisement is exactly the kind of contradiction that defined NEP. It was within this contradictory, hybrid context—part flag-waving socialism, part business-as-usual market economy—that Popova and Stepanova became textile designers.

In militaristic language paralleling the visual language of the striding, kicking woman of the propaganda poster, the Bolshevik art critic Iakov Tugendkhol'd wrote that with her textile design work Popova had made "a breach in the Bastille of our factory conservatism."[35] Most critical rhetoric cast Popova and Stepanova as pioneers; the Bolshevik rhetoric of the liberation of woman under socialism permeated public language,

---

35. Quoted in Adaskina, "Constructivist Fabrics and Dress Design," *Journal of Decorative and Propaganda Arts* 5 (Summer 1987): 157; hereafter abbreviated "CF."

Fig. 10.—"The New Everyday Life Is the Child of October," propaganda poster, 1923.

even if no one actually analyzed the role of women artists in the avant-garde with any seriousness.[36] But the "heroic" aspect of their entry into the factory as artist-productivists was tempered by the prosaic economic fact that they had been hired to help boost sales. The Russian Republic may have been socialist, but during NEP the First State Cotton-Printing Factory had to balance its budget and turn a profit. Hiring the Constructivists proved moderately successful in this regard; although they worked at the factory for less than a year, several dozen of their fabrics were printed and distributed throughout the Soviet Union and were seen widely on the streets of Moscow. Tugendkhol'd, who was by no means a constant supporter of Constructivism, also wrote, "Last spring, without even knowing it, all of Moscow was wearing fabrics which Popova had designed" (quoted in "CF," p. 157).

Popova and Stepanova were fully aware that their work at the First State Cotton-Printing Factory had to respond to the market; in the same memo to factory management in which they demanded participation in production, they also enumerated two final demands: "4. Contact with tailors, fashion ateliers and magazines. 5. Work on promoting the products of the factory in the press, advertising and magazines. Our participation could also take the form of work on designs for window displays."[37] They understood their productivist work in fabric design to be inseparable from broader questions of the market—and in the case of fabric designs, these questions specifically meant fashion.

Soviet women were routinely assailed with enormous images of emancipated women on propaganda posters, at the same time that Soviet publishing houses printed advertisements like the one for Mossukno fabrics and resumed the publication of prerevolutionary women's fashion magazines. *The Housewives' Magazine* (*Zhurnal dlia Khoziaek*), for example, had been started in 1913, combining practical and fashion advice for women with more weighty literary and political issues, including women's rights and the legalization of abortion; the magazine exemplified the tra-

---

36. There is a commonplace assumption among non-Soviet specialists that the early years of the Soviet Union were an unprecedented period of women's liberation and sexual emancipation. Sweeping legal reforms instituted by the Soviets immediately after the revolution did in fact accord women a level of equality before the law unrivalled in any country, and there was lively public debate in the 1920s about the possible forms of a new, communist sexuality. But recent scholarship in Soviet history is bursting this utopian bubble, demonstrating that actual sexual or women's liberation was very limited in the 1920s and was in many ways eliminated by the 1930s. See Eric Naiman, *Sex in Public: The Incarnation of Early Soviet Ideology* (Princeton, N.J., 1997); Wendy Z. Goldman, *Women, the State, and Revolution: Soviet Family Policy and Social Life, 1917–36* (Cambridge, 1993); and Frances Lee Bernstein, "'What Everyone Should Know about Sex': Gender, Sexual Enlightenment, and the Politics of Health in Revolutionary Russia, 1918–1931" (Ph.D. diss., Columbia University, 1998).

37. Quoted in Lavrentiev, "Poeziia graficheskogo dizaina v tvorchestve Varvary Stepanovoi," p. 25; trans. in *SCT,* p. 136; trans. mod. and expanded.

dition of bourgeois liberalism, clearly oriented toward the relatively small demographic group of literate, middle-class urban women. It ceased publication in 1917 due to the upheaval of the revolution but returned in 1922 as a publication of the State Publishing House. How did the Bolshevik press reconcile egalitarian socialist ideals with Parisian fashion trends? After all, Walter Benjamin, preeminent theorist of mass culture and socialism, would ask optimistically in his *Arcades Project:* "Does fashion die (as in Russia, for example) because it can no longer keep up the tempo?"[38] His question implies that only the tempo of actual social change brought about by revolution can obliterate finally the lure of fashion's endless cycle of novelty. Yet an editorial in the first postrevolutionary issue of *The Housewives' Magazine* in 1922 put the lie to his optimism, answering his question in a resounding negative: "our readers may think that fashion has died out . . . but our old friend fashion, powerfully ruling the female half of the human species, had no intention of dying!"[39] The editorial goes on to describe the length and pleating of the season's skirts, while other articles in the same issue offer serious discussion of the new Soviet laws on women's rights and the development of communal kitchens. This and all issues of the magazine carried several double-spread pages of Parisian fashion patterns, which were clearly its main selling point. The content of the magazine encompasses both socialist enlightenment and fashion, without attempting to theorize how the one might transform the other—how socialism might transform fashion. This was the question that preoccupied Popova and Stepanova.

The question of how socialism might transform consumer culture *in the context of NEP Russia* also preoccupied Arvatov. His essay "Everyday Life and the Culture of the Thing" had imagined industrial things in faraway America, but in 1925 he also wrote another essay, "Art and the Quality of Industrial Production," which was deeply embedded in the present conditions of the Soviet economy and therefore far more open to questions of actual consumer desire.[40] Soviet industry, he warns in this essay, is currently in a dismal state, lagging far behind the advances of Western industry. Factory design departments, when they exist, are staffed with old-fashioned, academic graphic artists who tend simply to replicate existing patterns, some ten or twenty years old. Before World War I, textile factories had relied primarily on patterns imported from Paris. With most trade agreements with the West nullified by the Bolshevik victory in the civil war, no new patterns were arriving from Paris in the early 1920s. For these reasons, Soviet mass-produced things lack the "'ele-

38. Walter Benjamin, *The Arcades Project,* trans. Howard Eiland and Kevin McLaughlin (Cambridge, Mass., 1999), p. 71; hereafter abbreviated *AP.*

39. Anon., "Modnaia khronika," *Zhurnal dlia Khoziaek,* no. 1 (1922): 3.

40. See Arvatov, "Iskusstvo i kachestvo promyshlennoi produktsii," *Sovetskoe Iskusstvo,* no. 7 (1925): 39–43; hereafter abbreviated "I."

gance,' 'fashion,' 'originality,' 'stylishness,' 'contemporaneity' (for example, in the English spirit, Americanized, etc.), 'chicness,' 'pleasantness,' and even 'opulence'" that consumers seek ("I," p. 40). Arvatov admits that satisfying consumers with the qualities they desire "is undoubtedly a question of the quality of production" ("I," p. 40). Therefore, even though it goes against his own theoretical convictions, Arvatov reluctantly endorses enlisting the help of applied artists—especially the new, left applied artist-Constructivists (and here he seems to have in mind Stepanova and Popova at the First State Factory), even if they are not yet functioning fully as Constructivist artist-engineers—to add the missing sense of "style" to Soviet commodities, raising their market value.

In this essay, then, Arvatov makes it clear that a *tselesoobraznyi* thing is one that succeeds in its purpose of satisfying consumer desires for fashion and stylishness as well as in the more standard Constructivist purpose of efficiently (transparently) performing its technical function. While some of the terms on his list of current Soviet consumer desires are negative for Arvatov—"elegant" and "chic" and "opulent" are unequivocally the adjectives of wealth—the other terms are not so distant from the supposedly more "rationalized" consumer desires that he associates with contemporary industrial development in America and Britain. Industrial production there, he claims, is represented by "the most convenient, comfortable, dynamic, everyday-economic, machinized thing" ("I," p. 41). Even if the Soviet-desired qualities are not yet quite as fully rational as these, they are clearly legitimate enough for Arvatov to harangue his imagined readers (managers of Soviet trusts or other government planners—unlikely readers, unfortunately for Arvatov, of the magazine *Soviet Art* in which he published this essay) to hire applied artist-constructivists in order to begin to satisfy them.

But this solution can only be temporary, he cautions, because using applied artists to beautify products is a "market oriented" approach that "indulg[es] the subjectively taste-determined, individualistic demands of the consumer" ("I," p. 41). He pulls back from fully endorsing the more open-ended understanding of the "purpose" served by *tselesoobraznost'*, calling for the eventual entry of true artist-productivists into industry in order to combat this "subjectively taste-determined" approach, which is causing Soviet industry to lag behind the more fully rationalized industry of the West. The artist must use her creativity not for "fantasizing," not for "decoration from without," but for "real technical construction" ("I," p. 41). These are of course the same terms that he uses in "Everyday Life and the Culture of the Thing"; the thing must be fully transparent in its construction rather than covered over by fantasy. He may point, in this essay, to the special circumstances of the present NEP economy, but he holds fast to his assertion that in the West, as in the Soviet Union, the future will lead "to the mass, collectivized calculation of the needs of society and their rational satisfaction, and thus to planned productive invention" ("I," p. 41). In my reading, the Constructivist thing falls somewhere between these two poles: acknowledging and aiming to satisfy the human desires of modernity, but committed to the belief that eventually, in some fully achieved socialist, industrial utopia, these desires can be fully rationalized to the benefit of all.

Stepanova and the Limits of Production Clothing

Stepanova's brief article "Today's Clothing Is Production Clothing," published in *Lef* in 1923, takes a typically hard Constructivist line against fashion; written by a woman artist, it serves as a powerful rebuttal to the return of NEP fashion magazines and their claims about the fashion desires of "the female half of the species." Store-window displays with their wax mannequins, Stepanova writes, will become a thing of the past because contemporary clothing can only be understood in action: "Fashion, which psychologically reflects our everyday life [*byt*], habits and aesthetic taste, is giving way to clothing organized for working in various branches of labor" (*CNM*, p. 181). This kind of utilitarian work clothing was called *prozodezhda* (production clothing), and it could be broken down into even more specialized categories, called *spetsodezhda* (special clothing). The form of this clothing should be determined exclusively by the "more precise and specific demands" posed by its function, with no decoration or ornamentation; to use Arvatov's term, the function and mode of making of this clothing will be transparent in its form. Stepanova names as examples "the clothing worn by surgeons, pilots, workers in acid factories, firemen and members of arctic expeditions" (*CNM*, p. 182).[41] With the exception of surgeons, all of these professions were exclusively male at that time. These examples buttress the strong antifeminine rhetoric of the entire article, as Stepanova scrambles to dissociate herself from anything culturally related to femininity—*byt*, the decorative, the store window, even the wax mannequin.

Stepanova's rhetoric mimes, in the avant-garde context of *Lef*, the language of Bolshevik economic planners and clothing industry specialists. Her terms appeared in the proclamation "On the Provision with *Prozodezhda* and *Spetsodezhda* of Workers in Coal Mines" of October 1920, signed by no less of a Bolshevik official than Lenin himself (see *SCT*, p. 53). Her essay has much in common with the technical publications of the textile and clothing industries of the time, which similarly promoted

41. In another section of the article she also lists the following kinds of specialized, primarily masculine clothing: "pilot's uniform, chauffeur's uniform, protective aprons for workers, football shoes, waterproof coat, military service jacket" (*CNM*, p. 181).

the eradication of handicraft production in favor of industrial mass production and the rationalization of clothing designs.[42] By allying her text
rhetorically with the technical language of the garment industry, Stepanova asserts the distance of her own artistic project from fashion. Here
as elsewhere in her practice, her vehement commitment to the engineering and production model of art, which was generally associated with masculine areas of experience, signals her desire to distance herself from the
usual expectations of her gender—expectations that we have already seen
revealed in the criticism her paintings suffered in 1920.[43]

Stepanova's article on production clothing was published before she
began to work at the First State Cotton-Printing Factory. She had not, at
that point, had any practical experience with mass-producing things to
be sold in the NEP marketplace nor with the possibility that her Constructivist designs would be used by consumers in their everyday lives in
non-Constructivist ways. A few years later, however, Stepanova wrote an
important text that takes up the question that the fashion magazines, and
she herself, had refused: how might socialism transform fashion? The
magazines had naively assumed that the two could coexist; she herself, in
1923, had claimed that socialism would obviously destroy fashion. This
1928 essay, "The Tasks of the Artist in the Textile Industry," conveys both
her continued commitment to the model of the artist-productivist and,
more surprisingly, a new understanding of fashion as an emblem of modernity and an object of socially meaningful consumer desire.[44] Stepanova's clothing designs maintain allegiance to the standard Constructivist
model of transparency; in this respect, she functions for me in this essay
as something of a foil to Popova, whose direct forays into fashion design
strain more fully, I will suggest, against the limits of that model. But in
her writings and her teaching Stepanova would manifest signs of acceptance of the broader understanding of the socialist thing as an object of

42. On the imperative within the garment industry to convince workers to give up
their handicraft mentality, see, for example, *Tekhnika i iskusstvo shveinoi promyshlennosti* [*Technology and Art of the Garment Industry*], no. 2 (1925).

43. In a diary entry from 1927, Stepanova reports on a meeting of the editorial board
of the journal *Novyi Lef,* in which the board attacks Dziga Vertov, and she comes to his defense. The other board members accuse her of defending him for personal reasons and laugh
at her even as she protests loudly. She writes that "they say I am 'that kind of woman'—I
drink vodka, I play mah-jong" (*CNM,* p. 206). This anecdote goes some way toward explaining why a woman artist would try to avoid calling attention to her gender, because it
could so easily be used against her.

44. See Stepanova, "Zadachi khudozhnika v tekstil'nom proizvodstve," in *Rodchenko-
Stepanova: Budushchee—Edinstvennaia Nasha Tsel',* ed. Peter Noever (Munich, 1991), pp.
190–93; hereafter abbreviated "Z." The manuscript is in the Rodchenko-Stepanova Archive,
Moscow. A significantly shortened version of the essay, with a different title, was published
in the newspaper *Vecherniaia Moskva* on 28 Febraury 1928; an English translation of this
shortened version was published in Lavrentiev, *Varvara Stepanova,* p. 180.

individual, opaque desires as well as collective, transparent ones—the kind of understanding that would come to the forefront in Popova's work.

Aside from a few garments that she made for her own use, Stepanova did not design clothes incorporating her mass-produced fabrics. This points to the contradictory nature of the fabric-design work for her. At the factory she was designing thin, printed cotton calicoes destined primarily for traditional women's garments such as dresses, skirts, and scarves, or for domestic objects like curtains and table cloths, but these were exactly the kinds of traditional objects of *byt* that she had criticized in 1923 because they "psychologically reflect" our "habits and aesthetic taste." In her 1928 article, she notes that printed cotton fabrics are already becoming obsolete and that the artist in the textile industry must concentrate on developing new kinds of fabrics, such as the knitted fabrics (*trikotazh*) that have already begun to proliferate in the West. She acknowledges, in effect, that even her own greatest Constructivist triumph, her work at the First State Cotton-Printing Factory, had been doomed from the perspective of her own larger goals of replacing traditional fashion with rationalized clothing. Her attempt to use optical designs to infuse calico cloth with the dynamism of production was therefore in retrospect merely a partial, applied-art contribution to improving the quality of Soviet fabric production rather than a total transformation of the object.

Stepanova's many clothing designs of the early 1920s did not, then, incorporate the draping effect of soft calico fabrics. They rather inclined toward stiff, even boxy, forms in simple geometric designs that stemmed from appliquéd fabrics rather than printed ones. They were for the most part not everyday clothes but rather clothes designed for specific utilitarian functions: sports costumes (through her involvement in staging agitational performances at the pedagogical faculty of the Academy of Social Education in Moscow); *prozodezhda* for actors in theatrical productions; and a few designs for women's "professional suits." Unlike her fabric designs, which were mass-produced in the here-and-now of Moscow in 1924, her clothing designs seemed to be destined for a different, Constructivist world. They do not address specific, historically experienced bodies, structured within deeply ingrained gender hierarchies; they rather bypass contemporary *byt* completely in favor of public spaces for the staging of an egalitarian, androgynous order.

Her designs for sports clothes that illustrated her 1923 article in *Lef* exemplify this imagined order (fig. 11). Their form was determined by function. Their bold graphic patterning was not decorative, she claimed, but was justified by the need to differentiate teams on the playing field; she classified them as a form of *spetsodezhda*. The drawings consist of flat planes of circles, triangles, and rectangles from the pictorial lexicon of suprematism. And, as in suprematism, these designs participate in the indexical rhetoric of modernism, reducing the visual image to the most

FIG. 11.—Varvara Stepanova, designs for sports clothes published in *Lef,* 1923.

FIG. 13.—Students in Stepanova sports costumes, in performance of *An Evening of the Book*, 1924.

FIG. 12.—Aleksandr Rodchenko, photograph of Zhemchuzh-naia in a Stepanova sports costume, 1924.

Fig. 14.—Students at the Academy of Social Education dressed in Stepanova sports costumes, 1924.

basic geometric shapes inherent in representation, so we can see how it is made. The drawings do not portray the body in action, which, according to her text, was the only way that production clothing could be seen. They rather evoke human bodies conforming to a geometric order—an appropriate visual metaphor for athletic bodies disciplined by the emerging ideology of proletarian *fizkul'tura* (physical culture). A photograph of Stepanova's friend Evgeniia Zhemchuzhnaia modelling a version of one of these costumes in Stepanova's studio attests to the ruin of these androgynous geometric lines when they enter into contact with a real body that gives off heat and has rounded limbs (fig. 12). Yet in photographs from the performance of *An Evening of the Book,* an agitational student theater piece promoting literacy designed by Stepanova in 1924 at the Academy of Communist Education, the multiplication of this same costume on a whole row of young female bodies of uniform height and size suddenly enables it to live up to the dynamism of the drawings (fig. 13). The costumes create a continuous geometric pattern from body to body, like a fabric design, suggesting a direct connection between Stepanova's optical designs and the futurist, mechanistic vision of the human body as a disciplined collective machine that is so often attributed to Constructivism.

This collective of young girls in Stepanova's sports costumes demonstrates a version of the body possible in performance, but not experienced in the everyday life of Moscow in 1924, in which females always wore skirts. Stepanova's androgynous vision is most evident in an evocative photograph of male and female students of the Academy of Social

Education in Moscow, all dressed in the same sports costume of her de-sign.[45] (fig. 14). The dark striped pattern of the pants, in particular, seems designed to override the conventional signs of gender difference. The illusion of a diamond-within-a-diamond design when the legs of the pants are pressed together makes the lower half of the students' bodies look like some completely third, hermaphroditic appendage—phallic in its form but distinctly vaginal in its patterning, with the lines emanating out from the "central core" of the diamond shape.[46] Throwing open the windows and filling them, their androgynous costumes minimizing natural differ-ences between bodies, the young students proclaim a hybrid, new con-structed order against the naturalism of the ornate ironwork vegetation of the window frames on the prerevolutionary building. It may be a coin-cidence that the students were photographed posing in the upper-storey windows of the school, of all places (it is an odd site for a group photo-graph), but this photograph might also stage Stepanova's explicit rebuttal of the class and gender hierarchies of the fashion displays of the contem-porary store window.

Critical as Stepanova may have been of the store window, her mass-produced fabrics, like the others produced by the factory, necessarily entered the commercial spaces of NEP Moscow. A photograph by Rod-chenko shows bolts of her optical fabric—the striped balls floating on a recessed lattice of stripes examined above—on display in a fabric store window in 1924 (fig. 15). Framed sketches of women's fashions are placed on top of the fabric, suggesting its availability for being sewn up into fashionable dresses rather than rational *prozodezhda*. Bunched together

45. Though there is no record of Stepanova's view of how gender difference would be affected by socialism, she does seem to suggest that the socialist future will be more androg-ynous, and more egalitarian, in a set of images from a poster that she made to advertise yet another agitational play performed at the Academy of Socialist Education: *Through Red and White Glasses*, 1923. On the lower left of the poster, under the phrase "through red glasses," she has drawn three fairly schematic red figures, two males and a female, dressed in three varieties of boxy "production clothing." The female figure is just as straight-edged and rectangular as her male counterparts; her gender is discernible only by the rounded line of her jaw and the slight fullness of the style of her short hair. The counterparts to these figures on the right side of the poster appear under the phrase "through white glasses." Here there are four white figures dressed in conventional, upper-class clothes, and again there is one female, but she is strongly differentiated from the male figures, drawn with a caricatured feminine body: she has enormous round breasts, a tiny waist, wide hips, and full thighs.

46. "Central core" imagery was the term invented by Judy Chicago to describe what she called the essentially female image of the vaginal form, and which she claimed to see in the work of most women artists. See Judy Chicago, *Through the Flower: My Struggle as a Woman Artist* (Garden City, N.Y., 1977). As further evidence that Stepanova was aware of the genital signification of the abstract patterning of her costume designs, see her double design for male and female costumes for *The Death of Tarelkin* that are identical except for a geomet-ric form at crotch level on the male costume that points upward, suggesting a phallic shape, while the same form on the female costume is placed pointing downwards, suggesting a vaginal shape.

FIG. 15.—Aleksandr Rodchenko, photograph of Stepanova's fabric in a store window, Moscow, 1924.

FIG. 16.—Fabric store window display, Passazh Arcade, Leningrad, 1924. Central State Archive of Film and Photographic Documents, St. Petersburg.

and softly draped in the typical style of Russian commercial displays of the time, the thin calico fabric loses some of its modernist optical effect. Compared, however, to another fabric store window display in the newly renovated Passazh Arcade in Leningrad in 1924—the kind of arcade that was the subject of Benjamin's opus—the geometries of Stepanova's pattern look markedly different from the formal and highly ornamental lace patterns and the array of old-fashioned floral prints on offer there, destined for the overcrowded bourgeois interiors that survived during the period of NEP (fig. 16).

A Soviet film from late 1924 provides some backhanded evidence that this contrast between Stepanova's fabric and its visual surroundings was recognized, that its offer of a visual sign of rationality, and even of modernity itself, was taken up by cultural producers beyond the confines of the *Lef* group. A film still from the comedy *The Cigarette Girl from Mossel'prom*, a big hit for the Soviet film industry, shows a female character wearing a dress made from the same Stepanova fabric in the store window, here with the light and dark colors reversed (fig. 17). In the main narrative of the movie, a young and pretty cigarette girl from the state-owned Mossel'prom company temporarily becomes the mistress of an evil visiting American capitalist, but she is thankfully brought back into the Bolshevik fold by the end through the intervention of the bumbling comic hero who adores her. He is shown kneeling before the woman wearing the Stepanova fabric, who is attempting to snag him for herself. The film gets exactly right the way that the fabric's bright optics rebel against the faded florals of the outdated wallpaper, against the impossibly primitive gas burner and bucket that announce the pathos of Russian *byt* and against the actresses's own full body, which is not conventionally flattered by the busy pattern. The film designers recognize that Stepanova's fabric is meant to signify dynamism, rationality, mechanization—even as these meanings are used to poke mean-spirited fun at this ungainly woman clutching her pot lid, the futuristic fabric rendering her almost clownish. By placing the fabric in a context that points up its clownishness, and by domesticating it into a fashionable flapper-style dress with a decorative white collar, the film designers most likely also got a chance to mock the productivist pretensions of the zany Constructivists. But they nonetheless utilized the dynamic meaning that the optical design was meant to offer, even if only in lampooning it.

While Stepanova's own utilitarian clothing designs signalled her desire to move toward a strictly rational form of clothing, there are other signs of her willingness to work within the market structures of fashion during NEP. Her work designing calico prints, despite her misgivings, emblematizes that willingness, and there are indications that she welcomed or even anticipated the uses to which her fabrics were put once they entered the NEP market. Her obvious pleasure in wearing a traditionally feminine dress made from her optical fabric—not a sports cos-

Fɪɢ. 17.—Film still from *The Cigarette Girl from Mossel'prom,* 1924. Courtesy British Film Institute.

tume or production suit—as she poses dreamily for a photograph by Rodchenko in 1924 might offer one indication (fig. 18). So does her interest in having Rodchenko *document* the presence of her fabric in a store window, as we saw above. In her 1928 article, she concludes that the fundamental task of the artist-textile worker is to stop making textile drawings as an abstraction and to take an active part in forming them into clothing—"to force his way into the *byt* and life of the consumer and find out what gets done with the fabric after it leaves the factory" ("Z," p. 192). This conclusion was based on a more elaborate plan from her teaching methods at Vkhutemas in 1925. She had students keep a notebook on them at all times for recording the fabrics and clothes that they observed on the streets. These were her requirements:

(a) direct observation of the current designs for fabrics produced by the Soviet textile industry, with sketches
(b) study of the evolution of changes in so-called "fashion" and analysis of it
(c) observation of the current situation, with the goal of devising methods for a conscious awareness of the demands imposed on us by new social conditions. [*CNM,* p. 185]

She acknowledges that the "current situation" of fashion must be studied, understood, and, to an extent, designed for. But she urges her students

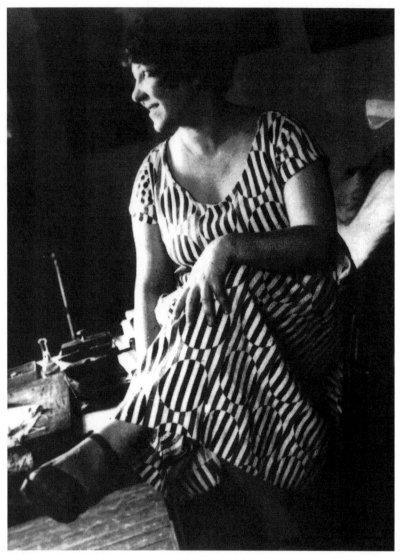

Fig. 18.—Aleksandr Rodchenko, photograph of Stepanova in a dress of her own fabric, 1924.

ultimately to move toward projects that will depart from the conventions of fashion and respond to the "new social condition" of an egalitarian socialist economy.

I emphasize Stepanova's conscious, if guarded, openness to exploring consumer desire in everyday life because Constructivism, and Leninism for that matter, are often criticized for replacing one harmful entity—the commodity fetish—with another one—the technological fetish—imposing a kind of enforced technological uniformity onto social life. I want to understand Constructivism, instead, as a practice that willingly adapted itself to the needs of everyday life, such as they were in the hybrid context of NEP Russia in the early 1920s, and I want to claim that this was a source of its strength as an avant-garde art-into-life practice rather than a sign of its failure. My argument is specifically meant to challenge Boris Groys's accusations that the Constructivists aimed for a "total work of art," a total restructuring of the lived environment according to avant-garde ideals of rationalization and utilitarianism, thus paving the way for the genocidal Stalinist *Gesamtkunstwerk*.[47]

Stepanova's guarded openness to fashion was only acceptable to her, however, as a part of the Constructivist insistence on the exalted role of the artist in improving Soviet industrial production, which she reiterated in her 1928 essay. She complains that the artist in the textile industry has been forced to remain a mere applied artist, a handicraft decorator, rather than an independent participant in production—someone who invents new dyes, for example, or new structures and materials for cloth. This complaint was fully justified, we know, by her own disappointing experience in the First State Cotton-Printing Factory. A reference to the automobile industry in her opening paragraph suggests just how industrial, and non–craft-oriented, her ambitions for artists in the textile industry are: "How many textile drawings of the last decade do we know," she asks, "that could be favorably compared to the exterior design of even only the latest model of the Ford automobile?" ("Z," p. 190).

This comparative lack of achievement on the part of the textile artist resulted not only from the applied-art tradition of the textile industry but also from the very character of textile production as an industrial form. The textile is a flat plane that resembles the surface of drawing or painting, trapping the textile artist within traditional artistic practices rather than encouraging her to develop the principle of *tselesoobraznost'* ("Z," p. 191)—to invent new ways of projecting the textiles into three-dimensional forms, as artists can do in other industries. The Soviet artist-textile worker must take an active part in this purposive forming of textiles into clothing, which will result in a new form of socialist fashion: "Fashion in a planned socialist economy will take a completely different form and will depend, not on competition in the market, but on the improvement and rationalization of the textile and garment industry" ("Z," pp. 191–92). Clothing under socialism will be responsive to history, not the market. Clothes will still fall out of use, not because they start to look funny when the market generates novel fashions, but rather because con-

---

47. See Boris Groys, *The Total Art of Stalinism: Avant-garde, Aesthetic Dictatorship, and Beyond,* trans. Charles Rougle (Princeton, N.J., 1992).

ditions of *byt* will have changed, necessitating new forms of clothing ("Z," p. 192). Yet the socialist rationalization of fashion will not mean the end of fashion:

> It would be a mistake to think that fashion can be eliminated, or that it is only an unnecessary appendage of a speculative character. Fashion accessibly offers a set of the predominant lines and forms of a given slice of time—the outer signs of an epoch. It never repeats the forms it has already found, but steadily and consistently takes the path of rationalization, just as, step by step, our *byt* is becoming increasingly rationalized. ["Z," p. 191]

She has not completely changed her hard-line view of 1923; the market structures that organize fashion must eventually cede to a more rational organization of clothing. But she acknowledges fashion as a valuable expression of the experience of modernity, and, in an even more surprising departure from the rigorously antifeminine as well as antifashion rhetoric of her earlier essay, she goes on to suggest that fashion is valuable because it both expresses and produces liberation from gender hierarchies.

Stepanova compares the development of men's and women's clothing over the past decade, in the West as well as in Russia. The influence of the uniform from World War I had temporarily rationalized men's clothing, she claims, but this tendency did not last, and it reverted to more traditional forms. In contrast, women's clothing changed dramatically; she does not have to remind her readers that, in the same ten years, short skirts and loose, long-waisted dresses replaced the long skirts, fitted waists, and even corsets that persisted through the 1910s. These empirical observations then lead her to make a statement that is extraordinary for a woman artist who never otherwise publicly expressed any views on gender: "The appearance of woman over the last decade exhibits an exceptional picture of her emancipation. In these ten years women's dress has been rationalized to such an extent that it has come to represent in and of itself almost the greatest achievement of contemporary urban *byt*" ("Z," p. 191). The unexpected passion with which she announces the importance of the changes in women's fashion that she has experienced in her own adult life (from age twenty-four to thirty-four) demonstrates her understanding of the significance of clothing for the individual female wearer as well as for the collective.

Popova's Flapper Dress

If Stepanova acknowledged the importance of fashion in her writings, if not directly in her practice, Popova's interest in fashion was more straightforward; she designed many fashionable dresses and even two window displays for a fashion store in Moscow. Unlike Stepanova, whose interest in designing stiff, androgynous clothing, primarily in the vein of sports and production clothing, precluded making designs that utilized the softer, more traditional cotton calico fabric that she designed at the First State Cotton-Printing Factory, Popova took up the role of the artist-productivist that Stepanova would recommend in her 1928 article. She took her two-dimensional fabric-design work to the next level of *tselesoobraznost'* by shaping it into three-dimensional objects to be used in everyday life. She attempted to intervene directly into the Soviet fashion industry in order to improve it (though unlike her fabrics, her dress designs were never mass-produced).

Popova's clothing designs based on her own fabrics aimed for the "chicness" that Soviet consumers wanted and that Soviet products lacked, according to the list of desirable consumer qualities that Arvatov had enumerated in his essay "Art and the Quality of Industrial Production." In Arvatov's terms, she would fall squarely into the category of the temporary fix offered by the left applied artist: improving the quality of backward Soviet production, first, by making dynamic designs for the already outmoded cotton calico fabrics and, second, by making these mass-produced Soviet fabrics appeal to consumers by projecting them into designs for "elegant" coats and "stylish" flapper dresses. (*Flapper dress* is my term, not Popova's; I use it to evoke the familiar vision of the loose-fitting, drop-waisted style of dresses from the 1920s rather than the figure of the flapper herself.)[48] I would like to propose that the "current" and ostensibly temporary interest in consumer desires that Arvatov allows for in his essay is not only a temporal condition of Popova's objects but a structural one. Popova's work shows Constructivism to be a practice that is as much about meeting the needs of consumption as about a fantasy of production.

Popova did not write about her fashion designs, so we can only analyze her theory of the Constructivist thing from the things themselves. These things do seem to set up a deliberate confrontation between the rational product of socialist industry and the commodity fetish. They point, in effect, to a fundamental problem in Marxist thought: how will our desire for the mass-produced objects of industry be organized under socialism? What happens to the individual fantasies and desires organized under capitalism by the commodity fetish and the market after the socialist revolution? How will consumers suddenly forget all of their fetishistic

48. Sarabianov and Adaskina claim that Popova's dress designs were oriented not toward the working woman (the office worker, teacher, sales clerk), and certainly not toward the proletarian woman worker, but rather toward "a more artistic type" from the "'gay twenties'. . . the artist, the film star" (*P*, p. 303)—in other words, the flapper. But there is much evidence to suggest that this style of dress was worn by a range of urban, working women in Russia, including proletarian women on special occasions. My claim, as will become clear, is that Popova was working against just such class hierarchies within fashion.

desires, inculcated by the capitalist market, and relate to objects in a purely rational way (Arvatov's "rational satisfaction")? The very idea of a Constructivist flapper dress addresses this question by proposing an object that would attempt to harness the power of the commodity fetish— its ability to solicit individual desires—*for socialism*. In this final portion of my essay, I will argue that Popova's flapper dresses are not merely routine commercial designs that are marginal to her "real" practice as a Constructivist but are important contributions to an expanded understanding of the Constructivist theory of the socialist thing, which takes seriously the desire of the consumer and realizes that capitalism, with its honing of the commodity form that endlessly organizes and gives form to this desire, has a profound weapon that socialism cannot simply cede to it.[49]

The Soviet garment industry was one of the most backward of Russian industries; in 1917, only three percent of all clothing was industrially produced, with the rest made in small artisanal workshops or at home (see *SCT*, p. 9). The many foreign dress patterns published in magazines like *The Housewives' Magazine* were directed at women sewing at home or ordering dresses from workshops; the idea of fashionable clothing available to everyone at mass-market prices was still largely utopian. Left artists like Popova were not alone in confronting the problem; the state-owned Moscow Garment-Producing Trust, for example, established an Atelier of Fashions to improve Soviet clothing production. In 1923 it briefly published a journal, *Atelier,* which illustrated sketches of Western European fashions (fig. 19). The magazine was discontinued after one issue for its elitist bias; the recommended textiles for the kinds of dresses it published—crepe de chine, cheviot, and cashmere—were available in Russia only to the well-connected few, and the complicated fluted and accordion-pleated skirts were beyond the skills of women at home or the capabilities of Soviet mass production.

In contrast to *Atelier,* Popova designed *tselesoobraznye* Constructivist dresses, the forms of which fully and appropriately *respond to* the limits imposed by the Soviet conditions of mass production. For example, she designed a dress out of the optical fabric that we examined above, on the

49. In its proximity to the commodity, this Constructivist object is closer to the products of mass culture than to art objects. Constructivism broke with the traditional model of autonomous avant-garde art not in order to establish a more effective space for art to resist the dominant institutions of society, but in order, on the contrary, to participate more fully in the political project of the Bolshevik state—including its commodity economy, mass culture, and propaganda. This gives Constructivism its strange, partially repressed status in Peter Bürger's theory of the avant-garde because while it is clearly a "historical avant-garde" that attempts to bring art into the praxis of life, it does so by turning art into a (new, Soviet) form of mass culture. For Bürger, under the influence of Adorno, when it does this "art becomes practical but it is an art that enthralls"—it enthralls and subjugates rather than emancipates (Peter Bürger, *Theory of the Avant-garde,* trans. Michael Shaw [Minneapolis, 1984], p. 54). On Bürger in relation to Constructivism, see Kiaer, introduction, *Imagine No Possessions.*

Fig. 19.—Sketch of a dress design in the journal *Atelier,* 1923.

cover of *Lef* (here in blue on black, rather than orange on black) (fig. 20). Its main visual interest stems not from the expensive fabrics and complex cuts of the fancy *Atelier* designs but from the bold geometric graphics of Popova's own fabric design based on her formal experience as an abstract painter. The dress has an elongated silhouette and a decorative collar, much like the dress made from Stepanova's fabric in the movie *The Ciga-rette Girl from Mossel'prom,* but Popova re-creates the stylish effects of Western fashion through highly simplified means. The dress is plainly and fully cut and is given its shape by being tied with a large simple sash rather than by tailoring; it is ornamented by an oversized collar that is attached to the top of the dress in a rudimentary way; and it is made from available, affordable, mass-produced printed cotton from the First State Cotton-Printing Factory. It is ready for mass production.

But Popova's flapper dress could also be described, in less flattering terms, as *clumsily* simple. The collar resembles a large bunched napkin, and the voluminous cheap printed cotton fabric does not drape as grace-fully as the flapper style demands. Compare it, for example, to a very similar dress toward the right of a spread of foreign fashions illustrated in *The Housewives' Magazine* in 1925, which has a more carefully measured and sewn collar, a more tailored cut, and a more discreet geometric print (fig. 21). The clumsiness of Popova's dress is even more painfully appar-ent in an extraordinary reconstruction of the design made in 1985 by Elena Khudiakova, an architecture student in Moscow who faithfully re-created a number of Popova and Stepanova designs (fig. 22).

Fig. 20.—Liubov' Popova, design for a dress, 1923–24.

My proposal is not, however, that Popova's design is a failure, a sign that she had ventured, in her Constructivist fervor, into an area of practice for which she was not trained—a criticism levelled frequently at the Constructivists.[50] I want to propose, instead, that this dress is an object that indexically shows us how it is made; it hides nothing, but rather renders its mode of production *transparent*. It wants to wear its Constructivist heart on its fashionable sleeve, as it were; it wants to incorporate the consumer fantasy of fashion into the Constructivist rhetoric of transparency or indexicality. The purpose or use-value of this flapper dress is not only to clothe a female body efficiently but to elicit the belief that, in wearing this dress instead of a Western or NEP-produced one, the woman who wears it is more rational and more emancipated (to use Stepanova's term) than nonsocialist wearers of flapper dresses. This belief is elicited *through*—and will eventually take the place of—the fantasies of femininity that normally function to give such a dress its exchange-value on the market. This understanding of Popova's dress design adds a layer of meaning to Arvatov's description of the ideal transparency of the industrial thing: "the mechanism of a thing, the connection between the elements of a thing and its purpose, were now transparent, compelling people practically, and thus also psychologically, to reckon with them" ("EL," p. 126). Popova's flapper dress project acknowledges addressing consumer fantasy as a necessary purpose of the socialist ob-

50. See, for example, Miklashevskii's criticism of Tatlin's attempt to design a winter coat, despite the fact that he possessed none of the qualifications of a professional coat-maker, in Konstantin Miklashevskii, *Gipertrofiia Iskusstva* (Petrograd, 1924), p. 61.

FIG. 21.—Foreign fashion patterns illustrated in *The Housewives' Magazine,* 1925.

FIG. 22.—Elena Khudiakova, reconstruction of Popova dress design, 1985. Modeled by Khudiakova.

ject, even if the goal is to direct the fantasy of the consumer (to "compel her psychologically") away from purposeless decoration and ornament and toward more *tselesoobraznye* and transparent objects that embody the creativity of industrial production.

Despite its obviously feminine and fashionable aspects, in its indexicality this flapper dress bears a surprising resemblance to Popova's most famous clothing designs, which are usually considered to be more properly Constructivist than her dresses: her *prozodezhda* costumes designed for Meierkhol'd's production of *The Magnanimous Cuckold* in 1922 (fig. 23). The flattened, highly simplified, and perfectly symmetrical drawing of an outfit of shirt, skirt, and apron for a female character called Actor No. 5, for example, is largely composed of the floating quadrilaterals that had made up Popova's suprematist paintings, rendering the construction of the clothing as transparent as the truth-to-materials ethos rendered her abstract paintings understandable as modernist works that were about the process of painting. The flat black rectangles of the apron have

Fig. 23.—Liubov' Popova, design for *prozodezhda* for actor no. 5, 1921.

been replaced, in the flapper dress, by the softer forms of the enormous sash and handkerchief collar, but the design is still an indexical one in which materials and parts speak for themselves and nothing is hidden.

For Marx, the industrially produced object becomes a commodity fetish when the real value of the object is replaced by its exchange-value on the market. Laura Mulvey clarifies this in semiotic terms when she writes that Marx's fetish derives from a failure of inscription; the sign of (labor) value should leave an indexical trace on the object, but the commodity's success depends on the erasure of the marks of production. The object must enter the market with a seductive sheen.[51] If the desirability of the capitalist commodity on the market is based on the *invisibility* of the industrial labor process, then by refusing to pull off the slickly accomplished sheen of fashion, Popova's dress "breaks the spell of the commodity," to use a Benjaminian phrase. Through its very material forms, the dress reveals its own recent birth as a hybrid socialist object in the conditions of the semisocialist, semimarket economy of the New Economic Policy.

Popova's dress challenges the usual function of the fashion commodity not only by succeeding in preserving the traces of labor but also by refusing to produce the seamless sheen of femininity—the glossy surface that, in the psychoanalytic scenario, covers over and disavows the fantasy of the lack of the female body.[52] Not just labor value, but the labored production of femininity, is made visible in the bunched-napkin collar of her dress. Unlike the similar collar on the dress in the fashion drawing in *The Housewives' Magazine,* which drapes delicately over the model's shoulders, calling attention to her throat and breastplate, Popova's massive collar broadens the model's shoulders and obliterates her chest; it becomes a sign for the failed attempt to produce an appropriately feminine surface armor. In this willful androgyny, the dress unexpectedly resembles the *prozodezhda* costumes for the *Magnanimous Cuckold* because we know that Popova considered her designs for these costumes to be androgynous. The men's and women's costumes were identical, except that women were given skirts instead of pants, and a text by Popova reveals that for her this distinction was so natural that she did not even notice it: "there was a fundamental disinclination to making any distinction between the men's and women's costumes; it just came down to changing the pants to a skirt."[53] Combined with Popova's embrace of mechanical drawing, mathematics, and industrialism, this interest in androgyny does

51. See Laura Mulvey, "Some Thoughts on Theories of Fetishism in the Context of Contemporary Culture," *October,* no. 65 (Summer 1993): 3–20, esp. pp. 9–11.

52. Mulvey makes this connection between the sheen of the commodity fetish and the glossy surface of the filmic or photographic image of the female movie icon, which covers over the threat of castration posed by the female body that "lacks" the phallus. See ibid.

53. Popova, "Introduction to the INKHUK Discussion of the *Magnanimous Cuckold*," in *P,* p. 379.

suggest a conscious will on her part to resist the conventional signs of sexual difference in her Constructivist things. Her flapper dress is best understood as a design that continues this utopian resistance to conventional gender hierarchies rather than temporarily deviating from it into conventional, commercialized femininity.

On the level of the unconscious, it is possible to read the optical pattern of the fabric itself as a refusal to make the female body cover over the fantasy of its lack, a refusal of the veil of femininity as Freudian fetish, as well as a refusal of the commodity fetish. Sewn up into this bizarre dress, the op-art design of receding black holes and protruding blue targets, which seems so abstract and anonymous when viewed as a flat image, begins to resemble an apotropaic proliferation of vaginal "central core" forms across the model's body, as if the dress deliberately fails to perform its role as the feminine fetish that allays male fears of castration. If we recall Stepanova's clownish sports costumes for the students at the Academy of Social Education, with the suggestively vaginal form created by the pattern on the pants, we find ourselves with examples in the work of both artists of the repressed sign of femininity bubbling up in the context of purportedly androgynous, Constructivist clothing designs. In the case of Stepanova, this eruption, along with the suggestively phallic shape of the pants design, might be read as a sign of the sexuality repressed from her clothing designs more generally. But, in the case of Popova, the errant sign of the repressed female body that surfaces here stands for the contradictions entailed in trying to combine a feminine fashion form with Constructivist transparency. The pressure of the attempt to hold both aspects in solution is made visible in the clumsy forms of the dress itself, which would most likely have been too antifetishistic to function as a commercially successful feminine commodity had it reached the NEP market in 1924. The dress addresses and resists that market, pushing at the limits of Constructivist transparency or truth-to-materials or indexicality, but also, like Stepanova's designs, upholding them.

What happens when the Constructivist flapper dress pushes so hard at the limits of transparency that it almost achieves the sheen of the commodity? I want to turn, finally, to Popova's most overtly commercial fashion imagery: a window display design of 1924 (fig. 24). It presents summer clothing in the window of a Moscow fashion studio in 1924; as in the fashion sketch from *The Housewives' Magazine,* the cyrillic word is *leto,* or summer. The earnest indexicality of the previous dress, and the demands of the strapped Soviet economy, seem long-forgotten, replaced by a stroke of montage, with a sinuous model, an elegant, flowing frock, and an ostentatious motorcar that appears to be speeding toward us. The patterned fabric of the dress is not one of Popova's more complex optical designs but a slightly more conventional horizontal stripe pattern contrasted with a decorative piping of vertical stripes. We seem to be far from

Fɪɢ. 24.—Liubov' Popova, design for a window display, 1924.

the young students dressed in Stepanova's androgynous sports costumes filling the windows of the Academy of Socialist Education, far from Stepanova's cautious relation to fashion as something to be studied and negotiated, but ultimately transcended. We seem to be, in fact, squarely inside what Benjamin called the "commodity phantasmagoria." How might this image be redeemed for socialism? Can there be such a thing as a Constructivist flapper dress?

For Benjamin, fashion was one of the dominant wish-images of modernity, occupying the entire Konvolut B of his *Arcades Project*.[54] This project attempted to imagine not just a Marxist revolution but the transition to socialism that would follow it, to imagine a form of socialist culture that would reactivate the original promise of the creativity of industrialism while delivering it from the commodity phantasmagoria of capitalism that prevented its realization.[55] Thus, the Constructivists and Benjamin share not only the core Marxist belief that a socialist future—once freed from the commodity phantasmagoria—would embrace the creative material abundance made possible by industrial modernity but the more specific, and stranger, belief that the success of this socialist culture would depend on the very *material forms* of modern things. Benjamin theorized the dialectical moment that would break the spell of the commodity; this break with the past will come when the presence of mythic wish-images of the ur-past—the myth of "a humane society of material abundance"—are made visible to the dreaming collective *in the newest technological forms*.[56]

Benjamin critiques the endless novelty of fashion as an instrument of capital that makes the subject—particularly the female subject—forgetful of history and so prevents historical change.[57] This forgetful subject, lulled by the phantasmagoria of capitalism, is precisely the subject of "the dreaming collective." Fashion reifies the human capacity for change into the inorganic commodity, the "realm of dead things," replacing the natural engendering of human life (the natural condition of birth) with novelty's inescapable cycle of eternal recurrence (*AP*, p. 70; trans. mod.).[58]

54. On the wish image, see *AP*, p. 4; on Marx and the "commodity phantasmagoria," see pp. 181–82, where Benjamin quotes Otto Rühle.

55. Susan Buck-Morss writes that the *Arcades Project* "put forth the notion that socialist culture would need to be constructed out of the embryonic, still-inadequate forms that preexisted in capitalism" (Susan Buck-Morss, *The Dialectics of Seeing: Walter Benjamin and the Arcades Project* [Cambridge, Mass., 1989], p. 123). Buck-Morss's synthesis and interpretation of the *Arcades Project* has been an invaluable guide for me to Benjamin's text, and it stands as a major contribution to the theory of modernity in its own right.

56. Buck-Morss, *The Dialectics of Seeing*, p. 274. See also pp. 146, 116–17.

57. "Fashions are a collective medicament for the ravages of oblivion. The more short-lived a period, the more susceptible it is to fashion" (*AP*, p. 80).

58. I have used Buck-Morss's translation here (see Buck-Morss, *The Dialectics of Seeing*, p. 101) in place of Eiland and McLaughlin's "world of the inorganic"; on the "overcoming" of birth and death, see *AP*, p. 79; on "the ridiculous superstition of novelty," see Paul Valéry, quoted in *AP*, p. 74.

But, in other entries in Konvolut B, Benjamin calls attention to the utopian promise of fashion. The mass-production of clothing beginning in the nineteenth century led to a democratization of style; the new industrial abundance of fashion challenges the "natural" social hierarchies of class based on the accidents of birth, making visible the mythic wish-image of, precisely, "a humane society of material abundance."[59] This is why Benjamin's question about fashion in Soviet Russia, which we have already considered, is phrased so uncertainly: "*Does* fashion die (as in Russia, for example)?" Perhaps it should not die, after all, because it is the locus of the wish-image that must be redeemed in the new material forms of modernity in order to engender a utopian future. Could the conditions of *actual* social change brought about in Russia by the defeat of capital and the "birth" of the revolution stop fashion's eternal cycle of repetition and reawaken its utopian promise as a force of social change?

The Constructivist thing is born from the rhetoric of transparency or indexicality, but it points, not just to its mode of making, but also to its historical situatedness, to its place within the wish-images of modernity. Popova's photomontage window display design could, for example, be analyzed within the standard rhetoric of transparency as a typically leftist avant-garde image that aims for a disruption or laying bare of the device of consumer fantasy. The argument that the pictorial technique of montage disrupts the sheen of the bourgeois spectacle, calling attention to the construction of ideology within it, is a familiar one from modernist art history. The obvious fragmentation of the woman's body in the window display—the way that it is cobbled together pictorially, its parts out of proportion—could serve well to illustrate Benjamin's critique of fashion as an inorganic commodity, the falsely animated dead forms of which turn the real, living woman into a "gaily decked-out corpse" (*AP,* p. 63; trans. mod.).[60] But I don't think, in the end, that it does so. It is, rather, an image that engages with the wish-image as something that must be redeemed by the form of the Constructivist dress. The dislocations of this montage work to make the body of the female figure more, rather than less, vital. Her elongated silhouette mimics those of the figures in the insipid fashion drawings of the time, such as the ones in *The Housewives' Magazine,* but she goes them one better. She has the same ridiculously tiny, pointed feet below and small head above, but, in between, a massive,

---

59. On the "revolution" in cotton prints and the changing dress of the lower classes: "Every woman used to wear a blue or black dress that she kept for ten years without washing, for fear it might tear to pieces. But now her husband, a poor worker, covers her with a robe of flowers for the price of a day's labor" (Jules Michelet [1846], quoted in *AP,* p. 78; see also p. 75). Buck-Morss cautions that the entries describing fashion as an indicator of social change are more predominant earlier on and that in the 1930s the entries on fashion become increasingly critical. See Buck-Morss, *The Dialectics of Seeing,* pp. 98, 403 n. 97.

60. I have used Buck-Morss's translation of this phrase; see Buck-Morss, *The Dialectics of Seeing,* p. 101.

sensual body explodes out of the picture, with immense rosy arms, one of them lifted in an autoerotic gesture to touch the bare flesh of the exposed pink shoulders. The dress swirls around her body, clinging to reveal its contours, and Popova has brushed in a ruddy, reddish glow to liven up the black-and-white cheeks of her cut-out photographic face. Through her sheer size and pictorial force, this vital figure broadcasts not only the dynamic qualities of the contrasting stripes of the Constructivist dress but the powerful wish-image of the bodily freedom and confidence of an urban woman in 1924, only recently freed from the tightly fitted waists and full-length skirts that Popova wore as a young woman.

Popova's window display can serve as an illustration of Stepanova's exhilarated statement that contemporary fashion represents the emancipation of woman, that it "represent[s] in and of itself almost the greatest achievement of contemporary urban *byt*." Although the elegantly subdued figures in the fashion spread in *The Housewives' Magazine* are technically wearing similarly comfortable clothing, Popova's giant, unfettered, collaged woman, disproportionate and bursting out of the frame, insists pictorially on her emancipation. As Benjamin wrote in "One-Way Street," the modern advertisement "all but hits us between the eyes with things as a car, growing to gigantic proportions, careens at us out of a film screen."[61] The juxtaposition of the female figure with the speeding car is almost ham-handedly insistent on the dynamism, activity, and contemporaneity of the woman and the dress. Like Stepanova, who invoked the artist-constructors at the Ford Motor Company as models for Constructivist textile worker-constructors, Popova's design syntagmatically borrows the veneer of industrial achievement of the motorcar to promote the modernity of her dress. (It is a more standard symbol of the "greatest achievement of contemporary urban *byt*" than Stepanova's—and Popova's—proposed symbol of women's fashion.) And while it might surprise us to see an expensive status commodity like a fancy car in a Constructivist image, even more than seeing a flapper dress, the motorcar at that time in the Soviet Union symbolized modernity and progress as much as wealth; Moscow in 1924 was, we should recall, still primarily a city of horse-drawn carriages.

For the Constructivists, who unbeknownst to Benjamin went further than any of his contemporaries toward realizing his theory, the mass-production of cheap, high-quality Constructivist textiles was meant to democratize fashion and disseminate the creative technological forms of modernist art throughout everyday life.[62] There is no shortage of proof

61. Benjamin, "One-Way Street," *Reflections: Essays, Aphorisms, Autobiographical Writings,* trans. Edmund Jephcott, ed. Peter Demetz (New York, 1978), p. 85.
62. I say "unbeknownst" to him because Benjamin, in his relationship with Asja Lacis and on his visit to Moscow, clearly became acquainted with the more straightforwardly agitational and ascetic practices of the literary and artistic avant-garde, yet does not seem to

to back up this claim about the Constructivist dedication to egalitarianism. The critic Ivan Aksenov, for example, reported that two days before her own death from scarlet fever, and deep in grief over the death of her child who had just succumbed to the same illness, Popova still "experienced great happiness upon ascertaining . . . that fabrics covered with her designs were selling widely in the countryside and in working-class neighborhoods."[63] According to Tugendkhol'd, Popova had said that "not one of her artistic successes ever gave her such deep satisfaction as the sight of a peasant woman and a worker buying lengths of her material" (quoted in "CF," p. 157). In the obituary he wrote for her, he noted that her fabrics were transforming the taste of working-class women: "This spring, the women of Moscow—not the Nepmankas, but the workers, the cooks, the service workers—began dressing themselves up. Instead of the former petite bourgeois little flowers, there appeared on the fabrics new and unexpectedly strong and clear patterns."[64]

In this window display, then, Popova deliberately invoked the capitalist language of fashion advertising in order to take up its wish-imagery of abundance and redeem it for socialism. Its redemptive quality stems from Popova's deeply personal investment in it. Montage, which Popova otherwise rarely used, is not deployed critically or disruptively, but, rather, parodically to emphasize the sheer overload of images available for the (her) investment of desire. Note the long cut-out rectangle of shiny green paper along the left border that picks up the green of the pom-pom on the hat and the numbers on the lower right; the curl of the sash that fits just so within the space framed by the car wheel and the vertical text; or the way that the tiny photograph of the model's face—the only element literally cut out from commercial advertising—is dwarfed by the freakish enormity of the shoulders and arms. Popova's choice to play with the montage technique can help us to understand the personal meaning of her Constructivist flapper dress. She has borrowed the montage technique here as a visual strategy—from Stepanova, as far as I can surmise—precisely for its personally parodic effect.

Popova seemed to be looking specifically at Stepanova's photomontage caricatures of herself and Rodchenko of 1924, which parody the kind of gender and class divisions that Constructivism tried to break down (fig. 25). On the right side of the image, Rodchenko's bespectacled photographic head sprouts a massive, drawn-in boxer's body in a pair of boxing shorts, spoofing the Constructivist as working-class strongman— a spoof sharpened by the conspicuous absence of male genitals

have been aware of the more commercial or everyday practices of the Constructivists, such as dress designs or advertisements, that I emphasize in my project.
    63. I. A. Aksenov, "Posmertnaia vystavka L. S. Popovoi," *Zhizn' Iskusstva*, 3 Feb. 1925, p. 5.
    64. Iakov Tugendkhol'd, "Pamiati L. Popovoi," *Khudozhnik i zritel'* 6, no. 7 (1924): 77.

FIG. 25.—Alexandr Rodchenko, photomontage caricature of Popova and Rodchenko in *Nash Gaz,* 1924.

revealed by the absurdly lacy boxer shorts and the oddly geometric, upward-pointing phallic shape formed by the space between his legs. On the left side and on the other side of a parodic gender divide, Popova's face is pasted onto a body striking a haughty pose in an elaborate flapper dress, complete with jumbo belt buckle and preposterously long sash—the female artist-Constructivist tricked out as bourgeois fashion plate. That the caricature took this particular form suggests that Popova was used to being teased by her colleagues for her style of dress and upper-class ways.[65]

Listen to Rodchenko, reminiscing about first meeting Popova in 1915 when they participated in an exhibition together:

> Popova, who was one of the rich, related to us with condescension and scorn, because she considered us to be unsuitable company, a class that she wanted nothing to do with. . . . She almost never talked with me, and came by only rarely, leaving behind her in the gallery the scent of expensive perfume and the memory of beautiful clothing."[66]

This is the Popova who emerges from Rodchenko's caricature, certainly, appropriately juxtaposed with a proletarian-boxer Rodchenko. But the crucial point is that Popova had a change of heart and committed herself to socialist goals and therefore began to disassociate herself from her previous self-presentation; as Rodchenko himself at the conclusion of the above passage in his memoirs: "later, after the revolution, she changed a lot and became a real comrade."[67] The figure in Popova's window display design mimics almost exactly the *Nash Gaz* caricature of her—right down to the position of the feet, the right arm on the hip, and the angle of the tilted head— suggesting that Popova's window display is shot through with a self-aware and self-mocking humor at her own investment in fashion, the unpreventably bubbling-up of her haute-bourgeois feminine upbringing that marks her difference from colleagues like Stepanova and Rodchenko.

Popova's ironic identification with the figure in the window design expands the Constructivist rhetoric of transparency, as it is usually understood. Popova's investment of personal desire in the thing does not immediately return it, however, to the structure of the fetish, which names the "incomprehensible mystery of the power of material things," according to William Pietz.[68] Constructivism insists, rather, that the power of material

65. In another caricature from this series—the one discussed above showing Popova and Stepanova taking their fabric designs to the factory—Popova is again depicted as fashionably dressed in a short, swingy skirt, angular jacket, tiny high-heeled black boots, and an elegant hat, an amusing getup for someone pushing a wheelbarrow down the street but, again, one that suggests that fashionable feminine attire was a reliable source of Popova jokes.

66. Rodchenko, *Opyty dlia budushchego: Dnevniki, stat'i, pisma, zapiski* (Moscow, 1996), p. 60.

67. Ibid.

68. William Pietz, "The Problem of the Fetish, I," *Res* 9 (Spring 1985): 14. In Pietz's important material and historical account of the fetish, it is a material object that is both deeply personal and collective. But I have attempted here to support the Constructivists' own assertions that their things, in their transparency, should no longer be understood in terms of the structure of the fetish.

Fig. 26.—Group photograph of Popova with her students at Vkhutemas, 1922.

things *can* be rendered comprehensible, to the benefit of makers and users alike, without diminishing it. It is of course always risky to exploit the recourse we have to biography, and I do not mean to imply that Popova's upper-class feminine identity can *explain* her Constructivist things.[69] But I do think that it gave her particular knowledge and experience that allowed her to produce the window display as such an extreme, but therefore also effective, example of the Constructivist thing as a transparent socialist counterpart to the commodity fetish. The *tselesoobraznost'* of Popova's window design is that it is formed in relation to the goal of confronting consumer desire. It gives form to consumer desire through forms gleaned from her own desires—which, as Rodchenko's memoirs show, are perhaps imperfectly socialist but are changing in a socialist direction—in order to encourage a similar socialist change in the desires of the mass of female consumers. The window design offers the mythic wish-images represented by the motorcar and the model, but it redeems them through the Constructivist dress, which is not mythic, but actually obtainable, because it is mass-produced by Soviet industry for the purpose of being affordable and easily available to working women. Possession is no longer exclusive.

As women Constructivists, Popova and Stepanova took different

69. On the uses and abuses of biography for reading the work of women artists, see the recent work of Anne Wagner, particularly *Three Artists (Three Women): Modernism and the Art of Hesse, Krasner, and O'Keeffe* (Berkeley, 1996). As she writes there, an artist's "position as a woman does not have fixed, predictable consequences" (p. 6).

paths with their Constructivist things. Stepanova's artistic successes derived from her embrace of the antisubjective language of technology, an embrace that was conditioned by her negative experiences as a woman painter. She upheld the standard Constructivist rhetoric of transparency, pushing at its limits only in her writings; her clothing designs stick tenaciously, and to my mind exhilaratingly, to a model of transparency and egalitarian androgyny that has no truck with commercial feminine fashions. Popova's willingness to risk experimenting in the feminized area of the fashion commodity led, by contrast, to the more surprising and densely layered meanings of the Constructivist flapper dresses. This willingness most likely resulted from her more secure artistic identity; she was less in need than Stepanova of the authority conferred by the technological model of artistic making. Her flapper dresses refute the parodic gender polarization of Stepanova's caricatures, suggesting that androgynous sports costumes are not the only alternative to the clothing of bourgeois femininity or proletarian masculinity.

I conclude with a photograph of Popova with her students at Vkhutemas in 1922 (fig. 26). She sits in the middle of the group, wearing a white pom-pom on her hat. This pom-pom, standing out defiantly from the drabness of a sea of Muscovites bundled against the indoor winter cold, functions for me as a *punctum,* reaching across a gulf to join with the green pom-pom perched on the hat of the female figure in her window display. We need both these images, I think, to make sense of the Constructivist project: the grim determination, out of the impossible material privations of the postrevolutionary years, to mass-produce transparent utilitarian things for use in everyday life—and the dream of creating a socialist form of modernity in which the phantasmatic power of things would be redeemed for the benefit of everyone.

The Romance of Caffeine and Aluminum

Jeffrey T. Schnapp

The title of my essay echoes that of one of late antiquity's most learned works: Martianus Capella's *Marriage of Mercury and Philology*. But whereas the fifth-century Neoplatonic philosopher was concerned with timeless nuptials of the intellect, allegorical nuptials joining the trivium to the quadrivium, eloquence to learning, I am interested instead in the convergence between two bodies in the accelerated time frame that corresponds to the advent of modernity. The first of these bodies is the active ingredient in coffee, isolated for the first time in 1820, a substance emblematic of the modern individual's striving for hyperproductivity and appetite for hyperstimulation. The second is the most important of the new metals embraced by twentieth-century industry: aluminum—a material discovered in 1854 but first produced on an industrial scale at the turn-of-the-century mark.

Viewed in hindsight, the coming together of coffee and aluminum seems inevitable. However divergent the time lines governing the rise to prominence of each substance, however different the uses to which each

This essay was originally composed on the occasion of a November 2000 conference held at the Carnegie Museum of Art to celebrate the opening of an exhibition entitled *Aluminum by Design: Jewelry to Jets*, curated by Sarah Nichols. I am grateful to the conference organizers for having granted me the opportunity to formulate these reflections before a lively audience of designers, curators, collectors, historians, and "aluminuts." I must also gratefully acknowledge the invaluable assistance provided me by the marketing division of Bialetti Industrie, in particular, by its director, Claudia Canesi, and by her assistant, Micaela Orizio.

Unless otherwise noted, all translations are my own.

is and was put, they shared certain common associations right from the start: associations with lightness, speed, mobility, strength, energy, and electricity. Fated or not, the meeting was long in coming. It had to wait until the mid-1930s, the golden era of aluminum designs for the kitchen and the beginning of fascist Italy's pursuit of economic autarchy, at which time it gave birth to a domestic object that can still be found in nearly every Italian home and in many a kitchen throughout the world: the Bialetti Moka Express (fig. 1).[1] The story that I would like to recount is that of this modest but characteristic product of Italy's design culture during the fascist decades. It is the story of the Moka's invention by Alfonso Bialetti in 1933, of its postwar marketing by his son Renato, and of its enormous success, indicated by global sales now closing in on the 220 million mark. Embedded within this tale is a web of other tales regarding the distinctive nature of Italian industrial development, the politics and symbolism of industrial materials, and the sociocultural significance of coffee and aluminum's movement back and forth between outdoors and indoors, between public and private consumption. In short, I hope to suggest that the romance of caffeine and aluminum is no less an allegory than the marriage of Mercury and Philology, though an allegory made up of distinctly this-worldly, sociohistorical object lessons. These lessons adhere so closely to the object under scrutiny that here allegory must be conceived of not in the Neoplatonic sense of truths veiled beneath the surface of a beautiful lie but rather in the incarnational sense of truths materially nested within other truths nested, in turn, within other truths. Industrial objects may appear forgetful and therefore reducible to function, whether understood as the emanation of a psyche or of practical needs and concerns, or subsumed within abstract (and sometimes analytically too facile) processes like rationalization and commodification. Yet such understandings strip away the actual density that characterizes the object world: the subtle incrustations of intention and invention, fantasy and ideology, tradition and accident that, like a family history that can be recovered only by means of exacting genealogical research, an object carries in the train of its existence. Things may be opaque, but they are

1. On aluminum's emergence as a domestic metal, see Penny Sparke, "Cookware to Cocktail Shakers: The Domestication of Aluminum in the United States, 1900–1939," *Aluminum by Design*, ed. Sarah Nichols (exhibition catalog, Carnegie Museum of Art, Pittsburgh, 2000), pp. 112–39.

Jeffrey T. Schnapp is the director of the Stanford Humanities Laboratory. Among his recent publications are *A Primer of Italian Fascism* (2000), *Gaetano Ciocca—Costruttore, inventore, agricoltore, scrittore* (2000), and *Vedette fiumane* (2000). *Ball and Hammer (Tenderenda the Fantast)* appeared in 2002.

Fig. 1.—Father and Son. The original 1933 Bialetti Moka Express accompanied by its 1950s descendant. Source: Bialetti.

rarely dull, and the stories of imaginary and material investments that they tell, like the story of the Bialetti Moka Express, conjoin the minutia of history to large-scale social processes, the actions of individuals to those of collectivities, in ways that expose the workings of history within everyday forms of communion like the morning cup of coffee that you and I imbibe before heading off to work.

Like chocolate and tea, coffee first reached Western Europe as an exotic commodity. It first appeared in the seventeenth century as Greek, Turkish, and Armenian vendors walked the streets of the major European capitals. But coffee drinking became fashionable only in the course of the eighteenth century, when it gave rise to what, in the West, was a novel institution: the coffeehouse. Like the product that they served up, usually in the Turkish fashion, coffeehouses at first proved controversial. Moralists called attention to their all-too-evident "oriental" derivation, suggesting that, as was imagined to be the case with its Turkish and Egyptian counterparts, coffeehouses were dens of iniquity, gambling, prostitution, and even pederasty.[2] Yet this insalubrious reputation altered both as coffee took hold in the royal courts and as coffeehouses proliferated to the point of becoming the defining feature of a newly emerging public sphere.[3] No longer the Western image of an Eastern other, the coffeehouse became a site increasingly associated with novelty and news, with present-centered, "modern" activities like the reading of newspapers, with commerce, advertising, the promiscuous mixing of social classes, contemporary culture, and, of course, politics, particularly revolutionary politics. In London, a coffeehouse founded in 1668 was at the origin of the insurance syndicate known as Lloyd's of London. By 1700 there were 2000 such establishments and such was their liveliness that Charles II banned them momentarily, fearing that they were hotbeds of freethinking and revolutionary fervor. By 1800, there were tens of thousands. The same proliferation may be found in Italy, France, Germany, and the United States, accompanied by the same functional link between public coffee consumption and trade, contemporary culture and politics.[4]

My purpose in briefly sketching out this backdrop, rendered in all its details by Heinrich Eduard Jacob in *The Saga of Coffee: The Biography of an Economic Product,* is to underline a couple of historical facts that will be substantially altered neither by the increasing grandeur and luxury of nineteenth-century and early twentieth-century cafés nor by the gradual spread of coffee drinking at home:

1. that coffee was a beverage to be consumed *publicly* well into the twentieth century; public consumption remained the norm, with private preparation and consumption tending to be restricted to the middle and upper classes until the second half of the nineteenth century;

2. that, accordingly, places of public consumption such as coffeehouses tended to dominate the coffee trade, functioning as wholesale buyers and retail sellers of beans, as well as serving as coffee bean roasters;

3. that coffee machines were typically devised with coffeehouses, not

2. On the coffeehouse and coffee consumption in the Near East, see Ralph S. Hattox, *Coffee and Coffeehouses: The Origins of a Social Beverage in the Medieval Near East* (Seattle, 1985), and Hélène Desmet-Gregoire, *Les Objets du café dans les societés du Proche-Orient et de la Mediterranée* (Paris, 1989).

3. Carlo Goldoni's *La bottega del caffè* (Milan, 1750) accurately depicts the transitional period, emphasizing as it does the coffeehouse's links to vice and virtue alike.

4. Among the sources that are worth consulting on this topic are Ulla Heise, *Kaffee und Kaffeehaus: Eine Kulturgeschichte* (Hildesheim, 1987); Emanoel Araujo et al., *O Café* (exhibition catalog, Praça do Banco Real, São Paulo, 28 Aug.–20 Oct. 2000); Antoinette Schnyder-von Waldkirch, *Kleine Kulturgeschichte des Kaffees* (exhibition catalog, Johann Jacobs Museum, Zürich, 1991); Heise et al., *Süsse muß der Coffee sein! Drei Jahrhunderte europäische Kaffeekultur und die Kaffeesachsen* (exhibition catalog, Stadtgeschichtliches Museum, Leipzig, 28 Apr.–12 June 1994); and Alberto Manodori et al., *Il caffè: Storia e cultura* (exhibition catalog, Biblioteca Vallicelliana, Rome, 16 Oct. 1989).

private users, in mind, domestic coffee machines remaining elementary by comparison;

4. that, due to the normativity of public consumption, coffee itself became closely identified both with processes of sociopolitical change (progress, reform, technological innovation, revolution) and with modern forms of individualism; and, finally,

5. that public consumption rendered coffee drinking a predominantly male practice with emancipatory significance for women as, in the course of the nineteenth and twentieth centuries, they struggled to conquer a place in the public sphere. (The obvious analogy would be with cigarette smoking in the twentieth century.)[5]

The gender divide is crucial for understanding the social and symbolic impact of twentieth-century inventions such as the Moka Express and may be traced back to the beginnings of European coffee consumption as indicated by such seventeenth-century tractates as "The Women's Petition against Coffee representing to public consideration the Grand Inconveniences to their SEX from the Excessive Use of that Drying, Enfeebling Liquor" and the male response "vindicating their own performances, and the Vertues of their Liquor" (fig. 2). But to what sort of "performances" was coffee thought to give rise as one approaches the turn-of-the-twentieth-century mark? There was general agreement that they were mental rather than carnal. In his 1825 classic, *The Physiology of Taste*, the gastronome Jean Anthelme Brillat-Savarin underscored coffee's role as an agent of cerebral excitement and perceptual sharpening, free from "the agitation and unhappiness which accompany insomnia brought on by any other cause."[6] But accelerated living contained the danger of accelerated aging; for instance, children were supposed to be reduced to "little dried-up machines, stunted and old at the age of twenty" (*PT*, p. 105).[7] Honoré de Balzac confirms the fear in his *Treatise on Modern Stimulants*, where coffee finds a place of honor alongside tobacco and distilled spirits. An immoderate coffee drinker (like myself), the great novelist erroneously assigns to tannin the role of *agent agitateur* with remarkable powers when ingested on an empty stomach. After an initial purgative

5. On this subject, in addition to Heinrich Jacob, *The Saga of Coffee: The Biography of an Economic Product*, trans. Eden and Cedar Paul (London, 1935), see Wolfgang Schivelbusch, *Tastes of Paradise: A Social History of Spices, Stimulants, and Intoxicants*, trans. David Jacobson (New York, 1992), pp. 62–84. Schivelbusch's emphasis upon coffee as "the great soberer" (that is, as an agent of antialcoholism and the Protestant ethic) is sometimes overdone, as indicated by the insistence in Balzac and others (see the subsequent quotation) upon coffee's intoxicating properties.

6. Jean Anthelme Brillat-Savarin, *The Physiology of Taste*, trans. Anne Drayton (London, 1994), p. 104; hereafter abbreviated *PT*.

7. Elsewhere Brillat-Savarin describes coffee's potentially toxic effects with reference to its figurative transformation of the brain into "a mill with all its wheels revolving, but nothing for them to grind" (*PT*, p. 106).

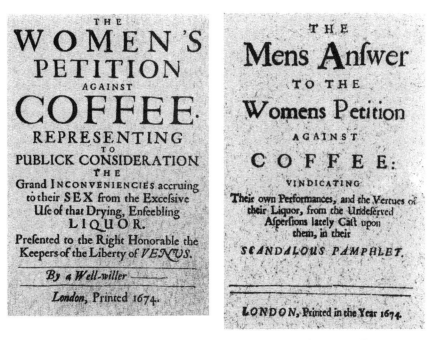

FIG. 2.—Two seventeenth-century English pamphlets for and against coffee consumption. Source: Stanford University Library.

effect, ferocious in nature, no less ferocious untapped powers are unleashed:

> Ideas surge forth like the battalions of a great army on the field of battle and the combat begins. Memories attack with their banners unfurled. The light cavalry of comparisons develops at a magnificent gallop. The artillery of logic comes to the rescue with its artillerymen and shells. Witticisms appear as sharpshooters. Figures begin to take shape. The paper covers itself with ink, since the evening begins and ends in torrents of black liquid, just like the battlefield in gunpowder.[8]

Balzac's description goes on and on (as if to prove that it was written under the influence). My point in citing it is to call attention to how the

8. Honoré de Balzac, *Traité des excitants modernes* (Paris, 1992), p. 44. At the conclusion of this chapter, Balzac connects the excess mental productivity fueled by tannin with sexual impotence: "Two young voyagers, Mssrs. Combes and Tamisier, found that Abyssinians are generally impotent and did not hesitate to ascribe the cause of this unfortunate state to the abuse of coffee, which the natives indulge in to the nth degree" (ibid., p. 46).

disruptive and creative effects attributed to coffee establish the framework for understanding provocative claims like that made some eighty-
five years later by Filippo Tommaso Marinetti that, as the founder and
evangelist of futurism, the first full-blown cultural-political avant-garde
movement, he was the *caffeine of Europe*. Marinetti styled himself the *caffeine* of Europe because he envisaged himself both as a purgative agent,
dedicated to freeing Europe from its idolatry of the past, and as a new
sort of industrial-era human being—a hyperactive multiplied man immune to the snares of romantic love . . . which is to say, a caffeinated man.
Such descriptions also help us to make sense of the meanings and urges
that gave rise the emergence, at the turn of the century, of that most
distinctive of Italian forms of coffee: *caffè espresso*.

Heretical though it may seem to admit it, espresso coffee is not an
Italian invention, experiments with steam pressure brewing having been
undertaken in Britain and France as far back as the early 1800s. Nor is
the word *espresso* a genuinely Italian word. The label was borrowed from
the English *express* via the French *exprès*, meaning something made to order and, by extension, produced and delivered with dispatch. This meaning was modified by the rise in mid–nineteenth-century England of
special trains running "expressly" to single locations without making intervening stops, trains that soon came to be known throughout Europe
as *expresses* (fig. 3).[9] The connection with coffee brewing may not appear
obvious. But it was prefigured by a subgenre of coffeemakers known as
coffee locomotives, manufactured between 1840 and 1870, that played
upon the functional analogy between the boilers of steam engines and
the boilers in coffee machines (fig. 4).[10] So when in 1901 Luigi Bezzera
filed his patent for the first restaurant-style espresso machine, a machine
consisting in a large boiler with four double pumps subsequently commercialized by the La Pavoni company, he could pretty much count on
the fact that consumers would understand the symbolic valences of drinking a product bearing the designation *caffè espresso*. As I have already
noted, coffee had been progressively entering ever larger numbers of private homes during the second half of the nineteenth century, and, when
and where it did so, at least on Italian soil, it was prepared by recourse
to one of two simple devices: either a *napoletana*—a reversible pot heated
on the stove and then flipped over so that the boiling water trickles down
through the coffee—or a *milanese*—in which water is boiled until it
seethes through the ground coffee held in a strainer near the pot's top

9. The picture is actually slightly more complex, inasmuch as the word *express* was,
before the era of trains, already associated with express messengers who could be counted
upon to deliver messages at speeds superior to those of the ordinary mail service. So "express" train services were themselves tapping into a prior usage.
10. On coffee locomotives, see Edward and Joan Bramah, *Coffeemakers: Three Hundred
Years of Art and Design* (London, 1989), pp. 104–9, which also contains a comprehensive
history of coffeemaker design.

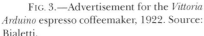

FIG. 4.—English coffee locomotive in silver based on design by Jean Baptiste To-selli, nineteenth century. Source: Bialetti.

FIG. 3.—Advertisement for the *Vittoria Arduino* espresso coffeemaker, 1922. Source: Bialetti.

(fig. 5). Unlike these domestic peers, the new espresso machines were designed to dazzle through their size and speed, with rumbling boilers, brass fittings, enameled ornaments, vulcanized rubber knobs, and gleaming metallic lines all at the command of the caffeinated double of the train conductor-engineer—the *barista* (fig. 6). They reinforced and reinterpreted the long-standing conviction that strong coffee was the virile liquor with which modern men powered their corporeal and corporate boilers. And even if the steam-brewed coffee that these behemoths turned out often tasted burnt, the brew was power-packed, intense, and quickly consumed. It translated the values of efficiency and excitement associated with the express train into an everyday beverage in comparison to which domestic coffee was but a slow and pallid imitation.

Enter Alfonso Bialetti, freshly returned from a decade-long stint of work in the French aluminum industry. In 1918 Bialetti founded a small metal and machine shop in Crusinallo, in his native Piedmont.[11] The region already had a long tradition of metal work and, in the wake of World

11. Although there is some confusion about the matter among current Bialetti employees, it may be that Bialetti's shop evolved into the firm known as Metallurgica Lombarda-Piemontese dei Fratelli Bialetti-Piedimulera, listed in the review *Metalli leggeri e loro applicazioni* 1 (May–June 1931) as specializing in "lathe-turned products in billet metal, stamped sheet metal, foundry services, laminates and metal wire; in particular, casting in molds, especially of items for the home and hotel supplies" (p. 27).

Fig. 5.—Napoletana (left) and Milanese (right) coffeemakers from the late nineteenth century. Source: Bialetti.

Fig. 6.—Luigi Bezzera company espresso stand manned by *baristi* at the Fiera di Milano (Milan Trade Fair), 1906. Source: Bialetti.

War I, had established itself as the principal manufacturing region for place settings, pots, and kitchen utensils and appliances (a role that it has maintained to the present day thanks to companies like Alessi).[12] As corporate lore would have it, Bialetti begins with a small industrial oven, an anvil, and a milling machine, fabricating pieces to order for industrial clients by making use of a technique he acquired in France: that of gravity casting aluminum in reusable cast iron molds. A decade passes during which he becomes intrigued with how local housewives boil their linens in tubs built around a central conduit that draws the boiling soapy water upwards and redistributes it across the linens through a radial opening. Lightning strikes: why not adapt this simple physical principle to coffee making? Why not transform the unwieldy and complex restaurant espresso machine into a light, trouble-free, inexpensive domestic appliance? Why not democratize espresso coffee by introducing it into every Italian home? Whether Bialetti was aware of it or not, the major manufacturers of espresso machines, La Pavia, Cremonesi, and Gaggia, were all beginning to experiment with ways of eliminating steam infusion in favor of hot water introduced under pressure by means of a piston pump. But they focused on costly, large-scale machines made of brass, copper, and steel. Bialetti's solution was more elegant and simple. Design an entirely self-contained aluminum unit made up of three principal pieces that, on the model of the *napolitana,* could be heated on a mere stovetop, but capable of making precisely the same intensely flavorful coffee heretofore limited to restaurants and cafés. The lower portion of the device would serve as a boiler, sealed off from the upper portion so that, when heated, the increased pressure would force hot water up through a conduit and

12. It is perhaps worth noting that the founder of Alessi, Alberto Alessi, was the grandson of Alfonso Bialetti (this according to Charlotte Higgins, "Cheat Chic: Alessi Kettle," *The Guardian,* 18 Sept. 1998, p. 17).

basket packed with ground coffee that, once sufficiently pressurized, would surge up into the upper chamber and spill over to fill a pot (fig. 7). The only recently uncovered original patent (filed in 1951) insists that "without requiring any ability whatsoever" the new device embodies an "organic simplicity, making it very easy to use, at a more than accessible cost."[13] So much for *barista*-showmen and ritual trips to the *caffè*. So much also for the humble *napolitana* and the *milanese*. Domestic coffee making would be raised to the dignity of the local coffeehouse; domestic coffeemakers, which is to say housewives, would be raised to the dignity of the *barista*.

For several years Bialetti tinkered with his invention. There were technical glitches to confront: among them, the need to achieve the proper flow of coffee through the apparatus and to overcome the tendency for boilers to crack under pressure or blow up (addressed by adjusting the alloy employed, altering wall thicknesses and adding a safety valve). There were also design questions to resolve. Bialetti may have been an expert aluminum craftsman, but he was no designer and worked largely on his own. Accordingly, when it came to designing the Moka Express, he did as so many others had done before him: he borrowed his designs from contemporary sources like the silver coffee services on display in the luxury emporia of Milan. In other words, he *copied* high-end designs by the likes of Hoffmann, Puiforcat, Genazzi, and Hénin, adopting the flared, symmetrical eight-faceted design that has remained the signature of the Moka Express (and, indeed, the signature of much of the subsequent family of Bialetti products that build on the Moka's legacy) (fig. 8).[14] Bialetti's very first design differed in two important respects from the later product: the original boiler was convex and not conical; and the lateral handle and lid cover handles were initially made out of wood (not plastic or vulcanized rubber) (fig. 9). Fabrication and strength considerations led to the abandonment of the former; durability problems led to a shift to plastic in the latter case, though it is worth noting that a slight design change was involved since the original lid handle had

13. "Progetti di oggetti-tipo: Brevetti di design in Italia 1946–1964," *Domus* (Apr. 1995): 141. Alfonso Bialetti hadn't apparently bothered to apply for a patent, so the formal patent application was drawn up in the immediate postwar in the course of Renato's reorganization of the family firm to protect it from imitators. The result was that competitors had to list their observance of the Bialetti patent in their advertising.

14. A *caffelatte* service by Hénin closely resembling the Moka Express was featured in *La casabella* 59 (Nov. 1932): 73, accompanied by the following text (written, most likely, by Giò Ponti):

We commend to our readers this *caffelatte* service by Hénin, the noted Milanese silversmith. Everyone is aware of the difficulties in locating objects on the market that harmonize with modern taste from the standpoint of style and execution. To run across objects as refined as those forged by Hénin, thus, means bringing to a happy resolution the problem of merging practicality and elegance (something all lovers of useful and beautiful objects take to heart) and the pursuit of a stylish contemporary habitat.

Fɪɢ. 8.—Announcement by Giò Ponti of Hénin's newest silver coffee service, published in *La casabella,* Nov. 1932. Source: author.

Fɪɢ. 7.—Internal diagram of 1960s Moka Express. Source: Bialetti.

Fɪɢ. 9.—Top sections, three generations of Moka Express coffeemakers (1930s, 1950s, 1960s). Source: author.

a hexagonal profile that, in the definitive version, is altered into a upwardly flaring octagonal stem.[15] Once these solutions were arrived at in 1933, the tinkering ended. The moral of the story is that, for all its current ubiquity, the Moka Express remains a characteristic design of the mid-1930s marooned in the 1950s and 1960s. That is, its triumph as a mass-market appliance would have to be delayed, for reasons that I will shortly adumbrate, until the Italian postwar "economic miracle."

The context within which Bialetti's invention came about had rendered aluminum no ordinary metal. From the standpoint of global production and the international market for aluminum, particularly in the

15. Also worth noting is the fact that the original top wasn't attached to the upper body of the coffeemaker in the original design. In the definitive design, the top hinges right above the handle.

domains of transportation, household products, furniture, and architecture, the thirties represent something of a golden age. And Italy aspired to be among the leaders of this golden age, despite its belated entry into aluminum production and despite the still relatively small scale of its national aluminum industry at the end of the 1920s. Even the official statistics furnished by the fascist Ministry of Corporations were unpromising: in 1929 the per capita annual consumption of aluminum in Italy was a mere .226 kilograms, three times less than the .62 kilograms consumed in France and Germany, and five times less than the 1.14 kilograms consumed in the United States. This implied that with a total production of eleven thousand tons (the estimate for 1931), Italian industry was able to exceed the needs of the entire domestic market. The fascist government set out to improve the situation by favoring the Montecatini group's gradual takeover from various American, Swiss, and German interests of the entire Italian aluminum industry, concentrated around production facilities in Mori and Marghera and bauxite mines in Istria, Campania, and Sicily. A de facto monopoly resulted by decade's end, with Italy rising to the modest rank of fourth largest European producer behind France, Hungary, and Yugoslavia. The governmental campaign hinged on the principle of autarchy, which is to say on the pursuit of economic self-sufficiency by means of a heroic overcoming of Italy's deficiencies in the domains of raw materials and natural resources. The population was mobilized for causes such as the so-called Battle for Grain aimed at reducing Italy's dependence on imported wheat. Likewise, new autarchic technologies and products were promoted so as to exploit available materials and to avoid imported ones.[16] Such was the framework within which magazines like Giò Ponti's *La casa bella* issued a call to designers, architects, and manufacturers to "organize aluminum" (*organizzare l'alluminio*). And organize they did (fig. 10).

Italy was poor in iron ore, coal, and petroleum. But it was far richer in bauxite and leucite. So, even before the League of Nations imposed trade sanctions in retribution for Mussolini's 1935 invasion of Ethiopia, leading to an intensification of the autarchy campaign, aluminum had emerged as the autarchic metal of choice. Two reviews were launched to promote its diffusion: *Metalli leggeri e loro applicazioni,* an industry review established in 1931; and a government counterpart, *Alluminio,* founded in the following year.[17] Both set out to codify what would become one

16. For a case in point, see my discussion of the rayon campaign in "The Fabric of Modern Times," *Critical Inquiry* 24 (Autumn 1997): 191–239.

17. *Metalli leggeri e loro applicazioni* had a silver foil cover and claimed that it was the "only Italian review exclusively dedicated to the development of light metal industries, product applications, and manufactured goods." Every issue had on its cover a quote from the engineer Giuseppe Belluzzo, formerly Minister of the National Economy (1925–1928) and of Public Instruction (1928–1929): "Italy has abundant raw materials, abundant enough to forge the new productive Civilization that is already shining on the horizon: a

of the defining propagandistic credos of the decade: aluminum is Italy's national metal, a populist metal, the "real material of the unreal velocities" and accelerated progress achieved thanks to the fascist revolution.[18] The July–August 1931 special issue of *Metalli leggeri e loro applicazioni,* for instance, opened with an editorial piece entitled "Rally!" (*Adunata*) that summoned all Italians:

> to acknowledge that a new and decisively important protagonist has emerged in the nation's economic life: ALUMINUM. An Italian metal, the abundance of which makes us the envy of the world. Thanks to its manifold applications, aluminum is sure to permit us to reduce to a bare minimum the importation of other metals, freeing the Fatherland from the onerous tributes that, to this day, continue to be exacted abroad. Aluminum is the inexhaustible Italian resource. It embodies Italy's unyielding destiny! . . . RALLY ROUND! Our rally is not only theoretical and spiritual, but effectual and practical as well. Every individual must assume his place in this overall renewal of mentalities and methods.[19]

A second example of this myth seems particularly apt inasmuch as it suggests (more realistically) that Italy's distinctive contribution to the use of aluminum will be to conjoin large-scale industrial production to small-scale craft traditions:

> It might be said that metals have their own physiognomy and character, just as there exist certain somatic attributes of nations that are present in all individuals. . . . [And] we would be tempted to assert the *Latinity* of aluminum to the degree that no other metal lends itself so well to the temperament of Latin peoples, in general, and of Italians, in particular. This, at least, can be deduced by the speed with which Italian craftsmen have assimilated the complex technical principles of working with light metals and by their mastery over the unprocessed material itself. The latter being the necessary precondition for achieving the sense of refinement and good taste that have always distinguished Italian craftsmanship when working with traditional metals. In the artistic and decorative domains one can declare

Civilization principally based upon the ubiquity of light metals and their alloys in everything including national defense." The full title of the second journal was *Alluminio: Rivista tecnica del gruppo metalli leggeri della Associazione Nazionale Fascista fra gli Industriali Metallurgici Italiani.*

18. The full text in Carlo Panseri, "Introduzione all'anno IV," *Alluminio* 4 (Jan. 1935): 1 reads:

> Aluminum is not only the *metal* of the Fatherland; it is also the metal of progress, the real material of unreal velocities [*la materia reale dell'irreale velocità*]. Above all, it is that metal which demands the highest degree of knowledge [*dottrina*], understanding and research in order to fully unveil the polyhedric character of the applications to which it lends itself [*il poliedrico aspetto della sua applicabilità*].

19. Anon., "Adunata," *Metalli leggeri e loro applicazioni* 1 (July–Aug. 1931): 73–74.

ORGANIZZARE L'ALLUMINIO

Poiché tutti ne parlano in questo momento, discorriamo anche noi delle «leghe leggere», non — si capisce — in rapporto a macchine od altre cose pesanti, bensì all'arredamento e alla decorazione, che son cose che interessano noi e i nostri lettori.

Sotto il nome cadenzato di «leghe leggere» si nasconde l'alluminio, ricchezza italiana, che incominciamo anche noi ad usare per facciate di negozi, parti di mobili e altro, seppur ancora timidamente, con incertezza e non di rado, se vogliamo esser sinceri, più per ragioni di moda o di stile che per convinzione.

Noi pensiamo invece che l'alluminio potrebbe vantaggiosamente portare la sua simpatica nota nei nostri interni, surrogando altri più costosi materiali e trovando la sua schietta indicazione, quando le nostre industrie dell'arredamento, poco informate di quanto è già stato realizzato in questo campo, ricevessero adeguate direttive generali. Da chi? Non sappiamo. Probabilmente dai produttori stessi dell'alluminio, *cui prodest*.

Non si tratta di soppiantare il legno che costa in Italia, malgrado le nostalgie stilistiche di tanti mobilieri, illustri tradizioni e possiede indicazioni insostituibili, ma di prescrivere l'impiego dell'alluminio dove appare inutile adoperare altri materiali d'importazione straniera. Il sediame curvato si fa in legno: perché non costruirlo in alluminio? Vi sono in Italia centinaia di fabbriche di mobili in ferro: perché non lavorerebbero esse il nuovo metallo?

Per l'impiego, poi, di esso nella decorazione e nell'arredamento vero e proprio, non vi sembra che la creazione di un organismo tecnico che ne studiasse le varie applicazioni e le rendesse note a cui potesse interessare, faciliterebbe lo svolgimento di un'opera fattiva ben più di cento articoli di giornale?

Si sa, sono idee buttate là e *les conseilleurs ne sont pas les payeurs*. Ma è certo che se si vorrà far qualcosa di serio perché l'alluminio, razionalmente adoperato da ogni specie di artisti della casa, porti anch'esso il suo contributo al benessere della nazione, bisognerà imboccar questa strada.

CASA BELLA

FIG. 10.—*Let's organize aluminum:* frontispiece of *La casa bella,* March 1931 issue. Source: author.

without hesitation that, although Italy possesses neither the colossal potential of the United States of America nor the meticulous technological precision of Germany, it has achieved a degree of aesthetic expressivity and a measured understanding of effects that place it in the forefront, even if the experiments and applications pursued thus far remain limited.[20]

The nineteenth century was the century of socialism and heavy metals; the twentieth century, the century of fascism and aluminum.[21] Comical as they may appear today, these were the sorts of equations that industry advertising and state propaganda sought to promote within the framework of fascism's claim that the March on Rome marked at once a radical rupture with Italy's past and a recovery of its ancient glory. The result was the interweaving of two distinct aluminum iconographies throughout the 1930s, simultaneously present in a two-page spread from the magazine *Domus*, which juxtaposes the image of a modern military aircraft with an Assyro-Babylonian bas-relief of warrior-charioteers (fig. 11). In keeping with this twofold emphasis, aluminum circulated under both modernist and traditionalist labels. *Avional* may serve as an example of the first. The term echoes the French and Spanish words for airplane (*avion*) and corresponds to a wide array of aluminum expressions of fascist modernity: from advertising images that link aluminum to abstract art; to Giò Ponti's brilliant 1937 showcase of aluminum applications, the Montecatini headquarters building in Milan; to the sequence of trade fair installations at the Fiera di Milano that began in 1930 and culminated in 1938 with the Autarchic Exhibition of Italian Minerals at the Circus Maximus held in Rome (100-plus exhibitors in an entire hall celebrating aluminum and magnesium designed according to the canons of rationalist architecture).[22] A second label, *anticorodal*, alluding as it does to the metal's resistance to corrosion, may be taken as referring to a parallel but alternative mythology that associated aluminum not with revolutionary change but with the preservation of the historical values of Italian art and/or the resurgence of ancient Roman glory. This "traditionalist" iconography may be observed in the advertising campaigns that accompa-

20. Anon., "La mostra dell'alluminio alla XIII Fiera di Milano," *Alluminio* 1 (Apr. 1932): 166. The text was meant to consecrate the aluminum hall mounted within the thirteenth Fiera di Milano, organized by the Montecatini group.

21. The notion was formulated by none other than Arnaldo Mussolini, il Duce's trusted brother: "We have often said: just like the nineteenth century was the century of iron, heavy metals, and carbon, so the twentieth century should be the century of light metals, electricity, and petroleum. In the course of history discoveries sometimes serve as the beneficiaries of peoples. If we [Italians] haven't iron, we have aluminum" (quoted by Nicola Parravano of the Italian Royal Academy, preface to the inaugural issue, *Alluminio* 1 [Jan.–Feb. 1932]: 1).

22. On the exhibition, see Partito nazionale fascista, *Mostra autarchica minerale italiano: Guida della mostra* (exhibition catalog, Rome, 18 Nov. 1938–9 May 1939).

.nied the construction of the Olympic Stadium in Rome or in sculptures like this *Fascist Victory* flanked by an ad in which one of the corroded bronze horses from Saint Mark's square is shadowed by an immaculate aluminum outline (figs. 12 and 13).[23] Many other examples could be cited: the decorative fountain in *anticorodal* forged by Dante Parini for the fourteenth Fiera di Milano and the gargantuan *Genius of Fascism* mounted horseman devised for the Italian pavilion at the Paris International Expo of 1937. But the key point remains that these two iconographic strains were really one. The values of lightness, agility, and speed emphasized in the first were coupled in the second to solidity, strength, monumentality, and duration in time; and vice versa (fig. 14).

Whether or not Alfonso Bialetti was susceptible to this decade-long campaign to establish the Latinity of aluminum, the earlier cited portrait of the Italian craftsman at ease with the complex technical principles of working with light metals fits him like a glove. Bialetti was a better craftsman, however, than a businessman, for the 1930s would prove a decade of limited success for his invention. The reasons had nothing to do with a decline in coffee drinking. The contrary was true, especially after 1935 when coffee came to figure ever more prominently in the mythology both of empire and of autarchy: of *empire* because Ethiopia, the nation Italy

23. The horses on Saint Mark's square were, of course, a particularly apt symbol inasmuch as they were already in danger due to centuries of corrosion thanks to Venice's sea air, pigeon droppings, and the like.

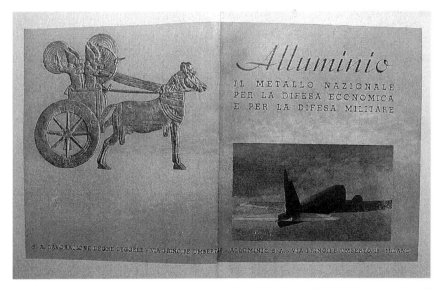

FIG. 11.—Advertisement for "Aluminum, the national metal for Italy's economic and military defense," published in *Domus*'s 1935 special issue on *Italians*. Source: author.

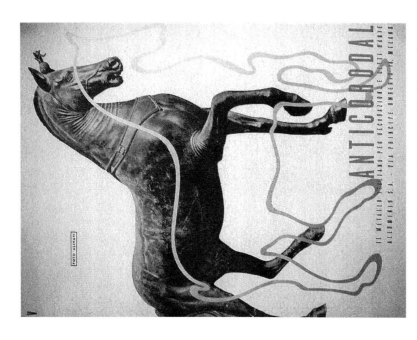

FIG. 12.—Advertisement featuring L. Arpesani's *Fascist Victory*, sculpture in cast and carved *anticorodal* alloy. *Domus* 70 (Oct. 1933): iv. Source: author.

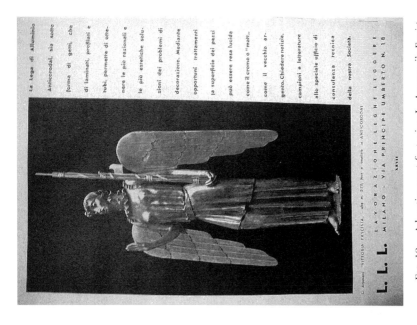

FIG. 13.—Advertisement for *anticorodal*, "the Italian metal for decoration and art objects," in *Domus*'s 1935 special issue on Roman art. Source: author.

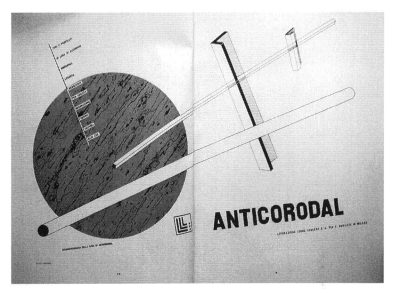

Fig. 14.—Advertisement designed by Luigi Veronesi for *anticorodal* published in various issues of *Domus* 1936. Source: author.

had invaded, was a major coffee producer of Moka-type coffee beans; of *autarchy* because Brazil refused to follow the League of Nations sanctions imposed by the world community and continued to furnish Italy with its coffee beans (fig. 15). Nor were fascism's regressive gender politics to blame, favoring as they did women's roles as housewives and mothers over public roles.[24] Rather, the problem was Bialetti's only partial understanding of the importance of marketing. Initially Moka Expresses were sold by the inventor himself, who set up stands at weekly public markets in the Piedmont region. Later, the coffeemakers were delivered directly from the factory to regional retailers. No effort to industrialize their production or to market them on a national (not to mention, international) scale was undertaken. Bialetti's shop continued to turn out an array of other products, all on an equally small scale. The result was that a mere 70,000 units were produced between 1934 and 1940. Then came the war. Imports ceased and Italy's national metal became Italy's military metal, unavailable for civilian purposes. Coffee too became scarce. Bialetti shut down his shop, oiled up his casting molds, and safely packed them away in the basement of his home for the duration of the conflict.

There exists a secondary reason for the difficulties encountered by the Moka Express: the relatively high cost of Italian aluminum until the 1950s. The industry had grown under the umbrella of autarchy and ex-

24. On this subject, see Victoria de Grazia, *How Fascism Ruled Women, Italy, 1922–1945* (Berkeley, 1992), esp. pp. 201–3.

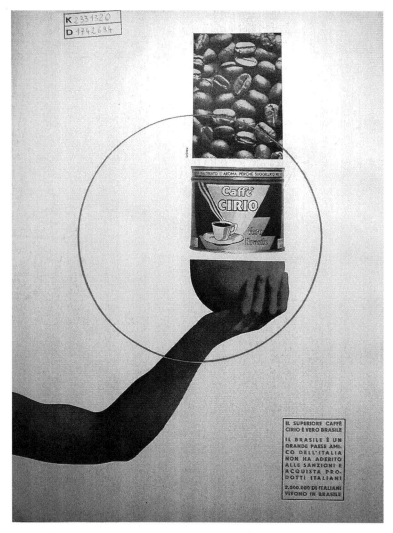

Fig. 15.—Advertisement for "Cirio's superior coffee, a true Brazilian coffee. Brazil is a great friend of Italy / it hasn't observed the sanctions and purchases Italian products / 2 million Italians live in Brazil." Published in *Domus*'s 1935 special issue on *Italians*. Source: author.

panded even more rapidly thanks to the war effort. But tariff barriers and Montecatini's virtual monopoly had eliminated pressures to contain costs or improve efficiency. As a result, in 1946 domestically produced aluminum averaged about 140 lire per kilo while American aluminum (including shipping costs to Genoa) was available at 42 lire per kilo. The alarm was sounded by Elio Vittorini's militant *Il politecnico,* a new review dedicated to the cultural, political, and economic reconstruction of post-war Italy. *Il politecnico* called for a true democratization of aluminum, in keeping with its antifascist program of institutional reforms. Calling the lie to fascism's assertion that aluminum was Italy's national metal, it entitled one polemical sally "Aluminum: An Aristocratic Product." The anonymous author went on to argue that "aluminum this expensive will never give rise to widespread popular consumption, whether for domestic or craft uses, for tools, bicycles, etc."[25] Structural inefficiencies were to blame as well for the elevated costs. Montecatini was also in the electrical power business, and it was channeling a significant portion of the aluminum it produced into its own (overpriced) power lines; Montecatini's competitors, not wanting to aid the industrial giant, were instead importing tin ones from abroad, thereby contributing to a mushrooming trade deficit.

This was the new republican Italy to which Alfonso's son, Renato, returned in 1946, after several years in a German prisoner-of-war camp, to take over his father's business. Renato was intimately acquainted with metallurgy, having worked alongside Alfonso before he was conscripted into the army. But he brought an entirely new sensibility and understanding to manufacturing and to marketing. Production was resumed in the same modest facility in Crusinallo in the late 1940s but with the Bialetti product line narrowed down to a single object: the Moka Express, now fabricated in a full range of sizes (from two cups to ten) and in larger numbers (up to 1,000 units per day). This exclusive focus on coffeemakers was buttressed by national advertising campaigns on billboards, in newspapers and magazines, on the radio, and, later, on television programs such as the wildly popular *Carosello*. The campaigns were initially financed by means of loans (daring for such a small concern) and strove to build a distinctive brand identity in the minds both of vendors and consumers, as well as to differentiate the Moka Express from the swarm of clones and competitors that were emerging as Italy's domestic market came back to life thanks to the postwar boom: rivals like the Columbia Crème (fig. 16).[26] Characteristic of the younger Bialetti's bold approach were the publicity blitzes undertaken during Italy's most important trade fair, the Fiera di Milano. Year after year, the company would purchase every available billboard in the entire city of Milan, literally saturating

25. The article reads: "American aluminum costs 42 lire a kilo in the port of Genoa. Italian aluminum costs from 130 to 150 lire a kilo. . . . Aluminum this expensive will never become the object of mass consumption [*di largo consumo popolare*], whether for purposes of household uses, crafts, tools, bicycles, etc." (anon., "L'alluminio, un prodotto aristocratico," *Il politecnico*, 5 Jan. 1946, p. 2).

26. The 1956 edition of the *Catalogo ufficiale, 34esima Fiera di Milano* (Milan, 1956), for example, includes yet another competitor: the "Nova Express" by Irmel, a company located (like Bialetti) in Omegna. The advertising copy reads: "the coffeemakers stamped out in a single piece of ultra-pure aluminum (99.5% pure) with a heavy base. Economical—Hygienic—Practical—Speedy" (p. 502).

FIG. 16.—A page from the catalog of the 1955 Fiera di Milano. Source: Bialetti.

the city with images of its coffeemaker (fig. 17). Bialetti's booths became legendary for their scale and inventiveness. In 1956, for instance, the indoor installation was paired with an outdoor sculpture consisting of a giant Moka Express suspended in the air by a stream of coffee above a cup sitting atop a faceted platform bearing its name (fig. 18). The forging of a brand identity was completed with the creation in 1953, at Renato's instigation, of the Bialetti mascot: the *omino con i baffi*, the formally attired mustachioed man with his index finger upraised as if hailing a cab or ordering an espresso (fig. 19). Originally a doodle by Paul Campari, the symbol was, in fact, a cartoon of Alfonso meant at once as humorous and familiar. Familiar in the literal sense that the *omino* was devised so that every Italian might relate to him with a mix of fondness and nostalgia: as the image of the sort of patriarch, be he a father, uncle, or grandfather, who, heretofore, had lived their lives in coffeehouses. Yet while evoking this past, the advertisements promised a radical innovation: "in casa un espresso come al bar" ("an espresso at home just like at a café"). By implication, they promised to bring the once itinerant patriarch back into the household. The home would become a café, instead of the café becoming a home away from home.

FIG. 19.—Paul Campari's drawing of the Bialetti trademark, the *omino con i baffi (mustachioed little man)*, early 1950s. Source: Bialetti.

FIG. 18.—Moka Express fountain display at entrance of 1956 Fiera di Milano. Source: Bialetti.

in casa
un espresso
come al bar
con

caffettiera
MOKA EXPRESS BIALETTI

FIG. 17.—Billboard-lined streets of Milan, during period of 1956 Fiera di Milano. Source: Bialetti.

Times had changed. Memories of the fascist debacle were conveniently fading, and consumerism was on the rise as Italian homes were increasing in comfort and size thanks to the economic boom of the 1950s. And a new American-influenced social imaginary envisaged them as activity and entertainment centers for a tightly knit nuclear family. Through Bialetti's advertising campaigns, the Moka Express placed itself at the center of these cross currents (figs. 20 and 21). It became the emblem of an increasingly egalitarian, do-it-yourself attitude. "Dove è papa"? ("Where is Daddy?") asks one ad, the answer being, "He's in the kitchen with the Moka Express," whose simplicity permits a reversal of conventional gender roles. The reversal corresponds, in turn, to the casting of Italian women in active, nondomestic roles: "for everyone, also for the female skier" reads another ad, adding that "at home, anywhere at all, an espresso just like at a café." Thanks to the "organic simplicity" of the Moka Express, Dad could be trusted in the kitchen and Mom was free to hit the slopes.

I conclude with the final step in the transformation of the Bialetti firm from craft workshop into a modern medium-scale industry: namely, with the construction between 1952 and 1956 of a state-of-the-art factory in Omegna. By now profits were rising, the price of aluminum was falling (due to a global aluminum glut), and the success of Bialetti's advertising blitzes was such that the old facility would suffice no more. Renato Bialetti set about the task like a true visionary, much like Adriano Olivetti in the prewar period, insisting upon the rationalization of every feature of the building and upon the streamlining of the Bialetti production line (fig. 22). A massive freight elevator was devised so that arriving trucks could dump their holds of aluminum ingots not on the ground floor, as in a conventional factory, but directly into cauldrons located up on the fifth floor. The entire production process consisted of a smooth lateral and downward motion floor by floor, ending with the inspection and packaging of every item right on the threshold of the ground-floor loading dock from which trucks could depart for their destinations. Workers were assigned individual lockers and showers, as well as provided with houses and with various other progressive amenities. Renato expanded the Bialetti product line to include other household appliances (toasters, vacuum cleaners, meat grinders), but the backbone of the company remained the production of a growing family of Moka Express machines, now being turned out at the rhythm of 18,000 per day or 4 million per year. Yet, for all this emphasis upon modernization, there remained a paradoxical, characteristically Italian touch that renders the romance between caffeine and aluminum also an enduring marriage between the new and the old.

At the sparkling new production facility in Omegna, the very heart of Alfonso Bialetti's remarkable little invention, the boiler, continued to be produced precisely as it was in 1933: that is, cast and then individually finished, inspected, and sorted not by a production line worker but in-

FIG. 20.—Late 1950s advertisement illustrating the ease with which espresso coffee can be made at home, even by men, thanks to the Moka Express; published in various popular magazines. Source: Bialetti.

FIG. 21.—Another late 1950s advertisement juxtaposing a captain (the Bialetti mascot) who is making himself an espresso and a housewife serving her husband an espresso at home 'better than that available at cafés"; published in various popular magazines. Source: Bialetti.

FIG. 22.—Renato Bialetti standing in front of the new rationalist factory (still under construction) in Crusinallo, Apr. 1955. The current Bialetti factory is a half-mile from this site. Source: Bialetti.

FIG. 23.—The forging of the boiler of a Moka Express, late 1950s. Today the molten aluminum and casting is mechanized, but the finishing of each piece is still carried out by an individual metal worker. Source: Bialetti.

stead by a skilled craftsman. Twenty years had passed and nothing had changed (fig. 23). Another forty-seven have transpired since then and, once again, nothing has changed. When I visited the current factory in the summer of 2000, I was amazed and requested an explanation. Bialetti's head engineer reassured me: automated pressure casting and finishing had been tried many times and the result was too many flaws; gravity casting and an intimate working knowledge of aluminum were required to ensure a resistant and reliable product. I was in no position to argue, given my limited understanding of materials science. But the contrast kept me company all the way back to Milan. On the one side, artisans; on the other, computer-actuated robots. The two working together on a hybrid artifact: an icon of the machine age that is a throwback to the era of manual production. In short, a portrait in aluminum of the original *omino con i baffi*.

Object, Relic, Fetish, Thing: Joseph Beuys and the Museum

Charity Scribner

"What I never had is being torn from me. / What I did not live, I will miss forever."[1] With these lines from the poem *Property* (1990) Volker Braun conveys the loss that attended the end of "real existing socialism" in Germany. Today, more than a decade after the Berlin Wall was reduced to rubble and swept away, there lingers the sense that something was lost with the disintegration of the Soviet Bloc—something more than the Trabant automobiles and Lenin statues, more than employment guarantees or the threat of environmental ruin. As the two Germanys unify into one, the customs and culture of the Western half are eclipsing those of the former GDR. After the postcommunist turn, or *Wende*, museum curators have begun to sort through the wreckage of East Germany's industrial debris and Marx's wasted ideals. But what do they want to find?

Taking stock of the GDR's fallout, these collectors have organized exhibitions such as "Commodities for Daily Use" and "Eastern Mix." They have founded the Center for the Documentation of Everyday Life, also known as the Open Depot (Offenes Depot). Their shows—which have sparked wide interest—enter into a dense mnemonic field that Braun and other writers and artists had already begun to till much earlier (fig. 1). In her 1996 drama *Melancholia I, or the Two Sisters* Judith Kuckart undertook

---

Unless otherwise indicated, all translations are mine.

1. Volker Braun, "Das Eigentum," in *Von einem Land und vom andern: Gedichte zur deutschen Wende*, ed. Karl Otto Conrady (Frankfurt am Main, 1993), ll. 8–9, p. 51. For an analysis of melancholia in Braun's writing, see Wolfgang Emmerich, "Status Melancholicus: Zur Transformation der Utopie in der DDR-Literatur," in *Literatur in der DDR: Rückblicke*, ed. Heinz-Ludwig Arnold and Frauke Meyer-Gosau (Munich, 1991), pp. 232–45, and Horst Domdey, "Volker Braun und die Sehnsucht nach der Grossen Kommunion: Zum Demokratiekonzept der Reformsozialisten," *Deutschland Archiv* 11 (Nov. 1990): 1771–74.

a diagnosis of the condition that Braun described in *Property*. One interlude in the play suggests the defeat and doubt of an aging and apparently unemployed couple (fig. 2). Sitting near a new department store in the depressed city of Magdeburg, they wait for a tram. "So where are the Russians?" the woman asks the man. "Didn't there used to be a red flag hanging there?" No response. She takes up a new tack: "Where did you lose that?" Again no response. What thing is "that?" Soon it appears that the woman herself does not know what she is asking after:

SHE: I would have seen it there when I was leaving.
HE: What?
SHE: Your thingamajig.
HE: So what.
SHE: But I didn't see it.
HE: Where?[2]

The couple's exchange discloses the disorientation that has beset many Germans after the *Wende*. Freud maintains that the melancholic grasps his condition "only in the sense that he knows *whom* he has lost but not *what* he has lost in him."[3] This is the case in both Braun's play and Kuckart's drama and perhaps in ex-GDR visual culture as well. The incoherence that manifests at the moment of depressive collapse can be expressed in these terms: "Before knowing what is missing, I know that I am missing 'I know not what.'"[4] "Your thingamajig," the woman from *Melancholia I* calls it—*dein Dingsda*, in German. Not quite a thing, nor entirely an object, the matter at hand thwarts her attempts to designate, to concretize.

In eastern Germany a thousand little things—produced by the *Volkseigene Betriebe* (VEB) or "people's own industries"—have outlasted both

2. Judith Kuckart, *Melancholie I, oder Die zwei Schwestern*, Berliner Ensemble, Berlin. Dir. Jörg Aufenanger, 18 Dec. 1996.

3. Sigmund Freud, "Mourning and Melancholia," *The Standard Edition of the Complete Psychological Works of Sigmund Freud*, trans. and ed. James Strachey, 24 vols. (London, 1953–74), 14:245.

4. In *La Cruauté mélancolique* Jacques Hassoun draws upon Freud's description of the melancholic's confusion, bringing it to bear on Vladimir Jankélévitch work on "'le je-ne-sais-quoi'" (Jacques Hassoun, *La Cruauté mélancolique* [Paris, 1995], p. 64); see Vladimir Jankélévitch, *Le Je-ne-sais-quoi et le presque-rien* (Paris, 1980), p. 11.

Charity Scribner organized Platforms I and II for Documenta 11 in Kassel. She is an assistant professor of European studies at the Massachusetts Institute of Technology. Her first book, *Requiem for Communism*, appeared in 2003, and her current research examines terrorism and militancy in European culture of the 1970s and 1980s.

FIG. 1.—Offenes Depot, Eisenhüttenstadt. Photo: Charity Scribner.

FIG. 2.—*Melancholie I, oder Die zwei Schwestern,* Berliner Ensemble, Berlin. Dir. Jörg Aufenanger, 18 Dec. 1996. Photo: Florian Zeyfang. Source: Nina Lorenz-Herting, Berlin.

the GDR's official literary forms and the ideology of Marxism-Leninism, which, in part, brought them into existence.[5] From the early fifties to the late eighties, authorities mandated the proliferation of light manufacture within the GDR. The plan: to let consumer goods play their small part in building the collective.[6] One such item was quick-cooking Tempo Peas, formulated in the sixties for the millions of working mothers in East Germany (fig. 3). When the Treuhand Anstalt corporation privatized the VEB Suppina Auerbach Food Processing Plant in the early nineties, Tempo Peas were discontinued. But some packets still lie around, waiting to prompt remembrances of things past. Recently, curator Andreas Ludwig exhibited Tempo Peas in a historical exhibition of the GDR quotidian at the Open Depot. (Andreas Ludwig and the Open Depot have no relationship to the Museum Ludwig or to its founders, Peter and Irene Ludwig.) He installed them into a scenario of a Konsum

5. "A Thousand Little Things" ("Tausend kleine Dinge"), a promotional jingle for the GDR's Konsum shops, featured frequently on East German television from the sixties on.
6. Drawing from the writings of Boris Arvatov, Christina Kiaer has documented the extent to which the Constructivists envisioned a political affinity between the consumer good and the human subject. See Boris Arvatov, "Everyday Life and the Culture of the Thing (Toward the Formulation of the Question)," trans. Christina Kiaer, *October,* no. 81 (Summer 1997): 119–28, and Kiaer, "Boris Arvatov's Socialist Objects," *October,* no. 81 (Summer 1997): 105–18. GDR industrial designers were similarly inclined to mobilize consumer goods toward the socialist project. See Neue Gesellschaft für Bildende Kunst, *Wunderwirtschaft: DDR-Konsumkultur in den 60er Jahren* (Cologne, 1996).

Fig. 3.—Tempo Erbsen, Sammlung Industrielle Gestaltung, Berlin. Source: Sammlung Industrielle Gestaltung, Berlin.

grocery store, where they share shelf space with other standard merchandise (fig. 4). The shop panorama gives viewers the chance to reflect upon daily life in the GDR and to survey the changed marketscape of the new Germany. Yet already in 1980 the packets had been displayed in a different context. Joseph Beuys integrated them into his installation *Economic Values (Wirtschafftswerte)*—an assemblage that combines VEB products with a small sculpture of Beuys's own design (fig. 5). Long before the workers' republics of Eastern Europe entered their final agonies, Beuys registered the odd charge of the communist commodity. As a prominent figure in West Germany's Oppositional scene, Beuys shared the Left's investment in the notion of a socialist alternative.[7] Taking up Tempo Peas, *Economic Values* did two things. It touched upon the question of the found object as art object, and it anticipated the current race to curate the socialist past.

Tempo Peas offer a juncture between current museal and artistic practices, one that exposes the function of the frame in assigning the meaning of objects, on one hand, and things, on the other. Here the curator and the artist pass different sentences on a single artifact. Ludwig reads Tempo Peas as an object in the narrative of the GDR; his Open Depot sets

7. For a reflection on Beuys's politics, see Heiner Müller and Jan Hoet, "Insight into the Process of Production—A Conversation," in *Documenta IX*, ed. Jan Hoet, 3 vols. (Stuttgart, 1991), 1:96.

Fig. 4.—Konsum display, Offenes Depot, Eisenhüttenstadt.
Photo: Charity Scribner.

apart the packets as relics of that lifeworld. Beuys, meanwhile, incorporates Tempo Peas as a fetish of his proto-Marxist ideals. The things in *Economic Values* exceed the object of Ludwig's study. They are its deficit and its surplus, at once.[8]

8. In his work toward a theory of things, Bill Brown posits a difference between objects and things. If the object is materialized and utilized, the thing exceeds these properties. Imbued with "sensuous" or "metaphysical presence," the thing can be cast with the spell of the fetish or totem. Applying Brown's logic to Tempo Peas, I would argue that Beuys's thing is "temporalized as the before and after of the object" (Bill Brown, "Thing Theory," p. 5).

Fig. 5.—Joseph Beuys, *Wirtschaftswerte*, 1980. © 2002 Artists Rights Society (ARS), New York / VG Bild-Kunst, Bonn.

The Open Depot

Ludwig's museum is located near Germany's border with Poland in the industrial town of Eisenhüttenstadt (formerly Stalinstadt). Developed in the nineteen-fifties to gird the workaday with freedom, equality, and unity, the concrete arcades of Eisenhüttenstadt have been abandoned to those who cannot (or do not want to) meet the exigencies of market competition. The Open Depot takes up residence in the defunct nursery unit that was once a vital organ of the city. Here Ludwig displays objects ranging from paper products to heavy machinery. The lightest collectibles—books, food wrappers, and the like—are of materials so fragile, so acidic, that they appear much older than their true fifteen or twenty years. In contrast, the leaden, but still functional office equipment and household appliances—adding machines that weigh ten pounds, blenders, twenty—seem built to last an eternity, whether carefully curated in the museum or wantonly abandoned to the rubbish bins of history.

With the post-*Wende* influx of Western consumer goods, many Eisenhüttenstadters have chosen to upgrade their homes and workplaces. Now, on rubbish collection days, possessions that were cast off to make room for new furnishings and appliances litter the local sidewalks. For some Eisenhüttenstadters, this gesture of jettisoning the outmoded seems arduous.

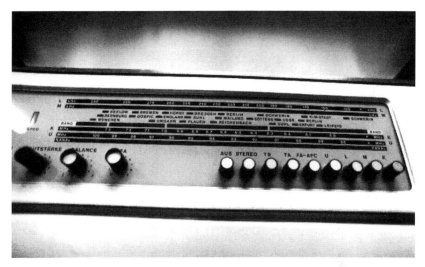

FIG. 6.—VEB Radio, Offenes Depot, Eisenhüttenstadt. Photo: Alan Chin.

Supplanting the trusty family radio with a Chinese-made stereo system is a freighted act for them. So, instead of leaving the radio, the face of which bears the names of satellite stations in Bucharest and Minsk, to wait for the sanitation workers, some opt to bequeath these artifacts to the Open Depot (fig. 6). In the acquisition process, a group of museum staff, trained by Ludwig in the methods of oral history, interview the donors. They pose questions not only about the provenance of the objects but also about the owners' memories of the way they once lived with them or among them. Although the interview records have not yet been made public, much of the collection is open to view, as are the densely inscribed guest books where visitors can record their responses and reflect upon the thoughts of those who have come before them.[9] The Open Depot sets memory work into play on a human scale by concentrating on household objects. Amassing and displaying these mundane artifacts, Ludwig creates a space where viewers not only can come together to debate their past and future but where they can also identify and insert their private lives, their own memories of countless detail, into the larger body of German history.

The GDR maintained its fair share of museums. Policy makers recognized the imperative to discern a heritage separate from that of West Germany and so directed funds toward memorials that would legitimate the new socialist nation. Exhibitions that highlighted the antifascist resistance

9. Guest books were a common sight in GDR museums, as were notebooks for recording comments and complaints for the managers of many institutions, such as schools, hospitals, and shops. Citizens were meant to understand that they played a decisive role in policy making and that administrators would take seriously their public criticism.

movement, the Soviet liberation, and the life of the proletariat filled both museums of fine art and the galleries of historical societies. But since unification much of this has changed, as many institutions of visual culture have been put under Western direction. Years before the Open Depot was established, Westerners had anticipated the impact that an exhibition of Second World material culture would have. In August 1989, West German curators had organized "SED: Stunning Eastern Design" at the Habernoll Gallery near Frankfurt am Main. But this show merely lampooned the "pallid universe" of démodé East German consumer goods.[10] The selection of GDR products depicted in the exhibition catalogue—from faded packets of vulcanized rubber condoms to cartons of Sprachlos (speechless) cigars—appears aimed to confirm the superior tastes of sophisticated Westerners. Later, in the early nineties, the Museum of German History on East Berlin's Unter den Linden underwent a massive overhaul that entailed the closeting of displays such as one that juxtaposed Hegel's spectacles with the first television set manufactured in the GDR. In 1996 the Museum of Working-Class Life packed up and relocated from the center of East Berlin to the peripheral district of Marzahn. To this day, most of its collection remains warehoused.

Economic Values

Beuys's *Economic Values* locates itself between the Eisenhüttenstadt and Habernoll exhibitions. Like "Stunning Eastern Design," *Economic Values* claims an exoticizing purchase on the wares it displays. But Beuys also enables the later, more earnest projects like the Open Depot, as he measures the exhibition value of ordinary artifacts. After Germany's postwar economic miracle (*Wirtschaftswunder*), after glasnost, *Economic Values* seems to activate a dialectic between these two strands of visual culture—high camp and sober documentary.

The Belgian curator Jan Hoet strongly favored *Economic Values* and acquired the assemblage for the permanent collection of the Museum of Contemporary Art in Ghent, which he directs. When Hoet was artistic director of the FRG's Documenta IX in 1992, he used *Economic Values* to catalyze the international exhibition. This was the first Documenta to be held after German unification. Hoet organized the event around the theme "Collective Memory" and ran it as a kind of conceptual lost-and-found department for the remainders of socialism.

A set of slightly askew metal shelves define the shape and dimensions of *Economic Values*. Stocked on each shelf are items of basic necessity—simple tools and staple foods. Although Beuys enjoyed a reputation as a defender

10. See *SED: Schönes Einheits Design,* ed. Georg C. Bertsch, Ernst Hedler, and Matthias Dietz (exhibition catalog, Habernoll Gallery, Dreieich, 27 Aug. 1989).

of social justice and an insider of Left-oriented political movements such as the Green Party and other socialist initiatives, he spent little time in the Eastern Bloc and so relied on colleagues to ferry Tempo Peas and other GDR products to his studio. From a massive collection of donated wares, Beuys selected only those that looked the most superannuated.[11] He passed over wares that evidenced the traces of sophisticated Western marketing strategies in favor of those packed in coarse, unbleached paper, printed with a single color, or perhaps two. Scant ornamentation illustrates the labels. In some cases all that is written is the name of the good—"Millet" or "Honey" (fig. 7). In an interview, Beuys characterized the design of the products he displayed as that of *Behelfsverpackung*—the provisional or makeshift packaging used in situations of duress, such as those produced for military and relief operations. (Well before conceiving *Economic Values*, Beuys had created works that spoke of the need to heal Germany's wounded postwar civilization, but none of these had identified Eastern Europe as the agent or accomplice of such a recovery. Consider *Stuhl mit Fett* [*Fat Chair* (1964)] and *Das Rudel* [*The Pack* (1969)]).[12] In *Economic Values* his selection process rendered the wares as poor things, that is, as examples of "die Reste" or remains that many saw as integral to East Germany during the cold war.[13] To such minds the letters DDR did not signify the *Deutsche Demokratische Republik*, but rather *der dumme Rest:* the meager remainder of Germany's division.

Economic Values sets the accent squarely on the "Easternness" of the found objects Beuys selects.[14] To Western eyes (to date, the piece has been exhibited only in Western Europe), the assemblage offers a glimpse of

11. For a description of Beuys's selection process, see *Joseph Beuys: Das Wirtschaftswertprinzip*, ed. Klaus Staeck and Gerhard Steidl (Heidelberg, 1990), p. 7.

12. For an inflected reading of Beuys's career that has informed this essay, see Benjamin H. D. Buchloh, "Reconsidering Beuys, Once Again" and "Beuys, the Twilight of the Idol," in *Joseph Beuys: Mapping the Legacy*, ed. Gene Ray (New York, 2001), pp. 75–89, 199–211. Bettina Funcke has recently made a series of compelling arguments that counter aspects of the Buchlovian take, shall we say, of Beuys. Drawing on Kierkegaard's *Entweder-Oder* and Boris Groys's *Unter Verdacht*, Funcke demonstrates that Beuys's self-idealization as artist, as hero, was a consciously ironic strategy of his work. Beuys pitched his project to performatively destabilize two notions of postwar subjectivity—that any German could remain under the sway of a Führer, Hitler or some other, and that any member of the art world could stay under the spell of abstract expressionism and its elected genius, Jackson Pollock. See Bettina Funcke, "Scharlatanerie als Strategie," unpublished manuscript, 2003.

13. In interviews Beuys emphasizes that the apparent simplicity of the goods assembled on his shelves betrays an inner richness and complexity. He links the installation to the aesthetics of *arte povera*, but still it is clear that Beuys imagines *Economic Values* as a bridge to Germany's "lost" other. See Ulrich Dietzel, "Gespräch mit Heiner Müller," in *Joseph Beuys: Das Wirtschaftwertsprinzip*, pp. 27–28. A longer version of this interview was first published as "Was gebraucht wird: Mehr Utopie, mehr Phantasie und mehr Freiräume für Phantasie. Ein Gespräch mit Ulrich Dietzel," *Sinn und Form* 4 (1985): 1193–217.

14. Although a few of the packages included in *Economic Values* were produced in the Federal Republic of Germany, packets from the GDR, Poland, and the Soviet Union form the bulk of the goods amassed on the shelves and make the greatest visual impact.

FIG. 7.—Joseph Beuys, *Wirtschaftswerte*, detail, 1980. © 2002 Artists Rights Society (ARS), New York / VG Bild-Kunst, Bonn.

what Beuys considered the quaint material culture of the other Europe. Perhaps Beuys was aware of the ethnographic risk undertaken in *Economic Values*, for he signals his foreignness to the state socialist world. Into the installation Beuys inserted a piece of his own sculpture, a blocklike plaster cast he had produced in the sixties (fig. 8). Several steps were necessary to integrate the cast with the other elements. Beuys daubed the block's chipped edges with butter in a deliberately futile attempt to repair them. (If anything, the butter would accelerate the sculpture's decomposition because its lipids would macerate the plaster.) He also marked each element of the assemblage with his own signature and the note "Economic Value 1," thereby elevating each element of the work into a readymade and integrating all the parts into a whole. But these interventions undermine themselves; Beuys's inscriptions partially erase the different histories of the elements. His sculpture, meanwhile, was resurrected from his own warehouse, an archival limbo that he himself had created. By eliding the "origins" of the various things collected, Beuys suggests that both his plaster cast and the (still extant) socialist material world have been disinterred from deep storage.

Soon after completing *Economic Values* the contents of Beuys's packages began to decay. As a measure of conservation, Beuys replaced the contents with more durable mixtures of sand and chalk that preserved the impression of weight and volume within the wrappers. Forestalling sedimentation, *Economic Values* holds its objects deep in its heart where they seem to both live and die, just beyond the edge of time. The dust gather-

FIG. 8.—Joseph Beuys, *Wirtschaftswerte*, detail, 1980. ©
2002 Artists Rights Society (ARS), New York / VG Bild-Kunst,
Bonn.

ing below the packet of peas takes on a life of its own, making the work paradoxically immortal in its own death, emanating like a halo of decay.

Like a mourner's relic, Beuys's things, in themselves, are only trivial remainders, almost absurd. Yet they are not relics. Beheld by a mourner, a proper relic takes on a specific meaning. It is instilled with the power to signify the death of the loved one and, moreover, to ward off his return. An authentic relic, Pierre Fédida speculates, cannot be thrown away. Because it can no longer circulate in an exchange economy, it also cannot be substituted by some other object (as is the case in Beuys's work). Depleted of use-value, the relic reminds the mourner of his power over the dead.[15] It fends off anxieties of death and the *ne plus* (no longer) that awaits mortals, Fédida argues, keeping at bay any haunting visions of rot. This reliquary logic defines and legitimates the bequest of possessions from generation to

15. See Pierre Fédida, "La Relique et le travail du deuil," *Nouvelle Revue de Psychanalyse* 2 (Fall 1970): 249–54, esp. p. 249.

generation; because the mourner can only appropriate the property of the mourned if he really *is* dead and gone, the relic's delivery marks the passing of time. *Economic Values* has little to do with the task of laying something to rest, however. Because Beuys's knowledge of these artifacts is second-hand, his installation does not preserve them as relics but rather confects them as false souvenirs.

Key for Beuys was the purported biological purity of the Eastern goods as well as the principles of recycling that he presumed to motivate the manufacturers.[16] But if these were the only messages he wanted to convey, Beuys need not have procured packages of Eastern provenance. *Economic Values* is not an ecological reflection on the transience of nature. It is about the spoils of state socialism—the idealized Marxist alternative that many, Beuys included, imagined to inhere in the East. Despite Beuys's attempt to critique the FRG's postwar economy, in the end *Economic Values* merely presents another gamut of commodity fetishes.[17] A problem arises with Beuys's handling of the GDR object world. "You never know what you have until you lose it"—this seems to be the thinking of the work. Fixating on loss, Beuys loses his grip on real history and so loses perspective on what real existing socialism really was.

Against this, the Open Depot offers an object lesson on the course of GDR history. Ludwig relates to his work as an engaged participant trying to come to terms with his own past. Beuys acts at one remove from actual lived experience. His touch sends the GDR hurtling toward a place outside of history. Effectively, Beuys transfers time onto a spatial plane where the past is another country, another Germany. Ludwig's mournful regard for Tempo Peas and other leftovers of the GDR becomes apparent when Beuys's handling of the identical materials is brought into the same scope. Whereas Ludwig seeks to place Tempo Peas in a specific moment on a real historical time line, Beuys betrays his romantic investment. He arrests his collection within an eternal present. *Economic Values* disavows the failure (then in progress) of the regime that produced its accumulated wares and languishes in the leftist melancholia that plagued many of Beuys's ilk. A study of loss, *Economic Values* remains a sullen stockroom, bereft of a compelling historical narrative.

16. In an interview with playwright Heiner Müller, Dietzel refers to a conversation he once had with Beuys. The artist explained that his attraction to the products of state socialist industry lay in the "voluptuous creativity" that they embodied. Müller agrees with this characterization and describes GDR material culture as a sort of "treasure trove" (*Fundgrube*) in which Beuys could explore and indulge his "material sensitivities" (Dietzel, "Gespräch mit Heiner Müller," pp. 27–28).

17. Psychoanalysis links the concept of disavowal closely to that of fetishism. The fetish embodies a disavowal. Without entering into the complex relationship between Marxist and Freudian notions of fetishism, one should nonetheless remark how the leap from concrete social analysis to the critique of instrumental reason impacts upon the status of commodity fetishism. See, for example, Wolfgang Fritz Haug, *Kritik der Warenästhetik* (Frankfurt, 1971).

Niche culture

Although Ludwig may rightfully mourn the GDR's passing, a number of temporal discontinuities nevertheless punctuate his account of German cultural memory. The Open Depot concentrates on the private and the domestic, the realm of what East Germans called niche culture. Ludwig affirms the private lives that were led within communism. But, significantly, his emphasis on niche culture comes over and against the documentation of larger, state-sanctioned practices. Ludwig does not illuminate the patterns of identification that connected the private to the monumental, the personal to the political in the GDR past. Indeed, his exhibition seems to provide refuge from the more difficult issues informing the Germans' collective heritage. What linked the first unification of German states in the nineteenth century, the legacy of National Socialism, and Soviet-style communism? What was the genealogy of Eastern Bloc intelligence agencies such as the Stasi and the KGB? Ludwig does not address these questions.

Despite the central role of the Stasi in GDR life, no vestiges of this bureau figure in the Open Depot. After the armed forces, the Stasi was East Germany's largest employer; its archives documented information on more than a quarter of its citizens. It cast an air of suspicion over relations between coworkers and neighbors and even, at times, between family members. The key to its archives—a master repertoire containing a single index card for each Stasi staff member, informer, and object of surveillance—extends for more than a mile. Following government directives, Stasi collaborators compiled classified reports, which recorded in minute detail the lives of millions of individuals whose daily actions were considered to bear upon matters of national security interest: 22.31 Telephone rings. No answer. The object continues to read. 22.40 The object converses briefly with spouse. 23.02 Object's spouse draws curtains in north-facing windows. 23.10 Lamps extinguished.

In the Open Depot Ludwig trains the viewer's attention away from Stasi operations as well as the official cultural events and customs that once engaged GDR citizens as a mass. He also employs different installation strategies for artifacts associated with private life and those associated with bureaucratic institutions. Whereas some rooms of the Open Depot contain case after case of barely distinguishable appliances, stacked catacombs of the GDR's industrial history, elsewhere Ludwig has staged the artifacts in panoramas of life as it was lived in the recent, but rapidly receding past. All things considered, the Open Depot merits credit; its activation of collective memory challenges the strictures of archival history. If Ludwig merely conserved and catalogued objects manufactured by the VEB, his museum would serve as a tomb—a fixture on the order of Lenin's and Stalin's refrigerated mausolea. Thus, Ludwig does not directly confront the Stasi legacy, but the Open Depot does initiate a more critical curatorial practice in Eastern Germany (fig. 9). (To wit, the Stasi headquarters on

FIG. 9.—Forschungs- und Gedenkstätte Normannenstraße, Berlin. Photo: Charity Scribner.

Berlin's Normannenstraße were recently converted into a museum.) Ludwig's strategies of coupling objects with memory samples and using guest books both break from the archival drive of the Stasi files and make the museal space more public. Where the Stasi sought to control the space of the GDR, the Open Depot exposes the alterity of history.

Given that the Stasi was foundational to every aspect of GDR life—not only the public sphere but also that of the domestic—its archives continue to inform the collective memory that is unfolding after the *Wende* in both the provincial museum and the mega-exhibition. For a crucial distinction separates the archives from the official histories disseminated in the GDR. Whereas academics, curators, and administrators of other state institutions presented affirmative accounts of the building of socialism, secret police files stored the largest records of actual politics and society. Despite the brute ideological censorship of Stasi data, this archive was (and remains) an accurate source of information about the times when things went out of order or *außer Betrieb*. Such failures and "factory seconds"—strikes, missed production goals, and moments of general discontent—were kept secret from the public. The Stasi held tight rein over its information, allowing access only to the highest ranks of the *nomenklatura*. The Stasi's existence was common knowledge, but its archives seemed to withhold mysteries. The files belonged neither to the patently public domain of official history nor to the exclusively private sphere. Rather, the Stasi reports functioned as a covert supplement to state-mandated discourse. These chronicles were recorded in an alienated, impersonal mode, yet they penetrated into the intimate recesses of private life. Since 1989, much of the archive has been opened to the public. As more details surface, many people struggle to figure these reports into their own memories of life in a divided Germany. The interest in the Open Depot and other GDR shows is a product of this struggle. So was Hoet's return to *Economic Values* in the 1992 Documenta.

The collaborative role of Tempo Peas in the project of realizing socialism registers in both displays. The Open Depot effectively preserves and exhibits the thousands of little things that gave weight and substance to everyday life in East Germany. And *Economic Values* also attends to a microhistory that was a critical element of European modernity. But Ludwig and Beuys leave other stories untold. For consumption also worked to distract Germans; it kept them from criticizing the tragic realities of state socialism.

What of the millions of bodies—German, Russian, Ukranian—buried in the mass graves of Soviet prison camps? a cynic might ask. This terrible truth subtended every aspect of state socialist practice, but the museums of this history are only just now being founded. One could read niche culture as both the GDR's enabling fiction and founding disavowal. From this perspective the Open Depot and *Economic Values* would merely extend the state's authoritarian legacy—plying VEB wares and diverting our gaze from the gulag, state socialism's most genuine artifact. The archeology of these deeper veins of material culture has only just begun. Although we cannot yet calculate the worth of these sites, at least we know their names. Kolyma, Vorkuta, Norilsk. The list goes on.

A Pebble, a Camera, a Man Who Turns into a Telegraph Pole

John Frow

Moving house while I was writing this paper, I have been working in an unusually intense way with physical things: sanding back wooden floors, shifting cartons of books, sealing a window frame with putty, tightening the rings on a washing machine hose . . . Callused on my fingers, this is a kind of knowledge different from intellectual knowing (which is, never-theless, always a matter of paper and ink and electric currents running through machinery). Old skills of understanding the world with my hands come back to me. And I experience the sheer singularity of its things: this nameless, almost indescribable Odradek of a thing, for ex-ample, an asymmetrical grooved and slotted bit of fractionally cylindrical metal that ties two planks of bookshelf together around a projecting, greased metal screw. Someone designed it, gave it its mysteriously precise logic, perhaps even has a name for it; but to me it's purely strange.

That sense of strangeness is one kind of beginning to an essay on things, but it's one that can get caught up all too easily in a supposition of the thing's ontological purity and in the nostalgia for a world of simple objects that talk about things so often betrays. That nostalgia permeates almost all contemporary thinking about things. It is classically located in Heidegger's harkening to the things of a stable and preindustrial rural world ('a stone, a clod of earth, a piece of wood . . . Lifeless beings of nature and objects of use')[1] and to the 'authentic experience' of thingness

---

1. Martin Heidegger, 'The Origin of the Work of Art', *Poetry, Language, Thought*, trans. Albert Hofstadter (New York, 1971), p. 21; hereafter abbreviated 'O'.

by the Greeks, an experience of 'the Being of beings in the sense of presence' which has been lost to Western philosophy in the process of translating Greek thought into the Latin categorization of thingness as the union of substance with accidents, or as the unity of a manifold of sensations, or as formed matter ('O', p. 23). If the impossible scope of this topic is in some sense imaginable, however, it's because it is narrowed by the way certain questions tend to press more urgently on us—to shape a certain corner of the amorphous space inhabited by the disciplines that think about cultural thingness. These questions have to do with our habitation of the aftermath of a theoretical paradigm which sought to imagine the world rigorously in terms of the play of representations and rigorously to exclude the sleight of hand by which a beyond of representation is posited in such a way that representation could be measured against it. Our problem is that beyond.

Which is perhaps above all a problem about the writing or imaging of things in texts. This is "Pebble," a poem by the Polish poet Zbigniew Herbert:

> The pebble
> is a perfect creature
>
> equal to itself
> mindful of its limits
>
> filled exactly
> with a pebbly meaning
>
> with a scent which does not remind one of anything
> does not frighten anything away does not arouse desire
>
> its ardour and coldness
> are just and full of dignity
>
> I feel a heavy remorse
> when I hold it in my hand
> and its noble body
> is permeated by false warmth

John Frow is Regius Professor of Rhetoric and English Literature and Director of the Institute for Advanced Studies in the Humanities at the University of Edinburgh. His most recent books are *Time and Commodity Culture* (1997) and (coauthored with Tony Bennett and Michael Emmison) *Accounting for Tastes: Australian Everyday Cultures* (1999).

> —Pebbles cannot be tamed
> to the end they will look at us
> with a calm and very clear eye[2]

Like the remote beloved of courtly poetry, the 'perfect creature' generates
a drama of longing, of attempted conquest, and of refusal. In the first act
the pebble is described through a series of divisions between subject and
predicate which are, however, in relations of such absolute equivalence
that the division again disappears. Thingness is the tautologous identity
of subject and predicate. If we are to understand its entelechy, the perfection of its necessary being, we must suppose it to have an intention regarding its disposition within its own (spatial and moral) limits, to have a
meaning which is exactly and entirely coextensive with it, to have a scent
which can be defined only as the negation of all the properties of scent,
to have equal and opposite emotions which entirely befit its status as an
emotionless entity. In the second act of the story, the speaker, whom we
must suppose to be disturbed by the inhuman perfection and thus inac-
cessibility of the pebble, seeks to impose his emotions on it but succeeds
only in transmitting a warmth which cannot touch the pebble's heart;
realizing this, the speaker feels remorse. The third act records this defeat:
the self-identity of the pebble renders it invulnerable to domination. It is
unresponsive to human emotion. It returns the human gaze without fear
and with a rationality that refuses the false warmth with which we try to
awaken it to a sense of our own existence. Like the remote beloved, the
pebble cannot care for us.

Why does the pebble return my gaze? But 'return' is the wrong way
of putting it: the pebble does no more than look at me, unseeing, and
it does so because to be so purely a thing, so deeply withdrawn from
capture by others, is to pass into that mode of irreducibility and unknow-
ability that we call the subject. Its look is the very form of that presence-
to-self which cannot, as such, be an object for another. This is the paradox
of any fascination with the thingness of things: that things posited in
themselves, in their distinctness from intention, representation, figuration, or relation, are thereby filled with an imputed interiority and, in
their very lack of meaning, with 'a pebbly meaning' which is at once full
and inaccessible. (Think of the final minutes of Antonioni's *L'Ellipse*, a
series of slow, wordless, stylized shots that shift us from a world of stories
to a world of things—scaffolding, a fence, a leaking bucket, a sprinkler, a
woman waiting for a bus, rustling leaves, a sodium light—which had until
then been the background for human action and which now, revealed in
the plenitude of their being, at once enigmatic and luminous, are seen to
be the point of the film, its true actors, the ones that look at us.) Sartre

---

2. Zbigniew Herbert, 'Pebble', *Selected Poems*, trans. Czeslaw Milosz and Peter Dale
Scott (Harmondsworth, 1968), p. 108. Reproduced by permission of Penguin Books Ltd.

expresses this paradox in the following way: being in-itself, he writes, 'does not refer to itself as self-consciousness does. It is this self. It is itself so completely that the perpetual reflection which constitutes the self is dissolved in an identity. That is why being is at bottom beyond the *self.*' Yet, at the same time, 'in fact being is opaque to itself precisely because it is filled with itself. This can be better expressed by saying that *being is what it is*':[3] 'equal to itself/mindful of its limits'.

This paradox and the drama that surrounds it constitute a discourse which flourished early in the last century, both in the phenomenological reduction which seeks to bracket things in their singularity and in a central tradition of poetic (and to a degree novelistic) writing which sought, in reaching back to the thingness of things, to free them from their merely instrumental status in a world of human uses: the poetry of Rilke's *Neue Gedichte,* of William Carlos Williams's imagism, of Neruda's *Odas Elementales,* of Ponge's *Le Parti pris des choses.* The thingness of things posited in this discourse—its stuff, its matter, whatever it is that subsists behind and beneath accident, contingency, time, and the weave of knowledges and uses that give them to me—is like a dream of immortality, of inherence and persistence beyond all change. That's why the vision of thingness so quickly becomes a vision of God (Stan's epiphanic glimpse of the numinous in a gob of spittle in *The Tree of Man,* for example).[4] And it's why the true role of Things, of underlying thingness, is to be the mirror of our souls, the object that makes us a subject, that makes us real. That's why the auratic thing returns my gaze: it is myself that I see, looking back in astonishment at *its* mirror image, myself. Hence Lacan's thesis that the gaze is inscribed in the world, always already looking at me; that the gaze 'imagined by me in the field of the Other' forms me as other to myself in the same movement as that in which I 'recognize' the Thing that sees me.[5]

Endowed with an interiority and a memory, things become stories. This is the description of a throwaway camera which, towards the end of Richard Powers's novel *Gain,* stands in for the heroine's death from cancer:

The camera jacket says: "Made In China With Film From Italy Or Germany." The film itself accretes from more places on the map than emulsion can cover. Silver halide, metal salts, dye couplers, bleach fixatives, ingredients gathered from Russia, Arizona, Brazil, and underwater seabeds, before being decanted in the former DDR. Camera in a pouch, the true multinational: trees from the Pacific Northwest and the southeastern coastal plain. Straw and recovered wood scrap from Canada. Synthetic adhesive from Korea. Bauxite

3. Jean-Paul Sartre, *Being and Nothingness: An Essay on Phenomenological Ontology,* trans. Hazel E. Barnes (London, 1957), p. lxv.

4. See Patrick White, *The Tree of Man* (Harmondsworth, 1961), p. 476.

5. Jacques Lacan, *The Four Fundamental Concepts of Psycho-Analysis,* trans. Alan Sheridan, ed. Jacques-Alain Miller (London, 1977), p. 84.

from Australia, Jamaica, Guinea. Oil from the Gulf of Mexico or North Sea Brent Blend, turned to plastic in the Republic of China before being shipped to its mortal enemies on the Mainland for moulding. Cinnabar from Spain. Nickel and titanium from South Africa. Flash elements stamped in Malaysia, electronics in Singapore. Design and colour transfers drawn up in New York. Assembled and shipped from that address in California by a merchant fleet beyond description, completing the most heavily choreographed conference in existence.[6]

Literally a black box, the camera unseals and unfolds itself as a matrix of histories and geographies. To recover things is to find again these lost stories, the lines of people and places that converge in them and that have been obscured by the thickening of the surfaces of things, the self-evidence that informs them with presence pure and simple.

The strongest version of this story of the bad enchantment of the world of things is the Marxist theory of commodity fetishism.[7] The concept displaces the enlightened critique of religion ('primitive' and especially animistic religion, but for enlightened thought all religion is primitive) into the critique of political economy.[8] With the advent of widespread commodification, the social relation between people which is the reality of human work and exchange comes to assume the 'fantastic' form of a relation between things. The structure of the commodity, in which the particularity of use-value is subordinated to the abstract universality of exchange-value, effects a mystified conversion of 'the social characteristics of men's own labour' into what seem to be 'objective characteristics of the products of labour themselves'.[9] Persons and things both become thinglike, and the causal relation between work and value is inverted. Whereas the related Marxist concept of alienation foregrounds a transcendental notion of the person, the concept of commodity fetishism turns its focus to the opposition between a simple and a complex social relation, to an opposition between the immediacy of relations among direct producers of use-values and the highly mediated and abstract structure of commodity relations. What characterizes things in capitalist production and exchange is thus not at all their thingness but the opposite, an abstractness which *takes the form of* a dense materiality. Insofar as the Marxist account of the commodity form is an analysis of semiotic value, its tendency is to oppose use-value to exchange-value as matter to representation and as immediacy to mediation. More broadly: despite the

6. Richard Powers, *Gain* (New York, 1998), pp. 347–48.

7. The following paragraph draws on an argument made in my *Time and Commodity Culture* (Oxford, 1997), pp. 141–42.

8. See William Pietz, 'Fetishism and Materialism: The Limits of Theory in Marx', in *Fetishism as Cultural Discourse*, ed. Emily Apter and Pietz (Ithaca, N.Y., 1993), pp. 130–31.

9. Karl Marx, *Capital: A Critique of Political Economy*, trans. Ben Fowkes, 3 vols. (London, 1976), 1:164–65.

force of its historical and relational conception of the commodity form, its conceptual ground is a myth of presence which leads it to understand this form on the one hand as the alienation of the integrity of the person and on the other as the replacement of the simplicity, transparency, and immediacy of the use-value of things with a complex system of representations.

Leah Hager Cohen spells out what we might take to be the consequences of this replacement. At the core of commodity fetishism is an 'erosion of objects' singularity' by the abstract equivalence of exchange-value.[10] Things are 'sealed off from their origins, ensconced from their own true stories, which are the stories of people, of work, of lives' (*G*, p. 13). Her own project of tracing the stories that lie hidden within the everyday commodities she consumes—paper, glass, coffee beans—is explicitly an act of restoration of a kind of knowledge of things that has been lost with the passing of traditional ways of life:

> Once, we could not help but know what piece of earth the potatoes on our dinner plate came from. We knew whose hand shaped and fired the plate. We knew who cobbled our shoes, and whose cow was slaughtered to provide the leather. We knew from which spring, or well, or rain barrel our water was dipped. In many parts of the world people still know these things, but in what we term the developed nations of the earth such facts have gone hazy, have taken on the properties, almost, of fairy tales: the notion of connections seems charming, but not quite real. [*G*, p. 13]

In that lost world the human is more human, things more thinglike because of the immanence of human stories to things. This is a knowledge that can be recovered by a labor of attention: 'Everywhere you rest your eyes, invisible stories blossom' (*G*, p. 289).

Such attention takes place within a discourse that is at once humanist and epistemological; to be fully human is to know that things are made up of human stories, is to penetrate the layers of abstraction beneath which these true stories are concealed. Persons and things are mutually constituted in the representations of things. Yet we might note an ambivalence in Cohen's argument: what she seeks to restore is precisely not the singularity of things (it is rather the fetish which is truly singular) but the network of human relations that compose them. Things, in her account, are entirely made up of the stories that thread them through with meaning and value, making them entirely reducible to human representations. The throwaway camera is at once so rich with convergent destinies that it can take the place of the novel's dying heroine and so trivial in itself that it is designed for nothing except to be discarded. All opposites are revers-

10. Leah Hager Cohen, *Glass, Paper, Beans: Revelations on the Nature and Value of Ordinary Things* (New York, 1997), p. 224; hereafter abbreviated *G*.

ible in this imaginary of the thing, stretched taut across the dialectic of abstract equivalence and human story, and of an otherness so complete that it becomes, again, the same. But might it be possible to evade this dialectic in order to imagine a world in which persons and things are partly strangers and partly kin? In which we recognize that 'the question of things, even the question whether they are, is inseparable from a question about what they do, or what can be done with them'?[11] Let us start again.

In a small town to the west of Sydney, a Greek owns a café in the main street. His daughter waits on the tables; she is said to have a wine-dark stain on her body, a secret 'so zealously guarded no man had managed to report its details'.[12] A travelling salesman comes to town; he is attracted to the sullenness of the waitress and to the secret of her body and decides not to leave town until he has seen it. One night he goes behind the café and watches through her bedroom window as she undresses. As she turns naked towards him he steps back and 'something solid met him from behind'; his arms disappear into his sides, and 'he felt himself merge into something altogether hard and straight; unusually tall.'[13] His head becomes cold, he begins to hear voices; he has turned into a telegraph pole, fashioned from karri and blackened at the base by the stain which has been transferred from the waitress, of whose intermittent nakedness he now has a clear view in all weathers.[14]

The story, from Murray Bail's *Eucalyptus*, fuses two myths from Ovid: the story of Actaeon and Diana (told earlier in the novel in a purer form as the story of Young Molloy who watches the novel's heroine, Ellen, pissing by the river, and who then has a smash on his motorbike and loses his sight),[15] and the story of Daphne and Apollo—in Horace Gregory's translation:[16]

> —as she spoke
> A soaring drowsiness possessed her; growing
> In earth she stood, white thighs embraced by climbing
> Bark, her white arms branches, her fair head swaying
> In a cloud of leaves; all that was Daphne bowed
> In the stirring of the wind, the glittering green
> Leaf twined within her hair and she was laurel—

which in turn is reminiscent of Rilke's 'Orpheus. Eurydice. Hermes.' where Eurydice, already growing more and more remote ('Sie war in

11. Bill Brown, 'How to Do Things with Things (A Toy Story)', *Critical Inquiry* 24 (Summer 1998): 936–37.

12. Murray Bail, *Eucalyptus* (Melbourne, 1998), p. 193.

13. Ibid., p. 194.

14. See ibid., p. 195.

15. See ibid., p. 48.

16. Ovid, *Metamorphoses*, trans. Horace Gregory (New York, 1958), 1.546–52, p. 46.

sich'), is 'so full of her great death . . . that she could understand nothing'. 'Sie war schon Wurzel'; Eurydice is transformed into the same remote otherness as Daphne and the commercial traveller.[17]

That otherness is what the discourse of thingness seeks and fails to apprehend as a mode of being not subject to human will. It seeks to free things from the instrumental status which ties them to human being and thus to endow them with a language of their own; and the effect of this is then to *return* them, as quasi subjects, to the human world. The pebble is endowed with a subjectivity, the camera with a historical and geographical memory. For Gadamer the problem of our relation to things is that 'we are not at all ready to hear things in their own being, that they are subjected to man's calculus and to his domination of nature through the rationality of science'.[18] 'Things' here implicitly means naturally occurring or at least simple things rather than complex technical or aesthetic objects. If thinking about thingness has, throughout the history of philosophy, been systematically distorted by the privilege given to such simple bounded entities—if stones, clods of earth, tables, and pots are taken to be somehow more thinglike than machines or buildings or works of art, or than immaterial entities such as time or a dream or the Chrysler corporation—this is above all a problem of examples and their role in foregrounding certain sets of logical entailments over others. Examples are pregnant particularities, 'cases' of the real proposed in such a way that certain more general conclusions can be drawn from their peculiar features; they constitute a 'paradigm' in the Aristotelian sense of an 'instance serv[ing] as vector pointing to a principle or conclusion' but also in the sense that they crowd out other ways of exemplifying some domain of reality.[19] Gadamer's world must satisfy two demands: that for the existence of an order of things independent of the order of the human and for the existence of a common sphere allowing for a passage between these two orders. What allows us to apprehend the purity of simple things in an otherness which nevertheless unfolds itself to us is language. Even in a world becoming increasingly technical, a world in which things 'are simply vanishing, and only the poet still remains true to them' ('N', p. 71), it is yet possible to speak of a language of things, as long as we 'remember what things really are, namely, not a material that is used and consumed, not a tool that is used and set aside, but something instead

17. Rainer Maria Rilke, 'Orpheus. Eurydike. Hermes.' *Neue Gedichte*, in *Werke*, 3 vols. (Frankfurt am Main, 1966), 1: 300, 301. Eurydice's becoming-root directly recalls the transformation of Daphne's feet into the roots of a tree: 'pes modo tam velox pigris radicibus haeret' (Ovid, *Metamorphoses*, 1.551, p. 46).

18. Hans-Georg Gadamer, 'The Nature of Things and the Language of Things', *Philosophical Hermeneutics*, trans. and ed. David E. Linge (Berkeley, 1976), p. 71; hereafter abbreviated 'N'.

19. Alexander Gelley, *Unruly Examples: On the Rhetoric of Exemplarity* (Stanford, Calif., 1995), p. 1.

that has existence in itself and is "not forced to do anything," as Heidegger says' ('N', pp. 71–72). There is a kind of lack of faith in the way we fail to attend to things, to their inherent speech, instead rendering them the mere instruments of our will. The metaphor of force here is a metaphor of rape: to use is to violate. Yet Gadamer has no wish to restore a simple dichotomy of the human and the nonhuman, a dualism of 'subjectivity and will, on the one hand, and object and being-in-itself, on the other' ('N', p. 74). Whereas classical metaphysics seeks a mediation of these poles in a theological notion of the preexistent correspondence of soul and world, and Marxism in the concept of praxis, Gadamer supposes that it is finally language which effects this mediation in its reconciliation of the language of things with the fact of the 'fundamentally linguistic character of our experience of the world' ('N', pp. 77–78).

Bail's story, however, posits no such separate but reconcilable being of things and speaking souls. It allegorises a world in which a commercial traveller is *also* a telegraph pole, and the telegraph pole takes on the human capacity to listen to the messages that pass through it and to peer through a bedroom window. Standing like the traveller's erect penis in the darkness outside, it looks and listens and desires and is neither wholly one thing nor the other. The fusion is never complete. Eurydice is constantly on the verge of becoming a root but does not lose her human shape. In the world of this story, the deep metaphysical opposition, the tied dichotomy of difference and mutual constitution as between things and representations and between humans and nonhumans, becomes flattened; difference in kind between commercial travellers and telegraph poles gives way to a mixing in which things and persons exchange properties and partly resemble and partly don't resemble each other. In this world you can still tell the difference between persons and things, but the difference is not an ontological absolute.

This flattening is the most striking move made by that set of collaborations in the sociology of science that is sometimes known as actor network theory. The explicit focus of this group is on the subclass of things that might be called technological: the instruments of scientific work, on the one hand, and on the other the functional objects produced by the conjunction of scientific work with industry, with money, with engineers and designers, with markets and marketing strategies, with end-users, with planning and regulation, with legal rights and obligations, and so on. But may it not be that in some sense all objects belong to this class? That all objects are inscribed within worlds of meaning and use, that even the pebble has its uses and its meanings, among them that of figuring the useless and the meaningless? If so much depends upon a red wheelbarrow glazed with rain water beside the white chickens, is this not above all because there is something to say about it—namely, that so much depends upon it? Certainly Latour will argue that *for all practical purposes* (including, I think, the practical purposes of poetry) the absolute things of the discourse of thingness have no meaningful or indeed meaningless existence:

> Objects that exist simply as objects, finished, not part of a collective life, are unknown, buried under soil. Real objects are always parts of institutions, trembling in their mixed status as mediators, mobilizing faraway lands and people, ready to become people or things, not knowing if they are composed of one or of many, of a black box counting for one or of a labyrinth concealing multitudes.[20]

It's not that, in the Marxist sense, things really are social relations which have become opaque; they both *are* and *affect* social relations, they are a partner in them, and all 'social' relations mix together chains of humans and nonhumans. Latour's exemplary objects—a speed bump, a hotel key with a weight attached to it, a door closer, a camera—are inscribed and programmed by human will and in turn, as nonhuman delegates, require humans to behave in certain ways. The speed bump 'is not made of matter, ultimately; it is full of engineers and chancellors and lawmakers, commingling their wills and their story lines with those of gravel, concrete, paint, and standard calculations.' Matter and persons connect and intermingle in a zone 'where some, though not all, of the characteristics of concrete become policemen, and some, though not all, of the characteristics of policemen become speed bumps'.[21]

The metaphor of the chain or network is a way of trying to conceptualize the kinds of social actors (or perhaps more precisely actants) there are, the links that tie them together, and the systemic processes which constitute and configure them as actors. But to put it like this is to suggest that the network is a structuring context working upon actors already in possession of stable dispositions and interests. The point rather is that networks are formed by the relations and interactions between actors and in turn crystallize a morphology which shapes and constrains their interests and actions. Latour gives the example of the widespread uptake of photography following Eastman's invention of removable roll film in the late 1880s and asks whether we can explain this diffusion in terms of the interests of the social groups involved. But these groups, he argues, were themselves deeply transformed by the technical innovations: 'The amateur market [in photography] was explored, extracted, and constructed from heterogeneous social groups which *did not* exist as such before Eastman. The new amateurs and Eastman's camera *co-produced* each other.'[22]

20. Bruno Latour, 'On Technical Mediation—Philosophy, Sociology, Genealogy', *Common Knowledge* 3 (Fall 1994): 46.

21. Ibid., p. 41.

22. Latour, 'Technology Is Society Made Durable', trans. Gabrielle Hecht, in *A Sociology of Monsters: Essays on Power, Technology, and Domination*, ed. John Law (London, 1991), p. 117.

The invention—in this case, Eastman's film stock and cameras—is an actor amongst others. It generates actions and changes relationships. But it doesn't do this by itself; it is not a determinant of change. The process is driven by all of the forces and interests involved—forces which are commercial, technological, legal, aesthetic, and so on—and which are invested unequally in players with different degrees of strength and persistence. If we think of an actor or actant in this sense as any entity with the power to associate chains of matter, text, humans and nonhumans, and money, then the reservation of the term to embodied human will becomes absurd; things, too, embody human will. The hotel key with a weight attached to it makes a polite request to me, on behalf of the hotelier, to hand it in at the desk before I go out. The speed bump gives me an instruction, on behalf of the police or some traffic control authority, to slow down on this stretch of road. To call these things, the key and the bump, 'nonhuman' is to ignore all the ways in which human will is translated into things and in which things in turn work as delegates which relay back to us these configurations of human will. 'Men and things exchange properties and replace one another':[23] the microprocessor that transforms the Aramis light rail project is neither fully on the side of human beings, since it is inert matter onto which human qualities—reasonings, programmes of action, obedience and control—have been transcribed, nor fully on the side of nonhumans, since that transcription has made it more and other than 'a bag of parts, a heap of pins, a pile of silicon' (*A*, p. 213). There are no such 'sides', such separate and self-contained series; there is only an endless mixing of the properties of persons with the properties of things.

An important model for this ontology of the social order as a composite of 'networks of heterogeneous materials' is Foucault's conception of discourse (or rather the discursive formation) as a matter not of language alone but of a complex of talk, texts, rules, bodies, authorisations, things, architectures, and so on.[24] The 'and so on' is important because the chains of relations that make up discourse and other institutions have no fixed composition and no predetermined effects. They are built from acts of translation—a process somewhat imprecisely defined in actor network theory but involving the recruitment and conversion of other (human or nonhuman) actors and chains of actors to one's own project in order to build more complex and more durable assemblages.[25] Things, in this

23. Latour, *Aramis, or The Love of Technology*, trans. Catherine Porter (Cambridge, Mass., 1996), p. 61; hereafter abbreviated *A*.

24. Law, 'Introduction: Monsters, Machines and Sociotechnical Relations', in *A Sociology of Monsters*, p. 10.

25. See in particular Michel Callon, 'Some Elements of a Sociology of Translation: Domestication of the Scallops and the Fishermen of St Brieuc Bay', in *Power, Action, and Belief: A New Sociology of Knowledge?* ed. Law (London, 1986), pp. 196–233.

model, never stand alone; they are bits of associative chains which form and re-form the hybrids of nature and culture of which our world is composed.

Things 'are simply vanishing', says Gadamer ('N', p. 71), but only if you mean 'a stone, a clod of earth, a piece of wood.' Is it really true that the world is becoming emptied of things? Karin Knorr Cetina makes precisely the opposite argument: that the modern world has seen an expansion not only of material things but of a 'sociality with objects' which has to some extent displaced forms of sociality centered on human beings.[26] The problem again is that of the example: if Gadamer defines things against use, then artefacts don't count as proper things and the world is indeed emptier. But all things have uses, even if they are not designed to be useful. And all things are inscribed with textuality. This is quite clear in the case of artefacts. Every designed object is the end product of a process of talking, writing, sketching, and calculation. It is accompanied by 'codes, checklists, maintenance manuals and user handbooks'.[27] And it bears within it the codes and programmes of action—the encoding of potential uses—that map its intended purposes. It goes without saying that these potential uses need not be realized. They may go astray, users may decline or be unable to recognize them, they may be deflected by other programmes, or they may be translated into contexts where they are unfamiliar or have no effective force.[28] But artefacts, 'carried on a wave of texts which bear testimony to the scars of the textualizations that accompanied their design and displacement,'[29] are 'souls through and through' (*A*, p. 223).

All this is true a fortiori of the semantically and pragmatically most complex artefacts, those which function as works of art. Two kinds of complexity are immediately relevant. The first is that which has to do with the unpredictability of the relation between inscription and uptake, the uncontrollability of the reading process (which doesn't mean that it is unstructured, of course). The second has to do with the fact that works of art both are themselves things and may at the same time represent things. The doubleness of this relation to thingness is the ground of possibility for a form of self-reference whereby a meditation on things can be taken as a meditation on the thingness of the work of art; hence, perhaps, the poignancy of such meditation, as well as its urgency in raising the problem of the different kinds of thingness that may inhere in complex

26. Karin Knorr Cetina, 'Sociality with Objects: Social Relations in Postsocial Knowledge Societies', *Theory, Culture, and Society* 14 (Nov. 1997): 2.

27. Callon, 'Techno-economic Networks and Irreversibility', in *A Sociology of Monsters,* p. 137.

28. See Law, 'Power, Discretion, and Strategy', in *A Sociology of Monsters,* pp. 175–76.

29. Callon, 'Techno-economic Networks and Irreversibility', p. 137.

functional artefacts, on the one hand, and simple or natural nonfunctional objects on the other.

If, privileging the latter, we were to reserve true thingness only to material entities, the problem of distinguishing the material from the immaterial dimensions of things would at once arise: are the programmes of action inscribed in a machine part of its thingness? Does the framing of a simple tool within a field or fields of possible uses detract from its materiality? Does the soul of the hawk, the biological coding of the thistle make it less thinglike than the pebble, 'equal to itself/mindful of its limits'? Can we distinguish meaningfully between objects which are fully cultural and objects which lack a cultural or at least artefactual dimension?

Alec McHoul tries to do so in a recent article. Defining the conditions of existence of the cultural object (by which he means 'whatever it is that people can produce-and-recognize *as* something', where 'recognize' means 'use-as' or 'know and use')[30] by way of a contrast with naturally occurring objects, he writes that the former 'has meaning; it is a statement; it belongs to a cultural constituency; it's borrowable by other such agents for their own practices; it is assembled from several different technologies; and so on' ('OH', p. 21). And he gives as an example of the difference between naturally occurring and cultural objects the distinction 'between two otherwise identical piles of stones where one is a minor avalanche and the other a cairn' ('OH', p. 21). We might recognize this as the classic aesthetic problem of the *Naturschönes*, the nonintentional object which can be read as though it were intentional, and the problem, conversely, of the transformation effected on the pile of stones (or bricks, for example) by the imputation to it of an aesthetic intention. This topos restates in a different way the question of whether artefacts can be made to stand for all objects, or whether there is a difference *in kind* between pebbles and artefacts.

But look a little more closely at McHoul's specification of the conditions under which cultural objects can be recognized. Centrally, he says, they are characterized by the possibility that their 'propriety', their 'proper' or inscribed or intended function can be reappropriated, turned to a different use. Thus cultural objects are marked 'by the fact that they can always come to mean things, to be recognized, to be used, to be known, to be governed, and cared for in *at least two* (frequently more) different cultural systems, different assemblages of production and recognition' ('OH', pp. 10–11). Cultural and functional hybridity is an ordinary condition of objects, and the most mundane thing, a teacup for example, must be readable in a number of different ways—as an aesthetic object, as a useful object, as the material product of certain highly evolved tech-

30. Alec McHoul, 'Ordinary Heterodoxies: Towards a Theory of Cultural Objects', *UTS Review* 3 (Nov. 1997): 8; hereafter abbreviated 'OH'.

nologies, and so on. The teacup is inherently complex; it 'can only be known, used, recognized, and so on, because it can be so in relation to the confluence of more than a single system'. Conversely, if such things 'were ever given as hypothetically pure and simple productions and recognitions from within a single system, they wouldn't be knowable, usable or recognizable for us at all. (If there were such things, they would be noumenal, natural in the purest sense, and no art or science could know them)' ('OH', p. 12).

But this is just why there can be no neat distinction between cultural objects and naturally occurring objects. The pile of stones formed by a minor avalanche carries equally with it the possibility of being otherwise recognized; it can, for example, be taken for a cairn or taken to be beautiful. The condition of possibility is the same in each case. The stones, the pebble, exist within the realm of that possibility. Is there a difference, then, between the pile and the cairn? Yes, but it's one that, like that between humans and nonhumans, needs to be flattened, read horizontally as a juxtaposition rather than vertically as a hierarchy of being. It's a feature of our world that we can and do distinguish between piles of strewn stone and cairns, between pebbles and cameras, between trees and telegraph poles—between unintended and intended things, things shaped and unshaped—just as we routinely and reasonably distinguish things from persons. But the sort of world we live in makes it constantly possible for these two sets of kinds to exchange properties, for the heap of stones to be read as an arrangement, for the dead matter of the camera to be understood as an inscription of human work and will. The difference that seems to be one of kind is one of use and recognition. Conversely, of course, persons *are* and can be read as things (as bodies, as flesh and bone, living or dead). A discarded camera lying broken at the roadside or discarded on a beach can seem like driftwood, like mere scattered matter. The conversion from simple to complex, functional to nonfunctional, can happen in both directions. Things are naturally shifty, and part of how we think about them should involve the processes of recognition and framing which govern their placing, their point, their uptake. (And it is here that we might begin to catch sight of the limits of the example of the artefact that informs the network model of the being of things: the explanatory form to which it lends itself is that of an economy of uses, and it rarely adumbrates, except at the most general level,[31] the historical dimensions of that economy.[32] Rather, different models of

31. Latour sketches out a genealogy of the modernist principle of 'purification' which radically distinguishes people from things. See Latour, *We Have Never Been Modern*, trans. Porter (Cambridge, Mass., 1993).

32. The beginnings of such a detailed history are being worked out in a number of studies of technological development, of which the most striking is still Steven Shapin and Simon Schaffer, *Leviathan and the Air-Pump: Hobbes, Boyle, and the Experimental Life* (Princeton, N.J., 1985).

the historicity of things are entailed by the example of the commodity, formed within a semiotic economy in which the mode of presence of things is deeply prestructured by the relation between model and series and between material things and their display or representation; or by the example of waste matter, formed by and formative of an economy of value for which it works as the exorbitant supplement that initiates change.)[33]

Much of the most interesting writing on material culture in recent years has been concerned with the conversion processes by which things pass from one state into another. This includes the work of Igor Kopytoff and Arjun Appadurai on the complex trajectories of things in their passage from one regime of value to another; of Nancy Munn, Annette Weiner, and others on the multiple social functions performed by shell tokens in kula exchange; Nicholas Thomas's argument about the 'entanglement' of things, and systems of things, in the colonial encounter; and Michael Thompson's account of the way the zero-degree of value that he calls 'rubbish' works as a generative dynamic in the destruction and formation of value.[34] These all lend support to Thomas's critique of 'the essentialist notion that the identity of material things is fixed in their structure and form'.[35] Things in any minimally complex system carry an indefinite number of actual or potential overlapping uses, significations, and values. No single game exhausts their function; no single description exhausts the uses to which their properties might appropriately or inappropriately lend themselves, and they are always shadowed by the traces of virtual uses and the complicated circuits of knowledge, need, and desire that map those virtualities.

A pebble, a camera, a man who turns into a telegraph pole. What kinds of things are these? The number of possible taxonomies is almost unlimited. Taxonomies inform and shape every sphere of life, from the plethora of folk classifications and the orderings of things by the law to the rigorous formal ontologies of the natural sciences and philosophy.[36]

33. See Frow, 'Invidious Distinction: Waste, Difference, and Classy Stuff', *UTS Review* (forthcoming).

34. See Igor Kopytoff, 'The Cultural Biography of Things: Commoditization as Process', in *The Social Life of Things: Commodities in Cultural Perspective*, ed. Arjun Appadurai (Cambridge, 1986), pp. 64–91; Appadurai, 'Introduction: Commodities and the Politics of Value', in *The Social Life of Things*, pp. 3–63; Nancy D. Munn, 'Gawan Kula: Spatiotemporal Control and the Symbolism of Influence', in *The Kula: New Perspectives on Massim Exchange*, ed. Jerry W. Leach and Edmund Leach (Cambridge, 1983), pp. 277–308; Annette B. Weiner, '"A World of Made Is Not a World of Born"': Doing Kula on Kiriwina', in *The Kula*, pp. 147–70; Nicholas Thomas, *Entangled Objects: Exchange, Material Culture, and Colonialism in the Pacific* (Cambridge, Mass., 1991); and Michael Thompson, *Rubbish Theory: The Creation and Destruction of Value* (Oxford, 1979).

35. Thomas, *Entangled Objects*, p. 28.

36. See Geoffrey C. Bowker and Susan Leigh Star, *Sorting Things Out: Classification and Its Consequences* (Cambridge, Mass., 1999).

But to speak briefly of the ways these things have appeared in the textual contexts in which I've cited them, we could say that if the pebble figures a fully nonhuman world, so entirely and indifferently other that it turns, by a familiar paradox, into a quasi subject in its own right; if the throwaway camera is a black box which opens out to reveal the weave of stories and travels and tracings of work and trade that compose it; and if the man who turns into a telegraph pole speaks to us of the passing of the human and the nonhuman backwards and forwards between and into each other, these three things do not belong to mutually exclusive classes. Rather than thinking in terms of an opposition of things to humans or of inanimate material entities to bodies endowed with consciousness and intention, it makes sense to recognize both the heterogeneity of things in the world—complexly ordered along intersecting scales running from the material to the immaterial, the simple to the complex, the functional to the nonfunctional, the living to the inert, the relatively immediate to the highly mediated—*and* the fluidity of the relations between these categories. Thingness and the kinds of thingness are not inherent in things; they are effects of recognitions and uses performed within frames of understanding (which may be markets or ad hoc negotiations of action or desire or bodily skills as much as they may be intellectual formattings or sedimented codes). And persons, too, count or can count as things. This is the real strangeness: that persons and things are kin; the world is many, not double.

Fateful Attachments: On Collecting, Fidelity, and Lao She

Rey Chow

Collectors are among the most suggestive characters in literary histories, East and West. What is intriguing about them is often not only what they collect but also the paradoxical movement, inscribed in their collecting behavior, from the frivolous to the serious, from the casual pleasures of accumulating nonessential objects to the most perverse kinds of addiction. This movement reveals a type of personality disorder that can be aesthetically fascinating. But aesthetic observations alone have far from exhausted the interpretative possibilities of the collector's obsession; other libidinal ramifications, albeit less frequently observed and explored, lurk behind what seems at first to be a matter of pure eccentric individualism. This is especially the case if a collector is faced not only with his or her collected objects but simultaneously with the forces of socialization, such as the moral imperative of self-sacrifice vis-à-vis a collective. At the juncture between the love for the inanimate as such and the demands of group identity, what might the act of collecting signify? What might an intimacy with inanimate objects do to one's sense of communal belonging, of being part of, say, a national community?

The first and preliminary version of this essay was delivered as a keynote speech at the workshop "China/Japan/Literature/Theory," coorganized by Michel Hockx and Ivo Smits, at the School of Oriental and African Studies, University of London, June 1999. A special note of thanks to Sarah Wei-ming Chen for bringing Lao She's story to my attention years ago and to Bill Brown for his very enabling comments and suggestions during the rewriting process.

Unless otherwise indicated, all translations are my own.

These questions are unveiled by the remarkable, little known short story "Lian" ("Attachment") by the modern Chinese author Lao She, the pen name of Shu Qingchun or Shu Sheyü (1899–1966).[1] In the discussion to follow, I suggest that inscribed in this narrative of an ordinary man's idiosyncratic obsession with collectibles is nothing less than an alternative way of thinking about what we nowadays call identity politics. Accordingly, the far-reaching implications concerning social identity and identification are illuminated not so much through the familiar light of human subjectivity as through the obscure allure of material objects, an allure that in turn tells us something about the passion with which such objects have characteristically been condemned in modern theory.

Often characterized as a humorous realist novelist, Lao She is among modern Chinese writers second perhaps only to Lu Xun in international renown, with works translated into some twenty languages other than Chinese.[2] Lao She had a prolific writing career that spanned over four decades from the 1920s (when he was a lecturer in Chinese at what was then known as the School of Oriental Studies, University of London) to the 1960s and included numerous novels, short story collections, essays, plays, and poems.[3] In the West, he is best known for his novel *Luotuo xiangzi* (*Rickshaw* [1936–37]), which features a lower-class laborer, a rickshaw puller. It is notable that Lao She had authored the first significant proletarian novel in China even as the Chinese Communist Party was gathering momentum and beginning to make propagandist declarations about writing for the people.[4] In "Attachment" we find a very different kind of story, one that returns us by an alternative route to the problematic of collective purpose and struggle in a modern political state.

First published in 1943 during China's War of Resistance against Japan, this story tells of the events that take place in the life of an unremarkable art collector, Zhuang Yiya. Lao She begins by observing that

1. See Lao She, "Lian," *Pinxue ji* (Wenjin chubanshe, 1944), pp. 110–21; trans. Sarah Wei-ming Chen, under the title "Attachment," *Blades of Grass: The Short Stories of Lao She,* trans. William A. Lyell and Chen (Honolulu, 1999), pp. 211–25; hereafter abbreviated "A." The story was first published in the journal *Shi yü chao wenyi,* 15 Mar. 1943, pp. 37–43.
2. For an account of the foreign translations of Lao's works, see Lao She, *Lao She shenghuo yü chuangzuo zishu,* ed. Hu Jieqing (Hong Kong, 1981), pp. 527–28.
3. For a list of Lao's works, see *Lao She,* ed. Shu Ji (Hong Kong, 1988), pp. 266–95.
4. "While the rest of the Chinese literary world debated hotly, and for years, the value of proletarian literature, Lao wrote the novel that the left wing insisted on but failed to produce" (quoted from the dust jacket of Lao She, *Rickshaw: The Novel Lo-t'o Hsiang Tzu,* trans. Jean M. James [Honolulu, 1979]).

Rey Chow is Andrew W. Mellon Professor of the Humanities at Brown University and the author of several books, including, most recently, *The Protestant Ethnic and the Spirit of Capitalism* (2002).

there are two kinds of collectors. The first are those who collect as a distraction. Typically, these collectors "have some learning which enables them to make an honest living" and who, "whenever they have spare money . . . will spend it on things that delight their hearts and enhance their sense of refinement." The second kind of collector is very different: "They collect, but they also peddle. They appear to be refined, but at core they are no different from merchants." These other collectors' collecting "is equivalent to hoarding" ("A," pp. 211–12).

Among theorists of modernity, Walter Benjamin's account of the book collector serves as a relevant intertext here because of its unabashed acknowledgment of the importance, in collecting, of ownership. For Benjamin's book collector, to acquire an old book is to give it rebirth, and collecting is thus part of an endeavor to renew the world by tearing things out of their original contexts and inserting them in the novel one of the collection. Ownership, Benjamin writes, "is the most intimate relationship that one can have to objects. Not that they come alive in him [the collector]; it is he who lives in them."[5] Approaching his topic at the historically transitional period from high bourgeois European society to the mass culture world of global modernity, Benjamin sees in collecting an intellectual practice that allows one to remain in touch with the past. What are being assembled through collecting are not just the things themselves but also memories: "Every passion borders on the chaotic, but the collector's passion borders on the chaos of memories" ("U," p. 60). Together, the twin obsessions with ownership and with memory suggest that collecting carries with it a desire for possessing history, even if such a possession can only come in fragmented, incomplete forms. At the same time, because of the often accidental nature of the encounter with objects—one can never be sure what might come one's way, when and where—the nostalgia for owning the past that is embedded in collecting is, arguably, inseparable from a utopian sense of anticipation, of looking forward to a future that is not yet entirely known.

Benjamin's stance on collecting is thought-provoking because it offers a significant shift from the stern critique of commodity fetishism that has, since Marx's *Capital,* been a predominant way of viewing material things in capitalist culture. In his analysis, Marx points out that commodities are artificial objects that hide the human labor that has gone into their making. To underscore his point that such commodities are false representations of the real relations of production, Marx mobilizes a series of terms—such as "mist-enveloped," "secret," "disguised," "hidden," "absurd"—that foregrounds the fabulous, beguiling nature of their ap-

---

5. Walter Benjamin, "Unpacking My Library: A Talk about Book Collecting," *Illuminations,* trans. Harry Zohn, ed. Hannah Arendt (New York, 1969), p. 67; hereafter abbreviated "U." For another interesting account of collecting, see Susan Stewart, *On Longing: Narratives of the Miniature, the Gigantic, the Souvenir, the Collection* (Baltimore, 1984), pp. 151–69.

peal. "The whole mystery of commodities, all the magic and necromancy that surrounds the products of labour as long as they take the form of commodities," he writes, "vanishes . . . so soon as we come to other forms of production."[6] Despite the ambiguities that may be detected in Marx's memorable portrayal, this portrayal has nonetheless given rise to a prevalent modernist intellectual tendency to regard things as superficial and morally suspect phenomena. In the 1920s, Georg Lukács, for instance, extended the implications of Marx's argument for his own theory of the reification of human consciousness in capitalist society. For Lukács, the thing-dominated relation between man and the world is what gives rise to ideology, an inverted, distorted understanding of history that could only be corrected through the proletarian revolution.[7] A few decades later, Roland Barthes attempted to rewrite the classic critique of false consciousness by way of the tools of semiology, so that reification—which Barthes at that time identified with petit-bourgeois French mass culture, from the advertisements of soap powders and detergents, to ornamental cooking, to toys and plastic—could be dissected through a "scientific" analysis of staggering sign systems working in collaboration with one another.[8] The novelty and fashionableness of his analysis (at the time he wrote) notwithstanding, Barthes was by and large still participating in the Marxist tradition of a deep distrust of the objects that saturate the commercial cultural environment of the industrialized modern world.

In view of this persistent sense of misgiving about things even within bourgeois Western society, it is not surprising that things were also among the evils that had to be purged in a self-consciously revolutionary political state such as Communist China. Among the popular representations of the traumatic happenings of the Cultural Revolution of the 1960s, for instance, is the burning of books and artifacts, the shameful reminders of bygone eras of ideological corruption. Such burning was characteristic of the "class struggle" that was officially launched against both China's feudalist tradition and Western imperialism. As such, the destruction of "bad" things became Communist China's way of honoring, in a literal manner, the critical revolutionary tradition of thing-phobia that arguably began with Marx. Ironically, in the retrospective assessments of the Cultural Revolution, scholars and writers have tended overwhelmingly to interpret such destruction of things as part of a larger violence against humanity—when, strictly speaking, such destruction was genealogically consistent with the Marxist critique of dehumanization as made manifest in the processes of reification and commodification. In the midst of this

6. Karl Marx, *Capital: A Critique of Political Economy,* trans. Samuel Moore and Edward Aveling, ed. Frederick Engels, 3 vols. (New York, 1906), 1:7.
7. See Georg Lukács, *History and Class Consciousness: Studies in Marxist Dialectics,* trans. Rodney Livingstone (Cambridge, Mass., 1971).
8. See Roland Barthes, *Mythologies,* trans. Annette Lavers (London, 1973).

theoretical confusion dominated by humanism (what is human and what is inhuman—preserving things or destroying them?), an interesting question is elided: If these remnants of the past are indeed so despicable, why not simply confiscate and dispose of them in secret? Why the visual, almost celebratory, public display of the act of destruction?

One possible answer, of course, is, So as to teach everyone a lesson. This displacement onto an altruistic, collective purpose is perhaps the most readily available—and "respectable"—antidote to any fascination with things in themselves, a fascination that is usually considered a symptom of selfishness. One reason Benjamin's work is so powerful, it follows, is that he manages to turn this entrenched discursive stereotyping of love-of-things-as-selfishness around by arguing that collecting, however private and selfish it may seem, can also be understood as a kind of historical-materialist practice.[9] He thus makes it possible to lavish attention on the "mist-enveloped" objects of bourgeois modernity while also maintaining Marx's emphasis on a critique of history. Indeed, by combining that emphasis with a sympathetic reading of the inorganic, Benjamin paves the way for a drastically different type of theoretical attitude to materialize toward the universe of objects. At the same time, his modes of inquiry, because they stem concretely from a historical materialism that specializes in the cultural sediments of high capitalist bourgeois Europe, do not necessarily provide answers for every kind of question that arises with the act of collecting and its existential implications—especially when such questions pertain to a non-Western culture in the throes of collective endeavors such as modernization and nationalist revolution. To return to the example of China, what kind of historical lesson is being taught in the Cultural Revolution's practice of setting piles of things on fire, and for what purpose? In the demonstrative spectacle of burning that is supposed to teach everyone a lesson, there seems to be something that exceeds the explicit rationale of the attributed pedagogical function and, for that matter, any attempt to redefine it within a strictly historical materialist framework. It is in this light—that is, the possible theoretical insufficiency of even the most sympathetic historical-materialist reader of things, such as Benjamin—that the work of a writer such as Lao She may, I believe, serve as a provocative alternative approach to the love of things in modern times.

In Lao She's protagonist Zhuang Yiya we see a good example of the Benjaminian passion for owning bits and pieces of history. History here appears in the form of culture—the cherished collectibles that, supposedly, enhance people's sense of their own refinement. Remarkably, Lao She depicts changing attitudes toward history by way of the changing

9. See, for instance, Benjamin, "Eduard Fuchs: Collector and Historian," in *The Essential Frankfurt School Reader,* ed. Andrew Arato and Eike Gebhardt (New York, 1978), pp. 225–53.

attitudes toward collecting and thereby incidentally introduces the issue of *class* understood in cultural rather than economic terms.[10] The first kind of collector, his story tells us, includes those who may be described as members of the new middle class in early twentieth-century urban China: "In terms of profession, these people are perhaps government employees, or perhaps middle school teachers. Sometimes we also find lawyers or doctors" ("A," p. 211). But in terms of the enjoyment of leisure, these people are members of an older society in which culture still means something pleasurable, something to be enjoyed or possessed for itself. Their behavior toward objects, the scraps and ruins of bygone years, contains an indulgent, lingering quality that is fast becoming out of step with their times. By contrast, the second kind of collector is merely opportunistic. Though these collectors may appear to be refined, they collect not for the sake of the pleasure given by the objects but rather in order to make money. Accumulating the bits and pieces of the past is for them simply a means to an end, the end of generating capital. To this extent, they belong to a newer order of society, a class whose ties with the past are strictly through the external relation of trade and exchange. Apart from its commodified forms, which offer themselves to be raided, these people have little or no use for history, which they suppose can be readily discarded in their march toward the future.

Its brevity notwithstanding, "Attachment" is carefully organized into three distinct narrative segments, each bearing a progressively different significance. The first of these segments concentrates on establishing Zhuang as a character with his special attachment. A member of the Jinan gentry, Zhuang is a college graduate and has worked as an administrator and middle school teacher. He began collecting by buying numerous inexpensive items, on which he bestows a rapt, ritualistic attention. Under his gaze, these items become personified, yet at the same time he has to subject them to an impersonal, methodical process of sorting and classifying before they can be safely put away:

> He will take home a couple of such eighty-cent treasures, full of insect holes, smudgy, smeared, and crinkled up like an old woman's face. Only at night, after locking the door to his room, will he savor the pleasures of his modest purchases, handling them over and over again. After numbering them, he will carefully press his seal on them,

10. Among modern Chinese writers, Xü Dishan has made use of the figure of a lower-class woman collector, an urban ragpicker, to point a moral about the hypocrisy of patriarchal society's investment in "cultural refinement" in his short story "Chuntao" ("Big Sister Liu" [1934]), trans. Sidney Shapiro, in *Stories from the Thirties*, 2 vols. (Beijing, 1982), pp. 111–41. I have offered a discussion of this story in *Woman and Chinese Modernity: The Politics of Reading between West and East* (Minneapolis, 1991), pp. 145–50. According to Lao She, Xü was the friend who encouraged him to become a writer; see his essay mourning Xü, "Jing-dao Xü Dishan Xiansheng," in *Lao She*, pp. 184–90.

then put them in a large cedar chest. This bit of exertion will send him to bed, happily weary and satisfied. Even his world of dreams will be quaintly ancient. ["A," p. 213]

As time goes by, Zhuang acquires the reputation—given in jest and with sarcasm by fellow collectors and shop owners—of being a "connoisseur of Shandong's minor artists" ("A," p. 215). Although he would like to earn more in order to buy better pieces of calligraphy and painting, Zhuang never considers using his collection to make money: "Selling his calligraphy and paintings to make some money is something he will not do. For better or for worse, this is *his* collection, and it will follow him to his grave. He will never sell it. He is not a merchant" ("A," p. 216).

The second segment of the narrative begins as Zhuang turns forty. It is 1937, the year in which China was invaded by the Japanese. By this time, Zhuang has fully internalized the idea that he is an expert; he understands the rituals that accompany the activity of collecting and wants to leave a name:

He has made no contribution to the world, but becoming a collector by a fluke isn't too bad an achievement. He hasn't lived in vain. After all, as the saying goes, When people die they leave behind their name; when wild geese fly away, they leave behind their cries!" ["A," p. 218]

Zhuang decides that he will purchase something that is truly worth money. By luck and circumstance, he comes into possession of a painting by the master Shi Qi. Because the authenticity of the piece is at first dubious, many collectors are unwilling to bid, and rumors are soon spread by Yang Kechang, a rival bidder, that Zhuang is a fool for having purchased it. The tables are turned, however, when a connoisseur of great reputation, Mr. Lu, certifies that the Shi Qi is indeed a bona fide work by the master. Since Mr. Lu's seal of approval enjoys credibility even among "European and American" collectors, Zhuang is completely vindicated ("A," p. 221).

It is important to remember that Lao She deliberately places this crowning achievement of collecting in the midst of a national catastrophe, Japan's invasion of China. In terms of symbolic significance, the acquisition and authentication of the painting by Shi Qi are simultaneously the acquisition and authentication of Zhuang's social identity; he is now no longer just fantasizing about being an expert collector but indeed has become one. He has taken on the identity that was previously awarded to him only in jest. The second segment ends at the point when even Yang Kechang, the person who once mocked Zhuang's credibility, is apologizing to him. Precisely at this point, however, Lao She inserts the historical reminder: "July seventh—war breaks out with Japan" ("A," p. 221). The following third and final segment then brings the entire narrative to a crux with the imminent arrival of the Japanese. We are now offered a shocking observation about Zhuang: "It isn't that he lacks patriotic feelings. . . . However, for the sake of his beloved objects, it seems to him that surrender is not necessarily impermissible" ("A," pp. 222–23). During a time of national crisis, Zhuang continues to be unswervingly faithful to his collection of strange old objects. Unlike everyone else, he has not fled and is not exactly sorry for not having done so: "Every day he waits for the Japanese, holding the Shi Qi in his arms and saying to himself, 'Come on then! The Shi Qi and I will die together!'" ("A," p. 223).

One day, Yang comes to inform Zhuang that the Japanese have arrived in town and would like to appoint him as the head of the education bureau. Zhuang's first reaction is that he can't work for the Japanese (see "A," p. 224). Then Yang explains the conditions: should Zhuang agree, he would save his collection and the Japanese would shower him with gifts. Should he refuse, however, his things would be confiscated and he would be punished, perhaps even killed. With tears in his eyes, Zhuang looks at the two chests of his collection and nods his head. The story ends at this point with the statement, "To be attached to something is to die with it" ("A," p. 225).

By the end of this story, the Benjaminian themes of ownership and remembrance, themes that foreground the collector's relationship with the past, have given way to another prominent one, namely, that of fidelity. What makes Lao She's story perplexing is not simply the collector's fetishization of his objects nor even the historical-materialist implications of such fetishization; it is, ultimately, the excessiveness and exclusiveness of his attachment in comparison with which other kinds of attachment do not seem to have any weight. If history is present, it is present by way of issues of identification and its social mediations, and by way of the seeming irreconcilability between the personal collection and the political collective as such.

Interestingly, Lao She took a diametrically opposite attitude toward attachment to things in the autobiographical essay "'Si da jia kong'" ["An Empty House"], which was also written in 1943 and dealt with the similar topic of personal possessions. Lao She describes how, having been forced to move from place to place and often since 1937 in a state of emergency, he has lost all his books, furniture, utensils, and savings, as well as precious gifts of calligraphy and paintings from friends. Despite such losses, his conclusion is an upbeat one. In sharp contrast to the fictional tale, the autobiographical essay ends with a morally unambiguous call to arms: "Let's not be sad over the loss of these books. To save [our] culture, we must [first] defeat the Japanese soldiers!"[11] The remarkable divergence in tone between these two pieces of work from the same period suggests

11. Lao She, "'Si da jia kong,'" *Lao she shenghuo yü chuangzuo zishu*, pp. 421–24.

that Lao She was profoundly ambivalent toward this topic and that he could handle this ambivalence only in the medium of fiction.

Whereas for Benjamin the critical interest of collecting lies in the impossibility of disentangling it from *re*collection, from an attempt to re-assemble the past at the border between tradition and modernity, for Lao She it is less a question of remembrance and nostalgia than a question of incommensurable loyalties, a question he stages explicitly through the confrontation between Zhuang's attachment to his collection and the impulse toward patriotism when one's homeland is besieged.[12] Rather than the temporal and historical transition emphasized by Benjamin, there-fore, the boundary highlighted by Lao She is an existential one, replete with the tensions between submitting to one's native culture and submit-ting to foreigners (in this case, when the foreigners are the enemies invad-ing and looting one's country). Lao She, who was Manchurian rather than Han Chinese, but who served as the secretary general for the All-China Resistance League of Writers and Artists during the eight-year war with Japan, could not but be sensitized to this very fraught, indeed ironic, complex of ethnic and national identification in modern China.[13]

If what the collector in Benjamin refuses to give up is an intimate, albeit outmoded, relationship with the past through its remnants, what is it that a character such as Zhuang refuses to give up?

To respond to this question, it would be necessary to discern the arguably Lacanian theoretical implications of the story's subtle narrative movements. In the first segment, it is possible to see Zhuang as purely rummaging around in the Imaginary: he is obviously attracted to the bric-a-brac; he is even neglecting his obligations to his wife because of his penchant for collecting, but he has not really grasped the meaning of what he is doing. It is almost as though what he is rummaging around

12. Even in real life, Lao She's nostalgia for the calligraphy and paintings he had lost was due primarily to the fact that they had been personal gifts from friends and elders. See Lao She, "'Si da jia kong.'"

13. Lao's interest in his own ethnic background is best seen in the unfinished, semiau-tobiographical novel *Zheng hong qi xia* (first published in 1979), which can be found in *Lao She shenghuo yü chuangzuo zishu,* pp. 179–350; trans. Don J. Cohn, under the title *Beneath the Red Banner* (Beijing, 1982). For a discussion of Lao She's use of his Manchu heritage in some of his works, see Peter Li, "Identity and Nationhood in Lao She's *Teahouse,*" *Chinese Studies* 13 (Dec. 1995): 275–97. One of the incidents that saddened him throughout his life was the manner in which his father was killed. A low-paid palace guard during the last days of the Manchu Dynasty, Lao She's father was carrying gunpowder during the Boxer Rebellion (1900), when the international Eight-Nation Allied Army invaded Beijing. Ignited by an incendiary bomb, the gunpowder exploded; with severe burns, Lao She's father crawled into a grain shop to await death. When his nephew discovered him by chance, his body had turned black and he was unable to speak. He handed the nephew a pair of socks he had removed from his swollen feet; these socks were later buried with some other possessions in his empty tomb. For an account of Lao She's involvement in the resistance against Japan, see *Lao She,* pp. 255–56; see also his own account of his activities during the war in "Bafang fengyü," *Lao She shenghuo yü chuangzuo zishu,* pp. 430–77.

for are not only the objects but also his own self-knowledge. In this regard, the objects may be seen as providing a kind of mirroring function, an external reflection of his groping efforts. This initial rummaging phase gives way next to Zhuang's determination as he reaches middle age to make something of his life by acquiring at least one worthy item. The purchase and possession of the Shi Qi, together with the expert recognition that follows, stands in effect as an entry into the Symbolic at large. If, in the rummaging phase, Zhuang is merely collecting curiosities for idle pleasure, by the time the Shi Qi is bought and authenticated he has found a definite purpose—a confirmed social status—for himself.

The difficult and traumatic question emerges in the third segment with the demand made by the Japanese, which leads to an unexpected encounter with the Real. The scenario around Zhuang at this point is a curious reminder of the well-known one-liner, Your money or your life! In terms of logic, the interest of this threat inheres in the impossibility of choice set up by the word *or,* for although the word gives the illusion of an equal choice between two things, it is in fact an impracticable one: one cannot hold onto money without holding onto life itself. The moral, it follows, is that one can in reality only "choose" life, that in fact this is not a real choice between detachable alternatives because one of the terms is the precondition for the other.

In Lao She's story the logic is quite different. The choice presented to Zhuang by the Japanese is, rather, You can have your collection *and* your life! Holding onto the material object and holding onto life belong in this command on the same plane rather than being separated by the dividing line *or.* But *from the perspective of being a Chinese citizen,* what would be lost, should one opt for this choice, is a crucial kind of value/possession, namely, one's identity as a member of the national community, a community in which *resistance* against the common enemy has to take priority as the definitive meaning of belonging. In this regard, the dilemma faced by Zhuang is more akin to the Confucian teaching of *she sheng qü yi,* to surrender one's physical life for moral righteousness.[14] If we translate this teaching into a form such as Moral righteousness or your life! the choice advocated by the ancients is clear: moral righteousness is more valuable than life and life itself should no longer be viewed as the ultimate possession, as something of which we cannot let go. The ancients were in effect saying: Be morally righteous or be dead. The person who holds onto his own life rather than moral righteousness, so their logic goes, would thus be a coward unworthy of the respect of his fellow human community.

During a national crisis when there is a clearly identifiable enemy, patriotism often occupies precisely the elevated place of "moral righteous-

14. *Yi* can also be translated as "a just cause" or "brotherhood." Its chief emphasis is that of loyalty of a social or communal nature.

ness" in the above imperative. Yet patriotism itself—and moral righteousness by implication—can function so resolutely only because it represses
the ideological mechanism that gives it its momentum. This ideological
mechanism works by polarizing external reality into an antagonism between "us" and "them," offering those who subscribe to patriotism an
unambiguous collective purpose in which to anchor themselves. As Slavoj
Žižek suggests, the reason ideology works is never simply because it tells
lies (*"ideology has nothing to do with 'illusion,'* with a mistaken, distorted representation of its social content") but rather because it serves a protective
function: the polarities, the antagonisms on which ideology depends for
its persuasiveness in fact help to shield us from the terror of a free field
of significatory possibilities and thus from complete identificatory chaos.[15]
Adhering to the ideology of patriotism during war, for instance, would
allow one the security of an epistemological closure (we are good, the
enemy evil), which in turn makes it possible to act without self-restraint
or compunction. Take the character Yang Kechang in Lao She's story. He
is not at all virtuous or likable, but he has internalized the imperative of
patriotism sufficiently to know how to act appropriately under the historical circumstances. While he is obviously working for the Japanese (who
send him to talk to Zhuang) and is thus a national traitor *(hanjian),* he can
act with a clear conscience because he believes that he is only superficially
subservient to the enemy. This is evident when he is contemplating buying the Shi Qi. Even though he doubts the authenticity of the painting,
Yang rationalizes his wish by way of a patriotic reflex, namely, that it is all
right to take advantage of the Japanese:

> He wants to secure the painting at the price of a fake painting, then
> turn around and sell it to the Japanese as genuine. There is no ques-
> tion that the painting is a fine piece. Moreover, even if it should be a
> fake, the Japanese will pay a hefty price for it, because in Japan Shi
> Qi pieces are highly marketable. ["A," p. 219]

When Zhuang refuses to act in accordance with patriotism, he is refusing precisely a socially endorsed ideological anchoring and the protection—the life—that it allows him. His refusal brings to the fore the
repressed fact that there is perhaps something *else* that is not entirely
reducible to the polarization between us and the enemy, that the closure
and security offered by national chauvinism are not necessarily satisfying
or final. But it is lethal to dare forsake such closure and security. Hence,
even though by his decision Zhuang gets to live, the concluding line suggests the opposite to be the case; his surrender to the Japanese is in effect
a kind of death, a suicidal annihilation of an existence that has been so-

---

15. Slavoj Žižek, "Introduction: The Spectre of Ideology," in *Mapping Ideology,* ed.
Žižek (London, 1994), p. 7; hereafter abbreviated "I." See also Žižek, "How Did Marx Invent
the Symptom?" in *Mapping Ideology,* pp. 296–331.

cially and culturally derived. When he was brutalized and humiliated by the Red Guards at the onset of the Cultural Revolution, Lao She, too, chose to commit suicide. (He thus became one of relatively few modern Chinese writers to do so, in contrast to the significant number of suicides among modern Japanese writers.) In retrospect, the narrative of "Attachment" seems to stand as an uncanny kind of foreboding.[16]

As a collector, then, what exactly is it that Zhuang refuses to give up? Is it the love of art itself? Lao She seems, according to at least one critic, to intend such a reading.[17] Consider again the manner in which he begins his tale, when he offers what appears to be a straightforward categorization of collectors into two types. Accordingly, Zhuang could be read as the artistic collector who, unlike his mercenary counterpart, refuses to give up his dedication to art. On closer examination, however, what Lao She has established is a familiar binary opposition between intrinsic and extrinsic relations, a binary opposition that recalls none other than the classical Marxist analysis of commodities in terms of use- and exchange-values (an analysis that, as I mentioned above, is inscribed in a deep-rooted suspicion of commodities as mendacious objects). The problems inherent in such an opposition have been effectively clarified by post-structuralist analysis, which has demonstrated that there can be no object of use- or intrinsic value that does not at some point come into relation with what is other than itself or outside itself.[18] Use- or intrinsic value, in other words, is always already an outcome—an aftereffect—of exchange

16. For a discussion of the clear sense of skepticism toward patriotism that runs throughout Lao She's writings, a skepticism that is accompanied by a recurrent fascination with self-destruction, see David Der-wei Wang, *Fictional Realism in Twentieth-Century China: Mao Dun, Lao She, Shen Congwen* (New York, 1992), pp. 157–200.

17.

> As a story about art, 'Attachment' is Lao She's strongest affirmation of art as the seed as well as the fruit of love; art gives meaning to man's existence. The war years seem to have consolidated Lao She's view of himself as a man of the pen and to have confirmed in his mind the validity and importance of art.
> The last line in 'Attachment' provides a possible reason why Lao She may have committed suicide at the beginning of the Cultural Revolution when he was attacked for his writings (Chen, "Pen or Sword: The Wen-Wu Conflict in the Short Stories of Lao She [1899–1966]" [Ph.D. diss., Stanford University, 1985], pp. 89–98).

18. For a well-known and helpful example of such an analysis, see Jean Baudrillard, *For a Critique of the Political Economy of the Sign,* trans. Charles Levin (St. Louis, 1981). This analysis of Marx enables Baudrillard to deconstruct, in a systematic manner, the hostility toward commodity fetishism that lies at the core of classical political economy. Unfortunately, in Baudrillard's case this perceptive understanding of the contradictions inherent in the traditional Marxist critique of "false consciousness" has led, in his subsequent writings, to the other theoretical extreme, an a priori cynical attitude that tends to scoff at any attempt at ideology-critique because everything is always already ideological. Žižek puts it succinctly:

> one should be careful to avoid the trap that makes us slide into ideology under the guise of stepping out of it. That is to say, when we denounce as ideological the very attempt to draw a clear line of demarcation between ideology and actual reality, this

and circulation. By extension, if art can only receive its value when it is inserted in a system of comparison, circulation, and exchange (however primitive), can there really be a kind of collector who collects purely for the pleasure (use- or intrinsic value) of the objects themselves?

The untenable nature of this binary opposition between the two kinds of collectors is clearly something sensed by Lao She also, for the rest of his narrative performs nothing short of a problematization or deconstruction of the opposition itself. Consequently, we see Zhuang, despite his initial classification, actively building a social life around his collecting habit (befriending antique shop owners, exchanging views with and offering advice to fellow buyers), gradually acquiring a reputation, and finally achieving professional recognition for owning the painting by Shi Qi. Throughout the story we are made aware of the presence of foreigners. When Yang brings two Japanese to look at Zhuang's collection the first time, Zhuang thinks to himself afterwards: "Even the Japanese have come for a viewing. Hm, so this little collection of his has already brought him international recognition!" ("A," p. 218). Already mentioned are the European and American antique collectors who are said to give credit to the connoisseur Mr. Lu's endorsements. These narrative details, which foreground the interpersonal and transcultural import of Zhuang's activities, offer an alternative understanding of the collector to the binary categorization that is set up at the beginning. Such details suggest that, however pure and secluded an object may be in its owner's fantasy, it is virtually impossible to avoid its coming into contact with a system of evaluation that is external to and other than itself (such as money, social recognition, or the professional approval of the connoisseur); the intrinsic or use-value of an object, that is, comes inevitably to be validated by what is foreign or extrinsic to it. By implication, the collector who only collects for the sake of the object (for the love of art) is at best a fantasy; in actual practice he is not entirely distinguishable from the peddling and hoarding ones.

The necessary bifurcation of the narrative into these two incongruent, indeed contradictory, versions of Zhuang (who is said to belong to the first kind of collector, only then to behave in a manner not entirely distinguishable from the second) is further amplified by the enigmatic ending. Let me trace again the narrative thread Lao She provides. According to the categorization at the beginning of the story, what distinguishes the two kinds of collectors is mercenariness, which is normally not considered a virtue. Unlike Yang, Zhuang is not interested in the money he can make from the Shi Qi or his collection. Yet precisely because of this—his lack of mercenariness—Zhuang turns out to be, by

---

inevitably seems to impose the conclusion that the only non-ideological position is to renounce the very notion of extra-ideological reality and accept that all we are dealing with are symbolic fictions, the plurality of discursive universes, never "reality"— *such a quick, slick "postmodern" solution, however, is ideology par excellence.* ["I," p. 17]

implication, the more extreme traitor. This is the unnerving part of the story, but it would be inaccurate to explain it purely by way of a collector's so-called love for art. (Such an explanation would justify a meticulous elaboration of art, things, and objects in the name of how history is really inscribed in them and so forth, but it would also leave intact the binary opposition—between art and reality, between intrinsic and exchange-value, between unworldly and worldly collectors—that is already challenged above.)

What makes Zhuang's decision provocative or scandalous, I think, is not simply that he surrenders (or pretends to surrender, as in the case of Yang) to the enemy for the sake of art but that he is faithfully attached to *something other than the national community itself.* If he "lacks" mercenariness, he nonetheless has not (as the more moralistically minded might expect) filled this lack with patriotism but instead has filled it with devotion to his objects. Though unthinkable under the political circumstances at the time, his surrender to the national enemy, a traitorous act to be sure, is still only symptomatic of a much deeper perversion, namely, that he does not desire to live at all without his objects. His reward of life, then, is only the incidental byproduct of this perversion, this other fidelity. To recall the terms of our argument, not only has Zhuang overturned the assumption that physical life is the ultimate possession (as in the threat, Your money or your life!); he has also substituted dedication to a grand collective meaning such as moral righteousness (as in the imperative *she sheng qü yi*) or love for one's nation with an idiotic and narcissistic dedication to material objects.

As Benjamin writes, "Not that [the objects] come alive in [the collector]; it is he who lives in them." The disturbing nature of Zhuang's behavior has less to do with the fact that he gets to keep his life by being a national traitor/moral coward than it has to do with his absurd feeling that life is worth nothing without his own collection of man-made things.[19] What Zhuang refuses to give up is therefore neither the pure pleasure provided by the objects nor the social recognition he has won through contacts with others; rather, it is the nonexchangeable, irreplaceable *bond* he has established with his collection as such. These inanimate things, which in one respect are mere baggage or garbage, have now been

19. In the semiautobiographical short story "Xiaorenwu zishu" ("Autobiography of a Minor Character") Lao She writes of private property in similar, albeit not identical, terms: "People with brains may consider abolishing private ownership. Some intellectuals may advocate the destruction of the family system. But in my mind, if all private ownership were like our rickety old house and our two jujube trees, I would be happy to declare myself a conservative. Because even though what we possessed didn't relieve us from our poverty, it did provide us that stability that made each blade of grass and each tree come alive in our hearts. At the very least, it made me a small blade of grass always securely rooted to its own turf. All that I am began here. My character was molded and cast here" (Lao She, "Autobiography of a Minor Character," trans. Chen, *Blades of Grass*, p. 244).

raised to a supreme status—not simply the status of physical life itself, which can still be destroyed, but indeed the status of that higher, indestructible sublime ideal, that something *to die for.* In the language of morals, these objects are now on a par and openly vying with *yi,* the intangible virtue of human *fellowship* and *communal belonging* for which—and only for which, it is thought—individual life should be sacrificed.

Lao She's story thus stands as a fascinating exploration of a kind of experience that borders on identificatory anarchy. Being Manchu in Han-dominated China and thus likely to be more alert than many around him to the artificial, that is, historically constructed, nature of patriotic submission, he found in the tale of an apparent betrayal the occasion to dramatize something that goes much further than the ever-shifting polarities of patriotic ideology. This occasion emerges in the most unremarkable of situations, in the humdrum collecting habits of a middle-class citizen who thinks he is simply gathering bric-a-brac for entertainment. In the midst of the objects appears a void that the man refuses to fill with his fellow citizens' belief in the nation. Lao She, who actively championed the cause of resistive patriotism during the war, did not allow the impending nihilism of such a revelation to disrupt the still predominantly realist surface of his storytelling; rather, he relies on the old-fashioned method of letting his story's plot do the work, bringing it to a stop precisely at the moment when the obsessiveness of Zhuang's attachment transforms into the moral horror of surrendering to the Japanese. *Yet which is the greater horror—surrendering to the Japanese, or surrendering to objects?* The matter-of-fact style of his light, descriptive prose notwithstanding, by the ending we are suddenly face to face with the starkest of existential questions: what kinds of attachments make life worth living; what kinds of attachments are worth dying for? Can these questions still be answered with the old moral imperatives? Should Zhuang come to his senses, give up his objects, and die a resistive patriot in the hands of the Japanese? Is he not in some way redeemed by his attachment to the objects—while others go on to destroy themselves as well as other people with the terror of patriotism? With the concluding line, a traumatic chasm has gaped open in the epistemologically indeterminate behavior of this most ordinary of *xiaorenwu* (minor characters).[20]

20. Again, the short story "Autobiography of a Minor Character" may be noted here for the similarly stark existential questions it poses. Consider a passage like the following:

Every time I saw a mangy dog . . . I had to ask, "Why the heck are you living? How the devil do you manage to go *on* living?" This bit of concern did not rise from contempt but from the commiseration of "One who pities another remembers himself." In this pathetic creature I saw my own shadow. Why the heck was I living? How had *I* managed to go on living? Like this dog, I had no answer but felt lost, afraid, and indescribably sad. Yes, my past—what I remembered, what I heard, and what I seemed to remember and seemed to forget—was a stretch of darkness. I did not know how I had groped my way out. [Ibid., p. 234]

The nuanced apprehension of such paradoxes of fidelity was obviously not admissible to the construction of national literature in the modern China of the mid-twentieth century. Instead, patriotism made great leaps forward in multiple performances with continual polarizations of us and them, coercively transforming old allies into new enemies in the years ahead, when communism forged its stronghold in the populace's imagination. Such polarizations fueled the Red Guards' torture and murder of writers and intellectuals such as Lao She in the name of class struggle. Yet Lao She's politically incorrect story from the 1940s teaches us something important about the frenzy of the Cultural Revolution itself. In Zhuang's absolute faithfulness to his objects, in his belief that he would be nothing without them, don't we in fact witness a familiar kind of libidinal investment—*exactly the kind that the party and the nation want of its people?* A passage from Žižek helps explain my point here:

> Why, precisely, does Marx choose the term *fetishism* in order to designate the "theological whimsy" of the universe of commodities? What one should bear in mind here is that "fetishism" is a *religious* term for (previous) false idolatry as opposed to (present) true belief: for the Jews, the fetish is the Golden Calf; for a partisan of pure spirituality, fetishism designates "primitive" superstition, the fear of ghosts and other spectral apparitions, and so on. And *the point of Marx is that the commodity universe provides the necessary fetishistic supplement to the "official" spirituality:* it may well be that the "official" ideology of our society is Christian spirituality, but its actual foundation is none the less the idolatry of the Golden Calf, money. ["I," p. 20; last emph. mine]

Rather than being the moral opposite of the altruistic ideal of class struggle, the loyalty to things—what Žižek calls false idolatry—stands in fact as class struggle's "fetishistic supplement," a supplement that rivals the "official spirituality" of the Cultural Revolution in its demand for the love of the people. The danger posed by this rival "spirituality," which is equally if not more capable of exerting a magical hold on the people, is conjured in the perverse collecting behavior of a minor character like Zhuang. For the party, in other words, things are not realities in themselves but rather symbols: to destroy them is to destroy the evil idea, ideology, tradition, or history behind them; the condemnation of the material is in the end still part of an idealist battle. This, ultimately, is the reason it is imperative, in the process of class struggle, to put on exaggerated performances of the destruction of things. The excessive, ritualistic nature of the burning of books and artifacts is tantamount to a form of exorcism, the point of which is not simply to dispense with objects but to combat—to tame by mimicry—a competing *illusion* in full potency. Nothing short of a deliberate display of violence, repeated at regular intervals for all to see, is deemed sufficient to ward off this competitor's fierce power. Only by such vehement gestures of a ritualized attack can an alibi of official ideology's difference from its enemy be safely established: "Since I (the Communist Party) denounce you (feudalist and imperialist objects), I must be completely different from what you stand for." And, once ritualized in this manner, violence and the loyalty it demands are turned into properties/possessions exclusive to the political state, which can henceforth legitimize, indeed normalize, the ruthless stamping out of an equal contender for popular submission in the name of the collective good. Class struggle, then, assumes in the Chinese Cultural Revolution exactly the function of that socially constructed antagonism, polarized between the purity of our own position and the culpability of an enemy who is not one of us simply because we are struggling against it. Such social antagonism is typically mobilized in such a manner as to allow one group (in this case the party and the state) the privilege of monopolizing violence and loyalty, thereby veiling the more fundamental, radical antagonism inherent to human nature that Lacanians such as Žižek refer to as the Real and that Lao She reveals through the love of objects.[21]

Writing books, Benjamin suggests, is the most praiseworthy method of acquiring them; the books written by an author are, accordingly, his most intimate possessions.[22] This subtle connection among collecting, ownership, and a writer's sense of self-identity—made by a German-Jewish author who chose to end his own life in 1940, when persecution by the Nazis seemed imminent—was well-understood by those in charge of the harassing agenda of the Cultural Revolution. For the latter, it was thus not enough only to demolish relics of the past and strip people of their collectibles; it was also peremptory to attack writers precisely for their most cherished possessions—their writings—and to wrest from them the loyalty that, it was thought, could only belong to the party.

Lao She's story of the art collector gives us a clue to the complex significance of his reported suicide by drowning in Beijing on 24 August 1966. According to the account by his son, Shu Yi, Lao She, who had been ill that summer, was subjected to the typical demeaning interrogations and physical torture and branded a counterrevolutionary by the Red Guards on 23 August. He was detained and abused until after midnight and ordered to report again to the authorities the next morning. When morning came, Lao She left home after saying goodbye to his wife, Hu Jieqing (who thought he was going to the authorities), and to their

21. I have offered a more extended discussion of Žižek's distinction between these two kinds of antagonisms; see my chapter "Ethics after Idealism," *Ethics after Idealism: Theory-Culture-Ethnicity-Reading* (Bloomington, Ind., 1998), pp. 32–54.

22. "Of all the ways of acquiring books, writing them oneself is regarded as the most praiseworthy method" ("U," p. 61).

three-year-old granddaughter. Apparently, he then headed for the small park around Taiping Lake, where, it was later reported by a gatekeeper, he sat motionless the entire day. It is believed that he drowned himself around midnight on 24 August. When his body was eventually collected by his wife and cremated, his family was not allowed to retain his ashes. More than a decade later, when blame for the terrors of the Cultural Revolution was officially laid on the so-called Gang of Four (the influential ultraleftist clique spearheaded by Mao's wife Jiang Qing), Lao She was exonerated by party leaders as one of modern China's greatest writers. In the container that should have held his ashes, his family placed a pair of glasses, a pen, a brush, and some jasmine tea leaves—the very things that had accompanied him in his life as a writer.[23]

During his last moments by the lake, Lao She must have come to the realization that his selfless devotion to his country and the party had come to nothing. For all his patriotism he had been branded an enemy of the people, someone who had to be eliminated. Was his suicide one last act of loyalty—of attachment—to the patriotic community by proving his innocence with his own life? Or was it an act of defiance and self-defense against that very community which had utterly betrayed him, by holding onto his ultimate collection—his *self-possession* as a writer and an intellectual? "To be attached to something is to die with it": the statement with which he had ended the story he wrote in the 1940s now stands as a fateful, if ever cryptic, emblem of the manner in which he ended his own life narrative.

The things that are the most relentlessly condemned have a way of getting their retribution. In the ideologically chaotic aftermath of the Cultural Revolution, in the period of disillusionment, from the late 1970s to the present time, with the altruistic pronouncements of official ideology, what are some of the obsessions that have aggressively (re)surfaced in the People's Republic? Aside from the McDonalds, Rolexes, Mercedes-Benzes, colonial Hong Kong pop music, and Western-style accommodations, it is, in elite and nonelite circles alike, the cosmopolitan culture of Shanghai of the 1920s, 1930s, and 1940s, the pinnacle of a decadent,

23. In a tragic coincidence, then, Lao She's bodyless burial came to resemble his own father's; see n. 13. For an account of the last couple of days of Lao She's life, see Shu Yi, *Lao She* (Beijing, 1986), pp. 178–81; see also Hu's moving account of the circumstances of Lao's death, including the manner in which she received notification to collect his body, documented by Wang Xingzhi, in *Lao She shenghuo yü chuangzuo zishu*, pp. 535–62. A somewhat different account, also citing Shu, is offered by Lyell; see Lyell, "Translator's Postscript: The Man and the Stories," *Blades of Grass*, esp. pp. 279–81. Paul Bady has suggested that Lao She's suicide was most closely paralleled by the suicide of the character Qi Tianyou in *Si shi tong tang (Four Generations under One Roof)*; see Paul Bady, "Death and the Novel: On Lao She's Suicide," in *Two Writers and the Cultural Revolution: Lao She and Chen Jo-hsi*, ed. George Kao (Hong Kong, 1980), pp. 5–14. Bady's view is shared by Shu and elaborated by Wang; see Wang, *Fictional Realism*, pp. 198–99.

commodities-studded materialist environment, that has returned to fasci-
nate the mainland populace with a vengeance, while the Golden Calf,
money, has to all appearances replaced communism as the object of be-
lief/idolatry. Such collective attachments to the "fetishistic supplements"
to "official spirituality" are perhaps simply the latest footnotes to the prophetic tale Lao She told more than half of a century ago.

—Written in 1999, the one-hundredth year of Lao She's birth

"Dying Is an Art, Like Everything Else"

Michael Taussig

I take my title from one of the *Ariel* poems Sylvia Plath was writing up to the day she took her life at the age of thirty, and it is with her preoccupation with death and memory that I am myself preoccupied, most especially when I feel her poems enter into the things they refer to and take me along with them. This I call mimesis, but call it what you will; it stops us in our tracks as a mighty magic come alive as death animates things. As such these things are not symbols or star points for a multitude of poetic associations. Nor are they signs of anything much. Rather they are things, just things, criss-crossing back and forth between the animate and inanimate with the poet as the point of mediation, the question insistently posed, the question that makes us seem no less foolish than wise: How is it that the distinction between subject and object, between me and things, is so crucially dependent on life and death? Why is death the harbinger and index of the thing-world, and how can it be, then, that death awakens life in things? Over there, death, the graveyard where things erupt like gravestones, the entity-place. Here, me and life in buzzing blooming confusion, antithesis of entification. It was not always like this. It needed the Great Awakening brought by Enlightenment for death to finalize things. In other times and places the debate rages.

Before me is a picture of a man with a monk's haircut, seated, with a dark blue shirt down over his knees. He is old but strong and bulky with the body of a farm laborer or forest Indian, bare toes wide splayed into artifacts not known to city dwellers, neither shoes nor feet anymore. If I say he looks crumpled I may give the wrong idea. In his left hand is a lit cigarette. In the other, a fan of yellowing leaves, crackling the air. Clothes are folded over a line, for cupboards are rare in these parts. On the rough-cut floorboards is an open bottle of brandy. A necklace of animal teeth hangs on the unpainted wall boards that run vertically, dark and mottled with age. The smoke from the cigarette catches rays of sunlight. In front of the man sits a young girl with a swathe of black hair almost hiding her face as she leans forward, clasping her hands inside her knees. Now I hear the music, back of the throat sounds, rising and falling, not words, but splintered sound, the sort Artaud appreciated from the body without organs and wrote about from his visit to the Tarahumara with whom he took peyote in northern Mexico and heard the shamans rasp their "mixture of dislocation." For a long time they have been like this. The old man may tell you the song comes from the spirits of a vine that grows where the forest is thick and moist. Is this a plant or a person? You may ask. Animate or inanimate? Maybe all drugs pose that question? The visions come and go. The body disintegrates and reforms. One remembers these things for a time and the memories become part of the real world. The old man and the girl are the epitome of relaxation, a relaxation that goes hand in hand with intense concentration. Whenever there was a moment, two or three times a day, over two or three days, they would do this, together. The girl had been brought here by her grandmother—here being just outside of the small town of Mocoa in the forested foothills of the mountains running down into the Amazon in southern Colombia, in 1983, a place I had visited yearly since 1975.

Not so long ago her father had died. Early morning fishing by the river with the mist still heavy a stranger approached him and he came home vomiting. He had been mixed up with magic, white man's magic. A little later her mother died. And now they were calling the daughter. It was the healer's job to keep her here—on our side, a place I have dwelt in for a long time, assuming all along there was no Other side. Until then, that day just out of Mocoa swept by clouds trailing through the forest. It was the matter-of-factness that took me by storm. It was all so unhurried without fuss, something practical, like planting corn or preparing a meal.

Michael Taussig teaches anthropology at Columbia University. His books include *The Devil and Commodity Fetishism in South America* (1990), *Shamanism, Colonialism, and the Wild Man* (1987), *The Nervous System* (1992), *Mimesis and Alterity* (1993), *The Magic of the State* (1997), and *Defacement* (1999).

Yet it amounted to a divine tug-of-war. Why would these dead have such power? Why would they want her to die?

There is more to tell, but let me refer you to the ethnologist Robert Hertz's turn-of-the-century essay on the collective representations of death (in what are sometimes called primitive or premodern societies), where he concluded his sixty-page essay by saying that for the collective consciousness, death is in normal circumstances merely a temporary exclusion of the individual from human society.[1] In other words what we call human society is here pictured as being human and as being a society by virtue of the fact that the dead are very much part of it.

I don't know if this can really sink in. Hertz, who died still young in the trenches in World War I, made us appreciate the doubleness of death by drawing attention to the two burials that caught his eye in many societies, the first burial being the immediate disposal of the matter of the corpse, the second burial being the disposal of the spirit, a grand affair with much feasting and ceremonial, occurring months if not years later. Hertz offers us a redemptive, or functionalist, approach to grief, pain, and conflict. First you suffer loss. Chaos reigns. Then comes the reward. Peace is established. Life triumphs once more over death and harmony reigns.

And of course it all makes sense, in the end, an old story steeped in the marrow of social science as well as Christianity. There is "temporary exclusion" while the corpse rots between the first, rather peremptory funeral, and the much later second funeral. But this temporariness and this fussing around with two funerals instead of one, and the elaborateness of the second, should drive home to us all the more firmly the inclusion of the dead in human society, thanks to the efforts invested in giving them a rousing send-off. It's not that easy to shove them out into the cold blue yonder. The *inclusion* to which Hertz refers us is likely to be a vexed state of affairs, so vexed, in fact, that it amounts to a fundamental flaw running through the core of society like the San Andreas fault. It would be nice if the dead could be tucked away, far away, so there would be two worlds, one for the living and one for the dead. It would be almost as nice if they were given visiting privileges, say one or two days a year, like the Mexican Day of the Dead, candies and grinning skulls with picnics in the cemetery, and as a result of this liberal attitude they then promised to keep well out of the way for the remaining 364 days. But what if they're uncontainable, like illegal immigrants in California and Texas? To force the issue a little, imagine the city of New York with an additional borough, and this extra borough is the borough of the dead, bigger than all the other boroughs

---

1. See Robert Hertz, "A Contribution to the Study of the Collective Representation of Death," *Death and the Right Hand,* trans. Rodney and Claudia Needham (London, 1960), p. 86.

put together. What lives might the dead there lead? How do they communicate with the living? Are they part of the bridge-and-tunnel crowd? Does the government grant them a super senior status, and can they get into the movies at a reduced rate? What is their substance as they pass invisibly through the subway turnstiles without tokens to the consternation of the disguised police waiting their prey? What power might they have over us and how could they be gotten rid of as has been achieved in any decent city in America? Are they like the homeless, or vice versa? Maybe the mayor, having dealt with the squeegee people looming out of the crossroads and entrances to the city, has the answer. And what of my comic manner?

"'Your job now is to find the Western Lands,'" William Burroughs instructs in his book of that name. "'Find out how the Western Lands are created.' . . . Just as the Old World Mariners suddenly glimpsed a round Earth to be circumnavigated and mapped, so awakened pilgrims catch hungry flashes of vast areas beyond Death to be created and discovered and charted, open to anyone ready to take a step into the unknown, a step as drastic and irretrievable as the transition from water to land."[2]

Burroughs sounds the alarm. As usual. It seems funny at first. Poking fun at the dead so as to normalize them to the extent they almost disappear. After all, that's what being dead is supposed to be about. Disappearance. But then there's this stuff that can't be quite contained creeping round the edges like Burroughs himself. He goes back in order to advance, just like his prose form, strung out on amputated lyricism.

Crowds saturate *The Western Lands,* the lands of the dead, along with the clash of scents and color, not to mention unseemly sex. Why crowds, you ask? Why indeed? And in *Crowds and Power,* written twenty years after his frightening experience in the crowd of workers marching on the police in Vienna in the mid 1930s, Elias Canetti said the crowd of preeminent importance, what we might call the ur-crowd, were "the invisible crowds" of the dead, and he suggests all religions begin with this crowd. They are like a force of nature, like the wind, like rain, pressing in, rivers, forest, sand, heaps haunting the earth, and one of their notable characteristics is to envy, even hate, you and me. "Passionately and continually they seek to get hold of the living."[3] He gets his ideas from ethnography from Scotland, Uganda, South Africa, China . . . you name it. And the implication seems to be that this crowd is very much with us still, even if it's dropped out of sight. Invisibility can be real or apparent.

What is needed here is a decisive alienation-effect that can whip us around the repressions death fosters, letting us see anew the magical powers human societies have lodged therein. Nietzsche does this, I think,

2. William S. Burroughs, *The Western Lands* (New York, 1987), pp. 74, 115.
3. Elias Canetti, *Crowds and Power,* trans. Carol Stewart (New York, 1963), pp. 42, 262.

when he remarks that "the living is merely a type of what is dead, and a very rare type."[4] Freud does the same in *Beyond the Pleasure Principle*, written back-to-back with his essay "The Uncanny," where he sees life as but a circuitous path to death.[5] Or take Marcel Mauss in his *General Theory of Magic* with his wide-eyed question, "What are magical spirits?" To which he answers that the first category of magical spirits "embraces the souls of the dead."[6] Death, it appears, is the fount of magic! A biting illustration is provided by one of the most detailed ethnographies of the 20th century, written by Alicia and Gerardo Reichel-Dolmatoff. They lived permanently in Colombia and spent over a year in a village of mestizos and Indians they call Aritama in the foothills of the majestic Sierra Nevada on the coast of northern Colombia in the 1940s (the mountain overlooking Joseph Conrad's *Nostromo*). They too found the dead there to be an awfully envious lot—envious of the prosperity of their descendants and of all the things they did not have and enjoy when they were alive. "So," the ethnographers went on to say, "if the living should boast of their health or luck or property, the spirits are likely to destroy it and take revenge by making its possessor poor and ill. Anything that might rise above the average will call their envious attention—a beautiful woman, a healthy child, a strong man, a tree laden with fruit, a new dress, a plentiful harvest. Sometimes the living even deem it necessary to destroy such obvious prosperity in order not to awaken the spirit's envy."[7]

Unlike Hertz, the Reichel-Dolmatoffs tell us the spirits of the dead are not disposable. You live in Aritama, they say, in "constant fear of annoying the spirits, either by failing to make sufficient offerings or by arousing their envy" (*PA*, p. 353). And boy! Are these dead capricious! At night they go dancing through the streets, singing and talking, and they will say, "Oh! Let us enter so and so's house, for they are so generous with their offerings." They go in, and that person dies. They pass another house and say, "Oh! Forget them, they're so mean! They never make offerings!" And so they pass by and that person lives. As the ethnographers say, "There seems to be no way out" (*PA*, p. 353).

These dead are not concerned with morals, with adultery or murder, for instance. They only want the living to share with them, and they control all individuals by the sending of illness. You might think they are like

4. Friedrich Nietzsche, *The Gay Science*, trans. Walter Kaufmann (New York, 1974), p. 168.

5. See Sigmund Freud, *Beyond the Pleasure Principle*, in *The Standard Edition of the Complete Psychological Works of Sigmund Freud*, trans. and ed. James Strachey, 24 vols. (London, 1953–74), 18:7–64.

6. Marcel Mauss, *A General Theory of Magic*, trans. Robert Brain (1902; New York, 1972), p. 82.

7. Gerardo and Alicia Reichel-Dolmatoff, *The People of Aritama: The Cultural Personality of a Colombian Mestizo Village* (Chicago, 1961), p. 352; hereafter abbreviated *PA*.

the saints, intermediaries between person and God. No way! They *are* the religion! Above all, how hard it is, I think, for ethnographers to convey the mix of toughness and tenderness. "There is no love for the ancestors," these anthropologists tell us about this Colombian village. There is "no real worship. They are essentially evil and dangerous, and so they are feared" (*PA*, p. 354). The ancestors appear in dreams and nightmares and can be heard singing and dancing in the night, or "moaning in the forest. . . . Old people, remembering the hard times they have seen, often speak of the revenge they can take out upon their enemies [once they are dead]. With ill-disguised bitterness they point out that their descendants, who at present pay scant attention to their needs," will be after death singing another tune once they are dead (*PA*, p. 354).

There must be more to the story, yet we all agree that something has happened to death with the modern age. It seems to have disappeared from sight, and there is an awkwardness all round about what to do and say other than wallow in death-kitsch. This makes it impossible for us to deal with the unsentimental view of death in Aritama or know what to think when a dead man and woman call their little daughter to join them in death just outside Mocoa. With the famous "disenchantment of the world" the spirits retreat, no longer singing and dancing in the streets or moaning in what's left of the forest. The spirits retreat, said Freud, into the unconscious; that was his view of mental history over the long haul. Or maybe the dead simply die and NYC shrinks to the five boroughs along with the expansion of prisons for first-time drug offenders, prisons being the preeminent form of the modern death-space for the young men of the inner city in the U.S. today, each prisoner, no doubt, with his own story.

I would like to say—from the fullness of my naivete—that poetry fills this vacuum, that poetry is forced to fill this vacuum, and that poetry does this because it is the most mimetically nuanced form of verbal representation and expression there is, breaking up language no less than composing it, exquisitely self-aware while at the same time resolutely on the march with something to say. Nietzsche refers to the emptiness after the death of God as filled with a presence, the breath of empty space, and so even if the storyteller falls on hard times this space of death might offer opportunities to a poet who can pick up on the alarming notion that "the living is merely a type of what is dead, and a very rare type." It is my argument, then, that the poetry in question will criss-cross the division between the living and the dead creating thereby *a state of living-death* that will bring the poet into full flood and language into its mimetic birthright. Benjamin may have lost hope for the storyteller, but he was quick to seize on the magic of the commodity, the congealed pulse of the market, as epitomizing thinghood itself. By virtue of such an epitome he constructed an extraordinary poetics of death. As a critic close to him pointed out, the cast of Benjamin's thought was one of "'natural history,'" guided by the need to become a thing in "order to break the catastrophic spell of things."[8]

"'I am writing the best poems of my life,'" she wrote her mother about the *Ariel* poems a few days before her death. "'They will make my name.'"[9] And only a fellow poet could come whistling out of Aritama— for example, Anne Sexton (reportedly): "Her suicide was her most brilliant career move."[10] But also consider the opinion of Alfred Alvarez, who, I believe, thought that the *Ariel* poems look like they were written posthumously. I felt this, too. Think about it. It's as if the spirit of the dead poet is already there installed in life—living-death did we not say?—installed in the poet right on schedule: "Dying/ is an art, like everything else./ I do it exceptionally well."[11] Death is the death of God, the Father, Otto, whose gangrenous influence spreads far and wide across the poet's discursive net.

> If I've killed one man, I've killed two—
> The vampire who said he was you
> And drank my blood for a year,
> Seven years, if you want to know.
> Daddy, you can lie back now.
>
> There's a stake in your fat black heart
> And the villagers never liked you.
> They are dancing and stamping on you.
> They always *knew* it was you.
> Daddy, daddy, you bastard, I'm through.[12]

Could an Aritama peasant do better, cursing the dead? And what does she mean by saying if I've killed one man, I've killed two?

Ask Ted Hughes, for he certainly felt he had become possessed by the spirit of old Otto in his wife's vision of things. Breaking thirty-five years of silence after her death, as the newspapers would have it, he published just before his recent, anticipated, death, his *Birthday Letters*, a history, a love song, a lament, eighty-six poems in a chronological order of events big and small that are also communications with the spirit of the dead person, written in a continuous past-present tense—the tense of

8. T. W. Adorno, "A Portrait of Walter Benjamin," *Prisms,* trans. Samuel and Shierry Weber (Cambridge, Mass., 1981), p. 233.

9. Diane Wood Middlebrook, "Poetic Justice for Sylvia Plath," 27 Jan. 1998, *New York Times,* p. A19.

10. Ibid., p. A20.

11. Sylvia Plath, "Lady Lazarus," *Ariel* (New York, 1966), ll. 43–45, p. 7.

12. Plath, "Daddy," *Ariel,* ll. 71–80, p. 51.

life-in-death. "Who will remember your fingers?/ Their winged life? They flew/ With the light in your look." These her fingers become independent, animated, objects, performing their own clowning with those other dead objects, the keys of the piano, to make music: "They performed an incidental clowning/Routine of their own, deadpan puppets." These same fingers that play on the keys of the typewriter, "Possessed by infant spirit."[13] Oh yes! Now read "Freedom of Speech" when Canetti's and Burroughs's invisible crowd of the dead, including Sylvia, gather for her sixtieth birthday party thirty years after her death where, in the cake's glow, she feeds Ariel grapes from between her pursed lips. Ariel is seated on her knuckle, she is so solemn. Everyone laughs. The late poppies—about which Sylvia wrote so often, red. Red, and more red—laugh, too, while the candles tremble, their tips trying to contain their joy. Do I need to point out that this is a rip-roaringly animated world, of things become animated *precisely because of the invocation of the dead*—in an age when this cannot, or should not be done, taking advantage, precisely, of what we like to call poetic license. What is that? "And your Mummy/Is laughing in her nursing home," while you father laughs too—all these ghosts and things intermingled and come alive—

> And the stars,
> Surely the stars, too, shake with laughter.
> And Ariel—
> What about Ariel?
> Ariel is happy to be here
>
> Only you and I do not smile.[14]

These birthday poems "break" the famous Hughes silence on his side of the story, says James Fenton, professor of poetry at Oxford who finds it of interest that the poetry is not only poetry but is "information" as well—a remark we could, without loss of naivete, also very much apply to Plath's poems, too, prior to taking her own life.[15] Yet I don't think *information* is the right word, although I see why he would say and be puzzled by this quality of history, setting history to rights and much more as well, a strange path for poetry but actually, as I have been arguing all along, it is what you should expect as poetry is sucked in by the breath of empty space. That's the point. "'They address her as if she's still alive, as if he can talk with her,'" writes another critic. "'I find it very moving.'"[16]

---

13. Ted Hughes, "Fingers," *Birthday Letters* (New York, 1998), ll. 1–3, 5–6, 20, p. 194.
14. Hughes, "Freedom of Speech," *Birthday Letters*, ll. 13–14, 16–21, p. 192.
15. Anon., "NB," *Times Literary Supplement*, 23 Jan. 1998, p. 16.
16. Sarah Lyall, "A Divided Response to Hughes's Poems," *New York Times*, 27 Jan. 1998, p. E7.

Another is quoted, "'The really amazing thing is that it's written in this continuing present tense, as if she'd just left the room or was just about to come back into the room.'"[17]

Once or twice the poet laureate talks to her father's spirit as well. Old Otto Plath is in fact most everywhere here, and to the people of Aritama that would be no surprise, I guess.

> Your ghost inseparable from my shadow
> As long as your daughter's words can stir a candle.
> She could hardly tell us apart in the end.
> Your portrait, here, could be my son's portrait.
>
> I understand—you never could have released her.
> I was a whole myth too late to replace you.
> This underworld, my friend, is her heart's home.
> Inseparable, here we must remain.[18]

This could almost be the old healer under the clothesline, smoke trailing. "Heh Otto! Give us a break! Let go man." The throat explodes in drum rolls and a quiet uneven hum fills the space. A song? A poem? A chant? A noise like the noise of animals and the wind? What is a song? Or a poem? The young girl looks like she's being reborn from between his legs, sitting as she is, her body between his knees with her hands clasped. She faces outwards, face so serious, her leg in its plastic sandal twisted slightly. The two of them, she in her white dress, he in dark blues and greens, form a third creature, almost a monster, two-headed, one above the other, a four-legged humming creation. What holds it in stasis, like a statue locked in ecstasy, is the seriousness of the faces. These faces bore through time. Of course cynics will say Hughes emphasizes the mythic and the Father so as to deal with his own debts. How Aritama!

The dead father was right there, right in the table the poet laureate made for his wife, the table into which her words driving down would meet the father rising.

> I wanted to make you a solid writing-table
> That would last a lifetime.
> I bought a broad elm plank two inches thick,
> The wild bark surfing along one edge of it,
> Rough-cut for coffin timber. Coffin elm
> Finds a new life, with its corpse,
> Drowned in the waters of earth. It gives the dead
> Protection for a slightly longer voyage

17. Lyall, "In Poetry, Ted Hughes Breaks His Silence on Sylvia Plath," *New York Times,* 19 Jan. 1998, p. E3.

18. Hughes, "A Picture of Otto," *Birthday Letters,* ll. 13–20, p. 193.

Than beech or ash or pine might. With a plane
I revealed the perfect landing pad
For your inspiration. I did not
Know I had made and fitted a door
Opening downwards into your Daddy's grave

You bent over it euphoric
With your Nescafé every morning.
Like an animal, smelling the wild air,
Listening into its own ailment,
Then finding the exact herb.
It did not take you long
To divine in the elm, following your pen,
The words that would open it. Incredulous
I saw rise through it, in broad daylight,
Your Daddy resurrected.[19]

Yet it would be a mistake, according to her teacher, Robert Lowell, to see her *Ariel* poems as fruit of a game of "Russian roulette with six cartridges in the cylinder." These poems, he says, "tell that life, even when disciplined, is simply not worth it."[20] Is this analogous to Dido Merwin's observation that Lowell "used words like a Tommy gun whereas [Plath] used silence like nerve gas?"[21]

Dido Merwin was wary of Plath's moods, and the silence she evokes refers to Plath's being, not her poems; but to the degree it is possible let us try to understand Plath's poetry as silence and vice versa, a "silence" I take to be the archaic fear that, following Georges Bataille, Julia Kristeva called *abjection,* a state of uneasy and incomplete separation of Self from Other, a state of blurred boundaries, what Heidegger would have delighted in thinking of as a delirious speed up in Being, given that as Being is foregrounded, so concrete beings recede, and vice versa in a crazy-making oscillation of unconcealment and concealment. For it was Kristeva's inspired idea that such abject status provokes a language of dizzying virtuosity as language substitutes for the object world in general, and for the feared, the phobic, object in particular.[22] Here everything hangs on what is meant by substitution. What I call mimesis. With hysteria, for instance, one's body "talks" as an illness spouting repressed history—the last refuge of Benjamin's storyteller (Anna O) perched on the ominous

19. Hughes, "The Table," *Birthday Letters,* ll. 1–23, p. 138.
20. Robert Lowell, foreword, Plath, *Ariel,* pp. x–xi.
21. Dido Merwin, "Vessel of Wrath: A Memoir of Sylvia Plath," in Anne Stevenson, *Bitter Fame: A Life of Sylvia Plath* (Boston, 1998), p. 336.
22. See Jacqueline Rose, *The Haunting of Sylvia Plath* (Cambridge, Mass., 1991), and Julia Kristeva, "Something to Be Scared Of," *Powers of Horror: An Essay on Abjection,* trans. Leon S. Roudiez (New York, 1982), pp. 32–55.

edge of the *case study*. With fetishism, objects "talk" through complex games they play with the phallus that is not there (Freud) or through the value accorded the misplaced concreteness of the commodity (Marx). But only with abjection, when boundaries between self and other become blurred and fearsomely up for grabs, does language soar because abjection is the preeminent state of living-death where subject and object stage their epistemic panic.

> The month of flowering's finished. The fruit's in,
> Eaten or rotten. I am all mouth.
> October's the month for storage[23]

The point is that such linguistic virtuosity should be called for what it is, namely, mimetic flux in which the thingness of things is there in your face criss-crossing perceiver and perceived, object with object.

> If only the wind would leave my lungs alone
> Dogbody noses the petals. They bloom upside down. . . .
> Cabbageheads: wormy purple, silver-glaze,
> A dressing of mule-ears, mothy pelts, but green-hearted,
> Their veins white as porkfat
>
> O the beauty of usage!
> > ["PB," ll. 12–13, 18–21, p. 131]

In the section called "Witch Burning" of this same poem we read:

> If I am a little one, I can do no harm.
> If I don't move about, I'll knock nothing over. So I said,
> Sitting under a potlid, tiny and inert as a rice grain.
> They are turning the burners up, ring after ring.
> We are full of starch, my small white fellows. We grow.
> It hurts at first. The red tongues will reach the truth.
> > ["PB," ll. 154–59, p. 135]

Linguistic overmastery indeed. But note how achieved: not by metaphor but through a mimetic burnout of metaphor fused at white heat into the referent—"Their veins white as porkfat"—in which language attains the status of witchcraft-substance, *mangu*, an organic substance in the abdomen of the Azande witch, no less than in the bodies of those who dance so as to undo the work of the witch. They are poets, too, all day long they dance in the African sun. They dance the question, said the ethnographer. Not only do they divine with their lips, but with their entire body, thanks to the medicines that their dancing activates, enabling

23. Plath, "Poem for a Birthday," *Sylvia Plath: Collected Poems*, ed. Hughes (London, 1981), ll. 1–3, p. 131; hereafter abbreviated "PB."

prophecy. These substances in the bodies of the witch no less than in the dancers are like persons. The medicine of the "poison oracle hears like a person and settles cases like a king, but it is neither a person nor a king, being simply a red powder."[24] Our ethnographer struggles manfully with the dilemma thus posed; a thing is like a person but is not one. Marx struggled, too, seeing people like things and vice versa as the trademark of capitalist epistemology following which Adorno describes the cast of Benjamin's thought as one of "natural history," guided in the materiality of its writing by "the need to become a thing in order to undo the catastrophic spell of things." This is more than an analysis. It's prescription. So we find ourselves back with spells and magic—Marxist magic, kabbalah magic, Zande magic, and of course death-magic, as Mauss and Hertz have instructed us this long century—the difference, the huge difference, between the poetry and the ethnography being that for poetry, death, like irony, is seductive, "an art, like everything else." Things and death criss-cross in (her) poetry, making amends for that world we have lost, whether of the folktale into which Hughes sinks to join wolves' singing for the two dead orphans, or what we anthropologists bring home from faraway seeming times and places, that world of the two funerals with its stories authorized, as Benjamin would say, by death; all these images and stories lie like ghosts in our modern world. There they sit in libraries and more often than you think in living speech. Here they are today with us heavy with literality because they are true, authorized and heavy with truth, waiting to be metamorphosed so as to energize our speech. And for this we are grateful, not least to the anthropologists and historians with their stories of sacrifice and ghosts. But then there is poetry because poetry is what after the death of God is the privileged form of mimetic language that can invoke the spirits of the dead as the ground for communion with things as people. "Eaten or rotten I am all mouth." The very "language of things" Benjamin was drawn to. "'If I could paint,'" she said the day before she died, "'I would want to paint things. I love the thinginess of things.'"[25]

24. E. E. Evans-Pritchard, *Witchcraft, Oracles, and Magic among the Azande* (Oxford, 1937), p. 321.
25. Stevenson, *Bitter Fame*, p. 295.

"Paths That Wind through the Thicket of Things"

Lesley Stern

Guided by film, then, we approach, if at all, ideas no longer on high-ways leading through the void but on paths that wind through the thicket of things.

—SIEGFRIED KRACAUER, *Theory of Film: The Redemption of Physical Reality*[1]

"Do you imagine/the bird desires *me?*" asks the speaker in a poem called *The Gutman Variations,* a poem inspired by *The Maltese Falcon* (John Huston, 1941). The speaker is clearly Caspar Gutman (or Sydney Green-street), but who is the addressee? Sam Spade (or Humphrey Bogart), we might surmise, or perhaps when Gutman interpellates an interlocutor he simply summons you who read and watch.

> Do you imagine
> the bird desires *me?* Entirely

This paper has benefited from exchanges with Jeffrey Minson, John Frow, Bill Brown, Miriam Hansen, Janet Bergstrom, Richard Smith, and my former film colleagues at the University of New South Wales: Jodi Brooks, Ross Harley, George Kouvaros, and Lisa Tra-here. Research and writing support was provided by the Getty Research Institute (the semi-nar on Gesture) and the Varuna Writer's Centre (Australia). Early versions were presented to the department of anthropology, Sydney University, and the Humanities Research Pro-gramme, University of New South Wales. I am grateful to the participants for their criti-cisms and suggestions.

1. Siegfried Kracauer, *Theory of Film: The Redemption of Physical Reality* (Princeton, N.J., 1997), p. 309; hereafter abbreviated *TF*.

        not. The bird is indifferent.
        The bird is a bird sir. And
        I mean to have it.[2]

It's an odd bird, a funny sort of a thing, that tired old Maltese falcon. Is it a bird, or is it a thing, or is it an object? It doesn't fly and it doesn't sing, it is by no means real and yet it is not, by any stretch of the imagination, simply imaginary. Although the film is called *The Maltese Falcon*, within the world of the film the falcon itself is referred to simply as "the black bird." But it is not really black (it is gold),[3] nor is it really a bird; it is of course, and as we all know, merely a statuette, and it is a long time before it materializes, within the diegesis, as a visible physical presence.[4] In this respect it is akin to Rosebud in *Citizen Kane* (Orson Welles, 1941). It is a thing that makes other things (things of a different order) happen; that is to say, its value is functional, and its function, inflected within an emblematic or hermeneutic register, is primarily narrative. But is this all? Gutman thinks not. When he says, "the bird is indifferent," he is not, à la Robbe-Grillet, arguing for the alterity of things, and neither is he concerned with nuance, with thirteen ways of looking at a blackbird. For him there is only one way. The bird is his desire, but it is desire objectified:

        Tell me the bird is unreal sir? It's
        my Desire. I have held the bird sir
        for just moments. Encrusted
        with diamonds from beak to claw.
        I held it against my chest. I felt it.
                      [*GV*, ll. 27–31]

So if it is desire objectified, is this merely to say it is a commodity? Well, this might be the case, but it is no ordinary, mass-produced commodity; it is more like a clandestine commodity, a nefarious luxury item.

    2. John Jenkins and Ken Bolton, *The Gutman Variations* (Adelaide, 1993); hereafter abbreviated *GV.*
    3. It looks black because it is encased in lead, but really it has a heart of gold. The fact that the bird in the film turns out to be *really* black (and therefore not the real bird) is in keeping with its fantasmatic identity. It is the true black heart of the *noir* drama.
    4. It does, however, appear in a sort of preface to the film. Presented as an iconic image, three-dimensional but isolated in space, it is accompanied by written text explaining its provenance and legendary status.

Lesley Stern (lfstern@ucsd.edu) is professor of visual arts at the University of California, San Diego. She is the author of *The Scorsese Connection* (1995) and *The Smoking Book* (1999) and editor, with George Kouvaros, of *Falling for You: Essays in Cinema and Performance* (1999). She is working on a book about things in the cinema.

Produced for purposes other than trade it becomes, to borrow a notion from Arjun Appadurai, diverted (as is often the case with works of art) into a trade trajectory.[5] It is a thing of value in circulation. Gutman understands the circulation of desire, but also the production and circulation of surplus-value. Invoking the presence of that notorious Lacanian Sam Spade/Humphrey Bogart, the poetic Gutman takes jovial if argumentative issue with the putative suggestion that between him and the thing there might be a touch of projection or cathexis:

> Identity and wholeness remain at the level
> of fantasy sir. Do they imagine sir
> that were I to bank the bird I would bank the *Other*
> [*GV,* ll. 155–57]

I'm reminded of another diverted object, an object that not only inaugurates a story, but also inaugurates the whole tradition of detective fiction. The *Maltese Falcon* is reminiscent of Wilkie Collins's *The Moonstone* (1868). The moonstone (as a thing, not a novel) is an accursed object—we know this from the very beginning—and it is cursed because it has been plundered, prized from its originary place and context. The same is true of the Maltese falcon (as a thing, not a movie), but we only discover that it is a fake at the end of the movie when it turns out to be not original at all, just one in a series. As accursed objects both the moonstone and the Maltese falcon generate narrative effects, but also—as accursed objects—they generate an excess of affect. Rather like those other famous cinematic birds, those malevolent Hitchcockian things par excellence.

"This Unreal Thing"

> I see what is not and I see this unreal thing exactly.
> —JEAN EPSTEIN, "Ciné-Mystique"[6]

Why begin a paper on things in the cinema with *The Gutman Variations,* a poem that, however hilarious it may be, can hardly stand as a comprehensive critique of *The Maltese Falcon?* First, this poetic apprehension of the film opens up a productive space for contemplating the mutability of things in the cinema. It gestures simultaneously towards the self-evidence of the object (in this case, one of the most clichéd of cinematic objects) and the difficulty of locating it or, perhaps we should say,

5. See Arjun Appadurai, "Introduction: Commodities and the Politics of Value," in *The Social Life of Things: Commodities in Cultural Perspective,* ed. Appadurai (Cambridge, 1986), pp. 3–63.

6. Jean Epstein, "Ciné-Mystique," trans. Stuart Liebman, *Millennium Film Journal* 10–11 (1984): 192.

of ascribing a value to it, to the thing. It is, as Sam Spade says, in the last line of the film, "the stuff that dreams are made of":[7] it is phenomenal and ephemeral, solid and phantasmatic,[8] it partakes of both a fictional and documentary identity, it is real and imaginary, a thing and a commodity, an object incarnated as a sign[9] and an unremarkable quotidian thing. But enough of the binaries; what is interesting about that odd bird, that funny sort of a thing, that tired old Maltese falcon, is its mutability. It is not fixed in its identity but has the capacity to be different things, sometimes simultaneously, but also at different times. It partakes of different temporalities. We might usefully borrow here from the language of contemporary anthropology to indicate how things move in and out of various "regimes of value" and "spheres of exchange" and to focus attention on both "the *cultural biography* and the *social history* of things."[10] But for all its usefulness this particular anthropological perspective cannot adequately apprehend something about the rendering of things that is particularly cinematic: the way in which the moving image (of the thing) has a capacity to move the spectator, to generate affect. This cannot be explained merely by invoking referentiality. More plausible is the proposition that while the indexicality of the cinematic image creates an effect of material presence, the movement of the image simultaneously renders that presence potentially unstable and ephemeral. This is not to say that only in the cinema are things charged with affect, nor that they are neces-

7. A line apparently contributed by Huston, not the hard-boiled Hammet. See James Naremore, *More Than Night: Film Noir in Its Contexts* (Berkeley, 1998), p. 61.

8. One could say that it is a marker of the "irreducible gap between the I of apperception and the noumenal Thing-that-thinks" (Slavoj Žižek, "'The Thing That Thinks': The Kantian Background of the *Noir* Subject," in *Shades of Noir: A Reader*, ed. Joan Copjec [London, 1993], p. 210). It is like the Thing-in-itself of the real, a fragment of the real that presents/materializes as a fantasmatic character.

9. See Appadurai, "Introduction," p. 38.

10. Ibid., p. 34. See also Igor Kopytoff, "The Cultural Biography of Things: Commoditization as Process," in *The Social Life of Things*, pp. 64–91, and Nicholas Thomas, *Entangled Objects: Exchange, Material Culture, and Colonialism in the Pacific* (Cambridge, Mass., 1991). Appadurai and Kopytoff both draw on the work of Paul Bohannan, "Some Principles of Exchange and Investment Among the Tiv," *American Anthropologist* 57 (1955): 60–70 and "The Impact of Money on an African Subsistence Economy," *Journal of Economic History* 19 [1959]: 491–503. There are limitations in borrowing from the language of anthropology. Clearly you can't simply map questions of, say, social and cultural exchange onto films (nor is it very productive to treat films as though they were straightforwardly ethnographic texts). Nevertheless, while it may be unwise to treat films *straightforwardly* as ethnographic texts, it might be surprisingly illuminating to treat them on occasion as *deviously intricate* ethnographic instantiations. Some recent moves in anthropology are suggestive from a methodological and theoretical aspect because they enable a move, in film studies, away from the constraints of a purely formalist or cognitive approach by, on the one hand, importing into the discussion questions about contexts and relations (among people, mediated by things, and among things themselves, mediated by a social dimension) and, on the other hand, by supplanting questions of representation by attending to notions of mimesis and performativity (and concomitantly looking at the life of things as mutating).

sarily more affective in the cinema, but, rather, that the *movement* of the image invests the delineation of things with a particular affectivity. In other words, a relation obtains between temporality and affectivity.

The second reason for beginning with *The Maltese Falcon* is that for all the bird's emblematic status the image that I remember most vividly does not present it as an alluring and mysterious object; rather, it renders the bird in a quotidian moment of banality. It is a close-up of Bogart's hands on a scruffy old bundle (configured so that we share his point of view). He holds in his hands something trussed up in old newspaper and tied with string. We know that it is the exotic black bird, and yet there is something about it at this moment that is decidedly ordinary, touching, and thingy. If Gutman claims to have felt it, so too at this moment do we feel it—the weight of it, its size, the feel of it all trussed up in paper and string.[11] The affect of the moment is the ability of the image to elicit from us a sensory response. This quotidian moment is also a moment of touch or a moment when the gestural and the object are brought into relation, when the thing elicits gestural attention. Or perhaps it is the other way around: gestural attention elicits a certain quality of thingness. This particular thing—this bird—mutates, partakes of different temporalities: narrative time and emotional duration (the temporality of touching) (fig. 1).

On the one hand, then, the mutability of things. On the other hand, a privileged moment: quotidian and involving a thing and gesture. This focus, however, is ghosted by a concatenation of intractable questions. When we speak of things in the cinema, do we mean solid things or something more like the force of things? Or do we mean things in the sense of "things happen" or "things I know" (and don't know) as in Godard's *Two or Three Things I Know about Her* (1966)? Do we mean to invoke all objects or only particular kinds of objects, what we might refer to as objects-becoming-things? These large questions will, like malevolent ghosts, keep breathing heavily, ruffling the feathers of this particular odd bird, this paper, as it jiggles *the* big question—what is a thing?—to ask instead: How do things acquire presence and meaning in the cinema? Through what cinematic means do they acquire value? How do things grab our attention? Is it a question of how they themselves are grabbed—by the camera, but in such a way that cinematic mediation inaugurates a circuit of touch and affect that is primordially human? Or do things have a life of their own, independent of the cinematic gaze and the cinematic touch? Is there a particularly cinematic class of things or a particularly cinematic way of rendering things?

Stanley Cavell casts the relation between things and their filmed projections as "a relation to be thought of as something's becoming some-

11. Béla Balázs: "one *feels the weight of objects and facts*. . . . It is easier to photograph things than emotions" (quoted in Gertrud Koch, "Béla Balázs: The Physiognomy of Things," *New German Critique* 40 [Winter 1987]: 175).

FIG. 1.—From *The Maltese Falcon.*

thing (say as a caterpillar becomes a butterfly, or as a prisoner becomes a count, or as an emotion becomes conscious, or as after a long night it becomes light)." The fact that objects on film are "always already displaced, *trouvé* (i.e. that we as viewers are always already displaced before them)" provides, he proposes, for "an undertaking that we might call film theory."[12] His emphasis on the fundamentally mutable nature of cinematic things is suggestive, but the path he proposes threads its way along higher ground than this essay or, rather, along a more philosophical trajectory (philosophy is brought to bear upon film and, in turn, film is used to illuminate philosophy). Cavell does indeed complain that on the whole philosophy has ignored the everyday, but his deployment of the concept is situated within a problematic of the modern human condition circumscribed by skepticism or alienated subjectivity. He posits film as an ontology that correlates to this human condition but that also, paradoxically, provides the means for dealing with it, for overcoming skepticism by offering everyday models and modes of relatedness.[13] My investigation is more akin to grubbing along in the hedgerows, messing about with things

12. Stanley Cavell, "What Becomes of Things on Film?" *Themes out of School: Effects and Causes* (Chicago, 1984), pp. 174, 183. See also Cavell, "The Uncanniness of the Ordinary," *In Quest of the Ordinary: Lines of Skepticism and Romanticism* (Chicago, 1988), pp. 153–78.

13. See Andrew Klevan, *Disclosure of the Everyday: Undramatic Achievement in Narrative Film* (Trowbridge, 2000).

in order to understand two or three things about the cinematic image and its capacity for rendering the material dimension of the everyday. As Henri Lefebvre put it—rhetorically resonating, albeit fortuitously, with Kracauer's "thicket of things"—in his 1968 *Everyday Life in the Modern World:*

> Behind us, as we stand at their point of intersection, are the way of philosophy and the road of everyday life. They are divided by a mountain range, but the path of philosophy keeps to the heights, thus overlooking that of everyday life; ahead the track winds, barely visible, through thickets, thornbushes and swamps.[14]

Horizons of Constraint

The Maltese Falcon and *The Gutman Variations* gave me a clue as to how to proceed, and in what follows in this paper I shall map out an approach that privileges the quotidian nature of things as a mode of cinematic instantiation. My claim is not that the quotidian is the only sphere or modality in which things materialize cinematically (as we have seen with reference to *The Maltese Falcon*) but that the quotidian provides a particularly illuminating way into understanding, first, certain cinematic operations and, second, the mutability of things in the cinema. In the latter part of this paper I will turn to an exemplary cinematic thing, the cigarette, and to smoking as a quotidian practice that recurs in film, that involves both a thing and gestural inflection, that spins a smoky web of connections between the movies and cultural history. However, in order to arrive at this point I need first to trace out a framework or modus operandi. My pursuit of the particular, of instantiations of cinematic thinginess, will unfold against a more general background or horizon of constraint. Actually this horizon is a mirage; it appears in double vision, two lines of disappearance called genre and taxonomy.

The pertinence of genre has already been invoked, for instance in the proposition that the cinematic thing partakes of both a fictional and documentary identity. The invocation of genre is useful not for drawing up exhaustive lists but because the filmic language of different genres alerts us both to different sorts of privileged object-things and to different ways of inflecting the material world. In other words it allows for differentiation; it provides the ground for elaborating a more detailed and nu-

14. Henri Lefebvre, *Everyday Life in the Modern World*, trans. Sacha Rabinovitch (London, 1971), p. 17. Lefebvre does not in fact dismiss philosophy, but he is rather engaged in a struggle to "reform" philosophical methodologies. His argument is that philosophy, in encountering everyday life, has to invent new methods and approaches. Particularly suggestive for film study is his recasting of the philosophical concept of recurrence within the everyday, involving as it does a turn towards questions of temporality and attention to gesturality and things (gestures of labor, gestures of leisure).

anced way of thinking about the mutability of things. Working within the spirit of genre, but avoiding the primacy of generic category, I mobilize two pairs of terms indicating, respectively, two cinematic propensities and two modes of cinematic operation: on the one hand *quotidian* and *histrionic;* and on the other hand *inflation* and *deflation.* The pertinence of a taxonomic approach is perhaps less self-evident than that of genre. Taxonomies can never produce watertight classifications and procedures, but methodologically their usefulness derives from a kind of failure endemic to the exercise. Leakage and infiltration are inevitable. A comprehensive taxonomic experiment would aim to illuminate both distinctions and tensions between individual, unique things (the *sense* of immediacy, the particularity of affect) and classes of things—either in the same film, or across films, or across that social terrain where movies in their quotidian dimension resonate with a larger cultural history.[15] In this paper I will attempt something more modest: a suggestion of what a particular (somewhat whimsical) classification—a list of particularly cinematically destined things—might look like.

The terms *quotidian* and *histrionic* serve to delineate two fundamental but paradoxical cinematic propensities.[16] My contention is not that these are two utterly distinct modalities but that they are two impulses always and to varying degrees present in cinema. On the one hand we can say that the cinema, since its inception, has always had a curiosity about the quotidian, a desire to scrutinize and capture the rhythms and nuances of everyday life, to capture (or be captured by) things. This is what Jean-Louis Comolli refers to as "the force of things,"[17] and Kracauer as "'the blind drive of things'" (*TF,* p. 58)[18] or the "urge for concretion" (*TF,* p. 297).[19] On the other hand, since its inception, the cinema has been

15. In anthropological terms this can be cast as the relation or distinction between individual, unique objects (cultural biography) and classes of objects (social history).

16. For further elaborations, see my *The Scorsese Connection* (London, 1995), particularly chap. 6; "Acting out of Character: *The King of Comedy* as a Histrionic Text," in *Falling for You: Essays on Cinema and Performance,* ed. Stern and George Kouvaros (Sydney, 1999), pp. 277–305; and "*The Tales of Hoffmann:* An Instance of Operality," in *Between Opera and Cinema,* ed. Jeongwon Joe and Rose Theresa (New York, 2001).

17. Jean-Louis Comolli, "Documentary Journey to the Land of the Head Shrinkers," trans. Annette Michelson, *October,* no. 90 (Fall 1999): 42. Comolli's idea is that "the force of things" captures cinematic representation, *not* that the cinema, as a representational medium, perforce captures the world.

18. Kracauer uses this phrase in the context of discussing the way in which the cinema, in dealing with sensational events, involving excesses of cruelty and suffering (whether fictional or actual) does more than simply imitate and depict: "it insists on rendering visible what is commonly drowned in inner agitation." He goes on: "The cinema, then, aims at transforming the agitated witness into a conscious observer. . . . Thus it keeps us from shutting our eyes to the 'blind drive of things'" (*TF,* p. 58). The phrase is taken from Laffay, "Les Grands Thèmes de l'écran," *La Revue du cinéma* 2 (Apr. 1948): 13.

19. Kracauer elaborates thus: "In experiencing an object, we not only broaden our knowledge of its diverse qualities but in a manner of speaking incorporate it into us so that

driven by a tendency to theatricalization, by a "properly cinematographic theatricality,"[20] by stylization, by processes of semiotic virtuosity. At the histrionic end of the spectrum we might locate the films of silent physical comedians like Keaton and Chaplin (where the democratization of people and things is a structural axiom generative of performance) and directors like Michael Powell and Emeric Pressburger (in particular a film like their *The Tales of Hoffmann* [1951], where things and people are similarly mobile and mimetic, where the diegesis elaborates a magical world removed from the quotidian, where all things are under the sign of the uncanny). At the quotidian end of the spectrum we might locate a range of early actuality films (including the Lumières films), examples of neorealism such as *Umberto D* (Vittorio de Sica, 1952), and directors like Ken Loach (from his early quasi-documentary *Family Life* [1971] to later dramas). But already we are running into trouble, into generic blurrings: think of all the fiction films that have tried to assimilate to themselves documentary tendencies and all the myriad ways that documentaries incorporate processes of fictionalization. Think of a film like Chantal Akerman's *Jeanne Dielman, 23 Quai du Commerce, 1080 Bruxelles* (1975), which is a fiction film preoccupied by the quotidian, a drama that assimilates to itself a range of documentary techniques but that is nevertheless far removed from "everyday" cinema, even though it dwells in detail on the daily chores, gestures, things, and movements of a Brussels housewife-cum-prostitute—peeling potatoes; kneading raw mince into a meat loaf; washing, drying, and putting away dishes; bathing, dressing, buttoning; cleaning the kitchen floor; polishing shoes; making beds; folding pajamas; taking out and putting away money in a blue-and-white soup tureen; making and eating wiener schnitzel; making and remaking coffee. . . . Even though Delphine Seyrig's performance is restrained, almost affectless—far from histrionic—Akerman's direction (despite its neorealist resonances) is more demonstrative, more ostensive. We need a critical vocabulary more attuned to the performative dimensions of cinema (including but not exhausted by 'acting').[21] The terms *histrionic* and *quotidian* go some of the way towards delineating different tendencies, but the terms *inflation* and *deflation* help us understand the peculiarly charged articulation of quotidian things.

These terms serve to designate cinematic operations, and their employment signals a shift away from a problematic of representation, an

---

we grasp its being and its dynamics from within—a sort of blood transfusion, as it were" (*TF,* p. 297).

   20. Gilles Deleuze uses this phrase, elaborating it as "the 'excess of theatricality' that Bazin spoke of" (Gilles Deleuze, *Cinema 2: The Time-Image,* trans. Hugh Tomlinson and Robert Galeta [London, 1989], p. 84; hereafter abbreviated *C*).

   21. For the most comprehensive study of Akerman's cinema, one that engages with these questions, see Ivone Margulies, *Nothing Happens: Chantal Akerman's Hyperrealist Everyday* (Durham, N.C., 1996).

orientation more towards rhetoric, towards the potentialities and actual-
izations of filmic language (how worlds are conjured into being, ideas
shaped, emotions solicited, viewers interpellated and touched). Inflation
involves an ostensive propensity, an exaggeration or foregrounding of the
cinematic codes (color, editing, camera movement, acting, and so on);
deflation, on the other hand, involves a playing down of the codes, an
intensive, rather than ostensive, propensity.[22] An economical illustration
of these terms can be found in a film from the early years of cinema. *An
Interesting Story* (James Williamson, 1905) begins in an ordinary way with
a domestic scene: a man is having breakfast and reading at the same time.
His gestures are mostly the routine gestures of eating, reading, pouring
coffee; in fact we would not even notice what he does as gestural if it were
not for two things: the book he holds, which absorbs him utterly, and the
fact that as a consequence of this he absentmindedly pours coffee into his
upturned bowler hat. This heralds a concatenation of events whereby one
thing (the book) serves as a trigger, detonating a series of collisions between another thing (the man's body) and a third group of things he
encounters on his way to work. Because he continues reading as he walks
he slips on the steps that the maid is washing, gets caught up in a skipping
rope, bumps into a donkey (to whom he doffs his hat apologetically), and
gets run over by a steamroller. After the accident a couple of men passing
by on bicycles survey the hero's flattened body. They scratch their heads,
and then they have an idea; they take their bicycle pumps, walk around
the body-thing in search of somewhere to attach them, and then begin
pumping. They inflate the man's body, he shakes hands with them, retrieves his book, and after finding his place continues on his way, reading
as usual. We see here not only the democracy of things and people in
early cinema but an illustration of both the quotidian and the histrionic
impulse. The cinema is about ordinary things, this film tells us—getting
up, having breakfast, going to work; but it also can conjure things out of
thin air, including human things. The histrionic dimension registers in
the sheer exuberance of the film, the showing off, if you like, of the capacity of cinema. Look what the cinema can do! it says, simultaneously illustrating the fact that bodies in cinema are not referential, but primarily
cinematic. On one level *An Interesting Story* is metacinematic, and the ges-

---

22. One inflection of this term can be found in Kracauer; he uses the term *dégonflage*.
Miriam Hansen contextualizes this within Kracauer's formula from the Marseilles notebooks: "film looks under the table." She writes that *dégonflage* (letting the air out) has the
effect of "deflating myths and ideals, conventions and hierarchies that have lost their material basis, if they ever had one, in social reality" (Hansen, "Introduction," *TF,* p. xvii; hereafter abbreviated "I.") In a footnote she observes that Kracauer often couples the term "with
the shorthand of 'Sancho Panza,' referring to the Cervantes character through the lens of
Kafka's 'The Truth on Sancho Panza': 'Insofar as film, by representing materiality, promotes
the work of disenchantment, it can be called the Sancho Panza who exposes the Donqui-
choteries of ideologies and intentional constructions'" ("I," p. xl n. 35).

tural activity of inflating the deflated body with a bicycle pump alludes to the cinematic operations that can similarly deflate and inflate things.

Those Things Which Provoke *the Gestures and Words*

Making coffee, drinking coffee, preparing breakfast, eating, reading: these are familiar gestural tropes in cinema, usually signalling a beginning of one sort or another—the beginning of a scene (a new day) or the beginning of a narrative. The function of this gestural regime is to establish quotidian routine as a springboard from which the drama can leap, a soaring deviation from the groundedness of the ordinary. But this doesn't always happen. Think of another starting-the-day scene, arguably made famous (it has become a magnet for critics and theorists) by André Bazin in his essay on *Umberto D.* In his vivid evocation of the scene featuring Maria, the maid, in the kitchen, he writes of

> the succession of concrete instants of life, no one of which can be said to be more important than another, for their ontological equality destroys drama at its very basis. . . . The camera confines itself to watching her doing her little chores: moving around the kitchen still half asleep, drowning the ants that have invaded the sink, grinding the coffee. . . . Thus, the unit event in a classical film would be "the maid's getting out of bed"; two or three brief shots would suffice to show this. De Sica replaces this narrative unit with a series of "smaller" events: she wakes up; she crosses the hall; she drowns the ants; and so on. But let us examine just one of these. We see how the grinding of the coffee is divided in turn into a series of independent moments; for example, when she shuts the door with the tip of her outstretched foot. As it goes in on her the camera follows the movement of her leg so that the image finally concentrates on her toes feeling the surface of the door.[23]

Bazin conjures the slow, sleepy sensuousness of this scene admirably. You flex the tip of your toes, can almost feel the door yourself; you go back and look at the scene again and can feel the sensation of the coffee grinding, the grinder held against your stomach (fig. 2). Bazin startlingly foregrounds the way in which the gestural and the object are brought into relation, though this is not the purpose of his analysis. His purpose is to demonstrate the way in which the expressive potential of editing is *deflated* in deference to the primacy of the real. This operation involves a temporal operation that we might describe as a minimal *inflation* of real time. In fact this scene does not strictly adhere to real time, but the ellip-

23. André Bazin, *"Umberto D:* A Great Work," *What Is Cinema?* trans. and ed. Hugh Gray, 2 vols. (Berkeley, 1972), 2:81–82.

Fig. 2.—From *Umberto D.*

ses are minimal compared to classic editing, and Bazin is concerned to draw attention to the way in which quotidian moments (and sensations, we might add) are allowed an "ontological equality which destroys drama."[24] Interestingly, although Bazin claims that the camera confines itself to watching he actually describes the way in which it does more than this: it "goes in on her" and "follows the movement of her leg." In other words, the gestural modality is framed, and, in turn, gesture frames things. Movement charges the image with a certain poignancy or affect. From this particular instance we might deduce something more general: the more that fiction films observe "documentary integrity"[25] and adhere to the quotidian propensity (deploying deflationary operations with regard to editing and narrative drama) the more likely they are to frame gesture, and this gestural attention is likely to elicit a certain quality of thingness (an inflation of gesture and of things).

Gestures migrate between everyday life and the movies, but where the gestural often goes unnoticed in the everyday, in the cinema (where

24. Klevan, in a section on *Umberto D*, connects this invocation of "ontological equality" to Cavell (Klevan, *Disclosure of the Everyday*, p. 49).

25. This phrase is used by Manny Farber and Patricia Patterson when they compare Gustav Leonhardt playing an entire harpsichord piece within one diagonal camera set-up in Jean-Marie Straub's *Chronicle of Anna Magdalena Bach* to Delphine Seyrig making a meat loaf in *Jeanne Dielman* (Manny Farber and Patricia Patterson, "Kitchen without Kitsch" [1977], *Negative Space: Manny Farber on the Movies* [New York, 1998], p. 347).

it travels between the quotidian and histrionic) it moves into visibility. Robert Bresson says,

> Gestures and words cannot form the substance of a film as they form the substance of a stage play. But the substance of a film can be that . . . thing or those things which *provoke* the gestures and words and which are produced in some obscure way in your models. Your camera *sees* them and records them. So one escapes from the photographic reproduction of actors performing a play; and cinematography, that new writing, becomes at the same time a method of discovery.

In a footnote he adds that it "does so because a mechanism gives rise to the unknown, and not because one has found this unknown in advance."[26] Bressonian cinema presents us with an ideal example of the generative tension between the two propensities I have outlined. In fact his cinema, particularly a film like *L'Argent* (Bresson, 1983), elicits discovery from the viewer precisely because it demonstrates its own cinematic performativity at the same time as it draws life from the quotidian world of things. *L'Argent*, as a histrionic version of neorealism, resonates with *Jeanne Dielman*, a hypostatization of neorealism.[27]

Consider three women: the maid starting her day in the kitchen in *Umberto D;* the older woman (who provides refuge for Yvon after he has committed his first two murders) in *L'Argent*, going about her daily chores prior to being murdered herself; and Jeanne Dielman—over the span of three days repeating her quotidian tasks precisely until small disturbances creep into her routines, culminating in her murder of a client. Certain things—like the accoutrements of coffee making—resonate, migrate, mutate across the three films. Jeanne makes coffee in the morning and keeps it in a flask; on the second day there's something wrong, she has to remake it, and we, with her, sharing her temporality, watch it slowly drip through the filter. The nameless woman in *L'Argent* carefully cradles in both hands a white porcelain bowl filled with coffee that she carefully carries across the grass for Yvon, until her father slaps her and there is a cut to a close-up of the dark hot coffee spilling over her hands.[28] *L'Argent*—of the three films the most systematically preoccupied with

---

26. Robert Bresson, *Notes on the Cinematographer,* trans. Jonathan Griffin (London, 1986), p. 59.

27. Margulies, early on in her study of Akerman, draws a connection between *Jeanne Dielman* and *Umberto D,* and she continues to thread the neorealist question throughout the book, in the process drawing *Two or Three Things I Know about Her* into the orbit of discussion; see Margulies, *Nothing Happens,* p. 8.

28. Kent Jones argues that "this scene serves as an excellent refutation of the lazy, commonly-held idea that Bresson is all about somnambulant, uninflected action. Every detail here is so specific, and every aspect of the film-making is devoted to rendering that specificity" (Kent Jones, *L'Argent* [London, 1999], p. 79).

things, with inflating the sensuous, tactile materiality of things—stands as an intermediate text between *Umberto D* and *Jeanne Dielman*. The acting is more pronouncedly affectless than in neorealism,[29] the relation between gestures and things more charged by time, more deliberately framed ("Make the objects look as if they want to be there," said Bresson).[30] But the duration of the image is not as stretched as in *Jeanne Dielman*. If the kitchen scene in *Umberto D* (according to Deleuze) possesses "the pace of a dream or nightmare" (*C*, p. 3),[31] in the light of *L'Argent* it is definitely a dream pace, and *Jeanne Dielman* is definitely at the nightmare end of the spectrum. This is partly because quotidian actions are rendered in literal time, but not just this.[32] All the cinematic codes are inflated. Seyrig, as actor, performs her repetitive actions not with habitual ease but with a constrained and constraining precision. Babette Mangolte's camera frames the action in a fixed, wide-angle view, rendering the muted colors of the apartment with disturbing sharpness and clarity.[33] Although things have a prominence, derived from the film's attention to quotidian moments, the camera seldom moves lovingly in on objects, tenderly following Jeanne's gestural inflections (as in Bazin's rendering of *Umberto D*). Rather, a diegetic obsessiveness is reiterated by several cinematic codes, the conflation serving to generate an incipiently histrionic propensity (arrived at through *conflation*, not through big acting, or fast editing, or excessive camera movement) (figs. 3–8).

"A fork falls, dishes remain sudsy, the brush flies as Jeanne shines the shoes, and she arrives either too early or too late to each of her routine

29. Rachel Moore, in the context of discussing *L'Argent,* provides an insightful analysis of "the brilliant objectness of things often found in films whose characters have a dulled or muted subjectivity. Things," she writes, "have the vibrance that characters do not possess" (Rachel O. Moore, *Savage Theory: Cinema as Modern Magic* [Durham, N.C., 2000], p. 82). Margulies makes a similar observation, but sees this tendency as a *displacement:* "The intensity produced by the cumulative actions of an initially affectless protagonist, is, in *Jeanne Dielman,* displaced onto the objects and domestic scene" (Margulies, *Nothing Happens,* p. 230 n. 45). I would stress, rather, a *circuitry,* in these films, of things and gestures.

30. Bresson, *Notes on the Cinematographer,* p. 101.

31. Deleuze (especially *C*, pp. 1–13) is illuminating on neorealism, which he situates as a transitional practice or moment between what he calls "the strong sensory-motor situations of traditional realism" and a "purely optical and sound situation" of a new kind of cinematic image (*C*, p. 5).

32. Jeanne's movements are "naturalized by the fiction, denaturalized by the duration" (Janet Bergstrom, "*Jeanne Dielman, 23 Quai Du Commerce, 1080 Bruxelles* by Chantal Akerman," *Camera Obscura* 2 [1977]: 117).

33. Laleen Jayamanne notes that "Jeanne/Delphine's performance has an energy which is derived from the concentrated doing of tasks rather than from any attempt to convey feeling," and she also notes that "it is interesting that Babette Mangolte, the cinematographer for *Jeanne Dielman,* was also Yvonne Rainer's in *Lives of Performers.* The way in which objects like chairs and tables are photographed in both films, within the overall structure, makes one attentive to these mundane objects which are usually devoured by the realist text" (Laleen Jayamanne, "Modes of Performance in Chantal Akerman's *Jeanne Dielman, 23 Quai de Commerce, 1080 Bruxelles,*" *Australian Journal of Screen Theory* 8 [1980]: 101, 110).

stations. Objects seem animistically fraught, with a will of their own."[34]
Things provoke a certain kind of gestural attention, or perhaps a woman's
touch animates all the things that come within her orbit. *Jeanne Dielman*
reminds me of *Pandora's Box* (G. W. Pabst, 1928) where Lulu's touch initiates a circuit whereby things (flowers, gun, knife) are animated and seem
to acquire a fateful will of their own. In *Umberto D* things are benign; in
Pandora's Box and *Jeanne Dielman* enchantment segues into accursedness.
In *L'Argent* the privileged thing, the forged banknote, takes on the status
of an accursed object—like the Maltese falcon and the moonstone—and
it is within this circuit that the quotidian life of the nameless woman gets
caught up and the relation between the banknote and the axe transpires.
In *Jeanne Dielman* "ontological equality" collapses under the strain of repetition and the cinematic inflation of quotidian duration, but the quotidian persists, quotidian things are dramatized. She murders, not according
to the gestural tropes of a western or a thriller or a melodrama, but rather
by inverting the Jack-the-Ripper scenario (as played out for instance in
Pandora's Box) and by using her kitchen scissors to slash the man's throat
(in a medium long shot, her back to the camera). In a final, very lengthy
shot, she sits immobile at the kitchen table, just like the blue-and-white
soup tureen on the right of the frame, that nodal thing in the commerce
(and drama) of the film.

"Tangled Like Old String"

> Wandering through cold streets tangled like old string,
> Coming on fountains rigid in the frost,
> Its formula escapes you; it has lost
> The certainty that constitutes a thing.
> —W. H. AUDEN, "Brussels in Winter"

The more you try to grasp the cinematic thing, to describe and clas-
sify it, the more its formula escapes you, the more certainty dissolves into
immateriality. From a certain perspective, then, following Ricciotto Canudo's early designation of cinema's faculty for representing immateriality, we might assume that a taxonomy of the thing, self-defeating exercise
though it may be, will take us to the heart of cinema.[35] But there is another reason for pursuing taxonomies, for constructing whimsical lists,
and that is to move away from the heart of the matter and, in a more
dispersive or crablike meandering, to concentrate (while remaining alert
to this immateriality) on the *matter* of cinema, the cinematic capacity for

34. Margulies, *Nothing Happens,* p. 78.
35. See Ricciotto Canudo, "Reflections on the Seventh Art," trans. Claudia Gorbman,
in Richard Abel, *French Film Criticism and Theory: A History/Anthology,* 2 vols. (Princeton, N.J.,
1988), 1:300.

Figs. 3–5.—From *L'Argent*.

FIGS. 6–8.—From *Jeanne Dielman*.

materialization. The filmic capacity to render the phenomenal world (or to enact, as Kracauer put it, "the process of materialization" [quoted in "I," p. xvii])[36] is equalled only by film's capacity to also unhinge the solidity and certainty of things. And it does so in many ways.

What follows is an experimental flight of taxonomic fancy. Provisional and suggestive, it proceeds by detailing certain objects that seem cinematically destined. (Another, and complementary, taxonomy might proceed according to modalities of thingness: things that look back; estranged things; the human skin of things.) It tacks between two precepts or extreme positions: "No ideas but in things"[37] and the notion of "real-life objects free of ideas."[38] I assume that while things are never without signifying power (taking signification to entail more than the semantic) nevertheless they carry affect and an indeterminacy that frequently derives at least in part from their indexical relationship to the real world. I pose this indeterminacy as simultaneously a resistance and an allure; at the very least it is an opportunity to shift the emphasis from the signifying potential of things to the sensuous, to the affect produced through tactility, the generation of a sense of touch (following Bill Brown's postulation that "sensuous praxis is inextricable from the resignifying praxis").[39]

A Banknote on Which Our Attention Is Riveted

"All our emotion exists for those dear old American adventure films," wrote Louis Aragon in 1918, "that speak of daily life and manage to raise to a dramatic level a banknote on which our attention is riveted, a table with a revolver on it, a bottle that on occasion becomes a weapon, a handkerchief that reveals a crime, a typewriter that's the horizon of a desk."[40] Here ordinary, functional things are cinematically charged, invested with drama, histrionically inflected. Those dear old American films are of course narrative films, and the drama invested in the objects has some-

36. Hansen points out that Kracauer's notion of the material dimension developed in the Marseilles notebooks gives way, in the later *Theory of Film*, to the less comprehensive term, "physical reality" ("I," p. xvi). Nevertheless, *Theory of Film* provides the most comprehensive approach to "things" in the cinema that we have, and it does so through its elaboration of a key concept: "the flow of life." Kracauer uses the phrase partly to distinguish films from still photography ("an emanation of the medium itself"), and to denote "a kind of life which is still intimately connected, as if by an umbilical cord, with the material phenomena from which its emotional and intellectual contents emerge" (*TF*, pp. 273, 71).

37. Quoted by Richard Roud, *Jean-Luc Godard* (London, 1967), p. 120.

38. Roger Cardinal, "Pausing Over Peripheral Detail," *Framework*, nos. 30–31 (1986): 126; hereafter abbreviated "PO."

39. Bill Brown, "How to Do Things with Things (A Toy Story)," *Critical Inquiry* 24 (Summer 1998): 954.

40. Louis Aragon, "On Decor" (1918), trans. Paul Hammond, in Abel, *French Film Theory and Criticism*, 1:166. Aragon used the term *remotivation* to describe what happens to these things on film.

thing to do with their narrative function—but not everything. Some objects seem to want, more than other objects, to be there. They look back at us, they want to be touched ("But when Ingrid Bergman hides a key in her hand, that key looks at you").[41] Just as there are clearly *films* that seem like paradigmatic cases for understanding the cinematic treatment of things, so too there are some *objects* that are paradigmatic, that seem cinematically destined. They include telephones, typewriters, banknotes, guns, dark glasses, coffee cups, raindrops and teardrops, leaves blowing in the wind, kettles, cigarettes. In materializing these objects the cinema invests them with pathos, renders them as moving. Cinematic apprehension simultaneously fills the objects with movement and contrives to move the viewer, to trigger a mode of knowing that is somatic, experienced through the duration of touch. This is often actualized mimetically via a gestural framing. But sometimes the cinematic thing has a capacity to touch us in more mysterious and circuitous ways, as is the case with raindrops and teardrops, and with leaves blowing in the wind, with kettles, and with cigarettes (fig. 9). These are the four cinematically destined things I will focus on, a discussion ghosted and informed by those tensions already elaborated between the quotidian and the histrionic and inflation and deflation.

41. Jean-Luc Godard, "Godard Makes [Hi]stories: Interview with Serge Daney," trans. Georgia Gurrieri, in *Jean-Luc Godard: Son + Image, 1974–1991,* trans Gurrieri, Rachel Bowlby, and Lynne Kirby, ed. Raymond Bellour and Mary Lea Bandy (exhibition catalog, Museum of Modern Art, New York, 30 Oct.–30 Nov. 1992), p. 164.

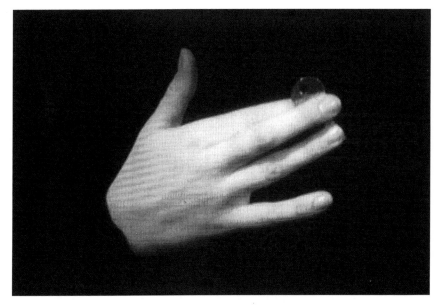

FIG. 9.—From *Notorious.*

Drops: Raindrops and Teardrops

Rain, and more specifically raindrops (as the thing manifestation of rain), exerts a general fascination. *The Voice of Things,* for instance, begins with "Rain."[42] In 1968, in *Everyday Life in the Modern World,* Lefebvre remarked on the blurring of the subject. "Now it is the object that plays the lead," he wrote,

> not in its objectivity (which had meaning only in relation to the subject) but as a thing, almost a pure form. If I want to write today— that is write fiction—I will start from an ordinary object, a mug, an orange, a fly of which I shall attempt a detailed description. . . . And why should I not choose that raindrop sliding down the window-pane? I could write a whole page, ten pages, on that raindrop; for me it will become the symbol of everyday life whilst avoiding every-day life; it will stand for time and space, or space within time; it will be the world and still only a vanishing raindrop.[43]

Lefebvre is writing about literature (specifically about description in the *nouveau roman*), but what he says about time and space pertains even more acutely to film. Think of all those movie scenes where narrative momentum is suspended, where time seems simultaneously to stand still and to pass, scenes where we are positioned with characters behind glass (so often in a car), watching raindrops fall and splatter and pass. Raindrops are not the same sort of cinematic things as guns or telephones, say, but they are quintessentially cinematic in that they embody (they do *not depict*) a kind of cinematic temporality to do with fascination and boredom. When you are waiting or hanging around wasting time you fixate on the minutiae and transformability of things, the shape of a paper clip with which one is fiddling, a wad of chewing gum (think of all that gum wad-ded and diverted in *Lolita*), a single raindrop. Where we tend to talk of *the* gun and *the* telephone we tend to talk of raindrops in the plural, they come in an avalanche, and yet we fixate on their singularity.

There is a contingency to raindrops that affords them a privileged thinginess and concomitant affectivity. Roger Cardinal, in "Pausing Over Peripheral Detail," describes a scene in Philippe Garrel's *Liberté, la nuit* (1983) where Emmanuelle Riva sits inside a parked car beside a lover who is explaining that he is leaving her. He writes:

> the rain beating on the wind screen is manifestly real rain. True, one can impute a symbolic significance to rain as a traditional concomi-

42. See Francis Ponge, *The Voice of Things,* trans. and ed. Beth Archer (New York, 1972).

43. Lefebvre, *Everyday Life in the Modern World,* pp. 7–8.

tant of grief; but any given individual raindrop sliding down the glass in front of Riva's stricken face is, logically, irrelevant to her emotion, circumstantial, unscripted. That is to say, there comes a point where material detail entirely escapes directorial sponsorship, to take its place before the viewer quite autonomously. . . . Figuratively, as well literally, the raindrop is *transparent;* neither informational nor symbolic, it is, simply, "obtusely," *itself.* ["PO," p. 122][44]

Cardinal captures the contingent force of the raindrop, but he underplays, I think, the way in which the raindrop-object (because of its very transparency) can be mobilized performatively, invested with affect. Consider the metonymic relation between raindrops and teardrops. Both are "natural" phenomena, and yet in film they acquire a performative dimension, spatially inflected, through the close-up. Think of that famous and much reproduced still of Renée Falconetti as Joan of Arc, the single tear glistening on her cheek, the frozen image implying time—the time it takes for a tear to emerge and flow. Balázs: "We cannot use glycerine tears in a close-up. What makes a deep impression is not a fat, oily tear rolling down a face—what moves us is to see the glance growing misty, and moisture gathering in the corner of the eye—moisture that as yet is scarcely a tear. This is moving, because this cannot be faked" (fig. 10).[45] But fat, oily tears can make a deep impression, as we see in *Necrologue* (1999) (number six of *The Phoenix Tapes,* by Christoph Girardet and Matthias Müller). For three minutes and forty seconds we watch, in slow motion, a close-up shot of Ingrid Bergman, in *Under Capricorn* (Alfred Hitchcock, 1949): moisture gathers in the corner of her eye, forming into a perfectly fat, oily teardrop. Her face is expressionless, a background, a stage for the performance of this thing in its slow roll down a cheek.

Leaves Blowing in the Wind

If there be an ontology of cinema (Bazin), it belongs to the documentary, insofar as despite all, and occasionally in spite of itself, it testifies to that which is not ourselves. I believe that in the first Lumière films it was already the force of things that captured cinematic representation; this force was equal to that of the form of representation that claimed to capture those things; it was this force of things as they assert themselves. For people were wonderstruck by the trembling of

44. His use of the term "obtusely" alludes to Roland Barthes's use of the term in his "The Third Meaning: Research Notes on Some Eisenstein Stills," *Image-Music-Text,* trans. and ed. Stephen Heath (New York, 1977), pp. 52–68.
45. Béla Balázs, *Theory of the Film: Character and Growth of a New Art,* trans. Edith Bone (New York, 1970), p. 77.

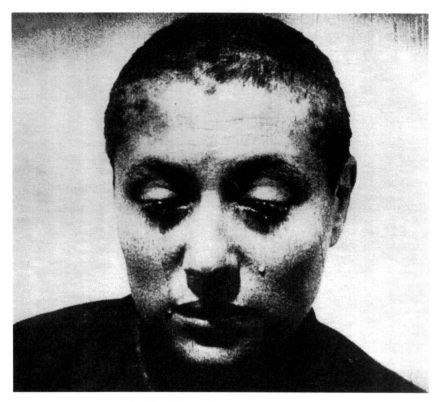

FIG. 10.—From *The Passion of Joan of Arc*.

leaves on the trees—a good example, since the wind bloweth where
it listeth—which produced an effect, an effect of the real.
                                                —JEAN-LOUIS COMOLLI[46]

In the beginning spectators were fascinated by incidental details such
as the foliage blowing in the wind behind the Lumières feeding their
baby. Gorky, in his famous account of visiting the cinema for the first time,
remarked: "Silently the ash-grey foliage of the trees sways in the wind."[47]
It was not the leaves as such that fascinated him. Rather, it was the uncanniness (which he found eery rather than fascinating) of the familiar
ghosted by the unfamiliar. But we can also read Gorky as registering, via

46. Jean-Louis Comolli, "Documentary Journey to the Land of the Head Shrinkers,"
pp. 41–42.
47. Maxim Gorky, "The Lumière Cinematograph (Extracts)," in *The Film Factory: Russian and Soviet Cinema in Documents*, trans. Richard Taylor, ed. Taylor and Ian Christie (Cambridge, Mass., 1988), p. 25.

the leaves, something quintessentially cinematic. Leaves register movement. Interestingly, for him the cinema "makes strange" the familiar, and he perceives this to be a component of the cinematic.

But leaves rustling (silently or otherwise) in the breeze can be read differently, as an acute example of cinema's capacity to register a world as if caught "'off-guard', unposed," in the words of Roger Cardinal. He describes a passage in Andrei Tarkovsky's *Mirror* (1974): "a lingering shot of undergrowth stirred by gusts of wind which seemed to affect only a small sector of the bushes at a time, brusquely animating and then immobilizing groups of leaves and twigs" ("PO," pp. 124–25). He finds the "phenomenal density" of such passages of film alluring since they embody the magic of real trees, and, furthermore, "they appeal to the non-visual senses as much as they appeal to the eye. . . . The gaze registers the sheer undifferentiated plenitude of undergrowth, apprehended not as formal configuration but as an exciting sensory presence in the raw state" ("PO," pp. 125–26). Here the foliage stands in for the phenomenal world, untouched by men.

But in other kinds of film, or in other kinds of criticism, almost the reverse obtains: "'And I? says the leaf which is falling.—And we? say the orange peel, the gust of wind. . . . Film, whether intentionally or not, is their mouthpiece'" (*TF*, p. 45). And from yet another angle, Godard begins *Two or Three Things I Know about Her* (1966) with a voice-over musing thus:

> It is 4.45.
> Should I speak of Juliette or of these leaves?
> Since it is impossible, in any case, really to do both together, let's say that both tremble gently in this beginning of the end of an October afternoon.

Here trembling leaves do not indicate nature and otherness but rather an image or device whereby an equivalence can be drawn between things (the leaves) and people (Juliette). Susan Sontag has argued that "in Godard's films things display a wholly alienated character. Characteristically, they are used with indifference, neither skillfully nor clumsily; they are simply there. "'Objects exist,'" Godard has written, "'and if one pays more attention to them than to people, it is precisely because they exist more than these people. Dead objects are still alive. Living people are often already dead.'"[48] Richard Roud, on the other hand, suggests an existen-

---

48. Cavell, quoting Susan Sontag who is quoting Elliot Rubenstein, quotes this passage in order to argue against it. The Godard voice, he suggests, as we know it through the narrator of *Two or Three Things I Know about Her*, is unreliable. He points to the "extraordinariness" of the filmed objects, particularly coffee and beer (Cavell, "What Becomes of Things on Film?" pp. 181–82).

tialist tracing to the things of "two or three things." He argues that Godard's model here is Francis Ponge, who during the last war began to write little prose poems, descriptions of objects, collected together in *The Voice of Things*. Philosophically his work was bound to appeal to the existentialists, and Sartre did much to promote him. Ponge himself insisted that the basic job of the poet was the naming of things, which incited Robbe-Grillet to a scabrous outburst: "Drowned in the *depth* of things, in the end man doesn't even see them any more; his role is soon limited to feeling, in their name, entirely *humanized* impressions and desires." He goes on to accuse both Ponge and Sartre of "thinking 'with things' and not *about them.*"[49] Which strikes me actually as an apposite way to approach *Two or Three Things I Know about Her.* I think that the leaves and Juliette provide Godard with a conceit for thinking about the cinema and epistemology. How do we come to know things cinematically? Is it purely through description? Not purely, though description matters because it renders an equivalence between things and people. But not all things are solid (though they may partake of materiality). Knowledge, for instance, is abstract, unstable, it trembles, like foliage in the wind.

Kettles

"'The kettle began it. . . .'" Thus Eisenstein opens his essay, "Dickens, Griffith, and the Film Today" (fig. 11).[50] He is quoting Dickens's opening to *The Cricket on the Hearth* (1845), and his argument is that the early American film aesthetic, forever linked with Griffith, derives from the Victorian novel, especially Dickens. It is the "'intimate'" Dickens, and the "'intimate' Griffith of contemporary or past American life" he focuses on ("DG," p. 198). "Certainly, this kettle," he writes, "is a typical Griffith-esque close-up. A close-up saturated, we now become aware, with typically Dickens-esque 'atmosphere'" ("DG," p. 199). He situates the function of such a close-up, then, within the realm of the descriptive, within a realm that we might now call the proaieretic. In distinguishing Soviet cinema from the American he argues that where Griffith, in his close-ups, never escapes *"representation and objectivity"* (showing and presenting, filling out character and atmosphere) the Soviet close-up is concerned "to *signify,* to *give meaning,* to *designate*" ("DG," pp. 240, 238). Eisenstein designates Dickens's method as cinematic because he isolates a thing (though Eisenstein does not use this term) from daily life that is in a sense part of

---

49. Alain Robbe-Grillet, "Towards a New Novel," *"Snapshots" and "Towards a New Novel,"* trans. Barbara Wright (London, 1965), pp. 89, 90.

50. Sergei Eisenstein, "Dickens, Griffith, and the Film Today," *Film Form: Essays in Film Theory,* trans. and ed. Jay Leyda (New York, 1949), p. 195; hereafter abbreviated "DG."

F<small>IG</small>. 11.—From *October.*

the scenery, does not have a narrative function, and yet by virtue of the close-up is lifted out of the mise-en-scène, framed, inflated we might say.

Kracauer argues—against Eisenstein—that Griffith's close-ups do more than just show or present; he stresses the importance of their "indeterminacy." He writes:

> To Griffith such huge images of small material phenomena are not only integral components of the narrative but disclosures of new aspects of physical reality. In representing them the way he does, he seems to have been guided by the conviction that the cinema is all the more cinematic if it acquaints us with the physical origins, ramifications, and connotations of all the emotional and intellectual events which comprise the plot; that it cannot adequately account for these inner developments unless it leads us through the thicket of material life from which they emerge and in which they are embedded. [*TF,* p. 48]

One way to designate such things is as props. Eisenstein, in developing his ideas, stressed the associational and went so far as to eradicate people in some sequences where he is indeed intent on filling out people or ideas about them. Yuri Tsivian persuasively argues, in a detailed analysis of sequences from *October* (Sergei Eisenstein, 1927) and *Intolerance* (D. W. Griffith, 1916), that "while in *Intolerance* props played up the actor, in *Oktyabr'* they upstaged him."[51] Instead of showing Lenin in exile, Eisenstein showed things designating his exile, including a simple kettle hanging over a bonfire that is juxtaposed, via a graphic cut, with Czar Alexander's crowned monogram, which a further cut reveals to be engraved on a plate. "Here," argues Tsivian, "Griffith's narrative economy turned into its opposite: a superfluity of props that makes *Oktyabr'* look like 'a Baroque film about the uprising of dishes,' as Victor Shklovsky dubbed it in his 1932 'Letter to Eisenstein'" ("HI," p. 53). With admirable subtlety Tsivian goes on to analyze and compare the plate smashing scene that detonated the mutiny on *Potemkin* (1925) and a domestic quarrel in Griffith's *True Heart Susie* (1919), in which Clarine Seymour breaks a plate. Although he concedes that the resemblance may only be coincidental, Tsivian makes the connection via the tropes of melodrama, pointing out that while Shklovsky stressed that new art forms emerge when old devices marry new material, so Eisenstein, with a similar pleasure in discovery of the new, "used to tell his students that the dramatic conflict underlying his *Potemkin*—the battleship, the city of Odessa, the Czarist troops—replicated the invariable 'love triangle' of the traditional melodrama" ("HI," p. 55). Thus the breaking of the plate by the sailor is described by Tsivian as "a 'feminine' gesture of revolt met with in melodramas and their real-life reenactments" ("HI," p. 55).

Tsivian, by invoking the tropes of melodrama, draws attention to resonances between texts that would normally be thought of as markedly distinctive. To find out more about things and the range of their cinematic modality we could build on his critique, but take it in a slightly different direction by sharpening the focus on the gesture-thing relation and examining in more detail the ways that Eisenstein and Griffith deploy both quotidian and histrionic propensities.

The kettle began it, and plates and dishes have joined in along the way. We have not, however, moved very far from the kitchen, and from Griffith and Eisenstein we can circle back into the orbit of *Umberto D, Jeanne Dielman, L'Argent,* and even *An Interesting Story* and their framing of the coffee pot as a kettle variant, and coffee making/pouring/drinking as a variant on plate throwing (and one could even circle back via a couple of small eddies, or excursuses: on the quivering plates in *The Wind* [1928], for instance, and on Ozu's red kettle, so beloved by the formalists for meaning nothing, and the auteurists for meaning everything).

51. Yuri Tsivian, "Homeless Images: D. W. Griffith in the Eye of Soviet Filmmakers," *Griffithiana* 60–61 (Oct. 1997): 53; hereafter abbreviated "HI."

Cigarettes

> The spectator cannot help laughing at the ridiculous hats, over-stuffed rooms, and obtrusive gestures impressed upon him by the veracious camera. As he laughs at them, however, he is bound to realize, shudderingly, that he has been spirited away into the lumber room of his private self. . . . In a flash the camera exposes the para-phernalia of our former existence, stripping them of the significance which originally transfigured them so that they changed from things in their own right into invisible conduits. . . .
>
> Film images encourage such a decomposition because of their emphatic concern with raw material not yet consumed. The thrill of these old films is that they bring us face to face with the inchoate, cocoon-like world whence we come—all the objects, or rather sediments of objects, that were our companions in a pupa state. . . . Numerous films . . . draw on the incomparable spell of those near and faraway days which mark the border region between the present and past. Beyond it the realm of history begins. [*TF,* pp. 56–57]

Remember Bette Davis—lips gleaming, head thrown back, brandishing a cigarette and blowing out smoke; remember Bogey—lifting a thumb to his lips, talking out of the side of his mouth, a cigarette hanging out the other, or cigarette between his fingers rubbing the back of his thumb around his lips; remember Judy Davis—edgily playing with a cigarette, speaking in a huskily smoky voice; remember Gena Rowlands, particularly in *Opening Night* (John Cassavetes, 1977), always a cigarette in hand, and if not a cigarette, a drink. A bit like Ray Milland in *The Lost Weekend* (Billy Wilder, 1945), except that he always puts the wrong end of the cigarette in his mouth and routinely, without batting an eyelid, takes it out, turns it, returns it to his mouth (or sometimes his long-suffering girlfriend does it for him). Remember, remember . . . I could have written: Think of Bette Davis, think of Bogey . . . But in fact when we recall these actors we do not exactly *think* of them with a cigarette; and yet it is hard to imagine them without. The cigarette (or cigarettes) seem simply to be there, they don't mean anything, and yet they are essential to the scene, to the idea we have of the actors, of the films.

If there is a class of objects that seems cinematically destined, there is a subclass that comes into view more obliquely than telephones and guns, say. On the one hand they are almost ubiquitous and therefore unimportant; we do not generally notice them as objects, they are merely there, quotidian things, part of the mise-en-scène, part of the gestural modality of the movie world. And yet, on the other hand, precisely because of this reticence they contain great power, the power or potential to mark out, first, cultural mores, rituals of exchange, the habitus that in day-to-day living goes unnoticed; and second, to shape movie conventions, to shape the gestural idiolects of particular actors, genres, dramatic configurations. Cigarettes fall into this category.

Smoking is (or was) a fact of life, a quotidian practice of, until recently, the majority of the adult population in many countries. Yet in film it acquires a particular valence. This is partly because of the glorious quality of smoke filtered through the light of black-and-white cinema. But it is also because the cinema in its neorealist propensity ferrets out and puts into play quotidian custom and in the process hypostatizes it, frames it, puts it into inverted commas, renders it as ritual. Which of course it is. In relation to cigarettes and smoking and the movies we are, at the beginning of this new millennium, living through an historical moment. Even a decade ago smoking in films was taken for granted; but now we notice it.

We notice it of course cinematically (for instance, in the way it might underline generic features), but this noticing also alerts us to things about the culture, about processes of exchange, romantic and erotic conventions, class, about the significance of things, about the circulation of commodities, and the transformation of commodities into mass ornaments.[52] If we become more finely attuned to the way in which individual actors and stars smoke (how they handle and use cigarettes, how they use cigarettes in orchestrating the nuances of relationships) this opens onto a more general knowledge: how idiosyncratic smoking gestures enter and shape the repertoire of cinematic language. But if the quotidian impresses itself in the cinematic, it is equally the case that the cinematic impinges upon the practices of everyday life. If the cinema hungrily inhales smoke from the culture at large, it also blows it out, in the process refining, framing, laying the grounds for repeatability so that the smoke circulates back into the practices of everyday life. How many of us learnt to smoke at the movies? And to kiss? And to make meatballs and wiener schnitzel?[53] Of course I don't just mean learnt to smoke in the sense of inhaling and exhaling smoke and feeling high (or sick). I mean all the rituals of sociality, all the accompanying gestural tropes of seduction and mercantilism and betrayal.

In a striking passage in his essay "Techniques of the Body," Marcel Mauss describes how he experienced a "kind of revelation" about his own culture, specifically about this process of reciprocity and exchange between the cinema and daily life. "I was ill in New York," he writes. "I wondered where previously I had seen girls walking as my nurses walked. I had the time to think about it. At last I realized that it was at the cinema. Returning to France, I noticed how common this gait was, especially in

52. See Kracauer, "The Mass Ornament," *The Mass Ornament: Weimar Essays,* trans. and ed. Thomas Y. Levin (Cambridge, Mass., 1995), pp. 75–86.
53. From Martin Scorsese's *Italianamerican* (1974) and *Jeanne Dielman* respectively.

Paris; the girls were French and they too were walking in this way. In fact, American walking fashions had begun to arrive over here, thanks to the cinema."[54] In the case of smoking (which we could add to his examples of swimming, walking, running) there is an entangled relation between the gestural habitus and the thing.

Perhaps Mauss's observations seem less striking today; however, it is not just a question of influence but of modes of incorporation, mimesis and performance. It is about the learning of techniques (how to manage body parts and other things), which also involves a forgetting. Although we didn't learn to smoke from instruction manuals, we did learn from somewhere, and, as in driving, as the process becomes habitual, we forget how and what we learnt. Smoking, like driving, belongs to what Bruno Latour describes as "a large *body* of skills that we have so well embodied or incorporated that the mediations of the written instructions are useless."[55]

Because of its ubiquity and quotidian nature the cigarette is a kind of charmed cinematic object. It is supremely deictic: used both to ground the subject in the here and now and also to function as a sign, a wand, as indexical. It is always solidly a thing, and yet it is also imaginary; as it is smoked and disappears it gestures both towards its own phenomenality and its genealogy: as one of a series, endlessly replaceable and repeatable. Its phenomenality is contingent; like the movies itself it passes before our eyes, disappears. Its existence—as a particular thing (this thing I hold between my fingers)—is finite. But then there will be another: another movie, another cigarette—to fondle and smoke and inhale. Just like the Maltese falcon. The revelation that the black bird is a fake, one in a series, without value, does not arrest Gutman's desire nor deflect him from his search. As the poetically incarnated Gutman says:

> We shall stop the circulation of
> language
> when we have the bird sir and we shall certainly stop the
> circulation
> of the bird!
>
> [*GV,* ll. 160–62]

54. Marcel Mauss, "Techniques of the Body," trans. Ben Brewster, *Economy and Society* 2 (Feb. 1973): 72. See also Mauss, *A General Theory of Magic,* trans. Robert Brain (New York, 1972) and *The Gift: The Form and Reason for Exchange in Archaic Societies,* trans. W. D. Halls (London, 1990). Kristin Ross, in *Fast Cars, Clean Bodies: Decolonization and the Reordering of French Culture* (Cambridge, Mass., 1995), says of Jacques Tati's films that "they make palpable a daily life that increasingly appeared to unfold in a space where objects tended to dictate to people their gestures and movements—gestures that had not yet congealed into any degree of rote familiarity, and that for the most part had to be learned from watching American films" (p. 5).

55. Bruno Latour, "Where Are the Missing Masses? The Sociology of a Few Mundane Artifacts," in *Shaping Technology/Building Society: Studies in Sociotechnical Change,* ed. Wiebe E. Bijker and John Law (Cambridge, Mass., 1992), p. 246. In this paper—humorously revolv-

Fig. 12.—From *The Big Sleep.*

So in fact the black bird and the cigarette are very similar sorts of things. There is no stopping their circulation.[56] Cigarettes mutate and circulate, in many different ways transmitting values, sensations, and meanings. Grounded in the quotidian, they are often deployed histrionically. Although cigarettes nearly always occur in a thingy capacity in film— that is to say, they are simply there as things, associated with daily habits and gestures—while being thingy they might also and simultaneously be and do other things. In this respect they are paradigmatic of cinematic things.

Imagine we are in the dark. At the beginning, before the credits roll (fig. 12).

Two names materialize on the screen, "Humphrey Bogart" and "Lauren Bacall," and behind the names stand two silhouettes: a man and

---

ing around a door hinge (or automatic groom as it is called in French) that goes on strike in a sociology department—Latour argues against easy distinctions (between the human and nonhuman, animate and inanimate, figurative and nonfigurative actors). People and things (in practicing techniques), he suggests, may, and do, exchange properties all the time.

56. The cigarette is not exactly a desirable object in the way the Maltese falcon is, and, although the profit from commercial tobacco trade is, of course, bankable, the cigarette itself is not a bankable object.

a woman. He lights her cigarette, and as the credits start rolling (for *The Big Sleep* [Howard Hawks, 1946]) the camera tilts down to an ashtray, a single cigarette brooding there, half consumed, smoking still. A second cigarette is placed beside it, smoke unfurls from the two, the strands entwining as they float silkily, dissipating eventually, absorbed into the velvety black background. Here the cigarette is a supercharged thing, and smoking is both sensuous, with material affect, and metaphoric. The cigarettes are real things and an index of desire. They metaphorize sexuality and an exchange; he lights her cigarette even before the story starts. Or perhaps it is the lighting of the cigarette that ignites the drama, a drama about—on one level—an exchange between two people. This moment, which charges the film, differs from the opening of *The Maltese Falcon* even though in both instances a thing (or things) are given precedence over human protagonists. In *The Maltese Falcon* the bird is presented as an extraordinary object, untouchable, legendary. Here, quotidian objects—eminently touchable and sensuous—are lifted out of the everyday, framed, dramatized, their presence inflated. Although they will revert to the quotidian, the histrionic charge of the opening will reverberate through the film, through a performative modality shaped by the stylized dialogue, by a register of arch innuendo.

Bogey was a tough guy, and for all the idiosyncracy of his style (smoking and otherwise) he came from a long line of tough guys. *The Musketeers of Pig Alley* (Griffith, 1912) is an early instance of the gangster genre. The film is remarkable both for the way it captures the density of street life, for its evocation of the real, the sense it creates of a story just happening to unfold before our eyes and within a milieu that exists independent of the drama. The Kipper Kid (who presages James Cagney in an almost uncanny fashion) and his small-time gangster cronies have a distinctive way of moving (and lounging or skulking), of holding a gun in their pocket, and, above all, of smoking. Cigarettes here constitute descriptive detail, but the gesturality involved in smoking also contributes to a performative register that begins to delineate generic features and a certain kind of heroism. If today you want to project the élan of a gangster you will probably cultivate a way of smoking that may well have its origins in the back alleys of New York City in the early years of the twentieth century; but it will be a way of smoking that has been developed, refined, and elaborated by the cinema as the gangster genre itself has developed and mutated (figs. 13 and 14).

Breathless (Godard, 1960) opens with Belmondo, in a fedora tipped low over his forehead, a cigarette hanging out of his mouth. He lifts his hand, removes the cigarette and holding it between his fingers he rubs the back of his thumb around his mouth. We have seen this gesture before, perhaps, like Mauss, in the streets of Paris, or perhaps in the movies. Very likely we recall it from *The Maltese Falcon* and *The Big Sleep*. This gesture immediately, in a very condensed way, rhetorically we might say,

FIG. 13.—From *Musketeers of Pig Alley.*

FIG. 14.—From *Breathless.*

evokes Bogey, but it also evokes the American B-grade gangster film and, for good measure, as though this wasn't enough, also a certain kind of American masculinity with which the French (from the surrealists to the cinephiles of Godard's generation) were enamored—a self-contained, laconic, stoical masculinity (which of course, as we know, is fading fast from the world). Once these things appear on film and are rendered performative through gestural modality, they (both the gestures and the things, though it is hard to prize them apart) can be reperformed, repeated, quoted by other performers.[57]

The Sentimental Bloke (Raymond Longford, 1918) opens with a long shot of the Kid coming out of his terrace cottage, a cigarette hanging from his mouth. Cut to a close-up; he pulls the cigarette from his mouth and exhales. The bloke looks a right bruiser. The street scene, his gesturality, the way he is dressed are an immediate index of class. And if we didn't know the story already—the film is based on an Australian verse classic—we could be forgiven for thinking that we were entering the Sydney equivalent of Pig Alley and the gangster genre. Before long the bloke finds himself in gaol, and when he gets out he sits forlornly on a park bench, lamenting the fact that he is, so the intertitles tell us, "Of 'ope, an' joy, an'/forchin destichoot." He searches in his pockets, but all he finds are a few strands of tobacco; he scans the grass where his eyes alight on a scrap of paper. He has the makings and proceeds to roll a cigarette, to light up and exhale. His whole body relaxes and the world is transformed:

> The little birds
>   is chirpin
> in the trees
> . . . .
> The parks and gardens
>   is a bosker sight.

And then he meets Doreen, "me ideel tart," and the reform process begins. On their first date he is waiting for her, leaning against a lamp post, fag hanging out of his mouth; when he becomes aware of her presence he promptly spits it out. At the end of the film, when they are married and settled bucolically in the country, he puffs a pipe. Here the cigarette-thing, initially barely noticeable in its thingness, is nevertheless in its cinematic rendering an index of class, milieu, and to some extent

57. The other figure quoted by Belmondo is Jean Gabin. As Dudley Andrew points out, "Belmondo's gestures may come from Jean Gabin, in Marcel Carné's *Daybreak* (*Le Jour se léve*, 1939), for both men measure out their final hours chain smoking, often lighting one cigarette from the butt of another and playing with the teddy bears of their winsome girlfriends" (Dudley Andrew, "*Breathless*: Old as New," in *Breathless*, ed. Andrew [New Brunswick, N.J., 1990], p. 15).

genre (particularly because it is so bound up with gesture); but later it
comes to serve a function more attendant on narrative, but rather than
effecting action it registers change, the progress of a kind of sentimental
education.

Trust (Hal Hartley, 1990) features a scene of Matthew (Martin Donovan) and Maria (Adrienne Shelly) at the abortion clinic. They sit still but
look anxious. A sequence of looped dialogue ensues, in which they deliver
their lines with complete indifference. Matthew has an unlit cigarette in
his mouth; it jumps up and down when he speaks.

MATTHEW: How long do you think it will take?
MARIA: I don't know. Not long, I guess.
She removes the cigarette from his mouth. He audibly sighs. He puts
another unlit cigarette in his mouth.
MATTHEW: Are you okay?
MARIA: Yeah, you?
She removes the cigarette from his mouth.
MATTHEW: I feel like smashing things up.
He audibly sighs.
    . . . .
MATTHEW: How long do you think it will take?
MARIA: I don't know. Not long, I guess.
She removes the cigarette from his mouth. He audibly sighs. He puts
another unlit cigarette in his mouth.
MATTHEW: Are you okay?
MARIA: Yeah, you?
She removes the cigarette from his mouth.
MATTHEW: I feel like tearing somebody's head off.[58]

The cigarette here, as associated with Donovan, is idiolectic (Donovan's way of smoking is as intrinsic to his mode of being as is Bogey's);
and in this instance it also appears to be a prop (a pretext for stage business, for indicating anxiety). But its function is not exclusively proppish,
nor simply indexical of character. It initiates a circuit: of things, words,
gestures. Hartley has said, "words can be gestures too."[59] Bearing in mind
the close relation between things and gestures, we might recast this apho-
ristic formulation as "words too can be things." The iteration of words
and gestures, and substitutability of cigarettes and words (both are put in
and taken out of the mouth, passed as it were from person to person)

58. Hal Hartley, *"Simple Men" and "Trust"* (London, 1992), p. 139. See also Sophie
Wise, "What I Like about Hal Hartley, or Rather, What Hal Hartley Likes about Me," in
Falling for You, pp. 259–61; I have borrowed Wise's visual descriptions.
59. Hartley, "Finding the Essential," interview with Graham Fuller, in *"Simple Men"
and "Trust,"* p. xli.

points to both the thinginess of words and the abstraction of things. One way of understanding the circuit and series of relations here is via Merleau-Ponty: "The spoken word is a gesture, and its meaning, a world."[60] He writes very persuasively about "life among things," bringing things and words into the same orbit—the orbit, that is, of my body and my apprehension of the world through gestural relations.[61] But there are other possible ways of reading this scene so it is rendered less in terms of phenomenological apprehension and more in terms of a reconfiguration of relations between words and things and people. One way would be to experiment with, on the one hand, Deleuzian categories, reading the scene through the classifications set up in chapter 8 of *Cinema 2*, "Cinema, Body and Brain, Thought," and, on the other hand, through Brechtian categories, reading the scene in terms of Brecht's extensive meditations on gesture and *gestus*.[62]

We are in the dark again. In the middle of a movie. Smoke swirls languorously, in impossibly slow motion, filtered through steamy light. Is the smoke in the theater, caught in the beam of the projector, or is it up there on the screen, contained by the diegesis? I can smell it, I reach out to touch it, but there is nothing there. Even if I could touch it there would be nothing there, this I know, but it does not prevent me from inhaling deeply. The screen is lit lowly in amber light, bathing a woman who sits on a table—her legs crossed, dressed in rich brown and umber—in a deeply saturated sepia wash. She has just stretched her neck back, blown smoke slowly into the air, and now, her head tilted forward, she looks out under her lashes. At me? At you? At a character off screen? At an imagined spectator?

The film is *Centre Stage* (Stanley Kwan, 1992), and the woman we are watching, who is watching us (the audience) watching her, is Maggie Cheung playing the role of the famous Chinese silent screen actress Ruan Ling-Yu, playing the part of a courtesan in a 1934 movie.[63] The layering in this film is intricate. The diegesis moves between rehearsals, shoots, the film within a film, intercut excerpts from Ruan's films (some authentic

60. Maurice Merleau-Ponty, *Phenomenology of Perception*, trans. Colin Smith (London, 1962), p. 184.

61. "I become involved in things with my body, they co-exist with me as an incarnate subject, and this life among things has nothing in common with the elaboration of scientifically conceived objects. In the same way, I do not understand the gestures of others by some act of intellectual interpretation. . . . It is through my body that I perceive 'things'. The meaning of a gesture thus 'understood' is not behind it, it is intermingled with the structure of the world outlined by the gesture, and which I take up on my own account" (ibid., pp. 185–86).

62. As in, for instance, Bertholt Brecht, *Brecht on Theatre: The Development of an Aesthetic*, trans. and ed. John Willet (New York, 1964).

63. My thanks to Miriam Hansen for first drawing my attention to this film some years ago and to Teri Silvio for reminding me of this scene more recently.

fragments, some reconstructions), a documentary element in which the actors and filmmakers talk about the project, and what we might term the intradiegetic, extra filmic drama of the present. Smoke infiltrates the different layers.

To repeat: gestures migrate between everyday life and the movies, but where the gestural often goes unnoticed in the everyday, in the cinema (where it travels between the quotidian and histrionic) it moves into visibility. Maggie Cheung, playing Ruan Ling-Yu, but not surrendering Maggie Cheung, is learning to smoke—both like a courtesan and like Ruan. Two fragments of old, scratched, black-and-white film are cut into the present: a woman is trying to pick up a man on the street at night, she sidles up to him, he blows smoke in the air and then contemptuously throws his cigarette on the ground at her feet and walks off. Immediately his place is taken by a scruffy down-and-out fellow who retrieves the cigarette butt and sucks on it greedily. The woman, humiliated, looks at the cigarette with some bemusement. In the other fragment the same woman sits on a table, her legs crossed and accepts a cigarette from a man who is trying to seduce her. The second fragment is played several times and replayed or reperformed several times, several different ways, by the fictional Ruan/Cheung (in dialogue with the director who also, amusingly, shows her how to blow smoke). Her gestures are slow, deliberate, but graceful; she sits on the table, crosses her leg, leans slightly to one side, elbow on knee, wrist falling languidly, cigarette held nonchalantly. When the man enters she puts her other hand on her hip, lifts her head, opens her mouth and breathes smoke into his face. Is it a demonstration of power, or an erotic gesture, or derisive? How does Cheung use the cigarette to both mimic and differentiate among different period styles, and the mores and political background entailed in enacting this difference? She conveys the voluptuous pleasure of smoking, the tactile gratification of holding a cigarette between your fingers, the way it liberates your wrist to move like a dancer, the way the body follows, lithe and sinuous. But this cigarette is also full of ideas. What are they? Suffice to say that the cigarette in *Centre Stage* is one of those things that provokes gestures because a mechanism gives rise to the unknown, and not because Cheung has found this unknown in advance (figs. 15 and 16).

She reminds us that the cigarette, as a cinematic thing par excellence, while being thingy might also and simultaneously be and do other things. It can function almost like the Maltese falcon or Rosebud: as a thing that makes other things happen and that enables knowledge by bringing into visibility the unknown. This can happen either on a narrative level (revelations about Rosebud and the falcon precipitate narrative closure even though they actually do not provide hermeneutic conclusions) or on an extradiegetic level (by opening onto and bringing into focus other times, other cultures, or even our own culture). In this essay I have mapped out an approach that privileges the quotidian nature of things as a mode of

Figs. 15 and 16.—From *Centre Stage*.

cinematic instantiation, arguing that attention to ways in which the material world is inflected might illuminate the affective dimension of the cinematic experience. But as soon as you turn to the quotidian your attention is caught by cinema's propensity for the histrionic. This is partly because in cinema the thing frequently elicits touch, and touch materializes in a gestural modality. Everyday, habitual gestures, caught by the moving camera, are potentially framed, put into quotation marks, hypostatized. Thus the quotidian is better understood if it is located within a dynamic matrix of performativity (in relation to the histrionic and located within an operational continuum between inflation and deflation). While the nature of cinematic affect certainly cannot be explained exhaustively by things or, rather, via the capacity of things to move us, nevertheless the phenomenon of thinginess provides a fortuitous entrée into the enigmatic realm of affect. It does this precisely because of an indeterminacy: the cinema evokes the solidity and tactility of things in the very moment of their passing, their ephemerality. In the cinema solid things turn into phantasms, touch turns into memory. It is the mutability of things that matters. At first it might seem that *The Maltese Falcon*—in which the apparently magnificent and priceless turns out to be merely mundane, worthless, mass-produced—reverses the more generalized case in which the mass-produced and mundane (the cigarette and the kettle) turn out to be enchanted, value-laden (meaning-laden) because of a certain kind of cinematic attention. But in fact value (the valuation of cinematic objects) is less straightforward, less sequentially manifested. Things do not turn out only in the end; they turn and turn, from moment to moment; as the effect of the real is conjured so it is unraveled. Affect derives its force not merely from the immediacy of touch but from the capacity of the object to elude the voracious grasp of the moment (and the narrative), to reverberate beyond the frame, to generate ideas within a cultural landscape not circumscribed by the diegesis.

Clearly it is a matter of potential and performativity. Certain film texts, certain cinematic objects, certain cinematic moments yield more value than others in this quest to understand the Thing. But they become rewarding not by virtue of certainty but, as Auden says, when the thing's "formula escapes you," when "it has lost / the certainty that constitutes a thing." Rosebud endures not because it is the key to understanding *Citizen Kane* but because, in the moment when the word materializes as a thing (at the end of the film), when it comes within reach, it burns up. Like a cigarette. Rather than closing down on the past it inaugurates a new process, it touches me somewhere between here and there, activating new memories, as is the case when Maggie Cheung holds her cigarette nonchalantly and blows smoke in my face. Guided by film, in these and other instances, we approach ideas no longer on highways leading through the void but on "paths that wind through the thicket of things."

Things on Film: Shadow and Voice in Wright Morris's Field of Vision

Alan Trachtenberg

> Leon Battista Alberti says,
> Some lights are from stars, some from the sun
> And moon, and other lights are from fires.
> The light from the stars makes the shadow equal to the body.
> Light from fire makes it greater,
> there, under the tongue, there, under the utterance.
> —CHARLES WRIGHT, "A Short History of the Shadow"

Wright Morris's photographs abound in things seen, standing or lying there for the eye's attention and the mind's endless play of seeking and inventing meanings. About his early camera work Morris wrote: "Apparently I had more than texture in mind on the evidence of the subjects I assembled. Doors and windows, gates, stoops, samples of litter, assorted junk, anything that appeared to have served its purpose. . . . Expressive fragments that managed to speak for the whole."[1] We begin with artifacts, inert, well-worn things that reflect light and project shade—objects chiefly of ordinary life on farms and in towns of the rural Midwest of the United States, in the 1930s and 1940s, the homely world of farmhouses, furniture, tools and implements and signs that mark everyday existence in that place at that time (figs. 1–5). Practical objects unmistakable, yes, but meanings ambiguous, imprecise, inciting the imagination to flights of memory, dreams, and wonder. The field of vision, the field of things, the field of reverie: Morris has made the convergence of these territories his own fictive domain. A Morris photograph is less a specific place than an idea of place arising from acts of creative imagining. To imagine means "to picture to oneself" with imagi-

1. Wright Morris, "Preface to the Second Edition," *The Inhabitants* (1946; New York, 1971), n.p.

FIG. 1.—Wright Morris, *Mailboxes, Western Nebraska,* 1947.

FIG. 2.—Wright Morris, *Farm House, Near McCook, Nebraska,* 1940.

FIG. 3.—Wright Morris, *Ed's Place,* 1947.

FIG. 4.—Wright Morris, *Clothes on Hook.* From *The Home Place,* 1947.

Alan Trachtenberg is Neil Gray Emeritus Professor of English and American studies at Yale University. Among his published works are *Brooklyn Bridge: Fact and Symbol* (1965), *The Incorporation of America: Culture and Society in the Gilded Age* (1982), *Reading American Photographs* (1989), and *Distinctly American: The Photography of Wright Morris* (2002). His next book, *Shades of Hiawatha: Staging Indians, Making Americans in the Early Twentieth Century,* is scheduled to appear in the fall of 2004.

FIG. 5.—Wright Morris, *Barber Pole, Weeping Water, Nebraska*, 1947.

FIG. 6.—Wright Morris, *Gano Grain Elevator, Western Kansas*, 1940.

FIG. 7.—Wright Morris, *Ed's Place. Near Norfolk, Nebraska*, 1947.

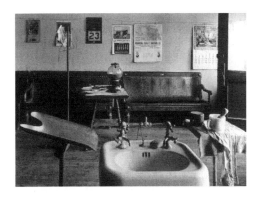

FIG. 8.—Wright Morris, *Barber Shop Interior. Cahow's Barber Shop*, 1947.

FIG. 9.—Wright Morris, *Bed, Shoes on Floor, Ed's Place,* 1947.

nation, that faculty of mind by which we conceive the absent as if it were present.[2] It's the means by which we make what is not present to the senses, what's *in*visible, seem as if it were present, there to touch as if it were real. It is the way of dreaming, making the unreal seem real enough to entice us, frighten us, move us with passion or hatred, perhaps awaken us in a sweat. The power of things in Morris's field of vision lies in how they simultaneously invite and elude us, how they incite and excite desire and need for certainty even as they flit away into shadowed uncertainty.

There's an excess of attention to things, an excess beyond what's needed to say what the objects are, what their uses might be for the people we don't see and can only imagine. While referentiality or identity—this is a house or a chair or a barber pole—may be their first effect, the pictures draw us further, beyond mere designation. Why are we given such things to see in just this way, from this perspective, in this light? Perspectives vary and multiply: we see buildings directly fronting the eye, erect and deco-

2. *Oxford English Dictionary,* 2d ed. (New York, 1989), s.v. "imagine."

FIG. 10.—Wright Morris, *Through the Glass Curtain.* From *The Home Place,* 1947.

FIG. 11.—Wright Morris, *Bedroom Dresser, Southern Indiana,* 1950.

rous and often mysterious (fig. 6); there are varying degrees of closeness in views of mundane things (figs. 7–8); or textures seem to detach themselves from surfaces, a jarring effect that raises questions about how we might understand what makes up a thing (fig. 9). Morris gives us a world that catches and holds our attention not by dramatic or quirky displays of human behavior—his pictures are almost entirely unpeopled—but by the attention of his roaming eye. "Anything that appeared to have served its purpose," Morris notes: "Except people. Only in their absence will the observer intuit, in full measure, their presence in the object."[3]

There's a resemblance here to both visual ethnography and 1930s documentary photography, but both categories come up short in accounting

FIG. 12.—Wright Morris, *Dresser Drawer. Ed's Place,* 1947.

3. Morris, "Preface to the Second Edition," n.p.

FIG. 13.—Wright Morris, *Bedroom (Horse Picture on Wall)*. From *The Home Place*, 1947.

for the effect of these pictures. Morris's photographs provoke us to put questions to and to think critically about photography itself, about the medium's implication in the way it pictures the world's physical body. What can the camera give us to see, for example, from a corner of one room into a corner of another, or through an intervening scrim curtain or as reflected in mirrors set at oblique angles to the objects registered there (figs. 10–11)? What comes into the camera's view when we open a drawer and linger

FIG. 14.—Wright Morris, *Front Door*. From *The Home Place*, 1947.
FIG. 15.—Wright Morris, *Screened Windows with Curtains*. From *The Home Place*, 1947.

closely, looking down on objects we normally pass without further thought (fig. 12)? What does it mean to look down rather than up or sideways or straight ahead? Consider the presence of photographs and other pictures: displayed on tables, hung on walls—things picturing other things, incorporated into the world's body (fig. 13). Morris sees pictures and picturing as integral to ordinary life: window frames, doorways; any opening through which the world frames itself (figs. 14–15); any mirror in a room apparently giving the place back to itself in exact and precise reversal (fig. 16).

Photographers are drawn to mirrors for many reasons: they can show what's behind the camera as well as what is in front of it; often they are interesting objects in their own right, coming in different sizes and shapes, framed in carved wood or unframed, inscribed with etched patterns. And a mirror can seem an emblem of photography itself, its glass surface reminding us of the glass eye of the camera (lens), and the reflection on the surface of the mirrored glass can stand for or even anticipate the picture that will eventu-

FIG. 16.—Wright Morris, *Front Room Reflected in Mirror.* From *The Home Place*, 1947.

ally come out of the camera. We can put it this way: what the photographed mirror shows is not exactly what the photograph itself shows, but is like it: an image fixed in time and space yet not dependent, as the mirror image is, on that time and space it depicts. The image in the mirror changes as we pass in front of it, come closer or back up. The mirror image depends on its immediate instrumental cause, what lies before it at whatever angle. The mirror image anticipates the photograph but is not identical to it. Once fixed on paper, the final photographic image is free to roam anywhere and nowhere; it's no longer dependent on what, in the real world, caused it to come into being.

We have a mirror in a room. Also in that room, visible neither in the photograph nor the mirror, is a camera. Mirrors and cameras have this in common: they are both instruments for the making of apparently exact and true images. Mirroring means exactitude, like the camera's vision. But the mirror's lateral reversal of the world it gives back plants a doubt. Is the image on the surface of the mirrored glass really a seamless transcription, or is it a transfiguration? We see here, too, mirrored pictures thrice removed, from original to mirror to photograph. The bow and vine and leafs engraved on the mirror's own surface tell us we are looking at both a flat, tangible surface and a fluid reflection on it that gives back the illusion of three-dimensional space. Everything seems fixed and still, yet we know, knowing how mirrors work, that if we take a step in any direction, everything will change. We know that the mirror cannot help but mirror, but also that what it mirrors counts as much on us, where we stand, as it does on what's there to be mirrored—the way, for example, this mirror shows a reversed image of what's behind us, things not present to us except as reflections. The door standing there mate-

FIG. 17.—From Walker Evans, *American Photographs* (1938).

FIG. 18.—From James Agee and Walker Evans, *Let Us Now Praise Famous Men* (1941).

rializes the doubt, its solidity as a substance giving way before our eyes into something unsteady, wavering, insubstantial, perhaps an effect of flaws on the mirror's surface—a standing door, unattached, simply there, its blank panels like picture frames waiting to be filled in. The entire mystery of things and their images flashes up before us in all their ambiguity.

Morris's work has often been compared with 1930s "documentary" photographs, Walker Evans's pictures especially, of weather-beaten shacks, country churches rising in elegance, furnishings giving off the dignity of honest purpose and use (figs. 17–18). It's right to note these resemblances, but it's mistaken to assume that resemblance means sameness. While it's both true and significant that his work in photography shared certain motives with 1930s documentary—not to show suffering but to reveal ordinariness—his pictures go toward different ends. He depicts many of the same sights, but with the difference (among others) that he calls heightened attention to the medium, to the act of seeing with the camera. Self-consciousness about perspective and angle of vision, moreover, goes along with an entirely different idea of the use of the photograph: not simply to show what's there but to elicit from the image something "hidden" or "concealed," as he often put it, something not immediately visible or legible. This intention to uncover what's concealed appears in Morris's experimental publications in the 1940s of images together with texts, "photo-texts"—about which I will have more to say further on. Another sign of a counterdocumentary motive is his omission of dates and places in the photo-texts, denying usual documentary reference. He has a different kind of work in mind for his pictures.[4]

On one of his earliest photographic trips across country, in 1938, Morris witnessed, as he recalled, "the American landscape crowded with ruins I wanted to salvage. The depression created a world of objects toward which I felt affectionate and possessive."[5] *Ruins* and *salvage*, words he uses repeatedly about his pictures, are double-edged terms: *salvage* in the sense of recover as well as preserve (recover from where? for what purposes?); *ruin* in the sense of runic as well as vestige or trace, a fragment, a riddle, something concealed in something revealed—as in an extraordinary close view from above, looking down upon an irreparably broken comb on a covered table next to a sewing kit, personal tools of self-mending in an oddly incongruent juxtaposition, the missing teeth seeming to mock any pretension toward restored or mended wholeness (fig. 19). Each thing disrupts the apparent meaning of the other.[6]

4. I discuss Wright and Evans in Alan Trachtenberg, "Wright Morris's 'Photo-Texts,'" *Yale Journal of Criticism* 9 (Spring 1996): 112–18 and "Wright Morris: American Photographer," in *Distinctly American: The Photography of Wright Morris*, ed. Trachtenberg and Ralph Lieberman (London, 2002), pp. 17–22. See also Trachtenberg, *Reading American Photographs: Images as History, Mathew Brady to Walker Evans* (New York, 1989), pp. 231–86.

5. Quoted in James Alinder, introduction to *Wright Morris: Photographs and Words*, ed. Alinder (Carmel, Calif., 1982), p. 8.

6. I am grateful for a stimulating conversation with Lance Duerfahrd regarding this imposing image and for his astute comments on an earlier version of this paper.

Can we take this as a comment on the other baffling remark, that "the depression created a world of objects?" In what sense "created a world"? A destructive event characterized by dispossession of property, of work, of place, of attachments, depression creates a "world" by these very forces, a world that elicits in Morris a sense of affectionate attachment and belonging: dispossession bringing possession. Is there an implication that photography, his photography—a medium for reattachment and repossession of the world—was also created by depression, brought about, provoked into being by the systemic collapse of the 1930s, photography as his way (like and unlike the New Deal) toward recovery by the salvaging of ruins? If by the effacement of date and place

Fig 19.—Wright Morris, *Comb on Dresser.* From *The Home Place,* 1947.

and the fictionalizing of the voice he attached to images in the photo-texts Morris seems to remove his pictures from historical reference, does this retrospective remark open a rift through which we can perceive kind of historicity? Made mostly in the late 1930s and the 1940s, are his photographs in some concealed but pervasive sense depression pictures after all?

"Vernacular as such is not concerned," Morris warned in 1940.[7] Vernacular implies the documenting of a culture, a pigeonhole (like ethnography) too cramped for *provocation,* a word that denotes an action of inciting, calling or drawing forth, an invitation, a summons. We are taken by the plain ordinariness of what Morris's pictures adduce, a world of things and their shadows, what John Crowe Ransom means by the "homely fulness of the world."[8] We are also taken by *how* he sees, his way of seeing that makes ruins or runic poems of things, that recovers as it uncovers, reveals as it conceals. Asking what the things in Morris's pictures provoke or summon us to is to ask about his conception and his personal, contingent uses of the medium of the provocation, photography.

What does it mean to say that photographs capture and mediate the world? Putting such a question risks claiming a privileged ontological status and function for the medium, as if there is a uniquely photographic way of standing toward the world. But if there were, and Morris (like all modernist photographers) was one who believed there is, how might we describe it? In his essay "What Photography Calls Thinking," Stanley Cavell wrote about "how little we know about what the photographic reveals," about the specific "transformative powers of the camera," what he calls "its original violence."[9] In an earlier essay, "What Becomes of Things on Film?" from which I draw the first part of my title, Cavell puts this question to cinema; his film, what passes through the projector on its way toward an image on the screen, is a positive version of a negative—a print on celluloid. Cavell speaks of cinema, but we might extend the trope to still photographs. Are they also acts of disruption? Cavell draws on Heidegger's notion that picturing "interrupts" the normal flow of work or play, turns attention elsewhere, hence disruption as the condition of picturing, enabling it. Things stand forth within sight, in Heidegger's words, paraphrased by Cavell, in "their conspicuousness, their obtrusiveness, and their obstinacy," insistent in the way they penetrate our field of vision.[10] At the same time and by the same act of presenting themselves to our eyes, things captured in light give us a doubled experience and a thought of doubleness; images of things on film are taken from things that remain behind. Left behind, they are irretrievably lost to our present tense, but remaining behind in actuality as a pastness they provoke a thought of their future. Will they change location, pass away, alter in small or large degree? Hence it is said that every photograph gives us a thought of what has been (as Roland Barthes famously put it) and what will yet be for that having-

7. Morris, "The Inhabitants: An Aspect of American Folkways," in *New Directions in Prose and Poetry, 1940,* ed. James Laughlin (Norfolk, Conn., 1940), p. 148; hereafter abbreviated "I."

8. John Crowe Ransom, *The World's Body* (New York, 1938), p. xi.

9. Stanley Cavell, "What Photography Calls Thinking," *Raritan* 4 (Spring 1985): 1. See also Cavell, "What Becomes of Things on Film?" *Themes Out of School: Effects and Causes* (San Francisco, 1984).

10. Cavell, "What Becomes of Things on Film?" p. 174.

been, something we cannot perfectly know: a future without a horizon, Barthes's *"without future."*[11] For reasons such as these, Cavell's idea that we worry or at least wonder about what happens to things on film wins assent.

I take "things on film" as apt for a discussion of still photographs for another reason. The phrase denotes the existence of a negative prior to the making of a positive image, as the stark black-white pattern in figure 20 denotes. In still photography what happens to things on film in the first instance is that they reappear on paper as positive images; their presence on film means they have undergone a process of negation, of reversal, as the condition for their reappearance in the recognizable form of a photographic picture. They are a negation of a negation, right side up, top to bottom and right to left, values matching those of normal vision. Photography negates or cancels the world in order to reproduce it, to present it as a *re*-presentation. And this process itself reproduces the most obvious observation to make about things in photographs: that they exist, as they do in the real world, as surfaces on which light falls; they reflect light, but also block light from passing through, producing shadow, the negation of light. Things on film declare their source in real-world space and time by the shadows they cast, negatives of themselves, producing the effect of three-dimensional volume (fig. 21). The mutually constitutive relations between a photographic negative and a photographic print are already signified in any real-world photograph by shadows falling beneath where light falls. The dance of light and dark tells us we are in the presence of things on film.

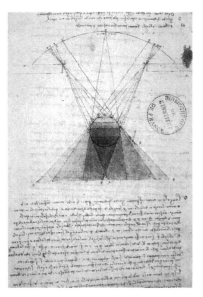

Light produces shadow—a truism first put into elegant theory in the late fifteenth century by Leonardo da Vinci. Light, he wrote (as paraphrased by Michael Baxandall) is "always accompanied by shadow." Just as there are luminous bodies that emit luminous rays, so there are "umbrous" bodies that emit shadowing rays (fig. 22). An umbrous body is something solid and dense that blocks and creates (casts or projects) shadow, an impenetrability we can only perceive because there is light. "Being dense," wrote Leonardo, "is the opponent of being luminous."

FIG. 22.—Leonardo da Vinci. Light from a window on an umbrous sphere.

11. Roland Barthes, *Camera Lucida*, trans. Richard Howard (New York, 1981), p. 90.

FIG. 20.—Wright Morris, *House in Winter, Near Lincoln, Nebraska,* 1941.

FIG. 21.—Wright Morris, *School House with Swings, Nebraska,* 1947.

The shadow, in Leonardo's studies, is the definitive mark or sign of light; without light, we cannot see; but darkness also enables sight. Light makes dark, and dark makes possible knowledge of a three-dimensional world.[12] Light and dark are, in Barthes's words in another connection, each other's "constitutive negativity."[13] Light brings shadow, shadow reveals light. By its automatic operations photography gives testimony to this plain yet unfathomable truth.

The play of opposites is immediately apparent in Morris's work: heavy projected shadows falling within intense areas of light, marking off edges (fig. 23); shadows that cling to their objects, the kind of shade sciographers call self-shadows (fig. 24); objects projecting negative pictures of themselves on other surfaces in the form of silhouetted shadows (fig. 25). A ladder against a wall was one of the commonest visual devices in eighteenth-century drawings (fig. 26), as here, of perspective and painting and architecture, an empirical illustration (fig. 27). The same trope appeared in one of the earliest photographs produced in the negative-positive process (fig. 28), *The Haystack* by William Henry Fox Talbot (inventor of the negative-positive process), from his *The Pencil of Nature* (1844), the first publication of photographs in book form, moreover with verbal commentary attached to each image—making Talbot, then, progenitor of Morris's photo-texts, as well as Morris's precursor in the photography of objects seen closely in bright light (including printed pages and bindings of books, pictures, and buildings). Shadows tell the life of things in photographs as in reality; by fixing shadows in place the photograph makes possible contemplation of the act of seeing, the simultaneity in perception of the light and the dark of things. Talbot wrote of *The Haystack:* "One advantage of the discovery of the Photographic Art will be, that it will enable us to introduce into our pictures a multitude of minute details [such as every accident of light and shade] which add to the truth and reality of the representation, but which no artist would take the trouble to copy faithfully from nature."[14] In the early days of the medium, "shadow" as in "fix the shadow ere the substance fade" or "fixing the shadow" means likeness, the image cast off or projected from dense light-reflecting and light-blocking things of the world. The coexistence of objects and their shadows in photographs such as Talbot's and Morris's can be taken as a self-reflective recognition that the medium defines itself within itself by its capture of the dual modality of objects in light and shade.

What does it mean to picture things on film, then, to picture things in a manner of picturing that is one of photography's capabilities? In painting or drawing, things appear as mimesis, handmade copies or imitations of things according to rules and systems (such as evolved, as Baxandall shows,

12. Michael Baxandall, *Shadows and Enlightenment* (New Haven, Conn., 1995), p. 152.

13. Barthes, "The Third Meaning: Research Notes on Some Eisenstein Stills," *Image, Music, Text,* trans. Stephen Heath (New York, 1977), p. 64; hereafter abbreviated "TM."

14. William Henry Fox Talbot, *The Pencil of Nature* (1844; New York, 1969), pl. 10, *The Haystack.*

FIG. 23.—Wright Morris, *Panama Depot (side view), Panama, Nebraska,* 1947.

FIG. 24.—Wright Morris, *Church near Truro, Cape Cod, Massachusetts,* 1939.

FIG. 25.—Wright Morris, *Abandoned House and Snow Drift, Near Lincoln, Nebraska,* 1940.

FIG. 26.—Wright Morris, *Wall, Wheel, and Ladder, New Mexico*, 1940.

FIG. 27.—Steps. Detail from Andrea Pozzo, *Perspettiva d'pittori e architetti, parte seconde,* 1700.

FIG. 28.—William Henry Fox Talbot, *The Haystack*, 1844–46.

in eighteenth-century rococo art) for creating on a flat surface the illusion of spatiality and, by use of shadow (along with color filtered with shade), of volume within space, as in Jean-Baptiste Oudry, *Hare, Sheldrake, Bottles, Bread and Cheese* (about 1742) (fig. 29). As Baxandall puts it, pictorial knowledge is itself an issue in this familiar kind of painting derived from seventeenth-century Dutch still-life. Reflections of the main light source (the window above and to the left) in the bottles on the shelf and caught in the drop of blood dripping from the hare's nose place the subjects in a space filled with light from a designated source. And shadows falling on lit surfaces—the hare's on the wall, a bottle's on the loaf of bread, the bread's on the shelf or table, the cheese on the crumpled paper wrapper—bring these surfaces in relation to the main objects on display, the unfortunate hare and its hanging companion, the duck killed in the act of lifting off. The whole performs an exercise in mimesis; we're not proffered food for nourishment or drink to quench thirst but an example of painterly representation. It is an empiricist abstraction from the work of light and shadow in real space.

Mimesis means the copying of the visible world, the world of things in light. It does not imply that the maker was necessarily present to that world at the time of the mimetic performance. Nor does it mean that the object

represented in any physical sense played a role in its own presentation, except, in Leonardo's trope, in that the rays of likeness given off by an object's surface in the "'radiant pyramid'" of perception can be said to be a "cause."[15] Photographs that capture those rays in an unconditionally physical act (chemical and mechanical) allow us to say that objects *present themselves* to the eye of the camera. Cavell puts it more succinctly: "A representation emphasizes the identity of its subject, hence it may be called a likeness; a photograph emphasizes the existence of its subject, hence it is that it may be called a transcription. One may also think of it as a transfiguration."[16]

All this goes almost without saying in discussions that assume that photography has a character unique to itself.[17] Nothing in a painting re-

FIG. 29.—Jean-Baptiste Oudry, *Hare, Sheldrake, Bottles, Bread and Cheese*, c. 1742.

15. Baxandall, *Shadows and Enlightenment*, p. 152.

16. Cavell, "What Photography Calls Thinking," p. 4.

17. But see the cogently argued counterview by Joel Snyder, "Picturing Vision," *Critical Inquiry* 6 (Spring 1980): 499–526 and, with Neil Walsh Allen, "Photography, Vision, and Representation," *Critical Inquiry* 2 (Autumn 1975): 143–69.

quires us to believe that the artist was there where his depicted objects were at that very moment, not in the way that it has seemed (pre–digital cameras) a necessity communicated by every unmodified photograph that the things in a photograph were once present to the recording lens, present in space and present in time. This is what we most commonly mean when we say *photograph,* an act of transcription so automatic, so self-performing, that what we see in a photographic picture, what we understand ourselves as seeing, is what the camera cannot help but see once the mechanism has been set in motion (the set-up gives us the margin of human will and choice). This is what we ordinarily believe every photograph wants us to know about itself, not as picture (that's something else) but as *photograph.* The powerful corollary of this knowledge is that the things displayed remain behind, outside the transcribed image; by the time we hold and view the image, the thing photographed may have become already something different. This is what we say about every real-life photograph: the thing was once there and now it is not, not precisely the same thing, not precisely in the same way; the picture saves it, salvages it—salvages it from the fate of what once stood before the lens (change of location, decay, decomposition, disappearance, ruination by depression). Every real-life photograph delivers itself as a past tense—a complication for the viewer, who stands then in a doubled relation to the pictured thing. We see it as something absent to us as we are absent to it; its presence now, in the picture, claims mutual absence (including absence from the future of the thing) as the defining condition of our role as viewers; this is what it most commonly means to look at photographs.

It's by subtraction, then, that such photographs put us in the presence of a real world. For Morris, pictures, whether actual photographs or mental images in the mind's eye of characters in his novels and stories, are always something salvaged from the flux of time, from the past and from their own condition of being past; they are always of the *present* even as they deliver traces of their past in signs of use and wear. In his photographs Morris looks at things as if they were already ruins, what's left over, and if they succeed as pictures they become "imaginary gains" recovered from "real losses," what remains and persists in the face of death. "Let me try and explain," Morris quotes Samuel Beckett: "From things about to disappear I turn away in time. To watch them out of sight, no, I can't do it."[18] It's the paradox of things appearing while disappearing, apprehended just in time, and *in* time.

It's in the space (a temporal zone) between what is found, what is salvaged, and what remains behind that Morris undertook his provocative experiment of photo-text, philosophically provocative in that it raises questions about itself. Linking image and words, his photo-texts are examples of how from the homely world of things sense can be derived—

---

18. Quoted as epigraph in Morris, *God's Country and My People* (New York, 1968), n.p.

how the hidden, secret life of things can be enhanced in such a way that the thing seen can be seen as if it were encountering us, eliciting our sight by looking back at us. Morris speaks of his photography as sacramental seeing; he speaks, quoting Henry James, of "mystic meanings" that things have "to give out."[19] The photo-text emerged for him as a way to summon from the image what is not entirely visible within it. Just as we can say that the photograph cancels or negates the world it envisions in order to make it visible, so the text cancels the photo in order to bring it into clearer, sharper focus, a focus legible enough to be articulated. He conceived of the form as a particular kind of labor, a labor of reading and refocusing.

> This material permits no compromise. It demands the legitimate range of both to communicate the full experience—what there is to be seen must be seen—to say must be said. Two separate mediums are employed for two distinct views. Only when refocused in the mind's eye will the third view result. The burden of *technique* is the reader's alone. His willingness to participate—rather than spectate—will determine his range. It makes no demands beyond a suspension of old formula. ["I," p. 147]

This is from Morris's note to a group of such texts that appeared under the title "The Inhabitants: An Aspect of American Folkways" in the 1940 number of James Laughlin's *New Directions,* in a section titled "The American Scene"; the same section included a selection of text and four photographs from James Agee and Walker Evans's *Let Us Now Praise Famous Men.* The date, the juxtaposition, and the reference to "American Folkways" show that Morris's experiments belong to the same modernist literary and photographic culture of the 1930s in which Agee and Evans worked.

Morris sought a presence in image to reverberate in conversation with someone's voice. "Have a good long look at *Kirby Lee* as you lend him your ears," he wrote in the introductory note. "The result is not a matter of invention, the element of technique is negligible—behind the novelty the *idea* is inherent, the two are the same" ("I," p. 148). The voice invites us to think not just about the adjoining picture but about photography itself; it makes the revelation of photography within the picture audible and legible at once, but there is nothing in the picture we can point to as the revelation (fig. 30).

Kirby Lee
Sittin here I'll just be looking at the cars when somethin turns my mind to somethin past. A street somewhere or bright lights in a store, or music comin from a phonograph. An I'll be there and not there,

19. Quoted as epigraph in Morris, *The Home Place* (New York, 1948). See also Morris, "Real Losses, Imaginary Gains," *Real Losses, Imaginary Gains: Stories by Wright Morris* (New York, 1976), pp. 1-6.

FIG. 30.—Wright Morris, *Meeting House, Southbury, Ct.,* 1938.

funny like. An it will be somethin common, somethin anybody's seen—a couple girls laughin or people millin in the square—or maybe just a light showin through a blind. But it ain't the thing, its what comes over it. Its like a no account scene just before somethin happens when you know somethin is bound to happen there. An yet nothin happens after all. Just people doin nothin, walkin around. Sometimes its Saturday night an there's a kindof quiet razzle, wimmen sittin in the buggies starin at the barber pole an the popcorn burner sparkin in their eyes. An yet its like people passin on a stage. Movin around before the curtain waitin for the thing to rise an the hero or the shero to come on. Only they don't an the millin just goes on. An yet I sit like a man caught in a spell. Like I was seein what nobody'd seen before an was a thing like the burnin of the bush—only I aint Moses an nobody calls. An yet in my own way I seen the light. I aint liked many an there aint many favored me. But I loved a thing an I know how it feels. An there's somethin over people that can touch a man deep, not just them you like through knowin, but the rest. There's somethin over people I can love. Seems they're just the same people but there's somethin in the air, softer kindof, like a secret was around. As if what I was seein was bigger than it was. Like what an In-jun summer haze does to the moon. ["I," p. 151]

As revealed in the voice-text, the photograph has become a scene of consciousness. The scene opens with a disruption in the present tense; the mind turns from looking at cars, things passing, toward "somethin past" already in the mind: an image like a photograph, which is always "past," a present pastness. The effect is a strange placelessness: "An I'll be there an not there," pastness and presentness fused in a single act. It's a past with a future yet unknown: "a no account scene just before somethin happens when you know somethin is bound to happen there. An yet nothin happens after all." Nothing happens but always something is about to happen—exactly the sense one gets in looking at photographs under the spell they cast.

In Morris's photo-texts voice and image stand in no definitive relation to each other; he often shuffled photos and texts, applying different voices to the same image and different images to the same voice, just as he often flipped the negative while printing to produce reversed images. The same picture often appeared on different occasions as a kind of positive-negative of each other—small but telling ways to unfix the apparent fixity of the photographed image. The relation of text to photo is contingent; one does not illustrate or authenticate the other; they are in fact disjunctive, and it's in the jolt that the attentive reader will find delight in having to *imagine* for one's self invisible connections, to seek associations within the image that give plausibility to the linkage. Each of two materialities, image and word, remain self-sufficient; paired together, they gain more than they lose. Each is, as Morris says, *enhanced*.

By 1946 the sequence of fifteen photo-texts had expanded to fifty-two in the book *The Inhabitants,* which retains some of the original texts, alters others, the introductory note dropped, and a new textual frame added—which is not of concern here. In both publications—and in the extraordinary *The Home Place* (1948), an extension of photo-text to the scale of a novel—all of Morris's photographs appeared untitled and undated, which is how they remained until republication in the catalogues of 1982 and 1992.[20] *Rural Schoolhouse, Eastern Kansas, 1939* appeared in *The Inhabitants* (1946) and reappeared in *God's Country and My People* (1968) with a different text. Here is the 1946 photo and text (fig. 31):

Shadows are the way things lay-me-down. Daddy can lay-me-down across the street. Mr. Clark's store can lay-me-down on the barn and the barn can lay-me-down on Mr. Clark. Everything that stands must lay-me-down. The fence, tracks in the road, birds that fly low, poles, trees, myself. Everything tall must lay-me-down like everything short. Everything hard as flat as everything soft. Everything as quiet as everything still. Even birds know why and have to lay-me-down too. Even the night must come and lay-me-down to sleep.[21]

Fig. 31.—Wright Morris, *Rural Schoolhouse, Eastern Kansas,* 1939.

20. See *Wright Morris,* and *Wright Morris: Origin of a Species,* ed. Sandra Phillips and John Szarkowski (exhibition catalog, San Francisco Museum of Modern Art, 3 Sept. 1992–1 Nov. 1992).

21. Morris, *God's Country and My People,* n.p.

A leafy field of play raked by low-falling shadows of trees lies between us and the austere pattern of whites and blacks on the elegantly plain structure in the upper third of the image. The spellbinding shadow of the pump handle makes a timepiece of the white, one-windowed, shingled wall, joining the shadows falling from the eaves and the invisible trees, the cast shadow of the post on the right, and the rectilinear self-shadows by which the clapboards define themselves. It's a moment in the sun before all goes dark (the long shadows imply dusk, though perhaps dawn), the teasing repetition of the old Puritan children's prayer echoing with thoughts, fears, certainties, and uncertainties of death: "Now I lay me down to sleep, I pray the Lord my soul to keep. If I should die before I wake, I pray the Lord my soul to take."

Morris's kind of photography reveals itself here as another laying-me-down of things of the world in a stillness evoking death but within which things can come to life again in the voices they summon. And the foregrounding in both text and image of shadow suggests quite powerfully that Morris's treatment of the trope (verbal and visual) verges toward an allegory for his entire project: shadows doubling things in real light; things and their shadows redoubled in pictures; a redoubling again of picture by words, by photo-text and yet again by sequences of photo-texts. By now the object-in-the-world and the picture-in-the-world each lose any privileged ontological status; separately and together they are given over to the utter contingency of perspective.[22]

Derived in part from the "Camera Eye" sections of *USA*, John Dos Passos's great experimental trilogy of the 1930s, the subjectivism of photo-text similarly declines the easy looking at photographs that are buttressed by textual translation (caption or gloss), replaces ease with difficulty for the sake of heightening the experience of the associative dimensions of things. Photo-text enacts a relation between eye and mind, photography and consciousness, a relation about which Morris writes at length in a remarkable group of some dozen essays and interviews on photography, collected in 1999 in a volume titled *Time Pieces: Photographs, Writing, and Memory*.[23] He repeatedly makes the point that photography gives access to the world, a way of connecting mind and matter, of affirming the real world toward which we stand as sensing, seeing creatures. Eyesight attaches us to things, the world's body, as if it were a kind of touch; seeing is the first step in the penetration of matter by mind, a way provisionally, momentarily, to overcome the alienation Emerson and other romantic thinkers attributed to consciousness itself—a way to join self to world in a "third view." Morris's "third view" that results from refocusing "in the mind's eye" the two "distinct views" of photo and text stands close to what Roland Barthes calls, in a reading of stills from films by Sergei Eisenstein, "the third meaning." Barthes talks about something left over in still photographs, something "evident, erratic, obstinate" ("TM," p. 53). The

22. My thanks to Bill Brown for help in clarifying this point.
23. See Morris, *Time Pieces: Photographs, Writing, and Memory* (New York, 1999).

third meaning follows from a first informational or communicative meaning, what the sign refers to, and the second or symbolic meaning. Analogous to the act of listening—of the classical five senses hearing is listed third—apprehension of the third meaning, Barthes writes, "compels an interrogative reading." In *Camera Lucida* he calls this a "punctum," that wounding mark in a picture that compels attention beyond the "studium," what the picture's communication and signification make *obvious*. The third meaning lies beyond the reach of intellection, a supplement in the form of something "fleeting, smooth and elusive." Barthes calls this "the obtuse meaning," "a meaning which seeks me out, me, the recipient of the message, the subject of the reading" ("TM," p. 54).

The fit may not be exact, but I think Barthes's "third meaning" helps us see what's up in Wright Morris's photo-texts. What Barthes calls a "mutation of reading" ("TM," p. 68) results in which photo and text cancel or negate each other in order to make visible and audible a third thing, a new "view" in the mode of a voice, a view in which text and image become each other's "constitutive negativity." Morris distinguishes between his photo-texts and typical word and image links in the daily press and most picture books; they show "a *technique* of translation," he writes, in which "the picture leans on the prose, the prose stiffens gallantly." Photo-text abandons "the lean-to picture, the translated prose" for the sake of a new "quality of experience" ("I," pp. 147, 148).

A gloss of these relations appears in an early picture never before exhibited or published (as far as I know), *Starfish and Portrait, Cleveland, Ohio*, and presumably never linked with a text—yet a picture that lends itself to a near diagrammatic interpretation of the relations embodied in photo-texts (fig. 32). A small framed portrait sits on one side of a table, just under a milk-glass vase whose stamped floral pattern echoes the leaves and flowers on the wallpaper behind the table. Neatly covering the table, its folds or ridges defined by self-shadows from an overhead source of light to the left, a white cloth lays down square frames on the surface of the table; pen and pencil in a stamped-glass goblet stand opposite, alone in one of those frames. In front of the portrait, three stamped and postmarked and apparently unsealed letters lie as if casually dropped, forming an ensemble of rectangulars; they may await reading or reply. In any case, they bring into the picture signs of an elsewhere (and the possibility of a message) to which the things in the picture bear some unarticulated relation. And we see, propped against the floral-patterned papered wall, the glorious five-pointed starfish. Reticulated veins or ridges on its surface form into a pattern of rays flowing as if by electrical energy toward each of the tips of the five points, emanating from the circle at the center of its surface. Something salvaged from a beach and placed as memento, an obdurate thing, once quick with life, now stiff in its afterlife as keepsake or souvenir, the starfish has been placed (we can only imagine it as intentionally placed, propped up as a standing object, though the decorative intention may not exhaust all

FIG. 32.—Wright Morris, *Starfish and Portrait, Cleveland, Ohio,* 1940s.

the implications of the placement) in such a way that its two bottom legs tri-angulate the pictured photograph and the writing tools. Every thing in the picture casts a shadow, on the table, on the wall, on itself.

A corner in a modest home transcribed by the camera reveals objects and an idea: photograph, personal letters (standing in for writing as such), and writing tools stand to each other in the form of a starfish, as if they form a third thing, something simple yet inexpressibly elegant, reminding us of the pleasure and thrill of a find, something rescued from tides and time, its name a metaphor yoking together two elements, star and fish, sky and sea, opposites yet similar in a way that signifies profundity (literally and figuratively: a vast depth). Tightly focussed, severely cropped or quoted from the space it shares with the camera, Morris's photograph gives the starfish a monumental scale. Standing between writing and picturing (the floral patterns of vase and wallpaper are also a form of picturing), this thing of nature, made into something supplemental by its capture on a beach and its transmutation into metaphor, points toward further possibilities of meaning, the cognition implied by the joining of photograph and writing. The starfish stands for that cognition, but in no obvious way. It's a gratuity, a mere compositional element (on the level of information); as a symbol we may take it to signify something found or salvaged from nature, cognate to the originals from which the floral wallpaper patterns were drawn and to this scene itself found by Morris's camera. Its five points might take us symbolically toward the five senses, but that's a stretch. Or we can see it as the sign of a rough kind of beauty cherished in this modest home where more lavish signs of beauty are likely very sparse. Everything else in the picture speaks of human history, including the cloth, probably retrieved from storage in a chest where its folds became as natural a deformation as the ridges of the starfish. The starfish too, in a sense, belongs to human history; it was brought here from somewhere else, a beach, a rocky shore, perhaps purchased in a gift shop. Its upright position stands for nature or the feral overcome by human will; it stands for death, the laying-me-down of something once alive and prone in the sea, facing up toward the sky; and its name bespeaks the human heritage of language and metaphoric naming. But something survives this humanizing of the object, something excessive beyond and outside what makes everything else in the picture signs within a signifying system: a third meaning. The dead thing awaits resurgence into new life, resurrection into unexpected and unspecified meaning.

What becomes of things in photographs, then, is that they expire into new life. They issue into a transfiguring voice, actual or imaginary, a voice that triangulates image and viewer. In the third view pictured things become sites of consciousness registered in speech. Like the starfish, photography joins opposites: *photo* and *grapheis*, light and writing, shadow and word. Yet the act of joining in metaphor has its own negative moment: what can be joined can also be disjoined; the hinge marks a rift as well as a joint, difference can insist upon itself even as it seems to be overcome. Photography makes its appearance at the hinge—a device that holds separate what it joins—between image and speech. It is an agent of a visibility that destabilizes by provocation. What happens to things on film is that they provoke and summon their opposite—shadow, word—in order to realize themselves as human experience. Photography shows that the quest for understanding is a dance of negativity. It is not so much a guide to reality as it is a uniquely modern means of questioning reality, helping us sort out what belongs to vision and what to mind and speech. It's an elusive visibility the camera lends to the world's body; as Wright Morris's pictures teach, it takes more than an eye to see what's there.

Index

machine, of poetry, 77
machines, animals as, 205; mathematical, see tools
Mackenzie, Henry, 220, 223
madness, defined, 208
magic, and commodity, 386; and death, 385; and film, 401; Marxist, 392; and see conjuration
Maillard, 102
Malevich, Kazimir, 255
Mallarmé, Stéphane, 77, 92
Maltese Falcon, 393–94, 397, 399, 423, 430
mammoth, and fossils, 234; as totem, 239
Man in a Red Cap (Titian), 183
Man Ray, 13
Man with a Ripped Glove (Titian), 181
Mandeville, Bernard, and sympathy, 198, 211–12, 214, 222
Mangolte, Babette, 406
Manual (Epictetus), 55
Maria of Austria, 180
Marinetti, Filippo Tommaso, 310
market, and fashion, 286; and see New Economic Plan
Marriage of Mercury and Philology (Capella), 304
Marvell, Andrew, 204, 210
Marx, Karl, 350, 355, 392; and commodities, 364–66, 373; and East Germany, 330, 333; and fetishism, 391; and praxis, 354; and romanticism, 229, 240, 243–44
Marxism, and art, 335, 342; and commodity fetish, 263–65; and fashion, 296; and modernism, 266; and production, 262, 293; see socialism
mass production, Soviet, 287–88, 297–98, 303
material culture, see materialism
Materialism (Graham), 87–88, 90, 92
materialism, 7, 97; of artifacts, 74–75; and literature, 97; in Locke, 217; and mechanism, 133; and obscurity, 83; and poetry, 76; and riddle, 79–81; and see constructivism; obscurity
materiality, see materialism
materiality-effect, 8
materialization, process of, in film, 410
materials, and simulation, 106–7
mathematical deduction, and knowledge, 62–63
mathematics, and imitation of ancients, 58; and knowledge, 40–41, 45; see algebra; geometry

Mauss, Marcel, 9, 385, 392, 420–21, 423
McHoul, Alec, 358
mechanical reproduction, 231
mechanism, theories of, 111–13
mediation, and immediacy, 350–51; and photography, 441; poet and, 381
Meditations (Descartes), 42
Medunetshkii, Konstantin, 258
Meierkhol'd, Vsevolod, 252, 291
Melancholia I, or the Two Sisters (Kuckart), 330–31
melancholia, 330–31; see loss
melodrama, 15, 407, 418
memento mori, 209
memorials, things as, 10
memory, and attention, 57; and cause, 60; and collecting, 364, 367, 369; collective, 338, 343–44; and death, 381–92; and knowledge, 57–58, 61–63; and machine, 130; and objects, 337
Merleau-Ponty, Maurice, 427
Merwin, Dido, 390
metamorphosis, 193–226; desire of slaves for, 225; and gold, 215; interspecies, 214
metaphor, in photography, 456; and things, 354
Metaphysical poetry, 78–79, 92
metaphysical, and physical, 231
metempsychosis, 193
Meteors (Descartes), 71
Methodus ad facilem historiarum cognitionem (Bodin), 55
Metzinger, Jean, 255
Middleton, Thomas, 187
milanese, 310, 313
Milland, Ray, 419
Milton, John, 82, 85, 88, 96
mimesis, 390–91; and automata, 125–27; and film performance, 421; in painting, 444–45; and poetry, 381; and repetition, 145; see also simulation
Mimesis (Auerbach), 82
Minsheu, John, 178
Mirror, 415
mirror, and camera, 437–39
mirroring, by objects, 371
Mitchell, W. J. T., 15
mob, and discipline, 47
modernism, 12–13; and photography, 449; see constructivism
modernist poetry, and riddle, 79
modernity, 12–14; and vanishing things, 10
montage, and advertising, 297, 299–301